Walden

I do not propose to write an ode to

dejection, but to brag as lustily as

chanticleer in the morning, standing on his roost,

if only to wake my neighbors up.

—Page 81

Walden

HENRY D. THOREAU

A FULLY ANNOTATED EDITION

Edited by Jeffrey S. Cramer

Yale University Press   New Haven and London

Edward Emerson's map on p. 151 courtesy of the
Thoreau Society (Raymond Adams Collection) and the
Thoreau Institute at Walden Woods

Designed by Sonia Shannon.
Set in Adobe Garamond type by Tseng Information
Systems, Inc.
Printed in the United States of America.

Library of Congress Cataloging-in-Publication Data
Thoreau, Henry David, 1817–1862.
Walden : a fully annotated edition / Henry D.
Thoreau ; edited by Jeffrey S. Cramer.
      p.   cm.
Includes bibliographical references (p.) and index.
ISBN 978-0-300-10466-0
1. Thoreau, Henry David, 1817–1862—Homes and
haunts—Massachusetts—Walden Woods.
2. Wilderness areas—Massachusetts—Walden Woods.
3. Natural history—Massachusetts—Walden Woods.
4. Walden Woods (Mass.)—Social life and customs.
5. Authors, American—19th century—Biography.
6. Solitude. I. Cramer, Jeffrey S., 1955- II. Title.
PS3048.A2C73   2004
818'.303—dc22   2004009596

A catalogue record for this book is available from the
British Library.

The paper in this book meets the guidelines for
permanence and durability of the Committee on
Production Guidelines for Book Longevity of the
Council on Library Resources.

10   9   8   7   6   5

Contents

Illustrations

Preface

In honor of the sesquicentennial of the publication of *Walden* in 1854, Thoreau's text has been newly edited and annotated. My main purpose has been twofold: to examine the text of *Walden* in light of the research and commentary that has been published in the past 150 years, and to present a reliable text with as comprehensive a series of annotations as possible. I have tried to correct errors and omissions of previous editions without creating new ones, but I feel like the traveler Thoreau described in his "Conclusion" to *Walden* who was told by a boy that the swamp before him had a hard bottom. On the traveler's horse sinking in up to the girths, he said, "I thought you said that this bog had a hard bottom." "So it has," answered the boy, "but you have not got half way to it yet." We may never get to the bottom of *Walden,* but I hope we have gotten that much closer.

Acknowledgments

It is difficult to begin without borrowing.
— Thoreau, in "Economy," Walden

I owe the greatest debt to the previous annotators of *Walden*—in particular, Walter Harding, Philip Van Doren Stern, and David Rohman. Without the foundations set by these three, this book could not have been made. I proceed humbly in their footsteps, but I proceed knowing that they would all agree with Emerson's words in "The Method of Nature": "Nothing solid is secure. . . . Even the scholar is not safe; he too is searched and revised."

A work like this could not have been made without the help of literally hundreds of people, known and unknown. Many are acknowledged below, but there are many who, I regret, have become anonymous and for these omissions of credit I apologize. There is generosity and enthusiasm in the world for which I am appreciative, and it is rewarding to know that such dedication and passion exists.

Among those I am especially grateful to are Bill Grealish, formerly of the Boston Public Library, reference librarian par excellence, and Nancy Browne, who came through in a pinch to locate and proof some last-minute resources; Thomas Knoles, American Antiquarian Society; Jeanne Bracken, Lincoln Public Library; Diane Ota and Janice Chadbourne of the Boston Public Library, who helped with questions about music and art; Russell A. Potter and Chas Cowing, for information on Kane and Franklin; Donald W. Linebaugh of the Program for Archaeological Research, The University of Kentucky, for questions about archaeology and nineteenth-century building practices; all the Stumpers-L wombats and, in particular, Denis Lien of the University of Minnesota Libraries; Jack Larkin, Director of Research, Collections, and

Library at Old Sturbridge Village; Austin Meredith; Ruth R. Rogers; and Jack MacLean for his help with Lincoln history. I have also been a beneficiary of the assistance of librarians at Houghton Library at Harvard University, the Henry E. Huntington Library in San Marino, California, and the Berg Collection of the New York Public Library.

My thanks to Robert Richardson and Wes Mott for their incisive readings of early drafts of, respectively, "Where I Lived, and What I Lived For" and "The Village"; Leslie Wilson, Concord Public Library, for her invaluable help in locating material and for her reading of an early draft of "Conclusion"; and Greg Joly, for the many enjoyable and informative hours of discussion over the meaning of a word or a phrase, and his casting the eye of a printer and a poet over "Economy."

I am grateful to Kathi Anderson, Executive Director of the Walden Woods Project and the Thoreau Institute at Walden Woods, for her support and flexibility in helping me to get this project done.

I am indebted to the various Thoreau scholars who have donated their research to the collections of the Thoreau Society and the Walden Woods Project. These collections, housed at the Thoreau Institute at Walden Woods, Lincoln, Massachusetts, and managed by Walden Woods Project, are an invaluable and unparalleled resource, without which this book could not have been completed.

Also, John Kulka of Yale University Press for his vision and confidence in bringing to fruition a project that was, in many ways, 150 years in the making.

Thanks also to my daughters, Kazia and Zoë, who had hoped that when this book was done, so would be my talking about Thoreau.

And finally, but always foremost in my heart and mind, my wife, Julia Berkley, who has been my toughest critic, staunchest supporter through everything Thoreauvian or not, and dearest friend.

Introduction

"'Walden' published." That is all that Thoreau wrote in his journal on 9 August 1854, the day of the publication of *Walden,* nine years and seven manuscript drafts after his move to Walden Pond. Several months earlier, when he received the first proofs, he simply wrote, "Got first proof of 'Walden.'" It seems like one of the most uneventful of occurrences, given the lack of notice in his journals. After the failure of his first book, *A Week on the Concord and Merrimack Rivers,* he may have been proceeding cautiously and without much hope of success.

The day he moved to Walden Pond was similarly minimalized in his journal: "*July 5. Saturday.* Walden. — Yesterday I came here to live." Perhaps the place itself was less important than being off on his own and he had not yet come to realize what that would mean to him. Although the name Walden, whether referring to the place or the book, is rife with symbol and meaning on both an intellectual and personal level for millions 150 years later, Thoreau had considered several other spots as sites for a possible residence. It didn't become a reality until Ralph Waldo Emerson purchased more than a dozen acres of land on the north side of Walden Pond, a 62-acre, 103-foot-deep glacial kettle-hole pond, and gave Thoreau permission to live there.

Ellery Channing wrote to Thoreau on 5 March 1845: "I see nothing for you in this earth but that field which I once christened 'Briars'; go out upon that, build yourself a hut, and there begin the grand process of devouring yourself alive." Whether Channing was suggesting or confirming the idea, the die was cast. Near the end of March Thoreau borrowed an axe to begin cutting down some white pines. In May his house was framed and he began clearing and plowing two and a half acres for planting.

One of the factors influencing Thoreau's decision to live by him-

Henry David Thoreau, from a daguerreotype by Benjamin D. Maxham, 18 June 1856, as published in *The Writings of Henry D. Thoreau* by Houghton Mifflin in 1906

self in the woods was the time he had spent with Charles Stearns Wheeler at Flint's Pond. Thoreau's friend and Harvard College roommate, Wheeler built a shanty near Flint's Pond in which he stayed at various times between 1836 and 1842. Thoreau stayed at the shanty, probably in 1837, but accounts differ as to the length of time. Although the exact location of Wheeler's shanty is unknown, it was in all probability built on land owned by his brother, William Francis Wheeler. If Thoreau did consider Flint's Pond as a possible site on which to live, it may have been to Francis Wheeler that he appealed.

Thomas Carlyle wrote in a letter to Emerson on 18 August 1841: "After a little groping, this little furnished Cottage, close by the beach of the Solway Firth, was got hold of: here we have been, in absolute seclusion, for a month,—. . . I fancy I feel myself considerably sounder of body and of mind." Having almost certainly read this letter—journals and correspondence were often shared and Thoreau was living in the Emerson household at the time—he would have felt affirmation in his desire to get away.

More significantly as a motivation, Thoreau's move to Walden answered the call Emerson promoted in "The American Scholar":

Young men of the fairest promise, who begin life upon our shores, inflated by the mountain winds, shined upon by all the stars of God, find the earth below not in unison with these, but are hindered from action by the disgust which the principles on which business is managed inspire, and turn drudges, or die of disgust, some of them suicides. What is the remedy? They did not yet see, and thousands of young men as hopeful now crowding to the barriers for the career do not yet see, that if the single man plant himself indomitably on his instincts, and there abide, the huge world will come round to him. Patience,—patience; with the shades of all the good and great for company; and for solace the perspective of your own infinite life; and for work the study and the communication of principles, the making those instincts prevalent, the conversion of the world. Is it not the chief disgrace in the world, not to be an unit;—not to be reckoned one character;—not to yield that peculiar fruit which each man was created to bear. . . . We will walk on our own feet; we will work with our own hands; we will speak our own minds.

On a larger scale, Thoreau was also responding to the challenges to society as suggested by the utopian communities springing up in the early 1840s, and in particular the two with which some of his friends were closely associated: Brook Farm and Fruitlands. He was conducting the same experiments in living that these communities were, but on a smaller scale and from a different direction. He was not trying to re-create society by reinventing how a community should work. Thoreau was questioning the individual's role and obligations, not to society only, but to himself: how should he live, how he should interact with his neighbors, how he should obligate himself to the laws of the society within which he lived. It was through the reform of the one that the many would be reformed. "Every revolution was first a thought in one man's mind," Emerson wrote in "History," "and when the same thought occurs to another man, it is the key to that era. Every reform was once a private opinion, and when it shall be a private opinion again it will solve the problem of the age." A year and a half before moving to Walden Pond, Thoreau wrote in "Paradise (to be) Regained," "We must first succeed alone, that we may enjoy our success together."

Regardless of how much each of the above forces acted on Thoreau, prompting and encouraging him, one of the primary motivations that sent him to Walden was a need for independence and space to work on what became *A Week on the Concord and Merrimack Rivers*. At Walden, Thoreau reexamined the manuscript he had started in 1842, following the sudden and shattering death of his brother, John, to commemorate the two brothers' friendship as embodied in a two-week boat excursion they had taken together in August and September 1839. The actual excursion became less important as it led to Thoreau's consideration of friendship, spirituality, society, and nature, as he incorporated those themes into the book.

Concurrently with his work on this manuscript, his living at the pond had prompted Thoreau's search for the fundamental facts of existence and a separation of the real from the actual. On his third day at Walden Thoreau wrote in his journal: "I wish to meet the facts of life—the vital facts, which are the phenomena or actuality the gods meant to show us—face to face, and so I came down here. Life! who knows what it is, what it does?"

As Thoreau stated in his journal, and repeated in *A Week on the Concord and Merrimack Rivers,* autobiography is preferred over biography: "If I am not I, who will be?" Or as he asked in a post-*Walden* entry of 21 October 1857: "Is not the poet bound to write his own biography? Is there any other work for him but a good journal? We do not wish to know how his imaginary hero, but how he, the actual hero, lived from day to day."

It was the poet's business, he explained in a journal entry on 19 August 1851, to be "continually watching the moods of his mind, as the astronomer watches the aspects of the heavens. What might we not expect from a long life faithfully spent in this wise? . . . As travellers go around the world and report natural objects and phenomena, so faithfully let another stay at home and report the phenomena of his own life."

It must be remembered, however, that *Walden* is not strict autobiography but a literary work in which Thoreau takes liberties for the sake of the artistic integrity of the mythic life he is creating. Differentiating between his actual and his ideal life, Thoreau wrote to Harrison Gray Otis Blake on 27 March 1848: "My actual life is a fact in view of which I have no occasion to congratulate myself, but for my faith and aspiration I have respect. It is from these that I speak." Similarly, he wrote to Calvin Greene on 10 February 1856:

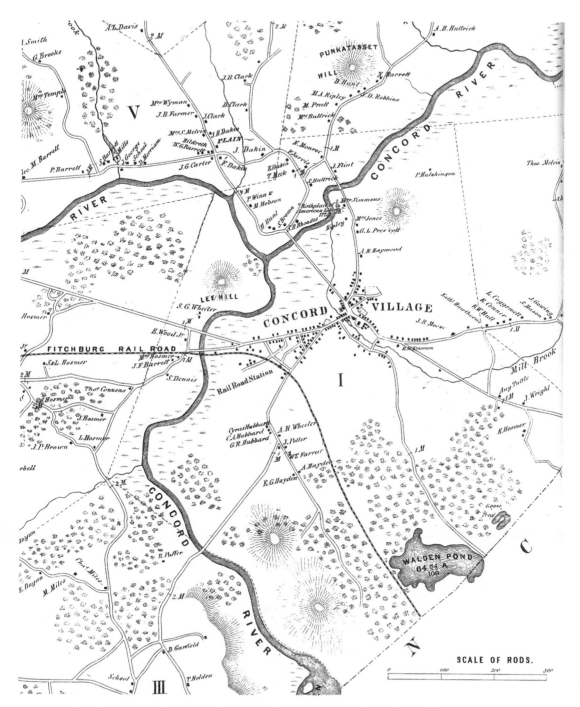

Detail from a map of Concord made in 1852 by Boston cartographer Henry Francis Walling (1825–1888),
with Walden Pond drawn from Thoreau's survey

"You may rely on it that you have the best of me in my books, and that I am not worth seeing personally—the stuttering, blundering, clod-hopper that I am. Even poetry, you know, is in one sense an infinite brag & exaggeration. Not that I do not stand on all that I have written—but what am I to the truth I feebly utter!"

Thoreau wrote about half of what became *Walden* while he was living at Walden Pond. Working his way through finishing and re-writing the manuscript later, on 9 November 1851, he wrote in his journal: "I, too, would fain set down something beside facts. Facts should only be as the frame to my pictures; they should be material to the mythology which I am writing. . . . My facts should be false-hoods to the common sense. I would so state facts that they shall be significant, shall be myths or mythologic."

Mythology was clearly what Thoreau was writing. If one reads *Walden* in any way other than the way it was intended to be read, the reader is predisposed to failure. "To read well, that is, to read true books in a true spirit, is a noble exercise, and one that will task the reader more than any exercise which the customs of the day esteem," Thoreau wrote in "Reading." "It requires a training such as the athletes underwent, the steady intention almost of the whole life to this object. Books must be read as deliberately and reserv-edly as they were written." If one thinks of *Walden* as the record of one man's stay at Walden Pond, reading it as autobiography, it be-comes easy to join the host of those who cavil at Thoreau, focusing on the dinners he ate with the Emersons or the laundry his mother and sisters did for him.

Thoreau is clear in his intentions and in the instructions he pre-sents in "Reading": "The heroic books, even if printed in the char-acter of our mother tongue, will always be in a language dead to degenerate times; and we must laboriously seek the meaning of each word and line, conjecturing a larger sense than common use permits out of what wisdom and valor and generosity we have." Thoreau is not writing about books from a distant past, the clas-sics of spiritual literature, both Eastern and Western. He is writing

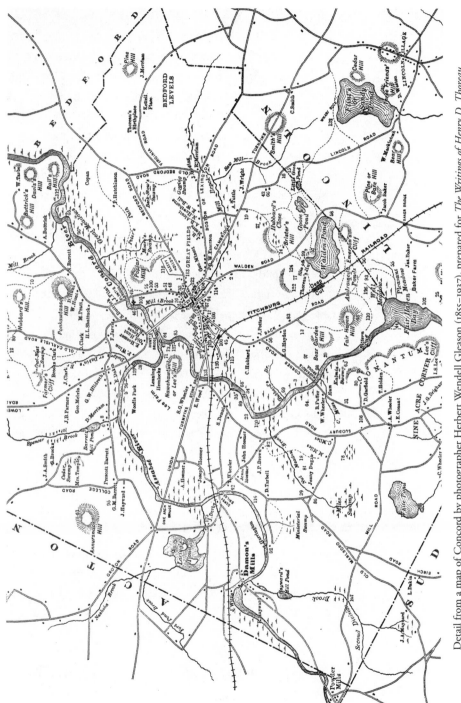

Detail from a map of Concord by photographer Herbert Wendell Gleason (1855–1937), prepared for *The Writings of Henry D. Thoreau,* published by Houghton Mifflin in 1906. Scale: 1″ = 1 mile

about the book you're holding in your hand. *Walden* is a heroic book because it is a book about a hero.

In "Thomas Carlyle and His Works," Thoreau wrote about both Carlyle's *On Heroes, Hero-Worship, and the Heroic in History* and Emerson's *Representative Men* that neither represents "the Man of the Age, come to be called working-man." He continued, "It is obvious that none yet speaks to his condition, for the speaker is not yet in his condition." He understood, as he would write in "Walking," that "the hero is commonly the simplest and obscurest of men." Consciously or not, Thoreau took up the challenge Carlyle wrote to Emerson on 29 August 1845: "I wish you would take an American hero, one whom you really love; and give us a History of him." Thoreau would redefine the heroic as he himself fulfilled the role of hero. By turning the experiment of life into a heroic task he was able to turn *Walden* from a philosophical tract of unattainable goals into a guide for the perplexed. He was able to make a representative man, not of the past, but of the present.

The experiment began on 4 July 1845 and ended on 6 September 1847; Thoreau lived at Walden for two years, two months, and two days. There was no epiphany, no great revelation. It does not make a good ending to the story to say that he left the pond because the Emersons needed him, but the fact remains that the immediate reason for his leaving the woods was Lidian Emerson's request that he care for the Emerson family and household while her husband was away on a lecture tour abroad. Although Emerson did not leave for Europe until the first week in October, Thoreau left the woods a week after being invited and moved directly into the Emerson household. This somewhat abrupt end to his stay at Walden may have prompted his journal entry of 22 January 1852: "I must say that I do not know what made me leave the pond. I left it as unaccountably as I went to it. To speak sincerely, I went there because I had got ready to go; I left it for the same reason."

Thoreau had also completed one of his primary tasks in moving to Walden, to write what would become *A Week on the Concord and Merrimack Rivers*. During his stay he had completed two drafts, the second of which Emerson described as "quite ready" for publication. In addition he had written versions of the essays "Ktaadn," "Thomas Carlyle and His Works," and "Resistance to Civil Government," as well as a 117-page version of *Walden*. (The manuscript went through seven drafts before it was finally published in 1854, nearly doubling in length in the process.)

The two years at the pond may have been the easy part. The task was to turn the experience of Walden into *Walden*. When he talked about the Walden experience in his lecture "History of Myself," he presented the economics of his life at the pond in the basic form that became the "Economy" chapter, but now he needed more.

When he read James Wilkinson's book *The Human Body* in 1851, Thoreau was impressed. "Wilkinson's book," he wrote in his journal, "to some extent realizes what I have dreamed of, — a return to the primitive analogical and derivative sense of words. His ability to trace analogies often leads to a truer word than more remarkable writers have found. . . . The faith he puts in old and current expressions as having sprung from an instinct wiser than science, and safely to be trusted if they can be interpreted. . . . Wilkinson finds a *home* for the imagination. . . . All perception of truth is the detection of an analogy; we reason from our hands to our heads." Understanding this was both a key and a confirmation of what he was trying to do in *Walden*.

"I am serene and satisfied," Thoreau wrote on 18 April 1852, "when the birds fly and the fishes swim as in fable, for the moral is not far off; when the migration of the goose is significant and has a moral to it; when the events of the day have a mythological character, and the most trivial is symbolized. . . . Every incident is a parable of the Great Teacher." It was perhaps this analogous nature of his writings that led to his objection, in "Conclusion," that "in this part of the world it is considered a ground for complaint if a man's writings admit of more than one interpretation."

Thoreau's method of exacting a truth out of an experience was told in a 16 November 1857 letter to Blake:

> Let me suggest a theme for you: to state to yourself precisely and completely what that walk over the mountains amounted to for you,—returning to this essay again and again, until you are satisfied that all that was important in your experience, is in it. Give this good reason to yourself for having gone over the mountains, for mankind is ever going over a mountain. Don't suppose that you can tell it precisely the first dozen times you try, but at 'em again, especially when, after a sufficient pause, you suspect that you are touching the heart or summit of the matter, reiterate your blows there, and account for the mountain to yourself. Not that the story need be long, but it will take a long while to make it short. It did not take very long to get over the mountain, you thought; but have you got over it indeed? If you have been to the top of Mount Washington, let me ask, what did you find there? That is the way they prove witnesses, you know. Going up there and being blown on is nothing. We never do much climbing while we are there, but we eat our luncheon, etc., very much as at home. It is after we get home that we really go over the mountain, if ever. What did the mountain say? What did the mountain do?

That same counsel may be directed to every reader of *Walden*. It may not take very long to read the book or get over the mountain, but then we must ask ourselves the questions: Have you got over it indeed? What did you find there?

Walden forces us to ask questions, and because the answers change, not only from generation to generation, but for each individual from year to year, we are still going over the mountain, going back to the pond, going back to the book. That 150 years later *Walden* is still a vital and relevant text is testimony to the universality of the parables of a great teacher and a tribute to the parable maker, the seer, and the poet that Thoreau was.

The following abbreviations for Thoreau's works are used in the notes:

C   *The Correspondence of Henry David Thoreau,* edited by Walter Harding and Carl Bode, 1958

CP   *Collected Poems of Henry Thoreau,* edited by Carl Bode, 1965

EEM   *Early Essays and Miscellanies,* edited by Joseph J. Moldenhauer and Edwin Moser, 1975

J   *The Journal of Henry Thoreau,* edited by Bradford Torrey and Francis H. Allen, 1906

PJ   *Journal,* edited by John C. Broderick, 1981–

W   *The Writings of Henry D. Thoreau,* Walden edition, 1906

Walden

Illustration from the title page of *Walden,* first edition, 1854

Economy

When I wrote the following pages, or rather the bulk of them, I lived alone, in the woods, a mile from any neighbor,[1] in a house which I had built myself, on the shore of Walden Pond, in Concord, Massachusetts, and earned my living by the labor of my hands only. I lived there two years and two months. At present I am a sojourner[2] in civilized life again.

I should not obtrude my affairs so much on the notice of my readers if very particular inquiries[3] had not been made by my townsmen concerning my mode of life, which some would call impertinent, though they do not appear to me at all impertinent, but, considering the circumstances, very natural and pertinent. Some have asked what I got to eat; if I did not feel lonesome; if I was not afraid; and the like. Others have been curious to learn what portion of my income I devoted to charitable purposes; and some, who have large families, how many poor children I maintained. I will therefore ask those of my readers who feel no particular interest in me to pardon me if I undertake to answer some of these questions in this book. In most books, the *I*, or first person, is omitted; in this it will be retained;[4] that, in respect to egotism, is the main difference. We commonly do not remember that it is, after all, always the first person that is speaking. I should not talk so much about myself if there were any

1 Much nearer than a mile were the Irish railroad laborers whom Thoreau saw on his daily walks, as he mentioned later in this chapter, along with the "shanties which everywhere border our railroads." Although the railroad was completed before he moved to Walden, and the shanties were being sold off, not all the railroad workers had moved on. Even as late as 31 December 1851 Thoreau "observed this afternoon the old Irishwoman at the shanty in the woods" [J 3:166]. Thoreau's residence at Walden also coincided for several months with that of Hugh Coyle, or Quoil. Thoreau noted his proximity in his journal: "I had one neighbor within half a mile for a short time when I first went to the woods, Hugh Quoil" [J 1:414]. In "Former Inhabitants" Thoreau claimed that he had "not remembered him as a neighbor" because of the limited overlap of their time there.

2 Thoreau looked at the stages of his life as temporary sojourns or experiments, and he wrote in an early journal entry, "I don't want to feel as if my life were a sojourn any longer" [J 1:299]. He may have felt this sense of temporariness from having had eight residences in the 12 years after graduating from Harvard in 1837.

3 Particular inquiries had been made even before Thoreau moved to Walden, as he noted in his journal for 24 December 1841, when he had been considering possible sites: "I want to go soon and live away by the pond. . . . But my friends ask what I will do when I get there" [J 1:299]. On 4 February 1846, Thoreau gave a lecture in Concord. "After I lectured here before, this winter," he wrote while at Walden, "I heard that some of my townsmen had expected of me some account of my life at the pond" [J 1:485]. It was probably shortly after that date when Thoreau began to make journal entries for a possible lecture: "I wish to say something to-night not of and concerning the Chinese and Sandwich-Islanders, but *to* and concerning you who hear me, who are said to live in New England" [J 1:395]. He did try to answer some of these inquiries in his Lyceum lectures of 10 and 17 February 1847, and possibly in the previous

month on 19 January, which formed the core of what became the first two chapters of *Walden*.

4 Thoreau wrote in his journal, and repeated in *A Week on the Concord and Merrimack Rivers,* that autobiography is preferred over biography. "If I am not I, who will be?" [J 1:270]. Or again, in a journal entry of 21 October 1857: "Is not the poet bound to write his own biography? Is there any other work for him but a good journal? We do not wish to know how his imaginary hero, but how he, the actual hero, lived from day to day" [J 10:115]. Other Transcendentalists shared the sentiment. Emerson wrote in his essay "The Transcendentalist": "I— this thought which is called I—is the mould into which the world is poured like melted wax." Margaret Fuller (1810–1850), in her essay on Goethe in *The Dial,* wrote: "Writing is worthless except as the record of life. . . . His book should be only an indication of himself."

5 In contrast to this call for a simple account, Thoreau wrote to the Emersons on 8 July 1843: "It is the height of art that on the first perusal plain common sense should appear—on the second severe truth—and on a third beauty—and having these warrants for its depth and reality, we may then enjoy the beauty forever more" [C 125].

6 Hawaiians; Captain James Cook (1728–1779) discovered the Hawaiian Islands in 1778 and named them after the Earl of Sandwich, his patron. Thoreau wrote similarly in "Life Without Principle": "Since *you* are my readers, and I have not been much of a traveler, I will not talk about people a thousand miles off, but come as near home as I can" [W 4:456].

7 Eighteen miles northwest of Boston, Concord was a village of approximately 2,200 people in Thoreau's day. Thoreau urged in his journal of 4 September 1851, "It is worth the while to see your native village thus sometimes, as if you were a traveller passing through it, commenting on your neighbors as strangers" [J 2:452]; but he also wrote: "To travel and 'descry new lands' is to think new thoughts, and have new imaginings. . . . The deepest and most original thinker is the farthest

body else whom I knew as well. Unfortunately, I am confined to this theme by the narrowness of my experience. Moreover, I, on my side, require of every writer, first or last, a simple and sincere account[5] of his own life, and not merely what he has heard of other men's lives; some such account as he would send to his kindred from a distant land; for if he has lived sincerely, it must have been in a distant land to me. Perhaps these pages are more particularly addressed to poor students. As for the rest of my readers, they will accept such portions as apply to them. I trust that none will stretch the seams in putting on the coat, for it may do good service to him whom it fits.

I would fain say something, not so much concerning the Chinese and Sandwich Islanders[6] as you who read these pages, who are said to live in New England; something about your condition, especially your outward condition or circumstances in this world, in this town, what it is, whether it is necessary that it be as bad as it is, whether it cannot be improved as well as not. I have travelled a good deal in Concord;[7] and every where, in shops, and offices, and fields, the inhabitants have appeared to me to be doing penance[8] in a thousand remarkable ways. What I have heard of Bramins[9] sitting exposed to four fires and looking in the face of the sun; or hanging suspended, with their heads downward, over flames; or looking at the heavens over their shoulders "until it becomes impossible for them to resume their natural position, while from the twist of the neck nothing but liquids can pass into the stomach;"[10] or dwelling, chained for life, at the foot of a tree; or measuring with their bodies, like caterpillars, the breadth of vast empires; or standing on one leg on the tops of pillars,—even these forms of conscious penance are hardly more incredible and astonishing than the scenes which I daily witness. The twelve labors of Hercules[11] were trifling in comparison with those which my neighbors have undertaken; for they were only twelve, and had an end; but I could never see that these men slew or captured any monster or finished any labor. They have no friend Iolas[12] to burn with a hot iron the root of the hydra's head, but as soon as one head is crushed, two spring up.[13]

I see young men, my townsmen, whose misfortune it is to have inherited farms, houses, barns, cattle, and farming tools; for these are more easily acquired than got rid of. Better if they had been born in the open pasture and suckled by a wolf,[14] that they might have seen with clearer eyes what field they were called to labor in. Who made them serfs of the soil? Why should they eat their sixty acres,[15] when man is condemned to eat only his peck of dirt?[16] Why should they begin digging their graves as soon as they are born? They have got to live a man's life,[17] pushing all these things before them, and get on as well as they can. How many a poor immortal soul have I met well nigh crushed and smothered under its load, creeping down the road of life, pushing before it a barn seventy-five feet by forty, its Augean stables never cleansed,[18] and one hundred acres of land, tillage, mowing, pasture, and wood-lot! The portionless, who struggle with no such unnecessary inherited encumbrances, find it labor enough to subdue and cultivate a few cubic feet of flesh.

But men labor under a mistake. The better part of the man[19] is soon ploughed into the soil for compost. By a seeming fate,[20] commonly called necessity, they are employed, as it says in an old book,[21] laying up treasures which moth and rust will corrupt and thieves break through and steal.[22] It is a fool's life, as they will find when they get to the end of it, if not before. It is said that Deucalion and Pyrrha created men by throwing stones over their heads behind them: — [23]

Inde genus durum sumus, experiensque laborum,
Et documenta damus quâ simus origine nati.[24]

travelled" [PJ 1:171]. Emerson, in "Self-Reliance," wrote: "The soul is no traveller; the wise man stays at home."

8 Thoreau did not believe in the Christian sacrament of penance. "Repentance is not a free and fair highway to God," he wrote in his 1850 journal. "A wise man will dispense with repentance. It is shocking and passionate. God prefers that you approach him thoughtful, not penitent, though you are the chief of sinners. It is only by forgetting yourself that you draw near to him" [J 2:3].

9 Brahmans, or Brahmins, are the highest of the four major Hindu castes: priest, warrior, merchant, and peasant.

10 This quotation (with minor variants in punctuation) and the other forms of penance Thoreau described are from James Mill (1773–1836), *The History of India* (1817), as published in *The Library of Entertaining Knowledge: The Hindoos* (London, 1834–35).

11 In Greek mythology, son of Zeus, known for his great strength. To be released from his servitude to Eurystheus, he had to complete twelve seemingly impossible labors.

12 Iolas: in Greek mythology, a son of Iphiclus, king of Thessaly, and friend of Hercules.

13 According to Thoreau's primary classical dictionary, John Lemprière's (1765?–1824) *Bibliotheca Classica*: "The second labour of Hercules was to destroy the Lernæan hydra, which had seven heads according to Apollodorus, 50 according to Simonides, and 100 according to Diodorus. This celebrated monster he attacked with his arrows, and soon after he came to a close engagement, and by means of his heavy club he destroyed the heads of his enemy. But this was productive of no advantage; for as soon as one head was beaten to pieces by the club, immediately two sprang up, and the labour of Hercules would have remained unfinished had not he commanded his friend Iolas to burn, with a hot iron, the root of the head which he had crushed to pieces."

14 The legendary founders of Rome, Romulus and Remus, were raised by a she-wolf after being abandoned as infants; Thoreau's February 1851 journal entry adds: "America is the she wolf to-day, and the children of exhausted Europe exposed on her uninhabited and savage shores are the Romulus and Remus who, having derived new life and vigor from her breast, have founded a new Rome in the West" [J 2:151].

15 Used to represent the average Concord farm size, although he used one hundred acres for the same purpose three sentences later.

16 Proverb dating back to at least the early 18th century: "We must all eat a peck of dirt before we die."

17 Possible allusion to William Ellery Channing's (1780–1842) "On the Elevation of the Laboring Classes": "Few men know, as yet, what a man is. They know his clothes, his complexion, his property, his rank, his follies, and his outward life. But the thought of his inward being, his proper humanity, has hardly dawned on multitudes; and yet, who can live a man's life that does not know what is the distinctive worth of a human being?"

18 The fifth of Hercules' twelve labors was to clean the Augean stables, which were home to three thousand oxen and had not been cleaned for many years. He accomplished it by redirecting the course of two rivers through the stables.

19 Allusion to St. Augustine's (354–430) *The City of God:* "This, indeed, is true, that the soul is not the whole man, but the better part of man; the body not the whole, but the inferior part of man."

20 It was a "seeming fate" in that Transcendentalists believed that people created their circumstances. As Thoreau wrote in his 1841 journal: "I make my own time, I make my own terms" [J 1:294]. He summed it up simply in a 20 May 1860 letter: "The principal, the only thing a man makes is his condition, or fate" [C 579]. Emerson had expressed similar views in "The Transcendentalist": "You think me the child of my circumstances: I make my circumstance. . . . You call it the power of circumstance, but it is the power of me."

21 For Thoreau, the Bible was an old book, with the same status as any other ancient scripture. In the "Sunday" chapter of *A Week on the Concord and Merrimack Rivers,* Thoreau grouped all such books together: "The reading which I love best is the scriptures of the several nations, though it happens that I am better acquainted with those of the Hindoos, the Chinese, and the Persians, than of the Hebrews, which I have come to last. Give me one of these bibles, and you have silenced me for a while" [W 1:72]. He clarified his position in an 1850 journal entry: "I do not prefer one religion or philosophy to another. I have no sympathy with the bigotry and ignorance which make transient and partial and puerile distinctions between one man's faith or form of faith and another's, — as Christian and heathen. I pray to be delivered from narrowness, partiality, exaggeration, bigotry. To the philosopher all sects, all nations, are alike. I like Brahma, Hari, Buddha, the Great Spirit, as well as God" [J 2:4].

22 Allusion to Matthew 6:19–20: "Lay not up for yourselves treasures upon earth, where moth and rust doth corrupt, and where thieves break through and steal." All biblical references are to the Authorized (King James) Version.

23 In Greek mythology, Deucalion and Pyrrha were the lone survivors of a great deluge brought upon earth by the wrath of Zeus. To repopulate the earth, they were directed by the oracle of Themis to throw stones behind themselves. Those Deucalion threw became men; those thrown by his wife, Pyrrha, became women.

24 Quoted from Ovid (Publius Ovidius Naso, 43 B.C.E.–17 C.E.), *Metamorphoses* 1.414–15, although Thoreau may have taken the Latin quotation from Sir Walter Raleigh's (1554–1618) *The History of the World.*

Or, as Raleigh rhymes it in his sonorous way, —

> "From thence our kind hard-hearted is, enduring
>   pain and care,
> Approving that our bodies of a stony nature
>   are."[25]

So much for a blind obedience to a blundering oracle, throwing the stones over their heads behind them, and not seeing where they fell.

Most men, even in this comparatively free country,[26] through mere ignorance and mistake, are so occupied with the factitious cares and superfluously coarse labors of life that its finer fruits cannot be plucked by them. Their fingers, from excessive toil, are too clumsy and tremble too much for that. Actually, the laboring man has not leisure for a true integrity day by day; he cannot afford to sustain the manliest relations to men; his labor would be depreciated in the market. He has no time to be any thing but a machine. How can he remember well his ignorance — which his growth requires — who has so often to use his knowledge? We should feed and clothe him gratuitously sometimes, and recruit him with our cordials,[27] before we judge of him. The finest qualities of our nature, like the bloom on fruits,[28] can be preserved only by the most delicate handling. Yet we do not treat ourselves nor one another thus tenderly.

Some of you, we all know, are poor, find it hard to live, are sometimes, as it were, gasping for breath. I have no doubt that some of you who read this book are unable to pay for all the dinners which you have actually eaten, or for the coats and shoes which are fast wearing or are already worn out, and have come to this page to spend borrowed or stolen time, robbing your creditors of an hour. It is very evident what mean and sneaking lives many of you live, for my sight has been whetted by ex-

25 Quoted, with one minor variant in punctuation, from Raleigh's *History of the World,* in which the lines are printed as a quatrain. Thoreau took an early interest in Raleigh: he gave a lecture on the subject before the Concord Lyceum on 8 February 1843, where he also quoted the lines from Ovid and Raleigh's translation [EEM 205]. He may have submitted the lecture for publication in *The Dial,* although it was not printed there, and several pages of it were incorporated into *A Week on the Concord and Merrimack Rivers.*

26 Comparatively free in relation to other countries. As Thoreau well knew, "The United States have a coffle of four millions of slaves" [W 4:430].

27 Something that invigorates, comforts, or raises the spirits; not yet, as in its modern usage, synonymous with liquor.

28 Bloom, a delicate powdery coating found on certain fruits, such as blueberries, grapes, and plums, is an indication of freshness.

29 "On the limits" was an expression for the restrictions placed on the freedom of people who had been jailed for debt. Concord resident Edward Jarvis (1803–1884) wrote in *Traditions and Reminiscences of Concord, Massachusetts:*

> Under the old law many poor debtors were brought to jail to remain there at least for a month or until they were willing to take the poor debtors' oath before a magistrate, or to "swear out." But the law allowed them to have "the liberty of the yard" by giving sureties that they would not transgress the prescribed limits. This was technically called "the liberty of the yard." Perhaps originally it only included the prison yard, but this privilege was extended. . . . This was in order that the debtors might obtain opportunity to work and support themselves. There were generally ten to twenty of these debtors, a few confined in prison, but most of them "out on the limits" as it was termed.

30 Refers to the Slough of Despond, the allegorical moral bog in John Bunyan's (1628–1688) *Pilgrim's Progress.*

31 Latin: another's bronze (i.e., money), although Thoreau translated it here as brass.

32 Habitual business patronage.

33 Felonies.

34 Possible allusion to Shakespeare's *Hamlet* 2.2.248–49: "I could be bounded in a nutshell and count myself a king of infinite space."

35 Ironic allusion to the financial panic of 1837 during which many banks failed.

36 Foreign to the Northern states, as it was a Southern institution, but also foreign or contrary to human nature.

37 It is possible that the idea of a Northern slavery came from Horace Greeley (1811–1872), political reformer, author, journalist, and founder of the New York *Tribune.* Greeley wrote in his 1845 essay "Slavery at Home": "*I understand by Slavery, that condition in which one human being exists*

perience; always on the limits,[29] trying to get into business and trying to get out of debt, a very ancient slough,[30] called by the Latins *æs alienum*,[31] another's brass, for some of their coins were made of brass; still living, and dying, and buried by this other's brass; always promising to pay, promising to pay, to-morrow, and dying to-day, insolvent; seeking to curry favor, to get custom,[32] by how many modes, only not state-prison offences;[33] lying, flattering, voting, contracting yourselves into a nutshell[34] of civility, or dilating into an atmosphere of thin and vaporous generosity, that you may persuade your neighbor to let you make his shoes, or his hat, or his coat, or his carriage, or import his groceries for him; making yourselves sick, that you may lay up something against a sick day, something to be tucked away in an old chest, or in a stocking behind the plastering, or, more safely, in the brick bank;[35] no matter where, no matter how much or how little.

I sometimes wonder that we can be so frivolous, I may almost say, as to attend to the gross but somewhat foreign[36] form of servitude called Negro Slavery, there are so many keen and subtle masters that enslave both north and south. It is hard to have a southern overseer; it is worse to have a northern one;[37] but worst of all when you are the slave-driver of yourself.[38] Talk of a divinity in man![39] Look at the teamster on the highway, wending to market by day or night; does any divinity stir within him?[40] His highest duty to fodder and water his horses! What is his destiny to him compared with the shipping interests? Does not he drive for Squire Make-a-stir?[41] How godlike, how immortal,[42] is he? See how he cowers and sneaks, how vaguely all the day he fears, not being immortal nor divine, but the slave and prisoner of his own opinion of himself, a fame won by his own deeds. Public opinion is a weak tyrant compared with our own private opinion. What a man thinks of himself, that it is which determines, or rather indicates, his fate. Self-emancipation even in the West Indian provinces[43] of the fancy and imagination,[44]—what Wilberforce[45] is there to bring that about? Think, also, of the ladies of the land weaving toilet cushions[46] against the last day, not to betray too green[47] an interest in their fates! As if you could kill time without injuring eternity.

The mass of men lead lives of quiet desperation.[48] What is called resignation is confirmed desperation. From the desperate city you go into the desperate country, and have to console yourself with the bravery of minks and muskrats. A stereotyped but unconscious despair is concealed even under what are called the games and amusements of mankind. There is no play in them, for this comes after work. But it is a characteristic of wisdom not to do desperate things.

When we consider what, to use the words of the catechism, is the chief end of man,[49] and what are the true necessaries and means of life, it appears as if men had deliberately[50] chosen the common mode of living because they preferred it to any other. Yet they honestly think there is no choice left. But alert and healthy natures remember that the sun rose clear. It is never too late to give up our prejudices. No way of thinking or doing, however ancient, can be trusted without proof. What every body echoes or in silence passes by as true to-day may turn out to be falsehood to-morrow, mere smoke of opinion, which some had trusted for a cloud that would sprinkle fertilizing rain on their fields. What old people say you cannot do you try and find that you can. Old deeds for old people, and new deeds for new. Old people did not know enough once, perchance, to fetch fresh fuel to keep the fire a-going; new people put a little dry wood under a pot,[51] and are whirled round the globe with the speed of birds, in a way to kill old people, as the phrase is. Age is no better, hardly so well, qualified for an instruc-

mainly as a convenience for other human beings. . . . You will readily understand, therefore, that if I regard your enterprise with less absorbing interest than you do, it is not that I deem Slavery a less but a greater evil. If I am less troubled concerning the Slavery in Charlestown or New-Orleans, it is because I see so much Slavery in New York, which appears to claim my first efforts. . . . Still less would I undertake to say that the Slavery of the South is not more hideous in kind and degree than that which prevails at the North."

38 This may have been in part influenced by William Ellery Channing's discourse "Spiritual Freedom": "The worst tyrants are those which establish themselves in our own breast. The man who wants force of principle and purpose is a slave, however free the air he breathes."

39 The "divinity within" is an idea prevalent in such writers as Sir Thomas Browne (1605–1682), in *Religio Medici* ("There is surely a peece of Divinity in us; something that was before the Elements, and owes no homage unto the Sun"), and John Milton (1608–1674) in *Paradise Lost* ("they feel / Divinity within them breeding wings" [9.1009–10]). It was this idea that allowed for a personal innate relationship with God and separated the Transcendentalists from the Unitarians, who were grounded in historical Christianity. In *Nature*, Emerson wrote simply: "I am part or particle of God." William Ellery Channing wrote in his sermon "Likeness to God": "Men, as by a natural inspiration, have agreed to speak of conscience as the voice of God, as the Divinity within us. This principle, reverently obeyed, makes us more and more partakers of the moral perfection of the Supreme Being, of that very excellence, which constitutes the rightfulness of his sceptre, and enthrones him over the universe."

40 Allusion to Joseph Addison's (1672–1719) *Cato* 5.1: "'Tis the Divinity that stirs within us; / 'Tis Heaven itself that points out an hereafter, / And intimates eternity to man."

41 Name created by Thoreau, although it may echo such names as Mr. Smooth-it-away and

Mr. Take-it-easy from Nathaniel Hawthorne's "The Celestial Railroad," published in 1843 in the *Democratic Review,* or Dr. Jonas Dryasdust, the fictitious antiquarian to whom Sir Walter Scott (1771–1832) dedicated some of his novels and whom Thoreau recalled in "Thomas Carlyle and His Works" [W 4:334].

42 Humans are godlike in that "God created man in his own image, in the image of God created he him; male and female created he them" [Genesis 1:27], but they can achieve godlike immortality only through "patient continuance in well doing" [Romans 2:7]. This may also be an allusion to Shakespeare's *Hamlet* 2.2.293–96: "What a piece of work is a man! . . . in apprehension how like a god."

43 Archipelago off Central America here used to symbolize something distant. This is also an allusion to Emerson's first public statement against slavery, "Emancipation in the British West Indies."

44 These two terms were used and defined synonymously until Samuel Taylor Coleridge (1772–1834) in *Biographia Literaria* began to develop a distinction between the two: "IMAGINATION I hold to be the living Power and prime Agent of all human Perception, and as a repetition in the finite mind of the eternal act of creation. . . . Fancy is indeed no other than a mode of Memory emancipated from the order of time and space." This distinction was adopted by the Transcendentalists, as when Emerson wrote in "History" that Greek fables are the "proper creations of the imagination and not of the fancy." One of the clearest definitions is by British art critic John Ruskin (1819–1900) in *Modern Painters:* "The fancy sees the outside, and is able to give a portrait of the outside, clear, brilliant, and full of detail. The imagination sees the heart and inner nature, and makes them felt, but is often obscure, mysterious, and interrupted, in its giving of outer detail."

45 William Wilberforce (1759–1833), sponsor of the Slavery Abolition Act, which was passed in 1833 and freed all the slaves in the British Empire. Wilberforce, who had a strong interest in abolition

after his conversion to evangelical Christianity in 1787, helped form the Anti-Slavery Society in England in 1823.

46 Popular in Thoreau's day, these were embroidered cushions women made for their dressing tables (toilets). This may be an allusion to Penelope, wife of Odysseus in Homer's *Odyssey.* To delay her unwanted suitors while waiting for her husband's return, Penelope promised to give an answer when she finished weaving a winding-sheet for Laërtes, Odysseus's father. To prevent the last day from arriving, at night she unwound what she had woven the previous day.

47 Immature, as in Shakespeare's *Hamlet* 1.3.101, in which Polonius referred to Ophelia as a "green girl."

48 The first three sentences of this paragraph first appeared at the end of two rejected manuscript leaves (ca. 1848) from *A Week on the Concord and Merrimack Rivers,* in which Thoreau described an organ-grinder he met in New Hampshire in 1838. A variant of the organ-grinder episode appeared in Version 4 of *Walden* before being ultimately dropped.

49 According to the Westminster Shorter Catechism in the *New England Primer,* the chief end of man is to glorify God and enjoy him forever. Later in this chapter Thoreau wrote: "Our hymn-books resound with a melodious cursing of God and enduring Him forever." In the "Where I Lived, And What I Lived For" chapter Thoreau wrote that people do not know whether life "is of the devil or of God, and have *somewhat hastily* concluded that it is the chief end of man here to 'glorify God and enjoy him forever.'"

50 Acting deliberately was crucial to Thoreau, as he wrote on 23 August 1851: "Resolve to read no book, to take no walk, to undertake no enterprise, but such as you can endure to give an account of to yourself. Live thus deliberately for the most part" [J 2:421].

51 Reference to the steam engine that powered ships and the railroads.

tor as youth, for it has not profited so much as it has lost. One may almost doubt if the wisest man has learned any thing of absolute value by living. Practically, the old have no very important advice to give the young, their own experience has been so partial, and their lives have been such miserable failures, for private reasons, as they must believe; and it may be that they have some faith left which belies that experience, and they are only less young than they were. I have lived some thirty years on this planet, and I have yet to hear the first syllable of valuable or even earnest advice from my seniors. They have told me nothing, and probably cannot tell me any thing, to the purpose. Here is life, an experiment to a great extent untried by me; but it does not avail me that they have tried it. If I have any experience which I think valuable, I am sure to reflect that this my Mentors[52] said nothing about.

One farmer says to me, "You cannot live on vegetable food solely, for it furnishes nothing to make bones with;" and so he religiously devotes a part of his day to supplying his system with the raw material of bones; walking all the while he talks behind his oxen, which, with vegetable-made bones, jerk him and his lumbering plough along in spite of every obstacle. Some things are really necessaries of life in some circles, the most helpless and diseased, which in others are luxuries merely, and in others still are entirely unknown.

The whole ground of human life seems to some to have been gone over by their predecessors, both the heights and the valleys, and all things to have been cared for. According to Evelyn,[53] "the wise Solomon[54] prescribed ordinances for the very distances of trees; and the Roman prætors have decided how often you may go into your neighbor's land to gather the acorns which fall on it without trespass, and what share belongs to that neighbor." Hippocrates[55] has even left directions how we should cut our nails; that is, even with the ends of the fin-

52 The specific reference, beyond the meaning of wise teacher or counselor, is to Mentor, the protector and teacher of Telemachus, son of Odysseus, in Homer's *Odyssey*.

53 John Evelyn (1620–1706), English diarist and horticulturist.

54 Solon, in Evelyn's *Sylva, or a Discourse of Forest-Trees*. The quotation is abridged from *Sylva*, where it begins: "Nay, the Wise *Solon* prescribed *Ordinances* for the very *distances* of *Trees*." Thoreau often emphasized his changes with underscoring, but he didn't here, so it is unclear whether he intentionally changed "Solon" to "Solomon." Solon (ca. 638–558 B.C.E.) was an Athenian statesman and poet who laid the foundations of Athenian democracy. Solomon (ca. 970–ca. 930 B.C.E.), a king of ancient Israel known for his wisdom, was the son of David and was traditionally associated with the Song of Solomon, Ecclesiastes, and Proverbs.

55 Greek physician (ca. 460–ca. 377 B.C.E.), known as the Father of Medicine.

56 Allusion to Hippocrates' "In the Surgery": "The nails neither to exceed nor come short of the finger tips."

57 Quoted from the Hindu scripture Vishnu Purana: "Be not afflicted, my child, for who shall efface what thou hast formerly done, or shall assign to thee what thou has left undone?" The Puranas refer to any of a class of Sanskrit sacred writings on Hindu mythology, folklore, etc., of varying date and origin. They are regarded as divinely inspired texts, each glorifying a particular god, but are also encyclopedias of secular as well as religious knowledge. There are eighteen main Puranas, coincidentally the same number of chapters as in *Walden*.

58 Pun: light from the sun, as well as a source of mental or spiritual inspiration and point of view.

59 The biblical allotted life span, as in Psalms 90:10: "The days of our years are threescore years and ten."

60 In the journal passage of 5 January 1851, on which this is based, Thoreau identified this voice as "the voice of my destiny" [J 2:137].

gers, neither shorter nor longer.[56] Undoubtedly the very tedium and ennui which presume to have exhausted the variety and the joys of life are as old as Adam. But man's capacities have never been measured; nor are we to judge of what he can do by any precedents, so little has been tried. Whatever have been thy failures hitherto, "be not afflicted, my child, for who shall assign to thee what thou hast left undone?"[57]

We might try our lives by a thousand simple tests; as, for instance, that the same sun which ripens my beans illumines at once a system of earths like ours. If I had remembered this it would have prevented some mistakes. This was not the light[58] in which I hoed them. The stars are the apexes of what wonderful triangles! What distant and different beings in the various mansions of the universe are contemplating the same one at the same moment! Nature and human life are as various as our several constitutions. Who shall say what prospect life offers to another? Could a greater miracle take place than for us to look through each other's eyes for an instant? We should live in all the ages of the world in an hour; ay, in all the worlds of the ages. History, Poetry, Mythology!—I know of no reading of another's experience so startling and informing as this would be.

The greater part of what my neighbors call good I believe in my soul to be bad, and if I repent of any thing, it is very likely to be my good behavior. What demon possessed me that I behaved so well? You may say the wisest thing you can old man,—you who have lived seventy years,[59] not without honor of a kind,—I hear an irresistible voice[60] which invites me away from all that. One generation abandons the enterprises of another like stranded vessels.

I think that we may safely trust a good deal more than we do. We may waive just so much care of ourselves as we honestly bestow elsewhere. Nature is as well adapted to our weakness as to our strength. The incessant anxiety and strain of some is a well nigh incurable form of disease. We are made to exaggerate the importance of what work we do; and yet how much is not done by us! or, what if we had been taken sick? How vigilant we are! determined not to live by faith if we can avoid it; all the day long on the alert, at night we unwillingly say our prayers and commit ourselves to uncertainties. So thoroughly and sincerely are we compelled to live, reverencing our life, and denying the possibility of change. This is the only way, we say; but there are as many ways as there can be drawn radii from one centre. All change is a miracle to contemplate; but it is a miracle which is taking place every instant.[61] Confucius said, "To know that we know what we know, and that we do not know what we do not know, that is true knowledge."[62] When one man has reduced a fact of the imagination to be a fact to his understanding,[63] I foresee that all men at length establish their lives on that basis.

Let us consider for a moment what most of the trouble and anxiety which I have referred to is about, and how much it is necessary that we be troubled, or, at least, careful. It would be some advantage to live a primitive and frontier life, though in the midst of an outward civilization, if only to learn what are the gross necessaries of life and what methods have been taken to obtain them; or even to look over the old day-books[64] of the merchants, to see what it was that men most commonly bought at the stores, what they stored, that is, what are the grossest groceries.[65] For the improvements of ages have had but little influence on the essential laws of man's existence; as our skeletons, probably, are not to be distinguished from those of our ancestors.

By the words, *necessary of life,* I mean whatever, of all that man obtains by his own exertions, has been from the first, or from long use has become, so important to

61 Unlike the Unitarians, who believed that the miracles of Jesus were performed as part of a special Providence that was not in the normal course of nature, Transcendentalists thought miracles were not relegated to the past. Emerson in his "Divinity School Address" wrote: "He [Jesus] spoke of miracles; for he felt that man's life was a miracle, and all that man doth, and he knew that this daily miracle shines, as the man is diviner. But the very word Miracle, as pronounced by Christian churches, gives a false impression; it is Monster. It is not one with the blowing clover and the falling rain." Thoreau wrote in his journal of 9 June 1850: "Men talk about Bible miracles because there is no miracle in their lives" [J 2:33].

62 Confucius (ca. 551?–478? B.C.E.), Chinese philosopher of ethical precepts for good management of family and society; quoted from Confucius, *Analects* 2.17. For the selection in *The Dial* (April 1843), Thoreau used, with a slight variant, the Joshua Marshman (1768–1837) translation from "Morals of Confucius" in *The Phenix: A Collection of Old and Rare Fragments:* "Having knowledge, to apply it; not having knowledge, to confess your ignorance; this is (real) knowledge." In *Walden* Thoreau used his own translation of Jean-Pierre-Guillaume Pauthier's (1801–1873) French translation found in *Confucius et Mencius: Les Quatre Livres de Philosophie Moral et Politique de la Chine* (Paris, 1841).

63 Transcendentalists made a distinction, not always commonly observed, between understanding and reason. The understanding examines what can be proved, while reason intuits what is beyond proof, which George Ripley (1802–1880) defined in *Discourses on the Philosophy of Religion* as "the immediate perception of Truth." Emerson explained the distinction in a letter to his brother in 1834: "Reason is the highest faculty of the soul—what we mean often by the soul itself; it never *reasons*, never proves, it simply perceives; it is vision. The Understanding toils all the time, compares, contrives, adds, argues, near sighted but strongsighted, dwelling in the present the expedient the customary. . . . Reason is potentially perfect in every man—Understanding in very different degrees of strength." Thoreau wrote in his journal of 23 July 1851 that his genius, or reason, "makes distinctions which my understanding cannot, and which my senses do not report" [J 2:337].

64 Thoreau enjoyed inspecting these old account books of business transactions. In an early journal entry he copied more than 20 entries from a fisherman's 1805 daybook [J 1:474], and in 1854 he copied entries from or commented on those of Ephraim Jones (1705–1756) from 1741 to 1750 [J 6:77–80, 88, 94–96, 101]. These were incorporated into a late draft of the "Winter Animals" chapter.

65 A pun Thoreau enjoyed enough to use twice in this chapter.

66 Habit, or learned behavior, as second nature has been expressed in the works of Diogenes (412–323 B.C.E.), Aristotle (384–322 B.C.E.), Marcus Tullius Cicero (ca. 106–43 B.C.E.), Plutarch (ca. 46–ca. 120), Michel de Montaigne (1533–1592), and others. First, or primary, nature would be behavior that is innate.

67 Charles Darwin (1809–1882), English naturalist, who visited South America in 1831 and published his account in 1839 as the third volume in *Narrative of the Surveying Voyages of his Majesty's Ships Adventure and Beagle.*

68 An archipelago off the southern tip of South America. Spanish: Land of fire.

69 Quoted from Darwin's *Narrative of the Surveying Voyages of his Majesty's Ships Adventure and Beagle.*

70 The aborigines of Australia, which, from its discovery in the 17th century by the Dutch, had been called New Holland.

71 Baron Justus von Liebig (1803–1873), German organic chemist, discovered that body heat is the result of combustion of foods in the body. In his works he referred to the human body as a furnace, and wrote of food burning in the body as it would in a fireplace. Thoreau's understanding of Liebig may have come from a review of "Liebig's Animal

human life that few, if any, whether from savageness, or poverty, or philosophy, ever attempt to do without it. To many creatures there is in this sense but one necessary of life, Food. To the bison of the prairie it is a few inches of palatable grass, with water to drink; unless he seeks the Shelter of the forest or the mountain's shadow. None of the brute creation requires more than Food and Shelter. The necessaries of life for man in this climate may, accurately enough, be distributed under the several heads of Food, Shelter, Clothing, and Fuel; for not till we have secured these are we prepared to entertain the true problems of life with freedom and a prospect of success. Man has invented, not only houses, but clothes and cooked food; and possibly from the accidental discovery of the warmth of fire, and the consequent use of it, at first a luxury, arose the present necessity to sit by it. We observe cats and dogs acquiring the same second nature.[66] By proper Shelter and Clothing we legitimately retain our own internal heat; but with an excess of these, or of Fuel, that is, with an external heat greater than our own internal, may not cookery properly be said to begin? Darwin,[67] the naturalist, says of the inhabitants of Tierra del Fuego,[68] that while his own party, who were well clothed and sitting close to a fire, were far from too warm, these naked savages, who were farther off, were observed, to his great surprise, "to be streaming with perspiration at undergoing such a roasting."[69] So, we are told, the New Hollander[70] goes naked with impunity, while the European shivers in his clothes. Is it impossible to combine the hardiness of these savages with the intellectualness of the civilized man? According to Liebig, man's body is a stove, and food the fuel which keeps up the internal combustion in the lungs.[71] In cold weather we eat more, in warm less. The animal heat[72] is the result of a slow combustion, and disease and death take place when this is too rapid; or for want of fuel, or from some defect in the draught, the fire goes out. Of course the vital heat[73] is not to be confounded with fire; but so much for analogy. It appears, therefore, from the above list, that the expression, *animal life,* is nearly synonymous with the expression, *animal heat;* for while Food may be regarded as the Fuel which keeps up the fire within us,—and Fuel serves only to prepare that Food or to increase the warmth of our bodies by addition from without,—Shelter and Clothing also serve only to retain the *heat* thus generated and absorbed.

The grand necessity, then, for our bodies, is to keep warm, to keep the vital heat in us. What pains we accordingly take, not only with our Food, and Clothing, and Shelter, but with our beds, which are our night-clothes, robbing the nests and breasts of birds to prepare this shelter within a shelter, as the mole has its bed of grass and leaves at the end of its burrow! The poor man is wont to complain that this is a cold world; and to cold, no less physical than social, we refer directly a great part of our ails. The summer, in some climates, makes possible to man a sort of Elysian life.[74] Fuel, except to cook his Food, is then unnecessary; the sun is his fire, and many of the fruits are sufficiently cooked by its rays; while Food generally is more various, and more easily obtained, and Clothing and Shelter are wholly or half unnecessary. At the present day, and in this country, as I find by my own experience, a few implements, a knife, an axe, a spade, a wheelbarrow, &c., and for the studious, lamplight, stationery, and access to a few books, rank next to necessaries, and can all be obtained at a trifling cost. Yet some, not wise, go to the other side of the globe, to barbarous and unhealthy regions, and devote themselves to trade for ten or twenty years, in order that they may live,—that is, keep comfortably warm,—and die in New England at last.[75] The luxuriously rich are not simply kept comfortably warm, but unnaturally hot; as I implied before, they are cooked,[76] of course *à la mode.*

Chemistry" in the October 1842 issue of *The North American Review:*

> With him, respiration is but a slow combustion. Oxygen is absorbed from the air into the blood, to support this combustion, and the different kinds of food, received into the body and digested, supply the fuel. These meet in the course of the circulation, and combine; and the carbonic acid and water which proceed from the combination, are carried off by the lungs; with processes and results precisely analogous to those of ordinary combustion, only that they are produced more slowly. Thus the lungs are both the hearth for the supply of air, or its oxygen, and the chimney for carrying away the smoke; while the stomach brings in the necessary chips and coal to keep up the flame. . . .
>
> To make use of a familiar, but not on that account a less just illustration, the animal body acts, in this respect, as a furnace, which we supply with fuel.

72 Heat generated in the body of a warm-blooded vertebrate as the result of physiological and metabolic processes.

73 From Aristotle, who, in "On Youth and Old Age, On Life and Death, On Breathing," developed the concept of heat as the vital force without which life cannot exist.

74 Reference to Elysium, in Greek mythology, where souls rested after death.

75 Reference to New Englanders involved in the China trade, which was then at its height.

76 Pun: both heated and ruined, as in the colloquialism "his goose is cooked."

Most of the luxuries, and many of the so called comforts of life, are not only not indispensable, but positive hinderances to the elevation of mankind. With respect to luxuries and comforts, the wisest have ever lived a more simple and meagre life than the poor.[77] The ancient philosophers, Chinese, Hindoo, Persian, and Greek, were a class than which none has been poorer in outward riches, none so rich in inward. We know not much about them. It is remarkable that *we* know so much of them as we do. The same is true of the more modern reformers and benefactors of their race. None can be an impartial or wise observer of human life but from the vantage ground of what *we* should call voluntary poverty. Of a life of luxury the fruit is luxury, whether in agriculture, or commerce, or literature, or art. There are nowadays professors of philosophy, but not philosophers. Yet it is admirable to profess because it was once admirable to live. To be a philosopher is not merely to have subtle thoughts, nor even to found a school, but so to love wisdom as to live according to its dictates, a life of simplicity, independence, magnanimity, and trust. It is to solve some of the problems of life, not only theoretically, but practically.[78] The success of great scholars and thinkers is commonly a courtier-like success, not kingly, not manly. They make shift to live merely by conformity, practically as their fathers did, and are in no sense the progenitors of a nobler race of men. But why do men degenerate ever? What makes families run out? What is the nature of the luxury which enervates and destroys nations? Are we sure that there is none of it in our own lives? The philosopher is in advance of his age even in the outward form of his life. He is not fed, sheltered, clothed, warmed, like his contemporaries. How can a man be a philosopher and not maintain his vital heat by better methods than other men?

When a man is warmed by the several modes which I have described, what does he want next? Surely not

---

77 Thoreau described his friend George Minott, sometimes Minot (1783–1861), as "not penurious but merely simple. . . . [Y]et he is not poor, for he does not want riches" [J 3:42].

78 It was central to Thoreau's philosophy that action follow thought. As Emerson wrote in "The Method of Nature": "The one condition coupled with the gift of truth is its use. That man shall be learned who reduceth his learning to practice."

more warmth of the same kind, as more and richer food, larger and more splendid houses, finer and more abundant clothing, more numerous incessant and hotter fires, and the like. When he has obtained those things which are necessary to life, there is another alternative than to obtain the superfluities; and that is, to adventure on life now, his vacation from humbler toil[79] having commenced. The soil, it appears, is suited to the seed, for it has sent its radicle[80] downward, and it may now send its shoot upward also with confidence. Why has man rooted himself thus firmly in the earth, but that he may rise in the same proportion into the heavens above? — for the nobler plants are valued for the fruit they bear at last in the air and light, far from the ground,[81] and are not treated like the humbler esculents,[82] which, though they may be biennials, are cultivated only till they have perfected their root, and often cut down at top for this purpose, so that most would not know them in their flowering season.

I do not mean to prescribe rules to strong and valiant natures, who will mind their own affairs whether in heaven or hell, and perchance build more magnificently and spend more lavishly than the richest, without ever impoverishing themselves, not knowing how they live, — if, indeed, there are any such, as has been dreamed; nor to those who find their encouragement and inspiration in precisely the present condition of things, and cherish it with the fondness and enthusiasm of lovers, — and, to some extent, I reckon myself in this number; I do not speak to those who are well employed, in whatever circumstances, and they know whether they are well employed or not; — but mainly to the mass of men who are discontented, and idly complaining of the hardness of their lot or of the times, when they might improve them. There are some who complain most energetically and inconsolably of any, because they are, as they say,

79 Thoreau is specific that this is a vacation from humble toil, not all toil, to free oneself for more significant labor. He wrote in his journal, "What is leisure but opportunity for more complete and entire action?" [J 1:293–94]. Or as Emerson wrote in *Nature:* "A man is fed, not that he may be fed, but that he may work."

80 The part of a plant embryo that develops into the root system.

81 Amos Bronson Alcott (1799–1888) made a distinction between vegetables that grew upward or aspired, such as wheat and apples, and those that grew downward, such as potatoes, beets, and radishes. Despite this distinction, the Alcotts did eat potatoes.

82 Edible plants.

83 Symbol of what attracts but also binds, as in Edmund Spenser's (1552–1599) *The Fairie Queene* 3.7: "A fool I to him firmly hold, that loves his fetters though they were of gold."

84 The Transcendentalists made a distinction between actual and real, or ideal, existence. Thoreau wrote in his journal: "On one side of man is the actual, and on the other the ideal. The former is the province of the reason" [J 1:360], and "I find the actual to be far less real to me than the imagined. Why this singular prominence and importance is given to the former, I do not know. In proportion as that which possesses my thoughts is removed from the actual, it impresses me. I have never met with anything so truly visionary and accidental as some actual events" [J 2:43].

85 The term originated in the 16th century as "in the nick," the now obsolete word "nick" meaning the critical moment, or from tallies marked with nicks or notches. If a man entered chapel just before the doors closed, he would be just in time to get nicked, and would therefore enter at the nick of time.

86 Although Thoreau often carried a notched stick for measuring, his allusion here is to Daniel Defoe's (1660–1731) Robinson Crusoe, who kept track of time by making notches on a wooden post. Thoreau noted in his journal: "We should make our notch every day on our characters, as Robinson Crusoe on his stick" [J 1:220]. The self-sufficient independence of Crusoe appealed to Thoreau, who referred to him in "Ktaadn" and *A Week on the Concord and Merrimack Rivers.*

87 Probable allusion to Thomas Moore's (1779–1852) *Lalla Rookh:* "This narrow isthmus 'twixt two boundless seas, / The past, the future,—two eternities!"

88 Toeing the line refers to the instructions sailors were given during muster to place their toes touching the seam between deck planks, ensuring a neat alignment of rows.

89 These three symbols have been subject to scholarly and personal interpretation and debate since publication, but no analysis has been gen-

doing their duty. I also have in my mind that seemingly wealthy, but most terribly impoverished class of all, who have accumulated dross, but know not how to use it, or get rid of it, and thus have forged their own golden or silver fetters.[83]

If I should attempt to tell how I have desired to spend my life in years past, it would probably surprise those of my readers who are somewhat acquainted with its actual history;[84] it would certainly astonish those who know nothing about it. I will only hint at some of the enterprises which I have cherished.

In any weather, at any hour of the day or night, I have been anxious to improve the nick of time,[85] and notch it on my stick[86] too; to stand on the meeting of two eternities,[87] the past and future, which is precisely the present moment; to toe that line.[88] You will pardon some obscurities, for there are more secrets in my trade than in most men's, and yet not voluntarily kept, but inseparable from its very nature. I would gladly tell all that I know about it, and never paint "No Admittance" on my gate.

I long ago lost a hound, a bay horse, and a turtle-dove,[89] and am still on their trail. Many are the travellers I have spoken concerning them, describing their tracks and what calls they answered to. I have met one or two who had heard the hound, and the tramp of the horse, and even seen the dove disappear behind a cloud, and they seemed as anxious to recover them as if they had lost them themselves.

To anticipate, not the sunrise and the dawn merely, but, if possible, Nature herself! How many mornings, summer and winter, before yet any neighbor was stirring about his business, have I been about mine! No doubt, many of my townsmen have met me returning from this enterprise, farmers starting for Boston in the twilight,[90] or woodchoppers going to their work. It is true, I never assisted the sun materially in his rising, but, doubt not, it was of the last importance only to be present at it.

So many autumn, ay, and winter days, spent outside the town, trying to hear what was in the wind, to hear and carry it express! I well nigh sunk all my capital in it, and lost my own breath into the bargain, running in the face of it. If it had concerned either of the political parties, depend upon it, it would have appeared in the Gazette[91] with the earliest intelligence. At other times watching from the observatory of some cliff or tree, to telegraph any new arrival;[92] or waiting at evening on the hill-tops for the sky to fall, that I might catch something, though I never caught much, and that, manna-wise, would dissolve again in the sun.[93]

For a long time I was reporter to a journal, of no very wide circulation, whose editor has never yet seen fit to print the bulk of my contributions,[94] and, as is too common with writers, I got only my labor for my pains. However, in this case my pains were their own reward.

For many years I was self-appointed inspector of snow storms and rain storms, and did my duty faithfully; surveyor,[95] if not of highways, then of forest paths and all across-lot[96] routes, keeping them open, and ravines bridged and passable at all seasons, where the public heel had testified to their utility.

I have looked after the wild stock of the town, which give a faithful herdsman a good deal of trouble by leaping fences; and I have had an eye to the unfrequented nooks and corners of the farm; though I did not always know whether Jonas or Solomon[97] worked in a particular field to-day; that was none of my business. I have watered[98] the red huckleberry, the sand cherry and the nettle tree, the red pine and the black ash, the white grape and the yellow violet, which might have withered else in dry seasons.

In short, I went on thus for a long time, I may say it

erally accepted as valid. Thoreau himself offered the following to Benjamin B. Wiley on 26 April 1857: "If others have their losses, which they are busy repairing, so have I *mine*, & their hound & horse may *perhaps* be the symbols of some of them. But also I have lost, or am in danger of losing, a far finer & more etherial treasure, which commonly no loss of which they are conscious will symbolize—this I answer hastily & with some hesitation, according as I now understand my own words" [C 478]. This may in part be related to the quotation from the Chinese philosopher Mencius (Meng-tse, 371–289? B.C.E.) in *A Week on the Concord and Merrimack Rivers:* "If one loses a fowl or a dog, he knows well how to seek them again; if one loses the sentiments of his heart, he does not know how to seek them again. . . . The duties of practical philosophy consist only in seeking after those sentiments of the heart which we have lost; that is all" [W 1:280].

90 Many Concord farmers brought their crops to market in Boston.

91 Possible reference to the *Yeoman's Gazette* published in Concord with variant titles from 1826 to 1840, although the term may refer to any gazette or newspaper.

92 Although electric telegraphy began in the 1830s and was being installed in Concord in 1851, here Thoreau is referring to the semaphore, as indicated by his journal of 25 July 1851 in which he referred to the telegraph as "movable signs on a pole with holes in them for the passage of the wind" [J 2:344].

93 Manna, which rained from the heavens, was the food God provided the children of Israel in the Sinai desert. According to Exodus 16:21: "When the sun waxed hot, it melted."

94 Probable reference to Thoreau's own journals, although possibly also referring to *The Dial* (1840–44). As editor of *The Dial*, Margaret Fuller had rejected Thoreau's submissions.

95 In 1840 Thoreau purchased a combination leveling instrument and circumferentor. His intention was to introduce surveying in the school he and his brother John ran, to give the study of mathematics a more practical and concrete application. This led to a lifelong source of income as a surveyor, and he made more than 150 surveys in the Concord area. The earliest extant record of a Thoreau survey is a receipt of 18 December 1845 from the Misses Hosmer.

96 It was part of Thoreau's enjoyment of the natural world to not be controlled by fences and property lines. When visiting Canada in 1850 he went "across lots in spite of numerous signs threatening the severest penalties to trespassers" [W 5:98]. On this preferred method of travel Thoreau wrote: "It is true we as yet take liberties and go across lots, and steal, or 'hook,' a good many things, but we naturally take fewer and fewer liberties every year, as we meet with more resistance. In old countries, as England, going across lots is out of the question. You must walk in some beaten path or other, though it may [be] a narrow one. We are tending to the same state of things here, when practically a few will have grounds of their own, but most will have none to walk over but what the few allow them" [J 14:305–6].

97 Laborers, but with an allusion to Matthew 12:41–42: "A greater than Jonas is here . . . a greater than Solomon is here."

98 Reference to urinating in the woods.

99 In a self-referencing pun, Thoreau wrote in "Paradise (to be) Regained": "A thoroughbred business man cannot enter heartily upon the business of life without first looking into his accounts" [W 4:283].

100 Strolling Indians were not an uncommon sight. In an early November 1850 journal entry Thoreau noted: "A squaw came to our door to-day with two pappooses, and said, 'Me want a pie.' Theirs is not common begging. You are merely the rich Indian who shares his goods with the poor. They merely offer you an opportunity to be generous and hospitable" [J 2:83].

101 Samuel Hoar (1778–1856), prominent lawyer and Concord's leading citizen. He was the father of Thoreau's friends Elizabeth (1814–1878) and

without boasting, faithfully minding my business, till it became more and more evident that my townsmen would not after all admit me into the list of town officers, nor make my place a sinecure with a moderate allowance. My accounts,[99] which I can swear to have kept faithfully, I have, indeed, never got audited, still less accepted, still less paid and settled. However, I have not set my heart on that.

Not long since, a strolling Indian[100] went to sell baskets at the house of a well-known lawyer[101] in my neighborhood. "Do you wish to buy any baskets?" he asked. "No, we do not want any," was the reply. "What!" exclaimed the Indian as he went out the gate, "do you mean to starve us?" Having seen his industrious white neighbors so well off,— that the lawyer had only to weave arguments, and by some magic wealth and standing followed, he had said to himself; I will go into business; I will weave baskets; it is a thing which I can do. Thinking that when he had made the baskets he would have done his part, and then it would be the white man's to buy them. He had not discovered that it was necessary for him to make it worth the other's while to buy them, or at least make him think that it was so, or to make something else which it would be worth his while to buy. I too had woven a kind of basket of a delicate texture, but I had not made it worth any one's while to buy them.[102] Yet not the less, in my case, did I think it worth my while to weave them, and instead of studying how to make it worth men's while to buy my baskets, I studied rather how to avoid the necessity of selling them. The life which men praise and regard as successful is but one kind. Why should we exaggerate any one kind at the expense of the others?

Finding that my fellow-citizens were not likely to offer me any room in the court house, or any curacy or living any where else, but I must shift for myself, I turned my face more exclusively than ever to the woods, where I was better known. I determined to go into business[103] at once, and not wait to acquire the usual capital, using such slender means as I had already got. My purpose in going to Walden Pond was not to live cheaply nor to live dearly there, but to transact some private business[104] with the fewest obstacles; to be hindered from accomplishing which for want of a little common sense, a little enterprise and business talent, appeared not so sad as foolish.

I have always endeavored to acquire strict business habits;[105] they are indispensable to every man. If your trade is with the Celestial Empire,[106] then some small counting house on the coast, in some Salem harbor,[107] will be fixture enough. You will export such articles as the country affords, purely native products, much ice and pine timber and a little granite,[108] always in native bottoms.[109] These will be good ventures. To oversee all the details yourself in person; to be at once pilot and captain, and owner and underwriter; to buy and sell and keep the accounts; to read every letter received, and write or read every letter sent; to superintend the discharge of imports night and day; to be upon many parts of the coast almost at the same time;—often the richest freight will be discharged upon a Jersey shore;[110]—to be your own telegraph, unweariedly sweeping the horizon, speaking all passing vessels bound coastwise; to keep up a steady despatch of commodities, for the supply of such a distant and exorbitant market; to keep yourself informed of the state of the markets, prospects of war and peace every where, and anticipate the tendencies of trade and civilization,—taking advantage of the results of all exploring expeditions, using new passages and all improvements in navigation;—charts to be studied, the position of reefs and new lights and buoys to be ascertained, and ever, and ever, the logarithmic tables to be corrected, for by the error of some calculator the vessel often splits upon a rock that should have reached a friendly pier,—there is

Edward (1823–1893) Hoar. This incident took place in early November 1850.

102 Reference to Thoreau's first book, *A Week on the Concord and Merrimack Rivers* (1849), which sold poorly; it took him four years to pay off his $290 debt to his publisher. In his journal of 27 October 1853 Thoreau wrote:

> For a year or two past, my *publisher*, falsely so called, has been writing from time to time to ask what disposition should be made of the copies of "A Week on the Concord and Merrimack Rivers" still on hand, and at last suggesting that he had use for the room they occupied in his cellar. So I had them all sent to me here, and they have arrived to-day by express, filling the man's wagon,—706 copies out of an edition of 1000 which I bought of Munroe four years ago and have been ever since paying for, and have not quite paid for yet. The wares are sent to me at last, and I have an opportunity to examine my purchase. They are something more substantial than fame, as my back knows, which has borne them up two flights of stairs to a place similar to that to which they trace their origin. Of the remaining two hundred and ninety and odd, seventy-five were given away, the rest sold. I have now a library of nearly nine hundred volumes, over seven hundred of which I wrote myself. Is it not well that the author should behold the fruits of his labor? My works are piled up on one side of my chamber half as high as my head, my *opera omnia*. This is authorship; these are the work of my brain. [J 5:459]

103 Not in the usual sense of employment for profit or improvement, but of being actively employed with a matter that engages a person's attention or requires care, as well as punning on the "private business" mentioned in the next sentence.

104 At least one of which was the writing of what would become *A Week on the Concord and Merri-*

mack Rivers, a memorial tribute to his brother, John, who died in 1842 from lockjaw.

105 Thoreau's management of his father's pencil and graphite business, as well as his work as a surveyor, showed his business acumen.

106 China, from the title "Tien Chao" (Heavenly Dynasty) given by the Chinese to their country, but also with reference to the spiritual world.

107 Salem, Massachusetts, was one of the major ports for the China trade. Thoreau's friend Hawthorne left Concord in 1846 to work in the Custom House in Salem until 1849.

108 Major raw products exported from Thoreau's New England.

109 Ships or vessels. Since independence the U.S. government had been trying to secure the American shipping industry through regulations encouraging the use of American bottoms, but such regulations often failed.

110 The New Jersey coast was the site of many shipwrecks, thus making the discharging of the richest freight, human life, a morbid pun.

111 Jean François de Galaup, Comte de la Pérouse (1741–ca. 1788), French navigator who was last heard from when his ships landed in 1788 at Botany Bay in Australia. Although his fate is unknown, it is probable that the natives of Vanikoro killed him when his ship was wrecked there.

112 Hanno was a Carthaginian explorer who traveled around the west coast of Africa in 480 B.C.E. and wrote the report "The Periplus of Hanno"; he is also mentioned in the "The Pond in Winter" chapter. Phoenicians were a Semitic people of the ancient Middle East and noted as early explorers.

113 Measures used in calculating the net weight of goods. Tare is a deduction for the weight of the wrapping or receptacle containing the goods; tret is a "good measure" allowance of 4 pounds in every 104 pounds for waste or damage.

114 The railroad from Boston to Fitchburg was built along the shore of Walden Pond shortly before Thoreau moved there; the line from Boston to Concord opened on 17 June 1844 and in Fitchburg on 5 March 1845. The ice trade was new to Walden

the untold fate of La Perouse;[111]—universal science to be kept pace with, studying the lives of all great discoverers and navigators, great adventurers and merchants, from Hanno and the Phœnicians[112] down to our day; in fine, account of stock to be taken from time to time, to know how you stand. It is a labor to task the faculties of a man,—such problems of profit and loss, of interest, of tare and tret,[113] and gauging of all kinds in it, as demand a universal knowledge.

I have thought that Walden Pond would be a good place for business, not solely on account of the railroad and the ice trade;[114] it offers advantages which it may not be good policy to divulge; it is a good port and a good foundation. No Neva marshes[115] to be filled; though you must every where build on piles of your own driving. It is said that a flood-tide, with a westerly wind, and ice in the Neva, would sweep St. Petersburg from the face of the earth.[116]

As this business was to be entered into without the usual capital, it may not be easy to conjecture where those means, that will still be indispensable to every such undertaking, were to be obtained. As for Clothing,[117] to come at once to the practical part of the question, perhaps we are led oftener by the love of novelty, and a regard for the opinions of men, in procuring it, than by a true utility. Let him who has work to do recollect that the object of clothing is, first, to retain the vital heat, and secondly, in this state of society, to cover nakedness,[118] and he may judge how much of any necessary or important work may be accomplished without adding to his wardrobe. Kings and queens who wear a suit but once, though made by some tailor or dress-maker to their majesties, cannot know the comfort of wearing a suit that fits. They are no better than wooden horses to hang the clean clothes on.[119] Every day our garments become more assimilated to ourselves, receiving the impress of the wearer's character, until we hesitate to lay them aside, without such delay and medical appliances and some such solemnity even as our bodies. No man ever stood the lower in my estimation for having a patch in his clothes; yet I am sure that there is greater anxiety, commonly, to have fashionable, or at least clean and unpatched clothes, than to have a sound conscience. But even if the rent is not mended, perhaps the worst vice betrayed is improvidence. I sometimes try my acquaintances by such tests as this;—who could wear a patch, or two extra seams only, over the knee? Most behave as if they believed that their prospects for life would be ruined if they should do it. It would be easier for them to hobble to town with a broken leg than with a broken pantaloon. Often if an accident happens to a gentleman's legs, they can be mended; but if a similar accident happens to the legs of his pantaloons, there is no help for it; for he considers, not what is truly respectable, but what is respected. We know but few men, a great many coats and breeches. Dress a scarecrow in your last shift, you standing shiftless[120] by, who would not soonest salute the scarecrow? Passing a corn-field the other day,[121] close by a hat and coat on a stake, I recognized the owner of the farm. He was only a little more weather-beaten than when I saw him last. I have heard of a dog that barked at every stranger who approached his master's premises with clothes on, but was easily quieted by a naked thief. It is an interesting question how far men would retain their relative rank if they were divested of their clothes. Could you, in such a case, tell surely of any company of civilized men, which belonged to the most respected class? When Madam Pfeiffer, in her adventurous travels round the world, from east to west, had got so near home as Asiatic Russia, she says that she felt the necessity of wearing other than a travelling dress, when she went to meet the authorities, for she "was now in a civilized country,

Pond when Thoreau lived there, and he described it in "The Pond in Winter" chapter.

115 At the delta of the Neva River in Russia.

116 Peter the Great (1672–1725) created the city of St. Petersburg (known as Leningrad, 1914–91) on the delta despite its being prone to destructive flooding. Although it was not swept from the face of the earth, the city has suffered from floods since it opened in 1703, the most destructive occurring in 1824.

117 The section on clothing was influenced by Thoreau's reading of Thomas Carlyle's (1795–1881) *Sartor Resartus,* which was published in Boston in 1836 as edited by Emerson. Thoreau viewed clothing as a symbolic outer layer with no true relation to the person underneath, as he explained in a letter of 21 January 1854 to Harrison Gray Otis Blake (1818–1898):

> My coat is at last done. . . . [A]nd the maker of it was not acquainted with any of my real depressions or elevations. . . . I expect a time when, or rather an integrity by which a man will get his coat as honestly, and as perfectly fitting as a tree its bark. Now our garments are typical of our conformity to the ways of the world, i.e. of the Devil, & to some extent react on us and poison us like that shirt which Hercules put on. . . .
>
> But (to return to the subject of coats), we are well nigh smothered under yet more fatal coats, which do not fit us, our whole lives long. Consider the cloak that our employment or station is—how rarely men treat each other for what in their true & naked characters they are. How we use & tolerate pretension; how the judge is clothed with dignity which does not belong to him, and the trembling witness with humility that does not belong to him, and the criminal perchance with shame or impudence which no more belong to him. It does not matter so much then what is the fashion of the cloak with which we cloak these cloaks. Change the coat—put the judge in the criminal box &

the criminal on the bench, and you might think that you had changed the men. [C 318–20]

118 Thoreau did not embrace conventional attitudes against nudity, as the following journal entry of 12 June 1852 shows: "Boys are bathing at Hubbard's Bend. . . . The color of their bodies in the sun at a distance is pleasing, the not often seen flesh-color. . . . As yet we have not man in nature. What a singular fact for an angel visitant to this earth to carry back in his note-book, that men were forbidden to expose their bodies under the severest penalties! . . . I wonder that the dog knows his master when he goes in to bathe and does not stay by his clothes" [J 4:92–93]. "I wonder," Thoreau wrote on 10 July 1852, "if any Roman emperor ever indulged in such luxury as this,—of walking up and down a river in torrid weather with only a hat to shade the head. What were the baths of Caracalla to this?" [J 4:214].

119 A wooden frame, known as a clothes horse, was used to air clothing.

120 Pun: slack, or lacking in energy and resource, as well as without a shift, a loosely fitting dress that hangs straight from the shoulder.

121 In September 1852. A contrasting incident is told in a 23 June 1853 passage: "The other day I saw what I took to be a scarecrow in a cultivated field, and noticing how unnaturally it was stuffed out here and there and how ungainly its arms and legs were, I thought to myself, 'Well, it is thus they make these things; they do not stand much about it;' but looking round again after I had gone by, I saw my scarecrow walking off with a real live man in it" [J 5:298].

122 Quoted from Ida Laura Pfeiffer (1797–1858), *A Lady's Voyage Round the World* (1850; published in America in 1852): "I had brought with me two letters, one to a German physician, and the other to the governor; but I did not wish to present myself to the latter in my travelling dress (for I was now in a civilized country, where of course people are judged by their clothes)."

123 Probable allusion to the proverb "Man may

where—— —people are judged of by their clothes."[122] Even in our democratic New England towns the accidental possession of wealth, and its manifestation in dress and equipage alone, obtain for the possessor almost universal respect. But they who yield such respect, numerous as they are, are so far heathen, and need to have a missionary sent to them. Beside, clothes introduced sewing, a kind of work which you may call endless; a woman's dress, at least, is never done.[123]

A man who has at length found something to do will not need to get a new suit to do it in; for him the old will do, that has lain dusty in the garret for an indeterminate period. Old shoes will serve a hero longer than they have served his valet,—if a hero ever has a valet,[124]—bare feet are older than shoes, and he can make them do. Only they who go to soirées and legislative halls must have new coats, coats to change as often as the man changes in them. But if my jacket and trousers, my hat and shoes, are fit to worship God in, they will do; will they not? Who ever saw his old clothes,—his old coat, actually worn out, resolved into its primitive elements, so that it was not a deed of charity to bestow it on some poor boy, by him perchance to be bestowed on some poorer still, or shall we say richer, who could do with less? I say, beware of all enterprises that require new clothes, and not rather a new wearer of clothes. If there is not a new man,[125] how can the new clothes be made to fit? If you have any enterprise before you, try it in your old clothes. All men want, not something to *do with*, but something to *do*, or rather something to *be*. Perhaps we should never procure a new suit, however ragged or dirty the old, until we have so conducted, so enterprised or sailed in some way, that we feel like new men in the old, and that to retain it would be like keeping new wine in old bottles.[126] Our moulting season, like that of the fowls, must be a crisis in our lives. The loon retires to solitary ponds to spend it. Thus also the snake casts its slough, and the caterpillar its wormy coat, by an internal industry and expansion; for clothes are but our outmost cuticle and mortal coil.[127] Otherwise we shall be found sailing under false colors,[128] and be inevitably cashiered at last by our own opinion, as well as that of mankind.

We don garment after garment, as if we grew like exogenous plants[129] by addition without. Our outside and often thin and fanciful clothes are our epidermis or false skin,[130] which partakes not of our life, and may be stripped off here and there without fatal injury; our thicker garments, constantly worn, are our cellular integument, or cortex; but our shirts are our liber[131] or true bark, which cannot be removed without girdling[132] and so destroying the man. I believe that all races at some seasons wear something equivalent to the shirt. It is desirable that a man be clad so simply that he can lay his hands on himself in the dark, and that he live in all respects so compactly and preparedly, that, if an enemy take the town, he can, like the old philosopher, walk out the gate empty-handed without anxiety.[133] While one thick garment is, for most purposes, as good as three thin ones, and cheap clothing can be obtained at prices really to suit customers; while a thick coat can be bought for five dollars, which will last as many years, thick pantaloons for two dollars, cowhide boots for a dollar and a half a pair, a summer hat for a quarter of a dollar, and a winter cap for sixty-two and a half cents, or a better be made at home at a nominal cost, where is he so poor that, clad in such a suit, *of his own earning,* there will not be found wise men to do him reverence?

When I ask for a garment of a particular form, my tailoress[134] tells me gravely, "They do not make them so now," not emphasizing the "They" at all, as if she quoted an authority as impersonal as the Fates,[135] and I find it difficult to get made what I want,[136] simply because she

work from sun to sun, but woman's work is never done."

124 Allusion to "No man is a hero to his valet," a variation of Michel de Montaigne's essay "Of Repentance": "Few men have been admired by their domestics." Thoreau may have known the saying through Carlyle's *On Heroes, Hero-Worship, and the Heroic in History:* "We will also take the liberty to deny altogether that of the witty Frenchman, That no man is a Hero to his valet-de-chambre."

125 Allusion to such New Testament passages as "And that ye put on the new man" [Ephesians 4:24] and "the new man, which is renewed in knowledge" [Colossians 3:10].

126 Allusion to Matthew 9:17: "Neither do men put new wine into old bottles: else the bottles break, and the wine runneth out . . . but they put new wine into new bottles, and both are preserved."

127 Allusion to Shakespeare's *Hamlet* 3.1.69: "When we have shuffled off this mortal coil."

128 Pirates would often sail under a false flag as a disguise to lure the unsuspecting.

129 Plants that grow an annual layer beneath the bark.

130 The surface of the skin, or epidermis, consists of dead cells, which are easily rubbed off and are sometimes referred to as false skin.

131 The inner bark of a tree, or of any exogenous stems, lying next the cambium and enveloped by the corky layer.

132 Cutting a belt through the bark and alburnum of a tree to disrupt flow of cambial sap so as to cause it to die, with a pun on girdle as a band or belt, usually linen, used to confine long flowing or loose garments.

133 Refers to Bias (ca. 6th century B.C.E.), one of the Seven Wise Men of Greece. Thoreau wrote in his journal of 12 July 1840: "In the sack of Priene, when the inhabitants with much hurry and bustle were carrying their effects to a place of safety, some one asked Bias, who remained tranquil amid the confusion, why he was not thinking how he should save something, as the others were. 'I do

so,' said Bias, 'for I carry all my effects with me'"
[J 1:169–70]. Thoreau probably read of Bias in
François de Salignac de La Mothe Fénelon's (1651–
1715) *The Lives and Most Remarkable Maxims of
the Antient Philosophers* (London, 1726), a copy of
which Bronson Alcott owned.

134 Mary Minott, sometimes Minot (1781–1861),
sister to Emerson's neighbor George Minott,
was seamstress for many Concordians. Horace
Hosmer (1830–1894) wrote in *Remembrances of
Concord and the Thoreaus:* "From the time I was 10
yrs old until old enough to buy my own clothes, I
used to go to the old Minot House and have my
clothes cut and made by Mary Minot, the maiden
sister of George Minot. She was a rather stern,
business like woman who ruled the household
alone." Franklin Sanborn (1831–1917) wrote in *The
Personality of Thoreau* that Thoreau's "garments
were usually cut by the village tailor, and made up
by Miss Mary Minot." Edward Jarvis wrote: "Mary
was a tailoress of the second-class, for working
men and boys. She was a faithful woman, much
respected."

135 In Greek mythology, the three Fates were
goddesses who controlled humans' lives: Clotho
spun the thread of life; Lachesis allotted each
person his destiny; and Atropos cut the thread.
Thoreau described the fates in a college essay
from 28 October 1836: "According to the belief of
the mass of the Greeks, 3 sisters, Clotho, Lachesis,
and Atropos, presided over the destinies of men.
They were acquainted with the past, the present,
and the future, and are represented with spindles
which they keep constantly in motion, spinning
the thread of human life, and singing the fate of
mortals. The Romans had their Parcae and the
Northerns their Nornen" [EEM 59].

136 According to his friend Franklin Sanborn's
journal, Thoreau "dresses very plainly," and "wore
almost constantly a kind of corduroy." His "whim
. . . of never blacking his boots," John Shepard
Keyes wrote to Francis Underwood, "gave him
an uncouth uncivilized look." Ellery Channing
(William Ellery Channing, the Younger, 1817–

cannot believe that I mean what I say, that I am so rash.
When I hear this oracular sentence, I am for a moment
absorbed in thought, emphasizing to myself each word
separately that I may come at the meaning of it, that I
may find out by what degree of consanguinity *They* are
related to *me*, and what authority they may have in an
affair which affects me so nearly; and, finally, I am inclined to answer her with equal mystery, and without any
more emphasis of the "they,"—"It is true, they did not
make them so recently, but they do now." Of what use
this measuring of me if she does not measure my character, but only the breadth of my shoulders, as it were a
peg to hang the coat on? We worship not the Graces,[137]
nor the Parcæ,[138] but Fashion. She spins and weaves and
cuts with full authority. The head monkey at Paris[139] puts
on a traveller's cap, and all the monkeys in America do
the same. I sometimes despair of getting any thing quite
simple and honest done in this world by the help of men.
They would have to be passed through a powerful press
first, to squeeze their old notions out of them, so that they
would not soon get upon their legs again, and then there
would be some one in the company with a maggot[140] in
his head, hatched from an egg deposited there nobody
knows when, for not even fire kills these things, and you
would have lost your labor. Nevertheless, we will not forget that some Egyptian wheat is said to have been handed
down to us by a mummy.[141]

On the whole, I think that it cannot be maintained
that dressing has in this or any country risen to the dignity
of an art. At present men make shift to wear what they
can get. Like shipwrecked sailors, they put on what they
can find on the beach, and at a little distance, whether
of space or time, laugh at each other's masquerade. Every
generation laughs at the old fashions, but follows religiously the new. We are amused at beholding the costume of Henry VIII., or Queen Elizabeth,[142] as much as

1901) said that Thoreau's coat pockets were large enough to hold a notebook and spyglass. Daniel Ricketson (1813–1898) wrote of his first encounter with Thoreau: "So unlike my ideal Thoreau, whom I had fancied, from the robust nature of his mind and habits of life, to be a man of unusual vigor and size, that I did not suspect, although I had expected him in the morning, that the slight, quaint-looking person before me was the Walden philosopher. There are few persons who had previously read his works that were not disappointed by his personal appearance."

In several places Thoreau described his sartorial preferences. His usual hat was "a straw one with a scaffold lining to it" [J 9:157]. When he traveled to Canada, he wore "over my coat one of those unspeakably cheap, as well as thin, brown linen sacks . . . because it looked better than the coat it covered, and last because two coats were warmer than one, though one was thin and dirty. . . . [T]he genuine traveler is going out to work hard and fare harder,—to eat a crust by the wayside whenever he can get it. Honest traveling is about as dirty work as you can do, and a man needs a pair of overalls for it" [W 5:31–32]. Of his corduroy pants, which he liked in a drab clay color, Thoreau wrote: "Anything but black clothes. I was pleased the other day to see a son of Concord return after an absence of eight years, not in a shining suit of black, with polished boots and a beaver or silk hat, as if on a furlough from human duties generally,—a mere clothes-horse,—but clad in an honest clay-colored suit and a snug every-day cap" [J 9:359–60]. His preferred drab color "is in harmony with nature, and you are less conspicuous in the fields and can get nearer to wild animals for it" [J 13:230]. Thoreau found shoes "commonly too narrow. If you should take off a gentleman's shoes, you would find that his foot was wider than his shoe. . . . Better moccasins, or sandals, or even bare feet, than a tight shoe" [J 2:5].

137 In Greek mythology, there were three Graces, minor goddesses who were the personification of grace and beauty: Aglaia (Splendor), Euphrosyne (Mirth), and Thalia (Good Cheer).

138 In Roman mythology, the three Parcae, Nona, Decuma, and Morta, were the equivalent of the Greek Fates.

139 Alfred Guillaume Gabriel, Count d'Orsay (1801–1852), a Frenchman, was the center of a fashionable artistic and literary circle in London and was considered the authority on matters of taste in English society. In 1849, to escape his creditors, he fled to Paris.

140 Whim or extravagant notion, but with a pun on the legless, soft-bodied, wormlike larva of flies, often found in decaying matter, and possibly an allusion to the story of the "bug which came out of the dry leaf of an old table of apple-tree wood" told in the "Conclusion" chapter.

141 Stories had circulated in Thoreau's day of wheat found among Egyptian mummies and sown in British soil. In the 1840s reports appeared in papers, including the *Concord Freeman* on 12 November 1841, about "mummy wheat" discovered in tombs up to 6,000 years old. The London *Times* carried a report on 14 August 1844 of a Mr. Reid's garden in which "we saw a quantity of Egyptian wheat in full ear, and giving promise of an abundant harvest, the seed of which was found in the folds of a mummy unrolled in 1840." Although every attempt to grow authentic mummy seed failed, the myth of mummy wheat would not die easily. After the publication of *Walden,* reports of the skepticism of botanists led Thoreau to correct "was handed down" in the first edition to "is said to have been handed down" in his copy of the book. He wrote in "The Succession of Forest Trees" in 1860: "The stories of wheat raised from seed buried with an ancient Egyptian, and of raspberries raised from seed found in the stomach of a man in England, who is supposed to have died sixteen or seventeen hundred years ago, are generally discredited, simply because the evidence is not conclusive" [W 5:200–201].

142 King of England, 1509–47, and queen of England, 1558–1603.

143 Generic term for islands inhabited by un-civilized natives, and specifically the Fiji Islands; possible allusion to the 19th-century song "King of the Cannibal Islands," which Thoreau would have read of in the first chapter to Herman Melville's (1819–1891) *Typee,* if he was not personally familiar with the song. Thoreau may have learned about *Typee* through one of three friends who were familiar with Melville's work: Hawthorne published a favorable review of it in the *Salem Advertiser* (25 March 1846), Bronson Alcott read it in December 1846, and Ellery Channing's poem "The Island Nukuheva" is about *Typee.*

144 From a journal passage regarding the visit to Concord on 3 February 1841 of the Rainers, a Tyrolese minstrel family forming a quartet of, at this time, three males and one female: "When these Swiss appear before me in gaiters and high-crowned hats with feathers, I am disposed to laugh, but soon I see that their serious eye becomes these and they it. It is the sincere life passed within it which consecrates the costume of any people" [J 1:196].

145 Standard character in old Italian comedy, often dressed in parti-colored apparel.

146 The color of royal garments.

147 Although Thoreau would have read about tattooing in several sources, including Charles Darwin's *Narrative of the Surveying Voyages of his Majesty's Ships Adventure and Beagle,* his use of the terms "hideous" and "barbarous" may refer to Melville's *Typee.* In the "Morning Visitors" chapter, Melville wrote of "the hideous blemish of tattoo-ing" and called it a "barbarous art," and in the "Tattooing and Tabooing" chapter he described the procedure in detail, as well as his being "horri-fied at the bare thought of being rendered hideous for life" if he were to have this art inflicted upon himself.

148 Thoreau referred to England as "the great workhouse of the world" later in this chapter.

if it was that of the King and Queen of the Cannibal Islands.[143] All costume off a man is pitiful or grotesque. It is only the serious eye peering from and the sincere life passed within it, which restrain laughter and consecrate the costume of any people.[144] Let Harlequin[145] be taken with a fit of the colic and his trappings will have to serve that mood too. When the soldier is hit by a cannon ball rags are as becoming as purple.[146]

The childish and savage taste of men and women for new patterns keeps how many shaking and squint-ing through kaleidoscopes that they may discover the particular figure which this generation requires to-day. The manufacturers have learned that this taste is merely whimsical. Of two patterns which differ only by a few threads more or less of a particular color, the one will be sold readily, the other lie on the shelf, though it frequently happens that after the lapse of a season the latter becomes the most fashionable. Comparatively, tattooing is not the hideous custom which it is called.[147] It is not barbarous merely because the printing is skin-deep and unalterable.

I cannot believe that our factory system is the best mode by which men may get clothing. The condition of the operatives is becoming every day more like that of the English;[148] and it cannot be wondered at, since, as far as I have heard or observed, the principal object is, not that mankind may be well and honestly clad, but, un-questionably, that the corporations may be enriched. In the long run men hit only what they aim at. Therefore, though they should fail immediately, they had better aim at something high.

As for a Shelter, I will not deny that this is now a nec-essary of life, though there are instances of men having done without it for long periods in colder countries than this. Samuel Laing says that "The Laplander in his skin dress, and in a skin bag which he puts over his head and

shoulders, will sleep night after night on the snow——
in a degree of cold which would extinguish the life of
one exposed to it in any woollen clothing."[149] He had
seen them asleep thus. Yet he adds, "They are not hardier
than other people." But, probably, man did not live long
on the earth without discovering the convenience which
there is in a house, the domestic comforts, which phrase
may have originally signified the satisfactions of the house
more than of the family; though these must be extremely
partial and occasional in those climates where the house
is associated in our thoughts with winter or the rainy season chiefly, and two thirds of the year, except for a parasol, is unnecessary. In our climate, in the summer, it was
formerly almost solely a covering at night. In the Indian
gazettes[150] a wigwam was the symbol of a day's march,
and a row of them cut or painted on the bark of a tree signified that so many times they had camped. Man was not
made so large limbed and robust but that he must seek to
narrow his world, and wall in a space such as fitted him.
He was at first bare and out of doors; but though this was
pleasant enough in serene and warm weather, by daylight,
the rainy season and the winter, to say nothing of the torrid sun, would perhaps have nipped his race in the bud if
he had not made haste to clothe himself with the shelter
of a house. Adam and Eve, according to the fable,[151] wore
the bower before other clothes.[152] Man wanted a home,
a place of warmth, or comfort, first of physical warmth,
then the warmth of the affections.

We may imagine a time when, in the infancy of the
human race, some enterprising mortal crept into a hollow
in a rock for shelter. Every child begins the world again,[153]
to some extent, and loves to stay out doors, even in wet
and cold. It plays house, as well as horse, having an instinct for it. Who does not remember the interest with
which when young he looked at shelving rocks, or any approach to a cave? It was the natural yearning of that por-

149 Quoted from Scottish traveler Samuel Laing
(1780–1868), *Journal of a Residence in Norway During the Years 1834, 1835, & 1836, Made with a View
to Enquire into the Moral and Political Economy of
that Country, and the Condition of its Inhabitants*
(London, 1837) 295. Thoreau's dashes replace: "in
the fjelde."

150 The Indian gazettes were engraved ideo-
grams and pictographs. In *The Maine Woods*
Thoreau wrote: "Our blankets being dry, we set out
again, the Indian as usual having left his gazette
on a tree" [W 3:298].

151 For Thoreau, the Judeo-Christian Bible was
as much a fable as any other ancient scripture.
He wrote in *A Week on the Concord and Merrimack Rivers:* "One memorable addition to the
old mythology is due to this era,—the Christian
fable. With what pains, and tears, and blood these
centuries have woven this and added it to the
mythology of mankind! The new Prometheus.
With what miraculous consent, and patience,
and persistency has this mythus been stamped
on the memory of the race! It would seem as if it
were in the progress of our mythology to dethrone
Jehovah, and crown Christ in his stead" [W 1:67].

152 On discovering that they were naked, Adam
and Eve "sewed fig leaves together, and made
themselves aprons" [Genesis 3:7].

153 One of several references to the English
Romantic and American Transcendentalist notion
that children stood closer to God and wisdom
than did adults, as in William Wordsworth's (1770–
1850) "Ode: Intimations of Immortality": "trailing
clouds of glory do we come / From God, who
is our home: / Heaven lies about us in our infancy!" [ll. 64–66]. The association of childhood
and wisdom is found in Thoreau's "Aulus Persius
Flaccus": "The life of a wise man is most extem-
poraneous, for he lives out of an eternity that
includes all time. He is a child each moment and
reflects wisdom. The far darting thought of the
child's mind tarries not for the development of
manhood; it lightens itself, and needs not draw
down lightning from the clouds" [*The Dial* (July

1840) 120]. He wrote in the last paragraph of the "Where I Lived, and What I Lived For" chapter: "I have always been regretting that I was not as wise as the day I was born."

154 Several of the senses of the word "domestic" from Noah Webster's 1828 *American Dictionary of the English Language:* belonging to the house, or home; pertaining to one's place of residence, and to the family; remaining much at home; living in retirement; living near the habitations of man; tame, not wild; pertaining to a nation considered as a family, or to one's own country; made in one's own house, nation or country.

155 Once considered a derogatory term, particularly as used by Confederate soldiers during the Civil War. In the "Sunday" chapter of *A Week on the Concord and Merrimack Rivers* Thoreau followed Webster's 1828 *American Dictionary* in deriving the epithet from the "New West Saxons, whom the red men call, not Angle-ish or English, but Yengeese, and so at last they are known for Yankees" [W 1:53].

156 Pun: a house in which work is carried on, as well as a poorhouse where the able-bodied poor were required to work in exchange for food, clothes, and shelter.

157 In Greek mythology the Minotaur, a monster with a bull's head and a man's body, was housed in a labyrinth. The Greek hero Theseus was able to kill the Minotaur and escape using the clew, a thread to follow, given him by Ariadne.

158 In an early journal entry Thoreau wrote: "I hate museums; there is nothing so weighs upon my spirits. They are the catacombs of nature. . . . They are dead nature collected by dead men. I know not whether I muse most at the bodies stuffed with cotton and sawdust or those stuffed with bowels and fleshy fibre outside the cases" [J 1:464].

159 A house could be a prison, according to Thoreau's 26 April 1841 journal, if a man "finds himself oppressed and confined, not sheltered and protected" [J 1:253].

160 An Algonquin tribe from the Penobscot Bay

tion of our most primitive ancestor which still survived in us. From the cave we have advanced to roofs of palm leaves, of bark and boughs, of linen woven and stretched, of grass and straw, of boards and shingles, of stones and tiles. At last, we know not what it is to live in the open air, and our lives are domestic in more senses than we think.[154] From the hearth to the field is a great distance. It would be well perhaps if we were to spend more of our days and nights without any obstruction between us and the celestial bodies, if the poet did not speak so much from under a roof, or the saint dwell there so long. Birds do not sing in caves, nor do doves cherish their innocence in dovecots.

However, if one designs to construct a dwelling house, it behooves him to exercise a little Yankee[155] shrewdness, lest after all he find himself in a workhouse,[156] a labyrinth without a clew,[157] a museum,[158] an almshouse, a prison,[159] or a splendid mausoleum instead. Consider first how slight a shelter is absolutely necessary. I have seen Penobscot Indians,[160] in this town, living in tents of thin cotton cloth, while the snow was nearly a foot deep around them, and I thought that they would be glad to have it deeper to keep out the wind. Formerly, when how to get my living honestly, with freedom left for my proper pursuits, was a question which vexed me even more than it does now, for unfortunately I am become somewhat callous, I used to see a large box by the railroad, six feet long by three wide, in which the laborers locked up their tools at night, and it suggested to me that every man who was hard pushed might get such a one for a dollar, and, having bored a few auger holes in it, to admit the air at least, get into it when it rained and at night, and hook down the lid, and so have freedom in his love, and in his soul be free.[161] This did not appear the worst, nor by any means a despicable alternative. You could sit up as late as you pleased, and, whenever you got up, go abroad without any landlord or house-lord dogging you for rent. Many a man is harassed to death to pay the rent of a larger and more luxurious box who would not have frozen to death in such a box as this. I am far from jesting. Economy[162] is a subject which admits of being treated with levity, but it cannot so be disposed of. A comfortable house for a rude and hardy race, that lived mostly out of doors, was once made here almost entirely of such materials as Nature furnished ready to their hands. Gookin,[163] who was superintendent of the Indians subject to the Massachusetts Colony, writing in 1674, says, "The best of their houses are covered very neatly, tight and warm, with barks of trees, slipped from their bodies at those seasons when the sap is up, and made into great flakes, with pressure of weighty timber, when they are green. . . . The meaner sort are covered with mats which they make of a kind of bulrush, and are also indifferently tight and warm, but not so good as the former. . . . Some I have seen, sixty or a hundred feet long and thirty feet broad. . . . I have often lodged in their wigwams, and found them as warm as the best English houses."[164] He adds, that they were commonly carpeted and lined within with well-wrought embroidered mats, and were furnished with various utensils. The Indians had advanced so far as to regulate the effect of the wind by a mat suspended over the hole in the roof and moved by a string. Such a lodge was in the first instance constructed in a day or two at most, and taken down and put up in a few hours; and every family owned one, or its apartment in one.

In the savage state every family owns a shelter as good as the best, and sufficient for its coarser and simpler wants; but I think that I speak within bounds when I say that, though the birds of the air have their nests, and the foxes their holes,[165] and the savages their wigwams, in modern civilized society not more than one half the families own

region of northern Maine, they frequently visited Concord to sell baskets and camped outside the town.

161 Allusion to Richard Lovelace's (1618–1657) "To Althea in Prison" ll.29–30: "If I have freedom in my love, / And in my soul am free." Thoreau quoted this phrase twice in his journal, on 21 July 1851 and 28 January 1852.

162 From the Greek *oikonomia*, meaning management of a household or of household affairs. In titling the chapter "Economy," Thoreau went beyond the word's common definitions—as a community's method of wealth creation or as frugality—and referred to its root meaning, as he often did. Emerson wrote in "Man the Reformer": "Economy is a high, humane office, a sacrament, when its aim is grand; when it is the prudence of simple tastes, when it is practiced for freedom, or love, or devotion." Thoreau wrote later in this chapter that the economy of living is "synonymous with philosophy."

163 Daniel Gookin (1612?–1687), a Virginia Puritan who moved to Massachusetts. He was made superintendent of Indians, to whom he showed a humane and intelligent interest. His protests against the retaliation of the whites in King Philip's War made him unpopular. He wrote two books on the Indians, *Historical Collections of the Indians in New England* and *The Doings and Sufferings of the Christian Indians,* both published posthumously.

164 Quoted, with several minor variations, from Gookin's *Historical Collections of the Indians in New England* of 1674 (Boston: Massachusetts Historical Society, 1792) 1:149–50.

165 Allusion to Matthew 8:20: "And Jesus saith unto him, The foxes have holes, and the birds of the air have nests; but the Son of man hath not where to lay his head."

166 The Rumford fireplace, invented by Benjamin Thompson, Count Rumford (1753–1814), used a smoke shelf that prevented downdrafts from carrying smoke into the room; back plastering was plaster applied between the studding; Venetian blinds at the time were made of thin wooden laths attached to strips of cloth; and a spring lock, also known as a latch-lock, used a spring to fasten automatically.

167 Standard rate at the time.

a shelter. In the large towns and cities, where civilization especially prevails, the number of those who own a shelter is a very small fraction of the whole. The rest pay an annual tax for this outside garment of all, become indispensable summer and winter, which would buy a village of Indian wigwams, but now helps to keep them poor as long as they live. I do not mean to insist here on the disadvantage of hiring compared with owning, but it is evident that the savage owns his shelter because it costs so little, while the civilized man hires his commonly because he cannot afford to own it; nor can he, in the long run, any better afford to hire. But, answers one, by merely paying this tax the poor civilized man secures an abode which is a palace compared with the savage's. An annual rent of from twenty-five to a hundred dollars, these are the country rates, entitles him to the benefit of the improvements of centuries, spacious apartments, clean paint and paper, Rumford fireplace, back plastering, Venetian blinds, copper pump, spring lock,[166] a commodious cellar, and many other things. But how happens it that he who is said to enjoy these things is so commonly a *poor* civilized man, while the savage, who has them not, is rich as a savage? If it is asserted that civilization is a real advance in the condition of man,—and I think that it is, though only the wise improve their advantages,—it must be shown that it has produced better dwellings without making them more costly; and the cost of a thing is the amount of what I will call life which is required to be exchanged for it, immediately or in the long run. An average house in this neighborhood costs perhaps eight hundred dollars, and to lay up this sum will take from ten to fifteen years of the laborer's life, even if he is not encumbered with a family;—estimating the pecuniary value of every man's labor at one dollar a day,[167] for if some receive more, others receive less;—so that he must have spent more than half his life commonly before *his* wigwam will be earned. If we suppose him to pay a rent instead, this is but a doubtful choice of evils. Would the savage have been wise to exchange his wigwam for a palace on these terms?

It may be guessed that I reduce almost the whole advantage of holding this superfluous property as a fund in store against the future, so far as the individual is concerned, mainly to the defraying of funeral expenses. But perhaps a man is not required to bury himself. Nevertheless this points to an important distinction between the civilized man and the savage; and, no doubt, they have designs on us for our benefit, in making the life of a civilized people an *institution,* in which the life of the individual is to a great extent absorbed, in order to preserve and perfect that of the race. But I wish to show at what a sacrifice this advantage is at present obtained, and to suggest that we may possibly so live as to secure all the advantage without suffering any of the disadvantage. What mean ye by saying that the poor ye have always with you,[168] or that the fathers have eaten sour grapes, and the children's teeth are set on edge?[169]

"As I live, saith the Lord God, ye shall not have occasion any more to use this proverb in Israel."

"Behold all souls are mine; as the soul of the father, so also the soul of the son is mine: the soul that sinneth it shall die."[170]

When I consider my neighbors, the farmers of Concord, who are at least as well off as the other classes, I find that for the most part they have been toiling twenty, thirty, or forty years, that they may become the real owners of their farms, which commonly they have inherited with encumbrances, or else bought with hired money,—and we may regard one third of that toil as the cost of their houses,—but commonly they have not paid for them

168 Allusion to Matthew 26:11: "For ye have the poor always with you; but me ye have not always," and its variants in Mark 14:17 and John 12:8.
169 Allusion to Ezekiel 18:2: "What mean ye, that ye use this proverb concerning the land of Israel, saying, fathers have eaten sour grapes, and the children's teeth are set on edge?" and to Jeremiah 31:29: "The fathers have eaten a sour grape, and the children's teeth have been set on edge."
170 These two sentences are quoted from Ezekiel 18:3 and 18:4.

171 In a letter to H. G. O. Blake on 16 November 1857, Thoreau wrote: "If our merchants did not most of them fail, and the banks too, my faith in the old laws of the world would be staggered. The statement that ninety-six in a hundred doing such business surely break down is perhaps the sweetest fact that statistics have revealed,—exhilarating as the fragrant of sallows in spring. . . . If thousands are thrown out of employment, it suggests that they were not well employed. Why don't they take the hint?" [C 496].

172 Somersaults.

173 The Middlesex Agricultural Society's annual agricultural fair, the Middlesex Cattle Show and Ploughing Match, later the Annual Exhibition of the Middlesex Agricultural Society, was held in Concord each September or October. Concord is in Middlesex County. Thoreau delivered his lecture "The Succession of Forest Trees" before the society at the 1860 fair.

174 Variant of "suant": even and uniform, and thereby running smoothly. Thoreau defined it in his journal for 3 February 1852 as "an expressive word, applied to machinery whose joints are worn, which has got into working order" [J 3:272].

175 Thoreau often praised the farmer and Jeffersonian freeholder, particularly as represented by his friend George Minott, but here is aware of the detrimental influence of commercialism on the agrarian life. In his journal of 8 February 1854 he wrote:

> The poets, philosophers, historians, and all writers have always been disposed to praise the life of the farmer and prefer it to that of the citizen. They have been inclined to regard trade and commerce as not merely uncertain modes of getting a living, but as running into the usurious and disreputable. . . .
>
> But now, by means of railroads and steamboats and telegraphs, the country is denaturalized, the old pious, stable, and unenvied gains of the farmer are liable to all the suspicion which only the merchant's formerly excited. All

yet. It is true, the encumbrances sometimes outweigh the value of the farm, so that the farm itself becomes one great encumbrance, and still a man is found to inherit it, being well acquainted with it, as he says. On applying to the assessors, I am surprised to learn that they cannot at once name a dozen in the town who own their farms free and clear. If you would know the history of these homesteads, inquire at the bank where they are mortgaged. The man who has actually paid for his farm with labor on it is so rare that every neighbor can point to him. I doubt if there are three such men in Concord. What has been said of the merchants, that a very large majority, even ninety-seven in a hundred, are sure to fail,[171] is equally true of the farmers. With regard to the merchants, however, one of them says pertinently that a great part of their failures are not genuine pecuniary failures, but merely failures to fulfil their engagements, because it is inconvenient; that is, it is the moral character that breaks down. But this puts an infinitely worse face on the matter, and suggests, beside, that probably not even the other three succeed in saving their souls, but are perchance bankrupt in a worse sense than they who fail honestly. Bankruptcy and repudiation are the spring-boards from which much of our civilization vaults and turns its somersets,[172] but the savage stands on the unelastic plank of famine. Yet the Middlesex Cattle Show[173] goes off here with *éclat* annually, as if all the joints of the agricultural machine were suent.[174]

The farmer[175] is endeavoring to solve the problem of a livelihood by a formula more complicated than the problem itself. To get his shoe-strings[176] he speculates in herds of cattle. With consummate skill he has set his trap with a hair springe[177] to catch comfort and independence, and then, as he turned away, got his own leg into it. This is the reason he is poor; and for a similar reason we are all poor in respect to a thousand savage comforts, though surrounded by luxuries. As Chapman sings,—

"The false society of men—
—for earthly greatness
All heavenly comforts rarefies to air."[178]

And when the farmer has got his house, he may not be the richer but the poorer for it, and it be the house that has got him. As I understand it, that was a valid objection urged by Momus against the house which Minerva made, that she "had not made it movable, by which means a bad neighborhood might be avoided;"[179] and it may still be urged, for our houses are such unwieldy property that we are often imprisoned rather than housed in them; and the bad neighborhood to be avoided is our own scurvy[180] selves. I know one or two families, at least, in this town, who, for nearly a generation, have been wishing to sell their houses in the outskirts and move into the village, but have not been able to accomplish it, and only death will set them free.

Granted that the *majority* are able at last either to own or hire the modern house with all its improvements. While civilization has been improving our houses, it has not equally improved the men who are to inhabit them. It has created palaces, but it was not so easy to create noblemen and kings. And *if the civilized man's pursuits are no worthier than the savage's, if he is employed the greater part of his life in obtaining gross necessaries and comforts merely, why should he have a better dwelling than the former?*

But how do the poor *minority* fare? Perhaps it will be found, that just in proportion as some have been placed in outward circumstances above the savage, others have been degraded below him. The luxury of one class is counterbalanced by the indigence of another. On the one side is the palace, on the other are the almshouse[181] and "silent poor."[182] The myriads who built the pyramids to be the tombs of the Pharaohs were fed on garlic,[183] and it may be were not decently buried themselves. The mason

milk-farms and fruit-farms, etc., are so many markets with their customs in the country. [J 6:106–8]

176 These were principally made of leather in Thoreau's day.

177 A noose or snare used for catching small game. It is possible that the word "springe" was an error not caught by Thoreau in the page proofs and that the word should be "spring," as he had in the early drafts of *Walden,* meaning that the trap is lightly set so that the slightest touch will trip it.

178 Abridged from George Chapman (1559?–1634), English dramatist, translator, and poet, in *The Tragedy of Caesar and Pompey* 5.2:

> ——I will stand no more
> On others' legs, nor build one joy without me.
> If ever I be worth a house again,
> I'll build all inward: not a light shall ope
> The common out-way; no expense, no art,
> No ornament, no door, will I use there;
> But raise all plain and rudely like a rampier,
> Against the false society of men,
> That still batters
> All reason piece-meal; and, for earthly
>   greatness
> All heavenly comforts rarifies to air,
> I'll therefore live in dark; and all my light
> Like ancient Temples, let in at my top.
> This were to turn one's back to all the world,
> And only look at heaven.

Thoreau may have gotten the quotation from Charles Lamb's (1775–1834) *Specimens of English Dramatic Poets Who Lived About the Time of Shakespeare,* where this excerpt was entitled "Inward Help the Best."

179 Quoted from Lemprière's *Bibliotheca Classica* 744, which also describes Momus in Greek mythology as "a god of pleasantry among the ancients, son of Nox, according to Hesiod. He was continually employed in satirising the gods, and

whatever they did was freely turned to ridicule."
In Roman mythology, Minerva was the goddess of
wisdom, known as Athena to the Greeks.

180 One cause of scurvy is long confinement.

181 The Concord almshouse was located on Walden Street, across the fields behind Emerson's
house.

182 Lemuel Shattuck (1793–1859) in *A History
of the Town of Concord* (1835) defined the silent
poor as "those individuals who are needy, but
do not wish to throw themselves on the town for
support." The *Reports of the Selectmen of Concord*
for 1844–45 showed that the town had money
for the support of the poor, but kept a separate
accounting for the silent poor, with the "income of
the several donations" being "paid out to sundry
persons."

183 Allusion to Herodotus (484?–425 B.C.E.):
"There are writings on the pyramids in Egyptian
characters showing how much was spent on
purges and onions and garlic for the workmen."
However, garlic is used here medicinally, not
nutritionally.

184 The Industrial Revolution started in the
mid-18th century in England, changing it from an
agricultural to an industrial economy.

185 Famine swept Ireland in the 1840s when the
potato crop failed, causing the death of approximately one million people. Hundreds of thousands
of Irish emigrated, many to the United States.

186 On maps, unexplored areas were marked in
white, but used here to pun on the word enlightened.

187 Reference to the breeding of slaves in the
South.

who finishes the cornice of the palace returns at night perchance to a hut not so good as a wigwam. It is a mistake to suppose that, in a country where the usual evidences of civilization exist, the condition of a very large body of the inhabitants may not be as degraded as that of savages. I refer to the degraded poor, not now to the degraded rich. To know this I should not need to look farther than to the shanties which every where border our railroads, that last improvement in civilization; where I see in my daily walks human beings living in sties, and all winter with an open door, for the sake of light, without any visible, often imaginable, wood pile, and the forms of both old and young are permanently contracted by the long habit of shrinking from cold and misery, and the development of all their limbs and faculties is checked. It certainly is fair to look at that class by whose labor the works which distinguish this generation are accomplished. Such too, to a greater or less extent, is the condition of the operatives of every denomination in England, which is the great workhouse of the world.[184] Or I could refer you to Ireland,[185] which is marked as one of the white or enlightened spots[186] on the map. Contrast the physical condition of the Irish with that of the North American Indian, or the South Sea Islander, or any other savage race before it was degraded by contact with the civilized man. Yet I have no doubt that that people's rulers are as wise as the average of civilized rulers. Their condition only proves what squalidness may consist with civilization. I hardly need refer now to the laborers in our Southern States who produce the staple exports of this country, and are themselves a staple production of the South.[187] But to confine myself to those who are said to be in *moderate* circumstances.

Most men appear never to have considered what a house is, and are actually though needlessly poor all their lives because they think that they must have such a one as their neighbors have. As if one were to wear any sort of coat which the tailor might cut out for him, or, gradually leaving off palmleaf hat[188] or cap of woodchuck skin,[189] complain of hard times because he could not afford to buy him a crown! It is possible to invent a house still more convenient and luxurious than we have, which yet all would admit that man could not afford to pay for. Shall we always study to obtain more of these things, and not sometimes to be content with less? Shall the respectable citizen thus gravely teach, by precept and example, the necessity of the young man's providing a certain number of superfluous glow-shoes,[190] and umbrellas, and empty guest chambers for empty guests, before he dies? Why should not our furniture be as simple as the Arab's or the Indian's? When I think of the benefactors of the race, whom we have apotheosized as messengers from heaven, bearers of divine gifts to man, I do not see in my mind any retinue at their heels, any car-load of fashionable furniture. Or what if I were to allow—would it not be a singular allowance?—that our furniture should be more complex than the Arab's, in proportion as we are morally and intellectually his superiors! At present our houses are cluttered and defiled with it, and a good housewife would sweep out the greater part into the dust hole,[191] and not leave her morning's work undone. Morning work! By the blushes of Aurora[192] and the music of Memnon,[193] what should be man's *morning work* in this world? I had three pieces of limestone[194] on my desk, but I was terrified to find that they required to be dusted daily, when the furniture of my mind was all undusted still, and I threw them out the window in disgust. How, then, could I have a furnished house? I would rather sit in the open air, for no dust gathers on the grass, unless where man has broken ground.

It is the luxurious and dissipated who set the fashions which the herd so diligently follow. The traveller who stops at the best houses, so called, soon discovers this, for

188 Inexpensive palm-leaf hats were popular summer wear. On his 1850 excursion to Canada, Thoreau wore "a thin palm-leaf hat without lining, that cost twenty-five cents" [W 5:31].

189 Woodchuck fur was used by hunters to make winter hats.

190 Galoshes, or rubbers: a corruption of gallo-shoes, as in "clean my Shoes and Galloshoes" found in Desiderius Erasmus (d. 1536), *Colloquia Concerning Men, Manners, and Things,* translated into English by Nathan Bailey (London, 1725).

191 Hole cut in the floor where dust and debris were swept.

192 In Roman mythology, goddess of the dawn.

193 A king of Ethiopia and son of Aurora and Tithonus. He was slain by Achilles in the Trojan War. According to Lemprière's *Bibliotheca Classica:* "The Æthiopians or Egyptians, over whom Memnon reigned, erected a celebrated statue to the honour of their monarch. This statue had the wonderful property of uttering a melodious sound every day, at sun-raising, like that which is heard at the breaking of the string of a harp when it is wound up. This was effected by the rays of the sun when they fell upon it."

194 Probably from the limestone quarries in the Easterbrook (now Estabrook) area north of Concord.

195 Greek form of Ashurbanipal (d. 822 B.C.E.), the last king of Assyria, a corrupt and effeminate ruler.

196 Allusion to Proverbs 12:10: "A righteous man regardeth the life of his beast: but the tender mercies of the wicked are cruel." Resigning oneself to someone's tender mercies is submitting to the power or discretion of an often unsympathetic individual.

197 Probable reference to either of two railroad cars made in 1845: the American passenger car or the Davenport and Bridges Car made in Cambridge, Massachusetts. Both were more spacious than previous cars, and were designed to lessen the jarring and swinging motion familiar to railroad passengers in Thoreau's day. The ladies' compartments had elegant sofas, dressing tables, mirrors, and a water closet.

198 The China trade inspired a vogue for Asian decor.

199 Common 19th-century name for an American, similar to the use of John Bull for the English, as when Thoreau wrote that a huckleberry pudding "is to Jonathan what his plum pudding is to John Bull" [*Huckleberries* 12]. Thoreau uses the name to mean someone "essentially provincial still, not metropolitan," in "Life Without Principle" [W 4:477].

200 Later in "Economy" Thoreau wrote: "None is so poor that he need sit on a pumpkin. That is shiftlessness."

201 Reference to Hawthorne's "The Celestial Railroad." Although Thoreau seldom read fiction, this story was called to his attention by Emerson, who wrote in a letter on 10 June 1843 that it "has a serene strength which one cannot afford not to praise,—in this low life."

202 Literally, "bad air," from the Italian *mala aria*, from the belief that malarial fever was caused by the bad air found in swamps.

203 Emphasizing the Latin root meaning: the tilling or culture of a field, with a pun on human culture. He made similar rhetorical emphasis

the publicans presume him to be a Sardanapalus,[195] and if he resigned himself to their tender mercies[196] he would soon be completely emasculated. I think that in the railroad car we are inclined to spend more on luxury[197] than on safety and convenience, and it threatens without attaining these to become no better than a modern drawing room, with its divans, and ottomans, and sunshades, and a hundred other oriental things, which we are taking west with us, invented for the ladies of the harem and the effeminate natives of the Celestial Empire,[198] which Jonathan[199] should be ashamed to know the names of. I would rather sit on a pumpkin[200] and have it all to myself, than be crowded on a velvet cushion. I would rather ride on earth in an ox cart with a free circulation, than go to heaven in the fancy car[201] of an excursion train and breathe a *malaria*[202] all the way.

The very simplicity and nakedness of man's life in the primitive ages imply this advantage at least, that they left him still but a sojourner in nature. When he was refreshed with food and sleep he contemplated his journey again. He dwelt, as it were, in a tent in this world, and was either threading the valleys, or crossing the plains, or climbing the mountain tops. But lo! men have become the tools of their tools. The man who independently plucked the fruits when he was hungry is become a farmer; and he who stood under a tree for shelter, a housekeeper. We now no longer camp as for a night, but have settled down on earth and forgotten heaven. We have adopted Christianity merely as an improved method of *agri*-culture.[203] We have built for this world a family mansion, and for the next a family tomb. The best works of art are the expression of man's struggle to free himself from this condition, but the effect of our art is merely to make this low state comfortable and that higher state to be forgotten. There is actually no place in this village for a work of *fine* art, if any had come down to us, to stand, for our lives, our houses and streets, furnish no proper pedestal for it. There is not a nail to hang a picture on, nor a shelf to receive the bust of a hero or a saint. When I consider how our houses are built and paid for, or not paid for, and their internal economy managed and sustained, I wonder that the floor does not give way under the visitor while he is admiring the gewgaws upon the mantel-piece, and let him through into the cellar, to some solid and honest though earthy foundation. I cannot but perceive that this so called rich and refined life is a thing jumped at, and I do not get on in the enjoyment of the *fine* arts which adorn it, my attention being wholly occupied with the jump; for I remember that the greatest genuine leap, due to human muscles alone, on record, is that of certain wandering Arabs, who are said to have cleared twenty-five feet on level ground.[204] Without factitious support, man is sure to come to earth again beyond that distance. The first question which I am tempted to put to the proprietor of such great impropriety is, Who bolsters you? Are you one of the ninety-seven who fail? or of the three who succeed? Answer me these questions, and then perhaps I may look at your bawbles and find them ornamental. The cart before the horse[205] is neither beautiful nor useful. Before we can adorn our houses with beautiful objects the walls must be stripped, and our lives must be stripped, and beautiful housekeeping and beautiful living be laid for a foundation: now, a taste for the beautiful is most cultivated out of doors, where there is no house and no housekeeper.

Old Johnson,[206] in his "Wonder-Working Providence," speaking of the first settlers of this town, with whom he was contemporary, tells us that "they burrow themselves in the earth for their first shelter under some hill-side, and, casting the soil aloft upon timber, they make a smoky fire against the earth, at the highest side." They did not "provide them houses," says he, "till the

in writing "phil-*anthropic*" in "Higher Laws" and "*extra-vagant*" in "Conclusion."

204 Unidentified. Reported in Thoreau's journal of 7 June 1851.

205 Found in English in John Heywood's (1497?–1580?) *Proverbs* (1546): "Set the cart before the horse," but also in Cicero's *Ad Atticum* 1.16: "Hysteron proteron."

206 Edward Johnson (1599?–1672) published *A History of New-England From the English Planting in the Yeere 1628 untill the Yeere 1652*, better known as *The Wonder-Working Providence of Sion's Saviour in New England*, in 1654. Thoreau also quoted "Old Johnson" in the "Concord River" chapter of *A Week on the Concord and Merrimack Rivers*.

207 Abridged from chapter 36, "Of the laborious worke Christ's people have in planting this wildernesse, set forth in the building the Towne of Concord, being the first in-land Towne," in *The Wonder-Working Providence:*

> Yet farther to tell of the hard labours this people found in Planting this Wildernesse . . . after they have thus found out a place of aboad, they burrow themselves in the Earth for their first shelter under some Hill-side, casting the earth aloft upon Timber; they make a smoaky fire against the Earth at the highest side, and thus these poore servants of Christ provide shelter for themselves, their Wives and little ones, keeping off the short showers from their Lodgings, but the long raines penetrate through, to their great disturbance in the night season: yet in these poore Wigwames they sing Psalmes, pray and praise their God, till they can provide them houses, which ordinarily was not wont to be with many till the Earth, by the Lords blessing, brought forth Bread to feed them, their Wives and little ones, which with sore labours they attaine every one that can lift a haw [hoe] to strike it into the Earth, standing stoutly to their labours, and teare up the Rootes and Bushes, which the first yeare beares them a very thin crop, till the soard [sward] of the Earth be rotten, and therefore they have been forced to cut their bread very thin for a long season.

208 Dutch colony in North America, established in 1613, renamed New York after its conquest by the English in 1664. The provincial secretary was Cornelis van Tienhoven (1610?–1656?).

209 The United Provinces of the Netherlands, also known as the Dutch Republic.

210 Quoted from Edmund Bailey O'Callaghan (1797–1880), *The Documentary History of the State of New York* (1851) 4:23.

earth, by the Lord's blessing, brought forth bread to feed them," and the first year's crop was so light that "they were forced to cut their bread very thin for a long season."[207] The secretary of the Province of New Netherland,[208] writing in Dutch, in 1650, for the information of those who wished to take up land there, states more particularly, that "those in New Netherland, and especially in New England, who have no means to build farm houses at first according to their wishes, dig a square pit in the ground, cellar fashion, six or seven feet deep, as long and as broad as they think proper, case the earth inside with wood all round the wall, and line the wood with the bark of trees or something else to prevent the caving in of the earth; floor this cellar with plank, and wainscot it overhead for a ceiling, raise a roof of spars clear up, and cover the spars with bark or green sods, so that they can live dry and warm in these houses with their entire families for two, three, and four years, it being understood that partitions are run through those cellars which are adapted to the size of the family. The wealthy and principal men in New England, in the beginning of the colonies, commenced their first dwelling houses in this fashion for two reasons; firstly, in order not to waste time in building, and not to want food the next season; secondly, in order not to discourage poor laboring people whom they brought over in numbers from Fatherland.[209] In the course of three or four years, when the country became adapted to agriculture, they built themselves handsome houses, spending on them several thousands."[210]

In this course which our ancestors took there was a show of prudence at least, as if their principle were to satisfy the more pressing wants first. But are the more pressing wants satisfied now? When I think of acquiring for myself one of our luxurious dwellings, I am deterred, for, so to speak, the country is not yet adapted to *human* culture,[211] and we are still forced to cut our *spiritual* bread far thinner than our forefathers did their wheaten. Not that all architectural ornament is to be neglected even in the rudest periods; but let our houses first be lined with beauty, where they come in contact with our lives, like the tenement of the shellfish, and not overlaid with it. But, alas! I have been inside one or two of them, and know what they are lined with.

Though we are not so degenerate but that we might possibly live in a cave or a wigwam or wear skins to-day, it certainly is better to accept the advantages, though so dearly bought, which the invention and industry of mankind offer. In such a neighborhood as this, boards and shingles, lime and bricks, are cheaper and more easily obtained than suitable caves, or whole logs, or bark in sufficient quantities, or even well-tempered clay or flat stones. I speak understandingly on this subject, for I have made myself acquainted with it both theoretically and practically. With a little more wit we might use these materials so as to become richer than the richest now are, and make our civilization a blessing. The civilized man is a more experienced and wiser savage. But to make haste to my own experiment.[212]

Near the end of March, 1845, I borrowed an axe[213] and went down to the woods by Walden Pond, nearest to where I intended to build my house,[214] and began to cut down some tall arrowy white pines, still in their youth, for timber. It is difficult to begin without borrowing, but perhaps it is the most generous course thus to permit your fellow-men to have an interest in your enterprise. The owner of the axe, as he released his hold on it, said that it was the apple of his eye;[215] but I returned it sharper than I received it. It was a pleasant hill-side where I worked, covered with pine woods, through which

211 Possible reference to Bronson Alcott's 1836 book *The Doctrine and Discipline of Human Culture.*

212 Given that Thoreau's move to Walden on 4 July establishes a connection with national independence, "experiment" may allude to Thomas Jefferson's (1743–1826) use of it in his inaugural address (1801), in which he called democracy a "successful experiment."

213 The borrowed axe was probably a broad axe, used to hew trees after cutting them down, and is different from the narrow, or felling, axe (referred to in the following paragraph), which Thoreau would have owned. The owner of the borrowed axe has been a disputed claim. There is no extant journal entry or other original source from Thoreau identifying the owner. Ellery Channing, in his copy of *Walden,* claimed ownership for himself. George Willis Cooke (1848–1923) and Townsend Scudder (1900–1988) both claimed it was Emerson's, but cited no authority. Henry S. Salt (1851–1939), Thoreau's first British biographer, claimed it was Bronson Alcott's, citing no authority, although he probably relied on Alcott's own statement reported in the *Concord Freeman* (19 August 1880): "When he projected the Walden cabin he came to me and said, 'Mr. Alcott, lend me an ax,' and with this he built the temple of a grand primeval man." Alcott had made the claim of ownership previously, as confirmed by a letter from C. C. Stearns to him on 18 March 1881 recalling a conversation during a visit with Alcott several years before in which Alcott told him of lending his axe to Thoreau.

214 Despite descriptions to the contrary by various authors, Thoreau, with few exceptions, referred to his domicile as a house, including in the first sentence of the book. He called it a homestead once, a cabin and a hut twice, a lodge and an apartment three times, and a dwelling four times.

215 Allusion to phrase found in several places in the Old Testament, as in Deuteronomy 32:10: "He kept him as the apple of his eye."

216 The Thoreau family home at the time was a two-story structure west of the railroad station, on Texas (now Belknap) Street. Thoreau and his father built the house, known as the Texas house, in September 1844 on a three-quarter-acre plot.

217 Meadowlark and Eastern phoebe (*Sayornis phoebe*). Phoebes, often called pewees or bridge pewees, arrive in early spring. The wood pewee (*Contopus virens*) does not arrive until May.

218 Allusion to Shakespeare's *Richard III* 1.1.1–2: "Now is the winter of our discontent / Made glorious summer by this son of York." It was an allusion Thoreau liked, as evidenced by his use of it in "Natural History of Massachusetts" [W 5:125] and his journal of 31 October 1857 [J 10:150].

219 Probably the Eastern ribbon snake (*Thamnophis sauritus*).

I looked out on the pond, and a small open field in the woods where pines and hickories were springing up. The ice in the pond was not yet dissolved, though there were some open spaces, and it was all dark colored and saturated with water. There were some slight flurries of snow during the days that I worked there; but for the most part when I came out on to the railroad, on my way home,[216] its yellow sand heap stretched away gleaming in the hazy atmosphere, and the rails shone in the spring sun, and I heard the lark and pewee[217] and other birds already come to commence another year with us. They were pleasant spring days, in which the winter of man's discontent[218] was thawing as well as the earth, and the life that had lain torpid began to stretch itself. One day, when my axe had come off and I had cut a green hickory for a wedge, driving it with a stone, and had placed the whole to soak in a pond hole in order to swell the wood, I saw a striped snake[219] run into the water, and he lay on the bottom, apparently without inconvenience, as long as I staid there, or more than a quarter of an hour; perhaps because he had not yet fairly come out of the torpid state. It appeared to me that for a like reason men remain in their present low and primitive condition; but if they should feel the influence of the spring of springs arousing them, they would of necessity rise to a higher and more ethereal life. I had previously seen the snakes in frosty mornings in my path with portions of their bodies still numb and inflexible, waiting for the sun to thaw them. On the 1st of April it rained and melted the ice, and in the early part of the day, which was very foggy, I heard a stray goose groping about over the pond and cackling as if lost, or like the spirit of the fog.

So I went on for some days cutting and hewing timber, and also studs and rafters, all with my narrow axe, not having many communicable or scholar-like thoughts, singing to myself, —

Men say they know many things;
But lo! they have taken wings,—
The arts and sciences,
And a thousand appliances;
The wind that blows
Is all that any body knows.[220]

I hewed the main timbers six inches square, most of the studs on two sides only, and the rafters and floor timbers on one side, leaving the rest of the bark on, so that they were just as straight and much stronger than sawed ones. Each stick was carefully mortised or tenoned by its stump, for I had borrowed other tools by this time. My days in the woods were not very long ones; yet I usually carried my dinner of bread and butter, and read the newspaper[221] in which it was wrapped, at noon, sitting amid the green pine boughs which I had cut off, and to my bread was imparted some of their fragrance, for my hands were covered with a thick coat of pitch. Before I had done I was more the friend than the foe of the pine tree, though I had cut down some of them, having become better acquainted with it. Sometimes a rambler in the wood was attracted by the sound of my axe, and we chatted pleasantly over the chips which I had made.

By the middle of April, for I made no haste in my work, but rather made the most of it,[222] my house was framed and ready for the raising. I had already bought the shanty of James Collins,[223] an Irishman who worked on the Fitchburg Railroad, for boards.[224] James Collins' shanty was considered an uncommonly fine one. When I called to see it he was not at home. I walked about the outside, at first unobserved from within, the window was so deep and high. It was of small dimensions, with a peaked cottage roof, and not much else to be seen, the dirt being raised five feet all around as if it were a compost heap. The roof was the soundest part, though a good deal warped

220 Thoreau's poem.

221 Thoreau was an avid reader of newspapers. In *A Week on the Concord and Merrimack Rivers,* he twice found himself immersed: "I sat up during the evening, reading by the light of the fire the scraps of newspapers in which some party had wrapped their luncheon" [W 1:194], and "With a bending sail we glided rapidly by Tyngsborough and Chelmsford, each holding in one hand half of a tart country apple pie which we had purchased to celebrate our return, and in the other a fragment of the newspaper in which it was wrapped, devouring these with divided relish, and learning the news which had transpired since we sailed" [W 1:384]. Franklin Sanborn, editor of the limited edition of *Walden* published by the Bibliophile Society in 1909, claimed that few Concordians "read the newspapers (particularly the New York *Tribune*) more eagerly than Thoreau." Despite his apparent fervor, he could also be equally dismissive, writing "Do not read the newspapers" [J 2:45] and:

I do not know but it is too much to read one newspaper in a week, for I now take the weekly *Tribune,* and for a few days past, it seems to me, I have not dwelt in Concord; the sun, the clouds, the snow, the trees say not so much to me. You cannot serve two masters. It requires more than a day's devotion to know and to possess the wealth of a day. To read of things distant and sounding betrays us into slighting these which are then apparently near and small. We learn to look abroad for our mind and spirit's daily nutriment, and what is this dull town to me? what are these plain fields and the aspects of this earth and these skies? All summer and far into the fall I unconsciously went by the newspapers and the news, and now I find it was because the morning and the evening were full of news to me. My walks were full of incidents. I attended not to the affairs of Europe, but to my own affairs in Concord fields. [J 3:208]

and made brittle by the sun. Door-sill there was none, but a perennial passage for the hens under the door board.[225] Mrs. C. came to the door and asked me to view it from the inside. The hens were driven in by my approach. It was dark, and had a dirt floor for the most part, dank, clammy, and aguish, only here a board and there a board which would not bear removal. She lighted a lamp to show me the inside of the roof and the walls, and also that the board floor extended under the bed, warning me not to step into the cellar, a sort of dust hole two feet deep. In her own words, they were "good boards overhead, good boards all around, and a good window," — of two whole squares originally, only the cat had passed out that way lately. There was a stove, a bed, and a place to sit, an infant in the house where it was born, a silk parasol, gilt-framed looking-glass, and a patent new coffee-mill nailed to an oak sapling, all told. The bargain was soon concluded, for James had in the mean while returned. I to pay four dollars and twenty-five cents to-night, he to vacate at five to-morrow morning, selling to nobody else meanwhile: I to take possession at six. It were well, he said, to be there early, and anticipate certain indistinct but wholly unjust claims on the score of ground rent and fuel. This he assured me was the only encumbrance. At six I passed him and his family on the road. One large bundle held their all, — bed, coffee-mill, looking-glass, hens, — all but the cat, she took to the woods and became a wild cat, and, as I learned afterward, trod in a trap set for woodchucks, and so became a dead cat at last.

I took down this dwelling the same morning, drawing the nails, and removed it to the pond side by small cartloads, spreading the boards on the grass there to bleach and warp back again in the sun. One early thrush gave me a note or two as I drove along the woodland path. I was informed treacherously by a young Patrick[226] that neighbor Seeley,[227] an Irishman, in the intervals of the carting,

222 Pun: use to the best advantage or to the uttermost, but also with the idea of making the most work out if it.

223 Unidentified further.

224 As the building of the railroad near Walden was completed, the shacks in which the laborers had lived were sold for a few dollars each, many of the laborers having moved on to look for work in the mills and factories. Thoreau's father had similarly purchased one or two shacks to construct the pencil shop attached to the family residence on Texas Street.

225 The door board is the door itself.

226 Common name for an Irishman, similar to John Bull for an Englishman.

227 Unidentified.

transferred the still tolerable, straight, and drivable nails, staples, and spikes to his pocket,[228] and then stood when I came back to pass the time of day, and look freshly up, unconcerned, with spring thoughts, at the devastation; there being a dearth of work, as he said. He was there to represent spectatordom, and help make this seemingly insignificant event one with the removal of the gods of Troy.[229]

I dug my cellar in the side of a hill sloping to the south, where a woodchuck had formerly dug his burrow, down through sumach and blackberry roots, and the lowest stain of vegetation, six feet square by seven deep, to a fine sand where potatoes would not freeze in any winter. The sides were left shelving,[230] and not stoned; but the sun having never shone on them, the sand still keeps its place. It was but two hours' work. I took particular pleasure in this breaking of ground, for in almost all latitudes men dig into the earth for an equable temperature. Under the most splendid house in the city is still to be found the cellar where they store their roots as of old, and long after the superstructure has disappeared posterity remark its dent in the earth. The house is still but a sort of porch at the entrance of a burrow.

At length, in the beginning of May, with the help of some of my acquaintances, rather to improve so good an occasion for neighborliness than from any necessity, I set up the frame of my house. No man was ever more honored in the character of his raisers[231] than I. They are destined, I trust, to assist at the raising of loftier structures one day. I began to occupy my house on the 4th of July,[232] as soon as it was boarded and roofed, for the boards were carefully feather-edged and lapped,[233] so that it was perfectly impervious to rain; but before boarding I laid the foundation of a chimney at one end, bringing two cartloads of stones up the hill from the pond in my arms. I built the chimney after my hoeing in the fall, be-

228 Nails were machine-made by this time and therefore less expensive than the ones formerly made by hand, but they still had value enough to make pocketing them desirable.

229 Possible allusion to the theft of the sacred image of Pallas Athena from Troy by the Greeks Odysseus and Diomedes, after they learned that the city could not be taken as long as it remained there, or perhaps to the rescue by Aeneas of his household gods.

230 Sloping or inclining gradually.

231 George Willis Cooke identified Thoreau's raisers as "Emerson, Alcott, W. E. Channing, Burrill and George Curtis, Edmund Hosmer and his sons, John, Edmund, and Andrew. Thoreau said that he wished the help of the young men because they had more strength than the older ones." Henry Seidel Canby (1878–1961) in *Thoreau* named only Channing, George Curtis, Alcott, and Hosmer but did not cite a source. Ralph Leslie Rusk (1888–1962) in *The Life of Ralph Waldo Emerson* did not refer to Emerson as a raiser, nor did Emerson himself ever refer to it. In his journals covering March to September 1845, however, Emerson made several references that may allude to the building of Thoreau's house: "Cultivated people cannot live in a shanty," "I can't see a house until it is built," and following a reference to Thoreau, "Is not a small house best?"

232 Used as a symbol of Thoreau's personal independence.

233 One thin edge of each overlapping the next.

234 The newspaper he wrapped his dinner in was its holder as well as his tablecloth when unwrapped.

235 Thoreau brought a copy of the *Iliad,* Homer's epic poem recounting the story of the Trojan War, with him to Walden, but it was stolen, as he mentioned in "The Village" chapter.

236 From an old English proverb dating back to at least the late 17th century: "Nine tailors make a man." Carlyle alluded to it in *Sartor Resartus* when he referred to tailors being "not Men, but fractional Parts of a Man," and again in telling the anecdote in which Queen Elizabeth, "receiving a deputation of Eighteen Tailors, addressed them with a: Good morning, gentlemen both!" The origin of the saying is believed to be from the old tradition of nine strokes, or tellers, of the church bell to indicate that the deceased was a man. Thoreau used the phrase also in the "The Pond in Winter" chapter.

fore a fire became necessary for warmth, doing my cooking in the mean while out of doors on the ground, early in the morning: which mode I still think is in some respects more convenient and agreeable than the usual one. When it stormed before my bread was baked, I fixed a few boards over the fire, and sat under them to watch my loaf, and passed some pleasant hours in that way. In those days, when my hands were much employed, I read but little, but the least scraps of paper which lay on the ground, my holder, or tablecloth,[234] afforded me as much entertainment, in fact answered the same purpose as the Iliad.[235]

It would be worth the while to build still more deliberately than I did, considering, for instance, what foundation a door, a window, a cellar, a garret, have in the nature of man, and perchance never raising any superstructure until we found a better reason for it than our temporal necessities even. There is some of the same fitness in a man's building his own house that there is in a bird's building its own nest. Who knows but if men constructed their dwellings with their own hands, and provided food for themselves and families simply and honestly enough, the poetic faculty would be universally developed, as birds universally sing when they are so engaged? But alas! we do like cowbirds and cuckoos, which lay their eggs in nests which other birds have built, and cheer no traveller with their chattering and unmusical notes. Shall we forever resign the pleasure of construction to the carpenter? What does architecture amount to in the experience of the mass of men? I never in all my walks came across a man engaged in so simple and natural an occupation as building his house. We belong to the community. It is not the tailor alone who is the ninth part of a man;[236] it is as much the preacher, and the merchant, and the farmer. Where is this division of labor to end? and what object does it finally serve? No doubt another *may* also think for me; but it is not therefore desirable that he should do so to the exclusion of my thinking for myself.

True, there are architects so called in this country, and I have heard of one at least possessed with the idea of making architectural ornaments have a core of truth, a necessity, and hence a beauty, as if it were a revelation to him.[237] All very well perhaps from his point of view, but only a little better than the common dilettantism. A sentimental reformer in architecture, he began at the cornice, not at the foundation. It was only how to put a core of truth within the ornaments, that every sugar plum in fact might have an almond or caraway seed in it, — though I hold that almonds are most wholesome without the sugar, — and not how the inhabitant, the indweller, might build truly within and without, and let the ornaments take care of themselves. What reasonable man ever supposed that ornaments were something outward and in the skin merely, — that the tortoise got his spotted shell, or the shellfish its mother-o'-pearl tints, by such a contract as the inhabitants of Broadway their Trinity Church?[238] But a man has no more to do with the style of architecture of his house than a tortoise with that of its shell: nor need the soldier be so idle as to try to paint the precise *color* of his virtue on his standard.[239] The enemy will find it out. He may turn pale when the trial comes. This man seemed to me to lean over the cornice, and timidly whisper his half truth to the rude occupants who really knew it better than he. What of architectural beauty I now see, I know has gradually grown from within outward, out of the necessities and character of the indweller, who is the only builder, — out of some unconscious truthfulness, and nobleness, without ever a thought for the appearance; and whatever additional beauty of this kind is

237 Horatio Greenough (1805–1852), sculptor, who was an early proponent of the idea of functional architectural decoration. Much of this passage came from Thoreau's journal of 11 January 1852, in which he was reacting not to Greenough's published papers on the subject but to a letter Greenough wrote to Emerson. Emerson, who liked the letter very much, showed it to Thoreau on 10 January 1852. The letter, written 28 December 1851, spoke of "a *beauty* which will never obey other than the call of genius." Thoreau was careful to remove all direct references to Greenough in *Walden*. It is possible that his reaction may have been written to oppose the enthusiastic response of Emerson, with whom Thoreau no longer had "solid seasons," as he indicated in the penultimate paragraph of the "Former Inhabitants; and Winter Visitors" chapter.

238 Gothic Revival-style church in New York built by Richard Upjohn (1802–1878) and rebuilt in 1846 after a fire.

239 On medieval standards and elsewhere, colors represented certain virtues, such as white for purity, red for loyalty, etc.

240 The picturesque school of landscape architecture, which was distinguished by wild ruggedness, irregularity, and textural variety, in imitation of the wild and uncultivated aspects of nature, promoted in the late 18th century by several writers, most prominently William Gilpin (1724–1804) in *Remarks on Forest Scenery and Other Woodland Views, Relative Chiefly to Picturesque Beauty* (1791) and *Three Essays: On Picturesque Beauty; On Picturesque Travel; and on Sketching Landscape* (1792).

241 Reference to the fable of the jay and the peacock as told by Aesop (ca. 620–560 B.C.E.) and Jean de la Fontaine (1621–1695).

242 French: esthetic or polite literature, and fine arts, respectively.

243 Not etymologically but by association: coffins were made by the local carpenter.

244 Sir Joshua Reynolds (1723–1792) used to say, according to William Wordsworth: "If you would fix upon the best colour for your house, turn up a stone, or pluck up a handful of grass by the roots, and see what is the colour of the soil where the house is to stand, and let that be your choice."

245 The grave. Thoreau used the same phrase in "Former Inhabitants." It was a common epithet used by several poets, including Wordsworth, Ossian (James MacPherson, 1736–1796), Robert Burns (1759–1796), and William Cullen Bryant (1794–1878).

246 Toss up a copper (a one-cent piece, which was made of copper) refers to tossing a coin to decide between two choices, and possibly also to the paying of Charon in Greek mythology to ferry spirits of the dead across the river Styx, the main river of Hades.

247 Thoreau's house at Walden was an example of the earliest form of English cottage architecture, which was transferred to America with the colonists: a house enclosing a single room with a fireplace at one end. This style was studied in such works as John Claudius Loudon's (1783–1843) *Encyclopedia of Cottage, Farm, and Villa Architecture* (London, 1835), Andrew Jackson Downing's

destined to be produced will be preceded by a like unconscious beauty of life. The most interesting dwellings in this country, as the painter knows, are the most unpretending, humble log huts and cottages of the poor commonly; it is the life of the inhabitants whose shells they are, and not any peculiarity in their surfaces merely, which makes them *picturesque;*[240] and equally interesting will be the citizen's suburban box, when his life shall be as simple and as agreeable to the imagination, and there is as little straining after effect in the style of his dwelling. A great proportion of architectural ornaments are literally hollow, and a September gale would strip them off, like borrowed plumes,[241] without injury to the substantials. They can do without *architecture* who have no olives nor wines in the cellar. What if an equal ado were made about the ornaments of style in literature, and the architects of our bibles spent as much time about their cornices as the architects of our churches do? So are made the *belles-lettres* and the *beaux-arts*[242] and their professors. Much it concerns a man, forsooth, how a few sticks are slanted over him or under him, and what colors are daubed upon his box. It would signify somewhat, if, in any earnest sense, *he* slanted them and daubed it; but the spirit having departed out of the tenant, it is of a piece with constructing his own coffin,—the architecture of the grave, and "carpenter" is but another name for "coffin-maker."[243] One man says, in his despair or indifference to life, take up a handful of the earth at your feet, and paint your house that color.[244] Is he thinking of his last and narrow house?[245] Toss up a copper[246] for it as well. What an abundance of leisure he must have! Why do you take up a handful of dirt? Better paint your house your own complexion; let it turn pale or blush for you. An enterprise to improve the style of cottage architecture![247] When you have got my ornaments ready I will wear them.

Before winter I built a chimney,[248] and shingled the

sides of my house, which were already impervious to rain, with imperfect and sappy shingles[249] made of the first slice of the log, whose edges I was obliged to straighten with a plane.

I have thus a tight shingled and plastered house, ten feet wide by fifteen long, and eight-feet posts, with a garret and a closet,[250] a large window on each side, two trap doors, one door at the end, and a brick fireplace opposite. The exact cost of my house, paying the usual price for such materials as I used, but not counting the work, all of which was done by myself, was as follows; and I give the details because very few are able to tell exactly what their houses cost, and fewer still, if any, the separate cost of the various materials which compose them: —

Boards, ...	$8 03½,	mostly shanty boards.[251]
Refuse shingles for roof		
and sides, ...	4 00	
Laths, ...	1 25	
Two second-hand windows with		
glass, ...	2 43	
One thousand old brick, ...	4 00	
Two casks of lime,[252]	2 40	That was high.
Hair,[253]	0 31	More than I needed.
Mantle-tree iron,[254]	0 15	
Nails,[255]	3 90	
Hinges and screws, ...	0 14	
Latch,[256]	0 10	
Chalk, ...	0 01	
Transportation, ...	1 40	} I carried a good part on my back.
In all, ...	$28 12½[257]	

These are all the materials excepting the timber, stones and sand, which I claimed by squatter's right.[258] I have also a small wood-shed adjoining, made chiefly of the stuff which was left after building the house.

I intend to build me a house which will surpass any

(1815–1852) *Treatise on the Theory and Practice of Landscape Gardening . . . With Remarks on Rural Architecture* (New York and Boston, 1841), and T. Thomas's *The Working-Man's Cottage Architecture, Containing Plans, Elevations, and Details, for the Erection of Cheap, Comfortable, and Neat Cottages* (New York, 1848).

248 Building the chimney is described in detail in the "House-Warming" chapter.

249 Less expensive and sufficient for his needs, although in a post-*Walden* journal entry Thoreau wrote that he could "detect all the poor or sappy shingles on my neighbor's low roof which I overlook, for they, absorbing much water and not drying for a long time, are so many black squares spotting the gray roof" [J 13:423]. Thoreau shingled his house in early October 1845.

250 There is no extant documentation identifying in which of the four corners of the house Thoreau's closet was located, but the most common place for one would be on one side of the fireplace, which projected into the room.

251 Thoreau paid $4.25 to James Collins for his shanty. It is unknown from whom he purchased the other boards. It is also unclear how much Thoreau paid for boards, for the page proofs read $8.35, not $8.03½. Half-cent coins were minted in the United States through 1857, although they were no longer very common in the 1840s.

252 Used in making plaster.

253 Hair, usually horsehair, was mixed into plaster as a binding agent to give it strength.

254 Mantle-tree, or mantletree: a wooden beam (although iron was often used instead) spanning the opening of a fireplace to serve as the lintel to support the chimney.

255 By 1842 machine-made nails were 3¢ a pound.

256 Thoreau helped forge the door latch.

257 In his journal Thoreau noted that an average house cost "perhaps 1500 dollars" [PJ 2:181], although earlier in "Economy" he wrote that the "average house in this neighborhood costs perhaps eight hundred dollars."

258 The American frontier was partly settled by squatting, occupying land without right or title, and then claiming right by virtue of occupation, not ownership. Although Thoreau liked to refer to himself as a squatter, he had permission to live on Emerson's land.

259 In the Roman Catholic Church, the Advocatus Diaboli, whose duty it was to put forward defects in a candidate's claim for canonization, but more generally one who argues against a cause or position, not as a committed opponent, but simply for the sake of argument.

260 Harvard College in Cambridge, Massachusetts, from which Thoreau graduated in 1837.

261 Thoreau occupied room 31 on the fourth floor in Hollis Hall at Harvard in 1835.

262 According to the *Catalogue of the Officers and Students of Harvard University for the Academical Year 1836–7*, Thoreau's final year, tuition was $90 for "instruction, library, lecture-rooms, steward's department, rent, and care of room." Other expenses included $94.50 for board for 42 weeks, $12.50 for textbooks, $3 for "special repairs," $3–$5 for washing, and, for heating, either $7.50 per cord of wood or $8 per ton of coal.

on the main street in Concord in grandeur and luxury, as soon as it pleases me as much and will cost me no more than my present one.

I thus found that the student who wishes for a shelter can obtain one for a lifetime at an expense not greater than the rent which he now pays annually. If I seem to boast more than is becoming, my excuse is that I brag for humanity rather than for myself; and my shortcomings and inconsistencies do not affect the truth of my statement. Notwithstanding much cant and hypocrisy, — chaff which I find it difficult to separate from my wheat, but for which I am as sorry as any man, — I will breathe freely and stretch myself in this respect, it is such a relief to both the moral and physical system; and I am resolved that I will not through humility become the devil's attorney.[259] I will endeavor to speak a good word for the truth. At Cambridge College[260] the mere rent of a student's room, which is only a little larger than my own, is thirty dollars each year, though the corporation had the advantage of building thirty-two side by side and under one roof, and the occupant suffers the inconvenience of many and noisy neighbors, and perhaps a residence in the fourth story.[261] I cannot but think that if we had more true wisdom in these respects, not only less education would be needed, because, forsooth, more would already have been acquired, but the pecuniary expense of getting an education would in a great measure vanish. Those conveniences which the student requires at Cambridge or elsewhere cost him or somebody else ten times as great a sacrifice of life as they would with proper management on both sides. Those things for which the most money is demanded are never the things which the student most wants. Tuition, for instance, is an important item in the term bill,[262] while for the far more valuable education which he gets by associating with the most cultivated of his contemporaries no charge is made. The mode of founding a college is, commonly, to get up a subscription of dollars and cents, and then following blindly the principles of a division of labor to its extreme, a principle which should never be followed but with circumspection, — to call in a contractor who makes this a subject of speculation, and he employs Irishmen[263] or other operatives actually to lay the foundations,[264] while the students that are to be are said to be fitting themselves for it; and for these oversights successive generations have to pay. I think that it would be *better than this,* for the students, or those who desire to be benefited by it, even to lay the foundation themselves. The student who secures his coveted leisure and retirement by systematically shirking any labor necessary to man obtains but an ignoble and unprofitable leisure, defrauding himself of the experience which alone can make leisure fruitful. "But," says one, "you do not mean that the students should go to work with their hands instead of their heads?"[265] I do not mean that exactly, but I mean something which he might think a good deal like that; I mean that they should not *play* life, or *study* it merely, while the community supports them at this expensive game, but earnestly *live* it from beginning to end. How could youths better learn to live than by at once trying the experiment of living? Methinks this would exercise their minds as much as mathematics. If I wished a boy to know something about the arts and sciences, for instance, I would not pursue the common course, which is merely to send him into the neighborhood of some professor, where any thing is professed and practised but the art of life; — to survey the world through a telescope or a microscope, and never with his natural eye; to study chemistry, and not learn how his bread is made, or mechanics, and not learn how it is earned; to discover new satellites to Neptune,[266] and not detect the motes in his eyes,[267] or to what vagabond he is a satellite himself; or to be devoured by the monsters that swarm all

263   Irish immigrants were primarily employed as menial laborers.
264   Pun on "founding" a college.
265   Possible allusion to the theories that both Brook Farm (1841–47) and Fruitlands (1843–44) attempted to put into practice. In a letter describing Brook Farm, George Ripley wrote to Emerson: "thought would preside over the operations of labor, and labor would contribute to the expansion of thought."
266   William Lassell (1799–1880), English astronomer, discovered a satellite of the planet Neptune in 1846.
267   Allusion to Matthew 7:3: "And why beholdest thou the mote that is in thy brother's eye, but considerest not the beam that is in thine own eye?" A similar passage is found in Luke 6:41.

268 In the 1840s, technological institutions were being established to help further the education of American workingmen, but Thoreau was probably referring specifically to the Lowell Institute in Boston, founded in 1836 as a lyceum for public lectures for Boston-area residents on the topics of philosophy, natural history, science, and the arts.

269 Manufactured by the noted cutlers, Joseph Rodgers & Sons, in Sheffield, England, founded in 1682, and used here as a symbol of high quality.

270 Nautical astronomy was one part of sophomore mathematics at Harvard in the 1830s.

271 Adam Smith (1723–1790), Scottish economist, author of *The Wealth of Nations;* David Ricardo (1772–1823), English economist, author of *Principles of Political Economy and Taxation;* and Jean-Baptiste Say (1767–1832), French economist, author of *Cours Complet d'Économie Politique Pratique.* Thoreau owned Say's *A Treatise on Political Economy, or, The Production, Distribution, and Consumption of Wealth* translated by C. R. Prinsey (Philadelphia, 1834).

272 A relatively new invention in Thoreau's day, Samuel Morse (1791–1872) having invented the magnetic telegraph in 1835 and patented his final model in 1837. During the following decade its use spread rapidly, although it did not reach Concord until August 1851.

273 Maine and Texas were the eastern and western limits, respectively, of the United States until California joined the Union in 1850. Thoreau used the same phrase in *A Week on the Concord and Merrimack Rivers:* "The States have leisure to laugh from Maine to Texas at some newspaper joke" [W 1:132].

274 Harriet Martineau (1802–1876), who had severe hearing loss and carried an ear trumpet with her at all times. She made a tour of America in 1834–35, from which experience she became an abolitionist and wrote two books highly critical of American life: *Society in America* (1837) and *A Retrospect of Western Travel* (1838).

275 For a telegraph cable between America and Europe, although the cable was laid on the ocean

around him, while contemplating the monsters in a drop of vinegar. Which would have advanced the most at the end of a month,—the boy who had made his own jack-knife from the ore which he had dug and smelted, reading as much as would be necessary for this,—or the boy who had attended the lectures on metallurgy at the Institute[268] in the mean while, and had received a Rodgers' pen-knife[269] from his father? Which would be most likely to cut his fingers? ... To my astonishment I was informed on leaving college that I had studied navigation![270]—why, if I had taken one turn down the harbor I should have known more about it. Even the *poor* student studies and is taught only *political* economy, while that economy of living which is synonymous with philosophy is not even sincerely professed in our colleges. The consequence is, that while he is reading Adam Smith, Ricardo, and Say,[271] he runs his father in debt irretrievably.

As with our colleges, so with a hundred "modern improvements;" there is an illusion about them; there is not always a positive advance. The devil goes on exacting compound interest to the last for his early share and numerous succeeding investments in them. Our inventions are wont to be pretty toys, which distract our attention from serious things. They are but improved means to an unimproved end, an end which it was already but too easy to arrive at; as railroads lead to Boston or New York. We are in great haste to construct a magnetic telegraph[272] from Maine to Texas;[273] but Maine and Texas, it may be, have nothing important to communicate. Either is in such a predicament as the man who was earnest to be introduced to a distinguished deaf woman,[274] but when he was presented, and one end of her ear trumpet was put into his hand, had nothing to say. As if the main object were to talk fast and not to talk sensibly. We are eager to tunnel under the Atlantic[275] and bring the old world some weeks nearer to the new; but perchance the first news that will leak through into the broad, flapping American ear will be that the Princess Adelaide[276] has the whooping cough. After all, the man whose horse trots a mile in a minute does not carry the most important messages; he is not an evangelist, nor does he come round eating locusts and wild honey.[277] I doubt if Flying Childers[278] ever carried a peck of corn to mill.

One says to me, "I wonder that you do not lay up money; you love to travel; you might take the cars and go to Fitchburg to-day and see the country." But I am wiser than that. I have learned that the swiftest traveller is he that goes afoot. I say to my friend, Suppose we try who will get there first. The distance is thirty miles; the fare ninety cents.[279] That is almost a day's wages. I remember when wages were sixty cents a day for laborers on this very road. Well, I start now on foot,[280] and get there before night; I have travelled at that rate by the week together. You will in the mean while have earned your fare, and arrive there some time to-morrow, or possibly this evening, if you are lucky enough to get a job in season. Instead of going to Fitchburg, you will be working here the greater part of the day. And so, if the railroad reached round the world, I think that I should keep ahead of you; and as for seeing the country and getting experience of that kind, I should have to cut your acquaintance altogether.

Such is the universal law, which no man can ever outwit, and with regard to the railroad even we may say it is as broad as it is long.[281] To make a railroad round the world available to all mankind is equivalent to grading the whole surface of the planet. Men have an indistinct notion that if they keep up this activity of joint stocks and spades[282] long enough all will at length ride somewhere, in next to no time, and for nothing; but though a crowd rushes to the depot, and the conductor shouts "All aboard!" when the smoke is blown away and the vapor condensed, it will be perceived that a few are riding, but

floor, not in a tunnel. *Scientific American* reported on 4 May 1850: "Transatlantic Telegraph. John A. Roebling, Esq., Civil Engineer, of Trenton, N. J., considers the construction of a line of telegraph wire across the Atlantic entirely practicable. . . . His design is to sink a strong wire rope upon the bottom of the ocean. . . . The wires being perfectly insulated and protected against the action of the sea water, quietly resting upon the bottom of the ocean, where nothing what ever can disturb them, their efficiency may at all times be depended on— they will remain free from those vexatious interruptions which are constantly interferring [sic] with land telegraph operations." The first, albeit briefly, successful transatlantic telegraph cable was laid in 1858; the first permanent cable was finished in 1866.

276 Adelaide Louisa Theresa Caroline Amelia (1792–1849), princess of Saxe-Meiningen.

277 Food of John the Baptist in the desert, from Matthew 3:4: "And the same John himself had his raiment of camel's hair, and a leathern girdle about his loins; and his meat was locusts and wild honey."

278 English racehorse, undefeated and purported to be the fastest in the world, bred by Leonard Childers (1673–1748) of Yorkshire.

279 Thoreau corrected this in the page proofs from seventy cents in the manuscript, noting to the printer: "They have changed the fare within the last week."

280 Possibly suggested by Thoreau's friend Isaac Hecker's (1819–1889) invitation to go on a pedestrian excursion in 1844: "a certain project which I have formed in which your influence has no slight share I imagine in forming. It is to work our passage to Europe, and to walk, work, and beg, if needs be, as far when there as we are inclined to do. . . . We desire to go without purse or staff, depending upon the all embracing love of God, Humanity, and the spark of courage imprisoned in us. . . . We shall prove the dollar is not almighty and the impossible moonshine."

the rest are run over,—and it will be called, and will be, "A melancholy accident."[283] No doubt they can ride at last who shall have earned their fare, that is, if they survive so long, but they will probably have lost their elasticity and desire to travel by that time. This spending of the best part of one's life earning money in order to enjoy a questionable liberty during the least valuable part of it, reminds me of the Englishman who went to India to make a fortune first, in order that he might return to England and live the life of a poet.[284] He should have gone up garret at once. "What!" exclaim a million Irishmen starting up from all the shanties in the land, "is not this railroad which we have built a good thing?" Yes, I answer, *comparatively* good, that is, you might have done worse; but I wish, as you are brothers of mine, that you could have spent your time better than digging in this dirt.

Before I finished my house, wishing to earn ten or twelve dollars by some honest and agreeable method, in order to meet my unusual expenses, I planted about two acres and a half of light and sandy soil near it chiefly with beans, but also a small part with potatoes, corn, peas, and turnips. The whole lot contains eleven acres, mostly growing up to pines and hickories, and was sold the preceding season for eight dollars and eight cents an acre.[285] One farmer said that it was "good for nothing but to raise cheeping squirrels on." I put no manure on this land, not being the owner, but merely a squatter,[286] and not expecting to cultivate so much again, and I did not quite hoe it all once. I got out several cords of stumps in ploughing, which supplied me with fuel for a long time, and left small circles of virgin mould, easily distinguishable through the summer by the greater luxuriance of the beans there. The dead and for the most part unmerchantable wood behind my house, and the driftwood from the pond, have supplied the remainder of my fuel. I was obliged to hire a

281 Popular phrase dating to at least the 17th century.

282 Pun on joint stock and trade, the stock or capital funds of a company held jointly or in common by its owners, and the spades used in grading the railroad beds.

283 Term used by newspapers in Thoreau's day to describe an accident, usually involving a steamship or railroad, in which many lives were lost.

284 Possibly either Robert Clive, 1st Baron Clive of Plassey (1725–1774), who established British rule in India with victories in Bengal, Calcutta, and Plassey, or Warren Hastings (1732–1818), first governor-general of British India. Although neither was primarily known as a poet, Clive did write some poetry and Hastings wrote an introduction to a contemporary translation of the Bhagavad Gita to which Thoreau referred in *A Week on the Concord and Merrimack Rivers* [W 1:142–44].

285 It was sold to Emerson, who wrote to his brother William on 4 October 1844: "In one of my solitary wood-walks by Walden Pond, I met two or three men who told me they had come thither to sell & to buy a field, on which they wished me to bid as purchaser. As it was on the shore of the pond, & now for years I had a sort of daily occupancy in it, I bid on it, & bought it, eleven acres for $8.10 per acre."

286 Pun on squatting to defecate, thus Thoreau did put manure on the land. Although it is probable that Thoreau had a privy, there is no extant record of one, nor did archaeologist Roland Robbins (1908–1987) find any evidence of one when he excavated the Walden house site in 1945.

team and a man[287] for the ploughing, though I held the plough myself. My farm outgoes for the first season were, for implements, seed, work, &c., $14 72½. The seed corn was given me.[288] This never costs any thing to speak of, unless you plant more than enough. I got twelve bushels of beans, and eighteen bushels of potatoes, beside some peas and sweet corn. The yellow corn and turnips were too late to come to any thing. My whole income from the farm was

	$23 44.
Deducting the outgoes, ...	14 72½
There are left, ...	$8 71½

beside produce consumed and on hand at the time this estimate was made of the value of $4 50,—the amount on hand much more than balancing a little grass which I did not raise. All things considered, that is, considering the importance of a man's soul and of to-day, notwithstanding the short time occupied by my experiment, nay, partly even because of its transient character, I believe that that was doing better than any farmer in Concord did that year.

The next year I did better still, for I spaded up all the land which I required, about a third of an acre,[289] and I learned from the experience of both years, not being in the least awed by many celebrated works on husbandry, Arthur Young[290] among the rest, that if one would live simply and eat only the crop which he raised, and raise no more than he ate, and not exchange it for an insufficient quantity of more luxurious and expensive things, he would need to cultivate only a few rods of ground, and that it would be cheaper to spade up that than to use oxen to plough it, and to select a fresh spot from time to time than to manure the old, and he could do all his necessary farm work as it were with his left hand at odd hours in the summer; and thus he would not be tied to an ox, or

287 Unidentified.

288 Probably by Edmund Hosmer (1798–1881). Franklin Sanborn identified Hosmer as "living on the Cambridge Turnpike, or a little off from that, along which his well-tilled farm extended. This made him one of Thoreau's nearest neighbors." Thoreau called Hosmer "the most intelligent farmer in Concord, and perchance in Middlesex . . . inclined to speculation in conversation—giving up any work to it for the time—and long-headed" [J 4:194].

289 Reduced from the 2½ acres he had planted the previous year. Despite his claim here that he did better in his second year at Walden, his journal noted a frost on the night of 12 June 1846 that killed his beans, tomatoes, squash, corn, and potatoes.

290 English agriculturist (1741–1820), who wrote such works as *Farmer's Guide in Hiring and Stocking Farms* (London, 1770) and *Rural Œconomy: or, Essays on the Practical Parts of Husbandry* (London, 1770).

291 Thoreau's use of the word "genius" is related to reason, which intuits what is beyond proof.

292 Possible reference to Jonathan Swift's (1667–1745) *Gulliver's Travels,* in which the horselike Houyhnhnms are the masters of the humanlike Yahoos. In 1843 Charles Lane (1800–1870) and Bronson Alcott wrote in "The Consociate Family Life": "So long as cattle are used in agriculture, it is very evident that man will remain a slave, whether he be proprietor or hireling. The driving of cattle beyond their natural and pleasurable exertion; the waiting upon them as cook and chambermaid three parts of the year; the excessive labor of mowing, curing and housing hay, and of collecting other fodder, and the large extra quantity of land needful to keep up this system, forms a combination of unfavorable circumstances."

293 Probable reference to the communal experiment Fruitlands, about which Lane and Alcott reported in the July 1843 issue of *The Dial* that it was "to supersede ultimately the labor of the plough and cattle, by the spade and the pruning knife."

294 Allusion to James Madison (1751–1836) in *Federalist* 49: "But a nation of philosophers is as little to be expected as the philosophical race of kings wished for by Plato."

horse, or cow, or pig, as at present. I desire to speak impartially on this point, and as one not interested in the success or failure of the present economical and social arrangements. I was more independent than any farmer in Concord, for I was not anchored to a house or farm, but could follow the bent of my genius,[291] which is a very crooked one, every moment. Beside being better off than they already, if my house had been burned or my crops had failed, I should have been nearly as well off as before.

I am wont to think that men are not so much the keepers of herds as herds are the keepers of men,[292] the former are so much the freer. Men and oxen exchange work; but if we consider necessary work only, the oxen will be seen to have greatly the advantage, their farm is so much the larger. Man does some of his part of the exchange work in his six weeks of haying, and it is no boy's play. Certainly no nation that lived simply in all respects, that is, no nation of philosophers, would commit so great a blunder as to use the labor of animals.[293] True, there never was and is not likely soon to be a nation of philosophers,[294] nor am I certain it is desirable that there should be. However, *I* should never have broken a horse or bull and taken him to board for any work he might do for me, for fear I should become a horse-man or a herds-man merely; and if society seems to be the gainer by so doing, are we certain that what is one man's gain is not another's loss, and that the stable-boy has equal cause with his master to be satisfied? Granted that some public works would not have been constructed without this aid, and let man share the glory of such with the ox and horse; does it follow that he could not have accomplished works yet more worthy of himself in that case? When men begin to do, not merely unnecessary or artistic, but luxurious and idle work, with their assistance, it is inevitable that a few do all the exchange work with the oxen, or, in other words, become the slaves of the strongest. Man thus not only works for the animal within him, but, for a symbol of this, he works for the animal without him. Though we have many substantial houses of brick or stone, the prosperity of the farmer is still measured by the degree to which the barn overshadows the house. This town is said to have the largest houses for oxen, cows, and horses hereabouts, and it is not behindhand in its public buildings; but there are very few halls for free worship or free speech[295] in this county. It should not be by their architecture, but why not even by their power of abstract thought, that nations should seek to commemorate themselves? How much more admirable the Bhagvat-Geeta[296] than all the ruins of the East! Towers and temples are the luxury of princes. A simple and independent mind does not toil at the bidding of any prince. Genius is not a retainer to any emperor, nor is its material silver, or gold, or marble, except to a trifling extent. To what end, pray, is so much stone hammered? In Arcadia,[297] when I was there, I did not see any hammering stone. Nations are possessed with an insane ambition to perpetuate the memory of themselves by the amount of hammered stone they leave. What if equal pains were taken to smooth and polish their manners? One piece of good sense would be more memorable than a monument as high as the moon. I love better to see stones in place. The grandeur of Thebes[298] was a vulgar grandeur. More sensible is a rod of stone wall that bounds an honest man's field than a hundred-gated Thebes[299] that has wandered farther from the true end of life. The religion and civilization which are barbaric and heathenish build splendid temples; but what you might call Christianity does not. Most of the stone a nation hammers goes toward its tomb only. It buries itself alive. As for the Pyramids,[300] there is nothing to wonder at in them so much as the fact that so many men could be found degraded enough to spend their lives constructing a tomb for some ambitious booby, whom it would have

295 Thoreau may be referring to the time in 1844 when Emerson, wishing to address a gathering of abolitionists on the anniversary of the emancipation of the slaves of the West Indies, was denied the use of the Concord churches. Thoreau finally got permission to use the courthouse and rang the bell himself to announce the meeting.

296 Also spelled Bhagavad Gita, a Sanskrit poem incorporated into the Mahabharata, one of the greatest religious classics of Hinduism. The Gita is presented as a dialogue between Lord Krishna and Prince Arjuna on the eve of the great battle of Kurukshetra. The main doctrines of the Gita are karma-yoga, the yoga of selfless action performed with inner detachment from its results; jnana-yoga, the yoga of knowledge and discrimination between the lower nature of man and the supreme self or soul; and bhakti yoga, the yoga of devotion to a particular god.

297 In ancient Greece, the home of pastoral simplicity and continuing happiness.

298 Ancient capital of Egypt under the 18th dynasty (ca. 1550–1290 B.C.E.). Its monuments were the richest in the land, with major temples at Luxor and Karnak on the east bank of the Nile and the necropolis, with tombs of royalty and nobles, on the west bank. Thebes was a testament to the grandeur of ancient Egypt.

299 Allusion to the *Iliad* 9:383, in which Thebes "pours her heroes through a hundred gates." Thebes was also called Hecatompylos for its hundred gates.

300 In his journal for 21 April 1852, Thoreau wrote: "We have heard enough nonsense about the Pyramids. If Congress should vote to rear such structures on the prairies to-day, I should not think it worth the while, nor be interested in the enterprise. It was the foolish undertaking of some tyrant. . . . The tower of Babel has been a good deal laughed at. It was just as sensible an undertaking as the Pyramids, which, because they were completed and have stood to this day, are admired" [J 3:453].

been wiser and manlier to have drowned in the Nile, and then given his body to the dogs. I might possibly invent some excuse for them and him, but I have no time for it. As for the religion and love of art of the builders, it is much the same all the world over, whether the building be an Egyptian temple or the United States Bank.[301] It costs more than it comes to. The mainspring is vanity, assisted by the love of garlic and bread and butter. Mr. Balcom,[302] a promising young architect, designs it on the back of his Vitruvius,[303] with hard pencil and ruler, and the job is let out to Dobson & Sons,[304] stonecutters. When the thirty centuries begin to look down on it,[305] mankind begin to look up at it. As for your high towers and monuments, there was a crazy fellow once in this town who undertook to dig through to China,[306] and he got so far that, as he said, he heard the Chinese pots and kettles rattle; but I think that I shall not go out of my way to admire the hole which he made. Many are concerned about the monuments of the West and the East,—to know who built them. For my part, I should like to know who in those days did not build them,—who were above such trifling. But to proceed with my statistics.

By surveying, carpentry, and day-labor of various other kinds[307] in the village in the mean while, for I have as many trades as fingers,[308] I had earned $13 34. The expense of food for eight months, namely, from July 4th to March 1st, the time when these estimates were made, though I lived there more than two years,—not counting potatoes, a little green corn, and some peas, which I had raised, nor considering the value of what was on hand at the last date, was

Rice, ...	$1 73½	
Molasses, ...	1 73	Cheapest form of the saccharine.
Rye meal, ...	1 04¾	
Indian meal, ...	0 99¾	Cheaper than rye.
Pork, ...	0 22	

301 The Bank of the United States was chartered in 1791 to provide a market for government bonds and a depository for government funds. Based in Philadelphia, it was established by Alexander Hamilton (1755–1804) and closed down in 1811. The Second Bank of the United States, which was established in 1816 with a 20-year charter that was not renewed, was built in the Egyptian style.

302 Unidentified.

303 Marcus Vitruvius Pollio (1st century B.C.E.), Roman architect and author of *De Architectura*.

304 Unidentified.

305 Allusion to Napoléon I (1769–1821), who told his soldiers that forty centuries were looking down upon them as they stood before the pyramids of Egypt. The remark is found in Napoléon's *Memoirs of the History of France,* but Thoreau's likely source was Emerson, who wrote in his journal in 1845: "Soldiers, from the tops of those pyramids forty centuries look down on you." Emerson also quoted it in "Napoleon, or the Man of the World."

306 In Concord's Estabrook Woods is a slight excavation referred to as the "hole to China." In a journal entry of 27 June 1860 Thoreau wrote that a neighbor named Farmer showed him "where his uncle (?) tried to dig through to the other side of the world. Dug more or less for three years. Used to dig nights, as long as one candle lasted. Left a stone just between him and the other side, not to be removed till he was ready to marry Washington's sister. The foxes now occupy his hole" [J 13:376].

307 Thoreau performed various carpentry tasks for Emerson: in October 1845 Emerson paid him for building a fence; in September 1846 he advanced Thoreau money for work to be done adding a barn room; in the summer of 1847 Thoreau, with Bronson Alcott, worked at building a summerhouse for Emerson; in the fall of 1847 he put shelves in a closet. He also lived in the Emerson household from April 1841 to May 1843, working in the garden and around the house in exchange for room and board. In October 1845 Emerson paid him for building a drain and laying a cellar floor,

Flour, ...	0 88	} Costs more than Indian meal, both money and trouble.
Sugar, ...	0 80	
Lard, ...	0 65	
Apples, ...	0 25	
Dried apple, ...	0 22	
Sweet potatoes, . . .	0 10	
One pumpkin, . . .	0 6	
One watermelon, . .	0 2	
Salt, ...	0 3	

All experiments which failed.

Yes, I did eat $8 74, all told; but I should not thus unblushingly publish my guilt, if I did not know that most of my readers were equally guilty with myself, and that their deeds would look no better in print. The next year I sometimes caught a mess of fish for my dinner, and once I went so far as to slaughter a woodchuck which ravaged my bean-field,—effect his transmigration, as a Tartar[309] would say,—and devour him, partly for experiment's sake; but though it afforded me a momentary enjoyment, notwithstanding a musky flavor, I saw that the longest use would not make that a good practice, however it might seem to have your woodchucks ready dressed by the village butcher.

Clothing and some incidental expenses within the same dates, though little can be inferred from this item, amounted to

$8 40¾

Oil and some household utensils, ... 2 00

So that all the pecuniary outgoes, excepting for washing and mending, which for the most part were done out of the house, and their bills have not yet been received,[310]— and these are all and more than all the ways by which money necessarily goes out in this part of the world,— were

and in March 1850 he wanted Thoreau "reestablish our fallen arbour in the great path and he may set new posts, if he will." In a 4 October 1857 journal entry Thoreau recalled some of the jobs he did while living at Walden: "While I lived in the woods I did various jobs about the town,—some fence-building, painting, gardening, carpentering, etc., etc. One day a man came from the east edge of the town and said he wanted to get me to brick up a fireplace, etc., etc., for him. I told him that I was not a mason, but he knew that I had built my own house entirely and would not take no for an answer. So I went. . . . I bricked up a fireplace, papered a chamber, but my principal work was whitewashing ceilings. . . . About the same time I also contracted to build a wood-shed of no mean size. . . . I built six fences" [J 10:61–63].

308 In a letter to the secretary of his Harvard class, Thoreau wrote, "I am a Schoolmaster—a Private Tutor, a Surveyor—a Gardener, a Farmer— a Painter, I mean a House Painter, a Carpenter, a Mason, a Day-Laborer, a Pencil-Maker, a Glass-paper Maker, a Writer, and sometimes a Poetaster" [C 186].

309 Less correct but more common spelling of Tatar: a member of a group of Turkic peoples primarily inhabiting Tartary, a vast region of eastern Europe and northern Asia controlled by the Mongols in the 13th and 14th centuries. Tatars believed in the transmigration of the soul at death from one body to another, human or animal, as part of the cycle of reincarnation. Reincarnation is fundamental to Hindu, Buddhist, and Jain conceptions of the world, although it appears in many cultures.

310 The washing and mending were done by Thoreau's family, so that his remark about not having received a bill was more an inside joke to his family than a literal reporting of his outgoing expenses.

House, ...	$28 12½
Farm one year, ...	14 72½
Food eight months, ...	8 74
Clothing, &c., eight months, ...	8 40¾
Oil, &c., eight months, ...	2 00
In all, ...	$61 99¾

I address myself now to those of my readers who have a living to get. And to meet this I have for farm produce sold

	$23 44
Earned by day-labor, ...	13 34
In all, ...	$36 78,

which subtracted from the sum of the outgoes leaves a balance of $25 21¾ on the one side, — this being very nearly the means with which I started, and the measure of expenses to be incurred, — and on the other, beside the leisure and independence and health thus secured, a comfortable house for me as long as I choose to occupy it.

These statistics, however accidental and therefore uninstructive they may appear, as they have a certain completeness, have a certain value also. Nothing was given me of which I have not rendered some account.[311] It appears from the above estimate, that my food alone cost me in money about twenty-seven cents a week. It was, for nearly two years after this, rye and Indian meal without yeast,[312] potatoes, rice, a very little salt pork, molasses, and salt, and my drink water. It was fit that I should live on rice, mainly, who loved so well the philosophy of India. To meet the objections of some inveterate cavillers, I may as well state, that if I dined out occasionally,[313] as I always had done, and I trust shall have opportunities to do again, it was frequently to the detriment of my domestic arrangements. But the dining out, being, as I have

311 Possible allusion to Matthew 12:36: "Give account thereof in the day of judgment."

312 According to Edward Jarvis: "Nearly the whole of the bread in farmers' (and other working) families was brown made of Indian corn and rye meal. Very little wheat flour or white bread was used."

313 While living at Walden, Thoreau still occasionally enjoyed eating at his family's home, dining with the Emersons on Sundays, or stopping by the Hosmer household for supper. Thoreau was neither the hermit many have believed him to be nor the hypocrite implied by Ellery Channing's statement that he "bivouacked" at Walden but "really lived at home, where he went every day."

stated, a constant element, does not in the least affect a comparative statement like this.[314]

I learned from my two years' experience that it would cost incredibly little trouble to obtain one's necessary food, even in this latitude; that a man may use as simple a diet as the animals, and yet retain health and strength. I have made a satisfactory dinner, satisfactory on several accounts, simply off a dish of purslane[315] (*Portulaca oleracea*) which I gathered in my corn-field, boiled and salted. I give the Latin on account of the savoriness of the trivial name.[316] And pray what more can a reasonable man desire, in peaceful times, in ordinary noons, than a sufficient number of ears of green sweet-corn boiled, with the addition of salt? Even the little variety which I used was a yielding to the demands of appetite, and not of health. Yet men have come to such a pass that they frequently starve, not for want of necessaries, but for want of luxuries; and I know a good woman who thinks that her son lost his life because he took to drinking water only.[317]

The reader will perceive that I am treating the subject rather from an economic than a dietetic point of view, and he will not venture to put my abstemiousness to the test unless he has a well-stocked larder.

Bread I at first made of pure Indian meal and salt, genuine hoe-cakes,[318] which I baked before my fire out of doors on a shingle or the end of a stick of timber sawed off in building my house; but it was wont to get smoked and to have a piny flavor. I tried flour also; but have at last found a mixture of rye and Indian meal most convenient and agreeable. In cold weather it was no little amusement to bake several small loaves of this in succession, tending and turning them as carefully as an Egyptian his hatching eggs.[319] They were a real cereal fruit which I ripened, and they had to my senses a fragrance like that of other noble fruits, which I kept in as long as possible by wrapping them in cloths. I made a study of the ancient and

314 Edward Emerson (1844–1930), Ralph Waldo Emerson's son, agreed that Thoreau's dining out did not affect the truth of his accounting: "The mighty indictment that he was not honest in his experiment, for he did not live exclusively on his own meal and rice, but often accepted one of his mother's pies, or chanced in at a friend's at supper-time, seems too frivolous to notice, but since it is so often made, I will say that Henry Thoreau, while he could have lived uncomplainingly where an Esquimau could, on *tripe de roche* lichen and blubber, if need were (for never was man less the slave of appetite and luxury), was not a prig, nor a man of so small pattern as to be tied to a rule-of-thumb in diet, and ungraciously thrust back on his loving mother her gift. Nor was there the slightest reason that he should forego his long-established habit of appearing from time to time at night-fall, a welcome guest at the fireside of friends. He came for friendship, not for food."

315 Native plant of India commonly used as a potherb or greens.

316 The trivial name is the second part of the scientific name, applied to the species (the first part is the genus), with a pun on the savoriness of the herb.

317 Unidentified.

318 Johnnycakes, made of cornmeal, salt, and either boiling water or cold milk, and called hoe-cakes because they were sometimes baked on the iron blade of a hoe.

319 Egyptians had been early practitioners of artificial incubation. Thoreau may have read about this in Sir Gardner Wilkinson's (1797–1875) *The Manners and Customs of the Ancient Egyptians,* which quotes Diodorus Siculus (1st century B.C.E.): "Dispensing with the incubation of the hens, they with their own hands bring the eggs to maturity."

320 Unidentified.

321 Latin: breath, spirit.

322 In ancient Rome, a fire was kept continually burning in the temple of Vesta, goddess of the blazing hearth. Vestal virgins tended the fire day and night and it was never allowed to die out, except on 1 March, the start of the new year, when it was ceremonially renewed.

323 Pertaining to cereal grasses, from Ceres, Roman goddess of agriculture, with a pun on cerulean: blue, azure.

324 Analytic thinking separates a whole into its elemental parts or basic principles, while synthetic thinking combines separate elements to form a coherent whole.

325 Crystallized sodium carbonate, used as a leavening agent.

indispensable art of bread-making, consulting such authorities as offered, going back to the primitive days and first invention of the unleavened kind, when from the wildness of nuts and meats men first reached the mildness and refinement of this diet, and travelling gradually down in my studies through that accidental souring of the dough which, it is supposed, taught the leavening process, and through the various fermentations thereafter, till I came to "good, sweet, wholesome bread,"[320] the staff of life. Leaven, which some deem the soul of bread, the *spiritus*[321] which fills its cellular tissue, which is religiously preserved like the vestal fire,[322] — some precious bottle-full, I suppose, first brought over in the May-flower, did the business for America, and its influence is still rising, swelling, spreading, in cerealian[323] billows over the land, — this seed I regularly and faithfully procured from the village, till at length one morning I forgot the rules, and scalded my yeast; by which accident I discovered that even this was not indispensable, — for my discoveries were not by the synthetic but analytic process,[324] — and I have gladly omitted it since, though most housewives earnestly assured me that safe and wholesome bread without yeast might not be, and elderly people prophesied a speedy decay of the vital forces. Yet I find it not to be an essential ingredient, and after going without it for a year am still in the land of the living; and I am glad to escape the trivialness of carrying a bottle-full in my pocket, which would sometimes pop and discharge its contents to my discomfiture. It is simpler and more respectable to omit it. Man is an animal who more than any other can adapt himself to all climates and circumstances. Neither did I put any sal soda,[325] or other acid or alkali, into my bread. It would seem that I made it according to the recipe which Marcus Porcius Cato gave about two centuries before Christ. "Panem depsti-

cium sic facito. Manus mortariumque bene lavato. Fari-
nam in mortarium indito, aquæ paulatim addito, subigi-
toque pulchre. Ubi bene subegeris, defingito, coquitoque
sub testu."[326] Which I take to mean—"Make kneaded
bread thus. Wash your hands and trough well. Put the
meal into the trough, add water gradually, and knead it
thoroughly. When you have kneaded it well, mould it,
and bake it under a cover," that is, in a baking-kettle. Not
a word about leaven. But I did not always use this staff of
life. At one time, owing to the emptiness of my purse, I
saw none of it for more than a month.

Every New Englander might easily raise all his own
breadstuffs in this land of rye and Indian corn, and not
depend on distant and fluctuating markets for them. Yet
so far are we from simplicity and independence that, in
Concord, fresh and sweet meal is rarely sold in the shops,
and hominy[327] and corn in a still coarser form are hardly
used by any. For the most part the farmer gives to his
cattle and hogs the grain of his own producing, and buys
flour, which is at least no more wholesome, at a greater
cost, at the store. I saw that I could easily raise my bushel
or two of rye and Indian corn, for the former will grow on
the poorest land, and the latter does not require the best,
and grind them in a hand-mill, and so do without rice
and pork; and if I must have some concentrated sweet,
I found by experiment that I could make a very good
molasses either of pumpkins or beets, and I knew that
I needed only to set out a few maples to obtain it more
easily still, and while these were growing I could use various substitutes beside those which I have named. "For,"
as the Forefathers sang,—

>   "we can make liquor to sweeten our lips
> Of pumpkins and parsnips and walnut-tree
>   chips."[328]

326 Quoted from Marcus Porcius Cato (234–149 B.C.E.), *De Agri Cultura* 74, a practical treatise on farming and country life.
327 Coarsely ground dry corn, after the hull and germ had been removed, which was boiled in water or milk.
328 Quotation from what was sometimes referred to as the "Forefathers' Song," also known as "New England Annoyances," written around 1630. Thoreau's source may have been John Warner Barber's (1798–1885) *Historical Collections, Being a General Collection of Interesting Facts, Traditions, Biographical Sketches, Anecdotes, &c., Relating to the History and Antiquities of Every Town in Massachusetts, with Geographical Description.*

329 According to Thomas Morton's (ca. 1579–1647) *Manners and Customs of the Indians (of New England)* (1637): "If they knew the benefit of salt (as they may in time), and the means to make salt meat fresh again, they would endeavor to preserve fish for winter, as well as corn; and that if anything bring them to civility, it will be the use of salt, to have food in store, which is a chief benefit in a civilized commonwealth. These people have begun already to incline to the use of salt. Many of them would beg salt of me to carry home with them, that had frequented our homes and had been acquainted with our salt meats; and salt I willingly gave them."

330 There is no record extant indicating in which farmer's family Thoreau's cloth was woven.

331 Allusion to Genesis 3:23: when Adam and Eve were driven out of Eden, it became Adam's lot to till the ground.

332 Reversal of "faith is the root," found in Matthew Henry's (1662–1714) *Commentary on the Whole Bible* and William Penn's (1644–1718) *Fruits of Solitude.*

333 Pun: board as wood and also as food or provisions. Thoreau was aware of the difficulty some of his statements would present to readers: "My facts shall be falsehoods to the common sense. I would so state facts that they shall be significant, shall be myths or mythologic" [J 3:99].

334 Probably Isaac Hecker (1819–1888), founder of the Paulist Fathers, who wrote in his diary on 30 August 1843: "If the past nine months or more are any evidence, I find that I can live on very simple diet. . . . So far I have had wheat ground and made into unleavened bread, but as soon as we get in a new lot, I shall try it in the grain."

335 English and American law granted a widow one-third of her husband's personal property should he die intestate and leave a child or descendant.

Finally, as for salt, that grossest of groceries, to obtain this might be a fit occasion for a visit to the seashore, or, if I did without it altogether, I should probably drink the less water. I do not learn that the Indians ever troubled themselves to go after it.[329]

Thus I could avoid all trade and barter, so far as my food was concerned, and having a shelter already, it would only remain to get clothing and fuel. The pantaloons which I now wear were woven in a farmer's family,[330]—thank Heaven there is so much virtue still in man; for I think the fall from the farmer to the operative as great and memorable as that from the man to the farmer;[331]—and in a new country fuel is an encumbrance. As for a habitat, if I were not permitted still to squat, I might purchase one acre at the same price for which the land I cultivated was sold—namely, eight dollars and eight cents. But as it was, I considered that I enhanced the value of the land by squatting on it.

There is a certain class of unbelievers who sometimes ask me such questions as, if I think that I can live on vegetable food alone; and to strike at the root of the matter at once,—for the root is faith,[332]—I am accustomed to answer such, that I can live on board nails.[333] If they cannot understand that, they cannot understand much that I have to say. For my part, I am glad to hear of experiments of this kind being tried; as that a young man tried for a fortnight to live on hard, raw corn on the ear, using his teeth for all mortar.[334] The squirrel tribe tried the same and succeeded. The human race is interested in these experiments, though a few old women who are incapacitated for them, or who own their thirds in mills,[335] may be alarmed.

My furniture, part of which I made myself, and the rest cost me nothing of which I have not rendered an account, consisted of a bed, a table, a desk, three chairs, a looking-glass three inches in diameter, a pair of tongs and andirons, a kettle, a skillet,[336] and a frying-pan, a dipper, a wash-bowl, two knives and forks, three plates, one cup, one spoon, a jug for oil, a jug for molasses, and a japanned[337] lamp. None is so poor that he need sit on a pumpkin. That is shiftlessness. There is a plenty of such chairs as I like best in the village garrets to be had for taking them away. Furniture! Thank God, I can sit and I can stand without the aid of a furniture warehouse. What man but a philosopher would not be ashamed to see his furniture packed in a cart[338] and going up country exposed to the light of heaven and the eyes of men, a beggarly account of empty boxes? That is Spaulding's[339] furniture. I could never tell from inspecting such a load whether it belonged to a so called rich man or a poor one; the owner always seemed poverty-stricken. Indeed, the more you have of such things the poorer you are. Each load looks as if it contained the contents of a dozen shanties; and if one shanty is poor, this is a dozen times as poor. Pray, for what do we *move* ever but to get rid of our furniture, our *exuviæ;*[340] at last to go from this world to another newly furnished, and leave this to be burned? It is the same as if all these traps[341] were buckled to a man's belt, and he could not move over the rough country where our lines are cast without dragging them,—dragging his trap. He was a lucky fox that left his tail in the trap.[342] The muskrat will gnaw his third leg off to be free.[343] No wonder man has lost his elasticity. How often he is at a dead set![344] "Sir, if I may be so bold, what do you mean by a dead set?" If you are a seer,[345] whenever you meet a man you will see all that he owns, ay, and much that he pretends to disown, behind him, even to his kitchen furniture and all the trumpery which he saves and will not burn, and he will appear to be harnessed to it and making what headway he can. I think that the man is at a dead set who has got through a knot hole or gateway where

336 In Thoreau's day, a small vessel of iron, copper, or other metal, somewhat deeper than a frying pan and raised on legs, used for heating and boiling water, stewing meat, etc.

337 Lacquerware.

338 Thoreau hauled his furniture to Walden in a cart: "It was on the 4th of July that I put a few articles of furniture into a hay-rigging, some of which I had made myself, and commenced housekeeping" [J 3:200]. This was probably the same cart he used earlier to haul boards to his building site.

339 Unidentified. Although Franklin Sanborn noted in his Bibliophile Edition of *Walden* that he believed the name to be fictitious, Thoreau added a penciled query to a "Dea. Spaulding" to an April 1841 journal entry [PJ 1:700].

340 Latin: cast-off objects.

341 Pun: traps as snares, and also as external ornamentation or trapping.

342 Allusion to Aesop's fable "The Fox Without a Tail," in which the fox lost his tail to free himself from a trap.

343 In his journal Thoreau quoted Concord trapper George Melvin: "Oh, the muskrats are the greatest fellows to gnaw their legs off. Why I caught one once that had just gnawed his third leg off, this being the third time he had been trapped; and he lay dead by the trap, for he could n't run on one leg." Thoreau commented: "Such tragedies are enacted even in this sphere and along our peaceful streams, and dignify at least the hunter's trade. Only courage does anywhere prolong life, whether in man or beast. . . . Man, even the hunter, naturally has sympathy with every brave effort, even in his game, to maintain that life it enjoys. The hunter regards with awe his game, and it becomes at last his medicine" [J 1:481]. He wrote about it again in a journal entry for 5 February 1854: "Shall we not have sympathy with the muskrat which gnaws its third leg off, not as pitying its sufferings, but through our kindred mortality, appreciating its majestic pains and its heroic virtue?" [J 6:98].

344 Fixed or stationary condition caused by an obstacle, thus an inability to continue or progress.

345 Literally one who sees, and by extension a prophet, but also a poet: "The bard has in a great measure lost the dignity and sacredness of his office. Formerly he was called a seer, but now it is thought that one man sees as much as another" [W 1:392]. Emerson in his "Divinity School Address" wrote: "Always the seer is a sayer. Somehow his dream is told; somehow he publishes it with solemn joy: sometimes with pencil on canvas, sometimes with chisel on stone, sometimes in towers and aisles of granite, his soul's worship is builded; sometimes in anthems of indefinite music; but clearest and most permanent, in words."

346 Trim, neat.

347 Allusion to John 5:8: "Take up thy bed, and walk."

348 Folk beliefs.

his sledge load of furniture cannot follow him. I cannot but feel compassion when I hear some trig,[346] compact-looking man, seemingly free, all girded and ready, speak of his "furniture," as whether it is insured or not. "But what shall I do with my furniture?" My gay butterfly is entangled in a spider's web then. Even those who seem for a long while not to have any, if you inquire more narrowly you will find have some stored in somebody's barn. I look upon England to-day as an old gentleman who is travelling with a great deal of baggage, trumpery which has accumulated from long housekeeping, which he has not the courage to burn; great trunk, little trunk, band-box and bundle. Throw away the first three at least. It would surpass the powers of a well man nowadays to take up his bed and walk,[347] and I should certainly advise a sick one to lay down his bed and run. When I have met an immigrant tottering under a bundle which contained his all—looking like an enormous wen which had grown out of the nape of his neck—I have pitied him, not because that was his all, but because he had all *that* to carry. If I have got to drag my trap, I will take care that it be a light one and do not nip me in a vital part. But perchance it would be wisest never to put one's paw into it.

I would observe, by the way, that it costs me nothing for curtains, for I have no gazers to shut out but the sun and moon, and I am willing that they should look in. The moon will not sour milk nor taint meat of mine,[348] nor will the sun injure my furniture or fade my carpet, and if he is sometimes too warm a friend, I find it still better economy to retreat behind some curtain which nature has provided, than to add a single item to the details of housekeeping. A lady once offered me a mat, but as I had no room to spare within the house, nor time to spare within or without to shake it, I declined it, preferring to wipe my feet on the sod before my door. It is best to avoid the beginnings of evil.

Not long since I was present at the auction of a deacon's effects,[349] for his life had not been ineffectual:[350]—

"The evil that men do lives after them."[351]

As usual, a great proportion was trumpery which had begun to accumulate in his father's day. Among the rest was a dried tapeworm. And now, after lying half a century in his garret and other dust holes, these things were not burned; instead of a *bonfire*,[352] or purifying destruction of them, there was an *auction*,[353] or increasing of them. The neighbors eagerly collected to view them, bought them all, and carefully transported them to their garrets and dust holes, to lie there till their estates are settled, when they will start again. When a man dies he kicks the dust.[354]

The customs of some savage nations might, perchance, be profitably imitated by us, for they at least go through the semblance of casting their slough annually; they have the idea of the thing, whether they have the reality or not. Would it not be well if we were to celebrate such a "busk,"[355] or "feast of first fruits," as Bartram[356] describes to have been the custom of the Mucclasse Indians?[357] "When a town celebrates the busk," says he, "having previously provided themselves with new clothes, new pots, pans, and other household utensils and furniture, they collect all their worn out clothes and other despicable things, sweep and cleanse their houses, squares, and the whole town, of their filth, which with all the remaining grain and other old provisions they cast together into one common heap, and consume it with fire. After having taken medicine, and fasted for three days, all the fire in the town is extinguished. During this fast they abstain from the gratification of every appetite and passion whatever. A general amnesty is proclaimed; all malefactors may return to their town. —"[358]

"On the fourth morning, the high priest, by rubbing

349 Deacon Reuben Brown (1781–1854). Thoreau attended the auction of Brown's belongings on 27 January 1854. Ellery Channing called the deacon "a penurious old curmudgeon, who lived next house to me in the middle of the town,—a human rat."

350 Pun on the deacon's "effects."

351 Quoted from Shakespeare's *Julius Caesar* 3.2.72.

352 Originally a purging fire for burning heretics, proscribed books, or corpses. Possible allusion, supported by Thoreau's use of the word "trumpery" earlier in this paragraph, to Hawthorne's story "Earth's Holocaust" (1844), which begins: "Once upon a time—but whether in the time past or time to come, is a matter of little or no moment—this wide world had become so overburthened with an accumulation of worn-out trumpery, that the inhabitants determined to rid themselves of it by a general bonfire."

353 From the Latin, *auctio*: an increasing.

354 Conflation of kick up the dust, meaning create a fuss, and bite the dust, to die.

355 Main festival of the Mucclasse Indians, celebrating the end of the old and the beginning of the new year.

356 William Bartram (1739–1823), American naturalist.

357 Mucclasse, or Muklasa, a town believed to have been a group affiliated with either the Alabama or Kosati Indians. "Muklasa," meaning friends or people of one nation, is an Alabama and Choctaw word. They moved from the Tallapoosa River region of Alabama to Florida in 1814.

358 This and the following quotations are from Bartram's *Travels Through North and South Carolina, Georgia, East and West Florida, the Cherokee Country, the Extensive Territories of the Muscogulges, or Creek Confederacy, and the Country of the Cherokees* (1791) 509–10. Bartram continued this sentence: "and they are absolved from their crimes, which are now forgotten, and they restored to favor."

359 Thoreau read in William Hickling Prescott's (1796–1859) *History of the Conquest of Mexico* (1843) of

> a remarkable festival, celebrated by the natives at the termination of the great cycle of fifty-two years. . . . The cycle would end in the latter part of December, and, as the dreary season of the winter solstice approached, and the diminished light of day gave melancholy presage of its speedy extinction, their apprehensions increased; and, on the arrival of the five "unlucky" days which closed the year, they abandoned themselves to despair. They broke in pieces the little images of their household gods, in whom they no longer trusted. The holy fires were suffered to go out in the temples, and none were lighted in their own dwellings. Their furniture and domestic utensils were destroyed; their garments torn in pieces; and every thing was thrown into disorder, for the coming of the evil genii who were to descend on the desolate earth.

360 Defined as such by St. Augustine and subsequently carried over to the *Book of Common Prayer* (1662) and such dictionaries as John Walker's 1822 *A Critical Pronouncing Dictionary, and Expositor of the English Language* and Webster's 1828 *American Dictionary*.

361 This works out to working approximately one day a week and resting six, a reversal of the biblical order. In the Harvard commencement exercises of 30 August 1837, Thoreau said: "The order of things should be somewhat reversed,—the seventh should be man's day of toil, wherein to earn his living by the sweat of his brow, and the other six his sabbath of the affections and the soul, in which to range this wide-spread garden, and drink in the soft influences and sublime revelations of Nature" [EEM 117].

362 Pun on his name. Thoreau taught school in Canton, Massachusetts, in early 1836, at the Center School in Concord briefly in 1837, and in the pri-

dry wood together, produces new fire in the public square, from whence every habitation in the town is supplied with the new and pure flame."

They then feast on the new corn and fruits and dance and sing for three days, "and the four following days they receive visits and rejoice with their friends from neighboring towns who have in like manner purified and prepared themselves."

The Mexicans also practised a similar purification at the end of every fifty-two years, in the belief that it was time for the world to come to an end.[359]

I have scarcely heard of a truer sacrament, that is, as the dictionary defines it, "outward and visible sign of an inward and spiritual grace,"[360] than this, and I have no doubt that they were originally inspired directly from Heaven to do thus, though they have no biblical record of the revelation.

For more than five years I maintained myself thus solely by the labor of my hands, and I found, that by working about six weeks in a year,[361] I could meet all the expenses of living. The whole of my winters, as well as most of my summers, I had free and clear for study. I have thoroughly[362] tried school-keeping, and found that my expenses were in proportion, or rather out of proportion, to my income, for I was obliged to dress and train, not to say think and believe, accordingly,[363] and I lost my time into the bargain. As I did not teach for the good of my fellow-men, but simply for a livelihood, this was a failure. I have tried trade;[364] but I found that it would take ten years to get under way in that, and that then I should probably be on my way to the devil. I was actually afraid that I might by that time be doing what is called a good business.[365] When formerly I was looking about to see what I could do for a living, some sad experience in conforming to the wishes of friends[366] being fresh in my mind to tax my ingenuity, I thought often and seriously of picking huckleberries; that surely I could do, and its small profits might suffice,—for my greatest skill has been to want but little,—so little capital it required, so little distraction from my wonted moods, I foolishly thought. While my acquaintances went unhesitatingly into trade or the professions, I contemplated this occupation as most like theirs; ranging the hills all summer to pick the berries which came in my way, and thereafter carelessly dispose of them; so, to keep the flocks of Admetus.[367] I also dreamed that I might gather the wild herbs, or carry evergreens to such villagers as loved to be reminded of the woods, even to the city, by hay-cart loads. But I have since learned that trade curses everything it handles; and though you trade in messages from heaven, the whole curse of trade attaches to the business.

As I preferred some things to others, and especially valued my freedom, as I could fare hard and yet succeed well, I did not wish to spend my time in earning rich carpets or other fine furniture, or delicate cookery, or a house in the Grecian or the Gothic[368] style just yet. If there are any to whom it is no interruption to acquire these things, and who know how to use them when acquired, I relinquish to them the pursuit. Some are "industrious," and appear to love labor for its own sake, or perhaps because it keeps them out of worse mischief; to such I have at present nothing to say. Those who would not know what to do with more leisure than they now enjoy, I might advise to work twice as hard as they do,—work till they pay for themselves, and get their free papers.[369] For myself I found that the occupation of a day-laborer was the most independent of any, especially as it required only thirty or forty days in a year to support one. The laborer's day ends with the going down of the sun, and he is then free to devote himself to his chosen pursuit, independent of his labor; but his employer, who speculates from month

vate school that he and his brother John ran from 1838 until March 1841, when it closed due to John's poor health from tuberculosis. He also served as a private tutor to the children of William Emerson on Staten Island from May through December 1843. His philosophy of education is explained in a 30 December 1837 letter to Orestes Brownson: "I would make education a pleasant thing both to the teacher and the scholar. This discipline, which we allow to be the end of life, should not be one thing in the schoolroom, and another in the street. We should seek to be fellow students with the pupil, and we should learn of, as well as with him, if we would be most helpful to him" [C 20].

363 At the end of his second week teaching at the Center School, school committee member Deacon Nehemiah Ball (b. 1791) observed that Thoreau did not use corporal punishment. Ball insisted that it was Thoreau's duty to flog his students regularly so the school's reputation would not be spoiled. Thoreau, acting accordingly, feruled several students, and that evening resigned. On flogging students he wrote: "I have even been disposed to regard the cowhide as a nonconductor. Methinks that, unlike the electric wire, not a single spark of truth is ever transmitted through its agency to the slumbering intellect it would address. I mistake, it may teach a truth in physics, but never a truth in morals" [C 20].

364 With the closing of his school in 1841, Thoreau helped out in the family graphite and pencil business.

365 On doing a good business Thoreau wrote in his journal of 20 April 1841: "There are certain current expressions and blasphemous moods of viewing things, as when we say 'he is doing a good business,' more prophane than cursing and swearing. There is death and sin in such words. Let not the children hear them" [J 1:251].

366 This was added in a late draft, circa 1853–54, and is a reference to Emerson's urging Thoreau to publish *A Week on the Concord and Merrimack Rivers* at his own expense. In October 1853 he had to buy back the unsold copies of the book.

367 In Greek mythology, Apollo, god of music and poetry, during his nine-year banishment from heaven, was forced to tend the flocks of the Pheraean king Admetus. Thoreau had several times identified himself with a god fallen, what Emerson called a "god in ruins." In one of several references in his correspondence, Thoreau wrote, "I, who am going to be a pencil-maker to-morrow, can sympathize with God Apollo, who served King Admetus for a while on earth" [C 47].

368 Architectural styles popular in the mid-19th century.

369 Immigrants in colonial times often went into debt, indenturing themselves, to pay for passage from Europe to America. When their debt was paid off in full, they were issued "free papers." Similarly, slaves who were manumitted or were able to purchase their own freedom were provided with free papers.

370 Allusion to Genesis 3:19, in which Adam was commanded: "In the sweat of thy face thou will eat bread, till thou return unto the ground."

371 Originally used in a letter to Horace Greeley on 19 May 1848 explaining his philosophy of economy: "The fact is man need not live by the sweat of his brow—unless he sweats easier than I do—he needs so little" [C 224].

372 Unidentified.

373 Possible reference to John Adolphus Etzler's *The Paradise Within Reach of All Men,* which urged the construction of large apartment houses; Charles Fourier's (1772–1837) self-sustaining co-operative community called phalansteries; or Harvard College, of which Thoreau wrote earlier in this chapter, regarding the student's rooms, that they were built "thirty-two side by side and under one roof."

374 Possible allusion to the proverbial phrase "Good fences make good neighbors," which appeared at least as early as the 1850 edition of *Blum's Farmer's and Planter's Almanac.*

to month, has no respite from one end of the year to the other.

In short, I am convinced, both by faith and experience, that to maintain one's self on this earth is not a hardship but a pastime, if we will live simply and wisely; as the pursuits of the simpler nations are still the sports of the more artificial. It is not necessary that a man should earn his living by the sweat of his brow,[370] unless he sweats easier than I do.[371]

One young man of my acquaintance,[372] who has inherited some acres, told me that he thought he should live as I did, *if he had the means.* I would not have any one adopt *my* mode of living on any account; for, beside that before he has fairly learned it I may have found out another for myself, I desire that there may be as many different persons in the world as possible; but I would have each one be very careful to find out and pursue *his own* way, and not his father's or his mother's or his neighbor's instead. The youth may build or plant or sail, only let him not be hindered from doing that which he tells me he would like to do. It is by a mathematical point only that we are wise, as the sailor or the fugitive slave keeps the polestar in his eye; but that is sufficient guidance for all our life. We may not arrive at our port within a calculable period, but we would preserve the true course.

Undoubtedly, in this case, what is true for one is truer still for a thousand, as a large house is not proportionally more expensive than a small one, since one roof may cover, one cellar underlie, and one wall separate several apartments.[373] But for my part, I preferred the solitary dwelling. Moreover, it will commonly be cheaper to build the whole yourself than to convince another of the advantage of the common wall; and when you have done this, the common partition, to be much cheaper, must be a thin one, and that other may prove a bad neighbor,[374] and also not keep his side in repair. The only coöperation which is commonly possible is exceedingly partial and superficial; and what little true coöperation there is, is as if it were not, being a harmony inaudible to men. If a man has faith he will coöperate with equal faith every where; if he has not faith, he will continue to live like the rest of the world, whatever company he is joined to. To coöperate, in the highest as well as the lowest sense, means *to get our living together.* I heard it proposed lately that two young men should travel together over the world, the one without money, earning his means as he went, before the mast[375] and behind the plough, the other carrying a bill of exchange[376] in his pocket. It was easy to see that they could not long be companions or coöperate, since one would not *operate* at all. They would part at the first interesting crisis in their adventures. Above all, as I have implied, the man who goes alone can start to-day; but he who travels with another must wait till that other is ready, and it may be a long time before they get off.

But all this is very selfish, I have heard some of my townsmen say. I confess that I have hitherto indulged very little in philanthropic enterprises.[377] I have made some sacrifices to a sense of duty, and among others have sacrificed this pleasure also. There are those who have used all their arts to persuade me to undertake the support of some poor family in the town; and if I had nothing to do, — for the devil finds employment for the idle, — I might try my hand at some such pastime as that. However, when I have thought to indulge myself in this respect, and lay their Heaven under an obligation by maintaining certain poor persons in all respects as comfortably as I maintain myself, and have even ventured so far as to make them the offer, they have one and all unhesitatingly preferred to remain poor. While my townsmen and women are devoted in so many ways to the good of their fellows, I trust that one at least may be spared to other and

375 As a common sailor.

376 Like a check, a document directing one person to pay a certain amount of money to another and charging it to the account of the originator.

377 One of his philanthropic activities was collecting money for a Michael Flannery, although on 12 October 1853 he noted in his journal some difficulties: "To-day I have had the experience of borrowing money for a poor Irishman who wishes to get his family to this country. One will never know his neighbors till he has carried a subscription paper among them. . . . To hear the selfish and cowardly excuses some make, —that *if* they help any they must help the Irishman who lives with them, — and him they are sure never to help! . . . What a satire in the fact that you are much more inclined to call on a certain slighted and so-called crazy woman in moderate circumstances rather than on the president of the bank!" [J 5:438–39]. Thoreau also contributed $1.00 to the Alcott fund, established by Emerson, as a life annuity for Bronson Alcott. It is probable that Emerson's journal entry about Thoreau asking "fairly enough, when is it that the man is to begin to provide for himself?" is in reference to this fund.

378 Possible reference to Cotton Mather's (1663–1728) *Bonifacius: An Essay upon the Good, that is to be Devised and Designed, by those Who Desire to Answer the Great End of Life and to Do Good While they Live,* commonly called *Essays to Do Good* (1710); or Benjamin Franklin's (1706–1790) *Dogood Papers.*

379 Reversal of the term "malice aforethought," used as a necessary state of mind to prove murder. Thoreau similarly reversed the phrase when he wrote of "goodness aforethought" in the "Conclusion" chapter.

380 In 1848 Thoreau attended one of Bronson Alcott's "conversations," at which James Freeman Clarke (1810–1888), the Unitarian minister, author, and editor, having read Silvio Pellico's (1789–1854) *My Prisons,* said, "Much is implied in the phrase 'going about doing good;' and still more when it reads 'going about *being* good.'"

381 In the system of classing stars according to their apparent brightness created by Hipparchus (ca. 170–ca. 120 B.C.E.), a Greek astronomer and geographer, the brightest stars belong to the first magnitude, and those just visible to the naked eye are in the sixth magnitude.

382 In English folklore, a mischievous sprite who appears as Puck in Shakespeare's *A Midsummer Night's Dream* and as Hobgoblin in Michael Drayton's (1563–1631) *Nimphidia.* Thoreau copied the ballad "The Mad Merry Pranks of Robin Goodfellow," sometimes attributed to Ben Jonson (1572–1637), into his commonplace book.

383 Allusion to Milton's *Paradise Lost* 1.63: "No light, but rather darkness visible."

less humane pursuits. You must have a genius for charity as well as for any thing else. As for Doing-good,[378] that is one of the professions which are full. Moreover, I have tried it fairly, and, strange as it may seem, am satisfied that it does not agree with my constitution. Probably I should not consciously and deliberately forsake my particular calling to do the good which society demands of me, to save the universe from annihilation; and I believe that a like but infinitely greater steadfastness elsewhere is all that now preserves it. But I would not stand between any man and his genius; and to him who does this work, which I decline, with his whole heart and soul and life, I would say, Persevere, even if the world call it doing evil, as it is most likely they will.

I am far from supposing that my case is a peculiar one; no doubt many of my readers would make a similar defence. At doing something,—I will not engage that my neighbors shall pronounce it good,—I do not hesitate to say that I should be a capital fellow to hire; but what that is, it is for my employer to find out. What *good* I do, in the common sense of that word, must be aside from my main path, and for the most part wholly unintended. Men say, practically, Begin where you are and such as you are, without aiming mainly to become of more worth, and with kindness aforethought[379] go about doing good. If I were to preach at all in this strain, I should say rather, Set about being good.[380] As if the sun should stop when he had kindled his fires up to the splendor of a moon or a star of the sixth magnitude,[381] and go about like a Robin Goodfellow,[382] peeping in at every cottage window, inspiring lunatics, and tainting meats, and making darkness visible,[383] instead of steadily increasing his genial heat and beneficence till he is of such brightness that no mortal can look him in the face, and then, and in the mean while too, going about the world in his own orbit, doing it good, or rather, as a truer philosophy has discovered, the world going about him getting good.[384] When Phaeton,[385] wishing to prove his heavenly birth by his beneficence, had the sun's chariot but one day, and drove out of the beaten track, he burned several blocks of houses in the lower streets of heaven, and scorched the surface of the earth, and dried up every spring, and made the great desert of Sahara, till at length Jupiter[386] hurled him headlong to the earth with a thunderbolt, and the sun, through grief at his death, did not shine for a year.[387]

There is no odor so bad as that which arises from goodness tainted. It is human, it is divine, carrion. If I knew for a certainty that a man was coming to my house with the conscious design of doing me good, I should run for my life, as from that dry and parching wind of the African deserts called the simoom, which fills the mouth and nose and ears and eyes with dust till you are suffocated, for fear that I should get some of his good done to me, — some of its virus mingled with my blood. No, — in this case I would rather suffer evil the natural way. A man is not a good *man* to me because he will feed me if I should be starving, or warm me if I should be freezing, or pull me out of a ditch if I should ever fall into one. I can find you a Newfoundland dog[388] that will do as much.[389] Philanthropy is not love for one's fellow-man in the broadest sense.[390] Howard[391] was no doubt an exceedingly kind and worthy man in his way, and has his reward;[392] but, comparatively speaking, what are a hundred Howards to *us,* if their philanthropy do not help *us* in our best estate, when we are most worthy to be helped? I never heard of a philanthropic meeting in which it was sincerely proposed to do any good to me, or the like of me.

The Jesuits[393] were quite balked by those Indians who, being burned at the stake, suggested new modes of torture to their tormentors. Being superior to physical suffering, it sometimes chanced that they were superior to any consolation which the missionaries could offer; and the

---

384 Pun: becoming virtuous, and acquiring effects or possessions.

385 In Greek mythology, son of Helios, the Sun.

386 In Roman mythology, the chief god, identified with the Greek god Zeus, originally a sky-god, associated with lightning and the thunderbolt.

387 Told in Ovid's *Metamorphoses* 2.1–400.

388 Ellery Channing owned a Newfoundland dog that would often accompany Thoreau and Channing on their walks together.

389 Echo of Richard Sheridan's (1751–1816) *The Rivals* 1.1: "Obligation; why a water spaniel would have done as much!"

390 In his journal of 11 February 1841, Thoreau called charity "the interference of a third person" [J 1:212].

391 John Howard (1726?–1790), English prison reformer.

392 Allusion to Matthew 5:12: "Rejoice, and be exceeding glad: for great is your reward in heaven."

393 Roman Catholic religious order, Society of Jesus, which attempted to convert the Native Americans to Christianity. This paragraph was added after Thoreau started reading *Jesuit Relations*, volumes of which he began borrowing from Harvard in 1852.

394 Known as the Golden Rule, versions of which are found in the New Testament (Matthew 5:44, 7:12, Luke 6:31), the Talmud, the Koran, the *Analects* of Confucius, and other religious and philosophical writings.

395 Allusions to Matthew 5:44: "Love your enemies."

396 Allusion to Luke 23:34: "Then said Jesus, Father, forgive them; for they know not what they do."

397 Latin: outer.

398 Latin: inner.

399 Pun: immersion in water and also clothes made of cotton or linen.

400 Store for slops: inexpensive, ready-made clothing.

401 Reference to the biblical injunction to tithing, donating one-tenth of one's income for the Lord.

402 Although far from a universal practice, some slaveholders would grant their slaves freedom from work on the Sabbath.

law to do as you would be done by[394] fell with less persuasiveness on the ears of those, who, for their part, did not care how they were done by, who loved their enemies[395] after a new fashion, and came very near freely forgiving them all they did.[396]

Be sure that you give the poor the aid they most need, though it be your example which leaves them far behind. If you give money, spend yourself with it, and do not merely abandon it to them. We make curious mistakes sometimes. Often the poor man is not so cold and hungry as he is dirty and ragged and gross. It is partly his taste, and not merely his misfortune. If you give him money, he will perhaps buy more rags with it. I was wont to pity the clumsy Irish laborers who cut ice on the pond, in such mean and ragged clothes, while I shivered in my more tidy and somewhat more fashionable garments, till, one bitter cold day, one who had slipped into the water came to my house to warm him, and I saw him strip off three pairs of pants and two pairs of stockings ere he got down to the skin, though they were dirty and ragged enough, it is true, and that he could afford to refuse the *extra*[397] garments which I offered him, he had so many *intra*[398] ones. This ducking[399] was the very thing he needed. Then I began to pity myself, and I saw that it would be a greater charity to bestow on me a flannel shirt than a whole slop-shop[400] on him. There are a thousand hacking at the branches of evil to one who is striking at the root, and it may be that he who bestows the largest amount of time and money on the needy is doing the most by his mode of life to produce that misery which he strives in vain to relieve. It is the pious slave-breeder devoting the proceeds of every tenth slave[401] to buy a Sunday's liberty[402] for the rest. Some show their kindness to the poor by employing them in their kitchens. Would they not be kinder if they employed themselves there? You boast of spending a tenth part of your income in charity; may be you should spend the nine tenths so, and done with it. Society recovers only a tenth part of the property then. Is this owing to the generosity of him in whose possession it is found, or to the remissness of the officers of justice?

Philanthropy is almost the only virtue which is sufficiently appreciated by mankind. Nay, it is greatly overrated; and it is our selfishness which overrates it. A robust poor man, one sunny day here in Concord, praised a fellow-townsman to me, because, as he said, he was kind to the poor; meaning himself. The kind uncles and aunts of the race are more esteemed than its true spiritual fathers and mothers. I once heard a reverend lecturer on England,[403] a man of learning and intelligence, after enumerating her scientific, literary, and political worthies, Shakespeare, Bacon, Cromwell,[404] Milton, Newton, and others, speak next of her Christian heroes, whom, as if his profession required it of him, he elevated to a place far above all the rest, as the greatest of the great. They were Penn, Howard, and Mrs. Fry.[405] Every one must feel the falsehood and cant of this. The last were not England's best men and women; only, perhaps, her best philanthropists.

I would not subtract any thing from the praise that is due to philanthropy, but merely demand justice for all who by their lives and works are a blessing to mankind. I do not value chiefly a man's uprightness and benevolence, which are, as it were, his stem and leaves. Those plants of whose greenness withered we make herb tea for the sick, serve but a humble use, and are most employed by quacks. I want the flower and fruit of a man; that some fragrance be wafted over from him to me, and some ripeness flavor our intercourse. His goodness must not be a partial and transitory act, but a constant superfluity, which costs him nothing and of which he is unconscious.

403 Possible reference to Rev. Frederick Henry Hedge, Transcendentalist and Unitarian minister from Bangor, Maine, who spoke on "The English Nation" at the Concord Lyceum on 16 January 1850.

404 Francis Bacon, 1st Baron Verulam (1561–1626), English statesman and philosopher; Oliver Cromwell (1599–1658), politician, general, and Lord Protector of England, 1653–58.

405 William Penn, Quaker humanitarian and reformer, founder of Pennsylvania; John Howard (mentioned above); Elizabeth Fry (1780–1845), English prison reformer, established soup kitchens and helped find employment for people.

406 Allusion to 1 Peter 4:8: "And above all things have fervent charity among yourselves: for charity shall cover the multitude of sins."

407 Southern slave states.

408 Allusion to Jeremiah 9:19: "For a voice of wailing is heard out of Zion, How are we spoiled! we are greatly confounded, because we have forsaken the land, because our dwellings have cast us out."

409 Pun: functions in relation to society, as well as bodily functions.

410 Seat or root of emotions, as in Isaiah 57:18: "As he has bowels to pity." With this connection in mind Thoreau wrote on 17 June 1853, referring to Rev. H. C. Wright (1797–1870), former Baptist minister, agent of the Massachusetts Anti-Slavery Society, and author of *A Kiss for a Blow:* "It was difficult to keep clear of his slimy benignity, with which he sought to cover you before he swallowed you and took you fairly into his bowels. It would have been far worse than the fate of Jonah" [J 5:264].

411 The 16th-century natural philosophers believed that the human was a microcosm, or miniature cosmos, while the earth was a living organism on a larger scale, the universe being a macrocosm.

412 Considered a source of indigestion.

413 Eskimos, inhabitants of northern Canada, Alaska, Greenland, and eastern Siberia, and Patagonians, who live on the southernmost tip of South America, representing extreme northern and southern points.

414 Covering western and eastern points of the globe.

415 Although "Son of God" was used specifically in the New Testament as an epithet for Jesus, in the Old Testament and in several places in the New Testament the word "son" was used to signify not only filiation but also any close connection or intimate relationship, and the term "son(s) of God" was used for persons having any special relationship with God: "But as many as received him, to them gave he power to become the sons

This is a charity that hides a multitude of sins.[406] The philanthropist too often surrounds mankind with the remembrance of his own cast-off griefs as an atmosphere, and calls it sympathy. We should impart our courage, and not our despair, our health and ease, and not our disease, and take care that this does not spread by contagion. From what southern plains[407] comes up the voice of wailing?[408] Under what latitudes reside the heathen to whom we would send light? Who is that intemperate and brutal man whom we would redeem? If any thing ail a man, so that he does not perform his functions,[409] if he have a pain in his bowels even,—for that is the seat of sympathy,[410]— he forthwith sets about reforming—the world. Being a microcosm[411] himself, he discovers, and it is a true discovery, and he is the man to make it,—that the world has been eating green apples;[412] to his eyes, in fact, the globe itself is a great green apple, which there is danger awful to think of that the children of men will nibble before it is ripe; and straightway his drastic philanthropy seeks out the Esquimaux and the Patagonian,[413] and embraces the populous Indian and Chinese villages;[414] and thus, by a few years of philanthropic activity, the powers in the mean while using him for their own ends, no doubt, he cures himself of his dyspepsia, the globe acquires a faint blush on one or both of its cheeks, as if it were beginning to be ripe, and life loses its crudity and is once more sweet and wholesome to live. I never dreamed of any enormity greater than I have committed. I never knew, and never shall know, a worse man than myself.

I believe that what so saddens the reformer is not his sympathy with his fellows in distress, but, though he be the holiest son of God,[415] is his private ail. Let this be righted, let the spring come to him, the morning rise over his couch, and he will forsake his generous companions without apology. My excuse for not lecturing against the use of tobacco is, that I never chewed it; that is a penalty which reformed tobacco-chewers have to pay; though there are things enough I have chewed, which I could lecture against. If you should ever be betrayed into any of these philanthropies, do not let your left hand know what your right hand does,[416] for it is not worth knowing. Rescue the drowning and tie your shoe-strings. Take your time, and set about some free labor.

Our manners have been corrupted by communication[417] with the saints. Our hymn-books resound with a melodious cursing of God and enduring him forever.[418] One would say that even the prophets and redeemers had rather consoled the fears than confirmed the hopes of man. There is nowhere recorded a simple and irrepressible satisfaction with the gift of life, any memorable praise of God. All health and success does me good, however far off and withdrawn it may appear; all disease and failure helps to make me sad and does me evil, however much sympathy it may have with me or I with it. If, then, we would indeed restore mankind by truly Indian, botanic, magnetic,[419] or natural means, let us first be as simple and well as Nature ourselves, dispel the clouds which hang over our own brows, and take up a little life into our pores. Do not stay to be an overseer of the poor,[420] but endeavor to become one of the worthies of the world.

I read in the Gulistan, or Flower Garden, of Sheik Sadi of Shiraz,[421] that "They asked a wise man, saying; Of the many celebrated trees which the Most High God has created lofty and umbrageous, they call none azad,[422] or free, excepting the cypress, which bears no fruit; what mystery is there in this? He replied; Each has its appropriate produce, and appointed season, during the continuance of which it is fresh and blooming, and during their absence dry and withered; to neither of which states is the cypress exposed, being always flourishing; and of this nature are

416 Allusion to Matthew 6:3: "But when thou doest alms, let not thy left hand know what thy right hand doeth."

417 Allusion to 1 Corinthians 15:33: "Be not deceived: evil communications corrupt good manners."

418 Satiric reversal and conflation of Job 2:9: "Curse God, and die!" and the Shorter Catechism of *The New England Primer:* "Man's chief End is to Glorify God, and to Enjoy Him for ever."

419 Indian here refers to various Native American remedies; botanic to natural remedies made from plants; and magnetic to animal magnetism, or mesmerism, a form of hypnotism proposed in 1775 by the German physician Friedrich Anton Mesmer (1733–1815).

420 A town official who administered to the poor, with a possible pun on "pores" in the previous line.

421 *The Gulistan, or Rose Garden,* a collection of poems, prose, and maxims concerning moral issues, was written by the Persian poet Sadi (or Saadi), born Sheikh Muslih Addin (1184–1291). Thoreau copied several extracts into his literary notebooks, using three of them in *A Week on the Concord and Merrimack Rivers* and one in *Walden.* Thoreau wrote in his journal of 8 August 1852: "Thought greets thought over the widest gulfs of time with unerring freemasonry. I know, for instance, that Sadi entertained once identically the same thought that I do, and thereafter I can find no essential difference between Sadi and myself. He is not Persian, he is not ancient, he is not strange to me. By the identity of his thoughts with mine he still survives" [J 4:290]. Emerson, too, was impressed with Sadi's work, writing a poem called "Saadi," translating many of his poems into English from a German translation, writing an essay on "Persian Poetry," and editing Francis Gladwin's translation of *The Gulistan* in 1865.

Reference 415 (continued from previous page): of God" [John 1:12], and "For as many as are led by the Spirit of God, they are the sons of God" [Romans 8:14].

422 Free man.

423 Dijlah is another name for the Tigris River in southwest Asia.

424 Muslim rulers, both secular and religious.

425 Quoted, with slight variations in punctuation, from *The Gulistan, or Flower-garden, of Shaikh Sadī of Shiraz* 473, translated by James Ross (1823).

426 The following poem is quoted from Thomas Carew's (1595?–1645) masque *Coelum Britannicum* (ll. 642–68). Thoreau added the title and self-satirizing subtitle and modernized the spelling. Of Carew, he wrote: "They say that Carew was a laborious writer, but his poems do not show it. They are finished, but do not show the marks of the chisel" [J 1:465]. The poem is complemental in that it completes, or supplies a deficiency in, the rest of the text by offering an opposing viewpoint. In the masque, this monologue, spoken by Mercury, is an attack on Poverty's pretentious claim of power. In his commonplace book Thoreau copied the following passage (ll. 609–16) from Poverty's monologue:

> But I decline those titles, and lay clayme
> To heaven by right of divine contemplation;
> She is my darling; I, in my soft lap,
> Free from disturbing cares, bargaines,
>   accounts,
> Leases, rents, stewards, and the feare of
>   theeves,
> That vex the rich, nurse her in calme repose,
> And with her all the vertues speculative,
> Which, but with me, find no secure retreat.
> [*Thoreau's Literary Notebooks* 296]

427 Thoreau mistranscribed "rigid" in the original as "right" in his commonplace book and then copied the mistake into *Walden*.

the azads, or religious independents. — Fix not thy heart on that which is transitory; for the Dijlah, or Tigris,[423] will continue to flow through Bagdad after the race of caliphs[424] is extinct: if thy hand has plenty, be liberal as the date tree; but if it affords nothing to give away, be an azad, or free man, like the cypress."[425]

COMPLEMENTAL VERSES.
THE PRETENSIONS OF POVERTY.[426]

"Thou dost presume too much, poor needy
    wretch,
To claim a station in the firmament,
Because thy humble cottage, or thy tub,
Nurses some lazy or pedantic virtue
In the cheap sunshine or by shady springs,
With roots and pot-herbs; where thy right[427]
    hand,
Tearing those humane passions from the mind,
Upon whose stocks fair blooming virtues
    flourish,
Degradeth nature, and benumbeth sense,
And, Gorgon-like, turns active men to stone.
We not require the dull society
Of your necessitated temperance,
Or that unnatural stupidity
That knows nor joy nor sorrow; nor your forc'd
Falsely exalted passive fortitude
Above the active. This low abject brood,
That fix their seats in mediocrity,
Become your servile minds; but we advance
Such virtues only as admit excess,
Brave, bounteous acts, regal magnificence,
All-seeing prudence, magnanimity

That knows no bound, and that heroic virtue
For which antiquity hath left no name,
But patterns only, such as Hercules,
Achilles, Theseus. Back to thy loath'd cell;
And when thou seest the new enlightened sphere,
Study to know but what those worthies were."

T. CAREW

1 Thoreau had considered sites other than Walden Pond. According to Ellery Channing, besides the Hollowell place referred to in the next paragraph, which was on the west side of the Sudbury River, below Hubbard's Bridge, Thoreau considered "Weird Dell, and one side of Fairhaven Hill, that of the orchard. He also thought of the Cliff Hill, and the Baker Farm." Fair Haven Hill was on the shore of the Sudbury River, about half a mile southwest of Walden, and was also known as The Cliffs. Baker Farm, in Lincoln, was on the east side of Fair Haven Bay, a half mile from Walden Pond, and the home of James Baker. According to his journal of 31 August 1851, he had "talked of buying Conantum once, but for want of money we did not come to terms. But I have farmed it in my own fashion every year since" [J 2:439]. Thoreau may also have considered Flint's Pond.

2 Pun: premises as property and as statements assumed to be true.

3 Thoreau's first written association of house and seat occurred in an August 1840 journal entry: "The rich man's house is a *sedes*—a place to sit in—the poor man's a *tectum*—a shelter. So in English we say a gentleman's *seat* or *residence,* but a poor man's *house* or *roof*" [PJ 1:169]. On 5 April 1841 Thoreau wrote: "I only ask a clean seat. I will build my lodge on the southern slope of some hill, and take there the life the gods send me" [J 1:244].

Where I Lived,
and What I Lived For

At a certain season of our life we are accustomed to consider every spot as the possible site of a house.[1] I have thus surveyed the country on every side within a dozen miles of where I live. In imagination I have bought all the farms in succession, for all were to be bought, and I knew their price. I walked over each farmer's premises,[2] tasted his wild apples, discoursed on husbandry with him, took his farm at his price, at any price, mortgaging it to him in my mind; even put a higher price on it,—took every thing but a deed of it,—took his word for his deed, for I dearly love to talk,—cultivated it, and him too to some extent, I trust, and withdrew when I had enjoyed it long enough, leaving him to carry it on. This experience entitled me to be regarded as a sort of real-estate broker by my friends. Wherever I sat, there I might live, and the landscape radiated from me accordingly. What is a house but a *sedes,*[3] a seat?—better if a country seat. I discovered many a site for a house not likely to be soon improved, which some might have thought too far from the village, but to my eyes the village was too far from it. Well, there I might live, I said; and there I did live, for an hour, a summer and a winter life; saw how I could let the years run off, buffet the winter through, and see the spring come in.

The future inhabitants of this region, wherever they may place their houses, may be sure that they have been anticipated. An afternoon sufficed to lay out the land into orchard, woodlot, and pasture, and to decide what fine oaks or pines should be left to stand before the door, and whence each blasted tree[4] could be seen to the best advantage; and then I let it lie, fallow perchance, for a man is rich in proportion to the number of things which he can afford to let alone.[5]

My imagination carried me so far that I even had the refusal of several farms,—the refusal was all I wanted,—but I never got my fingers burned by actual possession. The nearest that I came to actual possession was when I bought the Hollowell place, and had begun to sort my seeds, and collected materials with which to make a wheelbarrow to carry it on or off with; but before the owner gave me a deed of it, his wife—every man has such a wife—changed her mind and wished to keep it, and he offered me ten dollars to release him. Now, to speak the truth, I had but ten cents in the world, and it surpassed my arithmetic to tell, if I was that man who had ten cents, or who had a farm, or ten dollars, or all together. However, I let him keep the ten dollars and the farm too, for I had carried it[6] far enough; or rather, to be generous, I sold him the farm for just what I gave for it, and, as he was not a rich man, made him a present of ten dollars, and still had my ten cents, and seeds, and materials for a wheelbarrow left. I found thus that I had been a rich man without any damage to my poverty. But I retained the landscape, and I have since annually carried off what it yielded without a wheelbarrow. With respect to landscapes,—

"I am monarch of all I *survey*,
My right there is none to dispute."[7]

4 A withered or blighted tree. William Gilpin, in *Remarks on Forest Scenery and Other Woodland Views*, wrote: "The blasted tree has often a fine effect both in natural and in artificial landscape. In some scenes it is almost essential. When the dreary heath is spread before the eye, and ideas of wildness and desolation are required, what more suitable accompaniment can be imaged, than the blasted oak, ragged, scathed, and leafless, shooting its peeled white branches athwart the gathering blackness of some rising storm?"

5 The first, second, third, and fifth paragraphs of this chapter were first published, with variants, as "A Poet Buying a Farm" in *Sartain's Union Magazine* 11:127.

6 Pun: carried the joke (of buying the farm) and also carried the farm financially.

7 From William Cowper's (1731–1800) "Verses Supposed to be Written by Alexander Selkirk During His Solitary Abode in the Island of Juan Fernandez." Thoreau's italics emphasize his earning a living as a surveyor.

I have frequently seen a poet[8] withdraw, having enjoyed the most valuable part of a farm,[9] while the crusty farmer supposed that he had got a few wild apples only. Why, the owner does not know it for many years when a poet has put his farm in rhyme,[10] the most admirable kind of invisible fence, has fairly impounded it, milked it, skimmed it, and got all the cream, and left the farmer only the skimmed milk.

The real attractions of the Hollowell farm, to me, were; its complete retirement, being about two miles from the village, half a mile from the nearest neighbor, and separated from the highway by a broad field; its bounding on the river, which the owner said protected it by its fogs from frosts in the spring, though that was nothing to me; the gray color and ruinous state of the house and barn, and the dilapidated fences, which put such an interval between me and the last occupant; the hollow and lichen-covered apple trees, gnawed by rabbits, showing what kind of neighbors I should have; but above all, the recollection I had of it from my earliest voyages up the river, when the house was concealed behind a dense grove of red maples, through which I heard the house-dog bark. I was in haste to buy it, before the proprietor finished getting out some rocks, cutting down the hollow apple trees, and grubbing up some young birches which had sprung up in the pasture, or, in short, had made any more of his improvements. To enjoy these advantages I was ready to carry it on; like Atlas,[11] to take the world on my shoulders,—I never heard what compensation he received for that,—and do all those things which had no other motive or excuse but that I might pay for it and be unmolested in my possession of it; for I knew all the while that it would yield the most abundant crop of the kind I wanted if I could only afford to let it alone. But it turned out as I have said.

All that I could say, then, with respect to farming on a

8 Ellery Channing, who is called "Poet" in the "Brute Neighbors" chapter, and published seven volumes of poetry in his lifetime. He was also Thoreau's first biographer, publishing *Thoreau, the Poet-Naturalist* in 1873. He married Margaret Fuller's sister, Ellen, in 1842.

9 Possible echo of Emerson's *Nature:* "There is a property in the horizon which no man has but he whose eye can integrate all the parts, that is, the poet. This is the best part of these men's farms, yet to this their warranty-deeds give no title."

10 Ellery Channing put James Baker's farm "in rhyme" in his poem "Baker Farm," published in *The Woodman and Other Poems* (1849), part of which Thoreau quoted in the "Baker Farm" chapter.

11 In Greek mythology, Atlas carried the world on his shoulders.

large scale, (I have always cultivated a garden,)[12] was, that I had had my seeds ready.[13] Many think that seeds improve with age. I have no doubt that time discriminates between the good and the bad; and when at last I shall plant, I shall be less likely to be disappointed. But I would say to my fellows, once for all, As long as possible live free and uncommitted. It makes but little difference whether you are committed to a farm or the county jail.[14]

Old Cato, whose "De Re Rusticâ" is my "Cultivator,"[15] says, and the only translation I have seen makes sheer nonsense of the passage,[16] "When you think of getting a farm, turn it thus in your mind, not to buy greedily; nor spare your pains to look at it, and do not think it enough to go round it once. The oftener you go there the more it will please you, if it is good." I think I shall not buy greedily, but go round and round it as long as I live, and be buried in it first, that it may please me the more at last.

The present was my next experiment of this kind, which I purpose to describe more at length; for convenience, putting the experience of two years into one.[17] As I have said,[18] I do not propose to write an ode to dejection,[19] but to brag as lustily as chanticleer[20] in the morning, standing on his roost, if only to wake my neighbors up.

When first I took up my abode in the woods, that is, began to spend my nights as well as days there, which, by accident, was on Independence Day, or the fourth of July, 1845,[21] my house was not finished for winter, but was merely a defence against the rain, without plastering or chimney, the walls being of rough weather-stained boards, with wide chinks, which made it cool at night. The upright white hewn studs and freshly planed door and window casings gave it a clean and airy look, especially in the morning, when its timbers were saturated

12 The melons Thoreau grew were celebrated each autumn in his annual melon party. Edward Emerson wrote in *Henry Thoreau Remembered by a Young Man*: "He especially loved to raise melons. I once went to a melon-party at his mother's with various people, young and old, where his work had furnished the handsome and fragrant pink or salmon fruit on which alone we were regaled; and he, the gardener, came in to help entertain the guests."

13 Thoreau wrote in "The Succession of Forest Trees": "Though I do not believe that a plant will spring up where no seed has been, I have great faith in a seed. . . . Convince me that you have a seed there, and I am prepared to expect wonders" [W 5:203]. Thoreau believed that one has to be ready to succeed. He wrote in a post-*Walden* journal entry: "I think we may detect that some sort of preparation and faint expectation preceded every discovery we have made." [J 9:53].

14 Thoreau was committed to the county jail in July 1846 for nonpayment of taxes.

15 *Libri de re rustica* is the title of a collection of four Roman agricultural writers from the 2d century B.C.E. to the 4th century C.E. and often referred to as the *Scriptores rei rusticae*. Thoreau was reading Cato in this collection in 1851 from a copy borrowed from Bronson Alcott. "Cultivator" probably refers to the *Boston Cultivator*, a weekly agriculture newspaper published from 1839 to 1876, or to the general use of the name by such agricultural journals as the *New England Cultivator*, published in Boston, 1852–53, or the *Yankee Farmer and New England Cultivator*, published in Boston, 1835–41.

16 Alludes to the translation by Thomas Owen (1749–1812) in *M. Porcius Cato Concerning Agriculture* (London, 1803): "When you think of purchasing a farm, turn it thus in your mind; that you may not buy it greedily, nor spare to see your concerns, and that you may not have enough to go round it at once. As often as you go to see what is good, the more it will please you." Owen footnoted the phrase beginning "that you may not buy" and said he was not positive about his translation. The translation that follows, of Marcus Porcius Cato, *De Agri Cultura* 1.1, is Thoreau's.

17 This "convenience" was a literary device that freed Thoreau to follow the sequence of the seasons beginning with summer, which allowed him, among other things, to end his book with a spring-like feeling of renewal. Thoreau similarly shortened his two weeks on the river with his brother John into one in *A Week on the Concord and Merrimack Rivers* and three excursions into one in *Cape Cod*. It also serves as a reminder that *Walden* was a literary re-creation and not factual reportage.

18 In the motto on the half-title page. This motto, along with the final images of dawn in the "Conclusion," emphasizes that *Walden* was written as a wake-up call to his neighbors.

19 Allusion to Samuel Taylor Coleridge's "Ode to Dejection." Coleridge was a major influence on the Transcendentalists through such philosophical works as *The Friend* (1810) and *Aids to Reflection* (1825).

20 Rooster: from Chanticleer, the name of the rooster in *Reynard the Fox* and in Geoffrey Chaucer's (ca. 1343–1400) "The Nun's Priest's Tale," in which was written: "In all the land, for crowing, he'd no peer." Thoreau punned with the adverb "lustily": using it to mean energetically, but also, given that Chaucer's "gentle cock had in his governance / Seven hens to give him pride and all pleasance," it may also carry the meaning of sexual desire. Thoreau's essay "Walking" contains the following paean to the cock's crow: "Unless our philosophy hears the cock crow in every barnyard within our horizon, it is belated. That sound commonly reminds us that we are growing rusty and antique in our employments and habits of thought. His philosophy comes down to a more recent time than ours. There is something suggested by it that is a newer testament,—the gospel according to this moment. . . . It is an expression of the health and soundness of Nature, a brag for all the world,—healthiness as of a spring burst

with dew, so that I fancied that by noon some sweet gum would exude from them. To my imagination it retained throughout the day more or less of this auroral character, reminding me of a certain house on a mountain which I had visited the year before.[22] This was an airy and unplastered cabin,[23] fit to entertain a travelling god,[24] and where a goddess might trail her garments.[25] The winds which passed over my dwelling were such as sweep over the ridges of mountains, bearing the broken strains, or celestial parts only, of terrestrial music. The morning wind forever blows, the poem of creation is uninterrupted; but few are the ears that hear it. Olympus[26] is but the outside of the earth every where.

The only house I had been the owner of before, if I except a boat,[27] was a tent, which I used occasionally when making excursions in the summer, and this is still rolled up in my garret; but the boat, after passing from hand to hand, has gone down the stream of time.[28] With this more substantial shelter about me, I had made some progress toward settling in the world. This frame, so slightly clad, was a sort of crystallization around me, and reacted on the builder. It was suggestive somewhat as a picture in outlines. I did not need to go out doors to take the air, for the atmosphere within had lost none of its freshness. It was not so much within doors as behind a door where I sat, even in the rainiest weather. The Harivansa[29] says, "An abode without birds is like a meat without seasoning."[30] Such was not my abode, for I found myself suddenly neighbor to the birds; not by having imprisoned one, but having caged myself near them. I was not only nearer to some of those which commonly frequent the garden and the orchard, but to those wilder and more thrilling songsters of the forest which never, or rarely, serenade a villager,—the wood-thrush, the veery, the scarlet tanager, the field-sparrow,[31] the whippoorwill, and many others.

forth, a new fountain of the Muses, to celebrate this last instant of time" [W 5:246].

21 In a 17 January 1852 journal entry, Thoreau noted: "It was on the 4th of July that I . . . commenced housekeeping" [J 3:200]. In his journal of 5 July 1845 Thoreau had simply written: "Yesterday I came here to live" [J 1:361]. Friday, 4 July 1845, was a day of fair weather. The sun rose at 4:29 A.M. and set at 8 P.M.

22 The home of Ira Scribner (1800–1890), whom Thoreau and Ellery Channing had visited in August 1844. Thoreau recorded in his journal of 5 July 1845: "I lodged at the house of a saw-miller last summer, on the Caatskill Mountains, high up as Pine Orchard, in the blueberry and raspberry region, where the quiet and cleanliness and coolness seemed to be all one,—which had their ambrosial character. He was the miller of the Kaaterskill Falls. They were a clean and wholesome family, inside and out, like their house" [J 1:361].

23 One of Thoreau's three references to his Walden house as a cabin. The other two occur in "Visitors" and "The Village."

24 In Greek and other mythologies, the gods often traveled down to earth to play a part in mortal lives.

25 Possible allusion to Hector's description of the Trojan women, not goddesses, with their trailing robes or garments, in the *Iliad* 6.442.

26 In Greek mythology, the mountain where the gods resided.

27 Refers to the boat Thoreau and his brother John built for their 1839 river excursion. Thoreau described the boat, named "Musketaquid" after the Indian name for the Concord River, in *A Week on the Concord and Merrimack Rivers* [W 1:12–13].

28 Hawthorne wrote in a 1 September 1842 notebook entry that Thoreau, "being in want of money, the poor fellow was desirous of selling his boat, of which he is so fit a pilot, and which was built by his own hands; so I agreed to give him his price (only seven dollars) and accordingly became possessor of the Musketaquid." It later passed to Ellery Channing.

29 Hindu epic poem, ca. 5th century, about the god Krishna.

30 Thoreau's translation from the French edition of the *Harivansa, ou Histoire de la Famille de Hari,* translated into French by Simon Alexandre Langlois (1788–1854), 1:282.

31 The field sparrow is a bird not of the forest but of the fields, as Thoreau came to realize after publication of *Walden*. In a journal entry of 22 April 1859 he wrote: "As the pines gradually increase, and a wood-lot is formed, these birds will withdraw to new pastures. . . . They commonly place their nests here under the shelter of a little pine in the field" [J 12:155].

32 Site of the battle on 19 April 1775 marking the beginning of the American Revolution.

33 A mountain lake. Thoreau wrote similarly in his journal: "If there is no elevation in our spirits, the pond will not seem elevated like a mountain tarn, but a low pool, a silent muddy water, a place for fishermen" [J 1:377].

34 Secret or illegal religious meeting.

35 Pun: "around" as vicinity, and "a round," a partsong in which voices join until all are singing different parts of the song at the same time.

36 Ellery Channing identified this as Heywood's Peak, on the north side of Walden Pond. In several journal entries Thoreau observed the pond from the perspective of Heywood's Peak.

I was seated by the shore of a small pond, about a mile and a half south of the village of Concord and somewhat higher than it, in the midst of an extensive wood between that town and Lincoln, and about two miles south of that our only field known to fame, Concord Battle Ground;[32] but I was so low in the woods that the opposite shore, half a mile off, like the rest, covered with wood, was my most distant horizon. For the first week, whenever I looked out on the pond it impressed me like a tarn[33] high up on the side of a mountain, its bottom far above the surface of other lakes, and, as the sun arose, I saw it throwing off its nightly clothing of mist, and here and there, by degrees, its soft ripples or its smooth reflecting surface was revealed, while the mists, like ghosts, were stealthily withdrawing in every direction into the woods, as at the breaking up of some nocturnal conventicle.[34] The very dew seemed to hang upon the trees later into the day than usual, as on the sides of mountains.

This small lake was of most value as a neighbor in the intervals of a gentle rain storm in August, when, both air and water being perfectly still, but the sky overcast, mid-afternoon had all the serenity of evening, and the wood-thrush sang around,[35] and was heard from shore to shore. A lake like this is never smoother than at such a time; and the clear portion of the air above it being shallow and darkened by clouds, the water, full of light and reflections, becomes a lower heaven itself so much the more important. From a hill top near by,[36] where the wood had been recently cut off, there was a pleasing vista southward across the pond, through a wide indentation in the hills which form the shore there, where their opposite sides sloping toward each other suggested a stream flowing out in that direction through a wooded valley, but stream there was none. That way I looked between and over the near green hills to some distant and higher ones in the horizon, tinged with blue. Indeed, by standing on tiptoe I could catch a glimpse of some of the peaks of the still bluer and more distant mountain ranges in the north-west,[37] those true-blue coins from heaven's own mint, and also of some portion of the village. But in other directions, even from this point, I could not see over or beyond the woods which surrounded me. It is well to have some water in your neighborhood, to give buoyancy to and float the earth. One value even of the smallest well is, that when you look into it you see that earth is not continent but insular. This is as important as that it keeps butter cool.[38] When I looked across the pond from this peak toward the Sudbury meadows,[39] which in time of flood[40] I distinguished elevated perhaps by a mirage in their seething valley, like a coin in a basin, all the earth beyond the pond appeared like a thin crust insulated and floated even by this small sheet of intervening water, and I was reminded that this on which I dwelt was but *dry land*.[41]

Though the view from my door was still more contracted, I did not feel crowded or confined in the least. There was pasture enough for my imagination. The low shrub-oak[42] plateau to which the opposite shore arose, stretched away toward the prairies of the West and the steppes of Tartary,[43] affording ample room for all the roving families of men. "There are none happy in the world but beings who enjoy freely a vast horizon,"[44] — said Damodara,[45] when his herds required new and larger pastures.

Both place and time were changed, and I dwelt nearer to those parts of the universe and to those eras in history which had most attracted me. Where I lived was as far off as many a region viewed nightly by astronomers. We are wont to imagine rare and delectable places in some remote and more celestial corner of the system, behind the constellation of Cassiopeia's Chair,[46] far from noise and disturbance. I discovered that my house actu-

37 The Peterborough range in southern New Hampshire.

38 Submerging butter in wells during the summer was a method for keeping it cool.

39 The Sudbury meadows lay approximately three miles southwest of Walden Pond.

40 The Concord and Sudbury rivers overflow their banks during the spring.

41 Possible reference to Genesis 1:9: "And God said, Let the waters under the heaven be gathered together unto one place, and let the dry land appear: and it was so."

42 Also known as scrub oak. Thoreau wrote in a journal entry of 7 January 1857: "I should not be ashamed to have a shrub oak for my coat-of-arms" [J 9:207].

43 Grasslands in Asiatic Russia.

44 Thoreau's translation from Langlois' French edition of the *Harivansa, ou Histoire de la Famille de Hari* 1:283

45 Epithet for Krishna.

46 Group of five stars resembling a W in the constellation Cassiopeia.

47 Star clusters in the constellation Taurus.

48 Stars of the first magnitude in the constellations Taurus and Aquila, respectively.

49 From "The Shepherd's Love for Philiday," verses by an unknown author that were set to music by Robert Jones and published in 1610 in *The Muses Gardin of Delights, or the Fift Booke of Ayres,* and later collected in Thomas Evans's (1742–1784) four-volume *Old Ballads, Historical and Narrative,* rev. ed. (London, 1810) 1:248, Thoreau's source, from which he modernized the spelling.

50 Thoreau wrote in his journal: "My most sacred and memorable life is commonly on awaking in the morning. I frequently awake with an atmosphere about me as if my unremembered dreams had been divine, as if my spirit had journeyed to its native place, and, in the act of reentering its native body, had diffused an elysian fragrance around" [J 2:213]. Thoreau's use of morning as a symbol may have been influenced in part from *Nature,* in which Emerson wrote that "the knowledge of man is an evening knowledge, *vespertina cognitio,* but that of God is a morning knowledge, *matutina cognitio.*"

51 In Roman mythology, goddess of the dawn. Her name was Eos in Greek mythology.

52 Thoreau's morning bathing was as much ablution as hygiene. "I am inclined to think bathing almost one of the necessaries of life, but it is surprising how indifferent some are to it," he wrote in his journal of 8 July 1852. "What a coarse, foul, busy life we lead, compared even with the South-Sea-Islanders, in some respects. Truant boys steal away to bathe, but the farmers, who most need it, rarely dip their bodies into the streams or ponds" [J 4:201–2]. Books of hygiene from the 19th century indicate that bathing for cleanliness had not yet become a regular practice.

53 Ch'eng-t'ang, founder of the Shang, or Yin, dynasty, 1766–1122 B.C.E.

54 From Confucius, *The Great Learning* 2:1, "Commentary of the Philosopher Tsang"; this is Thoreau's translation from the French in Pauthier's *Confucius et Mencius* 44.

ally had its site in such a withdrawn, but forever new and unprofaned, part of the universe. If it were worth the while to settle in those parts near to the Pleiades or the Hyades,[47] to Aldebaran or Altair,[48] then I was really there, or at an equal remoteness from the life which I had left behind, dwindled and twinkling with as fine a ray to my nearest neighbor, and to be seen only in moonless nights by him. Such was that part of creation where I had squatted;—

> "There was a shepherd that did live,
>   And held his thoughts as high
> As were the mounts whereon his flocks
>   Did hourly feed him by."[49]

What should we think of the shepherd's life if his flocks always wandered to higher pastures than his thoughts?

Every morning[50] was a cheerful invitation to make my life of equal simplicity, and I may say innocence, with Nature herself. I have been as sincere a worshipper of Aurora[51] as the Greeks. I got up early and bathed in the pond;[52] that was a religious exercise, and one of the best things which I did. They say that characters were engraven on the bathing tub of king Tching-thang[53] to this effect: "Renew thyself completely each day; do it again, and again, and forever again."[54] I can understand that. Morning brings back the heroic ages.[55] I was as much affected by the faint hum of a mosquito making its invisible and unimaginable tour through my apartment at earliest dawn, when I was sitting with door and windows open, as I could be by any trumpet that ever sang of fame.[56] It was Homer's requiem;[57] itself an Iliad and Odyssey in the air, singing its own wrath and wanderings.[58] There was something cosmical about it; a standing advertisement, till forbidden,[59] of the everlasting vigor and fertility of the world. The morning, which is the most memorable season of the day, is the awakening hour. Then there is least somnolence in us; and for an hour, at least, some part of us awakes which slumbers all the rest of the day and night. Little is to be expected of that day, if it can be called a day, to which we are not awakened by our Genius,⁶⁰ but by the mechanical nudgings of some servitor, are not awakened by our own newly-acquired force and aspirations from within, accompanied by the undulations of celestial music, instead of factory bells, and a fragrance filling the air—to a higher life than we fell asleep from; and thus the darkness bear its fruit, and prove itself to be good, no less than the light. That man who does not believe that each day contains an earlier, more sacred, and auroral hour than he has yet profaned, has despaired of life, and is pursuing a descending and darkening way. After a partial cessation of his sensuous life, the soul of man, or its organs rather, are reinvigorated each day, and his Genius tries again what noble life it can make. All memorable events, I should say, transpire in morning time and in a morning atmosphere. The Vedas⁶¹ say, "All intelligences awake with the morning." Poetry and art, and the fairest and most memorable of the actions of men, date from such an hour. All poets and heroes, like Memnon,⁶² are the children of Aurora, and emit their music at sunrise. To him whose elastic and vigorous thought keeps pace with the sun, the day is a perpetual morning. It matters not what the clocks say or the attitudes and labors of men. Morning is when I am awake and there is a dawn in me. Moral reform is the effort to throw off sleep. Why is it that men give so poor an account of their day if they have not been slumbering? They are not such poor calculators. If they had not been overcome with drowsiness they would have performed something. The millions are awake enough for physical labor; but only one in a million is awake enough for effective intellectual exertion, only one in a hundred millions to a poetic or divine life. To be

55 Specifically, the period the Greek writer Hesiod (8th century B.C.E.) called the Heroic Age, before the Greeks returned from the Trojan War. The heroes were demigods, a race of noble warriors, who lived during the time of the wars in Thebes and Troy. In "Reading" Thoreau suggested that morning hours be consecrated to the reading of heroic books, the heroes of which the reader emulates.

56 Allusion to a poem by Felicia Dorothea Hemans (1793–1835), "The Landing of the Pilgrims": "And the trumpet that sings of fame" [l. 12].

57 Possible reference to Homer's praise of "the persistent daring of the mosquito who though it is driven hard away from a man's skin, even so, for the taste of human blood, persists in biting him," in *Iliad* 17.567–73, although this is alternately translated as a hornet and a fly.

58 Homer's *Iliad* opens with a reference to Achilles' wrath, and his *Odyssey* with a reference to Odysseus' wanderings.

59 Printer's term for a standing advertisement, abbreviated as TF.

60 From Latin, meaning "begetter," "genius" referred originally to an attendant spirit, and later as a personification of an individual's natural desires and appetites. Sampson Reed (1800–1880) wrote in "Oration on Genius" about its relation to "divine truth" and related the term to its original meaning: "Men say there is an inspiration in genius. The genius of the ancients was the good or evil spirit that attended the man." Emerson, in his early lecture "Genius," defined the word as "1. Genius, a man's natural bias or turn of mind. . . . 2. The second and popular sense of Genius is the intellect's spontaneous perception and exhibition of truth."

61 The most ancient and sacred literature of the Hindus, the product of divine revelation, handed down in four collections: the Rigveda (The Veda of Verses), the Yajurveda (The Veda of Sacrificial Texts), the Samaveda (The Veda of Chants), and the Atharvaveda (The Veda of the Fire-Priest). The impact of Thoreau's reading the Vedas is apparent by several references throughout his journals and other writings. In an 1850 journal entry he wrote: "What extracts from the Vedas I have read fall on me like the light of a higher and purer luminary, which describes a loftier course through a purer stratum,—free from particulars, simple, universal. It rises on me like the full moon after the stars have come out, wading through some far summer stratum of the sky" [J 2:4].

62 Son of Aurora, slain by Achilles in the Trojan War. Several giant statues of him were built near Thebes, from one of which, when warmed by the sun, music emanated.

63 Thoreau wrote in "Walking": "The Hottentots eagerly devour the marrow of the koodoo and other antelopes raw, as a matter of course. Some of our northern Indians eat raw the marrow of the Arctic reindeer, as well as various other parts, including the summits of the antlers, as long as they are soft. And herein, perchance they have stolen a march on the cooks of Paris. They get what usually goes to feed the fire. This is probably better than stall-fed beef and slaughter-house pork to make a man of. Give me a wildness whose glance no civilization can endure,—as if we lived on the marrow of koodoos devoured raw" [W 5:225].

64 The Spartans of ancient Greece were celebrated for their rigorous discipline and austerity, as well as their courage and military organization.

65 Thoreau's term for a travel essay, with a humorous reference to the afterlife.

awake is to be alive. I have never yet met a man who was quite awake. How could I have looked him in the face?

We must learn to reawaken and keep ourselves awake, not by mechanical aids, but by an infinite expectation of the dawn, which does not forsake us in our soundest sleep. I know of no more encouraging fact than the unquestionable ability of man to elevate his life by a conscious endeavor. It is something to be able to paint a particular picture, or to carve a statue, and so to make a few objects beautiful; but it is far more glorious to carve and paint the very atmosphere and medium through which we look, which morally we can do. To affect the quality of the day, that is the highest of arts. Every man is tasked to make his life, even in its details, worthy of the contemplation of his most elevated and critical hour. If we refused, or rather used up, such paltry information as we get, the oracles would distinctly inform us how this might be done.

I went to the woods because I wished to live deliberately, to front only the essential facts of life, and see if I could not learn what it had to teach, and not, when I came to die, discover that I had not lived. I did not wish to live what was not life, living is so dear; nor did I wish to practise resignation, unless it was quite necessary. I wanted to live deep and suck out all the marrow of life,[63] to live so sturdily and Spartan-like[64] as to put to rout all that was not life, to cut a broad swath and shave close, to drive life into a corner, and reduce it to its lowest terms, and, if it proved to be mean, why then to get the whole and genuine meanness of it, and publish its meanness to the world; or if it were sublime, to know it by experience, and be able to give a true account of it in my next excursion.[65] For most men, it appears to me, are in a strange uncertainty about it, whether it is of the devil or of God, and have *somewhat hastily* concluded that it is the chief end of man here to "glorify God and enjoy him forever."

Still we live meanly, like ants; though the fable tells

us that we were long ago changed into men;[66] like pygmies we fight with cranes;[67] it is error upon error, and
clout upon clout,[68] and our best virtue has for its occasion a superfluous and evitable wretchedness. Our life is
frittered away by detail. An honest man has hardly need
to count more than his ten fingers, or in extreme cases
he may add his ten toes, and lump the rest. Simplicity,
simplicity, simplicity![69] I say, let your affairs be as two or
three, and not a hundred or a thousand; instead of a million count half a dozen, and keep your accounts on your
thumb nail. In the midst of this chopping sea of civilized
life, such are the clouds and storms and quicksands and
thousand-and-one items to be allowed for, that a man has
to live, if he would not founder and go to the bottom and
not make his port at all, by dead reckoning,[70] and he must
be a great calculator indeed who succeeds. Simplify, simplify. Instead of three meals a day, if it be necessary eat but
one; instead of a hundred dishes, five; and reduce other
things in proportion. Our life is like a German Confederacy,[71] made up of petty states, with its boundary forever fluctuating, so that even a German cannot tell you
how it is bounded at any moment. The nation itself, with
all its so called internal improvements,[72] which, by the
way, are all external and superficial, is just such an unwieldy and overgrown establishment, cluttered with furniture and tripped up by its own traps, ruined by luxury and heedless expense, by want of calculation and a
worthy aim, as the million households in the land; and
the only cure for it as for them is in a rigid economy, a
stern and more than Spartan simplicity of life and elevation of purpose. It lives too fast. Men think that it is essential that the *Nation* have commerce, and export ice,[73] and
talk through a telegraph, and ride thirty miles an hour,[74]
without a doubt, whether *they* do or not; but whether we
should live like baboons or like men, is a little uncertain.
If we do not get out sleepers,[75] and forge rails, and devote

66 In Greek mythology, Aeacus, king of Oenopia,
when his subjects were destroyed by a pestilence,
entreated Zeus to repopulate his kingdom by
changing all the ants in an old oak tree into men.
Thoreau referred to this myth in *A Week on the
Concord and Merrimack Rivers:* "According to fable,
when the island of Ægina was depopulated by
sickness, at the instance of Æacus, Jupiter turned
the ants into men, that is, as some think, he made
men of the inhabitants who lived meanly like ants"
[W 1:58].

67 In the opening to Homer's *Iliad,* book 3, the
Trojans are compared to cranes fighting with
pygmies. Thoreau translated the passage in his
journal of 17 April 1846 as:

> The Trojans rushed with a clang & a shout like
>   birds;
> As when there is a clangor of cranes in the
>   heavens
> Who avoid winter & unspeakable rain,
> They fly with clangor toward the streams of
>   Ocean
> Bearing slaughter & Fate to Pygmaean men.
>   [PJ 2:234]

68 Blow upon blow, in context with pygmies fighting cranes, but also, in context with error upon
error, patch upon patch, i.e., endlessly patched
and mended, as in the "Forefathers' Song," part of
which Thoreau quoted in "Economy." His source
may have been Barber's *Historical Collections,*
where the verse is printed as:

> And now our old garments begin to grow thin,
> And wool is much wanted to card and to spin;
> If we can get a garment to cover without,
> Our other in-garments are clout upon clout.

69 In a letter to H. G. O. Blake dated 27 March
1848, Thoreau explained: "I do believe in simplicity.
It is astonishing as well as sad, how many trivial
affairs even the wisest man thinks he must attend
to in a day; how singular an affair he thinks he

must omit. When the mathematician would solve
a difficult problem, he first frees the equation of
all incumbrances, and reduces it to its simplest
terms. So simplify the problem of life, distinguish
the necessary and the real. Probe the earth to see
where your main roots run" [C 215]. In a journal
entry on 1 September 1853, Thoreau contrasted two
types of simplicity:

> The savage lives simply through ignorance
> and idleness or laziness, but the philosopher
> lives simply through wisdom. In the case of
> the savage, the accompaniment of simplicity
> is idleness with its attendant vices, but in
> the case of the philosopher, it is the highest
> employment and development. The fact for
> the savage, and for the mass of mankind, is
> that it is better to plant, weave, and build than
> do nothing or worse; but the fact for the phi-
> losopher, or a nation loving wisdom, is that
> it is most important to cultivate the highest
> faculties and spend as little time as possible
> in planting, weaving, building, etc. . . . The
> simple style is bad for the savage because he
> does worse than to obtain the luxuries of life;
> it is good for the philosopher because he does
> better than to work for them. The question is
> whether you can bear freedom. . . .
>
> There are two kinds of simplicity,—one that
> is akin to foolishness, the other to wisdom. The
> philosopher's style of living is only outwardly
> simple, but inwardly complex. [J 5:410–12]

70 Nautical term for reckoning a ship's position
by its course, speed, and last known position,
without direct reference to the position of the
stars.

71 A loose confederation of Germanic princi-
palities and minor kingdoms from 1815 to 1866,
before Germany was unified under Prince Otto von
Bismarck (1815–1898).

72 Extensive capital projects, such as railroads,
roadways, and waterways.

days and nights to the work, but go to tinkering upon
our *lives* to improve *them,* who will build railroads? And if
railroads are not built, how shall we get to heaven in season?[76] But if we stay at home and mind our business, who
will want railroads? We do not ride on the railroad; it rides
upon us. Did you ever think what those sleepers are that
underlie the railroad? Each one is a man, an Irish-man,
or a Yankee man. The rails are laid on them, and they are
covered with sand, and the cars run smoothly over them.
They are sound sleepers, I assure you. And every few years
a new lot is laid down and run over; so that, if some have
the pleasure of riding on a rail,[77] others have the misfortune to be ridden upon. And when they run over a man
that is walking in his sleep, a supernumerary sleeper in
the wrong position, and wake him up, they suddenly stop
the cars, and make a hue and cry about it, as if this were
an exception. I am glad to know that it takes a gang of
men for every five miles to keep the sleepers down and
level in their beds as it is, for this is a sign that they may
sometime get up again.

Why should we live with such hurry and waste of life?
We are determined to be starved before we are hungry.
Men say that a stitch in time saves nine, and so they take
a thousand stitches to-day to save nine to-morrow. As for
work, we haven't any of any consequence. We have the
Saint Vitus' dance,[78] and cannot possibly keep our heads
still. If I should only give a few pulls at the parish bell-
rope, as for a fire, that is, without setting the bell,[79] there is
hardly a man on his farm in the outskirts of Concord, notwithstanding that press of engagements which was his excuse so many times this morning, nor a boy, nor a woman,
I might almost say, but would forsake all and follow that
sound, not mainly to save property from the flames, but,
if we will confess the truth, much more to see it burn,
since burn it must, and we, be it known, did not set it

on fire,[80] — or to see it put out, and have a hand in it, if that is done as handsomely; yes, even if it were the parish church itself. Hardly a man takes a half hour's nap after dinner, but when he wakes he holds up his head and asks, "What's the news?" as if the rest of mankind had stood his sentinels. Some give directions to be waked every half hour, doubtless for no other purpose; and then, to pay for it, they tell what they have dreamed. After a night's sleep the news is as indispensable as the breakfast. "Pray tell me any thing new that has happened to a man any where on this globe," — and he reads it over his coffee and rolls, that a man has had his eyes gouged out[81] this morning on the Wachito River;[82] never dreaming the while that he lives in the dark unfathomed mammoth cave[83] of this world, and has but the rudiment of an eye[84] himself.

For my part, I could easily do without the post-office.[85] I think that there are very few important communications made through it. To speak critically, I never received more than one or two letters in my life — I wrote this some years ago[86] — that were worth the postage. The penny-post[87] is, commonly, an institution through which you seriously offer a man that penny for his thoughts[88] which is so often safely offered in jest. And I am sure that I never read any memorable news in a newspaper. If we read of one man robbed, or murdered, or killed by accident, or one house burned, or one vessel wrecked, or one steamboat blown up, or one cow run over on the Western Railroad,[89] or one mad dog killed, or one lot of grasshoppers in the winter, — we never need read of another. One is enough. If you are acquainted with the principle, what do you care for a myriad instances and applications? To a philosopher all *news,* as it is called, is gossip, and they who edit and read it are old women over their tea.[90] Yet not a few are greedy after this gossip. There was such a rush, as I hear, the other day at one of the offices to learn the foreign news

73 The shipping of New England ice to warmer regions was just beginning.

74 The railroad, which reached Concord the year before Thoreau's residence at Walden, was the first mode of transportation to reach that speed.

75 Wooden railroad ties upon which the tracks are laid.

76 Allusion to Hawthorne's "The Celestial Railroad."

77 Literally, as a passenger, but also with reference to the custom of removing an unwanted person by forcing him to straddle a wooden rail held aloft, often as a way of riding him out of town.

78 Chorea, a disease that affects the nervous system, causing spasmodic movements, depression, and emotional instability.

79 Pulling forcefully on a bell rope, hard enough to turn the bell mouth all the way upward with each pull, was known as setting the bell, or ringing high, and was the signal calling people to church. Ringing low, without setting it, sounds the bell faster and was used to give the fire alarm.

80 Thoreau had helped put out many fires, but this probably refers to his accidentally setting the woods on fire on 30 April 1844 with his companion Edward Hoar. A spark from their fire caught on the extremely dry grass nearby. Over 300 acres were burned, causing more than $2,000 in damage. The *Concord Freeman* reported on 3 May 1844: "The fire, we understand, was communicated to the woods through the thoughtlessness of two of our citizens, who kindled it in a *pine stump,* near the Pond, for the purpose of making a chowder. As every thing around them was as combustible almost as a fire-ship, the flames spread with rapidity, and hours elapsed before it could be subdued. It is to be hoped that this unfortunate result of sheer carelessness, will be borne in mind by those who may visit the woods in future for recreation." For years Thoreau had to endure being called "woods-burner" in whispers behind his back. His prolonged feelings of guilt caused him to write a lengthy journal account of the incident in June

1850, six years later (quoted in "House-Warming," note 57).

81 Along the Mississippi frontier, it was common in unarmed fights to attempt to gouge an opponent's eyes out by a distinct turn of the thumb. "I saw more than one man who wanted an eye, and ascertained that I was now in the region of 'gouging,'" wrote Timothy Flint (1780–1840) about his Louisiana missionary work in 1816.

82 The Ouachita (or Washito) River in southern Arkansas.

83 Conflation of Kentucky's Mammoth Cave with the "dark unfathomed caves of ocean" from Thomas Gray's (1716–1771) "Elegy Written in a Country Churchyard."

84 The fish in Kentucky's Mammoth Cave are blind and thus have only the "rudiment of an eye."

85 This may be more desire than actuality. According to Franklin Sanborn, "few residents of Concord frequented the Post Office more punctually." Thoreau wrote in "Life Without Principle": "In proportion as our inward life fails, we go more constantly and desperately to the post-office. You may depend on it, that the poor fellow who walks away with the greatest number of letters, proud of his extensive correspondence, has not heard from himself this long while" [W 4:471].

86 A reminder of the distance between Thoreau's residence at Walden and his writing of *Walden* and a caution about a slight change in attitude. He originally wrote "I could even dispense with the post office—I hardly receive more than one letter in a year" [PJ 2:374] in the winter of 1846–47 while still living at Walden, and yet several later journal references mention going to or returning from the post office, including one in January 1856 where he had been following for a week an ongoing conversation there—"Men have been talking now for a week at the post-office about the age of the great elm" [J 8:145].

87 Established in Great Britain in 1840 as a uniform postal fee. Postage was three cents in the United States in 1854 when *Walden* was published.

88 The earliest known use of this phrase in print is in John Heywood's *Proverbs:* "Freend (quoth the good man) a peny for your thought."

89 The Western Railroad of Massachusetts ran, in 1841, from Boston to the New York state line.

90 In "Life Without Principle" Thoreau also compared the news to teatime gossip: "Not without a slight shudder at the danger, I often perceive how near I had come to admitting into my mind the details of some trivial affair,—the news of the street; and I am astonished to observe how willing men are to lumber their minds with such rubbish,—to permit idle rumors and incidents of the most insignificant kind to intrude on ground which should be sacred to thought. Shall the mind be a public arena, where the affairs of the street and the gossip of the tea-table chiefly are discussed? Or shall it be a quarter of heaven itself,—an hypæthral temple, consecrated to the service of the gods?" [W 4:473].

by the last arrival, that several large squares of plate glass belonging to the establishment were broken by the pressure,—news which I seriously think a ready wit might write a twelvemonth or twelve years beforehand with sufficient accuracy. As for Spain, for instance, if you know how to throw in Don Carlos and the Infanta,[91] and Don Pedro and Seville and Granada,[92] from time to time in the right proportions,—they may have changed the names a little since I saw the papers,—and serve up a bull-fight when other entertainments fail, it will be true to the letter, and give us as good an idea of the exact state or ruin of things in Spain as the most succinct and lucid reports under this head in the newspapers: and as for England, almost the last significant scrap of news from that quarter was the revolution of 1649;[93] and if you have learned the history of her crops for an average year, you never need attend to that thing again, unless your speculations are of a merely pecuniary character. If one may judge who rarely looks into the newspapers, nothing new does ever happen in foreign parts, a French revolution not excepted.[94]

What news! how much more important to know what that is which was never old! "Kieou-pe-yu (great dignitary of the state of Wei) sent a man to Khoung-tseu to know his news. Khoung-tseu caused the messenger to be seated near him, and questioned him in these terms: What is your master doing? The messenger answered with respect: My master desires to diminish the number of his faults, but he cannot accomplish it. The messenger being gone, the philosopher remarked: What a worthy messenger! What a worthy messenger!"[95] The preacher, instead of vexing the ears of drowsy farmers on their day of rest at the end of the week,—for Sunday is the fit conclusion of an ill-spent week, and not the fresh and brave beginning of a new one,[96]—with this one other draggletail of a sermon, should shout with thundering voice,— "Pause! Avast![97] Why so seeming fast, but deadly slow?"

91 King Ferdinand VII of Spain (1784–1833) and his brother, Don Carlos (1788–1855), struggled for power in the 1830s. In 1843 Ferdinand's daughter, the thirteen-year-old Infanta (1830–1904), was crowned Queen Isabella II.

92 Don Pedro the Cruel of Seville (1334–1369) and his army subdued and killed Abu Said Muhammad VI (d. 1362) of Granada.

93 Beginning in 1642 and ending in 1649 with the establishment of the Puritan Commonwealth under Oliver Cromwell, temporarily replacing the British monarchy.

94 In his Bibliophile Edition of *Walden,* Sanborn published the following note by Thoreau: "This was written before the last (1848) Revolution broke out; but a revolution in France might be expected any day; and it would be as easy to tell where it would end, before it was born, as after it was five years old."

95 Thoreau's translation of Confucius' *Analects* 14.26, from the French translation in Pauthier's *Confucius et Mencius* 184.

96 In the Julian and Gregorian calendars, Sunday is the first day of the week. Thoreau, being somewhat anti-Sabbatarian, claimed otherwise. In the "Sunday" chapter of *A Week on the Concord and Merrimack Rivers,* he described being observed traveling on Sunday, and called himself and his brother "the truest observers of this sunny day. . . . [B]y our reckoning this was the seventh day of the week, and not the first" [W 1:64].

97 The nautical flavor is a possible allusion to Edward Thompson Taylor (1793–1871) of the Boston's Seamen's Bethel, the model for Father Mapple in Melville's *Moby-Dick,* whom Thoreau heard in Concord on 22 June 1845.

98 A 10th-century collection of ancient Persian, Indian, and Arabian tales, the most famous of which are those of Aladdin, Sinbad, and Ali Baba.
99 Quoted from *The Sankhya Karika, or Memorial Verses on the Sankhya Philosophy by Iswara Krishna,* translated by Henry Thomas Colebrooke (1765–1837) (Oxford, 1837) 72. Brahme, or Brahma, is the essence of spiritual being in Hindu philosophy.
100 Town center. Concord originated as a mill-dam site, a center of converging roads, from which a settlement grew.

Shams and delusions are esteemed for soundest truths, while reality is fabulous. If men would steadily observe realities only, and not allow themselves to be deluded, life, to compare it with such things as we know, would be like a fairy tale and the Arabian Nights' Entertainments.[98] If we respected only what is inevitable and has a right to be, music and poetry would resound along the streets. When we are unhurried and wise, we perceive that only great and worthy things have any permanent and absolute existence,—that petty fears and petty pleasures are but the shadow of the reality. This is always exhilarating and sublime. By closing the eyes and slumbering, and consenting to be deceived by shows, men establish and confirm their daily life of routine and habit every where, which still is built on purely illusory foundations. Children, who play life, discern its true law and relations more clearly than men, who fail to live it worthily, but who think that they are wiser by experience, that is, by failure. I have read in a Hindoo book, that "there was a king's son, who, being expelled in infancy from his native city, was brought up by a forester, and, growing up to maturity in that state, imagined himself to belong to the barbarous race with which he lived. One of his father's ministers having discovered him, revealed to him what he was, and the misconception of his character was removed, and he knew himself to be a prince. So soul," continues the Hindoo philosopher, "from the circumstances in which it is placed, mistakes its own character, until the truth is revealed to it by some holy teacher, and then it knows itself to be *Brahme*."[99] I perceive that we inhabitants of New England live this mean life that we do because our vision does not penetrate the surface of things. We think that that *is* which *appears* to be. If a man should walk through this town and see only the reality, where, think you, would the "Mill-dam"[100] go to? If he should give us an account of the realities he beheld there, we should not recognize the place in his description. Look at a meeting-house, or a court-house, or a jail, or a shop, or a dwelling-house, and say what that thing really is before a true gaze, and they would all go to pieces in your account of them. Men esteem truth remote, in the outskirts of the system, behind the farthest star, before Adam and after the last man. In eternity there is indeed something true and sublime. But all these times and places and occasions are now and here. God himself culminates in the present moment, and will never be more divine in the lapse of all the ages. And we are enabled to apprehend at all what is sublime and noble only by the perpetual instilling and drenching of the reality which surrounds us. The universe constantly and obediently answers to our conceptions; whether we travel fast or slow, the track is laid for us. Let us spend our lives in conceiving then. The poet or the artist never yet had so fair and noble a design but some of his posterity at least could accomplish it.

Let us spend one day as deliberately as Nature, and not be thrown off the track by every nutshell and mosquito's wing that falls on the rails.[101] Let us rise early and fast, or break fast, gently and without perturbation; let company come and let company go, let the bells ring and the children cry,—determined to make a day of it. Why should we knock under and go with the stream? Let us not be upset and overwhelmed in that terrible rapid and whirlpool called a dinner, situated in the meridian[102] shallows. Weather this danger and you are safe, for the rest of the way is down hill. With unrelaxed nerves, with morning vigor, sail by it, looking another way, tied to the mast like Ulysses.[103] If the engine whistles, let it whistle till it is hoarse for its pains. If the bell rings, why should we run? We will consider what kind of music they are like. Let us settle ourselves, and work and wedge our feet downward through the mud and slush of opinion, and prejudice, and tradition, and delusion, and appearance, that allu-

101 In the early days of the railroad, trains were easily and often derailed. *Scientific American* of 16 July 1853 quoted *The Railroad Journal* on the subject: "An engine and the front cars of a train will often go over a broken rail, or a cow, or stone, without derailment, while the last car, having nothing to draw it into the line of the train, is free to leave the track."

102 Noontime.

103 In Homer's *Odyssey*, book 12, Ulysses (Odysseus) tied himself to the mast so that he could hear the song of the Sirens without falling victim to them.

104 French: a point of support.

105 Instrument used in ancient Egypt to record the rise of the Nile River so cities could be warned of flooding, but with a pun on "nil" meaning "nothing."

106 Facts were a means to a higher or more mythological truth. In an early journal entry Thoreau wrote, "How indispensable to a correct study of Nature is a perception of her true meaning. The fact will one day flower out into a truth" [J 1:18].

107 Scimitar, a sword with a thin curved blade, known for its sharpness, in contrast to the heavier cleaver in the next paragraph.

vion which covers the globe, through Paris and London, through New York and Boston and Concord, through church and state, through poetry and philosophy and religion, till we come to a hard bottom and rocks in place, which we can call *reality,* and say, This is, and no mistake; and then begin, having a *point d'appui,*[104] below freshet and frost and fire, a place where you might found a wall or a state, or set a lamp-post safely, or perhaps a gauge, not a Nilometer,[105] but a Realometer, that future ages might know how deep a freshet of shams and appearances had gathered from time to time. If you stand right fronting and face to face to a fact,[106] you will see the sun glimmer on both its surfaces, as if it were a cimeter,[107] and feel its sweet edge dividing you through the heart and marrow, and so you will happily conclude your mortal career. Be it life or death, we crave only reality. If we are really dying, let us hear the rattle in our throats and feel cold in the extremities; if we are alive, let us go about our business.

Time is but the stream I go a-fishing in. I drink at it; but while I drink I see the sandy bottom and detect how shallow it is. Its thin current slides away, but eternity remains. I would drink deeper; fish in the sky, whose bottom is pebbly with stars. I cannot count one. I know not the first letter of the alphabet. I have always been regretting that I was not as wise as the day I was born. The intellect is a cleaver; it discerns and rifts its way into the secret of things. I do not wish to be any more busy with my hands than is necessary. My head is hands and feet. I feel all my best faculties concentrated in it. My instinct tells me that my head is an organ for burrowing, as some creatures use their snout and fore-paws, and with it I would mine and burrow my way through these hills. I think that the richest vein is somewhere hereabouts; so by the divining rod and thin rising vapors I judge; and here I will begin to mine.

Reading

With a little more deliberation in the choice of their pursuits, all men would perhaps become essentially students and observers, for certainly their nature and destiny are interesting to all alike. In accumulating property for ourselves or our posterity, in founding a family or a state, or acquiring fame even, we are mortal; but in dealing with truth we are immortal, and need fear no change nor accident. The oldest Egyptian or Hindoo philosopher raised a corner of the veil from the statue of the divinity;[1] and still the trembling robe remains raised, and I gaze upon as fresh a glory as he did, since it was I in him that was then so bold, and it is he in me that now reviews the vision. No dust has settled on that robe; no time has elapsed since that divinity was revealed. That time which we really improve, or which is improvable, is neither past, present, nor future.

My residence was more favorable, not only to thought, but to serious reading, than a university; and though I was beyond the range of the ordinary circulating library,[2] I had more than ever come within the influence of those books which circulate round the world, whose sentences were first written on bark, and are now merely copied from time to time on to linen paper. Says the poet Mîr Camar Uddîn Mast,[3] "Being seated to run through the region of the spiritual world; I have had this advantage in

1 Allusion to the lifting of the veil of Isis, in ancient Egypt, and the unveiling of Maya in Hindu religion.

2 This is an exaggeration; later in this chapter Thoreau referred to "a work in several volumes in our Circulating Library." The Concord Social Library, although not free, was available for a subscription fee. The Concord Town Library, beginning with the donated collections of the Concord Social Library, was established in 1851. Thoreau referred to it again in this chapter as "the puny beginning of a library." The town's first librarian, Albert Stacy (1821–1868), also owned a stationery store where he operated a small circulating library; his books were available for a rental fee and complemented, rather than duplicated, those in the town library. Thoreau had been borrowing books from Emerson's personal library since 1841, and later from Bronson Alcott and Ellery Channing, and in 1849 he obtained borrowing privileges from the Harvard College library.

3 Qamar-uddin Minnat, Persian and Urdu poet, a native of Delphi, who died in Calcutta in 1793.

4 Thoreau's translation of the French as found in Joseph Héliodore Garcin de Tassy's (1794–1878) *Histoire de la Littérature Hindoui et Hindoustani* (Paris, 1839–47) 1:331.

5 Thoreau had the Iliad in both Greek and English at Walden. His Greek text was *The Iliad of Homer, from the Text of Wolf with English Notes, and Flaxman's Designs*, edited by C. C. Felton (Boston, 1834), and his English text was the two-volume Alexander Pope (1688–1744) translation, *The Iliad of Homer* (Baltimore, 1812).

6 Travel literature was perhaps shallow, for the rhetorical purposes of *Walden*, but Thoreau read almost two hundred such works, and probably more, in his life. At this time he may have been reading travel literature as resource material for writing *A Week on the Concord and Merrimack Rivers*.

7 Aeschylus: Greek tragic poet (525–456 B.C.E.), author of more than 70 plays, only seven of which are extant.

books. To be intoxicated by a single glass of wine; I have experienced this pleasure when I have drunk the liquor of the esoteric doctrines."[4] I kept Homer's Iliad[5] on my table through the summer, though I looked at his page only now and then. Incessant labor with my hands, at first, for I had my house to finish and my beans to hoe at the same time, made more study impossible. Yet I sustained myself by the prospect of such reading in future. I read one or two shallow books of travel[6] in the intervals of my work, till that employment made me ashamed of myself, and I asked where it was then that *I* lived.

The student may read Homer or Æschylus[7] in the Greek without danger of dissipation or luxuriousness, for it implies that he in some measure emulate their heroes, and consecrate morning hours to their pages. The heroic books, even if printed in the character of our mother tongue, will always be in a language dead to degenerate times; and we must laboriously seek the meaning of each word and line, conjecturing a larger sense than common use permits out of what wisdom and valor and generosity we have. The modern cheap and fertile press, with all its translations, has done little to bring us nearer to the heroic writers of antiquity. They seem as solitary, and the letter in which they are printed as rare and curious, as ever. It is worth the expense of youthful days and costly hours, if you learn only some words of an ancient language, which are raised out of the trivialness of the street, to be perpetual suggestions and provocations. It is not in vain that the farmer remembers and repeats the few Latin words which he has heard. Men sometimes speak as if the study of the classics would at length make way for more modern and practical studies; but the adventurous student will always study classics, in whatever language they may be written and however ancient they may be. For what are the classics but the noblest recorded thoughts of man? They are the only oracles which are not decayed, and there are such answers to the most modern inquiry in them as Delphi and Dodona[8] never gave. We might as well omit to study Nature because she is old. To read well, that is, to read true books in a true spirit, is a noble exercise, and one that will task the reader more than any exercise which the customs of the day esteem. It requires a training such as the athletes underwent, the steady intention almost of the whole life to this object. Books must be read as deliberately and reservedly as they were written. It is not enough even to be able to speak the language of that nation by which they are written, for there is a memorable interval between the spoken and the written language, the language heard and the language read. The one is commonly transitory, a sound, a tongue, a dialect merely, almost brutish, and we learn it unconsciously, like the brutes, of our mothers. The other is the maturity and experience of that; if that is our mother tongue, this is our father tongue, a reserved and select expression, too significant to be heard by the ear, which we must be born again[9] in order to speak. The crowds of men who merely *spoke* the Greek and Latin tongues in the middle ages were not entitled by the accident of birth to *read* the works of genius written in those languages; for these were not written in that Greek or Latin which they knew, but in the select language of literature. They had not learned the nobler dialects of Greece and Rome, but the very materials on which they were written were waste paper to them,[10] and they prized instead a cheap contemporary literature. But when the several nations of Europe had acquired distinct though rude written languages of their own, sufficient for the purposes of their rising literatures, then first learning revived, and scholars were enabled to discern from that remoteness the treasures of antiquity. What the Roman and Grecian multitude could not *hear,* after the lapse of ages a few scholars *read,* and a few scholars only are still reading it.

8 The temples of Apollo at Delphi in Phocis and of Zeus at Dodona in Epirus were the two principal ancient Greek oracles.

9 Refers to religious conversion, as in John 3:3: "Jesus answered and said unto him, Verily, verily, I say unto thee, Except a man be born again, he cannot see the kingdom of God."

10 Medieval churchmen, not appreciating the value of the ancient classics, used the manuscripts as scrap paper (actually parchment) for their own sacred writings, ironically helping to preserve the writings they deemed worthless.

11 Xenophanes of Colophon (ca. 570–490 B.C.E.) theorized that the heavenly bodies had condensed into fiery clouds from earth's exhalations. Heraclitus of Ephesus (ca. 500 B.C.E.) expanded the idea of creation through balance of different substances and the process of condensation from fire. In this view, night was formed of murkier exhalations from earth, as from Tartarus, and day from exhalations ignited by the sun. Heraclitus and some of the Stoics believed that the stars depended for their illumination on exhalations from damp places on the earth.

12 Thoreau was aware of the demands to which an orator must yield to be successful. He wrote in his journal 6 December 1854:

> After lecturing twice this winter I feel that I am in danger of cheapening myself by trying to become a successful lecturer, *i.e.,* to interest my audiences. I am disappointed to find that the most that I am and value myself for is lost, or worse than lost, on my audience. I fail to get even the attention of the mass. I should suit them better if I suited myself less. I feel that the public demand an average man,—average thoughts and manners,—not originality, nor even absolute excellence. You cannot interest them except as you are like them and sympathize with them. I would rather that my audience come to me than that I should go to them, and so they be sifted; *i.e.,* I would rather write books than lectures. That is fine, this coarse. To read to a promiscuous audience who are at your mercy the fine thoughts you solaced yourself with far away is as violent as to fatten geese by cramming, and in this case they do not get fatter. [J 7:79–80]

13 Of Alexander the Great of Macedon (356–323 B.C.E.), Plutarch wrote in his *Lives:* "Among the treasures and other booty that was taken from Darius, there was a very precious casket, which being brought to Alexander for a great rarity, he asked those about him what they thought fittest to

However much we may admire the orator's occasional bursts of eloquence, the noblest written words are commonly as far behind or above the fleeting spoken language as the firmament with its stars is behind the clouds. *There* are the stars, and they who can may read them. The astronomers forever comment on and observe them. They are not exhalations[11] like our daily colloquies and vaporous breath. What is called eloquence in the forum is commonly found to be rhetoric in the study. The orator yields to the inspiration of a transient occasion, and speaks to the mob before him, to those who can *hear* him;[12] but the writer, whose more equable life is his occasion, and who would be distracted by the event and the crowd which inspire the orator, speaks to the intellect and heart of mankind, to all in any age who can *understand* him.

No wonder that Alexander carried the Iliad with him on his expeditions in a precious casket.[13] A written word is the choicest of relics. It is something at once more intimate with us and more universal than any other work of art. It is the work of art nearest to life itself. It may be translated into every language, and not only be read but actually breathed from all human lips;—not be represented on canvas or in marble only, but be carved out of the breath of life itself. The symbol of an ancient man's thought becomes a modern man's speech. Two thousand summers have imparted to the monuments of Grecian literature, as to her marbles, only a maturer golden and autumnal tint, for they have carried their own serene and celestial atmosphere into all lands to protect them against the corrosion of time. Books are the treasured wealth of the world and the fit inheritance of generations and nations. Books, the oldest and the best, stand naturally and rightfully on the shelves of every cottage. They have no cause of their own to plead, but while they enlighten and sustain the reader his common sense will not refuse them. Their authors are a natural and irresistible aristocracy in every society, and, more than kings or emperors, exert an influence on mankind. When the illiterate and perhaps scornful trader has earned by enterprise and industry his coveted leisure and independence, and is admitted to the circles of wealth and fashion, he turns inevitably at last to those still higher but yet inaccessible circles of intellect and genius, and is sensible only of the imperfection of his culture and the vanity and insufficiency of all his riches, and further proves his good sense by the pains which he takes to secure for his children that intellectual culture whose want he so keenly feels; and thus it is that he becomes the founder of a family.

Those who have not learned to read the ancient classics in the language in which they were written[14] must have a very imperfect knowledge of the history of the human race; for it is remarkable that no transcript of them has ever been made into any modern tongue, unless our civilization itself may be regarded as such a transcript. Homer has never yet been printed in English,[15] nor Æschylus,[16] nor Virgil[17] even,—works as refined, as solidly done, and as beautiful almost as the morning itself; for later writers, say what we will of their genius, have rarely, if ever, equalled the elaborate beauty and finish and the lifelong and heroic literary labors of the ancients. They only talk of forgetting them who never knew them. It will be soon enough to forget them when we have the learning and the genius which will enable us to attend to and appreciate them. That age will be rich indeed when those relics which we call Classics, and the still older and more than classic but even less known Scriptures of the nations, shall have still further accumulated, when the Vaticans[18] shall be filled with Vedas and Zendavestas[19] and Bibles, with Homers and Dantes[20] and Shakespeares, and all the centuries to come shall have successively deposited their trophies in the forum of the world. By such a pile[21] we may hope to scale heaven at last.[22]

be laid up in it; and when they had delivered their various opinions, he told them he should keep Homer's Iliad in it."

14 Although Thoreau could read Greek, he did not always read the Greek authors in the original, but would use Latin, French, or English translations.

15 Not literally but figuratively: i.e., the spirit of the original has never successfully been translated. Homer was first translated into English by George Chapman, begun in the early 1600s and published in 1624.

16 Aeschylus was first translated by Robert Potter (1721–1804) and published in 1777. Thoreau himself had made translations of Aeschylus' *Prometheus Bound* (published in the January 1843 issue of *The Dial*) and *The Seven Against Thebes* (posthumously published).

17 Publius Vergilius Maro (70–19 B.C.E.), Roman poet, author of the *Eclogues*, the *Georgics*, and the *Aeneid*. Gavin Douglas's (ca. 1475–1522) translation of Virgil was completed in July 1513.

18 Referring to the great library in the papal palace, the Vatican, in Rome.

19 Also called Avestas: the scriptures of Zoroastrianism, a religion of ancient Persia (modern-day Iran).

20 Dante Alighieri (1265–1321), Italian poet, author of the *Divina Commedia* and *Vita Nuova*.

21 Pun: stack of books and also pile, or structure.

22 Probable reference to the Tower of Babel (Genesis 11:1–9), a human attempt to reach heaven, and possibly to the mythological attempt of Otys and Ephialtes to scale heaven by piling Mount Ossa and then Mount Pelion upon Mount Olympus, referred to in Homer, Virgil, Plato (429–347 B.C.E.), and Dante.

The works of the great poets have never yet been read by mankind, for only great poets can read them. They have only been read as the multitude read the stars, at most astrologically, not astronomically.[23] Most men have learned to read to serve a paltry convenience, as they have learned to cipher in order to keep accounts and not be cheated in trade; but of reading as a noble intellectual exercise they know little or nothing; yet this only is reading, in a high sense, not that which lulls us as a luxury and suffers the nobler faculties to sleep the while, but what we have to stand on tip-toe to read and devote our most alert and wakeful hours to.

I think that having learned our letters we should read the best that is in literature,[24] and not be forever repeating our a b abs,[25] and words of one syllable, in the fourth or fifth classes, sitting on the lowest and foremost form[26] all our lives. Most men are satisfied if they read or hear read, and perchance have been convicted by the wisdom of one good book, the Bible,[27] and for the rest of their lives vegetate and dissipate their faculties in what is called easy reading. There is a work in several volumes in our Circulating Library entitled "Little Reading,"[28] which I thought referred to a town of that name[29] which I had not been to. There are those who, like cormorants and ostriches, can digest all sorts of this,[30] even after the fullest dinner of meats and vegetables, for they suffer nothing to be wasted. If others are the machines to provide this provender, they are the machines to read it. They read the nine thousandth tale about Zebulon and Sephronia,[31] and how they loved as none had ever loved before, and neither did the course of their true love run smooth,[32]—at any rate, how it did run and stumble, and get up again and go on! how some poor unfortunate got up on to a steeple, who had better never have gone up as far as the belfry; and then, having needlessly got him up there, the happy novelist rings the bell for all the world to come together and

---

23 On the difference between reading the stars astrologically and astronomically, Thoreau wrote in his journal of 21 January 1853:

A few good anecdotes is our science, with a few imposing statements respecting distance and size, and little or nothing about the stars as they concern man; teaching how he may survey a country or sail a ship, and not how he may steer his life. Astrology contained the germ of a higher truth than this. It may happen that the stars are more significant and truly celestial to the teamster than to the astronomer. . . . Though observatories are multiplied, the heavens receive very little attention. The naked eye may easily see farther than the armed. It depends on who looks through it. No superior telescope to this has been invented. In those big ones the recoil is equal to the force of the discharge. The poet's eye in a fine frenzy rolling ranges from earth to heaven, but this the astronomer's does not often do. It does not see far beyond the dome of the observatory. [J 4:470–71]

The astronomer, Thoreau wrote on 5 August 1851, "is as blind to the significant phenomena, or the significance of phenomena, as the wood-sawyer who wears glasses to defend his eyes from sawdust. The question is not what you look at, but what you see" [J 2:373].

24 In *A Week on the Concord and Merrimack Rivers* Thoreau wrote: "Read the best books first, or you may not have a chance to read them at all" [W 1:98].

25 Reference to the method of learning by rote.

26 Backless bench in the front of district schools for the youngest children.

27 The Christian Bible, which is often referred to as "the good book."

28 Allusion to the five-volume *Much Instruction from Little Reading: Extracts from Some of the Most Approved Authors, Ancient and Modern, to which are added, Some Biographical Sketches from the Earliest*

hear, O dear! how he did get down again![33] For my part, I think that they had better metamorphose all such aspiring heroes of universal noveldom into man weathercocks, as they used to put heroes among the constellations, and let them swing round there till they are rusty, and not come down at all to bother honest men with their pranks. The next time the novelist rings the bell I will not stir though the meeting-house burn down. "The Skip of the Tip-Toe-Hop,[34] a Romance of the Middle Ages, by the celebrated author of 'Tittle-Tol-Tan,'[35] to appear in monthly parts;[36] a great rush; don't all come together." All this they read with saucer eyes, and erect and primitive curiosity, and with unwearied gizzard, whose corrugations[37] even yet need no sharpening, just as some little four-year-old bencher[38] his two-cent gilt-covered edition of Cinderella,—without any improvement, that I can see, in the pronunciation, or accent, or emphasis, or any more skill in extracting or inserting the moral. The result is dulness of sight, a stagnation of the vital circulations, and a general deliquium[39] and sloughing off of all the intellectual faculties. This sort of gingerbread is baked daily and more sedulously than pure wheat or rye-and-Indian[40] in almost every oven, and finds a surer market.

The best books are not read even by those who are called good readers. What does our Concord culture amount to?[41] There is in this town, with a very few exceptions, no taste for the best or for very good books even in English literature, whose words all can read and spell. Even the college-bred and so called liberally educated men here and elsewhere have really little or no acquaintance with the English classics; and as for the recorded wisdom of mankind, the ancient classics and Bibles, which are accessible to all who will know of them, there are the feeblest efforts any where made to become acquainted with them. I know a woodchopper,[42] of middle age, who takes a French paper, not for news as he says,

Ages of the World to Nearly the Present Time, also, Extensive Scripture Lessons by "a friend to general improvement" (New York, 1827).

29 Reading is a town in Massachusetts, although Thoreau may have had in mind Reading, England.

30 Possible allusion to folklore as represented in Sir Thomas Browne's "That the Ostrich Digesteth Iron" in Pseudodoxia Epidemica, or, Enquiries into Very Many Received Tenents and Commonly Presumed Truths.

31 Zebulun (or Zebulon), in the Bible, was the sixth son of Jacob and Leah (Genesis 30:19–20). Sephronia is a possible variation on Sophronia, a character in the 16th-century poem Jerusalem Delivered by Tasso (1544–1595). Both names were used in the 18th and 19th centuries.

32 Allusion to Shakespeare's A Midsummer Night's Dream 1.1.134: "The course of true love never did run smooth."

33 Unidentified allusion.

34 Possible allusion to James Fenimore Cooper's (1789–1851) novel The Wept of Wish-ton-Wish (1829), although it was about King Philip's War, not the Middle Ages.

35 In "Walking" Thoreau referred to "the child's rigmarole, Iery wiery ichery van, tittle-tol-tan" [W 5:236].

36 Publishing a work serially in parts was a common 19th-century practice.

37 Seed-eating birds have muscular corrugated walls in their gizzards, to help with digestion.

38 Refers to the form, or bench, mentioned above.

39 Lack of vitality.

40 Dark bread made of rye and Indian (maize or corn) meal.

41 By common standards, Concord's culture amounted to much—most of the town's leading men were Harvard graduates, and the Lyceum had begun in 1829—but Thoreau is looking for a more transcendental perception.

42 Alek Therien, who is described more fully in the "Visitors" chapter.

43 Possible allusion to *Easy Reading for Little Folks* (Boston, n.d.).

44 Textbooks, respectively, for younger children and older children.

45 Terms for small persons, although in using "manikins" Thoreau may also have had in mind the artist's small wooden clay figure.

46 With the one exception of his *Apologia,* all of Plato's extant writings take the form of dialogues.

for he is above that, but to "keep himself in practice," he being a Canadian by birth; and when I ask him what he considers the best thing he can do in this world, he says, beside this, to keep up and add to his English. This is about as much as the college bred generally do or aspire to do, and they take an English paper for the purpose. One who has just come from reading perhaps one of the best English books will find how many with whom he can converse about it? Or suppose he comes from reading a Greek or Latin classic in the original, whose praises are familiar even to the so called illiterate; he will find nobody at all to speak to, but must keep silence about it. Indeed, there is hardly the professor in our colleges, who, if he has mastered the difficulties of the language, has proportionally mastered the difficulties of the wit and poetry of a Greek poet, and has any sympathy to impart to the alert and heroic reader; and as for the sacred Scriptures, or Bibles of mankind, who in this town can tell me even their titles? Most men do not know that any nation but the Hebrews have had a scripture. A man, any man, will go considerably out of his way to pick up a silver dollar; but here are golden words, which the wisest men of antiquity have uttered, and whose worth the wise of every succeeding age have assured us of;—and yet we learn to read only as far as Easy Reading,[43] the primers and class-books,[44] and when we leave school, the "Little Reading," and story books, which are for boys and beginners; and our reading, our conversation and thinking, are all on a very low level, worthy only of pygmies and manikins.[45]

I aspire to be acquainted with wiser men than this our Concord soil has produced, whose names are hardly known here. Or shall I hear the name of Plato and never read his book? As if Plato were my townsman and I never saw him, — my next neighbor and I never heard him speak or attended to the wisdom of his words. But how actually is it? His Dialogues,[46] which contain what was immortal in him, lie on the next shelf, and yet I never read them. We are under-bred and low-lived and illiterate; and in this respect I confess I do not make any very broad distinction between the illiterateness of my townsman who cannot read at all, and the illiterateness of him who has learned to read only what is for children and feeble intellects. We should be as good as the worthies of antiquity, but partly by first knowing how good they were. We are a race of titmen,[47] and soar but little higher in our intellectual flights than the columns of the daily paper.

It is not all books that are as dull as their readers. There are probably words addressed to our condition exactly, which, if we could really hear and understand, would be more salutary than the morning or the spring to our lives, and possibly put a new aspect on the face of things for us. How many a man has dated a new era in his life from the reading of a book. The book exists for us perchance which will explain our miracles and reveal new ones. The at present unutterable things we may find somewhere uttered. These same questions that disturb and puzzle and confound us have in their turn occurred to all the wise men; not one has been omitted; and each has answered them, according to his ability, by his words and his life. Moreover, with wisdom we shall learn liberality. The solitary hired man on a farm in the outskirts of Concord, who has had his second birth[48] and peculiar religious experience, and is driven as he believes into silent gravity and exclusiveness by his faith, may think it is not true; but Zoroaster,[49] thousands of years ago, travelled the same road and had the same experience; but he, being wise, knew it to be universal, and treated his neighbors accordingly, and is even said to have invented and established worship among men. Let him humbly commune with Zoroaster then, and, through the liberalizing influence of all the worthies, with Jesus Christ himself, and let "our church" go by the board.[50]

47 Stunted physically or mentally, here used to mean intellectually small, as "pygmies and manikins" in the previous paragraph, following the usage of the combining form to mean something small, as in titmouse, titlark, tomtit. The word appears to be unique to Thoreau, who used it elsewhere, as in "They are the titmans [?] of their race" [CP 158], and

> A finer race and finer fed
> Feast and revel o'er our head,
> And we titmen are only able
> To catch the fragments from their table.
>   [W 1:407–8]

48 Religious conversion.

49 Zoroaster, or Zarathustra (Greek form), the founder of the religion of Zoroastrianism in the 6th century B.C.E.

50 Fallen out of use or discarded, originally signifying something that has fallen overboard and been carried away.

51 Josiah Holbrook (1788–1854) started the first lyceum in the United States in 1826 as a local association for the discussion of topics of current interest. The Concord Lyceum began in 1829; Thoreau was elected secretary in October 1839 and curator in November 1839. In 1840 he was again elected curator and secretary but declined, retiring from the position in December 1840, though he was again elected curator several more times. As curator in 1843–44 he was allowed $109.20 to contract speakers; at the end of the season he had spent only $100 and had arranged for 25 speakers, including Emerson, Horace Greeley, and Theodore Parker (1810–1860). "How much might be done for this town with a hundred dollars!" Thoreau wrote in his journal. "I could provide a select course of lectures for the summer or winter with that sum, which would be an incalculable benefit to every inhabitant" [J 1:487]. Ten years later, in 1853, when he was again elected curator, Thoreau declined the position because he "did not know where to find good lecturers enough to make a course for the winter" [J 5:506]. He himself gave 21 lectures at the Lyceum, the first of which, "Society," was delivered on 11 April 1838, and the last, "Wild Apples," on 8 February 1860.

52 In 1851 the Commonwealth of Massachusetts authorized, but did little to assist, towns to establish public libraries. Concord was one of the first towns to establish such a library.

53 Thoreau is playing on the similarity of the words "aliment," nourishment, and "ailment," affliction, to emphasize his concern with nourishing the mind rather than the body.

54 As opposed to the common, or public, schools, the first of which was established in the United States in nearby Lexington in 1839 by Horace Mann (1796–1859). As secretary of the nation's first state board of education from 1837 to 1848, Mann advocated commonly controlled nonreligious schools attended by all people regardless of race, class, or sex, as an equalizer of educational opportunities.

55 The University of Paris and Oxford University.

56 Peter Abelard (1079–1142), French theologian, teacher, and philosopher, who taught at the University of Paris.

57 Allusion to Sir Thomas More's (1478–1535) *Utopia*, which described an ideal social state.

58 A Town House Building Committee was formed in 1850 to superintend construction of a large and durable building for municipal business and public meetings and to promote the interests of Concord. It was to be furnished and fenced, containing schoolrooms and offices as well as a hall with settees and chairs for meetings and public functions. According to town records (1851–1923), in addition to being used for town meetings the hall was hired out for such events as conventions, fairs, concerts, dances, plays, exhibitions, lectures, preaching, the Lyceum, and the Concord Artillery inspections. Thoreau surveyed the lot in 1850 for the "Court House Grounds and Adjacent Lots," which included the area for the Town House Building Committee in June 1850. The *Reports of the Selectmen of Concord* for the years 1852–53

We boast that we belong to the nineteenth century and are making the most rapid strides of any nation. But consider how little this village does for its own culture. I do not wish to flatter my townsmen, nor to be flattered by them, for that will not advance either of us. We need to be provoked,—goaded like oxen, as we are, into a trot. We have a comparatively decent system of common schools, schools for infants only; but excepting the half-starved Lyceum[51] in the winter, and latterly the puny beginning of a library suggested by the State,[52] no school for ourselves. We spend more on almost any article of bodily aliment or ailment[53] than on our mental aliment. It is time that we had uncommon schools,[54] that we did not leave off our education when we begin to be men and women. It is time that villages were universities, and their elder inhabitants the fellows of universities, with leisure—if they are indeed so well off—to pursue liberal studies the rest of their lives. Shall the world be confined to one Paris or one Oxford[55] forever? Cannot students be boarded here and get a liberal education under the skies of Concord? Can we not hire some Abelard[56] to lecture to us? Alas! what with foddering the cattle and tending the store, we are kept from school too long, and our education is sadly neglected. In this country, the village should in some respects take the place of the nobleman of Europe. It should be the patron of the fine arts. It is rich enough. It wants only the magnanimity and refinement. It can spend money enough on such things as farmers and traders value, but it is thought Utopian[57] to propose spending money for things which more intelligent men know to be of far more worth. This town has spent seventeen thousand dollars on a town-house,[58] thank fortune or politics, but probably it will not spend so much on living wit, the true meat to put into that shell, in a hundred years. The one hundred and twenty-five dollars annually subscribed for a Lyceum[59] in the winter is better spent than any other equal sum raised in the town. If we live in the nineteenth century, why should we not enjoy the advantages which the nineteenth century offers? Why should our life be in any respect provincial? If we will read newspapers, why not skip the gossip of Boston and take the best newspaper in the world at once? — not be sucking the pap of "neutral family" papers,[60] or browsing "Olive-Branches"[61] here in New England. Let the reports of all the learned societies come to us, and we will see if they know any thing. Why should we leave it to Harper & Brothers[62] and Redding & Co.[63] to select[64] our reading? As the nobleman of cultivated taste surrounds himself with whatever conduces to his culture, — genius — learning — wit — books — paintings — statuary — music — philosophical instruments,[65] and the like; so let the village do, — not stop short at a pedagogue, a parson, a sexton, a parish library, and three selectmen, because our pilgrim forefathers got through a cold winter once on a bleak rock with these. To act collectively is according to the spirit of our institutions; and I am confident that, as our circumstances are more flourishing, our means are greater than the nobleman's. New England can hire all the wise men in the world to come and teach her, and board them round[66] the while, and not be provincial at all. That is the *uncommon* school we want. Instead of noblemen, let us have noble villages of men. If it is necessary, omit one bridge over the river, go round a little there, and throw one arch at least over the darker gulf of ignorance[67] which surrounds us.

reported that the committee spent $19,253 for the Town Hall and that it included a hall, town offices, a safe for the preservation of town records, a room for a town library, and two classrooms.

59 In 1851 the Concord Lyceum raised its subscribed operating funds from $100 to $125.

60 Newspapers that avoided politics in favor of family reading matter.

61 *The Boston Olive Branch, Devoted to Christianity, Mutual Rights, Polite Literature, General Intelligence, Agriculture, and the Arts,* a Methodist weekly newspaper, began publication in Boston in 1836 under the editorship of Rev. Thomas F. Norris.

62 One of the foremost publishing firms in New York, established as a printing establishment in 1817, and publisher in 1850 of *Harper's New Monthly Magazine.*

63 The George W. Redding Company began as a newspaper depot in Boston in the 1830s, became a periodical depot in the 1840s, and by the 1850s was a book publisher and seller as well as a tea merchant.

64 Reference to Harper & Brothers' series "Select Library of Valuable Standard Literature."

65 Before the advent of modern science, the study of nature and the physical universe was termed natural philosophy. The instruments used by natural philosophers were of three types: mathematical (balances and weights), optical (telescopes and microscopes), and philosophical (electrical machines, air pumps, and other tools that manipulated the environment).

66 Teachers, particularly in rural areas, were often given room and board in the home of a student's parents in lieu of part of their salary. This often necessitated moving from home to home.

67 In Jonathan Swift's "An Essay on Modern Education": "There is one young lord in this town, who, by an unexampled piece of good fortune, was miraculously snatched out of the gulf of ignorance."

1 Thoreau used this device of referencing the previous chapter to create continuity. He also paired seemingly contrasting subjects: "Reading" and "Sounds"; "Solitude" and "Visitors"; "The Bean-Field" and "The Village." In an early journal entry Thoreau had already begun to link the written word and sound: "Books are to be attended to as new sounds merely. Most would be put to a sore trial if the reader should assume the attitude of a listener" [J 1:260].

2 Thoreau was aware that there were "manifold visions in the direction of every object" [W 1:47–48], and being the deliberate artist he was understood that he should "improve the opportunity to draw analogies. There are innumerable avenues to a perception of the truth" [J 2:457]. Following a brief description of ice on the river, Thoreau asked himself in his journal, "What is the analogy?" [J 2:111].

3 Made public.

4 Wooden window shutters were on pin hinges and could be completely removed.

5 In his journal of 31 March 1842 Thoreau wrote: "The really efficient laborer will be found not to crowd his day with work, but will saunter to his task surrounded by a wide halo of ease and leisure. There will be a wide margin for relaxation to his day. He is only earnest to secure the kernels of time, and does not exaggerate the value of the husk" [J 1:356].

6 As long as the water was warm enough, Thoreau bathed daily in the cove near his house. He stopped when the water got cold, as a journal entry from 26 September 1854 indicates: "Took my last bath the 24th. Probably shall not bathe again this year. It was chilling cold" [J 7:58].

Sounds

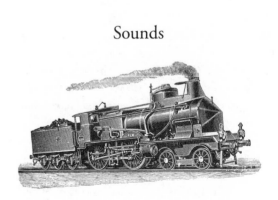

But while we are confined to books,[1] though the most select and classic, and read only particular written languages, which are themselves but dialects and provincial, we are in danger of forgetting the language which all things and events speak without metaphor,[2] which alone is copious and standard. Much is published,[3] but little printed. The rays which stream through the shutter will be no longer remembered when the shutter is wholly removed.[4] No method nor discipline can supersede the necessity of being forever on the alert. What is a course of history, or philosophy, or poetry, no matter how well selected, or the best society, or the most admirable routine of life, compared with the discipline of looking always at what is to be seen? Will you be a reader, a student merely, or a seer? Read your fate, see what is before you, and walk on into futurity.

I did not read books the first summer; I hoed beans. Nay, I often did better than this. There were times when I could not afford to sacrifice the bloom of the present moment to any work, whether of the head or hands. I love a broad margin[5] to my life. Sometimes, in a summer morning, having taken my accustomed bath,[6] I sat in my sunny doorway from sunrise till noon, rapt in a revery, amidst the pines and hickories and sumachs, in undisturbed solitude and stillness, while the birds sang around or flitted noiseless through the house, until by the sun falling in at my west window, or the noise of some traveller's wagon on the distant highway,[7] I was reminded of the lapse of time. I grew in those seasons like corn in the night,[8] and they were far better than any work of the hands would have been. They were not time subtracted from my life, but so much over and above my usual allowance. I realized what the Orientals mean by contemplation and the forsaking of works.[9] For the most part, I minded not how the hours went. The day advanced as if to light some work of mine; it was morning, and lo, now it is evening, and nothing memorable is accomplished. Instead of singing like the birds, I silently smiled at my incessant good fortune. As the sparrow had its trill, sitting on the hickory before my door, so had I my chuckle or suppressed warble which he might hear out of my nest. My days were not days of the week, bearing the stamp of any heathen deity,[10] nor were they minced into hours and fretted by the ticking of a clock; for I lived like the Puri Indians,[11] of whom it is said that "for yesterday, to-day, and to-morrow they have only one word, and they express the variety of meaning by pointing backward for yesterday, forward for to-morrow, and overhead for the passing day."[12] This was sheer idleness to my fellow-townsmen, no doubt; but if the birds and flowers had tried me by their standard, I should not have been found wanting.[13] A man must find his occasions in himself, it is true. The natural day is very calm, and will hardly reprove his indolence.

I had this advantage, at least, in my mode of life, over those who were obliged to look abroad for amusement, to society and the theatre, that my life itself was become my amusement and never ceased to be novel. It was a drama of many scenes and without an end. If we were always indeed getting our living, and regulating our lives according to the last and best mode we had learned, we should never be troubled with ennui. Follow your genius closely

7 The road from Concord to Lincoln, now Route 126.

8 Indian corn is said to grow quickly on warm summer nights. This image first appeared in Thoreau's journal for 26 February 1840: "Corn grows in the night" [J 1:124]. It reappeared twice in 1841: (on 23 January) "Our health requires that we should recline on it from time to time. When we are in it, the hand stands still on the face of the clock, and we grow like corn in the genial dankness and silence of the night" [J 1:174], and (on 7 June) "Methinks history will have to be tried by new tests to show what centuries were rapid and what slow. Corn grows in the night" [J 1:263].

9 Thoreau's understanding of contemplation and the forsaking of works comes from Charles Wilkins's (1750–1836) translation of *Mahābhārata: Bhagvat-gēētā, or Dialogues of Kreeshna and Arjoon.* In *A Week on the Concord and Merrimack Rivers* Thoreau wrote: "The Oriental philosophy approaches easily loftier themes than the modern aspires to; and no wonder if it sometimes prattle about them. It only assigns their due rank respectively to Action and Contemplation, or rather does full justice to the latter. Western philosophers have not conceived of the significance of Contemplation in their sense" [W 1:142–43].

10 Referring to the origin of the names of the days of the week: Wednesday for Woden, Thursday for Thor, Friday for Freya, etc.

11 A tribe of eastern Brazil.

12 Quoted from Ida Pfeiffer's *A Lady's Voyage Round the World* 36, with one variation: "overhead" for "over the head."

13 Allusion to Daniel 5:27: "Thou art weighed in the balances, and art found wanting."

14 A sack or bundle.

15 This inkstand was a gift from Elizabeth Hoar when Thoreau went to Staten Island in 1843 to tutor the children of Emerson's brother, William.

16 Creeping, slightly fragrant perennial, flowering from July to September (*Antennaria*, or *Gnaphalium, margaritaceum*).

17 Ellery Channing noted that there "is nothing like a hill here and never was" and that what was meant was a "small rise in the ground, but it is no hill, no 20 foot rise."

18 A rod is a surveyor's measure equaling 16$\frac{1}{2}$ feet. According to Thoreau's survey of Walden his house was more accurately twelve rods from the pond.

enough, and it will not fail to show you a fresh prospect every hour. Housework was a pleasant pastime. When my floor was dirty, I rose early, and, setting all my furniture out of doors on the grass, bed and bedstead making but one budget,[14] dashed water on the floor, and sprinkled white sand from the pond on it, and then with a broom scrubbed it clean and white; and by the time the villagers had broken their fast the morning sun had dried my house sufficiently to allow me to move in again, and my meditations were almost uninterrupted. It was pleasant to see my whole household effects out on the grass, making a little pile like a gypsy's pack, and my three-legged table, from which I did not remove the books and pen and ink,[15] standing amid the pines and hickories. They seemed glad to get out themselves, and as if unwilling to be brought in. I was sometimes tempted to stretch an awning over them and take my seat there. It was worth the while to see the sun shine on these things, and hear the free wind blow on them; so much more interesting most familiar objects look out of doors than in the house. A bird sits on the next bough, life-everlasting[16] grows under the table, and blackberry vines run round its legs; pine cones, chestnut burs, and strawberry leaves are strewn about. It looked as if this was the way these forms came to be transferred to our furniture, to tables, chairs, and bedsteads, — because they once stood in their midst.

My house was on the side of a hill,[17] immediately on the edge of the larger wood, in the midst of a young forest of pitch-pines and hickories, and half a dozen rods[18] from the pond, to which a narrow footpath led down the hill. In my front yard grew the strawberry, blackberry, and life-everlasting, johnswort and golden-rod, shrub-oaks and sand-cherry, blueberry and ground-nut. Near the end of May, the sand-cherry, (*Cerasus pumila,*) adorned the sides of the path with its delicate flowers arranged in umbels cylindrically about its short stems, which last, in the fall, weighed down with good sized and handsome cherries, fell over in wreaths like rays on every side. I tasted them out of compliment to Nature, though they were scarcely palatable. The sumach, (*Rhus glabra,*) grew luxuriantly about the house, pushing up through the embankment which I had made, and growing five or six feet the first season. Its broad pinnate tropical leaf was pleasant though strange to look on. The large buds, suddenly pushing out late in the spring from dry sticks which had seemed to be dead, developed themselves as by magic into graceful green and tender boughs, an inch in diameter; and sometimes, as I sat at my window, so heedlessly did they grow and tax their weak joints, I heard a fresh and tender bough suddenly fall like a fan to the ground, when there was not a breath of air stirring, broken off by its own weight. In August, the large masses of berries, which, when in flower, had attracted many wild bees, gradually assumed their bright velvety crimson hue, and by their weight again bent down and broke the tender limbs.

As I sit[19] at my window this summer afternoon, hawks are circling about my clearing; the tantivy of wild pigeons,[20] flying by two and threes athwart my view, or perching restless on the white-pine boughs behind my house, gives a voice to the air; a fishhawk dimples the glassy surface of the pond and brings up a fish; a mink steals out of the marsh before my door and seizes a frog by the shore; the sedge is bending under the weight of the reed-birds[21] flitting hither and thither; and for the last half hour I have heard the rattle of railroad cars,[22] now dying away and then reviving like the beat of a partridge, conveying travellers from Boston to the country. For I did not live so out of the world as that boy, who, as I hear, was put out to a farmer in the east part of the town, but ere long ran away and came home again, quite down at the heel and homesick. He had never seen such a dull and

19 This and the following nine paragraphs were first published in 1852, with variants, as "The Iron Horse" in *Sartain's Union Magazine* 11:66–68.

20 A tantivy is a rushing, galloping movement. Passenger, or wild, pigeons (*Ectopistes migratorius*) are extinct but were numerous in Thoreau's day. His journal of 12 September 1851 described pigeon-baiting:

> Saw a pigeon-place on George Heywood's cleared lot,—the six dead trees set up for the pigeons to alight on, and the brush house close by to conceal the man. I was rather startled to find such a thing going now in Concord. . . . The smooth sandy bed was covered with buckwheat, wheat or rye, and acorns. Sometimes they use corn. . . . Several men still take pigeons in Concord every year; by a method, methinks, extremely old and which I seem to have seen pictured in some old book of fables or symbols, and yet few in Concord know exactly how it is done. And yet it is all done for money and because the birds fetch a good price, just as the farmers raise corn and potatoes. I am always expecting that those engaged in such a pursuit will be somewhat less grovelling and mercenary than the regular trader or farmer, but I fear that it is not so. [J 2:499–500]

21 Bobolink (*Dolichonyx oryzivorous*).

22 According to Thoreau's journal of 26 January 1853, "five times a day I can be whirled to Boston within an hour" [J 4:479].

23 From Ellery Channing's "Walden Spring," in *The Woodman and Other Poems.*

24 Approximately one-third of a mile.

25 This would have been the shortest way to travel to the western side of town, where the Thoreau family was then living.

26 Allusion to Matthew 11:28: "Come unto me, all ye that labour and are heavy laden, and I will give you rest."

27 Pun on the timber in the previous line.

28 Hills where Indians had gathered huckleberries, a term that for Thoreau included the blueberry.

out-of-the-way place; the folks were all gone off; why, you couldn't even hear the whistle! I doubt if there is such a place in Massachusetts now: —

> "In truth, our village has become a butt
> For one of those fleet railroad shafts, and o'er
> Our peaceful plain its soothing sound is—
>   Concord." [23]

The Fitchburg Railroad touches the pond about a hundred rods [24] south of where I dwell. I usually go to the village along its causeway, [25] and am, as it were, related to society by this link. The men on the freight trains, who go over the whole length of the road, bow to me as to an old acquaintance, they pass me so often, and apparently they take me for an employee; and so I am. I too would fain be a track-repairer somewhere in the orbit of the earth.

The whistle of the locomotive penetrates my woods summer and winter, sounding like the scream of a hawk sailing over some farmer's yard, informing me that many restless city merchants are arriving within the circle of the town, or adventurous country traders from the other side. As they come under one horizon, they shout their warning to get off the track to the other, heard sometimes through the circles of two towns. Here come your groceries, country; your rations, countrymen! Nor is there any man so independent on his farm that he can say them nay. And here's your pay for them! screams the countryman's whistle; timber like long battering rams going twenty miles an hour against the city's walls, and chairs enough to seat all the weary and heavy laden [26] that dwell within them. With such huge and lumbering [27] civility the country hands a chair to the city. All the Indian huckleberry hills [28] are stripped, all the cranberry meadows are raked into the city. Up comes the cotton, down goes the woven cloth; up comes the silk, down goes the woollen; up come the books, but down goes the wit that writes them.

When I meet the engine with its train of cars moving off with planetary motion,—or, rather, like a comet, for the beholder knows not if with that velocity and with that direction it will ever revisit this system, since its orbit does not look like a returning curve,—with its steam cloud like a banner streaming behind in golden and silver wreaths, like many a downy cloud which I have seen, high in the heavens, unfolding its masses to the light,—as if this travelling demigod, this cloud-compeller,[29] would ere long take the sunset sky for the livery of his train; when I hear the iron horse make the hills echo with his snort like thunder, shaking the earth with his feet, and breathing fire and smoke from his nostrils, (what kind of winged horse or fiery dragon they will put into the new Mythology I don't know,) it seems as if the earth had got a race now worthy to inhabit it. If all were as it seems, and men made the elements their servants for noble ends! If the cloud that hangs over the engine were the perspiration of heroic deeds, or as beneficent to men as that which floats over the farmer's fields, then the elements and Nature herself would cheerfully accompany men on their errands and be their escort.

I watch the passage of the morning cars with the same feeling that I do the rising of the sun, which is hardly more regular. Their train of clouds stretching far behind and rising higher and higher, going to heaven while the cars are going to Boston, conceals the sun for a minute and casts my distant field into the shade, a celestial train[30] beside which the petty train of cars which hugs the earth[31] is but the barb of the spear. The stabler of the iron horse was up early this winter morning by the light of the stars amid the mountains, to fodder and harness his steed. Fire, too, was awakened thus early to put the vital heat in him and get him off. If the enterprise were as innocent as it is early!

29 Epithet applied to the Greek god Zeus as well as the Hindu Vedic god Indra.
30 Reference to Hawthorne's "The Celestial Railroad."
31 In "Walking" Thoreau wrote: "We hug the earth,—how rarely we mount! Methinks we might elevate ourselves a little more" [W 5:244].

32 A wheeled implement for planting seed evenly in drills or furrows. It was a relatively new agricultural machine; Jesse Buel (1778–1839), in *The Farmer's Companion, or, Essays on the Principles and Practice of American Husbandry* (1839), wrote of its "recent introduction in American husbandry." Manufacture of the seed drill in America did not begin until 1841.

33 Franklin Sanborn wrote: "Such a glen is in the woods south-east of Thoreau's hut, where the drifted snow sometimes stopped the heavy trains with light engines of that early period of railroading."

34 Any star visible in the morning, and most often used for the planet Venus.

35 Probable allusion to the phrase "iron sleep" found in several literary works, such as Thomas Gray's "The Descent of Odin: An Ode" ("To break my iron-sleep again" [l. 89]), and John Dryden's translation of Virgil's *Aeneid*, book 12, "oppressed with iron sleep."

36 Thoreau may not have had a specific swamp in mind, but there is a Dismal Swamp in southeastern Virginia and northeastern North Carolina. It appeared in William Byrd's (1674–1744) *History of the Dividing Line Betwixt Virginia and North Carolina*, Henry Wadsworth Longfellow's (1807–1882) "The Slave in the Dismal Swamp," Thomas Moore's "The Lake of the Dismal Swamp," and Harriet Beecher Stowe's (1811–1896) novel *Dred*.

37 The advent of the railroad imposed a precision in timekeeping in rural areas, leaving behind the previous method of telling time by the sun. Thoreau wrote in his journal on 8 June 1850 of reading in the newspaper that farmers on the western railroad set their clocks this way.

38 Pun: run well, and also referring to the conductors who drive trains.

39 Place for boarding horse-drawn stages.

If the snow lies deep, they strap on his snow-shoes, and with the giant plough, plough a furrow from the mountains to the seaboard, in which the cars, like a following drill-barrow,[32] sprinkle all the restless men and floating merchandise in the country for seed. All day the fire-steed flies over the country, stopping only that his master may rest, and I am awakened by his tramp and defiant snort at midnight, when in some remote glen in the woods[33] he fronts the elements incased in ice and snow; and he will reach his stall only with the morning star,[34] to start once more on his travels without rest or slumber. Or perchance, at evening, I hear him in his stable blowing off the superfluous energy of the day, that he may calm his nerves and cool his liver and brain for a few hours of iron slumber.[35] If the enterprise were as heroic and commanding as it is protracted and unwearied!

Far through unfrequented woods on the confines of towns, where once only the hunter penetrated by day, in the darkest night dart these bright saloons without the knowledge of their inhabitants; this moment stopping at some brilliant station-house in town or city, where a social crowd is gathered, the next in the Dismal Swamp,[36] scaring the owl and fox. The startings and arrivals of the cars are now the epochs in the village day. They go and come with such regularity and precision, and their whistle can be heard so far, that the farmers set their clocks by them,[37] and thus one well conducted[38] institution regulates a whole country. Have not men improved somewhat in punctuality since the railroad was invented? Do they not talk and think faster in the depot than they did in the stage-office?[39] There is something electrifying in the atmosphere of the former place. I have been astonished at the miracles it has wrought; that some of my neighbors, who, I should have prophesied, once for all, would never get to Boston by so prompt a conveyance, were on hand when the bell rang. To do things "railroad fashion" is now the by-word; and it is worth the while to be warned so often and so sincerely by any power to get off its track. There is no stopping to read the riot act,[40] no firing over the heads of the mob, in this case. We have constructed a fate, an *Atropos,* that never turns aside.[41] (Let that be the name of your engine.) Men are advertised that at a certain hour and minute these bolts will be shot toward particular points of the compass; yet it interferes with no man's business, and the children go to school on the other track. We live the steadier for it. We are all educated thus to be sons of Tell.[42] The air is full of invisible bolts. Every path but your own is the path of fate.[43] Keep on your own track, then.

What recommends commerce to me is its enterprise and bravery. It does not clasp its hands and pray to Jupiter. I see these men every day go about their business with more or less courage and content, doing more even than they suspect, and perchance better employed than they could have consciously devised. I am less affected by their heroism who stood up for half an hour in the front line at Buena Vista,[44] than by the steady and cheerful valor of the men who inhabit the snow-plough for their winter quarters; who have not merely the three-o'-clock in the morning courage, which Bonaparte thought was the rarest,[45] but whose courage does not go to rest so early, who go to sleep only when the storm sleeps or the sinews of their iron steed are frozen. On this morning of the Great Snow,[46] perchance, which is still raging and chilling men's blood, I hear the muffled tone of their engine bell from out the fog bank of their chilled breath, which announces that the cars *are coming,* without long delay, notwithstanding the veto of a New England north-east snow storm, and I behold the ploughmen covered with snow and rime, their heads peering above the mould-board[47]

40 The Riot Act, which became English law in 1715, asserted that if twelve or more individuals were found assembled and disturbing the peace, they must disperse or face charges of felony after having been read the law: "Our Sovereign Lord the King chargeth and commandeth all persons being assembled immediately to disperse themselves, and peaceably to depart to their habitations or to their lawful business, upon the pains contained in the act made in the first year of King George for preventing tumultuous and riotous assemblies. God save the King."

41 The name of Atropos, the third of the three Greek Fates, means "never turn aside."

42 Refers to the Swiss folk hero William Tell, whose son remained steady while Tell used a bow and arrow to shoot an apple from his head in 1307.

43 Possible allusion to Thomas Gray's "The Fatal Sisters: An Ode" ("As the paths of fate we tread" [l. 29]).

44 Site of a battle in the Mexican-American War where U.S. forces under General Zachary Taylor defeated the army of Antonio López de Santa Anna.

45 Reference to Napoléon I as quoted by Emerson in his 1838 journal from Count Emmanuel Augustin Dieudeonné de Las Cases, *Mémorial de Sainte Hélène: Journal of the Private Life and Conversation of the Emperor Napoleon at St. Helena* (Boston, 1823): "As to moral courage, I have rarely met with the *two o'clock in the morning kind.* I mean unprepared courage that which is necessary on an unexpected occasion & which in spite of the most unforeseen events leaves full freedom of judgment & decision." Emerson used this later in *Representative Men.*

Thoreau reworked this image several times, although misremembering the time of morning. It appeared first in an undated journal passage ("Buonaparte said that the three-o'clock-in-the-morning courage was the rarest, but I cannot agree with him. Fear does not awake so early. Few men are so degenerate as to balk nature by not beginning the day well" [J 1:462]) before it was revised for a deleted paragraph in the first draft of *A Week on the Concord and Merrimack Rivers.* Later, in "Walking," Thoreau wrote: "Bonaparte may talk of the three-o'clock-in-the-morning courage, but it is nothing to the courage which can sit down cheerfully at this hour in the afternoon over against one's self whom you have known all the morning, to starve out a garrison to whom you are bound by such strong ties of sympathy" [W 5:208].

46 Invokes the "Great Snow" of 17 February 1717 (mentioned again in the "Former Inhabitants" chapter), described by Cotton Mather in *Magnalia Christi Americana,* and used for any large snowstorm, as in Thoreau's 28 March 1856 journal entry: "Uncle Charles buried. He was born in February, 1780, the winter of the Great Snow, and he dies in the winter of another great snow, — a life bounded by great snows" [J 8:230].

47 Plow blade.

48 Possible allusion to two poems by Robert Burns: "To a Mountain Daisy" ("Stern Ruin's plough-share drives, elate / Full on thy bloom") and "To a Mouse" ("the cruel coulter past / Out thro' thy cell").

49 A major mountain range of western North America running along the eastern ridge of California.

50 Thoreau's allusion has not been identified.

51 In Boston. Thoreau wrote in *Cape Cod:* "Whoever has been down to the end of Long Wharf, and walked through Quincy Market, has seen Boston" [W 4:268].

52 Making palm straw hats and sandals was a common home industry during winter for New England farm families.

53 Coir, the fiber of the coconut husk, was used in making mats, particularly doormats.

54 Coarse material made from jute.

55 Old cloth was used in the making of rag, or linen, paper before the advent of cheap wood-fiber paper.

56 Pun: prepublication sheets of printed material to be checked and corrected, and sheets that hold the sails of a ship, so giving proof to the storm.

which is turning down other than daisies and the nests of field mice,[48] like bowlders of the Sierra Nevada,[49] that occupy an outside place in the universe.[50]

Commerce is unexpectedly confident and serene, alert, adventurous, and unwearied. It is very natural in its methods withal, far more so than many fantastic enterprises and sentimental experiments, and hence its singular success. I am refreshed and expanded when the freight train rattles past me, and I smell the stores which go dispensing their odors all the way from Long Wharf[51] to Lake Champlain, reminding me of foreign parts, of coral reefs, and Indian oceans, and tropical climes, and the extent of the globe. I feel more like a citizen of the world at the sight of the palm-leaf which will cover so many flaxen New England heads[52] the next summer, the Manilla hemp and cocoa-nut husks,[53] the old junk, gunny[54] bags, scrap iron, and rusty nails. This car-load of torn sails is more legible and interesting now than if they should be wrought into paper and printed books.[55] Who can write so graphically the history of the storms they have weathered as these rents have done? They are proof-sheets[56] which need no correction. Here goes lumber from the Maine woods, which did not go out to sea in the last freshet, risen four dollars on the thousand because of what did go out or was split up; pine, spruce, cedar, — first, second, third and fourth qualities, so lately all of one quality, to wave over the bear, and moose, and caribou. Next rolls Thomaston lime,[57] a prime lot, which will get far among the hills before it gets slacked.[58] These rags in bales, of all hues and qualities, the lowest condition to which cotton and linen descend, the final result of dress, — of patterns which are now no longer cried up,[59] unless it be in Milwaukie,[60] as those splendid articles, English, French, or American prints, ginghams, muslins, &c., gathered from all quarters both of fashion and poverty, going to become paper of one color or a few shades only, on which forsooth will be written tales of real life, high and low, and founded on fact! This closed car smells of salt fish,[61] the strong New England and commercial scent, reminding me of the Grand Banks[62] and the fisheries. Who has not seen a salt fish, thoroughly cured for this world, so that nothing can spoil it, and putting the perseverance of the saints[63] to the blush? with which you may sweep or pave the streets, and split your kindlings, and the teamster shelter himself and his lading against sun wind and rain behind it,—and the trader, as a Concord trader[64] once did, hang it up by his door for a sign when he commences business, until at last his oldest customer cannot tell surely whether it be animal, vegetable, or mineral, and yet it shall be as pure as a snowflake, and if it be put into a pot and boiled, will come out an excellent dun fish[65] for a Saturday's dinner. Next Spanish hides, with the tails still preserving their twist and the angle of elevation they had when the oxen that wore them were careering over the pampas of the Spanish main,[66]— a type of all obstinacy, and evincing how almost hopeless and incurable are all constitutional vices. I confess, that practically speaking, when I have learned a man's real disposition, I have no hopes of changing it for the better or worse in this state of existence. As the Orientals say, "A cur's tail may be warmed, and pressed, and bound round with ligatures, and after a twelve years' labor bestowed upon it, still it will retain its natural form."[67] The only effectual cure for such inveteracies as these tails exhibit is to make glue of them, which I believe is what is usually done with them, and then they will stay put and stick. Here is a hogshead of molasses or of brandy directed to John Smith, Cuttingsville, Vermont,[68] some trader among the Green Mountains, who imports for the farmers near his clearing, and now perchance stands over his bulk-head and thinks of the last arrivals on the coast, how they may affect the price for him, telling his cus-

57 Thomaston, Maine, was a major source of lime.

58 Slaked: the process of adding water to caustic quicklime to produce a more manageable powdered lime.

59 Praised publicly to increase value, as in the marketplace.

60 Milwaukee, Wisconsin, which in Thoreau's day was a rapidly growing city, but would not have had the same fashion sense as Boston or New York. Thoreau may have had in mind Margaret Fuller's *Summer on the Lakes, in 1843*, in which she wrote that Milwaukee "promises to be, some time, a fine one. . . . During the fine weather, the poor refugees arrive daily, in their national dresses, all travel-soiled and worn."

61 Salted and dried cod, haddock, and similar fish was sold locally but also had great commercial value and was shipped to Europe, or traded in the West Indies for sugar, cotton, molasses, and rum.

62 Off the southeast coast of Newfoundland, a major fishing region for New England fishermen.

63 The doctrine of the Perseverance of the Saints is, in the Westminster Confession of Faith, chapter 17: "They whom God hath accepted in His Beloved, effectually called and sanctified by His Spirit, can neither totally nor finally fall away from the state of grace; but shall certainly persevere therein to the end, and be eternally saved."

64 William Parkman (1741–1832), owner of a general store in Concord and deacon of the First Parish Church from 1788 until 1826, in whose house the Thoreau family lived shortly before Thoreau went to Walden. Parkman's shop was a small boxlike building next to his house on Main Street near where the Concord Free Public Library now stands. In a journal entry on 8 September 1838, Emerson wrote: "Henry Thoreau told a good story of Deacon Parkman, who lived in the house he now occupies, & kept a store close by. He hung out a salt fish for a sign, & it hung so long & grew so hard, black, & deformed, that the deacon forgot what thing it was, & nobody in town knew, but being examined chemically it proved to be salt fish. But duly every morning the deacon hung it on its peg."

65 Salt fish was so called for the dun coloring caused by the curing process.

66 Northeast coast of South America, between the Orinoco River and the Isthmus of Panama.

67 Quoted, with one minor variant in spelling, from the fable of the lion and the rabbit in *The Heetōpadēs of Veeshnoo-Sarmā, in a Series of Connected Fables, Interspersed with Moral, Prudential, and Political Maxims,* translated by Charles Wilkins (Bath, 1787), a selection from which was published in the July 1842 issue of *The Dial* (although this line is not there).

68 Village in Rutland County, Vermont, but here probably used to indicate any small town.

69 There is no extant record of a *Cuttingsville Times.*

70 Connecticut River, the longest river in New England, rising in northern New Hampshire and flowing south for 407 miles to Long Island Sound.

71 Quoted from John Milton's *Paradise Lost* 1.293–94. "Ammiral" is an older form of admiral, here meaning the flagship that carries the admiral.

72 Allusion to Psalms 50:10: "For every beast of the forest is mine, and the cattle upon a thousand hills."

73 Male sheep, the leader of a flock, on whose neck a bell is hung, but here referring to the locomotive.

74 Allusion to Psalms 114:4: "The mountains skipped like rams, and the little hills like lambs."

75 In southern New Hampshire, forming Concord's northwest horizon.

tomers this moment, as he has told them twenty times before this morning, that he expects some by the next train of prime quality. It is advertised in the Cuttingsville Times.[69]

While these things go up other things come down. Warned by the whizzing sound, I look up from my book and see some tall pine, hewn on far northern hills, which has winged its way over the Green Mountains and the Connecticut,[70] shot like an arrow through the township within ten minutes, and scarce another eye beholds it; going

> "to be the mast
> Of some great ammiral."[71]

And hark! here comes the cattle-train bearing the cattle of a thousand hills,[72] sheepcots, stables, and cow-yards in the air, drovers with their sticks, and shepherd boys in the midst of their flocks, all but the mountain pastures, whirled along like leaves blown from the mountains by the September gales. The air is filled with the bleating of calves and sheep, and the hustling of oxen, as if a pastoral valley were going by. When the old bell-wether[73] at the head rattles his bell, the mountains do indeed skip like rams and the little hills like lambs.[74] A car-load of drovers, too, in the midst, on a level with their droves now, their vocation gone, but still clinging to their useless sticks as their badge of office. But their dogs, where are they? It is a stampede to them; they are quite thrown out; they have lost the scent. Methinks I hear them barking behind the Peterboro' Hills,[75] or panting up the western slope of the Green Mountains. They will not be in at the death. Their vocation, too, is gone. Their fidelity and sagacity are below par now. They will slink back to their kennels in disgrace, or perchance run wild and strike a league with the wolf and the fox. So is your pastoral life whirled past and away. But the bell rings, and I must get off the track[76] and let the cars go by;—

Whats the railroad to me?
I never go to see
Where it ends.
It fills a few hollows,
And makes banks for the swallows,
It sets the sand a-blowing,
And the blackberries a-growing,[77]

but I cross it like a cart-path in the woods.[78] I will not have my eyes put out and my ears spoiled by its smoke and steam and hissing.

Now that the cars are gone by and all the restless world with them, and the fishes in the pond no longer feel their rumbling, I am more alone than ever. For the rest of the long afternoon, perhaps, my meditations are interrupted only by the faint rattle of a carriage or team along the distant highway.

Sometimes, on Sundays, I heard the bells,[79] the Lincoln, Acton, Bedford,[80] or Concord bell, when the wind was favorable, a faint, sweet, and, as it were, natural melody, worth importing into the wilderness. At a sufficient distance over the woods this sound acquires a certain vibratory hum, as if the pine needles in the horizon were the strings of a harp which it swept. All sound heard at the greatest possible distance produces one and the same effect, a vibration of the universal lyre, just as the intervening atmosphere makes a distant ridge of earth interesting to our eyes by the azure tint it imparts to it. There came to me in this case a melody which the air had strained, and which had conversed with every leaf and needle of the wood, that portion of the sound which the elements had taken up and modulated and echoed

76 Pun: railroad track, and track as a succession of ideas.

77 Thoreau's poem appeared in his journal in August 1850.

78 Thoreau often used the railroad tracks as a road—"The railroad is perhaps our pleasantest and wildest road" [J 3:342]—but here he has minimized its importance by reducing it in significance from the "causeway" it is earlier in this chapter to a mere cart-path.

79 In his journal of 9 May 1841, Thoreau wrote out a poem titled "The Echo of the Sabbath Bell Heard in the Woods," which began:

Dong, sounds the brass in the east,
As if for a civic feast,
But I like that sound the best
Out of the fluttering west. [J 1:259]

This poem also appeared without title and with variants in A Week on the Concord and Merrimack Rivers [W 1:50].

80 Neighboring towns to Concord.

from vale to vale. The echo is, to some extent, an original sound, and therein is the magic and charm of it. It is not merely a repetition of what was worth repeating in the bell, but partly the voice of the wood; the same trivial words and notes sung by a wood-nymph.

At evening, the distant lowing of some cow in the horizon[81] beyond the woods sounded sweet and melodious, and at first I would mistake it for the voices of certain minstrels by whom I was sometimes serenaded, who might be straying over hill and dale; but soon I was not unpleasantly disappointed when it was prolonged into the cheap and natural music of the cow. I do not mean to be satirical, but to express my appreciation of those youths' singing, when I state that I perceived clearly that it was akin to the music of the cow, and they were at length one articulation of Nature.

Regularly at half past seven, in one part of the summer, after the evening train had gone by, the whippoorwills[82] chanted their vespers for half an hour, sitting on a stump by my door, or upon the ridge pole of the house. They would begin to sing almost with as much precision as a clock, within five minutes of a particular time, referred to the setting of the sun, every evening. I had a rare opportunity to become acquainted with their habits. Sometimes I heard four or five at once in different parts of the wood, by accident one a bar behind another, and so near me that I distinguished not only the cluck after each note, but often that singular buzzing sound like a fly in a spider's web, only proportionally louder. Sometimes one would circle round and round me in the woods a few feet distant as if tethered by a string, when probably I was near its eggs. They sang at intervals throughout the night, and were again as musical as ever just before and about dawn.

When other birds are still the screech owls take up the strain, like mourning women their ancient u-lu-lu.[83]

81 Antiquated: on the horizon.

82 Nocturnal birds once common in New England.

83 Thoreau may have made the association of this sound with the word "ululate," to howl or wail loudly and sometimes specifically related to the screech of an owl, and with the name "ulula," a genus of owl.

Their dismal scream is truly Ben Jonsonian.[84] Wise midnight hags![85] It is no honest and blunt tu-whit tu-who[86] of the poets, but, without jesting, a most solemn graveyard ditty, the mutual consolations of suicide lovers remembering the pangs and the delights of supernal love in the infernal groves. Yet I love to hear their wailing, their doleful responses, trilled along the wood-side, reminding me sometimes of music and singing birds; as if it were the dark and tearful side of music, the regrets and sighs that would fain be sung. They are the spirits, the low spirits and melancholy forebodings, of fallen souls that once in human shape night-walked the earth and did the deeds of darkness, now expiating their sins with their wailing hymns or threnodies in the scenery of their transgressions. They give me a new sense of the variety and capacity of that nature which is our common dwelling. *Oh-o-o-o-o that I never had been bor-r-r-r-n!* [87] sighs one on this side of the pond, and circles with the restlessness of despair to some new perch on the gray oaks. Then—*that I never had been bor-r-r-r-n!* echoes another on the farther side with tremulous sincerity, and—*bor-r-r-r-n!* comes faintly from far in the Lincoln woods.

I was also serenaded by a hooting owl.[88] Near at hand you could fancy it the most melancholy sound in Nature, as if she meant by this to stereotype[89] and make permanent in her choir the dying moans of a human being,—some poor weak relic of mortality who has left hope behind,[90] and howls like an animal, yet with human sobs, on entering the dark valley, made more awful by a certain gurgling melodiousness,—I find myself beginning with the letters *gl* when I try to imitate it,—expressive of a mind which has reached the gelatinous mildewy stage in the mortification of all healthy and courageous thought. It reminded me of ghouls and idiots and insane howlings. But now one answers from far woods in a strain made really melodious by distance,—*Hoo hoo hoo, hoorer hoo;*

84 Allusion to Ben Jonson's "Witches' Song" from his *Masque of Queens* (1609) 2.317–18: "Wee give thee a shout: Hoo!"

85 Allusion to Shakespeare's *Macbeth* 4.1.64: "How now, you secret, black, and midnight hags."

86 Allusion to Shakespeare's *Love's Labour's Lost* 5.2.900–901: "Then nightly sings the staring owl: Tu-whit, tu-whoo!"

87 Possible reference to Chaucer's use of the phrase "Alas that I had been born" or a slight variant thereof in three works: *The Book of the Duchess*, "The Manciple's Tale," and *Troilus and Criseyde*.

88 Great horned owl (*Bubo Virginianus*), which Thoreau sometimes referred to as the cat owl.

89 Cast into a metal printing plate for permanent and repeated use, to protect the hand-set type.

90 Allusions to Euripides' (480–406 B.C.E.) *Electra*, in which Orestes said, "To which of thy friends, Electra, does this old relic of mortality belong?" and, elsewhere, the old man said to Orestes, "all hope is gone from thee."

91 Archaic: illuminates, but also with the more common meaning of elucidates.

92 The double, or black, spruce is the common spruce found in New England swamps. Thoreau originally had "single spruce"; however, the single spruce does not grow in Concord but does farther north. In his journal of 22 December 1853, Thoreau noted, after correcting a similar error: "It is remarkable how few inhabitants of Concord can tell a spruce from a fir, and probably not two a white from a black spruce, unless they are together" [J 6:22].

93 *Usnea barbata*: a greenish gray pendulous lichen growing on trees, sometimes referred to as beard moss or old man's beard.

94 Pun on the alcoholic beverages of the wine-bibbers and wassailers.

95 An unaccompanied round, often rhythmically intricate, for three or more voices, popular especially in the 17th and 18th centuries.

96 Refers to the river Styx in Greek mythology, the main river of Hades across which the souls of the dead were ferried by Charon.

97 Paunchy, corpulent. Aldermen were often caricatured as lovers of exotic food and having large bellies.

98 Floating heart (*Nymphoides lacunosum*).

and indeed for the most part it suggested only pleasing associations, whether heard by day or night, summer or winter.

I rejoice that there are owls. Let them do the idiotic and maniacal hooting for men. It is a sound admirably suited to swamps and twilight woods which no day illustrates,[91] suggesting a vast and undeveloped nature which men have not recognized. They represent the stark twilight and unsatisfied thoughts which all have. All day the sun has shone on the surface of some savage swamp, where the double spruce[92] stands hung with usnea lichens,[93] and small hawks circulate above, and the chicadee lisps amid the evergreens, and the partridge and rabbit skulk beneath; but now a more dismal and fitting day dawns, and a different race of creatures awakes to express the meaning of Nature there.

Late in the evening I heard the distant rumbling of wagons over bridges,—a sound heard farther than almost any other at night,—the baying of dogs, and sometimes again the lowing of some disconsolate cow in a distant barn-yard. In the mean while all the shore rang with the trump of bullfrogs, the sturdy spirits[94] of ancient wine-bibbers and wassailers, still unrepentant, trying to sing a catch[95] in their Stygian lake,[96]—if the Walden nymphs will pardon the comparison, for though there are almost no weeds, there are frogs there,—who would fain keep up the hilarious rules of their old festal tables, though their voices have waxed hoarse and solemnly grave, mocking at mirth, and the wine has lost its flavor, and become only liquor to distend their paunches, and sweet intoxication never comes to drown the memory of the past, but mere saturation and waterloggedness and distention. The most aldermanic,[97] with his chin upon a heart-leaf,[98] which serves for a napkin to his drooling chaps, under this northern shore quaffs a deep draught of the once scorned water, and passes round the cup with the ejaculation *tr-*

r-r-oonk, tr-r-r-oonk, tr-r-r-oonk! and straightway comes over the water from some distant cove the same password repeated, where the next in seniority and girth has gulped down to his mark;[99] and when this observance has made the circuit of the shores, then ejaculates the master of ceremonies, with satisfaction, *tr-r-r-oonk!* and each in his turn repeats the same down to the least distended, leakiest, and flabbiest paunched, that there be no mistake; and then the bowl goes round again and again, until the sun disperses the morning mist, and only the patriarch is not under the pond,[100] but vainly bellowing *troonk* from time to time, and pausing for a reply.

I am not sure that I ever heard the sound of cockcrowing from my clearing, and I thought that it might be worth the while to keep a cockerel[101] for his music merely, as a singing bird. The note of this once wild Indian pheasant[102] is certainly the most remarkable of any bird's, and if they could be naturalized without being domesticated, it would soon become the most famous sound in our woods, surpassing the clangor of the goose and the hooting of the owl; and then imagine the cackling of the hens to fill the pauses when their lords' clarions rested! No wonder that man added this bird to his tame stock, — to say nothing of the eggs and drumsticks.[103] To walk in a winter morning in a wood where these birds abounded, their native woods, and hear the wild cockerels crow on the trees, clear and shrill for miles over the resounding earth, drowning the feebler notes of other birds, — think of it! It would put nations on the alert. Who would not be early to rise, and rise earlier and earlier every successive day of his life, till he became unspeakably healthy, wealthy, and wise?[104] This foreign bird's note is celebrated by the poets of all countries along with the notes of their native songsters. All climates agree with brave Chanticleer. He is more indigenous even than the natives. His health is ever good, his lungs are sound, his spirits

99 A mark on a glass used in a drinking bout indicating the place to which each man was expected to drink.

100 Pun on those who have slipped under the table from inebriation.

101 Young rooster, under one year old.

102 The pheasant of India, from which the common domestic pheasant is descended. "As our domestic fowls are said to have their origin in the wild pheasant of India, sour domestic thoughts have their proto-types in the thoughts of her philosophers" [W 1:156].

103 Although this implied praise of drumsticks seems contradictory to Thoreau's more vegetarian-oriented statements elsewhere, his original journal passage of 11 July 1851 was clearer: "These birds are worth far more to me for their crowing and cackling than for their drumsticks and eggs" [J 2:301].

104 Allusion to Benjamin Franklin's "The Way to Wealth" in *Poor Richard's Almanack* (1757): "Early to bed and early to rise / Makes a man healthy, wealthy, and wise."

never flag. Even the sailor on the Atlantic and Pacific is awakened by his voice;[105] but its shrill sound never roused me from my slumbers. I kept neither dog, cat, cow, pig, nor hens, so that you would have said there was a deficiency of domestic sounds; neither the churn, nor the spinning wheel, nor even the singing of the kettle, nor the hissing of the urn, nor children crying, to comfort one. An old-fashioned man would have lost his senses or died of ennui before this. Not even rats in the wall, for they were starved out, or rather were never baited in,—only squirrels on the roof and under the floor, a whippoorwill on the ridge pole, a blue-jay screaming beneath the window, a hare or woodchuck under the house, a screech-owl or a cat-owl behind it, a flock of wild geese or a laughing loon on the pond, and a fox to bark in the night. Not even a lark or an oriole, those mild plantation birds, ever visited my clearing. No cockerels to crow nor hens to cackle in the yard. No yard! but unfenced Nature reaching up to your very sills. A young forest growing up under your windows, and wild sumachs and blackberry vines breaking through into your cellar; sturdy pitch-pines rubbing and creaking against the shingles for want of room, their roots reaching quite under the house. Instead of a scuttle[106] or a blind blown off in the gale,—a pine tree snapped off or torn up by the roots behind your house for fuel. Instead of no path to the front-yard gate in the Great Snow,—no gate,—no front-yard,—and no path to the civilized world!

105 Ships bound on long voyages often had cooped chickens on board to provide fresh eggs and meat. The roosters were necessary to fertilize the eggs.

106 Bucket commonly used for carrying coal.

Solitude

This is a delicious evening, when the whole body is one sense, and imbibes delight through every pore. I go and come with a strange liberty in Nature, a part of herself. As I walk along the stony shore of the pond in my shirt sleeves, though it is cool as well as cloudy and windy, and I see nothing special to attract me, all the elements are unusually congenial to me. The bullfrogs trump to usher in the night, and the note of the whippoorwill is borne on the rippling wind from over the water. Sympathy with the fluttering alder and poplar leaves almost takes away my breath; yet, like the lake, my serenity is rippled but not ruffled. These small waves raised by the evening wind are as remote from storm as the smooth reflecting surface. Though it is now dark, the wind still blows and roars in the wood, the waves still dash, and some creatures lull the rest with their notes. The repose is never complete. The wildest animals do not repose, but seek their prey now; the fox, and skunk, and rabbit, now roam the fields and woods without fear. They are Nature's watchmen,—links which connect the days of animated life.

When I return to my house I find that visitors have been there and left their cards, either a bunch of flowers, or a wreath of evergreen, or a name in pencil on a yellow walnut leaf or a chip. They who come rarely to the woods take some little piece of the forest into their hands to play

1 The railroad tracks were only one-third of a mile from Thoreau's Walden house. Where his family was living then, in the Texas house on the western side of Concord, the tracks were just beyond the backyard, so the distance at Walden may have seemed greater to him. As with placing his nearest neighbor a mile away, at the beginning of "Economy" and in the next paragraph here, his slightly inflated distances increased the impression of solitude for literary purposes.

2 Approximately one-fifth of a mile.

3 Thoreau wrote in "Walking": "I can easily walk ten, fifteen, twenty, any number of miles, commencing at my own door, without going by any house, without crossing a road except where the fox and the mink do: first along by the river, and then the brook, and then the meadow and the woodside. There are square miles in my vicinity which have no inhabitant." [W 5:212–13].

4 Possible echo of Virgil's *Aeneid* 6.641, which Thoreau translated "and they know their own sun and their own stars" [W 1:406].

5 Most likely the horned pout, about which Thoreau wrote in *A Week on the Concord and Merrimack Rivers:*

The horned pout (*Pimelodus nebulosus*), sometimes called Minister, from the peculiar squeaking noise it makes when drawn out of the water, is a dull and blundering fellow, and like the eel, vespertinal in his habits and fond of the mud. It bites deliberately, as if about its business. They are taken at night with a mass of worms strung on a thread, which catches in their teeth, sometimes three or four, with an eel, at one pull. They are extremely tenacious of life, opening and shutting their mouths for half an hour after their heads have been cut off; a bloodthirsty and bullying race of rangers, inhabiting the fertile river bottoms, with ever a lance in rest, and ready to do battle with their nearest neighbor. I have observed them in summer, when every other one had a long and bloody scar upon his back, where the skin

with by the way, which they leave, either intentionally or accidentally. One has peeled a willow wand, woven it into a ring, and dropped it on my table. I could always tell if visitors had called in my absence, either by the bended twigs or grass, or the print of their shoes, and generally of what sex or age or quality they were by some slight trace left, as a flower dropped, or a bunch of grass plucked and thrown away, even as far off as the railroad, half a mile distant,[1] or by the lingering odor of a cigar or pipe. Nay, I was frequently notified of the passage of a traveller along the highway sixty rods[2] off by the scent of his pipe.

There is commonly sufficient space about us. Our horizon is never quite at our elbows. The thick wood is not just at our door, nor the pond, but somewhat is always clearing, familiar and worn by us, appropriated and fenced in some way, and reclaimed from Nature. For what reason have I this vast range and circuit, some square miles of unfrequented forest, for my privacy, abandoned to me by men? My nearest neighbor is a mile distant, and no house is visible from any place but the hill-tops within half a mile of my own. I have my horizon bounded by woods all to myself; a distant view of the railroad where it touches the pond on the one hand, and of the fence which skirts the woodland road on the other. But for the most part it is as solitary where I live as on the prairies.[3] It is as much Asia or Africa as New England. I have, as it were, my own sun and moon and stars,[4] and a little world all to myself. At night there was never a traveller passed my house, or knocked at my door, more than if I were the first or last man; unless it were in the spring, when at long intervals some came from the village to fish for pouts,[5]—they plainly fished much more in the Walden Pond of their own natures, and baited their hooks with darkness,—but they soon retreated, usually with light baskets, and left "the world to darkness and to me,"[6] and the black kernel of the night was never profaned by any human neighborhood. I believe that men are generally still a little afraid of the dark, though the witches are all hung,[7] and Christianity and candles have been introduced.

Yet I experienced sometimes that the most sweet and tender, the most innocent and encouraging society may be found in any natural object, even for the poor misanthrope and most melancholy man. There can be no very black melancholy[8] to him who lives in the midst of Nature and has his senses still. There was never yet such a storm but it was Æolian music[9] to a healthy and innocent ear. Nothing can rightly compel a simple and brave man to a vulgar sadness. While I enjoy the friendship of the seasons I trust that nothing can make life a burden to me. The gentle rain which waters my beans and keeps me in the house to-day is not drear and melancholy, but good for me too. Though it prevents my hoeing them, it is of far more worth than my hoeing. If it should continue so long as to cause the seeds to rot in the ground and destroy the potatoes in the low lands, it would still be good for the grass on the uplands, and, being good for the grass, it would be good for me. Sometimes, when I compare myself with other men, it seems as if I were more favored by the gods than they, beyond any deserts that I am conscious of; as if I had a warrant and surety at their hands which my fellows have not, and were especially guided and guarded. I do not flatter myself, but if it be possible they flatter me. I have never felt lonesome, or in the least oppressed by a sense of solitude, but once, and that was a few weeks after I came to the woods, when, for an hour, I doubted if the near neighborhood of man was not essential to a serene and healthy life. To be alone was something unpleasant. But I was at the same time conscious of a slight insanity in my mood, and seemed to foresee my recovery. In the midst of a gentle rain while these thoughts prevailed,[10] I was suddenly sensible of such sweet and

was gone, the mark, perhaps, of some fierce encounter. Sometimes the fry, not an inch long, are seen darkening the shore with their myriads. [W 1:29–30]

6 Quoted from Thomas Gray's "Elegy Written in a Country Churchyard":

The curfew tolls the knell of parting day,
The lowing herd wind slowly o'er the lea,
The ploughman homeward plods his weary
way,
And leaves the world to darkness and to me.
[ll. 1–4]

7 The last person convicted during the Salem witch trials was hanged on 22 September 1692.
8 Melancholy was thought by ancient and medieval physiologists to be caused by a predominance of black bile, an imaginary secretion.
9 Music produced by the wind, from Aeolus, the Greek god of winds. An Aeolian harp, one of Thoreau's favorite instruments, was a stringed instrument placed in a window that produced music by the wind blowing across its strings.
10 The gentle rain occurred on 14 July 1845.

11 Quoted from Patrick MacGregor's version of the "Ossian" poem "Croma: A Poem" (ll. 52–54).

beneficent society in Nature, in the very pattering of the drops, and in every sound and sight around my house, an infinite and unaccountable friendliness all at once like an atmosphere sustaining me, as made the fancied advantages of human neighborhood insignificant, and I have never thought of them since. Every little pine needle expanded and swelled with sympathy and befriended me. I was so distinctly made aware of the presence of something kindred to me, even in scenes which we are accustomed to call wild and dreary, and also that the nearest of blood to me and humanest was not a person nor a villager, that I thought no place could ever be strange to me again. —

"Mourning untimely consumes the sad;
Few are their days in the land of the living,
Beautiful daughter of Toscar." [11]

Some of my pleasantest hours were during the long rain storms in the spring or fall, which confined me to the house for the afternoon as well as the forenoon, soothed by their ceaseless roar and pelting; when an early twilight ushered in a long evening in which many thoughts had time to take root and unfold themselves. In those driving north-east rains which tried the village houses so, when the maids stood ready with mop and pail in front entries to keep the deluge out, I sat behind my door in my little house, which was all entry, and thoroughly enjoyed its protection. In one heavy thunder shower the lightning struck a large pitch-pine across the pond, making a very conspicuous and perfectly regular spiral groove from top to bottom, an inch or more deep, and four or five inches wide, as you would groove a walking-stick. I passed it again the other day, and was struck with awe on looking up and beholding that mark, now more distinct than ever, where a terrific and resistless bolt came down out of the harmless sky eight years ago.[12] Men frequently say to me, "I should think you would feel lonesome down there, and want to be nearer to folks, rainy and snowy days and nights especially." I am tempted to reply to such,—This whole earth which we inhabit is but a point in space. How far apart, think you, dwell the two most distant inhabitants of yonder star, the breadth of whose disk cannot be appreciated by our instruments? Why should I feel lonely? is not our planet in the Milky Way? This which you put seems to me not to be the most important question. What sort of space is that which separates a man from his fellows and makes him solitary? I have found that no exertion of the legs can bring two minds much nearer to one another. What do we want most to dwell near to? Not to many men surely, the depot, the post-office, the bar-room, the meeting-house, the school-house, the grocery, Beacon Hill,[13] or the Five Points,[14] where men most congregate, but to the perennial source of our life, whence in all our experience we have found that to issue; as the willow stands near the water and sends out its roots in that direction. This will vary with different natures, but this is the place where a wise man will dig his cellar. . . . I one evening overtook one of my townsmen, who has accumulated what is called "a handsome property,"—though I never got a *fair* view[15] of it,—on the Walden road, driving a pair of cattle to market, who inquired of me how I could bring my mind to give up so many of the comforts of life. I answered that I was very sure I liked it passably well; I was not joking. And so I went home to my bed, and left him to pick his way through the darkness and the mud to Brighton,—or Bright-town,[16]—which place he would reach some time in the morning.

Any prospect of awakening or coming to life to a dead man makes indifferent all times and places. The place where that may occur is always the same, and indescrib-

12 The first part of the paragraph, to here, was added circa 1852–54 in the final two drafts. Thoreau may have in part been reminded of this tree by seeing on 27 June 1852 a white ash in Lincoln that had been struck by lightning the week before. His awe is apparent in this journal passage following a description of the stricken tree:

> All this was accomplished in an instant by a kind of fire out of the heavens called lightning, or a thunderbolt, accompanied by a crashing sound. For what purpose? The ancients called it Jove's bolt, with which he punished the guilty, and we moderns understand it no better. There was displayed a Titanic force, some of that force which made and can unmake the world. The brute forces are not yet wholly tamed. Is this of the character of a wild beast, or is it guided by intelligence and mercy? If we trust our natural impressions, it is a manifestation of brutish force or vengeance, more or less tempered with justice. Yet it is our own consciousness of sin, probably, which suggests the idea of vengeance, and to a righteous man it would be merely sublime without being awful. . . . Why should trees be struck? It is not enough to say because they are in the way. Science answers, *Non scio*, I am ignorant. All the phenomena of nature need [to] be seen from the point of view of wonder and awe, like lightning; and, on the other hand, the lightning itself needs to [be] regarded with serenity, as the most familiar and innocent phenomena. [J 4:156–58]

13 Location of the Massachusetts State House in Boston.

14 Section of lower Manhattan notorious in Thoreau's day for its jam-packed tenements, garbage-strewn streets, crime, prostitution, gambling, alcoholism, and disease. An intersection of streets forming five points gave it its name.

15 Pun: a just as well as a beautiful view.

16 Brighton was a town, now part of Boston, that

was home to slaughterhouses and farmers' markets. "Bright" was a common name for an ox, thus "Cattle-town."

17 These three paragraphs are Thoreau's translation of Confucius, *The Doctrine of the Mean* 16.1–3, from the French translation in Pauthier, *Confucius et Mencius* 77.

18 Thoreau's translation of Confucius, *Analects* 4.25, from the French translation in Pauthier, *Confucius et Mencius* 123.

19 Hindu god of air, wind, thunder, rain, and snow, who presides over the middle-realm deities.

ably pleasant to all our senses. For the most part we allow only outlying and transient circumstances to make our occasions. They are, in fact, the cause of our distraction. Nearest to all things is that power which fashions their being. *Next* to us the grandest laws are continually being executed. *Next* to us is not the workman whom we have hired, with whom we love so well to talk, but the workman whose work we are.

"How vast and profound is the influence of the subtile powers of Heaven and of Earth!"

"We seek to perceive them, and we do not see them; we seek to hear them, and we do not hear them; identified with the substance of things, they cannot be separated from them."

"They cause that in all the universe men purify and sanctify their hearts, and clothe themselves in their holiday garments to offer sacrifices and oblations to their ancestors. It is an ocean of subtile intelligences. They are every where, above us, on our left, on our right; they environ us on all sides."[17]

We are the subjects of an experiment which is not a little interesting to me. Can we not do without the society of our gossips a little while under these circumstances,— have our own thoughts to cheer us? Confucius says truly, "Virtue does not remain as an abandoned orphan; it must of necessity have neighbors."[18]

With thinking we may be beside ourselves in a sane sense. By a conscious effort of the mind we can stand aloof from actions and their consequences; and all things, good and bad, go by us like a torrent. We are not wholly involved in Nature. I may be either the driftwood in the stream, or Indra[19] in the sky looking down on it. I *may* be affected by a theatrical exhibition; on the other hand, I *may not* be affected by an actual event which appears to concern me much more. I only know myself as a human entity; the scene, so to speak, of thoughts and affections;

and am sensible of a certain doubleness by which I can stand as remote from myself as from another.[20] However intense my experience, I am conscious of the presence and criticism of a part of me, which, as it were, is not a part of me, but spectator, sharing no experience, but taking note of it; and that is no more I than it is you. When the play, it may be the tragedy, of life is over, the spectator goes his way. It was a kind of fiction, a work of the imagination only, so far as he was concerned. This doubleness may easily make us poor neighbors and friends sometimes.

I find it wholesome to be alone the greater part of the time. To be in company, even with the best, is soon wearisome and dissipating. I love to be alone. I never found the companion that was so companionable as solitude.[21] We are for the most part more lonely when we go abroad among men than when we stay in our chambers. A man thinking or working is always alone, let him be where he will. Solitude is not measured by the miles of space that intervene between a man and his fellows. The really diligent student in one of the crowded hives of Cambridge College is as solitary as a dervis[22] in the desert. The farmer can work alone in the field or the woods all day, hoeing or chopping, and not feel lonesome, because he is employed; but when he comes home at night he cannot sit down in a room alone, at the mercy of his thoughts, but must be where he can "see the folks," and recreate, and as he thinks remunerate himself for his day's solitude; and hence he wonders how the student can sit alone in the house all night and most of the day without ennui and "the blues;"[23] but he does not realize that the student, though in the house, is still at work in *his* field, and chopping in *his* woods, as the farmer in his, and in turn seeks the same recreation and society that the latter does, though it may be a more condensed form of it.

Society is commonly too cheap. We meet at very short

20 Thoreau expressed this duality in his journal when he wrote: "I am startled when I consider how little I am *actually* concerned about the things I write in my journal" [J 1:143]. In "Historic Notes of Life and Letters in New England," Emerson wrote: "The key to the period appeared to be that the mind had become aware of itself."

21 Echoing Wordsworth, Thoreau wrote in 1853: "Ah! The world is too much with us" [J 5:454]. In a post-*Walden* journal entry he explained his affinity for solitude:

There is nothing so sanative, so poetic, as a walk in the woods and fields even now, when I meet none abroad for pleasure. Nothing so inspires me and excites such serene and profitable thought. The objects are elevating. In the street and in society I am almost invariably cheap and dissipated, my life is unspeakably mean. No amount of gold or respectability would in the least redeem it,—dining with the Governor or a member of Congress! ! But alone in distant woods or fields, in unpretending sprout-lands or pastures tracked by rabbits, even in a bleak and, to most, cheerless day, like this, when a villager would be thinking of his inn, I come to myself, I once more feel myself grandly related, and that cold and solitude are friends of mine. I suppose that this value, in my case, is equivalent to what others get by churchgoing and prayer. I come to my solitary woodland walk as the homesick go home. I thus dispose of the superfluous and see things as they are, grand and beautiful. . . . I get away a mile or two from the town into the stillness and solitude of nature, with rocks, trees, weeds, snow about me. I enter some glade in the woods, perchance, where a few weeds and dry leaves alone lift themselves above the surface of the snow, and it is as if I had come to an open window. I see out and around myself. Our *skylights* are thus far away from the ordinary resorts of men. I am not satisfied with ordinary windows. I must have a true *skylight*. [J 9:208–9]

22 Dervish: a Sufi Muslim who has taken religious vows of poverty and austerity. Dervishes were noted for their ecstatic rituals and use of hypnotic trance-states, including dancing or ritual chanting, and were known as dancing, whirling, or howling dervishes according to the practice of their order. Although they were not necessarily known for leading solitary lives, story 28 in chapter 1 of the *Gulistan* of Sadi begins: "A solitary dervish was sitting in a corner of the desert."

23 The noun "blues," meaning low spirits, was first recorded in 1741 and may derive from "blue devil," a 17th-century term for a baleful demon.

24 Female workers in the Lowell mills slept in nearby dormitories. Their living situation is described in 14 November 1846 issue of *The Harbinger*: "The young women sleep upon an average six in a room, three beds to a room. There is no privacy, no retirement, here. It is almost impossible to read or write alone, as the parlor is full and so many sleep in the same chamber."

25 Unidentified.

26 A parhelion, or sundog: any one of several bright spots at the altitude of the sun, often tinged with color.

intervals, not having had time to acquire any new value for each other. We meet at meals three times a day, and give each other a new taste of that old musty cheese that we are. We have had to agree on a certain set of rules, called etiquette and politeness, to make this frequent meeting tolerable, and that we need not come to open war. We meet at the post-office, and at the sociable, and about the fire-side every night; we live thick and are in each other's way, and stumble over one another, and I think that we thus lose some respect for one another. Certainly less frequency would suffice for all important and hearty communications. Consider the girls in a factory,— never alone, hardly in their dreams.[24] It would be better if there were but one inhabitant to a square mile, as where I live. The value of a man is not in his skin, that we should touch him.

I have heard of a man lost in the woods and dying of famine and exhaustion at the foot of a tree, whose loneliness was relieved by the grotesque visions with which, owing to bodily weakness, his diseased imagination surrounded him, and which he believed to be real.[25] So also, owing to bodily and mental health and strength, we may be continually cheered by a like but more normal and natural society, and come to know that we are never alone.

I have a great deal of company in my house; especially in the morning, when nobody calls. Let me suggest a few comparisons, that some one may convey an idea of my situation. I am no more lonely than the loon in the pond that laughs so loud, or than Walden Pond itself. What company has that lonely lake, I pray? And yet it has not the blue devils, but the blue angels in it, in the azure tint of its waters. The sun is alone, except in thick weather, when there sometimes appear to be two, but one is a mock sun.[26] God is alone,—but the devil, he is far from being alone; he sees a great deal of company; he is legion.[27] I am no more lonely than a single mullein or dandelion in a pasture, or a bean leaf, or sorrel, or a horse-fly, or a humble-bee.[28] I am no more lonely than the Mill Brook,[29] or a weathercock, or the northstar, or the south wind, or an April shower, or a January thaw, or the first spider in a new house.

I have occasional visits in the long winter evenings, when the snow falls fast and the wind howls in the wood, from an old settler[30] and original proprietor, who is reported to have dug Walden Pond, and stoned it, and fringed it with pine woods; who tells me stories of old time and of new eternity; and between us we manage to pass a cheerful evening with social mirth and pleasant views of things, even without apples or cider,—a most wise and humorous friend, whom I love much, who keeps himself more secret than ever did Goffe or Whalley;[31] and though he is thought to be dead,[32] none can show where he is buried. An elderly dame,[33] too, dwells in my neighborhood, invisible to most persons, in whose odorous herb garden I love to stroll sometimes, gathering simples[34] and listening to her fables; for she has a genius of unequalled fertility, and her memory runs back farther than mythology, and she can tell me the original of every fable, and on what fact every one is founded, for the incidents occurred when she was young. A ruddy and lusty old dame, who delights in all weathers and seasons, and is likely to outlive all her children yet.

The indescribable innocence and beneficence of Nature,—of sun and wind and rain, of summer and winter,—such health, such cheer, they afford forever! and such sympathy have they ever with our race, that all Nature would be affected, and the sun's brightness fade, and the winds would sigh humanely, and the clouds rain tears, and the woods shed their leaves and put on mourning

27 Allusion to Luke 8:30–31: "Jesus asked him, saying, What is thy name? And he said, Legion: because many devils were entered into him."

28 Bumblebee.

29 A brook flowing through Concord that provided power for the mill at the Mill Dam.

30 The old settler is not identified further, beyond the idea that he represents a creative spirit or God. It may allude to Pan, although Pan is not a god of creation; in *A Week on the Concord and Merrimack Rivers* Thoreau wrote: "In my Pantheon, Pan still reigns in his pristine glory" [W 1:65]. Thoreau referred to the old settler two other times in *Walden*, in "The Ponds" and "Former Inhabitants; and Winter Visitors."

31 William Goffe (ca. 1605–ca. 1679), a Puritan general, and his father-in-law, Edward Whalley (d. ca. 1675), regicides who were held responsible for the execution of Charles I in 1642, fled to America, and lived in hiding in Connecticut and Massachusetts.

32 If Pan, then referring to the cry "Pan is dead!" from Plutarch's "Why the Oracles Cease to Give Answers." Thoreau wrote in *A Week on the Concord and Merrimack Rivers*: "for the great god Pan is not dead, as was rumored. No god ever dies" [W 1:65].

33 Possibly Mother Nature or Demeter, the Greek goddess of agriculture, health, and birth.

34 Medicinal herbs.

35 Communication.

36 Possible allusion to Morrison's Pill, described in Carlyle's *Past and Present* ("Brothers, I am sorry I have got no Morrison's Pill for curing the maladies of Society"), but more likely to such general cure-alls as Parr's Life Pills, Dr. Mainwaring's Pills, or Brandreth's Pills, which Thoreau referred to in *The Maine Woods:* "The Indian growing much worse, we stopped in the north part of Lincoln to get some brandy for him; but failing in this, an apothecary recommended Brandreth's pills" [W 3:319].

37 Terms used to advertise such remedies as Dr. George Stewart's Botanic Syrup and Vegetable Pills, Texan Universal Pills, or "Morrison's Pills — the celebrated Hygeian Universal Medicines of the Ertish College of Health."

38 Thomas Parr (1483–1635), an Englishman reputed to have lived to 152 years old, whose longevity lent his name to Parr's Life Pills.

39 The Souli River, which runs underground in some spots and so was thought to lead to Hades in Greek mythology.

40 Large salt lake on the Israel-Jordan border.

41 In Greek mythology, goddess of health.

42 In Greek mythology, Aesculapius was the god of medical arts.

43 In Greek mythology, goddess of youth, daughter of Zeus (Jupiter) and Hera (Juno); according to some myths she was conceived after Hera ate some wild lettuce.

in midsummer, if any man should ever for a just cause grieve. Shall I not have intelligence[35] with the earth? Am I not partly leaves and vegetable mould myself?

What is the pill[36] which will keep us well, serene, contented? Not my or thy great-grandfather's, but our great-grandmother Nature's universal, vegetable, botanic[37] medicines, by which she has kept herself young always, outlived so many old Parrs[38] in her day, and fed her health with their decaying fatness. For my panacea, instead of one of those quack vials of a mixture dipped from Acheron[39] and the Dead Sea,[40] which come out of those long shallow black-schooner looking wagons which we sometimes see made to carry bottles, let me have a draught of undiluted morning air. Morning air! If men will not drink of this at the fountain-head of the day, why, then, we must even bottle up some and sell it in the shops, for the benefit of those who have lost their subscription ticket to morning time in this world. But remember, it will not keep quite till noon-day even in the coolest cellar, but drive out the stopples long ere that and follow westward the steps of Aurora. I am no worshipper of Hygeia,[41] who was the daughter of that old herb-doctor Æsculapius,[42] and who is represented on monuments holding a serpent in one hand, and in the other a cup out of which the serpent sometimes drinks; but rather of Hebe,[43] cupbearer to Jupiter, who was the daughter of Juno and wild lettuce, and who had the power of restoring gods and men to the vigor of youth. She was probably the only thoroughly sound-conditioned, healthy, and robust young lady that ever walked the globe, and wherever she came it was spring.

Visitors

I think that I love society as much as most, and am ready enough to fasten myself like a bloodsucker for the time to any full-blooded man that comes in my way. I am naturally no hermit,[1] but might possibly sit out[2] the sturdiest frequenter of the bar-room, if my business called me thither.

I had three chairs in my house; one for solitude, two for friendship, three for society. When visitors came in larger and unexpected numbers there was but the third chair for them all, but they generally economized the room by standing up.[3] It is surprising how many great men and women a small house will contain. I have had twenty-five or thirty souls, with their bodies, at once under my roof, and yet we often parted without being aware that we had come very near to one another. Many of our houses, both public and private, with their almost innumerable apartments, their huge halls and their cellars for the storage of wines and other munitions of peace, appear to me extravagantly large for their inhabitants. They are so vast and magnificent that the latter seem to be only vermin which infest them. I am surprised when the herald blows his summons before some Tremont or Astor or Middlesex House,[4] to see come creeping out over the piazza for all inhabitants a ridiculous mouse,[5] which soon again slinks into some hole in the pavement.

1 That this was so is attested not only by his frequent walks into Concord but by the number of visitors to his Walden house. Mary Hosmer Brown (1856–1929), in *Memories of Concord,* recalled: "His life at Walden was never intended by him to be that of a hermit, nor was his sojourn there a very lonely one. When actually writing he refused to be disturbed; otherwise a chair set outside the door proclaimed his readiness for company." Horace Hosmer wrote in *Remembrances of Concord and the Thoreaus:* "We boys used to visit him on Saturday afternoons at his house by Walden, and he would show us interesting things in the woods near by."

2 Outlast, but literally stay seated as opposed to those who have drunk themselves under the table.

3 Even before living at Walden, this was Thoreau's method for entertaining visitors. In his journal for 8 June 1841, he wrote: "Having but one chair, I am obliged to receive my visitors standing, and, now I think of it, those old sages and heroes must always have met erectly" [J 1:264].

4 Hotels in Boston, New York, and Concord, respectively.

5 Allusion to Horace (65–8 B.C.E.), *Ars Poetica* 1.139: "Parturient montes, nascetur ridiculus mus" (Mountains will labor, to bring forth a ridiculous mouse).

One inconvenience I sometimes experienced in so small a house, the difficulty of getting to a sufficient distance from my guest when we began to utter the big thoughts in big words. You want room for your thoughts to get into sailing trim and run a course or two before they make their port. The bullet of your thought must have overcome its lateral and ricochet motion and fallen into its last and steady course before it reaches the ear of the hearer, else it may plough out again through the side of his head. Also, our sentences wanted room to unfold and form their columns[6] in the interval. Individuals, like nations, must have suitable broad and natural boundaries, even a considerable neutral ground, between them. I have found it a singular luxury to talk across the pond to a companion on the opposite side. In my house we were so near that we could not begin to hear,—we could not speak low enough to be heard; as when you throw two stones into calm water so near that they break each other's undulations. If we are merely loquacious and loud talkers, then we can afford to stand very near together, cheek by jowl, and feel each other's breath; but if we speak reservedly and thoughtfully, we want to be farther apart, that all animal heat and moisture may have a chance to evaporate. If we would enjoy the most intimate society with that in each of us which is without, or above, being spoken to, we must not only be silent, but commonly so far apart bodily that we cannot possibly hear each other's voice in any case. Referred to this standard, speech is for the convenience of those who are hard of hearing; but there are many fine things which we cannot say if we have to shout. As the conversation began to assume a loftier and grander tone, we gradually shoved our chairs farther apart till they touched the wall in opposite corners, and then commonly there was not room enough.

My "best" room,[7] however, my withdrawing room,[8]

---

6   Military term for making maneuvers, with a possible pun on the columns of a newspaper or magazine.

7   Parlor.

8   Originally a room where company withdraws after dining, particularly the ladies while the men drank and smoked, but later synonymous with parlor.

always ready for company, on whose carpet the sun rarely fell,[9] was the pine wood behind my house. Thither in summer days, when distinguished guests came, I took them, and a priceless domestic swept the floor and dusted the furniture and kept the things in order.

If one guest came he sometimes partook of my frugal meal, and it was no interruption to conversation to be stirring a hasty-pudding,[10] or watching the rising and maturing of a loaf of bread in the ashes, in the mean while. But if twenty came and sat in my house there was nothing said about dinner, though there might be bread enough for two, more than if eating were a forsaken habit; but we naturally practised abstinence; and this was never felt to be an offence against hospitality, but the most proper and considerate course. The waste and decay of physical life, which so often needs repair, seemed miraculously retarded in such a case, and the vital vigor stood its ground. I could entertain thus a thousand[11] as well as twenty; and if any ever went away disappointed or hungry from my house when they found me at home, they may depend upon it that I sympathized with them at least. So easy is it, though many housekeepers doubt it, to establish new and better customs in the place of the old. You need not rest your reputation on the dinners you give. For my own part, I was never so effectually deterred from frequenting a man's house, by any kind of Cerberus[12] whatever, as by the parade one made about dining me, which I took to be a very polite and roundabout hint never to trouble him so again. I think I shall never revisit those scenes. I should be proud to have for the motto of my cabin those lines of Spenser which one of my visitors inscribed on a yellow walnut leaf for a card:—

"Arrivéd there, the little house they fill,
　　Ne looke for entertainment where none was;

9　Except for Sundays and important occasions, such as weddings and funerals, it was the custom to keep the parlor closed and its curtains drawn, to prevent fading of carpets and furniture. Thoreau, of course, is talking about the floor of the forest.
10　Quickly cooked pudding made by stirring corn meal in boiling water or hot milk.
11　Echo of Jesus feeding the multitudes on seven loaves and a few small fishes, in Matthew 15:34–39.
12　In Greek mythology, a three-headed dog guarding the entrance to the land of the dead.

Rest is their feast, and all things at their will:
    The noblest mind the best contentment
has." [13]

When Winslow,[14] afterward governor of the Plymouth Colony, went with a companion on a visit of ceremony to Massasoit[15] on foot through the woods, and arrived tired and hungry at his lodge, they were well received by the king, but nothing was said about eating that day. When the night arrived, to quote their own words, — "He laid us on the bed with himself and his wife, they at the one end and we at the other, it being only plank, laid a foot from the ground, and a thin mat upon them. Two more of his chief men, for want of room, pressed by and upon us; so that we were worse weary of our lodging than of our journey."[16] At one o'clock the next day Massasoit "brought two fishes that he had shot," about thrice as big as a bream;[17] "these being boiled, there were at least forty looked for a share in them. The most ate of them. This meal only we had in two nights and a day; and had not one of us bought a partridge, we had taken our journey fasting." Fearing that they would be light-headed for want of food and also sleep, owing to "the savages' barbarous singing, (for they use to sing themselves asleep,)" and that they might get home while they had strength to travel, they departed. As for lodging, it is true they were but poorly entertained, though what they found an inconvenience was no doubt intended for an honor; but as far as eating was concerned, I do not see how the Indians could have done better. They had nothing to eat themselves, and they were wiser than to think that apologies could supply the place of food to their guests; so they drew their belts tighter and said nothing about it.[18] Another time when Winslow visited them, it being a season of plenty with them, there was no deficiency in this respect.

13 Quoted from Edmund Spenser's *The Faerie Queene* 1.1.35, with one minor variant.

14 Edward Winslow (1595–1655), a passenger on the *Mayflower* whose journals provide one of the earliest accounts of the Plymouth Colony.

15 Chief of the Wampanoags (1590–1661) who befriended the colonists.

16 Quoted, with minor variants, from Winslow's *A Relation or Journal of the Beginning and Proceedings of the English Plantation at Plimouth in New England* (1622), as found in Alexander Young's (1800–1854) *Chronicles of the Pilgrim Fathers of the Colony of Plymouth from 1602 to 1625* (1841) 210–13.

17 Freshwater sunfish, not the non-native true bream found in Europe.

18 Winslow noted that Massasoit was "both grieved and ashamed that he could no better entertain us."

As for men, they will hardly fail one any where. I had more visitors while I lived in the woods than at any other period in my life; I mean that I had some. I met several there under more favorable circumstances than I could any where else. But fewer came to see me upon trivial business. In this respect, my company was winnowed by my mere distance from town. I had withdrawn so far within the great ocean of solitude, into which the rivers of society empty, that for the most part, so far as my needs were concerned, only the finest sediment was deposited around me. Beside, there were wafted to me evidences of unexplored and uncultivated continents on the other side.

Who should come to my lodge this morning but a true Homeric or Paphlagonian[19] man,—he had so suitable and poetic a name that I am sorry I cannot print it here,[20]—a Canadian, a woodchopper and post-maker, who can hole fifty posts in a day, who made his last supper on a woodchuck which his dog caught. He, too, has heard of Homer, and, "if it were not for books," would "not know what to do rainy days," though perhaps he has not read one wholly through for many rainy seasons. Some priest who could pronounce the Greek itself taught him to read his verse in the testament in his native parish far away; and now I must translate to him, while he holds the book, Achilles' reproof to Patroclus[21] for his sad countenance.—"Why are you in tears, Patroclus, like a young girl?"—[22]

> "Or have you alone heard some news from
>   Phthia?
> They say that Menœtius lives yet, son of Actor,
> And Peleus lives, son of Æacus, among the
>   Myrmidons,[23]
> Either of whom having died, we should greatly
>   grieve."

19 Of Paphlagonia, an ancient country of Asia Minor on the Black Sea coast, rugged and mountainous with dense forests.

20 Alek Therien (1812–1885). In early versions Thoreau called him Alexander the Farmer, from the French word *terrien,* meaning landowner or countryman. According to Edward Emerson the name Therien, despite its French origin, was pronounced as in English, Thē'-ri-en. Thoreau described one of his encounters with Therien in a journal entry for 24 December 1853:

> Saw Therien yesterday afternoon chopping for Jacob Baker in the rain. I heard his axe half a mile off, and also saw the smoke of his fire, which I mistook for a part of the mist which was drifting about. . . . Asked him what time he started in the morning. The sun was up when he got out of the house that morning. He heard Flint's Pond whooping like cannon the moment he opened the door, but sometimes he could see stars after he got to his chopping-ground. He was working with his coat off in the rain. . . . He took a French paper to keep himself in practice,—not for news; he said he did n't want news. He had got twenty-three or twenty-four of them, had got them bound and paid a dollar for it, and would like to have me see it. He had n't read it half; there was a great deal of reading in it, by gorry. He wanted me to tell him the meaning of some of the hard words. How much had he cut? He was n't a-going to kill himself. He had got money enough. He cut enough to earn his board. A man could not do much more in the winter.

21 Achilles' closest friend.
22 This and the following are Thoreau's translation of Homer's *Iliad* 16.7, 16.13–16.
23 Phthia was the land ruled by Peleus, the father of Achilles; Menoetius was the father of Patroclus; Actor was a Theban hero; Aeacus was the son of Zeus and Aegina, the grandfather of Achilles, and king of the island of Aegina, which was named

after his mother. According to Greek mythology, when Aegina was depopulated by the plague, Aeacus prayed to Zeus to grant him new subjects. Zeus provided a new population by changing ants into people, the Myrmidons, who later took part in the Greek expedition against Troy with Achilles as their leader.

24 A powerful astringent, used both internally and topically.

25 On the Sabbath.

26 Therien was born in 1811, making him thirty-four when Thoreau went to Walden.

He says, "That's good." He has a great bundle of white-oak bark[24] under his arm for a sick man, gathered this Sunday morning. "I suppose there's no harm in going after such a thing to-day,"[25] says he. To him Homer was a great writer, though what his writing was about he did not know. A more simple and natural man it would be hard to find. Vice and disease, which cast such a sombre moral hue over the world, seemed to have hardly any existence for him. He was about twenty-eight years old,[26] and had left Canada and his father's house a dozen years before to work in the States, and earn money to buy a farm with at last, perhaps in his native country. He was cast in the coarsest mould; a stout but sluggish body, yet gracefully carried, with a thick sunburnt neck, dark bushy hair, and dull sleepy blue eyes, which were occasionally lit up with expression. He wore a flat gray cloth cap, a dingy wool-colored greatcoat, and cowhide boots. He was a great consumer of meat, usually carrying his dinner to his work a couple of miles past my house,—for he chopped all summer,—in a tin pail; cold meats, often cold woodchucks, and coffee in a stone bottle which dangled by a string from his belt; and sometimes he offered me a drink. He came along early, crossing my bean-field, though without anxiety or haste to get to his work, such as Yankees exhibit. He wasn't a-going to hurt himself. He didn't care if he only earned his board. Frequently he would leave his dinner in the bushes, when his dog had caught a woodchuck by the way, and go back a mile and a half to dress it and leave it in the cellar of the house where he boarded, after deliberating first for half an hour whether he could not sink it in the pond safely till nightfall,—loving to dwell long upon these themes. He would say, as he went by in the morning, "How thick the pigeons are! If working every day were not my trade, I could get all the meat I should want by hunting,—pigeons, woodchucks, rabbits, partridges,—by gosh! I could get all I should want for a week in one day."

He was a skilful chopper, and indulged in some flourishes and ornaments in his art. He cut his trees level and close to the ground, that the sprouts which came up afterward might be more vigorous and a sled might slide over the stumps; and instead of leaving a whole tree to support his corded wood, he would pare it away to a slender stake or splinter which you could break off with your hand at last.

He interested me because he was so quiet and solitary and so happy withal; a well of good humor and contentment which overflowed at his eyes. His mirth was without alloy. Sometimes I saw him at his work in the woods, felling trees, and he would greet me with a laugh of inexpressible satisfaction, and a salutation in Canadian French, though he spoke English as well. When I approached him he would suspend his work, and with half-suppressed mirth lie along the trunk of a pine which he had felled, and, peeling off the inner bark, roll it up into a ball and chew it while he laughed and talked. Such an exuberance of animal spirits had he that he sometimes tumbled down and rolled on the ground with laughter at any thing which made him think and tickled him. Looking round upon the trees he would exclaim,—"By George! I can enjoy myself well enough here chopping; I want no better sport." Sometimes, when at leisure, he amused himself all day in the woods with a pocket pistol, firing salutes to himself at regular intervals as he walked. In the winter he had a fire by which at noon he warmed his coffee in a kettle; and as he sat on a log to eat his dinner the chicadees would sometimes come round and alight on his arm and peck at the potato in his fingers; and he said that he "liked to have the little *fellers* about him."

In him the animal man chiefly was developed. In physical endurance and contentment he was cousin to the pine and the rock. I asked him once if he was not sometimes tired at night, after working all day; and he answered, with a sincere and serious look, "Gorrappit, I never was tired in my life." But the intellectual and what is called spiritual man in him were slumbering as in an infant. He had been instructed only in that innocent and ineffectual way in which the Catholic priests teach the aborigines, by which the pupil is never educated to the degree of consciousness, but only to the degree of trust and reverence, and a child is not made a man, but kept a child. When Nature made him, she gave him a strong body and contentment for his portion, and propped him on every side with reverence and reliance, that he might live out his threescore years and ten a child. He was so genuine and unsophisticated that no introduction would serve to introduce him, more than if you introduced a woodchuck to your neighbor. He had got to find him out as you did. He would not play any part. Men paid him wages for work, and so helped to feed and clothe him; but he never exchanged opinions with them. He was so simply and naturally humble — if he can be called humble who never aspires — that humility was no distinct quality in him, nor could he conceive of it. Wiser men were demigods to him. If you told him that such a one was coming, he did as if he thought that any thing so grand would expect nothing of himself, but take all the responsibility on itself, and let him be forgotten still. He never heard the sound of praise. He particularly reverenced the writer and the preacher. Their performances were miracles. When I told him that I wrote considerably, he thought for a long time that it was merely the handwriting which I meant, for he could write a remarkably good hand himself. I sometimes found the name of his native parish handsomely written in the snow by the highway, with the proper French accent, and knew that he had passed. I asked him if he ever wished to write his thoughts. He said that he had read and written letters for those who could not, but he never tried to write thoughts,—no, he could not, he could not tell what to put first, it would kill him, and then there was spelling to be attended to at the same time!

I heard that a distinguished wise man and reformer[27] asked him if he did not want the world to be changed; but he answered with a chuckle of surprise in his Canadian accent, not knowing that the question had ever been entertained before, "No, I like it well enough." It would have suggested many things to a philosopher to have dealings with him. To a stranger he appeared to know nothing of things in general; yet I sometimes saw in him a man whom I had not seen before, and I did not know whether he was as wise as Shakspeare or as simply ignorant as a child, whether to suspect him of a fine poetic consciousness or of stupidity. A townsman[28] told me that when he met him sauntering through the village in his small close-fitting cap, and whistling to himself, he reminded him of a prince in disguise.

His only books were an almanac and an arithmetic, in which last he was considerably expert. The former was a sort of cyclopædia to him, which he supposed to contain an abstract of human knowledge, as indeed it does to a considerable extent. I loved to sound him on the various reforms of the day, and he never failed to look at them in the most simple and practical light. He had never heard of such things before. Could he do without factories? I asked. He had worn the home-made Vermont gray,[29] he said, and that was good. Could he dispense with tea and coffee? Did this country afford any beverage beside water? He had soaked hemlock leaves[30] in water and drank it, and thought that was better than water in warm weather. When I asked him if he could do without money, he showed the convenience of money in such a way as to suggest and coincide with the most philosophical accounts of the origin of this institution, and the

27 Possible allusion to Emerson, who had hired Therien to do sawing, splitting, and stacking of wood.

28 Possible allusion to Emerson, who in a journal entry in 1851 commented on Therien's being "very inconspicuous in Beacon street."

29 Homespun cloth.

30 The needles of the hemlock spruce (*Tsuga canadensis*), not the leaves of the poisonous hemlock plant (*Conium macultatum* or *Cicuta macaluta*). Thoreau wrote in "Walking," "We require an infusion of hemlock spruce or arbor-vitæ in our tea" [W 5:225].

31 Latin: money, derived from *pecus* (cattle) as acknowledged in the next sentence.

32 Allusion to Plato's *Politicus* 266: "Man is the plume-less genus of bipeds, birds are the plumed."

33 Diogenes Laertius (ca. 3d century) plucked a fowl and brought it into the lecture room, exclaiming: "Here is Plato's man."

34 This conversation took place on 15 November 1851.

35 This conversation took place on 28 December 1853.

very derivation of the word *pecunia*.[31] If an ox were his property, and he wished to get needles and thread at the store, he thought it would be inconvenient and impossible soon to go on mortgaging some portion of the creature each time to that amount. He could defend many institutions better than any philosopher, because, in describing them as they concerned him, he gave the true reason for their prevalence, and speculation had not suggested to him any other. At another time, hearing Plato's definition of a man,—a biped without feathers,[32]—and that one[33] exhibited a cock plucked and called it Plato's man, he thought it an important difference that the *knees* bent the wrong way. He would sometimes exclaim, "How I love to talk! By George, I could talk all day!" I asked him once,[34] when I had not seen him for many months, if he had got a new idea this summer. "Good Lord," said he, "a man that has to work as I do, if he does not forget the ideas he has had, he will do well. May be the man you hoe with is inclined to race; then, by gorry, your mind must be there; you think of weeds." He would sometimes ask me first on such occasions, if I had made any improvement. One winter day[35] I asked him if he was always satisfied with himself, wishing to suggest a substitute within him for the priest without, and some higher motive for living. "Satisfied!" said he; "some men are satisfied with one thing, and some with another. One man, perhaps, if he has got enough, will be satisfied to sit all day with his back to the fire and his belly to the table, by George!" Yet I never, by any manœuvring, could get him to take the spiritual view of things; the highest that he appeared to conceive of was a simple expediency, such as you might expect an animal to appreciate; and this, practically, is true of most men. If I suggested any improvement in his mode of life, he merely answered, without expressing any regret, that it was too late. Yet he thoroughly believed in honesty and the like virtues.

There was a certain positive originality, however slight, to be detected in him, and I occasionally observed that he was thinking for himself and expressing his own opinion, a phenomenon so rare that I would any day walk ten miles to observe it, and it amounted to the re-origination of many of the institutions of society. Though he hesitated, and perhaps failed to express himself distinctly, he always had a presentable thought behind. Yet his thinking was so primitive and immersed in his animal life, that, though more promising than a merely learned man's, it rarely ripened to any thing which can be reported. He suggested that there might be men of genius in the lowest grades of life, however permanently humble and illiterate, who take their own view always, or do not pretend to see at all; who are as bottomless even as Walden Pond was thought to be, though they may be dark and muddy.

Many a traveller came out of his way to see me and the inside of my house, and, as an excuse for calling, asked for a glass of water. I told them that I drank at the pond, and pointed thither, offering to lend them a dipper.[36] Far off as I lived, I was not exempted from the annual visitation which occurs, methinks, about the first of April, when every body is on the move; and I had my share of good luck, though there were some curious specimens among my visitors. Half-witted men from the almshouse and elsewhere came to see me; but I endeavored to make them exercise all the wit they had, and make their confessions to me; in such cases making wit the theme of our conversation; and so was compensated. Indeed, I found some of them to be wiser than the so called *overseers* of the poor and selectmen of the town,[37] and thought it was time that the tables were turned. With respect to wit, I learned that there was not much difference between the half and the whole. One day, in particular, an inoffensive, simple-minded pauper,[38] whom with others I had often

36 In his journal of 17 January 1852, Thoreau reported: "One day two young women—a Sunday—stopped at the door of my hut and asked for some water. I answered that I had no cold water but I would lend them a dipper. They never returned the dipper, and I had a right to suppose that they came to steal. They were a disgrace to their sex and to humanity" [J 3:198].

37 Lemuel Shattuck wrote in *A History of the Town of Concord* that the selectmen "have acted as *Overseers of the Poor* and as *Assessors*, excepting from 1714 to 1725, when 5 overseers of the poor were chosen."

38 In the journal entry of 17 January 1852, Thoreau said the pauper was from the almshouse [J 3:198]. Ellery Channing suggested this might be a David Flint.

39 Allusion to Matthew 23:12: "Whosoever shall exalt himself shall be abased; and he that shall humble himself shall be exalted."

40 "Hospitalality" is a Thoreauism, relating it to hospital as an establishment for dispensing hospitality or care, as in a foundling hospital or the names of such institutions as Greenwich Hospital for retired seamen and Christ's Hospital (London) for the free education of boys.

41 Edward Emerson once asked Ann Bigelow (1813–1898), a close friend of the Thoreaus who was active in the Underground Railroad in Concord, about the use of the Walden house in helping runaway slaves to freedom, and wrote the following notes from their conversation:

> While Henry Thoreau was in the woods the slaves sometimes were brought to him there, but obviously there was no possible concealment in his house . . . so he would look after them by day, and at night-fall — no street lamps in Concord in those days — get them to his Mother's or other house of hiding. He was always ready to help with service and didn't count risk, and also, although he had little money always gave or advanced money to a slave who needed it. Sometimes this was repaid from the fund. It was no part of his *plan* in making the Walden hermitage to make there a refuge for fugitives. That was only incidental.

Although Thoreau referred to fugitive slaves being at his Walden house, and Bigelow concurred, Alfred Hosmer (1851–1903) wrote: "His hut was *not* used as a means of assisting escaping negroes, though he himself had helped many to escape. As one of the leading anti-slavery party here says, 'Why, we should not have thought of using his hut for a station, for it was too open, too readily searched, and we had houses in the village that were far better places of concealment, though Henry did help us in other ways.'" One of the houses in the village was that of Thoreau's par-

seen used as fencing stuff, standing or sitting on a bushel in the fields to keep cattle and himself from straying, visited me, and expressed a wish to live as I did. He told me, with the utmost simplicity and truth, quite superior, or rather *inferior,* to any thing that is called humility, that he was "deficient in intellect." These were his words. The Lord had made him so, yet he supposed the Lord cared as much for him as for another. "I have always been so," said he, "from my childhood; I never had much mind; I was not like other children; I am weak in the head. It was the Lord's will, I suppose." And there he was to prove the truth of his words. He was a metaphysical puzzle to me. I have rarely met a fellow-man on such promising ground, — it was so simple and sincere and so true all that he said. And, true enough, in proportion as he appeared to humble himself was he exalted.[39] I did not know at first but it was the result of a wise policy. It seemed that from such a basis of truth and frankness as the poor weakheaded pauper had laid, our intercourse might go forward to something better than the intercourse of sages.

I had some guests from those not reckoned commonly among the town's poor, but who should be; who are among the world's poor, at any rate; guests who appeal, not to your hospitality, but to your *hospitalality;*[40] who earnestly wish to be helped, and preface their appeal with the information that they are resolved, for one thing, never to help themselves. I require of a visitor that he be not actually starving, though he may have the very best appetite in the world, however he got it. Objects of charity are not guests. Men who did not know when their visit had terminated, though I went about my business again, answering them from greater and greater remoteness. Men of almost every degree of wit called on me in the migrating season. Some who had more wits than they knew what to do with; runaway slaves[41] with plantation manners, who listened from time to time, like the fox in the fable,[42] as if they heard the hounds a-baying on their track, and looked at me beseechingly, as much as to say, —

"O Christian, will you send me back?"[43]

One real runaway slave, among the rest, whom I helped to forward toward the northstar.[44] Men of one idea, like a hen with one chicken,[45] and that a duckling; men of a thousand ideas, and unkempt heads, like those hens which are made to take charge of a hundred chickens, all in pursuit of one bug, a score of them lost in every morning's dew, — and become frizzled and mangy in consequence; men of ideas instead of legs, a sort of intellectual centipede that made you crawl all over. One man proposed a book in which visitors should write their names, as at the White Mountains;[46] but, alas! I have too good a memory to make that necessary.

I could not but notice some of the peculiarities of my visitors. Girls and boys and young women generally seemed glad to be in the woods.[47] They looked in the pond and at the flowers, and improved their time. Men of business, even farmers, thought only of solitude and employment, and of the great distance at which I dwelt from something or other; and though they said that they loved a ramble in the woods occasionally, it was obvious that they did not. Restless committed men, whose time was all taken up in getting a living or keeping it; ministers who spoke of God as if they enjoyed a monopoly of the subject, who could not bear all kinds of opinions; doctors, lawyers, uneasy housekeepers who pried into my cupboard and bed when I was out, — how came Mrs. —— to know that my sheets were not as clean as hers? — young men who had ceased to be young, and had concluded that it was safest to follow the beaten track of the professions, — all these generally said that it was not possible to do so much good in my position. Ay! there was the rub.[48]

ents, which Moncure Daniel Conway (1832–1907) described visiting in 1853 in his *Autobiography:*

> He invited me to come next day for a walk, but in the morning I found the Thoreaus agitated by the arrival of a coloured fugitive slave from Virginia, who had come to their door at daybreak. Thoreau took me to a room where his excellent sister, Sophia, was ministering to the fugitive. . . . I observed the tender and lowly devotion of Thoreau to the African. He now and then drew near to the trembling man, and with a cheerful voice bade him feel at home, and have no fear that any power should again wrong him. That whole day he mounted guard over the fugitive, for it was slave-hunting time. But the guard had no weapon, and probably there was no such thing in the house.

42 There are several fables involving a pursued fox, including many in Aesop and Jean de la Fontaine, and retellings of the medieval French beast epic, *Le Roman de Renart* (ca. 1175–1250). It is unknown to which Thoreau may have been alluding.

43 Refrain ending each verse of Elizur Wright's (1804?–1885) "The Fugitive Slave to the Christian."

44 Ann Bigelow told Edward Emerson in 1892 that when fugitive slaves left on the railroad from Concord, "Henry Thoreau went as escort probably more often than any other man. He would look after the tickets, &c, but in the cars did not sit with the fugitive so as not to attract attention to the companionship."

45 Phrase found as early as the 18th century in Francis Grose's (1731–1791) *Lexicon Balatronicum: A Dictionary of Buckish Slang, University Wit, and Pickpocket Eloquence* and meaning overparticular and fussy. A hen with one chick is always pursuing one thing and never leaving it alone.

46 A register for visiting tourists was kept at the top of Mount Washington in the White Mountains as early as 1824. Thoreau wrote in his journal of 22 January 1852, from which this passage originated: "As if it were of any use, when a man failed to make any impression on you, for him to leave his name" [J 3:215].

47 Frederick Llewellyn Hovey Willis (1830–1914) described a visit to Thoreau with the Alcott family in July 1847 in his *Alcott Memoirs*:

> He was talking to Mr. Alcott of the wild flowers in Walden woods when, suddenly stopping, he said: "Keep very still and I will show you my family." Stepping quickly outside the cabin door, he gave a low and curious whistle; immediately a woodchuck came running towards him from a nearby burrow. With varying note, yet still low and strange, a pair of gray squirrels were summoned and approached him fearlessly. With still another note several birds, including two crows, flew towards him, one of the crows nestling upon his shoulder. I remember it was the crow resting close to his head that made the most vivid impression upon me, knowing how fearful of man this bird is. He fed them all from his hand, taking food from his pocket, and petted them gently before our delighted gaze; and then dismissed them by different whistling, always strange and low and short, each little wild thing departing instantly at hearing its special signal.
>
> Then he took us five children upon the Pond in his boat, ceasing his oars after a little distance from the shore and playing the flute he had brought with him, its music echoing over the still and beautifully clear water. He suddenly laid the flute down and told us stories of the Indians that "long ago" had lived about Walden and Concord; delighting us with simple, clear explanations of the wonders of Walden woods. Again he interrupted himself suddenly, speaking of the various kinds of lilies growing about Walden and calling the wood lilies, stately wild things. It was pond lily time and from the boat we gathered quantities of their pure white flowers and buds; upon our

The old and infirm and the timid, of whatever age or sex, thought most of sickness, and sudden accident and death; to them life seemed full of danger,—what danger is there if you don't think of any?—and they thought that a prudent man would carefully select the safest position, where Dr. B.[49] might be on hand at a moment's warning. To them the village was literally a *com-munity*,[50] a league for mutual defence, and you would suppose that they would not go a-huckleberrying without a medicine chest. The amount of it is, if a man is alive, there is always *danger* that he may die, though the danger must be allowed to be less in proportion as he is dead-and-alive to begin with. A man sits as many risks as he runs. Finally, there were the self-styled reformers, the greatest bores of all,[51] who thought that I was forever singing,—

> This is the house that I built;
> This is the man that lives in the house that I
> built;

but they did not know that the third line was,—

> These are the folks that worry the man
> That lives in the house that I built.[52]

I did not fear the hen-harriers,[53] for I kept no chickens; but I feared the men-harriers rather.

I had more cheering visitors than the last. Children come a-berrying, railroad men taking a Sunday morning walk in clean shirts, fishermen and hunters, poets and philosophers, in short, all honest pilgrims, who came out to the woods for freedom's sake, and really left the village behind, I was ready to greet with,—"Welcome, Englishmen! welcome, Englishmen!"[54] for I had had communication with that race.

return to the shore he helped us gather other flowers and laden with many sweet blossoms, we wended our way homewards rejoicingly.

48 Allusion to Shakespeare's *Hamlet* 3.1.67: "Ay, there's the rub."

49 Probable reference to Dr. Josiah Bartlett (1796–1878), a practicing physician in Concord for 57 years who had attended Thoreau's brother John during his final days.

50 Thoreau's splitting of the word is for emphasis, as elsewhere, stressing the derivation from the Latin *munio*, meaning to defend or fortify, prefixed by *com*, meaning together.

51 Thoreau met many such reformers at Emerson's house and elsewhere. He described one such meeting in a journal entry of 17 June 1853:

Here have been three ultra-reformers, lecturers on Slavery, Temperance, the Church, etc., in and about our house & Mrs. Brooks's the last three or four days,—A. D. Foss, once a Baptist minister in Hopkinton, N.H.; Loring Moody, a sort of travelling pattern-working chaplain; and H. C. Wright, who shocks all the old women with his infidel writings. Though Foss was a stranger to the others, you would have thought them old and familiar cronies. (They happened here together by accident.) They addressed each other constantly by their Christian names, and rubbed you continually with the greasy cheeks of their kindness. They would not keep their distance, but cuddle up and lie spoon-fashion with you, no matter how hot the weather nor how narrow the bed,— chiefly ——. I was awfully pestered with his benignity; feared I should get greased all over with it past restoration; tried to keep some starch in my clothes. He wrote a book called "A Kiss for a Blow," and he behaved as if there were no alternative between these, or as if I had given him a blow. I would have preferred the blow, but he was bent on giving me the

kiss, when there was neither quarrel nor agreement between us. . . . —— addressed me as "Henry" within one minute from the time I first laid eyes on him, and when I spoke, he said with drawling, sultry sympathy, "Henry, I know all you would say; I understand you perfectly; you need not explain anything to me;" and to another, "I am going to dive into Henry's inmost depths." I said, "I trust you will not strike your head against the bottom." . . . One of the most attractive things about the flowers is their beautiful reserve. The truly beautiful and noble puts its lover, as it were, at an infinite distance, while it attracts him more strongly than ever. [J 5:263–65]

52 Parody of the nursery rhyme "This is the house that Jack built."

53 English name for the Northern harrier (*Circus cyaneus*), also known in America as the marsh hawk, which seldom disturbs poultry, preferring instead small mammals, amphibians, reptiles, and birds, including the hen grouse, from which it may have received its name.

54 The greeting of Samoset (d. 1653) to the Pilgrims.

1 Thoreau planted 2¹/₂ acres of beans in rows 15 rods long and 3 feet apart, approximately 146 rows, which adds up to a total length just under seven miles. In his journal for 3 June 1851, Thoreau mentioned the common bean, *Phaseolus vulgaris*, which "includes several kinds of bush beans, of which those I raised were one" [J 2:227]. In this chapter he identified them more specifically as the "common small white bush bean." Edward Emerson said the bean field was located "in the square between the Lincoln Road and the wood roads"—now the corner of Routes 2 and 126—east of Thoreau's house [Edward Emerson to Harry McGraw, 22 October 1920].

2 Thoreau mentioned the beans in his journal of 7 July 1845, so he must have planted some in the spring before taking up residence at Walden, although he continued to plant into the summer.

3 "Small Herculean" was one of the oxymoronic literary devices Emerson complained of when he wrote in "Thoreau": "The habit of a realist to find things the reverse of their appearance inclined him to put every statement in a paradox. A certain habit of antagonism defaced his earlier writings,—a trick of rhetoric not quite outgrown in his later, of substituting for the obvious word and thought its diametrical opposite. He praised wild mountains and winter forests for their domestic air, in snow and ice he would find sultriness, and commended the wilderness for resembling Rome and Paris." Thoreau listed this device as a fault in his journal: "Paradoxes,—saying just the opposite,—a style which may be imitated" [J 7:7].

4 In Greek mythology, a giant who became stronger whenever he touched the earth, his mother. He was defeated by Hercules who, raising him so that he no longer made contact with the earth, squeezed him to death.

5 Plant of the rose family.

6 Edible seeds of leguminous plants, such as beans, chickpeas, lentils, etc., with a pun on pulse as drive.

7 Echo of Shakespeare's *Hamlet* 2.2.536: "What's Hecuba to him, or he to Hecuba . . . ?"

The Bean-Field

Meanwhile my beans, the length of whose rows, added together, was seven miles already planted,[1] were impatient to be hoed, for the earliest had grown considerably before the latest were in the ground;[2] indeed they were not easily to be put off. What was the meaning of this so steady and self-respecting, this small Herculean[3] labor, I knew not. I came to love my rows, my beans, though so many more than I wanted. They attached me to the earth, and so I got strength like Antæus.[4] But why should I raise them? Only Heaven knows. This was my curious labor all summer,—to make this portion of the earth's surface, which had yielded only cinquefoil,[5] blackberries, johnswort, and the like, before, sweet wild fruits and pleasant flowers, produce instead this pulse.[6] What shall I learn of beans or beans of me?[7] I cherish them, I hoe them, early and late I have an eye to them; and this is my day's work. It is a fine broad leaf[8] to look on. My auxiliaries are the dews and rains which water this dry soil, and what fertility is in the soil itself, which for the most part is lean and effete. My enemies are worms, cool days, and most of all woodchucks. The last have nibbled for me a quarter of an acre clean. But what right had I to oust johnswort and the rest, and break up their ancient herb garden? Soon, however, the remaining beans will be too tough for them, and go forward to meet new foes.

WALDEN

When I was four years old,[9] as I well remember, I was brought from Boston to this my native town,[10] through these very woods and this field, to the pond. It is one of the oldest scenes stamped on my memory. And now to-night my flute[11] has waked the echoes over that very water. The pines still stand here older than I; or, if some have fallen, I have cooked my supper with their stumps, and a new growth is rising all around, preparing another aspect for new infant eyes. Almost the same johnswort springs from the same perennial root in this pasture, and even I have at length helped to clothe that fabulous landscape of my infant dreams, and one of the results of my presence and influence is seen in these bean leaves, corn blades, and potato vines.

I planted about two acres and a half of upland; and as it was only about fifteen years since the land was cleared, and I myself had got out two or three cords of stumps, I did not give it any manure; but in the course of the summer it appeared by the arrow-heads[12] which I turned up in hoeing, that an extinct nation had anciently dwelt here and planted corn and beans ere white men came to clear the land, and so, to some extent, had exhausted the soil for this very crop.

Before yet any woodchuck or squirrel had run across the road, or the sun had got above the shrub-oaks, while all the dew was on, though the farmers warned me against it,—I would advise you to do all your work if possible while the dew is on,[13]—I began to level the ranks of haughty weeds in my bean-field and throw dust upon their heads.[14] Early in the morning I worked barefooted, dabbling like a plastic artist[15] in the dewy and crumbling sand, but later in the day the sun blistered my feet. There the sun lighted me to hoe beans, pacing slowly backward and forward over that yellow gravelly upland, between the long green rows, fifteen rods, the one end terminating in a shrub-oak copse where I could rest in the shade, the

8 Pun on the leaf (or page) that, as a writer, was also his day's work.

9 In an August 1845 journal entry, Thoreau noted that it was "Twenty-three years since, when I was 5 years old" that he first visited Walden Pond [J 1:380].

10 Thoreau was born in Concord on 12 July 1817. His family lived at 4 Pinckney Street in Boston from September 1821 to March 1823, following a brief stay in Boston's South End.

11 Thoreau, his brother, and his father played the flute. Franklin Sanborn wrote in *The Personality of Thoreau*, "Henry's favorite instrument was the flute, which his father had played before him; he was accompanied on the piano sometimes by one of his sisters; but the best place for hearing its pastoral note was on some hillside, or the edge of the wood or stream; and Emerson took pleasure in its strains upon those excursions to the Cliffs, or Walden, which were so frequent in the youth of the musician." Thoreau often would bring his flute to entertain the Alcott girls. After his death, Louisa

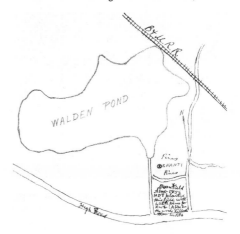

Edward Emerson's map, 1920. His note at lower right showing the location of Thoreau's bean field reads: "Bean Field. About 1856 HDT planted this field with white pines for RWE. A fire in the woods killed them in 1896."

May Alcott (1832–1888) reminisced about those days and published a poem, "Thoreau's Flute," in the September 1863 *Atlantic Monthly*.

12 Thoreau had accumulated a collection of approximately 900 Native American artifacts by the time he died. Hawthorne, in *Mosses from an Old Manse*, described Thoreau's "strange faculty of finding what the Indians have left behind them." Ellery Channing also reported, "In a walk, his companion, a citizen, said, 'I do not see where you find your Indian arrowheads.' Stooping to the ground, Henry picked one up, and presented it to him, crying, 'Here is one.'" Thoreau related a similar incident in his journal of 29 October 1837, in which, walking with his brother John, and extravagantly and humorously eulogizing the former inhabitants, Thoreau pointed to a spot, exclaiming that there was Tahatawan's arrowhead: "We instantly proceeded to sit down on the spot I had pointed to, and I, to carry out the joke, to lay bare an ordinary stone, which my whim had selected, when lo! the first I laid hands on, the grubbing stone that was to be, proved a most perfect arrowhead, as sharp as if just from the hands of the Indian fabricator!!!" [J 1:7–8]. Based on careful observation, Thoreau knew that autumn and spring offered the best chance of finding them: "The season for them began some time ago, as soon as farmers had sown their winter rye, but the spring, after the melting of the snow, is still better" [J 2:96].

13 On 16 July 1845 Thoreau discussed this issue with Alek Therien: "Therien said this morning (July 16th, Wednesday), 'If those beans were mine, I should n't like to hoe them till the dew was off.' He was going to his woodchopping. 'Ah!' said I, 'that is one of the notions the farmers have got, but I don't believe it'" [J 1:367].

14 Allusion to the symbol of mourning found in the Bible, as in Job 2:12 ("And sprinkled dust upon their heads towards heaven") and Lamentations 2:10 ("They have cast up dust upon their heads").

15 One who works in the three-dimensional arts, such as sculpture and ceramics.

other in a blackberry field where the green berries deepened their tints by the time I had made another bout. Removing the weeds, putting fresh soil about the bean stems, and encouraging this weed[16] which I had sown, making the yellow soil express its summer thought in bean leaves and blossoms rather than in wormwood[17] and piper[18] and millet grass,[19] making the earth say beans instead of grass,—this was my daily work. As I had little aid from horses or cattle, or hired men or boys, or improved implements of husbandry, I was much slower, and became much more intimate with my beans than usual. But labor of the hands, even when pursued to the verge of drudgery, is perhaps never the worst form of idleness. It has a constant and imperishable moral, and to the scholar it yields a classic result. A very *agricola laboriosus*[20] was I to travellers bound westward through Lincoln and Wayland[21] to nobody knows where; they sitting at their ease in gigs,[22] with elbows on knees, and reins loosely hanging in festoons; I the home-staying, laborious native of the soil. But soon my homestead was out of their sight and thought. It was the only open and cultivated field for a great distance on either side of the road; so they made the most of it; and sometimes the man in the field heard more of travellers' gossip and comment than was meant for his ear: "Beans so late! peas so late!"—for I continued to plant when others had begun to hoe,—the ministerial husbandman[23] had not suspected it. "Corn, my boy, for fodder; corn for fodder." "Does he *live* there?" asks the black bonnet of the gray coat; and the hard-featured farmer reins up his grateful dobbin[24] to inquire what you are doing where he sees no manure in the furrow, and recommends a little chip dirt,[25] or any little waste stuff, or it may be ashes or plaster. But here were two acres and a half of furrows, and only a hoe for cart and two hands to draw it,—there being an aversion to other carts and horses,—and chip dirt far away. Fellow-travellers as they rattled by compared it aloud with the fields which they had passed, so that I came to know how I stood in the agricultural world. This was one field not in Mr. Colman's report. And, by the way, who estimates the value of the crop which Nature yields in the still wilder fields unimproved by man? The crop of *English* hay[26] is carefully weighed, the moisture calculated, the silicates and the potash; but in all dells and pond holes in the woods and pastures and swamps grows a rich and various crop only unreaped by man. Mine was, as it were, the connecting link between wild and cultivated fields; as some states are civilized, and others half-civilized, and others savage or barbarous, so my field was, though not in a bad sense, a half-cultivated field. They were beans cheerfully returning to their wild and primitive state that I cultivated, and my hoe played the *Rans des Vaches*[27] for them.

Near at hand, upon the topmost spray of a birch, sings the brown-thrasher—or red mavis, as some love to call him—all the morning, glad of your society, that would find out another farmer's field if yours were not here. While you are planting the seed, he cries,—"Drop it, drop it,—cover it up, cover it up,—pull it up, pull it up, pull it up." But this was not corn, and so it was safe from such enemies as he. You may wonder what his rigmarole, his amateur Paganini[28] performances on one string or on twenty, have to do with your planting, and yet prefer it to leached ashes[29] or plaster. It was a cheap sort of top dressing[30] in which I had entire faith.

As I drew a still fresher soil about the rows with my hoe, I disturbed the ashes of unchronicled nations who in primeval years lived under these heavens, and their small implements of war and hunting were brought to the light of this modern day. They lay mingled with other natural stones, some of which bore the marks of having been burned by Indian fires, and some by the sun, and also bits

16 Thoreau here questioned the common use of the word "weed," although he later defined it in his journal as "uncultivated herbaceous plants which do not bear handsome flowers" [J 9:59].
17 Roman wormwood or ragweed (*Ambrosia artemisioefolia*).
18 Piper grass: quack grass (*Agropyron repens*) and slender wheat grass (*Agropyron trachycaulum*).
19 In his journal of 25 August 1858 Thoreau wrote: "*Setaria glauca,* glaucous panic grass, bottle grass, sometimes called fox-tail, tawny yellow, going to seed, Mrs. Hoar's garden. *Setaria viridis*, green bottle grass, in garden, some going to seed, but later than the last. These two I have called millet grass" [J 11:124].
20 Latin: hard-working farmer.
21 The road past Walden Pond, now Route 126, leads from Concord to Lincoln and Wayland.
22 Light, two-wheeled, one-horse carriages.
23 Rev. Henry Colman (1785–1849), who published *Report on the Agriculture of Massachusetts,* a series of four agricultural surveys, from 1838 to 1841.
24 Horse, especially a working farm horse, although sometimes used to describe a quiet plodding horse.
25 Chips or sawdust from an area where wood has been chopped or sawed.
26 Various imported crops, as timothy, redtop, and clover, cultivated in America as feed, and called English hay to distinguish it from the less valuable meadow hay harvested for bedding.
27 Swiss pastoral song for calling cows, more commonly spelled *Ranz des Vaches,* with a probable reference specifically to Friedrich von Schiller's (1759–1805) "Ranz des Vaches" from his 1804 *Wilhelm Tell,* as found in Charles Timothy Brooks (1813–1883), *Songs and Ballads: Translated from Uhland, Korner, and Other German Lyric Poets* (1842), published as volume 14 of George Ripley's *Specimens of Foreign Standard Literature.*
28 Niccolò Paganini (1782–1840), Italian violinist and composer noted for his ability to play entire passages on a single string.

29 Dampened ashes, used as topsoil.

30 A covering of fertilizer spread on soil without being plowed under, often applied after the crop is established.

31 Thoreau found music in the sounds around him. As he wrote in his journal: "Went into the woods by Holden Swamp and sat down to hear the wind roar amid the tree-tops. . . . It is a music that wears better than the opera, methinks. This reminds me how the telegraph-wire hummed coarsely in the tempest as we passed under it" [J 5:492]. "The commonest and cheapest sounds," Thoreau wrote in another journal entry, "as the barking of a dog, produce the same effect on fresh and healthy ears that the rarest music does. . . . It is better that these cheap sounds be music to us than that we have the rarest ears for music in any other sense. I have lain awake at night many a time to think of the barking of a dog which I had heard long before, bathing my being again in those waves of sound, as a frequenter of the opera might lie awake remembering the music he had heard" [J 10:227].

32 "One will lose no music by not attending the oratorios and operas" [J 2:379], Thoreau wrote in his journal in 1851. "My profession is . . . to attend all the oratorios, the operas in nature" [J 2:472].

33 *Chordediles minor:* a member of the goatsucker family, neither a hawk nor nocturnal, and a relative of the whippoorwill. During the breeding season, the male nighthawk makes a booming sound with its wings as it swerves upward following a dive.

34 Epithet for the sun used in Shakespeare's *Titus Andronicus* and *The Comedy of Errors*.

35 Common name for any large hawk, but especially the red-tailed hawk (*Buteo jamaicensis*).

36 Embodiment.

37 Concord celebrated two gala days, the anniversary of the battle there on 19 April 1775 and Independence Day on the Fourth of July.

of pottery and glass brought hither by the recent cultivators of the soil. When my hoe tinkled against the stones, that music[31] echoed to the woods and the sky, and was an accompaniment to my labor which yielded an instant and immeasurable crop. It was no longer beans that I hoed, nor I that hoed beans; and I remembered with as much pity as pride, if I remembered at all, my acquaintances who had gone to the city to attend the oratorios.[32] The night-hawk[33] circled overhead in the sunny afternoons — for I sometimes made a day of it — like a mote in the eye, or in heaven's eye,[34] falling from time to time with a swoop and a sound as if the heavens were rent, torn at last to very rags and tatters, and yet a seamless cope remained; small imps that fill the air and lay their eggs on the ground on bare sand or rocks on the tops of hills, where few have found them; graceful and slender like ripples caught up from the pond, as leaves are raised by the wind to float in the heavens; such kindredship is in Nature. The hawk is aerial brother of the wave which he sails over and surveys, those his perfect air-inflated wings answering to the elemental unfledged pinions of the sea. Or sometimes I watched a pair of hen-hawks[35] circling high in the sky, alternately soaring and descending, approaching and leaving one another, as if they were the imbodiment[36] of my own thoughts. Or I was attracted by the passage of wild pigeons from this wood to that, with a slight quivering winnowing sound and carrier haste; or from under a rotten stump my hoe turned up a sluggish portentous and outlandish spotted salamander, a trace of Egypt and the Nile, yet our contemporary. When I paused to lean on my hoe, these sounds and sights I heard and saw any where in the row, a part of the inexhaustible entertainment which the country offers.

On gala days[37] the town fires its great guns, which echo like popguns to these woods, and some waifs of martial music occasionally penetrate thus far. To me, away there in my bean-field at the other end of the town, the big guns sounded as if a puff ball[38] had burst; and when there was a military turnout of which I was ignorant, I have sometimes had a vague sense all the day of some sort of itching and disease in the horizon, as if some eruption would break out there soon, either scarlatina[39] or canker-rash,[40] until at length some more favorable puff of wind, making haste over the fields and up the Wayland road,[41] brought me information of the "trainers."[42] It seemed by the distant hum as if somebody's bees had swarmed, and that the neighbors, according to Virgil's advice, by a faint *tintinnabulum*[43] upon the most sonorous of their domestic utensils, were endeavoring to call them down into the hive again.[44] And when the sound died quite away, and the hum had ceased, and the most favorable breezes told no tale, I knew that they had got the last drone of them all safely into the Middlesex hive, and that now their minds were bent on the honey with which it was smeared.

I felt proud to know that the liberties of Massachusetts[45] and of our fatherland were in such safe keeping; and as I turned to my hoeing again I was filled with an inexpressible confidence, and pursued my labor cheerfully with a calm trust in the future.

When there were several bands of musicians, it sounded as if all the village was a vast bellows, and all the buildings expanded and collapsed alternately with a din. But sometimes it was a really noble and inspiring strain that reached these woods, and the trumpet that sings of fame, and I felt as if I could spit a Mexican with a good relish,[46]—for why should we always stand for trifles?—and looked round for a woodchuck or a skunk to exercise my chivalry upon. These martial strains seemed as far away as Palestine, and reminded me of a march of crusaders in the horizon, with a slight tantivy and tremulous motion of the elm-tree tops[47] which overhang the village. This was one of the *great* days; though the sky had from

38 Spore-bearing structure of fungi (order Lycoperdales) from which clouds of spores are emitted, with a hollow pop or report, when the ripe puffball is struck.

39 Scarlet fever, characterized by a scarlet skin eruption and high fever. Emerson's five-year-old son Waldo died of it in 1842.

40 A form of scarlet fever characterized by ulcerated or putrid sore throat.

41 Road between Concord and Wayland, a small town to the south.

42 Members of a "train band" training for service in the militia.

43 A ringing or tinkling of bells. The closest approximation to *tintinnabulum* in Virgil is the word *tinnitusque* (tinkling cymbals) in *Georgics* 4.64.

44 It was a folk belief that swarming bees could be called back to their hive by banging on pots and pans. Thomas Wildman's (d. 1781) *A Treatise on the Management of Bees* contained a brief description of this technique: "Whenever the bees of a swarm fly too high, they are made to descend lower, and disposed to settle, by throwing among them handfuls of sand or dust; probably the bees mistake this for rain. It is usual at the same time to beat on a kettle or frying-pan; perhaps from its being observed that the noise of thunder prompts such bees as are in the fields to return home." This may also be an allusion to the tinkling cymbals in Virgil's *Georgics*.

45 Allusion to *The Book of the General Lawes and Libertyes Concerning the Inhabitants of the Massachusetts*, first published in 1648.

46 The Mexican-American War (1846–48) began during Thoreau's stay at Walden. The pun here carries the idea of warfare, of spitting or impaling the enemy with enthusiasm, and also the idea of cooking, turning on a spit before a fire, with a good condiment; similar to "I could sometimes eat a fried rat with a good relish" in "House-Warming."

47 Although they have since been decimated by Dutch elm disease, during Thoreau's day elm trees lined most of Concord's streets.

my clearing only the same everlastingly great look that it wears daily, and I saw no difference in it.

It was a singular experience that long acquaintance which I cultivated with beans, what with planting, and hoeing, and harvesting, and threshing, and picking over, and selling them,—the last was the hardest of all,—I might add eating, for I did taste. I was determined to know beans.[48] When they were growing, I used to hoe from five o'clock in the morning till noon, and commonly spent the rest of the day about other affairs. Consider the intimate and curious acquaintance one makes with various kinds of weeds,—it will bear some iteration in the account, for there was no little iteration in the labor,—disturbing their delicate organizations so ruthlessly, and making such invidious distinctions with his hoe, levelling whole ranks of one species, and sedulously cultivating another. That's Roman wormwood,—that's pigweed,—that's sorrel,—that's piper-grass,—have at him, chop him up, turn his roots upward to the sun, don't let him have a fibre in the shade, if you do he'll turn himself t'other side up and be as green as a leek in two days. A long war, not with cranes, but with weeds, those Trojans who had sun and rain and dews on their side. Daily the beans saw me come to their rescue armed with a hoe, and thin the ranks of their enemies, filling up the trenches with weedy dead. Many a lusty crest-waving Hector,[49] that towered a whole foot above his crowding comrades, fell before my weapon and rolled in the dust.[50]

Those summer days which some of my contemporaries devoted to the fine arts in Boston or Rome, and others to contemplation in India, and others to trade in London or New York, I thus, with the other farmers of New England, devoted to husbandry. Not that I wanted beans to eat, for I am by nature a Pythagorean,[51] so far as beans are concerned, whether they mean porridge or voting,[52] and exchanged them for rice; but, perchance, as

48 Reversal of the common New England expression implying ignorance: "He doesn't know beans."

49 Son of King Priam and Hecuba, Hector was the bravest of the Trojan warriors.

50 Allusion to Homer's *Iliad* 22.403 (Alexander Pope translation): "At length he roll'd in dust."

51 Follower of Pythagoras (ca. 580–500 B.C.E.), ancient Greek philosopher and mathematician who told his students to abstain from beans. However, Joseph Hosmer, in describing a meal he ate with Thoreau at Walden in early September 1845, mentioned beans: "Our bill of fare included roasted horn pout, corn, beans, bread, salt, etc. . . . The beans had been previously cooked."

52 Beans were used as voting tallies in ancient times.

some must work in fields if only for the sake of tropes and expression, to serve a parable-maker one day. It was on the whole a rare amusement, which, continued too long, might have become a dissipation. Though I gave them no manure, and did not hoe them all once, I hoed them unusually well as far as I went, and was paid for it in the end, "there being in truth," as Evelyn says, "no compost or lætation[53] whatsoever comparable to this continual motion, repastination,[54] and turning of the mould with the spade."[55] "The earth," he adds elsewhere, "especially if fresh, has a certain magnetism in it, by which it attracts the salt, power, or virtue (call it either) which gives it life, and is the logic of all the labor and stir we keep about it, to sustain us; all dungings and other sordid temperings being but the vicars succedaneous[56] to this improvement." Moreover, this being one of those "worn-out and exhausted lay fields which enjoy their sabbath," had perchance, as Sir Kenelm Digby[57] thinks likely, attracted "vital spirits" from the air. I harvested twelve bushels of beans.

But to be more particular, for it is complained that Mr. Colman has reported chiefly the expensive experiments of gentlemen farmers, my outgoes were, —

For a hoe, ...	$0 54
Ploughing, harrowing, and furrowing, . . .	7 50, Too much.[58]
Beans for seed, ...	3 12½
Potatoes "	1 33
Peas "	0 40
Turnip seed, ...	0 06
White line for crow fence,[59]	0 02
Horse cultivator and boy three hours, . . .	1 00
Horse and cart to get crop, ...	0 75
In all, ...	$14 72½

My income was, (patrem familias vendacem, non emacem esse oportet,)[60] from

53 Manure.

54 Re-digging.

55 This, and the following, quoted from John Evelyn's *Terra: A Philosophical Discourse of Earth* (London, 1729) 14–16.

56 Pertaining to or acting as a substitute.

57 English philosopher and naturalist (1603–1665) who published *Discourse Concerning the Vegetation of Plants* in 1661, although Thoreau's fact-books indicate that he read Digby in John Evelyn's *Terra* 16: "in Sir Kenelm Digby's Discourse of Sympathetic Powder, he affirms, that the earth, in the Years of repose, recovers its Vigor, by the Attraction of the vital Spirits, which it receives from the Air, and those superior Irradiations, which endow simple Earth with Qualities promoting Fermentation."

58 According to Robert Gross, "The Great Bean Field Hoax: Thoreau and Agricultural Reformers" (1985), Thoreau paid only half the going rate.

59 A white string surrounding a field, for use as a scarecrow.

60 From Cato's *De Agri Cultura* 2.7: "The master should have the selling habit, not the buying habit."

61 In the "Economy" chapter.
62 Thoreau wrote in his journal in August 1845: "I will not plant beans another summer" [J 1:382].
63 Allusion to Jeremiah 8:20: "The harvest is past, the summer has ended, and we are not saved."

Nine bushels and twelve quarts of beans sold, ... $16 94
Five   "   large potatoes, ...   2 50
Nine   "   small   ". 2 25
Grass, ...   1 00
Stalks, ...   0 75

 In all, ... $23 44

Leaving a pecuniary profit, as I have elsewhere said,[61] of $8 71½.

This is the result of my experience in raising beans. Plant the common small white bush bean about the first of June, in rows three feet by eighteen inches apart, being careful to select fresh round and unmixed seed. First look out for worms, and supply vacancies by planting anew. Then look out for woodchucks, if it is an exposed place, for they will nibble off the earliest tender leaves almost clean as they go; and again, when the young tendrils make their appearance, they have notice of it, and will shear them off with both buds and young pods, sitting erect like a squirrel. But above all harvest as early as possible, if you would escape frosts and have a fair and salable crop; you may save much loss by this means.

This further experience also I gained. I said to myself, I will not plant beans and corn with so much industry another summer,[62] but such seeds, if the seed is not lost, as sincerity, truth, simplicity, faith, innocence, and the like, and see if they will not grow in this soil, even with less toil and manurance, and sustain me, for surely it has not been exhausted for these crops. Alas! I said this to myself; but now another summer is gone,[63] and another, and another, and I am obliged to say to you, Reader, that the seeds which I planted, if indeed they *were* the seeds of those virtues, were wormeaten or had lost their vitality, and so did not come up. Commonly men will only be brave as their fathers were brave, or timid. This generation is very sure to plant corn and beans each new year precisely as the Indians did centuries ago and taught the first settlers to do, as if there were a fate in it. I saw an old man the other day, to my astonishment, making the holes with a hoe for the seventieth time at least, and not for himself to lie down in! But why should not the New Englander try new adventures, and not lay so much stress on his grain, his potato and grass crop, and his orchards?—raise other crops than these? Why concern ourselves so much about our beans for seed, and not be concerned at all about a new generation of men? We should really be fed and cheered if when we met a man we were sure to see that some of the qualities which I have named, which we all prize more than those other productions, but which are for the most part broadcast and floating in the air, had taken root and grown in him. Here comes such a subtile and ineffable quality, for instance, as truth or justice, though the slightest amount or new variety of it, along the road. Our ambassadors should be instructed to send home such seeds as these,[64] and Congress help to distribute them over all the land.[65] We should never stand upon ceremony with sincerity. We should never cheat and insult and banish one another by our meanness, if there were present the kernel of worth and friendliness. We should not meet thus in haste. Most men I do not meet at all, for they seem not to have time; they are busy about their beans. We would not deal with a man thus plodding ever, leaning on a hoe or a spade as a staff between his work, not as a mushroom, but partially risen out of the earth, something more than erect, like swallows alighted and walking on the ground:—

"And as he spake, his wings would now and then
Spread, as he meant to fly, then close again,"[66]

so that we should suspect that we might be conversing with an angel. Bread may not always nourish us; but it always does us good, it even takes stiffness out of our

64 From a practice begun by Benjamin Franklin in England and Thomas Jefferson in France, both of whom collected rare seeds for distribution in America, and endorsed by John Quincy Adams (1767–1848), whose administration instructed all consuls to forward rare plants and seeds to Washington for distribution.

65 In 1839 Congress invested $1,000 in the Congressional Seed Distribution Program, administered by the U.S. Patent Office, to increase the amount of free seeds mailed to anyone requesting them.

66 Quoted from the fifth eclogue of Francis Quarles (1592–1644), "The Shepherd's Oracles."

67 Roman god of the earth, so called to distinguish him from Pluto, the Infernal Jove; also known as Jupiter and identified with the Greek god Zeus.

68 Greek god of agricultural prosperity, but also, with Thoreau's use of "infernal," a possible allusion to Pluto, god of the underworld.

69 Latin: "most highly respected," from the introduction to Cato's *De Agri Cultura*.

70 Marcus Terentius Varro (116–27 B.C.E.), Roman scholar and writer of more than 70 works, of which only *Rerum Rusticarum* is extant in complete form.

71 Thoreau's translation of Varro's *Rerum Rusticarum* 3.1.5. Saturn in Roman mythology was the god of agriculture and vegetation.

72 Allusion to Matthew 5:45: "For he maketh his sun to rise on the evil and on the good, and sendeth rain on the just and the unjust."

73 Joseph Hosmer, Thoreau's friend and a frequent visitor at Walden, wrote in his article "Henry D. Thoreau":

One of the axioms of his philosophy had been to take the life of nothing that breathed, if he could avoid it: but, it had now become a serious question with him, whether to allow the wood-chucks and rabbits to destroy his beans, or fight.

Having determined on the latter, he procured a steel trap, and soon caught a venerable old fellow to the "manor born," and one who had held undisputed possession there for all time.

After retaining the enemy of all beans in "durance vile" for a few hours, he pressed his foot on the spring of the trap and let him go — expecting and hoping never to see him more. Vain delusion!

In a few days after, on returning from the village post-office, on looking in the direction of the bean field, to his disgust and apprehension he saw the same old grey-back disappear behind some brush just outside the field.

On a reconnaissance he discovered that

joints, and makes us supple and buoyant, when we knew not what ailed us, to recognize any generosity in man or Nature, to share any unmixed and heroic joy.

Ancient poetry and mythology suggest, at least, that husbandry was once a sacred art; but it is pursued with irreverent haste and heedlessness by us, our object being to have large farms and large crops merely. We have no festival, nor procession, nor ceremony, not excepting our Cattle-shows and so called Thanksgivings, by which the farmer expresses a sense of the sacredness of his calling, or is reminded of its sacred origin. It is the premium and the feast which tempt him. He sacrifices not to Ceres and the Terrestrial Jove,[67] but to the infernal Plutus[68] rather. By avarice and selfishness, and a grovelling habit, from which none of us is free, of regarding the soil as property, or the means of acquiring property chiefly, the landscape is deformed, husbandry is degraded with us, and the farmer leads the meanest of lives. He knows Nature but as a robber. Cato says that the profits of agriculture are particularly pious or just, (*maximeque pius quæstus,*)[69] and according to Varro[70] the old Romans "called the same earth Mother and Ceres, and thought that they who cultivated it led a pious and useful life, and that they alone were left of the race of King Saturn."[71]

We are wont to forget that the sun looks on our cultivated fields and on the prairies and forests without distinction.[72] They all reflect and absorb his rays alike, and the former make but a small part of the glorious picture which he beholds in his daily course. In his view the earth is all equally cultivated like a garden. Therefore we should receive the benefit of his light and heat with a corresponding trust and magnanimity. What though I value the seed of these beans, and harvest that in the fall of the year? This broad field which I have looked at so long looks not to me as the principal cultivator, but away from me to influences more genial to it, which water and make it green.

These beans have results which are not harvested by me. Do they not grow for woodchucks partly?[73] The ear of wheat, (in Latin *spica,* obsoletely *speca,* from *spe,* hope,) should not be the only hope of the husbandman; its kernel or grain (*granum,* from *gerendo,* bearing,)[74] is not all that it bears. How, then, can our harvest fail? Shall I not rejoice also at the abundance of the weeds whose seeds are the granary of the birds? It matters little comparatively whether the fields fill the farmer's barns. The true husbandman will cease from anxiety, as the squirrels manifest no concern whether the woods will bear chestnuts this year or not, and finish his labor with every day, relinquishing all claim to the produce of his fields, and sacrificing in his mind not only his first[75] but his last fruits also.

the enemy had taken up a strategic position covered by some brush near his beans, and had entrenched himself by digging a "rifle pit," and otherwise made preparations for a determined siege. Accordingly he again set the trap and again caught the thief.

Now it so happened that those old knights of the shot gun, hook and line, Wesson, Pratt and Co., were on a piscatorial visit to the "devil's bar," equipped with all the necessary appliances to allure the finny tribe to destruction. A council of war was held at the "Bar," to determine what should be done with the wood-chuck.

A decision was rendered immediately by that old and popular landlord of the Middlesex, in his terse and laconic manner "knock his brains out."

This however was altogether too severe on the woodchuck, thought Henry; even woodchucks had some rights that "Squatter Sovereigns" should respect. Was he not the original occupant there? and had he not "jumped" the "wood-chucks claim[,]" destroyed his home, and built his "hut" upon the ruins? After considering the question carefully he took the woodchuck in his arms and carried him some two miles away; and then with a severe admonition at the end of a good stick, he opened the trap, and again let him "depart in peace"; and he never saw him more.

74 Allusion to Varro's *Rerum Rusticarum* 1.48.2–3: "The grain is so called from *gererre;* for the seed is planted that the ear may 'bear' (*gerat*) the grain. . . . The ear, however, which the peasants, in their old-fashioned way, call *speca,* seems to have got its name from *spes:* for it is because they hope (*sperant*) to have this grow that they plant."
75 As stipulated in Exodus 23:19, the first fruits of the ground were offered unto God by biblical injunction: "The first of the firstfruits of thy land thou shalt bring into the house of the Lord your God."

The Village

After hoeing, or perhaps reading and writing, in the forenoon, I usually bathed again in the pond, swimming across one of its coves for a stint, and washed the dust of labor from my person, or smoothed out the last wrinkle which study had made, and for the afternoon was absolutely free. Every day or two I strolled to the village to hear some of the gossip which is incessantly going on there, circulating either from mouth to mouth, or from newspaper to newspaper, and which, taken in homœopathic doses,[1] was really as refreshing in its way as the rustle of leaves and the peeping of frogs. As I walked in the woods to see the birds and squirrels, so I walked in the village to see the men and boys; instead of the wind among the pines I heard the carts rattle. In one direction from my house there was a colony of muskrats in the river meadows; under the grove of elms and buttonwoods in the other horizon was a village of busy men, as curious to me as if they had been prairie dogs, each sitting at the mouth of its burrow, or running over to a neighbor's to gossip. I went there frequently to observe their habits. The village appeared to me a great news room; and on one side, to support it, as once at Redding & Company's[2] on State Street, they kept nuts and raisins, or salt and meal and other groceries. Some have such a vast appetite for the former commodity, that is, the news, and such sound digestive organs, that they can sit forever in public avenues without stirring, and let it simmer and whisper through them like the Etesian winds,[3] or as if inhaling ether,[4] it only producing numbness and insensibility to pain, — otherwise it would often be painful to hear, — without affecting the consciousness. I hardly ever failed, when I rambled through the village, to see a row of such worthies, either sitting on a ladder sunning themselves, with their bodies inclined forward and their eyes glancing along the line this way and that, from time to time, with a voluptuous expression, or else leaning against a barn with their hands in their pockets, like caryatides,[5] as if to prop it up. They, being commonly out of doors, heard whatever was in the wind. These are the coarsest mills, in which all gossip is first rudely digested or cracked up before it is emptied into finer and more delicate hoppers within doors. I observed that the vitals of the village were the grocery, the bar-room, the post-office, and the bank; and, as a necessary part of the machinery, they kept a bell, a big gun, and a fire-engine, at convenient places; and the houses were so arranged as to make the most of mankind, in lanes and fronting one another, so that every traveller had to run the gantlet,[6] and every man, woman, and child might get a lick at him. Of course, those who were stationed nearest to the head of the line, where they could most see and be seen, and have the first blow at him, paid the highest prices for their places; and the few straggling inhabitants in the outskirts, where long gaps in the line began to occur, and the traveller could get over walls or turn aside into cow paths, and so escape, paid a very slight ground or window tax.[7] Signs were hung out on all sides to allure him; some to catch him by the appetite, as the tavern and victualling cellar;[8] some by the fancy, as the dry goods store and the jeweller's; and others by the hair or the feet or the skirts, as the barber, the shoemaker, or the tailor. Besides, there was a still more terrible stand-

3 Mediterranean winds; in particular, annual northerly summer winds lasting for about forty days.

4 The first inhalational anesthetic, a colorless, volatile, flammable liquid with a characteristic odor, first used in 1846. Thoreau experienced it during a visit to the dentist in 1851:

> By taking the ether the other day I was convinced how far asunder a man could be separated from his senses. You are told that it will make you unconscious, but no one can imagine what it is to be unconscious—how far removed from the state of consciousness and all that we call "this world"—until he has experienced it. The value of the experiment is that it does give you experience of an interval as between one life and another, —a greater space than you ever travelled. You are a sane mind without organs, —groping for organs, — which if it did not soon recover its old senses would get new ones. You expand like a seed in the ground. You exist in your roots, like a tree in the winter. If you have an inclination to travel, take the ether; you go beyond the furthest star. [J 2:194]

5 Statues of draped female figures used architecturally as supporting columns.

6 Thoreau would have been aware of Native Americans' use of the gantlet (sometimes spelled gauntlet) from such sources as the story of Hannah Dustan (b. 1657) in John Warner Barber's *Historical Collections:* "The gauntlet consisted of two files of Indians, of both sexes and of all ages, containing all that could be mustered in the village; and the unhappy prisoners were obliged to run between them, when they were scoffed at and beaten by each one as they passed, and were sometimes marks at which the younger Indians threw their hatchets. This cruel custom was often practised by many of the tribes, and not unfrequently the poor prisoner sunk beneath it." Thoreau told the story of Hannah Dustan in the

"Thursday" chapter of *A Week on the Concord and Merrimack Rivers*.

7 The Roman ground tax required payment to the government of one-tenth of the grain and one-fifth of the oil and wine a person produced; the British window tax, introduced in 1696, was levied on the number of windows in a dwelling.

8 A place where provision is made for strangers to eat.

9 In Greek mythology, the music of Orpheus had supernatural powers, and his singing could charm animals and inanimate objects. Although Lemprière's *Bibliotheca Classica* did not specifically link Orpheus and the Sirens, Apollonius Rhodius (fl. 3d century B.C.E.) did in book 4 of his *Argonautica*.

10 Translation, probably Thoreau's, of Francis Bacon's *De Sapienta Veterum* 31.

11 Of such an irruption Emerson wrote: "It is curious that Thoreau goes to a house to say with little preface what he has just read or observed, delivers it in lump, is quite inattentive to any comment or thought which any of the company offer on the matter, nay, is merely interrupted by it, &, when he has finished his report, departs with precipitation."

12 When visiting the Emersons, exiting through the back door would have been the most direct way back to Walden.

13 "Many walk by day; few walk by night. It is a very different season," Thoreau wrote in his journal in 1850 [J 2:41]. He elaborated in his journal on 5 August 1851:

> As the twilight deepens and the moonlight is more and more bright, I begin to distinguish myself, who I am and where; as my walls contract, I become more collected and composed, and sensible of my own existence, as when a lamp is brought into a dark apartment and I see who the company are. With the coolness and the mild silvery light, I recover some sanity, my thoughts are more distinct, moderated, and tempered. Reflection is more possible while the day goes by. The intense light of the sun unfits me for meditation,

ing invitation to call at every one of these houses, and company expected about these times. For the most part I escaped wonderfully from these dangers, either by proceeding at once boldly and without deliberation to the goal, as is recommended to those who run the gantlet, or by keeping my thoughts on high things, like Orpheus,[9] who, "loudly singing the praises of the gods to his lyre, drowned the voices of the Sirens, and kept out of danger."[10] Sometimes I bolted suddenly, and nobody could tell my whereabouts, for I did not stand much about gracefulness, and never hesitated at a gap in a fence. I was even accustomed to make an irruption[11] into some houses, where I was well entertained, and after learning the kernels and very last sieve-ful of news, what had subsided, the prospects of war and peace, and whether the world was likely to hold together much longer, I was let out through the rear avenues,[12] and so escaped to the woods again.

It was very pleasant, when I staid late in town, to launch myself into the night,[13] especially if it was dark and tempestuous, and set sail from some bright village parlor or lecture room, with a bag of rye or Indian meal upon my shoulder, for my snug harbor in the woods, having made all tight without and withdrawn under hatches with a merry crew of thoughts, leaving only my outer man at the helm, or even tying up the helm when it was plain sailing.[14] I had many a genial thought by the cabin[15] fire "as I sailed."[16] I was never cast away nor distressed in any weather, though I encountered some severe storms. It is darker in the woods, even in common nights, than most suppose. I frequently had to look up at the opening between the trees above the path in order to learn my route, and, where there was no cart-path, to feel with my feet the faint track which I had worn, or steer by the known relation of particular trees which I felt with my hands, passing between two pines for instance, not more than eighteen inches apart, in the midst of the woods, in-variably, in the darkest night. Sometimes, after coming home thus late in a dark and muggy night, when my feet felt the path which my eyes could not see, dreaming and absent-minded all the way, until I was aroused by having to raise my hand to lift the latch, I have not been able to recall a single step of my walk, and I have thought that perhaps my body would find its way home if its master should forsake it, as the hand finds its way to the mouth without assistance. Several times, when a visitor chanced to stay into evening, and it proved a dark night, I was obliged to conduct him to the cart-path in the rear of the house, and then point out to him the direction he was to pursue, and in keeping which he was to be guided rather by his feet than his eyes. One very dark night I directed thus on their way two young men who had been fish-ing in the pond.[17] They lived about a mile off through the woods, and were quite used to the route. A day or two after one of them told me that they wandered about the greater part of the night, close by their own prem-ises, and did not get home till toward morning, by which time, as there had been several heavy showers in the mean while, and the leaves were very wet, they were drenched to their skins. I have heard of many going astray even in the village streets, when the darkness was so thick that you could cut it with a knife, as the saying is. Some who live in the outskirts, having come to town a-shopping in their wagons, have been obliged to put up for the night; and gentlemen and ladies making a call have gone half a mile out of their way, feeling the sidewalk only with their feet, and not knowing when they turned. It is a surprising and memorable, as well as valuable experience, to be lost in the woods any time. Often in a snow storm, even by day, one will come out upon a well-known road and yet find it impossible to tell which way leads to the village. Though he knows that he has travelled it a thousand times, he can-

makes me wander in my thought; my life is too diffuse and dissipated; routine succeeds and prevails over us; the trivial has greater power then, and most at noonday, the most trivial hour of the twenty-four. I am sobered by the moonlight. I bethink myself. It is like a cup of cold water to a thirsty man. The moonlight is more favorable to meditation than sunlight. [J 2:372]

14 Originally "plane sailing," which is a method of navigation in which the earth's curvature is ignored, treating the earth's surface as a plane, but colloquially it is used to describe easy or uncomplicated progress.
15 The third of Thoreau's references to his Wal-den house as a cabin, and also a pun on the cabin of a ship, following the previous nautical images.
16 Refrain in several of the verses from the American "Ballad of Captain Robert Kidd."
17 Possibly George William Curtis (1824–1892) and James Burrill Curtis (1822–1895), who in 1845 were living at the Hosmer farmhouse on Lincoln Road.

18 Allusion to Matthew 10:39: "He that findeth his life shall lose it: and he that loseth his life for my sake shall find it."

19 Unidentified.

20 Thoreau had stopped paying his poll tax several years earlier to protest the involvement of Massachusetts with the institution of slavery and later the war with Mexico, which began in 1845. On 23 or 24 July 1846 (Thoreau's second summer at Walden Pond), Concord tax collector and jailer Sam Staples (d. 1895) stopped him and asked him to pay his tax. When Thoreau refused, Staples offered to pay it himself, which Thoreau would not allow, so he was taken to jail. That evening an unidentified person paid the tax to Staples's daughter. Although Thoreau should have been released at that point, Staples had already taken his boots off and was relaxing by the fire, so he decided to let Thoreau remain in jail for the night. When he was released the next day, Thoreau was angry at the intervention of the anonymous benefactor. Bronson Alcott had been similarly arrested for refusing to pay his taxes two and a half years earlier. Thoreau's essay "Resistance to Civil Government" was originally published in Elizabeth Peabody's (1804–1894) *Aesthetic Papers* in May 1849 and collected posthumously as "Civil Disobedience" in *A Yankee in Canada with Anti-Slavery and Reform Papers*. He also delivered it as a lecture at the Concord Lyceum on 26 January and 16 February 1848, and he related the incident briefly in *A Week on the Concord and Merrimack Rivers*.

21 Allusion to the fraternal organization the Independent Order of Odd Fellows, the purpose of which was to give aid to those in need and to pursue projects for the benefit of all. Thoreau also referred to it in "Paradise (to be) Regained": "Ay, this last may be what we want mainly,—a company of 'odd fellows' indeed" [W 4:299].

22 A few pages after noting Thoreau's arrest in his journal, Emerson wrote: "Don't run amuck against the world." The term was introduced into English through traders to the Eastern Archipelago, from the Malaysian adjective *amoq*,

not recognize a feature in it, but it is as strange to him as if it were a road in Siberia. By night, of course, the perplexity is infinitely greater. In our most trivial walks, we are constantly, though unconsciously, steering like pilots by certain well-known beacons and headlands, and if we go beyond our usual course we still carry in our minds the bearing of some neighboring cape; and not till we are completely lost, or turned round,—for a man needs only to be turned round once with his eyes shut in this world to be lost,—do we appreciate the vastness and strangeness of Nature. Every man has to learn the points of compass again as often as he awakes, whether from sleep or any abstraction. Not till we are lost, in other words, not till we have lost the world, do we begin to find ourselves,[18] and realize where we are and the infinite extent of our relations.

One afternoon, near the end of the first summer, when I went to the village to get a shoe from the cobbler's,[19] I was seized and put into jail, because, as I have elsewhere related, I did not pay a tax to, or recognize the authority of, the state which buys and sells men, women, and children, like cattle at the door of its senate-house.[20] I had gone down to the woods for other purposes. But, wherever a man goes, men will pursue and paw him with their dirty institutions, and, if they can, constrain him to belong to their desperate odd-fellow society.[21] It is true, I might have resisted forcibly with more or less effect, might have run "amok"[22] against society; but I preferred that society should run "amok" against me, it being the desperate party. However, I was released the next day, obtained my mended shoe, and returned to the woods in season to get my dinner of huckleberries on Fair Haven Hill.[23] I was never molested by any person but those who represented the state. I had no lock nor bolt but for the desk which held my papers, not even a nail to put over my latch or windows. I never fastened my door night or day, though I was to be absent several days; not even when the next fall I spent a fortnight in the woods of Maine.[24] And yet my house was more respected than if it had been surrounded by a file of soldiers. The tired rambler could rest and warm himself by my fire, the literary amuse himself with the few books on my table, or the curious, by opening my closet door, see what was left of my dinner, and what prospect I had of a supper. Yet, though many people of every class came this way to the pond, I suffered no serious inconvenience from these sources, and I never missed any thing but one small book, a volume of Homer,[25] which perhaps was improperly gilded,[26] and this I trust a soldier of our camp has found by this time.[27] I am convinced, that if all men were to live as simply as I then did, thieving and robbery would be unknown. These take place only in communities where some have got more than is sufficient while others have not enough. The Pope's Homers[28] would soon get properly distributed. —

<blockquote>
"Nec bella fuerunt,
Faginus astabat dum scyphus ante dapes."[29]
"Nor wars did men molest,
When only beechen bowls were in request."
</blockquote>

"You who govern public affairs, what need have you to employ punishments? Love virtue, and the people will be virtuous. The virtues of a superior man are like the wind; the virtues of a common man are like the grass; the grass, when the wind passes over it, bends."[30]

meaning rushing in a frenzy to commit acts of indiscriminate murder.

23 Fair Haven Hill, a half mile southwest of Walden on the Sudbury River, was one of Thoreau's favorite spots, and he wrote on 12 May 1850: "In all my rambles I have seen no landscape which can make me forget Fair Haven. I still sit on its Cliff in a new spring day, and look over the awakening woods and the river, and hear the new birds sing, with the same delight as ever. It is as sweet a mystery to me as ever, what this world is" [J 2:9].

24 Thoreau left Walden on 31 August 1846 and returned mid-September. This journey is recounted in "Ktaadn" in *The Maine Woods*.

25 Alek Therien had surreptitiously "borrowed" volume 1 of Thoreau's copy of Pope's translation of *The Iliad of Homer*. At Walden Thoreau had read to Therien out of this volume.

26 Gilt-edged, thus making it appear of more monetary worth, and attracting a thief. Thoreau may have been playing with the adverb "improperly" to mean both poorly gilded as well as inappropriately gilded and thus detracting from the real value of the written words.

27 Allusion to "Morals of Confucius" in *The Phenix: A Collection of Old and Rare Fragments* (New York, 1835) 83. Thoreau wrote in "Sayings of Confucius" in the April 1843 issue of *The Dial*: "A soldier of the kingdom of Ci lost his buckler; and having sought after it a long time in vain; he comforted himself with this reflection: 'A soldier has lost his buckler, but a soldier in our camp will find it; he will use it.'"

28 Translation of Homer into heroic couplets by the English poet Alexander Pope, translator of the volume Thoreau had owned.

29 Quoted from Albius Tibullus (ca. 55–ca. 19 B.C.E.), *Elegies* 1.10.7–8, but the error of "dum" for "cum" indicates that Thoreau's source was John Evelyn's *Sylva*. The translation that follows is Thoreau's.

30 Thoreau's translation of Confucius, *Analects* 12.19, from the French translation in Pauthier, *Confucius et Mencius* 169.

1 Quoted from John Milton's poem "Lycidas" (l. 193).

2 Not the cowboy of the American West, but a boy who drives cows to and from pasture.

3 Echo of Johann Wolfgang von Goethe's (1749–1832) statement recorded in Margaret Fuller's translation of *Conversations with Goethe in the Last Years of His Life Translated from the German of Eckermann* (Boston, 1839), published as volume 4 of George Ripley's *Specimens of Foreign Standard Literature:* "'Ask children and birds,' said he, 'how cherries and strawberries taste.'"

4 Boston was founded on three hills: Copps, Fort, and Beacon.

The Ponds

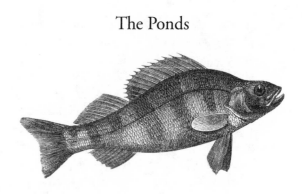

Sometimes, having had a surfeit of human society and gossip, and worn out all my village friends, I rambled still farther westward than I habitually dwell, into yet more unfrequented parts of the town, "to fresh woods and pastures new,"[1] or, while the sun was setting, made my supper of huckleberries and blueberries on Fair Haven Hill, and laid up a store for several days. The fruits do not yield their true flavor to the purchaser of them, nor to him who raises them for the market. There is but one way to obtain it, yet few take that way. If you would know the flavor of huckleberries, ask the cow-boy[2] or the partridge.[3] It is a vulgar error to suppose that you have tasted huckleberries who never plucked them. A huckleberry never reaches Boston; they have not been known there since they grew on her three hills.[4] The ambrosial and essential part of the fruit is lost with the bloom which is rubbed off in the market cart, and they become mere provender. As long as Eternal Justice reigns, not one innocent huckleberry can be transported thither from the country's hills.

Occasionally, after my hoeing was done for the day, I joined some impatient companion who had been fishing on the pond since morning, as silent and motionless as a duck or a floating leaf, and, after practising various kinds of philosophy, had concluded commonly, by the time I arrived, that he belonged to the ancient sect of

Cœnobites.[5] There was one older man,[6] an excellent fisher and skilled in all kinds of woodcraft, who was pleased to look upon my house as a building erected for the convenience of fishermen; and I was equally pleased when he sat in my doorway to arrange his lines. Once in a while we sat together on the pond, he at one end of the boat, and I at the other; but not many words passed between us, for he had grown deaf in his later years, but he occasionally hummed a psalm, which harmonized well enough with my philosophy. Our intercourse was thus altogether one of unbroken harmony, far more pleasing to remember than if it had been carried on by speech. When, as was commonly the case, I had none to commune with, I used to raise the echoes by striking with a paddle on the side of my boat, filling the surrounding woods with circling and dilating sound, stirring them up as the keeper of a menagerie his wild beasts, until I elicited a growl from every wooded vale and hill-side.[7]

In warm evenings I frequently sat in the boat playing the flute,[8] and saw the perch, which I seem to have charmed, hovering around me, and the moon travelling over the ribbed bottom, which was strewed with the wrecks of the forest. Formerly I had come to this pond adventurously, from time to time, in dark summer nights, with a companion,[9] and making a fire close to the water's edge,[10] which we thought attracted the fishes, we caught pouts with a bunch of worms strung on a thread; and when we had done, far in the night, threw the burning brands high into the air like skyrockets, which, coming down into the pond, were quenched with a loud hissing, and we were suddenly groping in total darkness. Through this, whistling a tune, we took our way to the haunts of men again. But now I had made my home by the shore.

Sometimes, after staying in a village parlor till the family had all retired, I have returned to the woods, and, partly with a view to the next day's dinner, spent the

5 A monastic religious order, with a pun: "See no bites."
6 Unidentified.
7 Edward Emerson recalled Thoreau showing him and other boys "especially how, at still midnight, in the middle of Walden, to strike the boat with an oar,—and, in another minute, the hills around awoke, cried out, one after another with incredible and startling *crash*, so that the Lincoln Hill and Fairhaven, and even Conantum, took up the tale of the outrage done to their quiet sleep."
8 The origin of this passage is from a journal entry of 27 May 1841.
9 Unidentified.
10 George William Curtis told of a similar nighttime experience in the July 1874 issue of *Harper's New Monthly Magazine*: "The Easy Chair remembers a weird night with Thoreau in his boat upon the Concord River, the Musketaquid. . . . An iron crate was built out from the bow of the boat and filled with the dead roots of old pine-trees—fat pine—and when this was kindled the blaze threw a broad glare for some distance upon the water, shutting out every thing else, and slowly drifting with the stream we could see clearly every thing below us."

hours of midnight fishing from a boat by moonlight, serenaded by owls and foxes, and hearing, from time to time, the creaking note of some unknown bird close at hand. These experiences were very memorable and valuable to me,—anchored in forty feet of water, and twenty or thirty rods from the shore, surrounded sometimes by thousands of small perch and shiners, dimpling the surface with their tails in the moonlight, and communicating by a long flaxen line with mysterious nocturnal fishes which had their dwelling forty feet below, or sometimes dragging sixty feet of line about the pond as I drifted in the gentle night breeze, now and then feeling a slight vibration along it, indicative of some life prowling about its extremity, of dull uncertain blundering purpose there, and slow to make up its mind. At length you slowly raise, pulling hand over hand, some horned pout squeaking and squirming to the upper air. It was very queer, especially in dark nights, when your thoughts had wandered to vast and cosmogonal themes in other spheres, to feel this faint jerk, which came to interrupt your dreams and link you to Nature again. It seemed as if I might next cast my line upward into the air, as well as downward into this element which was scarcely more dense. Thus I caught two fishes as it were with one hook.

The scenery of Walden is on a humble scale, and, though very beautiful, does not approach to grandeur, nor can it much concern one who has not long frequented it or lived by its shore; yet this pond is so remarkable for its depth and purity as to merit a particular description. It is a clear and deep green well, half a mile long and a mile and three quarters in circumference, and contains about sixty-one and a half acres; a perennial spring in the midst of pine and oak woods, without any visible inlet or outlet except by the clouds and evaporation.[11] The surrounding hills rise abruptly from the water to the height

11 Walden Pond is a flow-through lake, gaining water from the aquifer, a layer of rock or soil able to hold or transmit water, along its eastern perimeter and losing water to the aquifer along its western perimeter.

of forty to eighty feet, though on the south-east and east they attain to about one hundred and one hundred and fifty feet respectively, within a quarter and a third of a mile. They are exclusively woodland. All our Concord waters have two colors at least, one when viewed at a distance, and another, more proper, close at hand. The first depends more on the light, and follows the sky. In clear weather, in summer, they appear blue at a little distance, especially if agitated, and at a great distance all appear alike. In stormy weather they are sometimes of a dark slate color. The sea, however, is said to be blue one day and green another without any perceptible change in the atmosphere. I have seen our river, when, the landscape being covered with snow, both water and ice were almost as green as grass. Some consider blue "to be the color of pure water, whether liquid or solid."[12] But, looking directly down into our waters from a boat, they are seen to be of very different colors. Walden is blue at one time and green at another, even from the same point of view. Lying between the earth and the heavens, it partakes of the color of both. Viewed from a hill-top it reflects the color of the sky, but near at hand it is of a yellowish tint next the shore where you can see the sand, then a light green, which gradually deepens to a uniform dark green in the body of the pond. In some lights, viewed even from a hill-top, it is of a vivid green next the shore. Some have referred this to the reflection of the verdure; but it is equally green there against the railroad sand-bank, and in the spring, before the leaves are expanded, and it may be simply the result of the prevailing blue mixed with the yellow of the sand. Such is the color of its iris.[13] This is that portion, also, where in the spring, the ice being warmed by the heat of the sun reflected from the bottom, and also transmitted through the earth, melts first and forms a narrow canal about the still frozen middle. Like the rest of our waters, when much agitated, in clear weather, so that the

12 Quoted, with one minor variant in spelling, from James D. Forbes (1809–1868), *Travels Through the Alps of Savoy* 71: "The ice here is remarkably pure, and the fine blue caverns and crevasses may be as well studied as in almost any glacier in Switzerland. Of the cause of this colour I may observe once for all, that I consider it to be the colour of pure water, whether liquid or solid; though there are no doubt conditions of aggregation which give it more or less intensity, or change its hue."

13 Thoreau referred later in this chapter to a lake being the "earth's eye."

14 Michelangelo Buonarroti (1475–1564), Italian artist known for his paintings and sculptures of large and muscular figures.

surface of the waves may reflect the sky at the right angle, or because there is more light mixed with it, it appears at a little distance of a darker blue than the sky itself; and at such a time, being on its surface, and looking with divided vision, so as to see the reflection, I have discerned a matchless and indescribable light blue, such as watered or changeable silks and sword blades suggest, more cerulean than the sky itself, alternating with the original dark green on the opposite sides of the waves, which last appeared but muddy in comparison. It is a vitreous greenish blue, as I remember it, like those patches of the winter sky seen through cloud vistas in the west before sundown. Yet a single glass of its water held up to the light is as colorless as an equal quantity of air. It is well known that a large plate of glass will have a green tint, owing, as the makers say, to its "body," but a small piece of the same will be colorless. How large a body of Walden water would be required to reflect a green tint I have never proved. The water of our river is black or a very dark brown to one looking directly down on it, and, like that of most ponds, imparts to the body of one bathing in it a yellowish tinge; but this water is of such crystalline purity that the body of the bather appears of an alabaster whiteness, still more unnatural, which, as the limbs are magnified and distorted withal, produces a monstrous effect, making fit studies for a Michael Angelo.[14]

The water is so transparent that the bottom can easily be discerned at the depth of twenty-five or thirty feet. Paddling over it, you may see many feet beneath the surface the schools of perch and shiners, perhaps only an inch long, yet the former easily distinguished by their transverse bars, and you think that they must be ascetic fish that find a subsistence there. Once, in the winter, many years ago, when I had been cutting holes through the ice in order to catch pickerel, as I stepped ashore I tossed my axe back on to the ice, but, as if some evil genius had directed it, it slid four or five rods directly into one of the holes, where the water was twenty-five feet deep. Out of curiosity, I lay down on the ice and looked through the hole, until I saw the axe a little on one side, standing on its head, with its helve erect and gently swaying to and fro with the pulse of the pond; and there it might have stood erect and swaying till in the course of time the handle rotted off, if I had not disturbed it. Making another hole directly over it with an ice chisel which I had, and cutting down the longest birch which I could find in the neighborhood with my knife, I made a slip-noose, which I attached to its end, and, letting it down carefully, passed it over the knob of the handle, and drew it by a line along the birch, and so pulled the axe out again.

The shore is composed of a belt of smooth rounded white stones like paving stones,[15] excepting one or two short sand beaches, and is so steep that in many places a single leap will carry you into water over your head; and were it not for its remarkable transparency, that would be the last to be seen of its bottom till it rose on the opposite side. Some think it is bottomless. It is nowhere muddy, and a casual observer would say that there were no weeds at all in it; and of noticeable plants, except in the little meadows recently overflowed, which do not properly belong to it, a closer scrutiny does not detect a flag nor a bulrush, nor even a lily, yellow or white, but only a few small heart-leaves and potamogetons,[16] and perhaps a water-target[17] or two; all which however a bather might not perceive; and these plants are clean and bright like the element they grow in. The stones extend a rod or two into the water, and then the bottom is pure sand, except in the deepest parts, where there is usually a little sediment, probably from the decay of the leaves which have been wafted on to it so many successive falls, and a bright green weed is brought up on anchors even in midwinter.

We have one other pond just like this, White Pond[18]

15 No such stones remain on the shore.

16 Pondweeds, aquatic herbs with floating leaves.

17 Water-shield (*Brasenia peltata*), an aquatic plant with floating peltate leaves and jelly-covered stems.

18 A 43-acre pond approximately one mile southwest of Walden Pond.

19 A small settlement on the Sudbury Road between White Pond and Fair Haven Pond.
20 A spring that falls dry several times or is dry for most of the year.
21 In Greek mythology, a fountain on Mount Parnassus sacred to the Muses, and a source of inspiration.
22 Ancient Greek and Roman writers divided the history of the universe into a number of ages. The Golden Age was a time of perfection. The Greek poet Hesiod wrote in *Works and Days* of an ideal golden age in the past from which period there had been a progressive decline.
23 Of the highest quality. In the gem trade, the clarity of diamonds is assessed by their translucence: the more translucent, the higher the quality. Clear white diamonds are called diamonds of the first water.

in Nine Acre Corner,[19] about two and a half miles westerly; but, though I am acquainted with most of the ponds within a dozen miles of this centre, I do not know a third of this pure and well-like character. Successive nations perchance have drank at, admired, and fathomed it, and passed away, and still its water is green and pellucid as ever. Not an intermitting spring![20] Perhaps on that spring morning when Adam and Eve were driven out of Eden Walden Pond was already in existence, and even then breaking up in a gentle spring rain accompanied with mist and a southerly wind, and covered with myriads of ducks and geese, which had not heard of the fall, when still such pure lakes sufficed them. Even then it had commenced to rise and fall, and had clarified its waters and colored them of the hue they now wear, and obtained a patent of heaven to be the only Walden Pond in the world and distiller of celestial dews. Who knows in how many unremembered nations' literatures this has been the Castalian Fountain?[21] or what nymphs presided over it in the Golden Age?[22] It is a gem of the first water[23] which Concord wears in her coronet.

Yet perchance the first who came to this well have left some trace of their footsteps. I have been surprised to detect encircling the pond, even where a thick wood has just been cut down on the shore, a narrow shelf-like path in the steep hill-side, alternately rising and falling, approaching and receding from the water's edge, as old probably as the race of man here, worn by the feet of aboriginal hunters, and still from time to time unwittingly trodden by the present occupants of the land. This is particularly distinct to one standing on the middle of the pond in winter, just after a light snow has fallen, appearing as a clear undulating white line, unobscured by weeds and twigs, and very obvious a quarter of a mile off in many places where in summer it is hardly distinguishable close at hand. The snow reprints it, as it were, in clear white type alto-relievo.[24] The ornamented grounds of villas which will one day be built here may still preserve some trace of this.

The pond rises and falls, but whether regularly or not, and within what period, nobody knows, though, as usual, many pretend to know.[25] It is commonly higher in the winter and lower in the summer, though not corresponding to the general wet and dryness. I can remember when it was a foot or two lower, and also when it was at least five feet higher, than when I lived by it. There is a narrow sand-bar running into it, with very deep water on one side, on which I helped boil a kettle of chowder, some six rods from the main shore, about the year 1824,[26] which it has not been possible to do for twenty-five years; and on the other hand, my friends used to listen with incredulity when I told them, that a few years later I was accustomed to fish from a boat in a secluded cove in the woods, fifteen rods from the only shore they knew, which place was long since converted into a meadow.[27] But the pond has risen steadily for two years, and now, in the summer of '52,[28] is just five feet higher than when I lived there, or as high as it was thirty years ago, and fishing goes on again in the meadow. This makes a difference of level, at the outside, of six or seven feet; and yet the water shed by the surrounding hills is insignificant in amount, and this overflow must be referred to causes which affect the deep springs. This same summer the pond has begun to fall again. It is remarkable that this fluctuation, whether periodical or not, appears thus to require many years for its accomplishment. I have observed one rise and a part of two falls, and I expect that a dozen or fifteen years hence the water will again be as low as I have ever known it. Flint's Pond,[29] a mile eastward, allowing for the disturbance occasioned by its inlets and outlets, and the smaller intermediate ponds also, sympathize with Walden, and recently attained their greatest height at the same time

24 Degree of sculptured high relief of which the projection of a figure from the background is half or more the circumference.

25 The pond rises and falls in coincidence with the water table of the area.

26 In his journal of 27 August 1852, Thoreau originally wrote that he had boiled the chowder on the sand bar "more than twenty years ago" [J 4:321].

27 Wyman Meadow, or Pout's Nest, a few rods southeast of Thoreau's house site. Depending on the water level of the pond, it is either meadow or cove.

28 One of many indications that *Walden* was not written entirely during Thoreau's stay at Walden Pond.

29 Approximately one mile southeast of Walden Pond.

with the latter. The same is true, as far as my observation goes, of White Pond.

This rise and fall of Walden at long intervals serves this use at least; the water standing at this great height for a year or more, though it makes it difficult to walk round it, kills the shrubs and trees which have sprung up about its edge since the last rise, pitch-pines, birches, alders, aspens, and others, and, falling again, leaves an unobstructed shore; for, unlike many ponds and all waters which are subject to a daily tide, its shore is cleanest when the water is lowest. On the side of the pond next my house, a row of pitch-pines fifteen feet high has been killed and tipped over as if by a lever, and thus a stop put to their encroachments; and their size indicates how many years have elapsed since the last rise to this height. By this fluctuation the pond asserts its title to a shore, and thus the *shore* is *shorn,* and the trees cannot hold it by right of possession. These are the lips of the lake on which no beard grows. It licks its chaps from time to time. When the water is at its height, the alders, willows, and maples send forth a mass of fibrous red roots several feet long from all sides of their stems in the water, and to the height of three or four feet from the ground, in the effort to maintain themselves; and I have known the high-blueberry bushes about the shore, which commonly produce no fruit, bear an abundant crop under these circumstances.

Some have been puzzled to tell how the shore became so regularly paved. My townsmen have all heard the tradition, the oldest people tell me that they heard it in their youth, that anciently the Indians were holding a pow-wow upon a hill here, which rose as high into the heavens as the pond now sinks deep into the earth, and they used much profanity, as the story goes, though this vice is one of which the Indians were never guilty, and while they were thus engaged the hill shook and suddenly sank, and only one old squaw, named Walden, escaped, and from her the pond was named.[30] It has been conjectured that when the hill shook these stones rolled down its side and became the present shore. It is very certain, at any rate, that once there was no pond here, and now there is one; and this Indian fable does not in any respect conflict with the account of that ancient settler whom I have mentioned,[31] who remembers so well when he first came here with his divining rod, saw a thin vapor rising from the sward, and the hazel pointed steadily downward, and he concluded to dig a well here. As for the stones, many still think that they are hardly to be accounted for by the action of the waves on these hills; but I observe that the surrounding hills are remarkably full of the same kind of stones, so that they have been obliged to pile them up in walls on both sides of the railroad cut nearest the pond; and, moreover, there are most stones where the shore is most abrupt; so that, unfortunately, it is no longer a mystery to me. I detect the paver.[32] If the name was not derived from that of some English locality,—Saffron Walden, for instance,—one might suppose that it was called, originally, *Walled-in* Pond.[33]

The pond was my well ready dug. For four months in the year its water is as cold as it is pure at all times; and I think that it is then as good as any, if not the best, in the town. In the winter, all water which is exposed to the air is colder than springs and wells which are protected from it. The temperature of the pond water which had stood in the room where I sat from five o'clock in the afternoon till noon the next day, the sixth of March, 1846, the thermometer having been up to 65° or 70° some of the time, owing partly to the sun on the roof, was 42°, or one degree colder than the water of one of the coldest wells in the village just drawn.[34] The temperature of the Boiling Spring[35] the same day was 45°, or the warmest of any water tried, though it is the coldest that I know of in summer, when, beside, shallow and stagnant sur-

30 Thoreau noted in his copy of *Walden:* "This is told of Alexander's Lake in Killingly Ct. by Barber. v *his* Con. Hist. Coll." He was referring to John Warner Barber's *Connecticut Historical Collections* (New Haven, 1838), which recounts a similar tale of Native Americans being punished by the Great Spirit for their "licentiousness" at a festival: "While the red people in immense numbers were capering about upon the summit of the mountain, it suddenly 'gave way' beneath them and sunk to a great depth, when the water from below rushed up and covered them all except *one good old squaw,* who occupied one of the peaks, which now bears the name of Loon's Island." The story was also told specifically about Walden Pond in the 11 August 1821 issue of *Middlesex Gazette:*

> It is said that the place which now contains a body of water, was once a high hill—that on this hill the Indians assembled at certain season to celebrate their religious festivals, and at other times, to burn and torture prisoners taken in the wars with the early settlers of the country; it was on a meeting of numerous chiefs and tribes for the latter purpose, that this celebrated hill disappeared in the midst of their barbarous rejoicings, and sunk with all its savage inhabitants upon it. And on account of the remarkable depth of the water, which has never been fathomed, it was supposed to have continued to sink to such an amazing depth, that *the bottom dropped out one day.*

31 In "Solitude," where he is referred to as "an old settler" (note 30).

32 The paver was a glacier, which deposited boulders and drift. Glacial theory of land development began in the early 19th century and was pushed forward in 1840 when Louis Agassiz (1807–1873) published *Études sur les Glaciers,* the first book on glaciology and glacial geomorphology. In 1848 Agassiz became a professor of zoology and geology at Harvard.

33 On 4 June 1853 Thoreau examined land-grant

records at the town clerk's office and was "surprised to find such names as 'Wallden Pond' & 'Fair Haven' as early as 1653" [PJ 6:178]. Thoreau later noted in his copy of *Walden:* "Evelyn in his Diary (1654) mentioned 'the parish of Saffron Walden, famous for the abundance of Saffron there cultivated, and esteemed the best of any foreign country.'" Years later Thoreau was excited to discover that the Minott family of Concord was "descended from Thomas Minott, who, according to Shattuck, was secretary of the Abbott of Walden (!) in Essex, and whose son George was born at Saffron Walden (!)" [J 10:219]. A similar association to Walden being "walled in" was made in a bracketed reference in a brief article on the "Middlesex Map" in the 21 August 1830 issue of the Concord *Yeoman's Gazette:* "*Walden* [Wall'd in] *Pond* which is on the map indeed, but is left nameless."

34 Thoreau was sometimes concerned about his fact-gathering, as acknowledged in this 1851 journal entry: "I fear that the character of my knowledge is from year to year becoming more distinct and scientific; that, in exchange for views as wide as heaven's cope, I am being narrowed down to the field of the microscope. I see details, not wholes nor the shadow of the whole" [J 2:406].

35 Located a half mile west of Walden Pond, the Boiling Spring is a bubbling, not a hot, spring.

36 Brister's Spring, northeast of Walden Pond.

37 Chub (*Semotilus bullaris*).

38 Small freshwater fish, including, in Thoreau's day, the shiner, dace, roach, and minnow. In *A Week on the Concord and Merrimack Rivers,* Thoreau wrote:

> The chivin, dace, roach, cousin trout, or whatever else it is called (*Leuciscus pulchellus*), white and red, always an unexpected prize, which, however, any angler is glad to hook for its rarity;—a name that reminds us of many an unsuccessful ramble by swift streams, when the wind rose to disappoint the fisher. It is commonly a silvery soft-scaled fish, of grace-

face water is not mingled with it. Moreover, in summer, Walden never becomes so warm as most water which is exposed to the sun, on account of its depth. In the warmest weather I usually placed a pailful in my cellar, where it became cool in the night, and remained so during the day; though I also resorted to a spring in the neighborhood.[36] It was as good when a week old as the day it was dipped, and had no taste of the pump. Whoever camps for a week in summer by the shore of a pond, needs only bury a pail of water a few feet deep in the shade of his camp to be independent on the luxury of ice.

There have been caught in Walden, pickerel, one weighing seven pounds, to say nothing of another which carried off a reel with great velocity, which the fisherman safely set down at eight pounds because he did not see him, perch and pouts, some of each weighing over two pounds, shiners, chivins[37] or roach, (*Leuciscus pulchellus,*)[38] a very few breams, (*Pomotis obesus,*) and a couple of eels,[39] one weighing four pounds,—I am thus particular because the weight of a fish is commonly its only title to fame, and these are the only eels I have heard of here;—also, I have a faint recollection of a little fish some five inches long, with silvery sides and a greenish back, somewhat dace-like in its character, which I mention here chiefly to link my facts to fable. Nevertheless, this pond is not very fertile in fish.[40] Its pickerel, though not abundant, are its chief boast. I have seen at one time[41] lying on the ice pickerel of at least three different kinds; a long and shallow one, steel-colored, most like those caught in the river; a bright golden kind, with greenish reflections and remarkably deep, which is the most common here; and another, golden-colored, and shaped like the last, but peppered on the sides with small dark brown or black spots, intermixed with a few faint blood-red ones, very much like a trout. The specific name *reticulatus*[42] would not apply to this; it should be *guttatus*[43] rather.

These are all very firm fish, and weigh more than their size promises. The shiners, pouts, and perch also, and indeed all the fishes which inhabit this pond, are much cleaner, handsomer, and firmer fleshed than those in the river and most other ponds, as the water is purer, and they can easily be distinguished from them. Probably many ichthyologists would make new varieties of some of them. There are also a clean race of frogs and tortoises, and a few muscles[44] in it; muskrats and minks leave their traces about it, and occasionally a travelling mud-turtle[45] visits it. Sometimes, when I pushed off my boat in the morning, I disturbed a great mud-turtle which had secreted himself under the boat in the night. Ducks and geese frequent it in the spring and fall, the white-bellied swallows (*Hirundo bicolor*)[46] skim over it, kingfishers dart away from its coves, and the peetweets (*Totanus macularius*)[47] "teeter" along its stony shores all summer. I have sometimes disturbed a fishhawk[48] sitting on a white-pine over the water; but I doubt if it is ever profaned by the wing of a gull, like Fair Haven.[49] At most, it tolerates one annual loon. These are all the animals of consequence which frequent it now.

You may see from a boat, in calm weather, near the sandy eastern shore, where the water is eight or ten feet deep, and also in some other parts of the pond, some circular heaps half a dozen feet in diameter by a foot in height, consisting of small stones less than a hen's egg in size, where all around is bare sand. At first you wonder if the Indians could have formed them on the ice for any purpose, and so, when the ice melted, they sank to the bottom; but they are too regular and some of them plainly too fresh for that. They are similar to those found in rivers; but as there are no suckers[50] nor lampreys[51] here, I know not by what fish they could be made. Perhaps they are the nests of the chivin.[52] These lend a pleasing mystery to the bottom.

ful, scholarlike, and classical look, like many a picture in an English book. . . .

The dace (*Leuciscus argenteus*) is a slight silvery minnow, found generally in the middle of the stream where the current is most rapid. . . .

The shiner (*Leuciscus chrysoleucus*) is a soft-scaled and tender fish, the victim of its stronger neighbors, found in all places, deep and shallow, clear and turbid; generally the first nibbler at the bait, but, with its small mouth and nibbling propensities, not easily caught. It is a gold or silver bit that passes current in the river. [W 1:27–28]

39 In *A Week on the Concord and Merrimack Rivers* Thoreau referred to the common eel (*Muraena bostoniensis*) as "the only species of eel known in the State" [W 1:31]. The eels pass overland from the river to the pond.

40 Lemuel Shattuck wrote in *A History of the Town of Concord*, regarding fish in Walden Pond: "It is said no fish were caught in it, till they were transplanted there from other waters. Pickerel and other fish are now plenty there."

41 On 29 January 1853.

42 Latin: netlike. Reference to the pond pickerel's scientific name, *Esox reticulatus*.

43 Latin: speckled; spotted; marked by drops.

44 Mussels: freshwater clams (*Unio*).

45 Snapping turtle (*Chelonura serpentina*).

46 Now known as *Iridoprocne bicolor*, more commonly called the tree swallow. John James Audubon (1785–1851) used the name white-bellied swallow in *Birds of America*.

47 Now *Actitis macularia*, more commonly known as the spotted sandpiper.

48 Osprey (*Pandion haliaetus*).

49 Fair Haven Bay is a widening of the Sudbury River, a little less than one mile southwest of Walden Pond.

50 Common river fish in New England: *Catostomidae*. According to his journal of 3 June 1852, Thoreau learned from John Downes (1799–1882) that Downes "once saw the common sucker in numbers piling up stones as big as his fist (like the pile which I have seen), taking them up or moving them with his mouth" [J 2:224].

51 An eel-like fish, many of which are parasitic, with a circular sucking mouth, of which Thoreau wrote in *A Week on the Concord and Merrimack Rivers:* "You may sometimes see the curious circular nests of the lamprey eel (*Petromyzon americanus*), the American stone-sucker, as large as a cart-wheel, a foot or two in height, and sometimes rising half a foot above the surface of the water. They collect these stones, of the size of a hen's egg, with their mouths, as their name implies, and are said to fashion them into circles with their tails" [W 1:31].

52 Thoreau's theory is correct, as corroborated by William Converse Kendall and Edmund Lee Goldsborough, *The Fishes of the Connecticut Lakes and Neighboring Waters, with Notes on the Plankton Environment* (United States Bureau of Fisheries document, no. 633, Washington, D.C.: Government Printing Office, 1908).

53 Woven edging to prevent cloth from fraying.

54 A method used sometimes by artists and often by Thoreau of bending over and looking through the legs. Thoreau referred to this technique in several journal passages: "I look between my legs up the river across Fair Haven" [J 3:333], and "What shall we make of the fact that you have only to stand on your head a moment to be enchanted with the beauty of the landscape" [J 2:51]. Emerson suggested in *Nature:* "Turn the eyes upside down, by looking at the landscape through your legs, and how agreeable is the picture, though you have seen it any time these twenty years!" Emerson also told Thoreau in late 1853, "W. H. Channing conjectured that the landscape looked fairer when we turned our heads, because we beheld it with nerves of the eye unused before" [J 6:17].

The shore is irregular enough not to be monotonous. I have in my mind's eye the western indented with deep bays, the bolder northern, and the beautifully scolloped southern shore, where successive capes overlap each other and suggest unexplored coves between. The forest has never so good a setting, nor is so distinctly beautiful, as when seen from the middle of a small lake amid hills which rise from the water's edge; for the water in which it is reflected not only makes the best foreground in such a case, but, with its winding shore, the most natural and agreeable boundary to it. There is no rawness nor imperfection in its edge there, as where the axe has cleared a part, or a cultivated field abuts on it. The trees have ample room to expand on the water side, and each sends forth its most vigorous branch in that direction. There Nature has woven a natural selvage,[53] and the eye rises by just gradations from the low shrubs of the shore to the highest trees. There are few traces of man's hand to be seen. The water laves the shore as it did a thousand years ago.

A lake is the landscape's most beautiful and expressive feature. It is earth's eye; looking into which the beholder measures the depth of his own nature. The fluviatile trees next the shore are the slender eyelashes which fringe it, and the wooded hills and cliffs around are its overhanging brows.

Standing on the smooth sandy beach at the east end of the pond, in a calm September afternoon, when a slight haze makes the opposite shore line indistinct, I have seen whence came the expression, "the glassy surface of a lake." When you invert your head,[54] it looks like a thread of finest gossamer stretched across the valley, and gleaming against the distant pine woods, separating one stratum of the atmosphere from another. You would think that you could walk dry under it to the opposite hills, and that the swallows which skim over might perch on it. Indeed, they sometimes dive below the line, as it were by mistake, and are undeceived. As you look over the pond westward you are obliged to employ both your hands to defend your eyes against the reflected as well as the true sun, for they are equally bright; and if, between the two, you survey its surface critically, it is literally as smooth as glass, except where the skater insects, at equal intervals scattered over its whole extent, by their motions in the sun produce the finest imaginable sparkle on it, or, perchance, a duck plumes itself, or, as I have said, a swallow skims so low as to touch it. It may be that in the distance a fish describes an arc of three or four feet in the air, and there is one bright flash where it emerges, and another where it strikes the water; sometimes the whole silvery arc is revealed; or here and there, perhaps, is a thistle-down floating on its surface, which the fishes dart at and so dimple it again. It is like molten glass cooled but not congealed, and the few motes in it are pure and beautiful like the imperfections in glass. You may often detect a yet smoother and darker water, separated from the rest as if by an invisible cobweb, boom[55] of the water nymphs, resting on it. From a hill-top you can see a fish leap in almost any part; for not a pickerel or shiner picks an insect from this smooth surface but it manifestly disturbs the equilibrium of the whole lake. It is wonderful with what elaborateness this simple fact is advertised,—this piscine murder will out,[56]—and from my distant perch I distinguish the circling undulations when they are half a dozen rods in diameter. You can even detect a water-bug (*Gyrinus*)[57] ceaselessly progressing over the smooth surface a quarter of a mile off; for they furrow the water slightly, making a conspicuous ripple bounded by two diverging lines, but the skaters glide over it without rippling it perceptibly. When the surface is considerably agitated there are no skaters nor water-bugs on it, but apparently, in calm days, they leave their havens and adventurously glide forth from the shore by short impulses till they com-

55 Pole set in water, or a barrier, used to mark a channel or a boundary, although sometimes a strong barrier of beams or an iron chain or cable fastened to spars, extended across a river or the mouth of a harbor, to prevent an enemy's ships from passing.

56 Allusion to the phrase "Mordre wol out" in Chaucer's "The Prioresses Tale" and "The Nonne Prestes Tale."

57 Whirligig beetles: from the Gyrinidae family of insects, they can move across the water in inches without making even a ripple on the surface. When disturbed they begin whirling around in the movement for which they are named.

58 Possible allusion to the song "Oh, Boatman, Haste!" (1843), which has the line: "How silvery sweet the echo falls, / Like music dripping from the oar!" or to Thomas Moore's "Echo":

How sweet the Echo makes
To music at night,
When, roused by lute or horn, she wakes,
And, far away, o'er lawns and lakes,
Goes answering light.

pletely cover it. It is a soothing employment, on one of those fine days in the fall when all the warmth of the sun is fully appreciated, to sit on a stump on such a height as this, overlooking the pond, and study the dimpling circles which are incessantly inscribed on its otherwise invisible surface amid the reflected skies and trees. Over this great expanse there is no disturbance but it is thus at once gently smoothed away and assuaged, as, when a vase of water is jarred, the trembling circles seek the shore and all is smooth again. Not a fish can leap or an insect fall on the pond but it is thus reported in circling dimples, in lines of beauty, as it were the constant welling up of its fountain, the gentle pulsing of its life, the heaving of its breast. The thrills of joy and thrills of pain are undistinguishable. How peaceful the phenomena of the lake! Again the works of man shine as in the spring. Ay, every leaf and twig and stone and cobweb sparkles now at midafternoon as when covered with dew in a spring morning. Every motion of an oar or an insect produces a flash of light; and if an oar falls, how sweet the echo![58]

In such a day, in September or October, Walden is a perfect forest mirror, set round with stones as precious to my eye as if fewer or rarer. Nothing so fair, so pure, and at the same time so large, as a lake, perchance, lies on the surface of the earth. Sky water. It needs no fence. Nations come and go without defiling it. It is a mirror which no stone can crack, whose quicksilver will never wear off, whose gilding Nature continually repairs; no storms, no dust, can dim its surface ever fresh;—a mirror in which all impurity presented to it sinks, swept and dusted by the sun's hazy brush,—this the light dust-cloth,—which retains no breath that is breathed on it, but sends its own to float as clouds high above its surface, and be reflected in its bosom still.

A field of water betrays the spirit that is in the air. It is continually receiving new life and motion from above.

It is intermediate in its nature between land and sky. On land only the grass and trees wave, but the water itself is rippled by the wind. I see where the breeze dashes across it by the streaks or flakes of light. It is remarkable that we can look down on its surface. We shall, perhaps, look down thus on the surface of air at length,[59] and mark where a still subtler spirit sweeps over it.

The skaters and water-bugs finally disappear in the latter part of October, when the severe frosts have come; and then and in November, usually, in a calm day, there is absolutely nothing to ripple the surface. One November afternoon, in the calm at the end of a rain storm of several days' duration, when the sky was still completely overcast and the air was full of mist, I observed that the pond was remarkably smooth, so that it was difficult to distinguish its surface; though it no longer reflected the bright tints of October, but the sombre November colors of the surrounding hills. Though I passed over it as gently as possible, the slight undulations produced by my boat extended almost as far as I could see, and gave a ribbed appearance to the reflections. But, as I was looking over the surface, I saw here and there at a distance a faint glimmer, as if some skater insects which had escaped the frosts might be collected there, or, perchance, the surface, being so smooth, betrayed where a spring welled up from the bottom. Paddling gently to one of these places, I was surprised to find myself surrounded by myriads of small perch, about five inches long, of a rich bronze color in the green water, sporting there and constantly rising to the surface and dimpling it, sometimes leaving bubbles on it. In such transparent and seemingly bottomless water, reflecting the clouds, I seemed to be floating through the air as in a balloon, and their swimming impressed me as a kind of flight or hovering, as if they were a compact flock of birds passing just beneath my level on the right or left, their fins, like sails, set all around them.

59 From heaven, for eternity.

There were many such schools in the pond, apparently improving the short season before winter would draw an icy shutter over their broad skylight, sometimes giving to the surface an appearance as if a slight breeze struck it, or a few rain-drops fell there. When I approached carelessly and alarmed them, they made a sudden plash and rippling with their tails, as if one had struck the water with a brushy bough, and instantly took refuge in the depths. At length the wind rose, the mist increased, and the waves began to run, and the perch leaped much higher than before, half out of water, a hundred black points, three inches long, at once above the surface. Even as late as the fifth of December, one year,[60] I saw some dimples on the surface, and thinking it was going to rain hard immediately, the air being full of mist, I made haste to take my place at the oars and row homeward; already the rain seemed rapidly increasing, though I felt none on my cheek, and I anticipated a thorough soaking. But suddenly the dimples ceased, for they were produced by the perch, which the noise of my oars had scared into the depths, and I saw their schools dimly disappearing; so I spent a dry afternoon after all.

An old man who used to frequent this pond nearly sixty years ago,[61] when it was dark with surrounding forests, tells me that in those days he sometimes saw it all alive with ducks and other water fowl, and that there were many eagles about it. He came here a-fishing, and used an old log canoe which he found on the shore. It was made of two white-pine logs dug out and pinned together, and was cut off square at the ends. It was very clumsy, but lasted a great many years before it became water-logged and perhaps sank to the bottom. He did not know whose it was; it belonged to the pond. He used to make a cable for his anchor of strips of hickory bark tied together. An old man, a potter,[62] who lived by the pond before the Revolution, told him once that there was an iron chest at the bottom,

60 In 1852.

61 Unidentified. In Thoreau's original journal passage of 16 June 1853 the old man frequented the pond "fifty-five years ago" [J 5:260].

62 John Wyman, sometimes Wayman or Wyeman (1730?–1800), who built his house at Walden Pond in 1787 on land then owned by Dr. Abel Prescott (1718–1805). Wyman is also mentioned in "Former Inhabitants."

and that he had seen it. Sometimes it would come floating up to the shore; but when you went toward it, it would go back into deep water and disappear. I was pleased to hear of the old log canoe, which took the place of an Indian one of the same material but more graceful construction, which perchance had first been a tree on the bank, and then, as it were, fell into the water, to float there for a generation, the most proper vessel for the lake. I remember that when I first looked into these depths there were many large trunks to be seen indistinctly lying on the bottom, which had either been blown over formerly, or left on the ice at the last cutting, when wood was cheaper; but now they have mostly disappeared.

When I first paddled a boat on Walden, it was completely surrounded by thick and lofty pine and oak woods, and in some of its coves grape vines had run over the trees next the water and formed bowers under which a boat could pass. The hills which form its shores are so steep, and the woods on them were then so high, that, as you looked down from the west end, it had the appearance of an amphitheatre for some kind of sylvan spectacle. I have spent many an hour, when I was younger, floating over its surface as the zephyr willed, having paddled my boat to the middle, and lying on my back across the seats, in a summer forenoon, dreaming awake, until I was aroused by the boat touching the sand, and I arose to see what shore my fates had impelled me to; days when idleness was the most attractive and productive industry. Many a forenoon have I stolen away, preferring to spend thus the most valued part of the day; for I was rich, if not in money, in sunny hours and summer days, and spent them lavishly; nor do I regret that I did not waste more of them in the workshop or the teacher's desk. But since I left those shores the woodchoppers have still further laid them waste, and now for many a year there will be no more rambling through the aisles of the wood,

63 River in northern India held sacred by the Hindus.

64 According to Franklin Sanborn this plan was given up during Thoreau's lifetime. Flint's Pond was eventually used for this purpose.

65 To feed the steam engine, and also to make room for the laying of tracks and to supply railroad ties.

66 In the Trojan War, the Greeks were able to pierce Troy's defenses by hiding in a large wooden horse that they left as an ostensible gift, which the Trojans brought into the city.

67 Plutarch used this term in his life of Alexander: "But the enemy hardly sustaining the first onset soon gave ground and fled, all but the mercenary Greeks, who, making a stand upon a rising ground, desired quarter, which Alexander, guided rather by passion than judgment, refused to grant, and charging them himself first, had his horse (not Bucephalus, but another) killed under him."

68 More of More-Hall: hero in the English ballad "The Dragon of Wantley" who slew the beast by giving it a kick or a blow on its only mortally vulnerable spot, in some versions its mouth and in others its backside. The dragon in this ballad is also compared with the Trojan Horse:

> Have you not heard how the Trojan horse
> Held seventy men in his belly?
> This dragon was not quite so big,
> But very near, I'll tell ye;

And like Thoreau's Iron Horse the dragon browsed off the woods:

> All sorts of cattle this dragon would eat,
> Some say he ate up trees,
> And that the forests sure he would
> Devour up by degrees.

Thoreau's spelling, Moore of Moore Hall, apparently comes from the libretto by Henry Carey (1689–1743) to a burlesque comic opera also called *The Dragon of Wantley*. In the 18th cen-

with occasional vistas through which you see the water. My Muse may be excused if she is silent henceforth. How can you expect the birds to sing when their groves are cut down?

Now the trunks of trees on the bottom, and the old log canoe, and the dark surrounding woods, are gone, and the villagers, who scarcely know where it lies, instead of going to the pond to bathe or drink, are thinking to bring its water, which should be as sacred as the Ganges[63] at least, to the village in a pipe,[64] to wash their dishes with!—to earn their Walden by the turning of a cock or drawing of a plug! That devilish Iron Horse, whose ear-rending neigh is heard throughout the town, has muddied the Boiling Spring with his foot, and he it is that has browsed off all the woods on Walden shore;[65] that Trojan horse,[66] with a thousand men in his belly, introduced by mercenary Greeks![67] Where is the country's champion, the Moore of Moore Hall,[68] to meet him at the Deep Cut[69] and thrust an avenging lance between the ribs of the bloated pest?

Nevertheless, of all the characters I have known, perhaps Walden wears best, and best preserves its purity. Many men have been likened to it, but few deserve that honor. Though the woodchoppers have laid bare first this shore and then that, and the Irish have built their sties by it, and the railroad has infringed on its border, and the ice-men have skimmed it once, it is itself unchanged, the same water which my youthful eyes fell on; all the change is in me. It has not acquired one permanent wrinkle after all its ripples. It is perennially young, and I may stand and see a swallow dip apparently to pick an insect from its surface as of yore. It struck me again to-night, as if I had not seen it almost daily for more than twenty years,—Why, here is Walden, the same woodland lake that I discovered so many years ago; where a forest was cut down last winter another is springing up by its shore as lustily as ever;[70] the same thought is welling up to its surface that was then;

it is the same liquid joy and happiness to itself and its Maker, ay, and it *may* be to me. It is the work of a brave man surely, in whom there was no guile![71] He rounded this water with his hand, deepened and clarified it in his thought, and in his will bequeathed it to Concord. I see by its face that it is visited by the same reflection; and I can almost say, Walden, is it you?

> It is no dream of mine,
> To ornament a line;
> I cannot come nearer to God and Heaven
> Than I live to Walden even.
> I am its stony shore,
> And the breeze that passes o'er;
> In the hollow of my hand
> Are its water and its sand,
> And its deepest resort
> Lies high in my thought.[72]

The cars never pause to look at it; yet I fancy that the engineers and firemen and brakemen, and those passengers who have a season ticket and see it often, are better men for the sight. The engineer does not forget at night, or his nature does not, that he has beheld this vision of serenity and purity once at least during the day. Though seen but once, it helps to wash out State Street[73] and the engine's soot. One proposes that it be called "God's Drop."[74]

I have said that Walden has no visible inlet nor outlet, but it is on the one hand distantly and indirectly related to Flint's Pond, which is more elevated, by a chain of small ponds coming from that quarter, and on the other directly and manifestly to Concord River, which is lower, by a similar chain of ponds through which in some other geological period it may have flowed, and by a little digging, which God forbid, it can be made to flow thither

tury its popularity was second only to John Gay's (1685–1732) *The Beggars' Opera,* so Thoreau likely was aware of it.

69 Spot northwest of Walden Pond where the earth had been cut away to make level tracks for the railroad.

70 In "The Succession of Forest Trees" Thoreau explained: "The shade of a dense pine wood is more unfavorable to the springing up of pines of the same species than of oaks within it, though the former may come up abundantly when the pines are cut, if there chance to be sound seed in the ground" [W 5:190].

71 Allusion to John 1:47: "Jesus saw Nathanael coming to him, and saith of him, Behold an Israelite indeed, in whom is no guile!"

72 Thoreau's poem.

73 Financial and mercantile district of Boston, representative of business and material wealth. Emerson commented in his 1841 journal: "The view taken of Transcendentalism in State Street is that it threatens to invalidate contracts."

74 Possibly from Emerson who, in his journal of 9 April 1840, referred to Goose Pond as "the Drop or God's Pond." In his journal after 11 September 1849 Thoreau listed "Yellow pine lake" and "Hygae's Water" as two other suggestions for new names for Walden [PJ 3:24].

Allusion to Andrew Marvell's (1621–1678) "An Horatian Ode": "He lived reserved and austere" [l. 34].
76 Allusion to Thomas Gray's "Elegy in a Country Churchyard": "Full many a flower is born to blush unseen, / And waste its sweetness on the desert air" [ll. 55–56].
77 Thoreau's friend and Harvard College roommate Charles Stearns Wheeler (1816–1843) built a shanty near Flint's Pond in which he stayed at various times between 1836 and 1842. Thoreau stayed at the shanty, probably in 1837, but accounts differ as to the length of time. Although the exact location of Wheeler's shanty is unknown, it was in all probability built on the land owned by his brother, William Francis Wheeler (1812–1890).
78 Lilypad.
79 In his journal of 4 September 1851, Thoreau referred to the Indian walking "in single file, more solitary,—not side by side, chatting as he went" [J 2:457].
80 Moorball (*Cladophora aegagropila*): a fresh-water alga that forms a globular mass.

again. If by living thus reserved and austere,[75] like a hermit in the woods, so long, it has acquired such wonderful purity, who would not regret that the comparatively impure waters of Flint's Pond should be mingled with it, or itself should ever go to waste its sweetness[76] in the ocean wave?

Flint's, or Sandy Pond, in Lincoln,[77] our greatest lake and inland sea, lies about a mile east of Walden. It is much larger, being said to contain one hundred and ninety-seven acres, and is more fertile in fish; but it is comparatively shallow, and not remarkably pure. A walk through the woods thither was often my recreation. It was worth the while, if only to feel the wind blow on your cheek freely, and see the waves run, and remember the life of mariners. I went a-chestnutting there in the fall, on windy days, when the nuts were dropping into the water and were washed to my feet; and one day, as I crept along its sedgy shore, the fresh spray blowing in my face, I came upon the mouldering wreck of a boat, the sides gone, and hardly more than the impression of its flat bottom left amid the rushes; yet its model was sharply defined, as if it were a large decayed pad,[78] with its veins. It was as impressive a wreck as one could imagine on the sea-shore, and had as good a moral. It is by this time mere vegetable mould and undistinguishable pond shore, through which rushes and flags have pushed up. I used to admire the ripple marks on the sandy bottom, at the north end of this pond, made firm and hard to the feet of the wader by the pressure of the water, and the rushes which grew in Indian file,[79] in waving lines, corresponding to these marks, rank behind rank, as if the waves had planted them. There also I have found, in considerable quantities, curious balls,[80] composed apparently of fine grass or roots, of pipewort perhaps, from half an inch to four inches in diameter, and perfectly spherical. These wash back and forth in shallow water on a sandy bottom, and are sometimes cast on the shore. They are either solid grass, or have a little sand in the middle. At first you would say that they were formed by the action of the waves, like a pebble; yet the smallest are made of equally coarse materials, half an inch long, and they are produced only at one season of the year. Moreover, the waves, I suspect, do not so much construct as wear down a material which has already acquired consistency. They preserve their form when dry for an indefinite period.

Flint's Pond! Such is the poverty of our nomenclature. What right had the unclean and stupid farmer, whose farm abutted on this sky water, whose shores he has ruthlessly laid bare, to give his name to it?[81] Some skin-flint, who loved better the reflecting surface of a dollar, or a bright cent, in which he could see his own brazen face; who regarded even the wild ducks which settled in it as trespassers; his fingers grown into crooked and horny talons from the long habit of grasping harpy-like;[82]—so it is not named for me.[83] I go not there to see him nor to hear of him; who never *saw* it, who never bathed in it, who never loved it, who never protected it, who never spoke a good word for it, nor thanked God that he had made it. Rather let it be named from the fishes that swim in it, the wild fowl or quadrupeds which frequent it, the wild flowers which grow by its shores, or some wild man or child the thread of whose history is interwoven with its own; not from him who could show no title to it but the deed which a like-minded neighbor or legislature gave him,—him who thought only of its money value; whose presence perchance cursed all the shore; who exhausted the land around it, and would fain have exhausted the waters within it; who regretted only that it was not English hay or cranberry meadow,—there was nothing to redeem it, forsooth, in his eyes,—and would have drained and sold it for the mud at its bottom. It did not turn his

81 Flint's Pond in Lincoln was named after the original owner of the land, Thomas Flint (1603–1653). It was also known as Mr. Flint's Pond, Mrs. Flint's Pond, and Great Pond in the 17th century and Sandy Pond since the beginning of the 18th century. Based on his association with Flint's Pond through Charles Stearns Wheeler there is conjecture that Thoreau had originally wished to build his house there but had been denied the privilege, inciting his punning invective on some "skin-flint," but there is no evidence to support this and the story may be apocryphal.

82 In Greek mythology, a filthy, hideous winged monster.

83 To Thoreau, a pond should not be named for its owner.

84 Privilege granting right to use water for turning mill machinery or other private purposes.

85 Part of the Aegean Sea named after Icarus. According to Greek mythology, Icarus used wings of wax made by his father, Daedalus, to escape Crete. His wings melted when he flew too near the sun, and Icarus fell into the sea.

86 Quoted from William Drummond of Hawthornden's (1585–1649) "Icarus": "For still the shore my brave attempt resounds."

87 Small pond east of Walden Pond.

88 Although Goose Pond does not lie directly between Thoreau's Walden house and Flint's Pond in Lincoln, this was his preferred route, as indicated by this journal entry from the fall or winter of 1845–46: "Flints—going to which you cross Goose pond—where a whole colony of muskrats inhabits & have raised their cabins high above the ice—but not one is seen abroad" [PJ 2:141]. On 12 September 1851 he wrote: "return *via* east of Flint's Pond via, Goose Pond and my old home to railroad" [J 2:496]. This route is mentioned also in "Winter Animals."

89 Reference to the Lake District in the northwest of England, associated with Wordsworth, Coleridge, and Robert Southey (1774–1843).

90 Thoreau would be referring to a privilege to use these waters for his "private business."

mill, and it was no *privilege*[84] to him to behold it. I respect not his labors, his farm where every thing has its price; who would carry the landscape, who would carry his God, to market, if he could get any thing for him; who goes to market *for* his god as it is; on whose farm nothing grows free, whose fields bear no crops, whose meadows no flowers, whose trees no fruits, but dollars; who loves not the beauty of his fruits, whose fruits are not ripe for him till they are turned to dollars. Give me the poverty that enjoys true wealth. Farmers are respectable and interesting to me in proportion as they are poor,—poor farmers. A model farm! where the house stands like a fungus in a muck-heap, chambers for men, horses, oxen, and swine, cleansed and uncleansed, all contiguous to one another! Stocked with men! A great grease-spot, redolent of manures and buttermilk! Under a high state of cultivation, being manured with the hearts and brains of men! As if you were to raise your potatoes in the church-yard! Such is a model farm.

No, no; if the fairest features of the landscape are to be named after men, let them be the noblest and worthiest men alone. Let our lakes receive as true names at least as the Icarian Sea,[85] where "still the shore" a "brave attempt resounds."[86]

Goose Pond,[87] of small extent, is on my way to Flint's;[88] Fair Haven, an expansion of Concord River, said to contain some seventy acres, is a mile south-west; and White Pond, of about forty acres, is a mile and a half beyond Fair Haven. This is my lake country.[89] These, with Concord River, are my water privileges;[90] and night and day, year in year out, they grind such grist as I carry to them.

Since the woodcutters, and the railroad, and I myself have profaned Walden, perhaps the most attractive, if not the most beautiful, of all our lakes, the gem of the

woods, is White Pond;—a poor name from its common-
ness, whether derived from the remarkable purity of its
waters or the color of its sands. In these as in other respects, however, it is a lesser twin of Walden. They are
so much alike that you would say they must be connected under ground. It has the same stony shore, and its
waters are of the same hue. As at Walden, in sultry dog-
day weather,[91] looking down through the woods on some
of its bays which are not so deep but that the reflection
from the bottom tinges them, its waters are of a misty
bluish-green or glaucous[92] color. Many years since I used
to go there to collect the sand by cart-loads, to make sandpaper with,[93] and I have continued to visit it ever since.
One who frequents it proposes to call it Virid[94] Lake. Perhaps it might be called Yellow-Pine Lake, from the following circumstance. About fifteen years ago you could see
the top of a pitch-pine, of the kind called yellow-pine[95]
hereabouts, though it is not a distinct species, projecting above the surface in deep water, many rods from the
shore. It was even supposed by some that the pond had
sunk, and this was one of the primitive forest that formerly stood there. I find that even so long ago as 1792, in a
"Topographical Description of the Town of Concord," by
one of its citizens, in the Collections of the Massachusetts
Historical Society, the author, after speaking of Walden
and White Ponds, adds, "In the middle of the latter may
be seen, when the water is very low, a tree which appears
as if it grew in the place where it now stands, although the
roots are fifty feet below the surface of the water; the top
of this tree is broken off, and at that place measures fourteen inches in diameter."[96] In the spring of '49 I talked
with the man who lives nearest the pond in Sudbury, who
told me that it was he who got out this tree ten or fifteen years before.[97] As near as he could remember, it stood
twelve or fifteen rods from the shore, where the water was
thirty or forty feet deep. It was in the winter, and he had

91 Hottest days of summer, so named for Sirius, the Dog Star, which rises with the sun at that time of year.
92 Light blue.
93 The Thoreau family business included manufacturing sandpaper along with its pencils and graphite.
94 Green. Franklin Sanborn suggested in *Recollections of Seventy Years* that Ellery Channing had proposed this idea.
95 First-growth white pines have a yellowish color to their wood. In "Former Inhabitants" Thoreau used the colloquial name Pumpkin Pine.
96 Quoted from William Jones, "A Topographical Description of the Town of Concord, August 20, 1792" in *Massachusetts Historical Society Collections* 1:238. The Massachusetts Historical Society was founded in 1791 as a repository and publisher for collecting, preserving, and disseminating resources for the study of American history. Jones (1772–1813) presented this paper on 20 August 1792 while a student at Harvard.
97 Josiah (Joshua) Haynes, Jr. (1800–1884).

98 Tree trunk, particularly the portion immediately above the ground.

99 Water lily.

been getting out ice in the forenoon, and had resolved that in the afternoon, with the aid of his neighbors, he would take out the old yellow-pine. He sawed a channel in the ice toward the shore, and hauled it over and along and out on to the ice with oxen; but, before he had gone far in his work, he was surprised to find that it was wrong end upward, with the stumps of the branches pointing down, and the small end firmly fastened in the sandy bottom. It was about a foot in diameter at the big end, and he had expected to get a good saw-log, but it was so rotten as to be fit only for fuel, if for that. He had some of it in his shed then. There were marks of an axe and of woodpeckers on the but.[98] He thought that it might have been a dead tree on the shore, but was finally blown over into the pond, and after the top had become waterlogged, while the but-end was still dry and light, had drifted out and sunk wrong end up. His father, eighty years old, could not remember when it was not there. Several pretty large logs may still be seen lying on the bottom, where, owing to the undulation of the surface, they look like huge water snakes in motion.

This pond has rarely been profaned by a boat, for there is little in it to tempt a fisherman. Instead of the white lily,[99] which requires mud, or the common sweet flag, the blue flag (*Iris versicolor*) grows thinly in the pure water, rising from the stony bottom all around the shore, where it is visited by humming birds in June, and the color both of its bluish blades and its flowers, and especially their reflections, are in singular harmony with the glaucous water.

White Pond and Walden are great crystals on the surface of the earth, Lakes of Light. If they were permanently congealed, and small enough to be clutched, they would, perchance, be carried off by slaves, like precious stones, to adorn the heads of emperors; but being liquid, and ample, and secured to us and our successors forever, we disregard them, and run after the diamond of Kohi-noor.[100] They are too pure to have a market value; they contain no muck. How much more beautiful than our lives, how much more transparent than our characters, are they! We never learned meanness of them. How much fairer than the pool before the farmer's door, in which his ducks swim! Hither the clean wild ducks come. Nature has no human inhabitant who appreciates her. The birds with their plumage and their notes are in harmony with the flowers, but what youth or maiden conspires with the wild luxuriant beauty of Nature? She flourishes most alone, far from the towns where they reside. Talk of heaven! ye disgrace earth.

100 A 186-carat diamond from India, also known as the "mountain of light." In 1850 the East India Company presented it to Queen Victoria, who had it recut to 108.93 carats.

1 Ancient Celtic priesthood to whom the oak was sacred. The Roman historian and naturalist Pliny the Elder (Gaius Plinius Secundus, 23–79) reported that the Druids "held nothing more sacred than the mistletoe and the oak and they never perform any of their rites except in the presence of a branch of it. They choose groves formed of oaks for the sake of the tree alone."

2 The Eastern red cedar (*Juniperus virginiana*), the female of which produces waxy-blue berries.

3 In Norse mythology, Odin's great hall in which the souls of slain heroes reside eternally.

4 Not the true creeping juniper (*Juniperus horizontalis*) but the common juniper (*Juniperus communis*, var. *depressa*).

5 Inedible or poisonous mushroomlike fungus with an umbrella-shaped fruiting body.

6 More commonly periwinkle, a small edible sea snail.

7 Swamp azalea (*Rhododendron viscosum*).

8 Poison dogwood or sumac (*Rhus vernix*), of which Thoreau wrote in his journal: "The dogwood and its berries in the *swamp* by the railroad, just above the red house, pendent on long stems which hang short down as if broken. . . . Ah, give me to walk in the dogwood swamp, with its few coarse branches! Beautiful as Satan" [J 3:147].

9 The red berry of the winterberry, or black alder, which is not an alder at all but a species of holly (*Ilex verticillat*).

10 Climbing bittersweet (*Celastrus scandens*).

11 Mountain holly (*Nemopanthus mucronata*).

Baker Farm

Sometimes I rambled to pine groves, standing like temples, or like fleets at sea, full-rigged, with wavy boughs, and rippling with light, so soft and green and shady that the Druids[1] would have forsaken their oaks to worship in them; or to the cedar wood beyond Flint's Pond, where the trees, covered with hoary blue berries,[2] spiring higher and higher, are fit to stand before Valhalla,[3] and the creeping juniper[4] covers the ground with wreaths full of fruit; or to swamps where the usnea lichen hangs in festoons from the black-spruce trees, and toad-stools,[5] round tables of the swamp gods, cover the ground, and more beautiful fungi adorn the stumps, like butterflies or shells, vegetable winkles;[6] where the swamp-pink[7] and dogwood[8] grow, the red alder-berry[9] glows like eyes of imps, the waxwork[10] grooves and crushes the hardest woods in its folds, and the wild-holly[11] berries make the beholder forget his home with their beauty, and he is dazzled and tempted by nameless other wild forbidden fruits, too fair for mortal taste. Instead of calling on some scholar, I paid many a visit to particular trees, of kinds which are rare in this neighborhood, standing far away in the middle of some pasture, or in the depths of a wood or swamp, or on a hill-top; such as the black-birch, of which we have some handsome specimens two feet in diameter; its cousin the yellow-birch, with its loose golden vest, perfumed like the first; the beech, which has so neat a bole[12] and beautifully lichen-painted, perfect in all its details, of which, excepting scattered specimens, I know but one small grove of sizable trees left in the township, supposed by some to have been planted by the pigeons that were once baited with beech nuts near by; it is worth the while to see the silver grain sparkle when you split this wood; the bass; the hornbeam; the *Celtis occidentalis,* or false elm, of which we have but one well-grown; some taller mast of a pine,[13] a shingle tree,[14] or a more perfect hemlock than usual, standing like a pagoda in the midst of the woods; and many others I could mention. These were the shrines I visited both summer and winter.

Once it chanced that I stood in the very abutment of a rainbow's arch,[15] which filled the lower stratum of the atmosphere, tinging the grass and leaves around, and dazzling me as if I looked through colored crystal. It was a lake of rainbow light, in which, for a short while, I lived like a dolphin.[16] If it had lasted longer it might have tinged my employments and life. As I walked on the railroad causeway, I used to wonder at the halo of light around my shadow, and would fain fancy myself one of the elect.[17] One who visited me declared that the shadows of some Irishmen before him had no halo about them, that it was only natives that were so distinguished. Benvenuto Cellini[18] tells us in his memoirs, that, after a certain terrible dream or vision which he had during his confinement in the castle of St. Angelo,[19] a resplendent light appeared over the shadow of his head at morning and evening, whether he was in Italy or France, and it was particularly conspicuous when the grass was moist with dew.[20] This was probably the same phenomenon to which I have referred, which is especially observed in the morning, but also at other times, and even by moonlight. Though a constant one, it is not commonly noticed, and, in the case of an excitable imagination like Cellini's, it

12 Trunk of a tree before the first major branch.
13 White pine, which was the only tall species growing in Concord.
14 A tree with wood good for making shingles, and not the East Indian timber tree (*Arcocarpus fraxinifolius*), also known as the shingle tree, with a hard durable wood used for tea boxes. A shingle tree would be selected by chopping into the side of a tree, splitting out a block and trying it to see if it would split free.
15 Thoreau noted this phenomenon twice in his journals, once on 9 August 1851: "We were in the westernmost edge of the shower at the moment the sun was setting, and its rays shone through the cloud and the falling rain. We were, in fact, in a rainbow and it was here its arch rested on the earth" [J 2:382–83]. And on 7 August 1852 he wrote: "We see the rainbow apparently when we are on the edge of the rain, just as the sun is setting. If we are deep in the rain, then it will appear dim. Sometimes it is so near that I see a portion of its arch this side of the woods in the horizon, tingeing them. Sometimes we are completely within it, enveloped by it, and experience the realization of the child's wish" [J 4:288]. Despite Thoreau's claim that he stood within the abutment, this is not possible. The law of physics dictates that the rainbow must appear opposite the sun at 42° from the observer, the "rainbow angle," to be visible. It is unclear what natural phenomenon Thoreau experienced.
16 It was believed that the dolphin, in dying, assumes beautiful colors, although it is not the aquatic mammal of the order Cetacea that does so, but the dolphin fish (*Coryphaena hippurus*). Thoreau may have read of it in Lord Byron's (1788–1824) *Childe Harold's Pilgrimage* 4.29.6–9:

> Parting day
> Dies like the dolphin, whom each pang imbues
> With a new colour as it gasps away—
> The last still loveliest,—

17 The Puritans believed in God's electing certain

individuals for redemption. More generally, anyone saved from damnation by Divine Grace.

18 Italian artist and goldsmith (1500–1571), now known for his *Autobiography*.

19 In Rome, where Cellini was imprisoned on charges, possibly false, of having stolen the gems of the pontifical tiara.

20 In his journal of 12 September 1851, Thoreau wrote:

> Benvenuto Cellini relates in his Memoirs that, during his confinement in the castle of St Angelo in Rome, he had a terrible dream or vision in which certain events were communicated to him which afterward came to pass, and he adds: "From the very moment that I beheld the phenomenon, there appeared (strange to relate!) a resplendent light over my head, which has displayed itself conspicuously to all that I have thought proper to show it to, but those were very few. This shining light is to be seen in the morning over my shadow till two o'clock in the afternoon, and it appears to the greatest advantage when the grass is moist with dew: it is likewise visible in the evening at sunset. This phenomenon I took notice of when I was at Paris, because the air is exceedingly clear in that climate, so that I could distinguish it there much plainer than in Italy, where mists are much more frequent; but I can still see it even here, and show it to others, though not to the same advantage as in France." This reminds me of the halo around my shadow which I notice from the causeway in the morning,—also by moonlight,—as if, in the case of a man of an excitable imagination, this were basis enough for his superstition.
> [J 2:494–95]

Thoreau had read Thomas Roscoe's (1791–1871) translation of *Memoirs of Benvenuto Cellini, a Florentine Artist, written by Himself, Containing a Variety of Information Respecting Arts and the*

would be basis enough for superstition. Beside, he tells us that he showed it to very few. But are they not indeed distinguished who are conscious that they are regarded at all?

I set out one afternoon to go a-fishing to Fair Haven, through the woods, to eke out my scanty fare of vegetables. My way led through Pleasant Meadow,[21] an adjunct of the Baker Farm, that retreat of which a poet[22] has since sung, beginning,—

> "Thy entry is a pleasant field,
> Which some mossy fruit trees yield
> Partly to a ruddy brook,
> By gliding musquash[23] undertook,
> And mercurial trout,
> Darting about."[24]

I thought of living there before I went to Walden. I "hooked"[25] the apples, leaped the brook, and scared the musquash and the trout. It was one of those afternoons which seem indefinitely long before one, in which many events may happen, a large portion of our natural life, though it was already half spent when I started. By the way there came up a shower, which compelled me to stand half an hour under a pine, piling boughs over my head, and wearing my handkerchief for a shed;[26] and when at length I had made one cast over the pickerel-weed,[27] standing up to my middle in water, I found myself suddenly in the shadow of a cloud, and the thunder began to rumble with such emphasis that I could do no more than listen to it. The gods must be proud, thought I, with such forked flashes to rout a poor unarmed fisherman. So I made haste for shelter to the nearest hut, which stood half a mile from any road, but so much the nearer to the pond, and had long been uninhabited:—

"And here a poet builded,
  In the completed years,
For behold a trivial cabin
  That to destruction steers."[28]

So the Muse fables. But therein, as I found, dwelt now John Field,[29] an Irishman, and his wife, and several children, from the broad-faced boy who assisted his father at his work, and now came running by his side from the bog to escape the rain, to the wrinkled, sibyl-like,[30] cone-headed infant that sat upon its father's knee as in the palaces of nobles, and looked out from its home in the midst of wet and hunger inquisitively upon the stranger, with the privilege of infancy, not knowing but it was the last of a noble line, and the hope and cynosure of the world, instead of John Field's poor starveling brat. There we sat together under that part of the roof which leaked the least, while it showered and thundered without. I had sat there many times of old before the ship was built that floated this family to America. An honest, hard-working, but shiftless man plainly was John Field; and his wife, she too was brave to cook so many successive dinners in the recesses of that lofty stove; with round greasy face and bare breast, still thinking to improve her condition one day; with the never absent mop in one hand, and yet no effects of it visible any where. The chickens, which had also taken shelter here from the rain, stalked about the room like members of the family, too humanized methought to roast well. They stood and looked in my eye or pecked at my shoe significantly. Meanwhile my host told me his story, how hard he worked "bogging" for a neighboring farmer, turning up a meadow with a spade or bog hoe at the rate of ten dollars an acre and the use of the land with manure for one year, and his little broad-faced son worked cheerfully at his father's side the while, not knowing how poor a bargain the latter had made. I

History of the Sixteenth Century, with notes and observations by G. P. Carpani (New York, 1845).

21 South of Walden Pond, on the shore of Fair Haven Bay.

22 Ellery Channing, who is also the poet mentioned in the "Brute Neighbors" and "House-Warming" chapters.

23 Muskrat.

24 Quoted, with one minor variant in punctuation, from Ellery Channing's "Baker Farm," in *The Woodman and Other Poems.*

25 Stole.

26 The internal rhymes in this sentence suggest that it may have been part of an aborted poem.

27 Common name for a freshwater plant (*Pontederia cordata*) found in shallow waters of eastern North America, having heart-shaped leaves and spikes of violet-blue flowers.

28 Quoted, with one minor variant in punctuation, from Ellery Channing's "Baker Farm." Channing noted in his copy of *Walden* that by the word "poet" he meant "simply a maker or mechanic."

29 Beyond John Field's identification as an Irish laborer in *The Vital Records of Lincoln, Massachusetts,* his wife's name, Mary, and their daughter Mary's birth in May 1844, nothing is known of him. Thoreau visited John Field on 23 August 1845. The part of their meeting in which Thoreau tried to secure some water to drink is told in his "Fall 1845" journal about a John Frost. According to the Concord Registers there was a John N. Frost and Mary E. Colby of Lexington who were married on 27 July 1841, although it is unlikely that this is the same John Frost. Field and Frost are treated as the same person in *The Writings of Henry D. Thoreau.* It seems more likely, however, that Thoreau was using the Frost episode to enhance his meeting with the Irishman's family. If the John and Mary Frost who married in July 1841 were the same as John and Mary Field, and assuming their first child was born at least nine months after they married, then the "broad-faced boy who assisted his father" would be only slightly over three years old. Another indication that these are probably different people is that in the original journal passage about Frost there is no suggestion of either a family or other persons present, but when transferred to *Walden*, Thoreau inserted that there was a "consultation" about the water.

30 In Greek mythology, a Sybil was a fortune-teller who was granted years of life equal to the number of grains of sand she could hold in her hand. As she aged, she grew more decrepit.

31 English proverb traced back at least to the 17th century.

tried to help him with my experience, telling him that he was one of my nearest neighbors, and that I too, who came a-fishing here, and looked like a loafer, was getting my living like himself; that I lived in a tight, light, and clean house, which hardly cost more than the annual rent of such a ruin as his commonly amounts to; and how, if he chose, he might in a month or two build himself a palace of his own; that I did not use tea, nor coffee, nor butter, nor milk, nor fresh meat, and so did not have to work to get them; again, as I did not work hard, I did not have to eat hard, and it cost me but a trifle for my food; but as he began with tea, and coffee, and butter, and milk, and beef, he had to work hard to pay for them, and when he had worked hard he had to eat hard again to repair the waste of his system, — and so it was as broad as it was long,[31] indeed it was broader than it was long, for he was discontented and wasted his life into the bargain; and yet he had rated it as a gain in coming to America, that here you could get tea, and coffee, and meat every day. But the only true America is that country where you are at liberty to pursue such a mode of life as may enable you to do without these, and where the state does not endeavor to compel you to sustain the slavery and war and other superfluous expenses which directly or indirectly result from the use of such things. For I purposely talked to him as if he were a philosopher, or desired to be one. I should be glad if all the meadows on the earth were left in a wild state, if that were the consequence of men's beginning to redeem themselves. A man will not need to study history to find out what is best for his own culture. But alas! the culture of an Irishman is an enterprise to be undertaken with a sort of moral bog hoe. I told him, that as he worked so hard at bogging, he required thick boots and stout clothing, which yet were soon soiled and worn out, but I wore light shoes and thin clothing, which cost not half so much, though he might think that I was dressed like a gentleman, (which, however, was not the case,) and in an hour or two, without labor, but as a recreation, I could, if I wished, catch as many fish as I should want for two days, or earn enough money to support me a week. If he and his family would live simply, they might all go a-huckleberrying in the summer for their amusement. John heaved a sigh at this, and his wife stared with arms a-kimbo, and both appeared to be wondering if they had capital enough to begin such a course with, or arithmetic enough to carry it through. It was sailing by dead reckoning to them, and they saw not clearly how to make their port so; therefore I suppose they still take life bravely, after their fashion, face to face, giving it tooth and nail,[32] not having skill to split its massive columns with any fine entering wedge, and rout it in detail;—thinking to deal with it roughly, as one should handle a thistle. But they fight at an overwhelming disadvantage,—living, John Field, alas! without arithmetic, and failing so.

"Do you ever fish?" I asked. "O yes, I catch a mess now and then when I am lying by; good perch[33] I catch." "What's your bait?" "I catch shiners with fish-worms, and bait the perch with them." "You'd better go now, John," said his wife with glistening and hopeful face; but John demurred.

The shower was now over, and a rainbow above the eastern woods promised a fair evening; so I took my departure. When I had got without I asked for a dish, hoping to get a sight of the well bottom, to complete my survey of the premises; but there, alas! are shallows and quicksands, and rope broken withal, and bucket irrecoverable. Meanwhile the right culinary vessel was selected, water was seemingly distilled, and after consultation and long delay passed out to the thirsty one,—not yet suffered to cool, not yet to settle. Such gruel sustains life here, I thought; so, shutting my eyes, and excluding the motes by a skil-

32 Common phrase traceable back to classical times, meaning with all strength and means.
33 Yellow perch (*Perca flavescens*).

34 Thoreau often criticized his formal education. "What does education often do? It makes a straight-cut ditch of a free, meandering brook," he recorded in his journal [J 2:83]. John Albee (1833–1915) wrote in his *Reminiscences of Emerson:*

> I observed also that Emerson continually deferred to him and seemed to anticipate his view, preparing himself obviously for a quiet laugh at Thoreau's negative and biting criticisms, especially in regard to education and educational institutions. . . .
>
> As soon as I could I introduced the problem I came to propound—what course a young man must take to get the best kind of education. Emerson pleaded always for the college; said he himself entered at fourteen. This aroused the wrath of Thoreau, who would not allow any good to the college course. And here it seemed to me Emerson said things on purpose to draw Thoreau's fire and to amuse himself. When the curriculum at Cambridge was alluded to, and Emerson casually remarked that most of the branches were taught there, Thoreau seized one of his opportunities and replied: "Yes, indeed, all the branches and none of the roots." At this Emerson laughed heartily.

35 Allusion to Ecclesiastes 12:1: "Remember now thy Creator in the days of thy youth."

fully directed under-current, I drank to genuine hospitality the heartiest draught I could. I am not squeamish in such cases when manners are concerned.

As I was leaving the Irishman's roof after the rain, bending my steps again to the pond, my haste to catch pickerel, wading in retired meadows, in sloughs and bog-holes, in forlorn and savage places, appeared for an instant trivial to me who had been sent to school and college;[34] but as I ran down the hill toward the reddening west, with the rainbow over my shoulder, and some faint tinkling sounds borne to my ear through the cleansed air, from I know not what quarter, my Good Genius seemed to say,—Go fish and hunt far and wide day by day,—farther and wider,—and rest thee by many brooks and hearth-sides without misgiving. Remember thy Creator in the days of thy youth.[35] Rise free from care before the dawn, and seek adventures. Let the noon find thee by other lakes, and the night overtake thee every where at home. There are no larger fields than these, no worthier games than may here be played. Grow wild according to thy nature, like these sedges and brakes, which will never become English hay. Let the thunder rumble; what if it threaten ruin to farmers' crops? that is not its errand to thee. Take shelter under the cloud, while they flee to carts and sheds. Let not to get a living be thy trade, but thy sport. Enjoy the land, but own it not. Through want of enterprise and faith men are where they are, buying and selling, and spending their lives like serfs.

O Baker Farm!

"Landscape where the richest element
Is a little sunshine innocent." * *

"No one runs to revel
On thy rail-fenced lea." * *

"Debate with no man hast thou,
  With questions art never perplexed,
As tame at the first sight as now,
  In thy plain russet gabardine dressed." * *

"Come ye who love,
  And ye who hate,
Children of the Holy Dove,
  And Guy Faux[36] of the state,
And hang conspiracies
From the tough rafters of the trees!"[37]

Men come tamely home at night only from the next field or street, where their household echoes haunt, and their life pines because it breathes its own breath over again; their shadows morning and evening reach farther than their daily steps. We should come home from far, from adventures, and perils, and discoveries every day, with new experience and character.

Before I had reached the pond some fresh impulse had brought out John Field, with altered mind, letting go "bogging" ere this sunset. But he, poor man, disturbed only a couple of fins while I was catching a fair string, and he said it was his luck; but when we changed seats in the boat luck changed seats too. Poor John Field! — I trust he does not read this, unless he will improve by it, — thinking to live by some derivative old country mode in this primitive new country, — to catch perch with shiners.[38] It is good bait sometimes, I allow. With his horizon all his own, yet he a poor man, born to be poor, with his inherited Irish poverty or poor life, his Adam's grandmother[39] and boggy[40] ways, not to rise in this world, he nor his posterity, till their wading webbed bog-trotting[41] feet get *talaria*[42] to their heels.[43]

36 Guy Fawkes (1570–1606), English Catholic, who conspired to blow up the Parliament's House of Lords on 5 November 1605 and was hanged on 31 January 1606.

37 Quoted, with minor variants in punctuation, from Ellery Channing's "Baker Farm." The double asterisks were used to indicate deleted stanzas.

38 Yellow perch can be caught with earthworms, so Field's using worms to catch shiners as bait for the perch was unnecessary labor.

39 As Adam was the biblical first man and therefore had no grandmother, this refers to something that is ancient or seems to have existed for all time, but it also makes Field appear like an old woman in manner and habit.

40 Like a bog, and therefore something in which one could get stuck or bogged down, but also a reference to the "bog Irish" who were considered to be from the countryside and without much experience or understanding of life anywhere else.

41 Dating back to the 17th century, a "bog-trotter" was originally a British pejorative term for the Irish.

42 Winged sandals worn by, or wings growing directly from the ankles of, several minor Greek gods, giving them swift and unimpeded flight.

43 Field's inability to rise recalls the journal passage about the hawk, where Thoreau wrote of it "faithfully creeping on the ground as a reptile in a former state of existence. You must creep before you can run; you must run before you can fly" [J 3:108].

Thoreau's "Civil Disobedience" was an appeal to a higher law than constitutions or the statutes of society. In it he wrote: "Thus the State never intentionally confronts a man's sense, intellectual or moral, but only his body, his senses. It is not armed with superior wit or honesty, but with superior physical strength. I was not born to be forced. I will breathe after my own fashion. Let us see who is the strongest. What force has a multitude? They only can force me who obey a higher law than I" [W 4:376]. The term was popularized by the New York senator William Henry Seward (1801–1872) in his argument against the Fugitive Slave Bill on 11 March 1850: "The Constitution devotes the national domain to union, to justice, to defence, to welfare and to liberty. But there is a higher law than the Constitution." Echoing Seward, Thoreau wrote in "Slavery in Massachusetts": "What is wanted is men, not of policy, but of probity,—who recognize a higher law than the Constitution, or the decision of the majority" [W 4:403].

1 On primal instinct, Thoreau wrote: "What is peculiar in the life of a man consists not in his obedience, but his opposition, to his instincts" [J 2:46]. As he explained in "Economy," Thoreau did once make a meal of a woodchuck, although not raw.
2 Wildness was not synonymous with wilderness or nature but was what they represented: uncontrolled freedom. "I wish to speak a word for Nature," Thoreau wrote in the opening to "Walking," "for absolute freedom and wildness, as contrasted with a freedom and culture merely civil,—to regard man as an inhabitant, or a part and parcel of Nature, rather than a member of society" [W 5:205]. "Whatever has not come under the sway of man is wild. In this sense original and independent men are wild,—not tamed and broken by society," Thoreau wrote in his journal [J 2:448].
3 Usually means deer meat, but also, as here, any game meat.

Higher Laws

As I came home through the woods with my string of fish, trailing my pole, it being now quite dark, I caught a glimpse of a woodchuck stealing across my path, and felt a strange thrill of savage delight, and was strongly tempted to seize and devour him raw;[1] not that I was hungry then, except for that wildness which he represented.[2] Once or twice, however, while I lived at the pond, I found myself ranging the woods, like a half-starved hound, with a strange abandonment, seeking some kind of venison[3] which I might devour, and no morsel could have been too savage for me. The wildest scenes had become unaccountably familiar. I found in myself, and still find, an instinct toward a higher, or, as it is named, spiritual life, as do most men, and another toward a primitive rank and savage one, and I reverence them both. I love the wild not less than the good. The wildness and adventure that are in fishing still recommended it to me. I like sometimes to take rank hold on life and spend my day more as the animals do. Perhaps I have owed to this employment and to hunting, when quite young, my closest acquaintance with Nature. They early introduce us to and detain us in scenery with which otherwise, at that age, we should have little acquaintance. Fishermen, hunters, woodchoppers, and others, spending their lives in the fields and woods, in a peculiar sense a part of Nature themselves, are often in a more favorable mood for observing her, in the intervals of their pursuits, than philosophers or poets even, who approach her with expectation. She is not afraid to exhibit herself to them. The traveller on the prairie is naturally a hunter, on the head waters of the Missouri and Columbia[4] a trapper, and at the Falls of St. Mary[5] a fisherman. He who is only a traveller learns things at second-hand and by the halves, and is poor authority. We are most interested when science reports what those men already know practically or instinctively, for that alone is a true *humanity*, or account of human experience.

They mistake who assert that the Yankee has few amusements, because he has not so many public holidays, and men and boys do not play so many games as they do in England, for here the more primitive but solitary amusements of hunting fishing and the like have not yet given place to the former. Almost every New England boy among my contemporaries shouldered a fowling piece between the ages of ten and fourteen; and his hunting and fishing grounds were not limited like the preserves of an English nobleman, but were more boundless even than those of a savage. No wonder, then, that he did not oftener stay to play on the common.[6] But already a change is taking place, owing, not to an increased humanity, but to an increased scarcity of game, for perhaps the hunter is the greatest friend of the animals hunted, not excepting the Humane Society.[7]

Moreover, when at the pond, I wished sometimes to add fish to my fare for variety. I have actually fished from the same kind of necessity that the first fishers did. Whatever humanity I might conjure up against it was all factitious, and concerned my philosophy more than my feelings. I speak of fishing only now, for I had long felt differently about fowling, and sold my gun before I went to the woods.[8] Not that I am less humane than others, but I did not perceive that my feelings were much af-

4 The Missouri River in the central United States and the Columbia River in the Far West.

5 Probably the falls southeast from Lake Superior to Lake Huron, forming part of the border between Canada and the United States, but there are several falls with this name in North America.

6 Near the center of most New England towns and used for the common pasturing of farm animals.

7 Generic name for any charitable organization for protecting animals. Originally organized for the relief of human suffering, as in the Royal Humane Society in London, founded in 1770, but later given to protecting the helpless, including children, the elderly, and animals. The English Society for the Prevention of Cruelty to Animals was founded in 1824. The American Society for the Prevention of Cruelty to Animals was not founded until 1866, four years after Thoreau's death.

8 At the time of his river excursion with his brother, Thoreau still carried a gun. Gliding out of Concord, "we did unbend so far as to let our guns speak for us, when at length we had swept out of sight, and thus left the woods to ring again with their echoes" [W 1:14]. Later, in listing "a good outfit for one who wishes to make an excursion of *twelve* days into the Maine woods," he wrote: "A gun is not worth the carriage, unless you go as hunters" [W 3:350–51]. But in a draft, ca. 1848, from the opening of the "Wednesday" chapter of *A Week on the Concord and Merrimack Rivers*, Thoreau wrote: "Indeed, there are few tools to be compared with a gun for efficiency and compactness. We do not know of another so complete an arm" [*Thoreau's Complex Weave* 463].

9 Possible allusion to Emerson's poem "Forbearance," which begins: "Hast thou named all the birds without a gun?"

10 Allusion to Mark 1:17: "And Jesus said unto them, Come ye after me, and I will make you to become fishers of men."

11 From the prologue to Chaucer's *The Canterbury Tales* (ll. 177–78), which Thoreau quoted from Alexander Chalmers (1759–1834), *The Works of the English Poets from Chaucer to Cowper* 1:4. Thoreau confused the nun with the monk about whom the couplet was written.

12 Native American tribe of Canada, formerly inhabiting the area north of the St. Lawrence River.

13 Thoreau made several references to taking an animal's life as murder. In a letter of 16 February 1847 he wrote: "I confess to a little squeamishness on the score of robbing their [birds'] nests, though I could easily go to the length of abstracting an egg or two gently, now and then, and if the advancement of science obviously demanded it might be carried to the extreme of deliberate murder" [C 175]. Thoreau also used the word "murder" in *The Maine Woods* when referring to the killing of the moose [W 3:134].

14 As elsewhere, Thoreau was making a point in splitting the word (*philos*, to love, and *anthropos*, man); here his emphasis shows that his love was not confined to humans only. He made a similar distinction in *A Week on the Concord and Merrimack Rivers*: "Away with the superficial and selfish phil-*anthropy* of men" [W 1:36].

fected. I did not pity the fishes nor the worms. This was habit. As for fowling, during the last years that I carried a gun my excuse was that I was studying ornithology, and sought only new or rare birds. But I confess that I am now inclined to think that there is a finer way of studying ornithology than this. It requires so much closer attention to the habits of the birds, that, if for that reason only, I have been willing to omit the gun.⁹ Yet notwithstanding the objection on the score of humanity, I am compelled to doubt if equally valuable sports are ever substituted for these; and when some of my friends have asked me anxiously about their boys, whether they should let them hunt, I have answered, yes, — remembering that it was one of the best parts of my education, — *make* them hunters, though sportsmen only at first, if possible, mighty hunters at last, so that they shall not find game large enough for them in this or any vegetable wilderness, — hunters as well as fishers of men.¹⁰ Thus far I am of the opinion of Chaucer's nun, who

> "yave not of the text a pulled hen
> That saith that hunters ben not holy men."¹¹

There is a period in the history of the individual, as of the race, when the hunters are the "best men," as the Algonquins¹² called them. We cannot but pity the boy who has never fired a gun; he is no more humane, while his education has been sadly neglected. This was my answer with respect to those youths who were bent on this pursuit, trusting that they would soon outgrow it. No humane being, past the thoughtless age of boyhood, will wantonly murder¹³ any creature, which holds its life by the same tenure that he does. The hare in its extremity cries like a child. I warn you, mothers, that my sympathies do not always make the usual phil-*anthropic*¹⁴ distinctions.

Such is oftenest the young man's introduction to the

forest, and the most original part of himself. He goes thither at first as a hunter and fisher, until at last, if he has the seeds of a better life in him, he distinguishes his proper objects, as a poet or naturalist it may be, and leaves the gun and fish-pole behind. The mass of men are still and always young in this respect. In some countries a hunting parson is no uncommon sight. Such a one might make a good shepherd's dog, but is far from being the Good Shepherd.[15] I have been surprised to consider that the only obvious employment, except wood-chopping, ice-cutting, or the like business, which ever to my knowledge detained at Walden Pond for a whole half day any of my fellow-citizens, whether fathers or children of the town, with just one exception, was fishing. Commonly they did not think that they were lucky, or well paid for their time, unless they got a long string of fish, though they had the opportunity of seeing the pond all the while. They might go there a thousand times before the sediment of fishing would sink to the bottom and leave their purpose pure; but no doubt such a clarifying process would be going on all the while. The governor and his council[16] faintly remember the pond, for they went a-fishing there when they were boys; but now they are too old and dignified to go a-fishing, and so they know it no more forever. Yet even they expect to go to heaven at last. If the legislature regards it, it is chiefly to regulate the number of hooks to be used there;[17] but they know nothing about the hook of hooks with which to angle for the pond itself, impaling the legislature for a bait. Thus, even in civilized communities, the embryo man passes through the hunter stage of development.

I have found repeatedly, of late years, that I cannot fish without falling a little in self-respect. I have tried it again and again. I have skill at it, and, like many of my fellows, a certain instinct for it, which revives from time to time, but always when I have done I feel that it would

15 Allusion to John 10:11: "I am the good shepherd: the good shepherd giveth his life for the sheep."
16 The Governor's Council in Massachusetts is elected to advise the governor in affairs of state.
17 As a conservation measure to prevent overfishing.

18 Kitchen helper who washes dishes and performs other menial tasks.

19 Thoreau's original journal entry of 27 November 1852 for this passage showed a slightly changed disposition, but that change was not included in *Walden:* "Like many of my contemporaries I had rarely for many years used animal food, or tea or coffee, etc., etc., not so much because of any ill effects which I had traced to them in my own case, though I could theorize extensively in that direction, as because it was not agreeable to my imagination" [J 4:417]. Although he was not a strict vegetarian, Thoreau ate meat rarely, usually when it was a matter of convention or practicality. He wrote in his journal on 22 December 1853: "Left to my chosen pursuits, I should never . . . eat meat" [J 6:20]. He listed pork among his provisions in the "Economy" chapter, and in a 28 January 1858 letter he mentioned the moose meat he brought on one of his Maine excursions [C 508]. These examples, however, may have been a matter of a social convention and ease, as Moncure Conway wrote in his *Autobiography:* "Thoreau ate no meat; he told me his only reason was a feeling of the filthiness of flesh-eating. A bear huntsman he thought was entitled to his steak. He had never attempted to make any general principle on the subject, and later in life ate meat in order not to cause inconvenience to the family."

20 William Kirby (1759–1850) and William Spence (1783–1860), authors of *An Introduction to Entomology, or Elements of the Natural History of Insects,* the first edition of which was published in 1815.

have been better if I had not fished. I think that I do not mistake. It is a faint intimation, yet so are the first streaks of morning. There is unquestionably this instinct in me which belongs to the lower orders of creation; yet with every year I am less a fisherman, though without more humanity or even wisdom; at present I am no fisherman at all. But I see that if I were to live in a wilderness I should again be tempted to become a fisher and hunter in earnest. Beside, there is something essentially unclean about this diet and all flesh, and I began to see where housework commences, and whence the endeavor, which costs so much, to wear a tidy and respectable appearance each day, to keep the house sweet and free from all ill odors and sights. Having been my own butcher and scullion[18] and cook, as well as the gentleman for whom the dishes were served up, I can speak from an unusually complete experience. The practical objection to animal food in my case was its uncleanness; and, besides, when I had caught and cleaned and cooked and eaten my fish, they seemed not to have fed me essentially. It was insignificant and unnecessary, and cost more than it came to. A little bread or a few potatoes would have done as well, with less trouble and filth. Like many of my contemporaries, I had rarely for many years used animal food, or tea, or coffee, &c.; not so much because of any ill effects which I had traced to them, as because they were not agreeable to my imagination.[19] The repugnance to animal food is not the effect of experience, but is an instinct. It appeared more beautiful to live low and fare hard in many respects; and though I never did so, I went far enough to please my imagination. I believe that every man who has ever been earnest to preserve his higher or poetic faculties in the best condition has been particularly inclined to abstain from animal food, and from much food of any kind. It is a significant fact, stated by entomologists, I find it in Kirby and Spence,[20] that "some insects in their perfect state, though furnished with organs of feeding, make no use of them;" and they lay it down as "a general rule, that almost all insects in this state eat much less than in that of larvæ. The voracious caterpillar when transformed into a butterfly," . . . "and the gluttonous maggot when become a fly," [21] content themselves with a drop or two of honey or some other sweet liquid. The abdomen under the wings of the butterfly still represents the larva. This is the tid-bit which tempts his insectivorous fate. The gross feeder is a man in the larva state; and there are whole nations in that condition, nations without fancy or imagination, whose vast abdomens betray them.

It is hard to provide and cook so simple and clean a diet as will not offend the imagination; but this, I think, is to be fed when we feed the body; they should both sit down at the same table. Yet perhaps this may be done. The fruits eaten temperately need not make us ashamed of our appetites, nor interrupt the worthiest pursuits. But put an extra condiment into your dish, and it will poison you. It is not worth the while to live by rich cookery. Most men would feel shame if caught preparing with their own hands precisely such a dinner, whether of animal or vegetable food, as is every day prepared for them by others. Yet till this is otherwise we are not civilized, and, if gentlemen and ladies, are not true men and women. This certainly suggests what change is to be made. It may be vain to ask why the imagination will not be reconciled to flesh and fat. I am satisfied that it is not. Is it not a reproach that man is a carnivorous animal? True, he can and does live, in a great measure, by preying on other animals; but this is a miserable way,—as any one who will go to snaring rabbits, or slaughtering lambs, may learn,—and he will be regarded as a benefactor of his race who shall teach man to confine himself to a more innocent and wholesome diet. Whatever my own practice may be,[22] I have no doubt that it is a part of the destiny of the human race,

21 Quoted from Kirby and Spence's *Introduction to Entomology* (Philadelphia, 1846) 258.
22 This qualifier is another indication that Thoreau was aware of the myth-making aspects of *Walden* and the difference between his actual practices, or the facts, and the ideal possibilities. As he wrote later in this chapter, "My practice is 'nowhere,' my opinion is here."

23 Literally, cosmic dust that falls on the earth from space, but also, as here, a magical or dream-like feeling.

24 Probably muskrat.

25 Probable allusion to Thomas De Quincey's (1785–1859) *Confessions of an English Opium-eater* (1822), although opium was commonly available, for it was sold legally and at low prices throughout the 19th century, including in patent medicines such as McMunn's Elixir of Opium. A New England physician-druggist wrote circa 1870: "In this town I began business twenty years since. The population then at 10,000 has increased only inconsiderably, but my sales have advanced from 50 pounds of opium the first year to 300 pounds now." Most 19th-century users, although called opium eaters in the medical literature, were actually opium drinkers, using laudanum or other opiate liquids.

26 Thoreau wrote in his journal: "What kind of fowl would they be and new kind of bats and owls . . . [that] took a dish of tea or hot coffee before they began to sing?" [J 2:316]. (In his day people poured their tea from the cup into the saucer or dish to cool before drinking it.) His idea here followed Emerson's tenet regarding inspiration and the habits of the poet: "That is not an inspiration which we owe to narcotics, but some counterfeit excitement and fury."

in its gradual improvement, to leave off eating animals, as surely as the savage tribes have left off eating each other when they came in contact with the more civilized.

If one listens to the faintest but constant suggestions of his genius, which are certainly true, he sees not to what extremes, or even insanity, it may lead him; and yet that way, as he grows more resolute and faithful, his road lies. The faintest assured objection which one healthy man feels will at length prevail over the arguments and customs of mankind. No man ever followed his genius till it misled him. Though the result were bodily weakness, yet perhaps no one can say that the consequences were to be regretted, for these were a life in conformity to higher principles. If the day and the night are such that you greet them with joy, and life emits a fragrance like flowers and sweet-scented herbs, is more elastic, more starry, more immortal,—that is your success. All nature is your congratulation, and you have cause momentarily to bless yourself. The greatest gains and values are farthest from being appreciated. We easily come to doubt if they exist. We soon forget them. They are the highest reality. Perhaps the facts most astounding and most real are never communicated by man to man. The true harvest of my daily life is somewhat as intangible and indescribable as the tints of morning or evening. It is a little star-dust [23] caught, a segment of the rainbow which I have clutched.

Yet, for my part, I was never unusually squeamish; I could sometimes eat a fried rat [24] with a good relish, if it were necessary. I am glad to have drunk water so long, for the same reason that I prefer the natural sky to an opium-eater's heaven. [25] I would fain keep sober always; and there are infinite degrees of drunkenness. I believe that water is the only drink for a wise man; wine is not so noble a liquor; and think of dashing the hopes of a morning with a cup of warm coffee, or of an evening with a dish of tea! [26] Ah, how low I fall when I am tempted by them! Even music may be intoxicating. Such apparently slight causes destroyed Greece and Rome, and will destroy England and America. Of all ebriosity,[27] who does not prefer to be intoxicated by the air he breathes?[28] I have found it to be the most serious objection to coarse labors long continued, that they compelled me to eat and drink coarsely also. But to tell the truth, I find myself at present somewhat less particular in these respects. I carry less religion to the table, ask no blessing; not because I am wiser than I was, but, I am obliged to confess, because, however much it is to be regretted, with years I have grown more coarse and indifferent. Perhaps these questions are entertained only in youth, as most believe of poetry. My practice is "nowhere," my opinion is here. Nevertheless I am far from regarding myself as one of those privileged ones to whom the Ved[29] refers when it says, that "he who has true faith in the Omnipresent Supreme Being may eat all that exists," that is, is not bound to inquire what is his food, or who prepares it; and even in their case it is to be observed, as a Hindoo commentator has remarked, that the Vedant limits this privilege to "the time of distress."[30]

Who has not sometimes derived an inexpressible satisfaction from his food in which appetite had no share? I have been thrilled to think that I owed a mental perception to the commonly gross sense of taste, that I have been inspired through the palate, that some berries which I had eaten on a hill-side had fed my genius.[31] "The soul not being mistress of herself," says Thseng-tseu,[32] "one looks, and one does not see; one listens, and one does not hear; one eats, and one does not know the savor of food."[33] He who distinguishes the true savor of his food can never be a glutton; he who does not cannot be otherwise. A puritan may go to his brown-bread crust with as gross an appetite as ever an alderman to his turtle.[34] Not that food which entereth into the mouth defileth a man,[35] but the appetite with which it is eaten. It is neither the quality nor the

27 Drunkenness.

28 Thoreau wrote in his journal: "Oh, if I could be intoxicated on air and water!" [J 2:72].

29 The Vedas.

30 From Rajah Rammohun Roy's *Translation of Several Principal Books, Passages, and Texts of the Veds and of Some Controversial Works of Brahmunical Theology* (London, 1832) 21.

31 Franklin Sanborn's Bibliophile Edition of *Walden* included Ellery Channing's report that Thoreau "could never pass a berry without picking it. For huckleberries, wild strawberries, chestnuts, acorns and wild apples he had a snatch of veneration almost superstitious." Thoreau referred to the hills as "a table constantly spread" [J 5:330].

32 Tseng Tzu, sometimes Tseng Tsan, major disciple of Confucius.

33 Thoreau's translation of Confucius, *The Great Learning* 7:2, "Commentary of the Philosopher Tsang," from the French translation in Pauthier's *Confucius et Mencius* 51.

34 Aldermen were often caricatured as lovers of exotic food. Thoreau may be referring to the terrapin, or saddleback, an edible freshwater turtle, or to turtle soup. Turtle-fed aldermen was a common image in several contemporary or earlier sources, such as Washington Irving's *The Sketch Book of Geoffrey Crayon;* the anonymous "Passages from the Life of a Medical Eclectic" in *The American Whig Review* (April 1846); William Makepeace Thackeray's (1811–1863) *Vanity Fair;* and the "Introduction to the Giant Chronicles" section of Charles Dickens's (1812–1870) *Master Humphrey's Clock.*

35 Allusion to Matthew 15:11: "Not that which goeth into the mouth defileth a man; but that which cometh out of the mouth, this defileth a man."

36 Jelly was made by boiling calves' feet to extract the natural gelatin, combining the strained liquid with wine, lemon juice, and spices, adding sugar, and cooling until set.

37 A lever on an organ or harpsichord that controls the use of pipes or strings.

38 Thoreau found the jawbone sometime between 15 June and 20 June 1850. Franklin Sanborn recalled in the Bibliophile Edition of *Walden* that this "was in Plymouth, while rambling with Marston Watson" but that episode took place in June 1857 and yielded only hog bristles.

quantity, but the devotion to sensual savors; when that which is eaten is not a viand to sustain our animal, or inspire our spiritual life, but food for the worms that possess us. If the hunter has a taste for mud-turtles, muskrats, and other such savage tid-bits, the fine lady indulges a taste for jelly made of a calf's foot,[36] or for sardines from over the sea, and they are even. He goes to the mill-pond, she to her preserve-pot. The wonder is how they, how you and I, can live this slimy beastly life, eating and drinking.

Our whole life is startlingly moral. There is never an instant's truce between virtue and vice. Goodness is the only investment that never fails. In the music of the harp which trembles round the world it is the insisting on this which thrills us. The harp is the travelling patterer for the Universe's Insurance Company, recommending its laws, and our little goodness is all the assessment that we pay. Though the youth at last grows indifferent, the laws of the universe are not indifferent, but are forever on the side of the most sensitive. Listen to every zephyr for some reproof, for it is surely there, and he is unfortunate who does not hear it. We cannot touch a string or move a stop[37] but the charming moral transfixes us. Many an irksome noise, go a long way off, is heard as music, a proud sweet satire on the meanness of our lives.

We are conscious of an animal in us, which awakens in proportion as our higher nature slumbers. It is reptile and sensual, and perhaps cannot be wholly expelled; like the worms which, even in life and health, occupy our bodies. Possibly we may withdraw from it, but never change its nature. I fear that it may enjoy a certain health of its own; that we may be well, yet not pure. The other day I picked up the lower jaw of a hog, with white and sound teeth and tusks,[38] which suggested that there was an animal health and vigor distinct from the spiritual. This creature succeeded by other means than temperance and purity. "That in which men differ from brute beasts," says Mencius, "is a thing very inconsiderable; the common herd lose it very soon; superior men preserve it carefully." [39] Who knows what sort of life would result if we had attained to purity? If I knew so wise a man as could teach me purity I would go to seek him forthwith. "A command over our passions, and over the external senses of the body, and good acts, are declared by the Ved to be indispensable in the mind's approximation to God." [40] Yet the spirit can for the time pervade and control every member and function of the body, and transmute what in form is the grossest sensuality into purity and devotion. The generative energy, which, when we are loose, dissipates and makes us unclean, when we are continent invigorates and inspires us. Chastity is the flowering of man; and what are called Genius, Heroism, Holiness, and the like, are but various fruits which succeed it. Man flows at once to God when the channel of purity is open. By turns our purity inspires and our impurity casts us down. He is blessed who is assured that the animal is dying out in him day by day, and the divine being established. Perhaps there is none but has cause for shame on account of the inferior and brutish nature to which he is allied. I fear that we are such gods or demigods only as fauns and satyrs, [41] the divine allied to beasts, the creatures of appetite, and that, to some extent, our very life is our disgrace. —

"How happy's he who hath due place assigned
To his beasts and disaforested [42] his mind!

     *   *   *   *   *

Can use his horse, goat, wolf, and ev'ry beast,
And is not ass himself to all the rest!
Else man not only is the herd of swine,
But he's those devils too which did incline
Them to a headlong rage, and made them
    worse." [43]

39 Thoreau's translation of Mencius from the French translation in Pauthier's *Confucius et Mencius* 349.

40 Abridged from Roy's *Translation of Several Principal Books, Passages, and Texts of the Veds* 19.

41 In Roman and Greek mythology, respectively, half human, half beast (often goat) deities of the woods and mountains, lustful and fond of revelry.

42 In English law, to free from the restrictions of forest laws, i.e., change to common land, but also to defoliate, or make from forest to arable land. Thoreau quoted the phrase "disafforested his mind" in a fall 1846 journal passage.

43 Lines 9–10 and 13–17 of John Donne's (1572–1631) "To Sir Edward Herbert at Julyers," in the modernized spelling found in Chalmers, *The Works of the English Poets, from Chaucer to Cowper* 5:165. Donne's allusion is to Mark 5:11–14: "Now there was there nigh unto the mountains a great herd of swine feeding. And all the devils besought him, saying, Send us into the swine, that we may enter into them. And forthwith Jesus gave them leave. And the unclean spirits went out, and entered into the swine: and the herd ran violently down a steep place into the sea, (they were about two thousand;) and were choked in the sea."

All sensuality is one, though it takes many forms; all purity is one. It is the same whether a man eat, or drink, or cohabit, or sleep sensually. They are but one appetite, and we only need to see a person do any one of these things to know how great a sensualist he is. The impure can neither stand nor sit with purity. When the reptile is attacked at one mouth of his burrow, he shows himself at another. If you would be chaste, you must be temperate. What is chastity?[44] How shall a man know if he is chaste? He shall not know it. We have heard of this virtue, but we know not what it is. We speak conformably to the rumor which we have heard. From exertion come wisdom and purity; from sloth ignorance and sensuality. In the student sensuality is a sluggish habit of mind. An unclean person is universally a slothful one, one who sits by a stove, whom the sun shines on prostrate, who reposes without being fatigued. If you would avoid uncleanness, and all the sins, work earnestly, though it be at cleaning a stable.[45] Nature is hard to be overcome, but she must be overcome. What avails it that you are Christian, if you are not purer than the heathen, if you deny yourself no more, if you are not more religious? I know of many systems of religion esteemed heathenish whose precepts fill the reader with shame, and provoke him to new endeavors, though it be to the performance of rites merely.

I hesitate to say these things, but it is not because of the subject,—I care not how obscene my *words* are,—but because I cannot speak of them without betraying my impurity. We discourse freely without shame of one form of sensuality, and are silent about another. We are so degraded that we cannot speak simply of the necessary functions of human nature. In earlier ages, in some countries, every function was reverently spoken of and regulated by law. Nothing was too trivial for the Hindoo lawgiver,[46] however offensive it may be to modern taste. He teaches how to eat, drink, cohabit, void excrement

44 In a September 1852 letter to his friend H. G. O. Blake, Thoreau enclosed an essay, "Chastity & Sensuality," prefaced by the remark: "I send you the thoughts on Chastity and Sensuality with diffidence and shame, not knowing how far I speak to the condition of men generally, or how far I betray my peculiar defects." In the essay Thoreau wrote:

> If it is the result of a pure love, there can be nothing sensual in marriage. Chastity is something positive, not negative. It is the virtue of the married especially. All lusts or base pleasures must give place to loftier delights. They who meet as superior beings cannot perform the deeds of inferior ones. The deeds of love are less questionable than any action of an individual can be, for, it being founded on the rarest mutual respect, the parties incessantly stimulate each other to a loftier and purer life, and the act in which they are associated must be pure and noble indeed, for innocence and purity can have no equal. In this relation we deal with one whom we respect more religiously even than we respect our better selves, and we shall necessarily conduct as in the presence of God. [W 6:197, 205–6]

45 In his journal of 20 April 1841 Thoreau noted: "To-day I earned seventy-five cents heaving manure out of a pen, and made a good bargain of it. If the ditcher muses the while how he may live uprightly, the ditching spade and turf knife may be engraved on the coat-of-arms of his posterity" [J 1:250–51].

46 Manu, or Menu, was the legendary author of the Hindu code of religious law, *Manusmitri*, compiled in Sanskrit in the 1st century B.C.E. Manu is also the Hindu archetypal first man, survivor of the flood and father of the human race. Thoreau compiled a selection, "The Laws of Menu," for the January 1843 issue of *The Dial* from the *Institutes of Hindu Law, or, The Ordinances of Menu, According to the Gloss of Culluca, Comprising the Indian Sys-

and urine, and the like, elevating what is mean, and does not falsely excuse himself by calling these things trifles.

Every man is the builder of a temple,[47] called his body, to the god he worships, after a style purely his own, nor can he get off by hammering marble instead. We are all sculptors and painters, and our material is our own flesh and blood and bones. Any nobleness begins at once to refine a man's features, any meanness or sensuality to imbrute them.

John Farmer[48] sat at his door one September evening, after a hard day's work, his mind still running on his labor more or less. Having bathed he sat down to recreate his intellectual man. It was a rather cool evening, and some of his neighbors were apprehending a frost. He had not attended to the train of his thoughts long when he heard some one playing on a flute,[49] and that sound harmonized with his mood. Still he thought of his work; but the burden of his thought was, that though this kept running in his head, and he found himself planning and contriving it against his will, yet it concerned him very little. It was no more than the scurf[50] of his skin, which was constantly shuffled off. But the notes of the flute came home to his ears out of a different sphere from that he worked in, and suggested work for certain faculties which slumbered in him. They gently did away with the street, and the village, and the state[51] in which he lived. A voice said to him,— Why do you stay here and live this mean moiling[52] life, when a glorious existence is possible for you? Those same stars twinkle over other fields than these.—But how to come out of this condition and actually migrate thither? All that he could think of was to practise some new austerity, to let his mind descend into his body and redeem it, and treat himself with ever increasing respect.

tem of Duties, Religious and Civil, translated by Sir William Jones (1746–1794) (London, 1825).

47 Possible allusion to 1 Corinthians 3:16: "Know ye not that ye are the temple of God, and that the Spirit of God dwelleth in you?" Thoreau may have had in mind the version by Novalis (Friedrich Leopold, Freiherr von Hardenberg, 1772–1801), which he read in Carlyle's *Sartor Resartus:* "'There is but one Temple in the world,' says Novalis, 'and that Temple is the Body of Man.'"

48 Possibly used as a generic name, although in the manuscript drafts, beginning with Version 4, the farmer was identified as John Spaulding.

49 Possibly Thoreau himself, who often played his flute in his boat on the pond or the river ("I sit in my boat on Walden, playing the flute this evening" [J 1:260]; "I sailed on the North River last night with my flute, and my music was a tinkling stream which meandered with the river, and fell from note to note as a brook from rock to rock" [J 1:271–72]). Thoreau may also have been recalling his own reactions to the sound of a flute, as in his journal of 25 June 1852: "The flute I now hear from the Depot Field does not find such caverns to echo and resound in in my mind,—no such answering depths. . . . Now his day's work is done, the laborer plays his flute,—only possible at this hour. Contrasted with his work, what an accomplishment! Some drink and gamble. He plays some well-known march. But the music is not in the tune; it is in the sound" [J 4:144].

50 Thin flake of dead epidermis shed from the surface of the skin.

51 Pun: the state of Massachusetts, and also his condition or mode of being with regard to his circumstances.

52 Drudging.

Thoreau wrote in a journal entry of 23 March 1856: "I spend a considerable portion of my time observing the habits of the wild animals, my brute neighbors. By their various movements and migrations they fetch the year about to me" [J 8:220].

1 His companion was Ellery Channing, who is the poet in the dialogue below and in the "House-Warming" chapter. Channing lived on Punkatasset (sometimes Ponkawtasset) Hill, six miles north of Walden Pond, at this time.

2 Thoreau was not being literal in naming himself Hermit here, as has already been demonstrated in "The Village" and "Visitors." The dialogue between the Hermit and the Poet may be modeled after "A Conference betwixt an Angler, a Falconer, and a Hunter, each commending his Recreation" in Izaak Walton's (1593–1683) *The Compleat Angler or, the Contemplative Man's Recreation.*

3 To call field hands in for meals.

4 Bread made of corn meal.

5 Allusion to John Smith's (1580–1631) charge to his fellow colonists in Virginia: "You must obay this for a law, that he that will not worke, shall not eate, except by sicknesse he be disabled."

6 Common name for a dog.

7 Bread sweetened with molasses and raisins.

Brute Neighbors

Sometimes I had a companion in my fishing, who came through the village to my house from the other side of the town, and the catching of the dinner was as much a social exercise as the eating of it.[1]

Hermit.[2] I wonder what the world is doing now. I have not heard so much as a locust over the sweet-fern these three hours. The pigeons are all asleep upon their roosts,—no flutter from them. Was that a farmer's noon horn[3] which sounded from beyond the woods just now? The hands are coming in to boiled salt beef and cider and Indian bread.[4] Why will men worry themselves so? He that does not eat need not work.[5] I wonder how much they have reaped. Who would live there where a body can never think for the barking of Bose?[6] And O, the housekeeping! to keep bright the devil's door-knobs, and scour his tubs this bright day! Better not keep a house. Say, some hollow tree; and then for morning calls and dinner-parties! Only a woodpecker tapping. O, they swarm; the sun is too warm there; they are born too far into life for me. I have water from the spring, and a loaf of brown bread[7] on the shelf.—Hark! I hear a rustling of the leaves. Is it some ill-fed village hound yielding to the instinct of the chase? or the lost pig which is said to be in these woods, whose tracks I saw after the rain? It comes on apace; my sumachs and sweet-briars tremble. — Eh, Mr. Poet, is it you? How do you like the world to-day?

Poet. See those clouds; how they hang! That's the greatest thing I have seen to-day. There's nothing like it in old paintings, nothing like it in foreign lands, — unless when we were off the coast of Spain.[8] That's a true Mediterranean sky. I thought, as I have my living to get, and have not eaten to-day, that I might go a-fishing. That's the true industry for poets. It is the only trade I have learned. Come, let's along.

Hermit. I cannot resist. My brown bread will soon be gone. I will go with you gladly soon, but I am just concluding a serious meditation. I think that I am near the end of it. Leave me alone, then, for a while. But that we may not be delayed, you shall be digging the bait meanwhile. Angle-worms are rarely to be met with in these parts, where the soil was never fattened with manure; the race is nearly extinct. The sport of digging the bait is nearly equal to that of catching the fish, when one's appetite is not too keen; and this you may have all to yourself to-day. I would advise you to set in the spade down yonder among the ground-nuts, where you see the johnswort[9] waving. I think that I may warrant you one worm to every three sods you turn up, if you look well in among the roots of the grass, as if you were weeding. Or, if you choose to go farther, it will not be unwise, for I have found the increase of fair bait to be very nearly as the squares of the distances.

Hermit alone. Let me see; where was I? Methinks I was nearly in this frame of mind; the world lay about at this angle. Shall I go to heaven or a-fishing? If I should soon bring this meditation to an end, would another so sweet occasion be likely to offer? I was as near being resolved into the essence of things as ever I was in my life. I fear my thoughts will not come back to me. If it would do any good, I would whistle for them. When they make us an

8 In 1846, with financial support from Emerson, Ellery Channing voyaged through the Straits of Gibraltar along the Spanish coast on his way to Italy.

9 *Hypericum:* St. Johns wort, a perennial herb or shrub.

10 Thoreau's spelling of the Latinization, Kong-fuzi, for K'ung Futzu or Confucius. Thoreau did not use this form of the name anywhere else in his writings.

11 Memorandum.

12 New England term for any small freshwater fish.

13 Concord River.

14 Pilpai, or Bidpai, supposed author of a collection of Sanskrit fables, the *Hitopadesa*. Bidpai is a corruption of *bidbah*, the appellation of the chief scholar at the court of an Indian prince. Thoreau would have known Pilpai through the Charles Wilkins translation of *The Heetōpadēs of Veeshnoo-Sarmā*, a selection from which was published in July 1842 issue of *The Dial* (an earlier quotation from it appears in "Sounds").

15 Other collectors of fables, such as Aesop or Jean de La Fontaine.

16 Thoreau noted in his copy of *Walden* that this was *Mus leucopus*, the common house mouse, although a description in his journal would imply otherwise: "Like a squirrel, which [it] resembles, coming between the house mouse and the former. Its belly is a little reddish, and its ears a little longer" [J 1:368]. Thoreau, as shown in an 1855 journal passage, used the term mistakenly to mean *Peromyscus leucopus*, the white-bellied or deer mouse [J 7:345].

17 During the late 1840s Thoreau occasionally sent specimens to the Swiss naturalist Louis Agassiz, who came to the United States in 1846. In a letter of 1 June 1847 to James Elliot Cabot (1821–1903), Agassiz's assistant, Thoreau mentioned sending him "one dormouse? caught last night in my cellar" [C 182]. Cabot replied that Agassiz "seemed to know your mouse, and called it the white-bellied mouse. It was the first specimen he had seen" [C 183].

offer, is it wise to say, We will think of it? My thoughts have left no track, and I cannot find the path again. What was it that I was thinking of? It was a very hazy day. I will just try these three sentences of Con-fut-see;[10] they may fetch that state about again. I know not whether it was the dumps or a budding ecstasy. Mem.[11] There never is but one opportunity of a kind.

Poet. How now, Hermit, is it too soon? I have got just thirteen whole ones, beside several which are imperfect or undersized; but they will do for the smaller fry; they do not cover up the hook so much. Those village worms are quite too large; a shiner[12] may make a meal off one without finding the skewer.

Hermit. Well, then, let's be off. Shall we to the Concord?[13] There's good sport there if the water be not too high.

Why do precisely these objects which we behold make a world? Why has man just these species of animals for his neighbors; as if nothing but a mouse could have filled this crevice? I suspect that Pilpay[14] & Co.[15] have put animals to their best use, for they are all beasts of burden, in a sense, made to carry some portion of our thoughts.

The mice which haunted my house were not the common ones, which are said to have been introduced into the country, but a wild native kind[16] not found in the village. I sent one to a distinguished naturalist, and it interested him much.[17] When I was building, one of these had its nest underneath the house, and before I had laid the second floor, and swept out the shavings, would come out regularly at lunch time and pick up the crumbs at my feet. It probably had never seen a man before; and it soon became quite familiar, and would run over my shoes and up my clothes. It could readily ascend the sides of the room by short impulses, like a squirrel, which it resembled in its motions. At length, as I leaned with my elbow on the bench[18] one day, it ran up my clothes, and along my sleeve, and round and round the paper which held my dinner, while I kept the latter close, and dodged and played at bo-peep[19] with it; and when at last I held still a piece of cheese between my thumb and finger, it came and nibbled it, sitting in my hand, and afterward cleaned its face and paws, like a fly, and walked away.[20]

A phœbe soon built in my shed, and a robin for protection in a pine which grew against the house. In June the partridge, (*Tetrao umbellus,*)[21] which is so shy a bird, led her brood past my windows, from the woods in the rear to the front of my house, clucking and calling to them like a hen, and in all her behavior proving herself the hen of the woods. The young suddenly disperse on your approach, at a signal from the mother, as if a whirlwind had swept them away, and they so exactly resemble the dried leaves and twigs that many a traveller has placed his foot in the midst of a brood, and heard the whir of the old bird as she flew off, and her anxious calls and mewing, or seen her trail her wings to attract his attention, without suspecting their neighborhood. The parent will sometimes roll and spin round before you in such a dishabille, that you cannot, for a few moments, detect what kind of creature it is. The young squat still and flat, often running their heads under a leaf, and mind only their mother's directions given from a distance, nor will your approach make them run again and betray themselves. You may even tread on them, or have your eyes on them for a minute, without discovering them. I have held them in my open hand at such a time, and still their only care, obedient to their mother and their instinct, was to squat there without fear or trembling. So perfect is this instinct, that once, when I had laid them on the leaves again, and one accidentally fell on its side, it was found with the rest in exactly the same position ten minutes afterward. They are not callow like the young of most birds, but more per-

18 Not a seat but a workbench or long table, as in a carpenter's bench.

19 Peek-a-boo. The name "bo-peep" for this children's game is at least as old as Shakespeare's *King Lear* 1.4.143–44: "That such a king should play *bo-peep,* / And go the fools among."

20 Thoreau "was very much disappointed in not being able to present to me one of his little companions—a mouse," Joseph Hosmer wrote after visiting him at Walden in early September 1845. "He described it to me by saying that it had come upon his back as he leaned against the wall of the building, ran down his arm to his hand, and ate the cheese while holding it in his fingers; also, when he played upon the flute, it would come and listen from its hiding place, and remain there while he continued to play the same tune, but when he changed the tune, the little visitor would immediately disappear."

21 The ruffed grouse (*Bonasa umbellus*), which is often called a partridge.

fectly developed and precocious even than chickens. The remarkably adult yet innocent expression of their open and serene eyes is very memorable. All intelligence seems reflected in them. They suggest not merely the purity of infancy, but a wisdom clarified by experience. Such an eye was not born when the bird was, but is coeval with the sky it reflects. The woods do not yield another such a gem. The traveller does not often look into such a limpid well. The ignorant or reckless sportsman often shoots the parent at such a time, and leaves these innocents to fall a prey to some prowling beast or bird, or gradually mingle with the decaying leaves which they so much resemble. It is said that when hatched by a hen they will directly disperse on some alarm, and so are lost, for they never hear the mother's call which gathers them again. These were my hens and chickens.

It is remarkable how many creatures live wild and free though secret in the woods, and still sustain themselves in the neighborhood of towns, suspected by hunters only. How retired the otter manages to live here! He grows to be four feet long, as big as a small boy, perhaps without any human being getting a glimpse of him. I formerly saw the raccoon in the woods behind where my house is built, and probably still heard their whinnering[22] at night. Commonly I rested an hour or two in the shade at noon, after planting, and ate my lunch, and read a little by a spring which was the source of a swamp and of a brook, oozing from under Brister's Hill,[23] half a mile from my field. The approach to this was through a succession of descending grassy hollows, full of young pitch-pines, into a larger wood about the swamp. There, in a very secluded and shaded spot, under a spreading white-pine, there was yet a clean firm sward to sit on. I had dug out the spring and made a well of clear gray water, where I could dip up a pailful without roiling it, and thither I went for this purpose almost every day in midsummer, when the pond was warmest. Thither too the wood-cock led her brood, to probe the mud for worms, flying but a foot above them down the bank, while they ran in a troop beneath; but at last, spying me, she would leave her young and circle round and round me, nearer and nearer, till within four or five feet, pretending broken wings and legs, to attract my attention and get off her young, who would already have taken up their march, with faint wiry peep, single file through the swamp, as she directed. Or I heard the peep of the young when I could not see the parent bird. There too the turtle-doves[24] sat over the spring, or fluttered from bough to bough of the soft white-pines over my head; or the red squirrel, coursing down the nearest bough, was particularly familiar and inquisitive. You only need sit still long enough in some attractive spot in the woods that all its inhabitants may exhibit themselves to you by turns.

I was witness to events of a less peaceful character. One day when I went out to my wood-pile, or rather my pile of stumps, I observed two large ants, the one red, the other much larger, nearly half an inch long, and black, fiercely contending with one another. Having once got hold they never let go, but struggled and wrestled and rolled on the chips incessantly. Looking farther, I was surprised to find that the chips were covered with such combatants, that it was not a *duellum,* but a *bellum,*[25] a war between two races of ants, the red always pitted against the black, and frequently two red ones to one black. The legions of these Myrmidons[26] covered all the hills and vales in my wood-yard, and the ground was already strewn with the dead and dying, both red and black. It was the only battle which I have ever witnessed, the only battle-field I ever trod while the battle was raging; internecine war; the red republicans on the one hand, and the black imperialists on the other. On every side they were engaged in deadly combat, yet without any noise that I could hear,

24 Mourning doves; the true turtledove is not native to America.

25 Latin for duel and war, respectively.

26 Warlike people of ancient Thessaly who fought under Achilles in the Trojan War. Lemprière's *Bibliotheca Classica* has: "According to some the Myrmidons received their name from their having been originally ants." Thoreau may have been reminded of this connection from Pierre Huber (1777–1840), a Swiss entomologist who was quoted by Kirby and Spence in *An Introduction to Entomology* (Philadelphia, 1846) 362: "As the exploits of frogs and mice were the theme of Homer's muse, so, were I gifted like him, might I celebrate on this occasion the exhibition of Myrmidonian valor. . . . I trust you will not complain if, being unable to ascertain the name of any one of my heroes, my *Myrmidonomachia* be perfectly anonymous."

27 This phrase originally signified falling overboard, but also with a pun here of falling off the board on which they were fighting.

28 The motto of the Duke of Kent, which was also emblazoned in Latin on the flag of the Bedford Minutemen. Thoreau may have also known it through a poem by Felicia Hemans, "The Spartan Mother and Her Son," which closed with the son saying:

> Adieu ! my mother, if with glory crown'd
> Home I return not, scarr'd with many a wound,
> I'll bravely fall in battle's rushing tide;
> Conquer or die — "as my brave father died !"

29 According to Plutarch's "Apothegms of the Laconian Women" ("Sayings of Spartan Women" 16): A Spartan mother, "on handing her boy his shield, exhorting him, said, 'My son, either this or upon this.'"

30 Pope's translation of Homer's *Iliad* begins:

> Achilles' wrath, to Greece the direful spring
> Of woes unnumber'd, heavenly goddess, sing!
> That wrath which hurl'd to Pluto's gloomy
>   reign
> The souls of mighty chiefs untimely slain.

The wrath of Achilles caused him to refuse to join in the Trojan War; the death of his friend Patroclus finally forced the Greek hero into battle.

and human soldiers never fought so resolutely. I watched a couple that were fast locked in each other's embraces, in a little sunny valley amid the chips, now at noon-day prepared to fight till the sun went down, or life went out. The smaller red champion had fastened himself like a vice to his adversary's front, and through all the tumblings on that field never for an instant ceased to gnaw at one of his feelers near the root, having already caused the other to go by the board;[27] while the stronger black one dashed him from side to side, and, as I saw on looking nearer, had already divested him of several of his members. They fought with more pertinacity than bull-dogs. Neither manifested the least disposition to retreat. It was evident that their battle-cry was Conquer or die.[28] In the mean while there came along a single red ant on the hill-side of this valley, evidently full of excitement, who either had despatched his foe, or had not yet taken part in the battle; probably the latter, for he had lost none of his limbs; whose mother had charged him to return with his shield or upon it.[29] Or perchance he was some Achilles, who had nourished his wrath apart, and had now come to avenge or rescue his Patroclus.[30] He saw this unequal combat from afar, — for the blacks were nearly twice the size of the red, — he drew near with rapid pace till he stood on his guard within half an inch of the combatants; then, watching his opportunity, he sprang upon the black warrior, and commenced his operations near the root of his right fore-leg, leaving the foe to select among his own members; and so there were three united for life, as if a new kind of attraction had been invented which put all other locks and cements to shame. I should not have wondered by this time to find that they had their respective musical bands stationed on some eminent chip, and playing their national airs the while, to excite the slow and cheer the dying combatants. I was myself excited somewhat even as if they had been men. The more you think of it, the less the difference. And certainly there is not the fight recorded in Concord history, at least, if in the history of America, that will bear a moment's comparison with this, whether for the numbers engaged in it, or for the patriotism and heroism displayed. For numbers and for carnage it was an Austerlitz or Dresden.[31] Concord Fight! Two killed on the patriots' side, and Luther Blanchard[32] wounded! Why here every ant was a Buttrick,—"Fire! for God's sake fire!"[33]—and thousands shared the fate of Davis and Hosmer.[34] There was not one hireling there.[35] I have no doubt that it was a principle they fought for, as much as our ancestors, and not to avoid a three-penny tax on their tea;[36] and the results of this battle will be as important and memorable to those whom it concerns as those of the battle of Bunker Hill,[37] at least.

I took up the chip on which the three I have particularly described were struggling, carried it into my house, and placed it under a tumbler on my window-sill, in order to see the issue. Holding a microscope to the first-mentioned red ant, I saw that, though he was assiduously gnawing at the near fore-leg of his enemy, having severed his remaining feeler, his own breast was all torn away, exposing what vitals he had there to the jaws of the black warrior, whose breast-plate was apparently too thick for him to pierce; and the dark carbuncles of the sufferer's eyes shone with ferocity such as war only could excite. They struggled half an hour longer under the tumbler, and when I looked again the black soldier had severed the heads of his foes from their bodies, and the still living heads were hanging on either side of him like ghastly trophies at his saddle-bow,[38] still apparently as firmly fastened as ever, and he was endeavoring with feeble struggles, being without feelers and with only the remnant of a leg, and I know not how many other wounds, to divest himself of them; which at length, after half an hour more, he accomplished. I raised the glass,

31 Battles of the Napoleonic Wars, on 2 December 1805 and 26–27 August 1813, respectively, with losses totaling over eighty thousand troops.

32 A fifer from Acton, Massachusetts, who was possibly the first American wounded when the British opened fire in the battle of 19 April 1775 in Concord.

33 Major John Buttrick led the five hundred Minutemen in the Concord battle. The Patriots had been ordered not to fire, but once the British started shooting Buttrick yelled, "Fire, fellow soldiers, for God's sake, fire!"

34 Captain Isaac Davis and Abner Hosmer were the only two Americans killed in this battle.

35 Refers to the Hessian mercenaries hired by the British to fight in the American Revolution.

36 British tax on colonists that increased their resentment and led to the Boston Tea Party and the Revolution.

37 Battle of 17 June 1775 that was actually fought on Breed's Hill in Charlestown, Massachusetts, not on its neighboring Bunker Hill.

38 Arched front part of a saddle.

39 Hospital in Paris built by Louis XIV in the 1670s for veterans.

40 Kirby and Spence wrote of the "fury and carnage" of the ant battles in *An Introduction to Entomology* 363.

41 According to Kirby and Spence in *An Introduction to Entomology* 361: "Their battles have long been celebrated; and the date of them, as if it were an event of the first importance, has been formally recorded."

42 Swiss entomologist Pierre Huber; Kirby and Spence wrote in *An Introduction to Entomology* 362: "M. P. Huber is the only modern author that appears to have been witness to these combats." Huber's *Natural History of Ants* (London, 1820) contained a three-page account of a battle between red and black ants. A review of *Walden* in *The Churchman* (New York), 2 September 1854, mentioned that "a rather poetical account, rivalling the combats of Turks and Russians, was once given by a M. HANHART, an improvement upon HUBER which LEIGH HUNT has pleasantly commented upon and the original of which may be found in the *Edinburgh Journal of Science* for 1828." There is no indication that Thoreau was aware of Hanhart's account.

43 Literary name of Enea Silvio de' Piccolomini (1405–1464; Pope Pius II, 1458–64), who was also a poet, geographer, and historian.

44 Gabriel Condulmaro (1383–1447; Pope Eugene IV, 1431–47).

45 Swedish Catholic ecclesiastic and historian (1490–1558), titular archbishop of Upsala, and author of *Historia de Gentibus Septentrialibus*.

46 Christian II (1481–1559), cruel king of Denmark, Norway, and Sweden. His subjects revolted in 1532, imprisoning him for life.

47 Quoted, slightly edited and with variant punctuation, from Kirby and Spence's *Introduction to Entomology* 361–62.

48 James K. Polk (1795–1849), U.S. president, 1845–49.

49 Associated with Daniel Webster (1782–1852), senator from Massachusetts and supporter of

and he went off over the window-sill in that crippled state. Whether he finally survived that combat, and spent the remainder of his days in some Hotel des Invalides,[39] I do not know; but I thought that his industry would not be worth much thereafter. I never learned which party was victorious, nor the cause of the war; but I felt for the rest of that day as if I had had my feelings excited and harrowed by witnessing the struggle, the ferocity and carnage,[40] of a human battle before my door.

Kirby and Spence tell us that the battles of ants have long been celebrated and the date of them recorded,[41] though they say that Huber[42] is the only modern author who appears to have witnessed them. "Æneas Sylvius,"[43] say they, "after giving a very circumstantial account of one contested with great obstinacy by a great and small species on the trunk of a pear tree," adds that "'This action was fought in the pontificate of Eugenius the Fourth,[44] in the presence of Nicholas Pistoriensis, an eminent lawyer, who related the whole history of the battle with the greatest fidelity.' A similar engagement between great and small ants is recorded by Olaus Magnus,[45] in which the small ones, being victorious, are said to have buried the bodies of their own soldiers, but left those of their giant enemies a prey to the birds. This event happened previous to the expulsion of the tyrant Christiern the Second[46] from Sweden."[47] The battle which I witnessed took place in the Presidency of Polk,[48] five years before the passage of Webster's Fugitive-Slave Bill.[49]

Many a village Bose, fit only to course[50] a mud-turtle in a victualling cellar, sported his heavy quarters in the woods, without the knowledge of his master, and ineffectually smelled at old fox burrows and woodchucks' holes; led perchance by some slight cur which nimbly threaded the wood, and might still inspire a natural terror in its denizens;—now far behind his guide, barking like a canine bull toward some small squirrel which had treed itself for scrutiny, then, cantering off, bending the bushes with his weight, imagining that he is on the track of some stray member of the jerbilla[51] family. Once I was surprised to see a cat walking along the stony shore of the pond, for they rarely wander so far from home. The surprise was mutual. Nevertheless the most domestic cat, which has lain on a rug all her days, appears quite at home in the woods, and, by her sly and stealthy behavior, proves herself more native there than the regular inhabitants. Once, when berrying, I met with a cat with young kittens in the woods, quite wild, and they all, like their mother, had their backs up and were fiercely spitting at me. A few years before I lived in the woods there was what was called a "winged cat"[52] in one of the farmhouses in Lincoln nearest the pond, Mr. Gilian Baker's.[53] When I called to see her in June, 1842,[54] she was gone a-hunting in the woods, as was her wont, (I am not sure whether it was a male or female, and so use the more common pronoun,) but her mistress told me that she came into the neighborhood a little more than a year before, in April, and was finally taken into their house; that she was of a dark brownish-gray color, with a white spot on her throat, and white feet, and had a large bushy tail like a fox; that in the winter the fur grew thick and flatted out along her sides, forming strips ten or twelve inches long by two and a half wide, and under her chin like a muff, the upper side loose, the under matted like felt, and in the spring these appendages dropped off. They gave me a pair of her "wings," which I keep still. There is no appearance of a membrane about them. Some thought it was part flying-squirrel or some other wild animal, which is not impossible, for, according to naturalists, prolific hybrids have been produced by the union of the marten[55] and domestic cat. This would have been the right kind of cat for me to keep, if I had kept any; for why should not a poet's cat be winged as well as his horse?[56]

the Compromise of 1850 reaffirming fugitive slave laws, although it was James M. Mason (1798–1871), senator from Virginia, who authored the bill. The bill called for the return of fugitive slaves found in free states. So strong was the sentiment against Webster in Massachusetts that Emerson wrote several diatribes in his journal, including: "Pho! Let Mr Webster for decency's sake shut his lips once & forever on this word. The word *liberty* in the mouth of Mr Webster sounds like the word *love* in the mouth of a courtesan." Thoreau wrote in "Slavery in Massachusetts": "I hear a good deal said about trampling this law under foot. Why, one need not go out of his way to do that. This law rises not to the level of the head or the reason; its natural habitat is in the dirt. It was born and bred, and has its life, only in the dust and mire, on a level with the feet; and he who walks with freedom, and does not with Hindoo mercy avoid treading on every venomous reptile, will inevitably tread on it, and so trample it under foot,—and Webster, its maker, with it, like the dirt-bug and its ball" [W 4:394−95].

50 Pursue.

51 Unknown, but perhaps a variant of jerboa, a jumping mouse. Although the jumping mouse (family Zapodidae) found in North America is not of the same family as the jerboa (family Dipodidae), it is possible Thoreau confused the two. Thoreau used this term in drafts 6 and 7 of *Walden,* and did not correct it in the page proofs.

52 Caused as a result of feline cutaneous asthenia, a genetic skin disorder making the skin across the shoulders, back, and hindquarters extremely elastic; a winglike appearance can also occur if a longhaired breed becomes heavily matted, which would be the case here as Thoreau was given a pair of the cat's wings.

53 Given the location, the farm would have to be Baker Farm, although no Gilian Baker has been identified.

54 No journal entry is extant to corroborate this date.

55 A carnivore of the genus *Martes,* which also

includes weasels, stoats, otters, and badgers. There are eight species, which occur throughout temperate regions of the Northern Hemisphere. They hunt in trees, squirrels being their favorite prey, although they will take any other small mammal or bird. There are two species in America: the fisher, *Martes pennanti,* and the American marten, *M. americana.* Although a hybrid with a domestic cat is genetically impossible, Thoreau read about them in Richard Harlan's (1796–1843) *Fauna Americana, Being a Description of the Mammiferous Animals Inhabiting North America* (Philadelphia, 1825) 77–78. After a brief description of the successful union of a jackal and a dog, Harlan wrote: "In corroboration of the above, we may add that prolific hybrids have been produced by the union of animals *generically* distinct, between the martin, (*Mustela Martes*) and the domestic cat."

56   Reference to Pegasus, the winged horse of Greek mythology, who was a favorite of the Muses and so associated with poetic inspiration.

57   This phrase also appeared in "Natural History of Massachusetts": "And still later in the autumn, when the frosts have tinged the leaves, a solitary loon pays a visit to our retired ponds, where he may lurk undisturbed till the season of moulting is passed, making the woods ring with his wild laughter" [W 5:114].

58   Two-wheeled open carriages.

59   In "Natural History of Massachusetts" Thoreau wrote of the loon: "This bird, the Great Northern Diver, well deserves its name; for when pursued with a boat, it will dive, and swim like a fish under water, for sixty rods or more, as fast as a boat can be paddled, and its pursuer, if he would discover his game again, must put his ear to the surface to hear where it comes up" [W 5:114].

60   On 8 October 1852.

In the fall the loon (*Colymbus glacialis*) came, as usual, to moult and bathe in the pond, making the woods ring with his wild laughter[57] before I had risen. At rumor of his arrival all the Mill-dam sportsmen are on the alert, in gigs[58] and on foot, two by two and three by three, with patent rifles and conical balls and spy-glasses. They come rustling through the woods like autumn leaves, at least ten men to one loon. Some station themselves on this side of the pond, some on that, for the poor bird cannot be omnipresent; if he dive here he must come up there. But now the kind October wind rises, rustling the leaves and rippling the surface of the water, so that no loon can be heard or seen, though his foes sweep the pond with spy-glasses, and make the woods resound with their discharges. The waves generously rise and dash angrily, taking sides with all waterfowl, and our sportsmen must beat a retreat to town and shop and unfinished jobs. But they were too often successful. When I went to get a pail of water early in the morning I frequently saw this stately bird sailing out of my cove within a few rods. If I endeavored to overtake him in a boat, in order to see how he would manœuvre, he would dive and be completely lost, so that I did not discover him again, sometimes, till the latter part of the day.[59] But I was more than a match for him on the surface. He commonly went off in a rain.

As I was paddling along the north shore one very calm October afternoon,[60] for such days especially they settle on to the lakes, like the milkweed down, having looked in vain over the pond for a loon, suddenly one, sailing out from the shore toward the middle a few rods in front of me, set up his wild laugh and betrayed himself. I pursued with a paddle and he dived, but when he came up I was nearer than before. He dived again, but I miscalculated the direction he would take, and we were fifty rods apart when he came to the surface this time, for I had helped to widen the interval; and again he laughed long and loud, and with more reason than before. He manœuvred so cunningly that I could not get within half a dozen rods of him. Each time, when he came to the surface, turning his head this way and that, he coolly surveyed the water and the land, and apparently chose his course so that he might come up where there was the widest expanse of water and at the greatest distance from the boat. It was surprising how quickly he made up his mind and put his resolve into execution. He led me at once to the widest part of the pond, and could not be driven from it. While he was thinking one thing in his brain, I was endeavoring to divine his thought in mine. It was a pretty game, played on the smooth surface of the pond, a man against a loon. Suddenly your adversary's checker disappears beneath the board,[61] and the problem is to place yours nearest to where his will appear again. Sometimes he would come up unexpectedly on the opposite side of me, having apparently passed directly under the boat. So long-winded was he and so unweariable, that when he had swum farthest he would immediately plunge again, nevertheless; and then no wit could divine where in the deep pond, beneath the smooth surface, he might be speeding his way like a fish, for he had time and ability to visit the bottom of the pond in its deepest part. It is said that loons have been caught in the New York lakes eighty feet beneath the surface, with hooks set for trout,[62] — though Walden is deeper than that. How surprised must the fishes be to see this ungainly visitor from another sphere speeding his way amid their schools! Yet he appeared to know his course[63] as surely under water as on the surface, and swam much faster there. Once or twice I saw a ripple where he approached the surface, just put his head out to reconnoitre, and instantly dived again. I found that it was as well for me to rest on my oars and wait his reappearing as to endeavor to calculate where he would rise; for again and again, when I was strain-

61 In gaming, as in cards or checkers, to slip something under the board or table would be cheating, the opposite of what is "above board," or straightforward and not deceptive.

62 Thoreau's journal of 8 October 1852 reads: "A newspaper authority says a fisherman—giving his name—has caught loon in Seneca Lake, N.Y., eighty feet beneath the surface, with hooks set for trout. Miss Cooper has said the same" [J 4:380]. The newspaper authority was a letter to the editor, by "A Traveller," in the *Geneva Gazette* of 20 August 1852:

> I saw in a Geneva paper last year, some remarks respecting the Loon or great Northern Diver, being taken by hooks 80 or 90 feet under the surface of the water of Seneca Lake, as mentioned by Miss Cooper, in her "Rural Hours," and expressing a belief in the correctness of the statement, but there was no assertion from any knowledge of the editor.
>
> I lately met Mr. William Ormond, a boatman living at Geneva, on the northern shore of Seneca Lake, by the plank road, who says he lived here fifteen years, and has himself taken the Loon from hooks 80 feet under water, where they had been sunk for lake Trout.

Susan Fenimore Cooper (1813–1894), eldest daughter of James Fenimore Cooper, wrote in *Rural Hours*: "Not long since we saw one of these birds [loons] of unusual size, weighing nineteen pounds; it had been caught in Seneca Lake on the hook of what fishermen call a set-line, dropped to the depth of ninety-five feet, the birds having dived that distance to reach bait. Several others have been caught in the same manner in Seneca Lake upon lines sunk from eighty to one hundred feet." As Thoreau did not record any other information from Cooper's account in his journals or elsewhere, other that what was derived from the *Geneva Gazette*, it is unlikely that he had read her work.

63 Pun: course as in direction, and also, in relation to school in the previous line, a series of lessons or study.

64 Apparently a Thoreauism, the term does not appear in any pre-*Walden* dictionary, and Thoreau is cited as the source in the *The Century Dictionary* of 1889. He used the term in *The Maine Woods*:

> This of the loon—I do not mean its laugh, but its looning,—is a long-drawn call, as it were, sometimes singularly human to my ear,—*hoo-hoo-ooooo*, like the hallooing of a man on a very high key, having thrown his voice into his head. I have heard a sound exactly like it when breathing heavily through my own nostrils, half awake at ten at night, suggesting my affinity to the loon; as if its language were but a dialect of my own, after all. Formerly, when lying awake at midnight in those woods, I had listened to hear some words or syllables of their language, but it chanced that I listened in vain until I heard the cry of the loon. I have heard it occasionally on the ponds of my native town, but there its wildness is not enhanced by the surrounding scenery. [W 3:248]

ing my eyes over the surface one way, I would suddenly be startled by his unearthly laugh behind me. But why, after displaying so much cunning, did he invariably betray himself the moment he came up by that loud laugh? Did not his white breast enough betray him? He was indeed a silly loon, I thought. I could commonly hear the plash of the water when he came up, and so also detected him. But after an hour he seemed as fresh as ever, dived as willingly and swam yet farther than at first. It was surprising to see how serenely he sailed off with unruffled breast when he came to the surface, doing all the work with his webbed feet beneath. His usual note was this demoniac laughter, yet somewhat like that of a water-fowl; but occasionally, when he had balked me most successfully and come up a long way off, he uttered a long-drawn unearthly howl, probably more like that of a wolf than any bird; as when a beast puts his muzzle to the ground and deliberately howls. This was his looning,[64]—perhaps the wildest sound that is ever heard here, making the woods ring far and wide. I concluded that he laughed in derision of my efforts, confident of his own resources. Though the sky was by this time overcast, the pond was so smooth that I could see where he broke the surface when I did not hear him. His white breast, the stillness of the air, and the smoothness of the water were all against him. At length, having come up fifty rods off, he uttered one of those prolonged howls, as if calling on the god of loons to aid him, and immediately there came a wind from the east and rippled the surface, and filled the whole air with misty rain, and I was impressed as if it were the prayer of the loon answered, and his god was angry with me; and so I left him disappearing far away on the tumultuous surface.

For hours, in fall days, I watched the ducks cunningly tack and veer and hold the middle of the pond, far from the sportsman; tricks which they will have less need to practise in Louisiana bayous. When compelled to rise they would sometimes circle round and round and over the pond at a considerable height, from which they could easily see to other ponds and the river, like black motes in the sky; and, when I thought they had gone off thither long since, they would settle down by a slanting flight of a quarter of a mile on to a distant part which was left free; but what beside safety they got by sailing in the middle of Walden I do not know, unless they love its water for the same reason that I do.

Pun: house-warming as a celebration of a move into a new house, and the literal warming of his house for winter.

1 October, Thoreau wrote in his journal, "answers to that period in the life of man when he is no longer dependent on his transient moods, when all his experience ripens into wisdom, but every root, branch, leaf of him glows with maturity. What he has been and done in his spring and summer appears. He bears his fruit" [J 5:502]. There are several references to Thoreau's autumn graping expeditions in his journals. On 13 September 1859 he reminisced: "I remember my earliest going a-graping. (It was a wonder that we ever hit upon the ripe season.) There was more fun in finding and eying the big purple clusters high on the trees and climbing to them than in eating them. We used to take care not to chew the skins long lest they should make our mouths sore" [J 12:324]. He most often gathered the *Vitis labrusca*, the northern fox grape, a common wild grape.

2 Although Thoreau here abstained from gathering cranberries, his journals contain several passages describing the pleasures of going cranberrying: "I enjoyed this cranberrying very much, notwithstanding the wet and cold, and the swamp seemed to be yielding its crop to me alone. . . . I fill a basket with them and keep it several days by my side. . . . I have not garnered any rye or oats, but I gathered the wild vine of the Assabet" [J 9:40–41].

3 In November 1853 Thoreau described his experience with raking cranberries: "I find my best way of getting cranberries is to go forth in time of flood, just before the water begins to fall and after strong winds, and, choosing the thickest places, let one, with an instrument like a large coarse dung-fork, hold down the floating grass and other coarser part of the wreck mixed with [it], while another, with a common iron garden rake, rakes them into the boat, there being just enough chaff left to enable you to get them into the boat, yet with little water" [J 5:514].

4 Bison, also mistakenly called buffalo, grazed

House-Warming

In October I went a-graping to the river meadows, and loaded myself with clusters more precious for their beauty and fragrance than for food.[1] There too I admired, though I did not gather, the cranberries,[2] small waxen gems, pendants of the meadow grass, pearly and red, which the farmer plucks with an ugly rake,[3] leaving the smooth meadow in a snarl, heedlessly measuring them by the bushel and the dollar only, and sells the spoils of the meads to Boston and New York; destined to be *jammed*, to satisfy the tastes of lovers of Nature there. So butchers rake the tongues of bison[4] out of the prairie grass, regardless of the torn and drooping plant. The barberry's brilliant fruit was likewise food for my eyes merely;[5] but I collected a small store of wild apples for coddling,[6] which the proprietor and travellers had overlooked. When chestnuts were ripe[7] I laid up half a bushel for winter. It was very exciting at that season to roam the then boundless chestnut woods of Lincoln,[8]—they now sleep their long sleep under the railroad,[9]—with a bag on my shoulder, and a stick to open burrs with in my hand, for I did not always wait for the frost,[10] amid the rustling of leaves and the loud reproofs of the red squirrels and the jays,[11] whose half-consumed nuts I sometimes stole, for the burrs which they had selected were sure to contain sound ones. Occasionally I climbed and shook the trees.[12]

on prairie grass and were prized for their tongues, which were considered a delicacy. The July 1851 issue of *Harper's* included an article, "A Brush with the Bison," explaining that "it has been known for vast herds to be exterminated merely for their tongues."

5 Thoreau wrote in his journal of 25 May 1853, "That barberry bush near the bars on Conantum is methinks now the most beautiful, light, and graceful bush that I ever saw in bloom" [J 5:191], but he also thought barberries were better than a crop of apples because they would be "on the table daily all winter, while the two barrels of apples which we lay up will not amount to so much" [J 9:86].

6 To gently cook in hot, but not boiling, water; or to treat tenderly. In "Wild Apples" Thoreau wrote:

> Going up the side of a cliff about the first of November, I saw a vigorous young apple tree, which, planted by birds or cows, had shot up amid the rocks and open woods there, and had now much fruit on it, uninjured by the frosts, when all cultivated apples were gathered. It was a rank, wild growth, with many green leaves on it still, and made an impression of thorniness. The fruit was hard and green, but looked as if it would be palatable in the winter. Some was dangling on the twigs, but more half buried in the wet leaves under the tree, or rolled far down the hill amid the rocks. The owner knows nothing of it. . . .

> Nevertheless, *our* wild apple is wild only like myself, perchance, who belong not to the aboriginal race here, but have strayed into the woods from the cultivated stock. . . .

> Almost all wild apples are handsome. They cannot be too gnarly and crabbed and rusty to look at. The gnarliest will have some redeeming traits even to the eye. . . .

> The era of the Wild Apple will soon be past. It is a fruit which will probably become extinct in New England. . . . I fear that he who walks over these fields a century hence will not know the pleasure of knocking off wild apples. Ah,

poor man, there are many pleasures which he will not know. [W 5:299–301, 314, 321]

7 Mid-October, according to Thoreau's journal entries for 23 October 1855 [J 7:514] and 22 October 1857 ("Now is just the time for chestnuts") [J 10:119].

8 Thoreau was concerned about overuse and that the once "boundless" woods were becoming less abundant. He wrote in a journal entry of 17 October 1860: "It is well known that the chestnut timber of this vicinity has rapidly disappeared within fifteen years, having been used for railroad sleepers, for rails, and for planks, so that there is danger that this part of our forest will become extinct. . . . The last chestnut tracts of any size were on the side of Lincoln" [J 14:137].

9 Pun: railroad ties are called sleepers.

10 Chestnut burrs open with the onset of frost. Thoreau wrote in his journal of 22 October 1857: "At last Frost comes to unlock his chest; it alone holds the true key. Its lids straightway gape open, and the October air rushes in" [J 10:121].

11 "The jays scream, and the red squirrels scold," Thoreau wrote in an October 1852 journal entry, "while you are clubbing and shaking the trees" [J 4:382].

12 Thoreau was not pleased with shaking as a method for gathering chestnuts. He wrote in his journal that "it is a barbarous way to jar the tree, and I trust I do repent of it. Gently shake it only, or let the wind shake it for you" [J 10:123].

They grew also behind my house, and one large tree which almost overshadowed it, was, when in flower,[13] a bouquet which scented the whole neighborhood, but the squirrels and the jays got most of its fruit; the last coming in flocks early in the morning and picking the nuts out of the burrs before they fell. I relinquished these trees to them and visited the more distant woods composed wholly of chestnut. These nuts, as far as they went, were a good substitute for bread.[14] Many other substitutes might, perhaps, be found. Digging one day for fish-worms I discovered the ground-nut (*Apios tuberosa*)[15] on its string, the potato of the aborigines, a sort of fabulous fruit, which I had begun to doubt if I had ever dug and eaten in childhood, as I had told,[16] and had not dreamed it. I had often since seen its crimpled red velvety blossom supported by the stems of other plants without knowing it to be the same. Cultivation has well nigh exterminated it. It has a sweetish taste, much like that of a frostbitten potato, and I found it better boiled than roasted.[17] This tuber seemed like a faint promise of Nature to rear her own children and feed them simply here at some future period. In these days of fatted cattle and waving grain-fields, this humble root, which was once the *totem* of an Indian tribe,[18] is quite forgotten, or known only by its flowering vine; but let wild Nature reign here once more, and the tender and luxurious English grains will probably disappear before a myriad of foes, and without the care of man the crow may carry back even the last seed of corn to the great corn-field of the Indian's God in the south-west, whence he is said to have brought it;[19] but the now almost exterminated ground-nut will perhaps revive and flourish in spite of frosts and wildness, prove itself indigenous, and resume its ancient importance and dignity as the diet of the hunter tribe. Some Indian Ceres or Minerva must have been the inventor and bestower of it; and when the reign

---

13 The chestnut trees flower in June and July.

14 Like bread, they have high starch content. In medieval days, the chestnut was ground and used as a grain substitute when making bread. In parts of Asia and southern Europe, many still grind chestnuts into a meal for bread making. The chestnut tree has often been called the "bread tree."

15 Also known as *Apios americana,* a perennial herb with edible tuberous thickenings and stems, commonly known as the wild bean, pomme-de-terre, Indian potato, wild sweet potato, pea vines, and other names.

16 There is nothing extant in Thoreau's writings in which he told of eating groundnuts in his childhood. Although contextually it is possible he may have meant "as I had *been* told," there is no indication in an extant draft version of the passage to support this.

17 Thoreau wrote of the difference between roasted and boiled groundnuts in his journal of October 1852: "Roasted, they have an agreeable taste very much like a potato, though somewhat fibrous in texture. With my eyes shut, I should not know but I was eating a rather soggy potato. Boiled, they were unexpectedly quite dry, and though in this instance a little strong, had a more nutty flavor. With a little salt, a hungry man would make a very palatable meal on them" [J 4:384].

18 O'Callaghan's *Documentary History of the State of New York* includes a French document from 1666 in which the potato is referred to as a totem for the Iroquois "Potatoe tribe," or "La famille de la Pomme de Terre."

19 Roger Williams (1603?-1683) wrote in *A Key into the Language of America* that the Indians of New England "have a tradition, that the crow brought them at first an Indian grain of corn in one ear, and an Indian or French bean in another, from the great God Cawtantowwits's field in the southwest, from whence they hold came all their corn and beans." Thoreau referred to this legend again in his journal of 9 May 1852: "These are the

of poetry commences here, its leaves and string of nuts may be represented on our works of art.

Already, by the first of September,[20] I had seen two or three small maples turned scarlet across the pond, beneath where the white stems of three aspens diverged, at the point of a promontory, next the water. Ah, many a tale their color told![21] And gradually from week to week the character of each tree came out, and it admired itself reflected in the smooth mirror of the lake. Each morning the manager of this gallery substituted some new picture, distinguished by more brilliant or harmonious coloring, for the old upon the walls.[22]

The wasps came by thousands to my lodge in October,[23] as to winter quarters, and settled on my windows within and on the walls over-head, sometimes deterring visitors from entering. Each morning, when they were numbed with cold, I swept some of them out, but I did not trouble myself much to get rid of them; I even felt complimented by their regarding my house as a desirable shelter. They never molested me seriously, though they bedded with me; and they gradually disappeared, into what crevices I do not know, avoiding winter and unspeakable cold.[24]

Like the wasps, before I finally went into winter quarters in November, I used to resort to the north-east side of Walden, which the sun, reflected from the pitch-pine woods and the stony shore, made the fire-side of the pond; it is so much pleasanter and wholesomer to be warmed by the sun while you can be, than by an artificial fire.[25] I thus warmed myself by the still glowing embers which the summer, like a departed hunter, had left.

When I came to build my chimney[26] I studied masonry. My bricks being second-hand ones required to be cleaned with a trowel, so that I learned more than usual

warm-west-wind, dream-frog, leafing-out, willowy, haze days. . . . It was in such a season and such a wind that the crow brought the corn from the southwest" [J 4:43].

20 In 1852.

21 Possible allusion to Thomas Moore's "Those Evening Bells": "Those evening bells! Those evening bells! / How many a tale their music tells." Thoreau's journal passage of 1 September 1852 rhymingly extended this to: "Ah, many a tale their color tells of Indian times—and autumn wells [?]—primeval dells" [J 4:337].

22 In February 1859 Thoreau gave a lecture on "Autumnal Tints," which was published posthumously in the October 1862 issue of the *Atlantic Monthly*.

23 The original journal entry (8 November 1850) has November as the month of the wasps coming to his house [J 2:86].

24 Possible confusion with "the unspeakable rain of the Greek winter" [J 3:437], which Thoreau referred to in his journal of 18 April 1852. He may have received his impression of the Greek winter from Aratus's (ca. 315–ca. 245 B.C.E.) *Phaenomena*, Virgil's *Georgic I*, or Pliny's *Naturalis Historia*.

25 In an early spring journal entry from 1853, Thoreau wrote "That is an interesting morning when one first uses the warmth of the sun instead of fire; bathes in the sun, as anon in the river; eschewing fire, draws up to a garret window and warms his thoughts at natures great central fire, as does the buzzing fly by his side" [J 5:38].

26 Toward the end of summer 1845.

27 Ancient city in Mesopotamia, on the Euphrates River.

28 Chaldean king of Babylon, 605–562 B.C.E., whose people were skilled at making sun-baked mud-brick. That the bricks found at the ruins of Babylon have Nebuchadnezzar's name stamped on them was determined by Edward Hincks (1792–1866).

29 Possible allusion to Jacob's pillow in Genesis 28:11: Jacob "lighted upon a certain place, and tarried there all night, because the sun was set. And he took one of the stones of the place, and put it under his head, and lay down in that place to sleep."

30 Ellery Channing stayed with Thoreau in the fall of 1845, sleeping on the floor.

of the qualities of bricks and trowels. The mortar on them was fifty years old, and was said to be still growing harder; but this is one of those sayings which men love to repeat whether they are true or not. Such sayings themselves grow harder and adhere more firmly with age, and it would take many blows with a trowel to clean an old wiseacre of them. Many of the villages of Mesopotamia are built of second-hand bricks of a very good quality, obtained from the ruins of Babylon,[27] and the cement on them is older and probably harder still. However that may be, I was struck by the peculiar toughness of the steel which bore so many violent blows without being worn out. As my bricks had been in a chimney before, though I did not read the name of Nebuchadnezzar[28] on them, I picked out as many fireplace bricks as I could find, to save work and waste, and I filled the spaces between the bricks about the fireplace with stones from the pond shore, and also made my mortar with the white sand from the same place. I lingered most about the fireplace, as the most vital part of the house. Indeed, I worked so deliberately, that though I commenced at the ground in the morning, a course of bricks raised a few inches above the floor served for my pillow at night;[29] yet I did not get a stiff neck for it that I remember; my stiff neck is of older date. I took a poet to board for a fortnight about those times, which caused me to be put to it for room.[30] He brought his own knife, though I had two, and we used to scour them by thrusting them into the earth. He shared with me the labors of cooking. I was pleased to see my work rising so square and solid by degrees, and reflected, that, if it proceeded slowly, it was calculated to endure a long time. The chimney is to some extent an independent structure, standing on the ground and rising through the house to the heavens; even after the house is burned it still stands sometimes, and its importance and independence are apparent. This was toward the end of summer. It was now November.

The north wind had already begun to cool the pond, though it took many weeks of steady blowing to accomplish it, it is so deep. When I began to have a fire at evening, before I plastered my house, the chimney carried smoke particularly well, because of the numerous chinks between the boards. Yet I passed some cheerful evenings in that cool and airy apartment, surrounded by the rough brown boards full of knots, and rafters with the bark on high over-head. My house never pleased my eye so much after it was plastered, though I was obliged to confess that it was more comfortable. Should not every apartment in which man dwells be lofty enough to create some obscurity over-head, where flickering shadows may play at evening about the rafters? These forms are more agreeable to the fancy and imagination than fresco paintings or other the most expensive furniture. I now first began to inhabit my house, I may say, when I began to use it for warmth as well as shelter. I had got a couple of old fire-dogs[31] to keep the wood from the hearth, and it did me good to see the soot form on the back of the chimney which I had built, and I poked the fire with more right and more satisfaction than usual. My dwelling was small, and I could hardly entertain an echo in it; but it seemed larger for being a single apartment and remote from neighbors. All the attractions of a house were concentrated in one room; it was kitchen, chamber, parlor, and keeping-room;[32] and whatever satisfaction parent or child, master or servant, derive from living in a house, I enjoyed it all. Cato says, the master of a family (*patremfamilias*) must have in his rustic villa "cellam oleariam, vinariam, dolia multa, uti lubeat caritatem expectare, et rei, et virtuti, et gloriæ erit," that is, "an oil and wine cellar, many casks, so that it may

31 Andirons.
32 Term used in New England for a sitting room.

33 Quoted from Cato's *De Agri Cultura* 3, with Thoreau's translation.

34 Small wooden vessel that holds a quarter barrel.

35 Insect of the beetle family that feeds on grain.

36 Architectural decoration of rococo scrollwork, popular in Thoreau's day.

37 The king post in a gable roof is the vertical member connecting the apex of a triangular truss with the base. The queen posts are the two vertical tie posts in a roof truss that do not go to the apex.

38 In Roman mythology, ruler of the universe after deposing his father, Uranus. He was himself overthrown by his son, Jupiter, and fled to Rome, where he ushered in the Golden Age.

be pleasant to expect hard times; it will be for his advantage, and virtue, and glory."[33] I had in my cellar a firkin[34] of potatoes, about two quarts of peas with the weevil[35] in them, and on my shelf a little rice, a jug of molasses, and of rye and Indian meal a peck each.

I sometimes dream of a larger and more populous house, standing in a golden age, of enduring materials, and without ginger-bread work,[36] which shall still consist of only one room, a vast, rude, substantial, primitive hall, without ceiling or plastering, with bare rafters and purlins supporting a sort of lower heaven over one's head, — useful to keep off rain and snow; where the king and queen posts[37] stand out to receive your homage, when you have done reverence to the prostrate Saturn[38] of an older dynasty on stepping over the sill; a cavernous house, wherein you must reach up a torch upon a pole to see the roof; where some may live in the fireplace, some in the recess of a window, and some on settles, some at one end of the hall, some at another, and some aloft on rafters with the spiders, if they choose; a house which you have got into when you have opened the outside door, and the ceremony is over; where the weary traveller may wash, and eat, and converse, and sleep, without further journey; such a shelter as you would be glad to reach in a tempestuous night, containing all the essentials of a house, and nothing for house-keeping; where you can see all the treasures of the house at one view, and every thing hangs upon its peg that a man should use; at once kitchen, pantry, parlor, chamber, store-house, and garret; where you can see so necessary a thing as a barrel or a ladder, so convenient a thing as a cupboard, and hear the pot boil, and pay your respects to the fire that cooks your dinner and the oven that bakes your bread, and the necessary furniture and utensils are the chief ornaments; where the washing is not put out, nor the fire, nor the mistress, and perhaps you are sometimes requested to move from off the trap-door, when the cook would descend into the cellar, and so learn whether the ground is solid or hollow beneath you without stamping. A house whose inside is as open and manifest as a bird's nest, and you cannot go in at the front door and out at the back without seeing some of its inhabitants; where to be a guest is to be presented with the freedom of the house, and not to be carefully excluded from seven eighths of it, shut up in a particular cell, and told to make yourself at home there,—in solitary confinement. Nowadays the host does not admit you to *his* hearth, but has got the mason to build one for yourself somewhere in his alley,[39] and hospitality is the art of *keeping* you at the greatest distance. There is as much secrecy about the cooking as if he had a design to poison you. I am aware that I have been on many a man's premises, and might have been legally ordered off, but I am not aware that I have been in many men's houses. I might visit in my old clothes a king and queen who lived simply in such a house as I have described, if I were going their way; but backing out of a modern palace will be all that I shall desire to learn, if ever I am caught in one.[40]

It would seem as if the very language of our parlors would lose all its nerve and degenerate into *parlaver*[41] wholly, our lives pass at such remoteness from its symbols, and its metaphors and tropes are necessarily so far fetched, through slides and dumb-waiters, as it were; in other words, the parlor is so far from the kitchen and workshop. The dinner even is only the parable of a dinner, commonly. As if only the savage dwelt near enough to Nature and Truth to borrow a trope from them. How can the scholar, who dwells away in the North West Territory[42] or the Isle of Man,[43] tell what is parliamentary in the kitchen?

However, only one or two of my guests were ever bold enough to stay and eat a hasty-pudding with me; but when they saw that crisis approaching they beat a hasty

39 An aisle or narrow passageway.
40 Court etiquette requires subjects to back out when leaving royalty, not turning one's back toward them.
41 Conflation of parlor and palaver.
42 Acquired in 1783, this territory was considered the frontier in Thoreau's youth, covering the area that became the states of Ohio, Indiana, Illinois, Michigan, Wisconsin, and part of Minnesota.
43 British island in the Irish Sea.

44 In late autumn 1845. He left the house from 12 November to 6 December to allow the plaster to dry.

45 Common freshwater river mussel (family Unionidae), to which Thoreau referred in "Natural History of Massachusetts": "That common muscle, the *Unio complanatus,* or more properly *fluviatilis*" [W 5:129].

46 Limestone was mined in the Estabrook area north of Concord.

retreat rather, as if it would shake the house to its foundations. Nevertheless, it stood through a great many hasty-puddings.

I did not plaster till it was freezing weather.[44] I brought over some whiter and cleaner sand for this purpose from the opposite shore of the pond in a boat, a sort of conveyance which would have tempted me to go much farther if necessary. My house had in the mean while been shingled down to the ground on every side. In lathing I was pleased to be able to send home each nail with a single blow of the hammer, and it was my ambition to transfer the plaster from the board to the wall neatly and rapidly. I remembered the story of a conceited fellow, who, in fine clothes, was wont to lounge about the village once, giving advice to workmen. Venturing one day to substitute deeds for words, he turned up his cuffs, seized a plasterer's board, and having loaded his trowel without mishap, with a complacent look toward the lathing overhead, made a bold gesture thitherward; and straightway, to his complete discomfiture, received the whole contents in his ruffled bosom. I admired anew the economy and convenience of plastering, which so effectually shuts out the cold and takes a handsome finish, and I learned the various casualties to which the plasterer is liable. I was surprised to see how thirsty the bricks were which drank up all the moisture in my plaster before I had smoothed it, and how many pailfuls of water it takes to christen a new hearth. I had the previous winter made a small quantity of lime by burning the shells of the *Unio fluviatilis,*[45] which our river affords, for the sake of the experiment; so that I knew where my materials came from. I might have got good limestone within a mile or two and burned it myself, if I had cared to do so.[46]

The pond had in the mean while skimmed over in the shadiest and shallowest coves, some days or even weeks before the general freezing. The first ice is especially interesting and perfect, being hard, dark, and transparent, and affords the best opportunity that ever offers for examining the bottom where it is shallow; for you can lie at your length on ice only an inch thick, like a skater insect on the surface of the water, and study the bottom at your leisure, only two or three inches distant, like a picture behind a glass, and the water is necessarily always smooth then. There are many furrows in the sand where some creature has travelled about and doubled on its tracks; and, for wrecks, it is strewn with the cases of cadis worms[47] made of minute grains of white quartz. Perhaps these have creased it, for you find some of their cases in the furrows, though they are deep and broad for them to make. But the ice itself is the object of most interest, though you must improve the earliest opportunity to study it. If you examine it closely the morning after it freezes, you find that the greater part of the bubbles, which at first appeared to be within it, are against its under surface, and that more are continually rising from the bottom; while the ice is as yet comparatively solid and dark, that is, you see the water through it. These bubbles are from an eightieth to an eighth of an inch in diameter, very clear and beautiful, and you see your face reflected in them through the ice. There may be thirty or forty of them to a square inch. There are also already within the ice narrow oblong perpendicular bubbles about half an inch long, sharp cones with the apex upward; or oftener, if the ice is quite fresh, minute spherical bubbles one directly above another, like a string of beads. But these within the ice are not so numerous nor obvious as those beneath. I sometimes used to cast on stones to try the strength of the ice, and those which broke through carried in air with them, which formed very large and conspicuous white bubbles beneath. One day when I came to the same place forty-eight hours afterward, I found that those large bubbles

47 Larvae of the cadis, or, as is more commonly spelled now, caddis fly.

were still perfect, though an inch more of ice had formed, as I could see distinctly by the seam in the edge of a cake. But as the last two days had been very warm, like an Indian summer,[48] the ice was not now transparent, showing the dark green color of the water, and the bottom, but opaque and whitish or gray, and though twice as thick was hardly stronger than before, for the air bubbles had greatly expanded under this heat and run together, and lost their regularity; they were no longer one directly over another, but often like silvery coins poured from a bag, one overlapping another, or in thin flakes, as if occupying slight cleavages. The beauty of the ice was gone, and it was too late to study the bottom. Being curious to know what position my great bubbles occupied with regard to the new ice, I broke out a cake containing a middling sized one, and turned it bottom upward. The new ice had formed around and under the bubble, so that it was included between the two ices. It was wholly in the lower ice, but close against the upper, and was flattish, or perhaps slightly lenticular, with a rounded edge, a quarter of an inch deep by four inches in diameter; and I was surprised to find that directly under the bubble the ice was melted with great regularity in the form of a saucer reversed, to the height of five eighths of an inch in the middle, leaving a thin partition there between the water and the bubble, hardly an eighth of an inch thick; and in many places the small bubbles in this partition had burst out downward, and probably there was no ice at all under the largest bubbles, which were a foot in diameter. I inferred that the infinite number of minute bubbles which I had first seen against the under surface of the ice were now frozen in likewise, and that each, in its degree, had operated like a burning glass[49] on the ice beneath to melt and rot it. These are the little air-guns which contribute to make the ice crack and whoop.

48 On 31 October 1850, Thoreau called Indian summer "the finest season of the year" [J 2:76].
49 Magnifying glass used to start a fire.

At length the winter set in in good earnest, just as I had finished plastering, and the wind began to howl around the house as if it had not had permission to do so till then. Night after night the geese came lumbering in in the dark with a clangor and a whistling of wings, even after the ground was covered with snow, some to alight in Walden, and some flying low over the woods toward Fair Haven, bound for Mexico. Several times, when returning from the village at ten or eleven o'clock at night, I heard the tread of a flock of geese, or else ducks, on the dry leaves in the woods by a pond-hole behind my dwelling, where they had come up to feed, and the faint honk or quack of their leader as they hurried off. In 1845 Walden froze entirely over for the first time on the night of the 22d of December, Flint's and other shallower ponds and the river having been frozen ten days or more; in '46, the 16th; in '49, about the 31st; and in '50, about the 27th of December; in '52, the 5th of January; in '53, the 31st of December.[50] The snow had already covered the ground since the 25th of November, and surrounded me suddenly with the scenery of winter. I withdrew yet farther into my shell, and endeavored to keep a bright fire both within my house and within my breast. My employment out of doors now was to collect the dead wood in the forest, bringing it in my hands or on my shoulders, or sometimes trailing a dead pine tree under each arm to my shed. An old forest fence which had seen its best days was a great haul for me. I sacrificed it to Vulcan,[51] for it was past serving the god Terminus.[52] How much more interesting an event is that man's supper who has just been forth in the snow to hunt, nay, you might say, steal,[53] the fuel to cook it with! His bread and meat are sweet.[54] There are enough fagots and waste wood of all kinds in the forests of most of our towns to support many fires, but which at present warm none, and, some think, hinder the growth of the young wood. There was also the drift-

50 Thoreau often recorded such natural phenomena. His December 1845 journal has the following entries:

> Dec. 12. Friday. The pond skimmed over on the night of this day, excepting a strip from the bar to the northwest shore. Flint's Pond has been frozen for some time.
> Dec. 16. 17. 18, 19, 20. Pond *quite free* from ice, not yet having been frozen quite over.
> Dec. 23. Tuesday. The pond froze over last night entirely for the first time, yet so as not to be safe to walk upon. [J 1:394–95]

51 In Roman mythology, god of fire.
52 In Roman mythology, god of boundaries. The wood that was not good for fencing material was burned.
53 Emerson's journals described a walk with Thoreau in November 1838: "Suppose, he said, some great proprietor, before he was born, had bought up the whole globe. So had he been hustled out of nature. Not having been privy to any of these arrangements, he does not feel called on to consent to them, and so cuts fishpoles in the woods without asking who had a better title to the wood than he."
54 Allusion to Proverbs 9:17: "Stolen waters are sweet, and bread eaten in secret is pleasant."

55 Quoted from William Gilpin's *Remarks on Forest Scenery and Other Woodland Views* 1:122. Thoreau's notes on his readings in Gilpin appear in his journal of 12 April 1852.

56 Echo of Gilpin's *Remarks on Forest Scenery* 2:100–101, which explains that under the Lord Warden "are two distinct appointments of officers, the one to preserve the venison of the forest, and the other to preserve the vert. The former term, in the language of forest law, includes all species of game; the latter respects the woods and lawns which harbour and feed them." The Lord Warden in England was responsible for protecting the forest wildlife and greenery. In his journal on 12 April 1852 Thoreau wrote, in part quoting Gilpin: "In the New Forest in Hampshire they had a chief officer called the Lord Warden and under him two distinct officers, one to preserve the *venison* of the forest, another to preserve its *vert, i.e.* woods, lawns, etc. Does not our Walden need such? The Lord Warden was a person of distinction, as the Duke of Gloucester" [J 3:407–8].

57 Thoreau's long grief over the woods-burning episode can be seen in the journal entry he wrote in June 1850, six years after the accident:

> It burned over a hundred acres or more and destroyed much young wood. When I returned home late in the day, with others of my townsmen, I could not help noticing that the crowd who were so ready to condemn the individual who had kindled the fire did not sympathize with the owners of the wood, but were in fact highly elate [*sic*] and as it were thankful for the opportunity which had afforded them so much sport; and it was only half a dozen owners, so called, though not all of them, who looked sour or grieved, and I felt that I had a deeper interest in the woods, knew them better and should feel their loss more, than any or all of them. The farmer whom I had first conducted to the woods was obliged to ask me the shortest way back, through his own lot. Why, then, should the half-dozen owners [and] the indi-

wood of the pond. In the course of the summer I had discovered a raft of pitch-pine logs with the bark on, pinned together by the Irish when the railroad was built. This I hauled up partly on the shore. After soaking two years and then lying high six months it was perfectly sound, though waterlogged past drying. I amused myself one winter day with sliding this piecemeal across the pond, nearly half a mile, skating behind with one end of a log fifteen feet long on my shoulder, and the other on the ice; or I tied several logs together with a birch withe, and then, with a longer birch or alder which had a hook at the end, dragged them across. Though completely waterlogged and almost as heavy as lead, they not only burned long, but made a very hot fire; nay, I thought that they burned better for the soaking, as if the pitch, being confined by the water, burned longer as in a lamp.

Gilpin, in his account of the forest borderers of England, says that "the encroachments of trespassers, and the houses and fences thus raised on the borders of the forest," were "considered as great nuisances by the old forest law, and were severely punished under the name of *purprestures,* as tending *ad terrorem ferarum—ad nocumentum forestæ,* &c.,"[55] to the frightening of the game and the detriment of the forest. But I was interested in the preservation of the venison and the vert[56] more than the hunters or woodchoppers, and as much as though I had been the Lord Warden himself; and if any part was burned, though I burned it myself by accident, I grieved with a grief that lasted longer and was more inconsolable than that of the proprietors;[57] nay, I grieved when it was cut down by the proprietors themselves. I would that our farmers when they cut down a forest felt some of that awe which the old Romans did when they came to thin, or let in the light to, a consecrated grove, (*lucum conlucare,*) that is, would believe that it is sacred to some god. The Roman made an expiatory offering, and prayed, Whatever god or goddess thou art to whom this grove is sacred, be propitious to me, my family, and children, &c.[58]

It is remarkable what a value is still put upon wood even in this age and in this new country, a value more permanent and universal than that of gold. After all our discoveries and inventions no man will go by a pile of wood. It is as precious to us as it was to our Saxon and Norman ancestors. If they made their bows of it, we make our gunstocks of it. Michaux,[59] more than thirty years ago, says that the price of wood for fuel in New York and Philadelphia "nearly equals, and sometimes exceeds, that of the best wood in Paris, though this immense capital annually requires more than three hundred thousand cords, and is surrounded to the distance of three hundred miles by cultivated plains."[60] In this town the price of wood rises almost steadily, and the only question is, how much higher it is to be this year than it was the last. Mechanics and tradesmen who come in person to the forest on no other errand, are sure to attend the wood auction, and even pay a high price for the privilege of gleaning after the woodchopper. It is now many years that men have resorted to the forest for fuel and the materials of the arts; the New Englander and the New Hollander, the Parisian and the Celt,[61] the farmer and Robinhood,[62] Goody Blake and Harry Gill,[63] in most parts of the world the prince and the peasant, the scholar and the savage, equally require still a few sticks from the forest to warm them and cook their food. Neither could I do without them.

Every man looks at his wood-pile with a kind of affection. I love to have mine before my window, and the more chips the better to remind me of my pleasing work. I had an old axe which nobody claimed, with which by spells in winter days, on the sunny side of the house, I played about the stumps which I had got out of my bean-field. As my driver[64] prophesied when I was ploughing, they warmed me twice, once while I was splitting them, and

viduals who set the fire alone feel sorrow for the loss of the woods, while the rest of the town have their spirits raised? Some of the owners, however, bore their loss like men, but other some declared behind my back that I was a "damned rascal;" and a flibbertigibbet or two, who crowed like the old cock, shouted some reminiscences of "burnt woods" from safe recesses for some years after. I have had nothing to say to any of them. The locomotive engine has since burned over nearly all the same ground and more, and in some measure blotted out the memory of the previous fire. For a long time after I had learned this lesson I marvelled that while matches and tinder were contemporaries that the world was not consumed; why the houses that have hearths were not burned before another day; if the flames were not as hungry now as when I waked them. I at once ceased to regard the owners and my own fault, — if fault there was any in the matter, — and attended to the phenomenon before me, determined to make the most of it. [J 2:24–25]

58 Allusion to, and Thoreau's translation of, Cato's *De Agri Cultura* 139.
59 François André Michaux (1770–1855), French naturalist.
60 Quoted from Michaux's *The North American Sylva, or a Description of the Forest Trees of the United States, Canada, and Nova Scotia*, translated by Augustus L. Hillhouse (Paris, 1817–19), 3:269, with minor variants. Thoreau excerpted several passages from Michaux, including this quotation with slight variants, in his journal of 18 May 1851.
61 Earliest known people in what is now England.
62 Robin Hood, the legendary English outlaw of Sherwood Forest of whom there were many ballads written.
63 Goody Blake, in William Wordsworth's poem "Goody Blake and Harry Gill," cursed Harry Gill for denying her firewood: "That, live as long as live he may, / He never will be warm again."

64 One who drives draft animals to pull a vehicle, such as a plow. The individual driver here is unidentified.

65 To flatten, thicken, enlarge, or sharpen by hammering with endwise blows on white-hot iron.

66 Beat him to it.

67 Pine that is full of pitch or resin.

again when they were on the fire, so that no fuel could give out more heat. As for the axe, I was advised to get the village blacksmith to "jump"[65] it; but I jumped him,[66] and, putting a hickory helve from the woods into it, made it do. If it was dull, it was at least hung true.

A few pieces of fat pine[67] were a great treasure. It is interesting to remember how much of this food for fire is still concealed in the bowels of the earth. In previous years I had often gone "prospecting" over some bare hillside, where a pitch-pine wood had formerly stood, and got out the fat pine roots. They are almost indestructible. Stumps thirty or forty years old, at least, will still be sound at the core, though the sap-wood has all become vegetable mould, as appears by the scales of the thick bark forming a ring level with the earth four or five inches distant from the heart. With axe and shovel you explore this mine, and follow the marrowy store, yellow as beef tallow, or as if you had struck on a vein of gold, deep into the earth. But commonly I kindled my fire with the dry leaves of the forest, which I had stored up in my shed before the snow came. Green hickory finely split makes the wood-chopper's kindlings, when he has a camp in the woods. Once in a while I got a little of this. When the villagers were lighting their fires beyond the horizon, I too gave notice to the various wild inhabitants of Walden vale, by a smoky streamer from my chimney, that I was awake. —

Light-winged Smoke, Icarian bird,
Melting thy pinions in thy upward flight,
Lark without song, and messenger of dawn,
Circling above the hamlets as thy nest;
Or else, departing dream, and shadowy form
Of midnight vision, gathering up thy skirts;
By night star-veiling, and by day
Darkening the light and blotting out the sun;

Go thou my incense upward from this hearth,
And ask the gods to pardon this clear flame.[68]

Hard green wood just cut, though I used but little of that, answered my purpose better than any other. I sometimes left a good fire when I went to take a walk in a winter afternoon; and when I returned, three or four hours afterward, it would be still alive and glowing. My house was not empty though I was gone. It was as if I had left a cheerful housekeeper behind. It was I and Fire that lived there; and commonly my housekeeper proved trustworthy. One day, however, as I was splitting wood, I thought that I would just look in at the window and see if the house was not on fire; it was the only time I remember to have been particularly anxious on this score; so I looked and saw that a spark had caught my bed, and I went in and extinguished it when it had burned a place as big as my hand. But my house occupied so sunny and sheltered a position, and its roof was so low, that I could afford to let the fire go out in the middle of almost any winter day.

The moles nested in my cellar, nibbling every third potato,[69] and making a snug bed even there of some hair left after plastering and of brown paper; for even the wildest animals love comfort and warmth as well as man, and they survive the winter only because they are so careful to secure them. Some of my friends spoke as if I was coming to the woods on purpose to freeze myself. The animal merely makes a bed, which he warms with his body in a sheltered place; but man, having discovered fire, boxes up some air in a spacious apartment, and warms that, instead of robbing himself, makes that his bed, in which he can move about divested of more cumbrous clothing, maintain a kind of summer in the midst of winter, and by means of windows even admit the light, and with a lamp

68 Thoreau's poem, which originally appeared as "Smoke" in the April 1843 issue of *The Dial*.
69 Moles feed almost exclusively on soil insects, such as earthworms and grubs; roots, bulbs, and tubers of plants are not a food source but may be damaged indirectly as moles dig through the ground. It is likely that Thoreau's potatoes were eaten by mice, which use mole tunnels for protection and as avenues to food supplies. In "Brute Neighbors" Thoreau described the "mice which haunted my house."

70 Allusion to Atropos, the Fate who cuts the thread of life.

71 On 19 January 1810, when New England experienced gale winds and a sudden overnight drop of 50 degrees to subzero temperatures. Thoreau mentioned it twice in his journals: "Mother remembers the Cold Friday very well. She lived in the house where I was born. The people in the kitchen . . . drew up close to the fire, but the dishes which the Hardy girl was washing froze as fast as she washed them, close to the fire. They managed to keep warm in the parlor by their great fires" [J 9:213]; and "I asked M[inott] about the Cold Friday. He said, 'It was plaguy cold; it stung like a wasp.' He remembers seeing them toss up water in a shoemaker's shop, usually a very warm place, and when it struck the floor it was frozen, and rattled like so many shot" [J 9:230].

72 Possible reference to the "Great Snow" of 17 February 1717.

lengthen out the day. Thus he goes a step or two beyond instinct, and saves a little time for the fine arts. Though, when I had been exposed to the rudest blasts a long time, my whole body began to grow torpid, when I reached the genial atmosphere of my house I soon recovered my faculties and prolonged my life. But the most luxuriously housed has little to boast of in this respect, nor need we trouble ourselves to speculate how the human race may be at last destroyed. It would be easy to cut their threads[70] any time with a little sharper blast from the north. We go on dating from Cold Fridays[71] and Great Snows;[72] but a little colder Friday, or greater snow, would put a period to man's existence on the globe.

The next winter I used a small cooking-stove for economy, since I did not own the forest; but it did not keep fire so well as the open fireplace. Cooking was then, for the most part, no longer a poetic, but merely a chemic process. It will soon be forgotten, in these days of stoves, that we used to roast potatoes in the ashes, after the Indian fashion. The stove not only took up room and scented the house, but it concealed the fire, and I felt as if I had lost a companion. You can always see a face in the fire. The laborer, looking into it at evening, purifies his thoughts of the dross and earthiness which they have accumulated during the day. But I could no longer sit and look into the fire, and the pertinent words of a poet recurred to me with new force.—

> "Never, bright flame, may be denied to me
> Thy dear, life imaging, close sympathy.
> What but my hopes shot upward e'er so bright?
> What but my fortunes sunk so low in night?
>
> Why art thou banished from our hearth and hall,
> Thou who art welcomed and beloved by all?
> Was thy existence then too fanciful

For our life's common light, who are so dull?
Did thy bright gleam mysterious converse hold
With our congenial souls? secrets too bold?
Well, we are safe and strong, for now we sit
Beside a hearth where no dim shadows flit,
Where nothing cheers nor saddens, but a fire
Warms feet and hands—nor does to more aspire;
By whose compact utilitarian heap
The present may sit down and go to sleep,
Nor fear the ghosts who from the dim past
    walked,
And with us by the unequal light of the old wood
    fire talked."[73]

                            Mrs. Hooper

73 From the American poet Ellen Sturgis Hooper's (1812–1848) "The Wood-Fire," with slight variations in punctuation. This poem was first published in the second number of *The Dial* (October 1840).

1 Franklin Sanborn, in the Bibliophile Edition of *Walden*, described the woods as "the abode of denizens who rather shunned publicity, like the freed slaves of the eighteenth century, and white persons who had an affinity more than normal for ardent spirits. Something of the same inhabitation prevailed along the Old Marlboro Road on the other side of the Walden woods."

2 The road nearest to Thoreau's house, between Concord and Lincoln, was a makeshift route through Walden Woods for access to the woods and ponds.

3 The road through the woods was a shorter route between Concord and Lincoln than the Lincoln Road (now Route 126).

Former Inhabitants; and Winter Visitors

I weathered some merry snow storms, and spent some cheerful winter evenings by my fire-side, while the snow whirled wildly without, and even the hooting of the owl was hushed. For many weeks I met no one in my walks but those who came occasionally to cut wood and sled it to the village. The elements, however, abetted me in making a path through the deepest snow in the woods, for when I had once gone through the wind blew the oak leaves into my tracks, where they lodged, and by absorbing the rays of the sun melted the snow, and so not only made a dry bed for my feet, but in the night their dark line was my guide. For human society I was obliged to conjure up the former occupants of these woods.[1] Within the memory of many of my townsmen the road near which my house stands[2] resounded with the laugh and gossip of inhabitants, and the woods which border it were notched and dotted here and there with their little gardens and dwellings, though it was then much more shut in by the forest than now. In some places, within my own remembrance, the pines would scrape both sides of a chaise at once, and women and children who were compelled to go this way to Lincoln[3] alone and on foot did it with fear, and often ran a good part of the distance. Though mainly but a humble route to neighboring villages, or for the woodman's team, it once amused the traveller more than now by its variety, and lingered longer in his memory. Where now firm open fields stretch from the village to the woods, it then ran through a maple swamp on a foundation of logs,[4] the remnants of which, doubtless, still underlie the present dusty highway, from the Stratton, now the Alms House,[5] Farm, to Brister's Hill.

East of my bean-field, across the road, lived Cato Ingraham,[6] slave of Duncan Ingraham,[7] Esquire, gentleman of Concord village; who built his slave a house, and gave him permission to live in Walden Woods;—Cato, not Uticensis,[8] but Concordiensis.[9] Some say that he was a Guinea Negro.[10] There are a few who remember his little patch among the walnuts, which he let grow up till he should be old and need them; but a younger and whiter speculator[11] got them at last. He too, however, occupies an equally narrow house[12] at present. Cato's half-obliterated cellar hole still remains,[13] though known to few, being concealed from the traveller by a fringe of pines. It is now filled with the smooth sumach, (*Rhus glabra*,) and one of the earliest species of golden-rod (*Solidago stricta*)[14] grows there luxuriantly.

Here, by the very corner of my field, still nearer to town, Zilpha,[15] a colored woman, had her little house, where she spun linen for the townsfolk, making the Walden Woods ring with her shrill singing, for she had a loud and notable voice. At length, in the war of 1812,[16] her dwelling was set on fire by English soldiers, prisoners on parole,[17] when she was away, and her cat and dog and hens were all burned up together. She led a hard life, and somewhat inhumane. One old frequenter of these woods remembers, that as he passed her house one noon he heard her muttering to herself over her gurgling pot,— "Ye are all bones, bones!" I have seen bricks amid the oak copse there.

Down the road, on the right hand, on Brister's Hill,

4 A corduroy road formed by laying logs side by side transversely across a swampy area on a cart path or backwoods road.

5 The Stratton family at the end of the 17th century owned most of the land from the west side of Walden Street to Walden Pond. According to Lemuel Shattuck's *History of the Town of Concord*, "Mr. Hugh Cargill bequeathed to the town the 'Stratton Farm,' so called, which was valued, in 1800, at $1,360, 'to be improved as a poor-house, and the land to be improved by, and for the benefit of the poor.'"

6 Cato Ingraham died 23 August 1805, at age 54. According to Walter Harding, "Cato worked as a day laborer. He and his wife apparently kept a guest room for transients."

7 Duncan Ingraham was Concord's wealthiest citizen in the late 18th century, making much money in the slave trade. According to Franklin Sanborn's Bibliophile Edition: "Duncan Ingraham, Cato's master, was a sea captain and Surinam merchant, who had made a fortune and retired to live on it in Concord village, near where the Library now stands. He was an ancestor of Captain Marryat, the novelist, and of Captain Ingraham, of the U.S. Navy, who distinguished himself by refusing to give up a Hungarian refugee on board his vessel in 1854. Cato was one of the slaves in which Ingraham occasionally dealt; when he married, his master freed him and he went to live near Walden. He died in 1805, and his master in 1811."

8 Latin: of Utica. This refers to Marcus Porcius Cato Uticensis (95–46 B.C.E.), Roman statesman who died in Utica, in North Africa, and not to be confused with his great-grandfather, Marcus Porcius Cato.

9 Latin: of Concord.

10 From the north shore of the Gulf of Guinea, on the east coast of Africa, which was the principal source of slaves from the 16th to the 18th centuries, as opposed to born of slaves in America.

11 Unidentified.

12 The grave. Thoreau used the same phrase in "Economy."

13 Ellery Channing noted in his copy of *Walden* that this cellar hole was "directly at the opening of the path from the Walden road to Goose pond."

14 This species is unknown in New England. Thoreau substituted "arguta?" for "stricta" in his copy of *Walden*. Although the *Solidago arguta* is a common New England species, it is not an early species. According to botanist Ray Angelo: "It is evident that Thoreau applied this name to *Solidago juncea* (Early goldenrod), owing to a statement about the early flowering time of *Solidago stricta* in *Gray's Manual of Botany* (2nd ed.) and certain other superficial resemblances between the two species."

15 Zilpha, sometimes Zilphah or Zilpah, White (d. 1820), former slave. Her obituary appeared in the *Middlesex Gazette* of 22 April 1820: "Died. In this town, Zilphah White, a woman of color, aged 72—For a number of years, she has led a life of a hermitess, in a small place, which scarcely would bear the name of a hovel, and though nearly blind the latter part of her life, was a constant attendant on public worship." She is listed in the Concord Registers as: "(a black) belonging to Spencer, died April 16, 1820" at age 82. It is unknown which age of death, 72 or 82, is correct.

16 War declared on Britain by the United States (1812–14) prompted by British restrictions on U.S. trade during the Napoleonic Wars, impressments of American sailors for British ships, and British and Canadian support of the cause of the American Indians in the West.

17 Sanborn wrote in the Bibliophile Edition of *Walden*: "Concord was an inland town, and therefore chosen for the residence of paroled prisoners in our two wars with England, while awaiting their exchange. Among those received in the war of 1812 were some officers and sailors of the *Guerrière*, captured by 'Old Ironsides' not far from the Massachusetts coast; and these may have been the incendiaries of poor Zilpha's cottage."

18 Brister (sometimes Bristol) Freeman, a Concord resident and freed slave, died on 31 January 1822. In his earliest mentions of Freeman in his

lived Brister Freeman,[18] "a handy Negro," slave of Squire Cummings[19] once,—there where grow still the apple-trees which Brister planted and tended; large old trees now, but their fruit still wild and ciderish to my taste. Not long since I read his epitaph[20] in the old Lincoln burying-ground,[21] a little on one side, near the unmarked graves of some British grenadiers who fell in the retreat from Concord,[22]—where he is styled "Sippio Brister,"—Scipio Africanus[23] he had some title to be called,—"a man of color," as if he were discolored. It also told me, with staring emphasis, when he died; which was but an indirect way of informing me that he ever lived. With him dwelt Fenda, his hospitable wife, who told fortunes, yet pleasantly,—large, round, and black, blacker than any of the children of night,[24] such a dusky orb as never rose on Concord before or since.

Farther down the hill, on the left, on the old road in the woods, are marks of some homestead of the Stratton family;[25] whose orchard once covered all the slope of Brister's Hill, but was long since killed out by pitch-pines, excepting a few stumps, whose old roots furnish still the wild stocks of many a thrifty village tree.[26]

Nearer yet to town, you come to Breed's location,[27] on the other side of the way, just on the edge of the wood; ground famous for the pranks of a demon[28] not distinctly named in old mythology, who has acted a prominent and astounding part in our New England life,[29] and deserves, as much as any mythological character, to have his biography written one day; who first comes in the guise of a friend or hired man, and then robs and murders the whole family,—New-England Rum. But history must not yet tell the tragedies enacted here; let time intervene in some measure to assuage and lend an azure tint to them. Here the most indistinct and dubious tradition says that once a tavern[30] stood; the well the same, which tempered the traveller's beverage and refreshed his steed. Here then

journals Thoreau spelled his name as Bristow. Edward Jarvis wrote in *Traditions and Reminiscences of Concord, Massachusetts*: "Brister Freeman was a passionate negro, profane and suspicious. He was said to have once stolen a haddock and was therefore tormented and hooted by boys. Then he would swear and storm. This gathered boys and men about him who insulted and violated him to greater passion." According to Sanborn's Bibliophile Edition of *Walden*:

Brister was probably born about that time [1749], and long survived his master, he was an active and thrifty Negro, but the victim of those rude jokes that men often play on his race. The town butcher, Peter Wheeler, having a ferocious bull to slaughter, was rather afraid to bring him to the bull-ring. Seeing Brister passing his place on his way from Walden, Wheeler asked him to go into the slaughter-house and bring an axe,—with which he should have a job to do. He entered, unsuspecting, and the bull came at him,—then, finding the axe, he bravely defended himself and finally slew the bull. But when he came out, full of horror and indignation, he fled to the woods without waiting to be paid. His wife, Fenda (and perhaps himself as well), was a Guinea Negro.

19 John Cuming or Cummings (1728–1788). In his original journal passage Thoreau placed a question mark after the name, indicating that he was unsure about either the squire's surname or whether Freeman had been a slave of Cummings [J 1:429].

20 Thoreau here confused Brister Freeman of Concord with Brister Hoar (1756?–1820) of Lincoln, a slave of the John Hoar family. He changed his name to Scipio (sometimes Sippio or Sippeo) Brister around 1791 after receiving his freedom. Thoreau commented in his journal after seeing Brister's epitaph—"In memory of Sippio Brister a man of Colour who died Nov. 1. 1820. Æt. 64"—that it "is not telling us that he lived" [J 2:20].

21 The old Precinct Burial Ground is a one-acre section of what is now the Lincoln Cemetery on Lexington Road.

22 Thoreau wrote in his journal of 31 May 1850: "I visited a retired, now almost unused, graveyard in Lincoln to-day, where five British soldiers lie buried who fell on the 19th April, '75" [J 2:19].

23 Scipio of Africa; there was also a historical Scipio Africanus whose name Thoreau had in mind: Scipio Africanus Publius Cornelius (237–183 B.C.E.), also called Scipio the Elder, Roman general who led the invasion of Carthage, defeating Hannibal, after which he was given the honorary name Africanus.

24 Possible allusion to the Children of Night from Hesiod's *Theogony*: "And there the children of dark Night have their dwellings."

25 The homestead of the Stratton family was located at the current intersection of Walden Street and Brister's Hill Road. It was destroyed in 1770.

26 At the end of the paragraph, Thoreau added in his copy of *Walden*: "Surveying for Cyrus Jarvis Dec. 23 '56—he shows me a deed of this lot containing 6 A. 52 rods all on the W. of the Wayland Road—& 'consisting of plowland, orcharding & woodland'—sold by Joseph Stratton to Samuel Swan of Concord In holder Aug. 11th 1777."

27 John Breed (d. 1824), a barber, whose sign according to Thoreau's journal read: "Tailoring and barbering done with speed / By John C Newell & John C Breed" [J 2:20]. John Groves Hales (1785–1832), in "A Plan of the Town of Concord, Mass.," placed Breed's house site on the north side of the Walden Road, west of what is now the Hapgood Wright Town Forest. Edward Jarvis wrote:

There were a few drunkards in town, lost to all sense of self-respect, who might be seen, at any time, intoxicated, staggering with difficulty in the road, or even lying powerless on the ground. Chief among them was Breed, the barber, with whom rum was the all-absorbing want and motive of action. He would do anything, try any art, to get it. . . . If he could get a chance to shave or cut hair and thus earn six cents, he would expend one cent for a cracker and five for rum. It was a frequent sight to see him lying dead drunk in the highway, and if in the carriage path and in danger of injury, people would haul him to the grassy side, as they would a log or any other obstacle to travel, and then leave him to recover consciousness and power of motion sufficient to carry him home. He was found dead in the road, Sept. 1824, died of drunkenness.

28 Allusion to the term "demon rum" or "demon alcohol" used by moral reformers, in particular those in the temperance movement.

29 Rum played such a part in the lives of not only those who drank it but also those who produced it. By the early 19th century there were forty rum-producing distilleries in Boston alone, with others in Hartford and Newport. In the 17th and 18th centuries, rum was used to pay for slaves on the Guinea Coast, who were then taken to the West Indies and traded for molasses; the molasses was taken to New England for, among other things, producing rum, which was sent to the Guinea Coast to purchase more slaves. Many New England families in the pro-abolition North made much of their wealth from the slavery triangle.

30 There is no extant documentation that confirms this "indistinct and dubious tradition."

31 Wednesday, 26 May 1841.

32 Thoreau was living at the Emersons' house from April 1841 to May 1843.

33 Sir William D'Avenant (1606–1668), English poet, and poet laureate in 1638, whose *Gondibert, an Heroick Poem* remained unfinished. It was published in 1651.

34 Of this proclivity toward sleepiness, Thoreau wrote in a letter to his mother from Staten Island on 7 July 1843: "The demon which is said to haunt the Jones family—hovering over their eyelids with wings steeped in juice of poppies—has commenced another campaign against me" [C 122].

men saluted one another, and heard and told the news, and went their ways again.

Breed's hut was standing only a dozen years ago, though it had long been unoccupied. It was about the size of mine. It was set on fire by mischievous boys, one Election night,[31] if I do not mistake. I lived on the edge of the village then,[32] and had just lost myself over Davenant's Gondibert,[33] that winter that I labored with a lethargy, —which, by the way, I never knew whether to regard as a family complaint,[34] having an uncle who goes to sleep shaving himself,[35] and is obliged to sprout potatoes[36] in a cellar Sundays, in order to keep awake and keep the Sabbath, or as the consequence of my attempt to read Chalmers' collection of English poetry[37] without skipping. It fairly overcame my Nervii.[38] I had just sunk my head on this when the bells rung fire,[39] and in hot haste the engines rolled that way, led by a straggling troop of men and boys, and I among the foremost, for I had leaped the brook.[40] We thought it was far south over the woods,—we who had run to fires before,[41]—barn, shop, or dwelling-house, or all together. "It's Baker's barn," cried one.[42] "It is the Codman Place," affirmed another.[43] And then fresh sparks went up above the wood, as if the roof fell in, and we all shouted "Concord to the rescue!" Wagons shot past with furious speed and crushing loads, bearing, perchance, among the rest, the agent of the Insurance Company,[44] who was bound to go however far; and ever and anon the engine bell tinkled behind, more slow and sure, and rearmost of all, as it was afterward whispered, came they who set the fire and gave the alarm. Thus we kept on like true idealists, rejecting the evidence of our senses, until at a turn in the road we heard the crackling and actually felt the heat of the fire from over the wall, and realized, alas! that we were there. The very nearness of the fire but cooled our ardor. At first we thought to throw a frog-pond on to it; but concluded

The Joneses were Thoreau's mother's maternal grandparents.

35 Charles Dunbar (1780–1856), Thoreau's maternal uncle, who discovered a deposit of plumbago in Bristol, New Hampshire, in 1821 and later went into the pencil business with his brother-in-law, John Thoreau. In his journal of 3 April 1856, shortly after his uncle's death, Thoreau wrote:

> People are talking about my Uncle Charles. Minott tells how he heard Tilly Brown once asking him to show him a peculiar (inside?) lock in wrestling. "Now, don't hurt me, don't throw me hard." He struck his antagonist inside his knees with his feet, and so deprived him of his legs. Hosmer remembers his tricks in the barroom, shuffling cards, etc. He could do anything with cards, yet he did not gamble. He would toss up his hat, twirling it over and over, and catch it on his head invariably. . . .
>
> He had a strong head and never got drunk; would drink gin sometimes, but not to excess. Did not use tobacco, except snuff out of another's box sometimes. Was very neat in his person. Was not profane, though vulgar. . . .
>
> Uncle Charles used to say that he had n't a single tooth in his head. The fact was they were all double, and I have heard that he lost about all of them by the time he was twenty-one. Ever since I knew him he could swallow his nose.
> [J 8:245–46]

36 Remove the sprouts from potatoes.

37 Alexander Chalmers published his 21-volume *The Works of the English Poets from Chaucer to Cowper* in 1810.

38 Pun on the Nervii, an ancient Celto-Germanic tribe subdued by Caesar in 57 B.C.E. during the Gallic wars, and on nerves, with an allusion to Shakespeare's *Julius Caesar* 3.2.167: "That day he overcame the Nervii."

39 The fire bells were not rung until midnight, according to the *Concord Republican* of 28 May 1841.

40 The Mill Brook, which ran between the Emerson and Breed properties.

41 Despite the destructive power of a fire, and the civic-minded rush to help put it out, Thoreau was aware of its entertainment value. On 5 June 1850 he wrote in his journal: "Men go to a fire for entertainment. When I see how eagerly men will run to a fire, whether in warm or in cold weather, by day or by night, dragging an engine at their heels, I am astonished to perceive how good a purpose the love of excitement is made to serve. What other force, pray, what offered pay, what disinterested neighborliness could ever effect so much?" [J 2:30].

42 Both Jacob and James Baker lived south of Walden.

43 The Codman Farm, also known as the Grange, home of Lincoln's wealthiest family. It was built in the mid-1730s as the estate of the town's principal founder, Chambers Russell (1713–1766), and was enlarged in the 1790s by John Codman (1755–1803) from a Georgian mansion to a Federal-style country seat.

44 The Middlesex Mutual Fire Insurance Company, which was established in Concord in March 1826.

45 Standard equipment for amplifying commands during firefighting.

46 The Bascom & Cole English and West Indian Shop in Concord had a fire on the night of 25 April 1828. The *Yeoman's Gazette* for 3 May 1828 carried a "card" from the firm presenting "their grateful acknowledgements to the members of the Fire Society, to the Engine men, and to the other Citizens of this town."

47 Hand-drawn fire engines used in many small 19th-century American towns.

48 Allusion to the "day of the Lord" in 2 Peter 3:10: "But the day of the Lord will come as a thief in the night, in the which the heavens shall pass away with a great noise, and the elements shall melt with fervent heat, the earth also and the works that are therein shall be burned up."

49 Allusion to the deluge of Noah from Genesis 6–7.

50 Quoted from D'Avenant's preface to *Gondibert*: "*Wit* is not only the luck and labour, but also the dexterity of thought. . . . It is the Souls *Powder*, . . . (but most of mankind are strangers to *Wit*, as *Indians* are to *Powder*)." *Gondibert* was considered extremely dull, hence Thoreau's linking it with sleep. Jonathan Swift described it in *The Battle of the Books* as "clad in heavy Armor, and mounted on a staid sober Gelding, not so famed for his Speed as his Docility in kneeling, whenever his Rider would mount or alight."

51 Sanborn noted in his Bibliophile Edition that John Breed "had been dead for years when this fire occurred. . . . It was his son, also a toper, whom Thoreau found at the ruins the next day." In his copy of *Walden*, Ellery Channing called this Breed "a semi-idiot."

52 Lever used to raise water.

to let it burn, it was so far gone and so worthless. So we stood round our engine, jostled one another, expressed our sentiments through speaking trumpets,[45] or in lower tone referred to the great conflagrations which the world has witnessed, including Bascom's shop,[46] and, between ourselves, we thought that, were we there in season with our "tub,"[47] and a full frog-pond by, we could turn that threatened last and universal one[48] into another flood.[49] We finally retreated without doing any mischief,—returned to sleep and Gondibert. But as for Gondibert, I would except that passage in the preface about wit being the soul's powder,—"but most of mankind are strangers to wit, as Indians are to powder."[50]

It chanced that I walked that way across the fields the following night, about the same hour, and hearing a low moaning at this spot, I drew near in the dark, and discovered the only survivor of the family that I know, the heir of both its virtues and its vices,[51] who alone was interested in this burning, lying on his stomach and looking over the cellar wall at the still smouldering cinders beneath, muttering to himself, as is his wont. He had been working far off in the river meadows all day, and had improved the first moments that he could call his own to visit the home of his fathers and his youth. He gazed into the cellar from all sides and points of view by turns, always lying down to it, as if there was some treasure, which he remembered, concealed between the stones, where there was absolutely nothing but a heap of bricks and ashes. The house being gone, he looked at what there was left. He was soothed by the sympathy which my mere presence implied, and showed me, as well as the darkness permitted, where the well was covered up; which, thank Heaven, could never be burned; and he groped long about the wall to find the well-sweep[52] which his father had cut and mounted, feeling for the iron hook or staple by which a burden had been fastened to the heavy end,—all that he could now cling to,—to convince me that it was no common "rider."[53] I felt it, and still remark it almost daily in my walks, for by it hangs the history of a family.

Once more, on the left, where are seen the well and lilac bushes by the wall, in the now open field, lived Nutting and Le Grosse.[54] But to return toward Lincoln.

Farther in the woods than any of these, where the road approaches nearest to the pond, Wyman the potter[55] squatted, and furnished his townsmen with earthen ware, and left descendants to succeed him. Neither were they rich in worldly goods, holding the land by sufferance while they lived; and there often the sheriff came in vain to collect the taxes, and "attached a chip,"[56] for form's sake, as I have read in his accounts, there being nothing else that he could lay his hands on. One day in midsummer, when I was hoeing, a man who was carrying a load of pottery to market stopped his horse against my field and inquired concerning Wyman the younger.[57] He had long ago bought a potter's wheel of him, and wished to know what had become of him. I had read of the potter's clay and wheel in Scripture,[58] but it had never occurred to me that the pots we use were not such as had come down unbroken from those days, or grown on trees like gourds somewhere, and I was pleased to hear that so fictile an art was ever practised in my neighborhood.

The last inhabitant of these woods before me was an Irishman, Hugh Quoil,[59] (if I have spelt his name with coil enough,) who occupied Wyman's tenement,—Col. Quoil, he was called. Rumor said that he had been a soldier at Waterloo.[60] If he had lived I should have made him fight his battles over again. His trade here was that of a ditcher.[61] Napoleon went to St. Helena; Quoil came to Walden Woods. All I know of him is tragic. He was a man of manners, like one who had seen the world, and was capable of more civil speech than you could well attend to. He wore a great coat in mid-summer, being affected

53 Something mounted or attached, as the top rail of a stake-and-rider fence.

54 Stephen Nutting (b. 1768), who purchased a house, barn, and 113 acres of land on 1 April 1792; and Francis Le Grosse (ca. 1764–1809), who rented a small plot of land, including a house and barn, from a Peter Wheeler.

55 John Wyman, the potter mentioned in "The Ponds."

56 Legal gesture giving proof of an official effort to collect an uncollectable debt by attaching or confiscating a worthless item.

57 Thomas Wyman (1774?–1843), John's son, from whose estate Emerson purchased the Walden parcel on which Thoreau built his house. Emerson wrote of him: "Tom Wyman will be the saint & pattern of the time." In his autobiography, George Hoar (1826–1904) wrote:

> When I was a small boy a party of us went down to Walden woods. . . . There was an old fellow named Tommy Wyman, who lived in a hut near the pond, who did not like the idea of having the huckleberry-fields near him invaded by the boys. He told us it was not safe for us to go there. He said there was an Indian doctor in the woods who caught small boys and cut out their livers to make medicine. We were terribly frightened, and all went home in a hurry.
>
> When we got near town, we met old John Thoreau, with his son Henry, and I remember his amusement when I told him the story. He said, "If I meet him, I will run this key down his throat," producing a key from his pocket.

58 Allusion to Jeremiah 18:3–6: "Then I went down to the potter's house, and, behold, he wrought a work on the wheels. And the vessel that he made of clay was marred in the hand of the potter: so he made it again another vessel, as seemed good to the potter to make it. Then the word of the LORD came to me, saying, O house of Israel, cannot I do with you as this potter? saith the LORD. Behold, as the clay in the potter's hand, so are ye in mine hand, O house of Israel."

59 Hugh Coyle (1784?–1845). A longer character sketch, from which this paragraph was condensed, appeared in Thoreau's Walden-period journal, part of which is as follows:

I had one neighbor within half a mile for a short time when I first went to the woods, Hugh Quoil, an Irishman who had been a soldier at Waterloo, Colonel Quoil, as he was called, — I believe that he had killed a colonel and ridden off his horse, — who lived from hand — sometimes to mouth, — though it was commonly a glass of rum that the hand carried. He and his wife awaited their fate together in an old ruin in Walden woods. What life he got — or what means of death — he got by ditching. . . .

He was thirstier than I, and drank more, probably, but not out of the pond. That was never lower for him. Perhaps I ate more than he. The last time I met him, the only time I spoke with him, was at the foot of the hill on the highway as I was crossing to the spring one summer afternoon, the pond water being too warm for me. I was crossing the road with a pail in my hand, when Quoil came down the hill, wearing his snuff-colored coat, as if it were winter, and shaking with delirium tremens. I hailed him and told him that my errand was to get water at a spring close by, only at the foot of the hill over the fence. He answered, with stuttering and parched lips, bloodshot eye, and staggering gesture, he'd like to see it. "Follow me there, then." But I had got my pail full and back before he scaled the fence. And he, drawing his coat about him, to warm him, or to cool him, answered in delirium-tremens, hydrophobia dialect, which is not easy to be written here, he'd heard of it, but had never seen it; and so shivered his way along to town, — to liquor and to oblivion.

On Sundays, brother Irishmen and others,

---

with the trembling delirium, and his face was the color of carmine. He died in the road at the foot of Brister's Hill shortly after I came to the woods, so that I have not remembered him as a neighbor.[62] Before his house was pulled down, when his comrades avoided it as "an unlucky castle,"[63] I visited it. There lay his old clothes curled[64] up by use, as if they were himself, upon his raised plank bed. His pipe lay broken on the hearth, instead of a bowl broken at the fountain.[65] The last could never have been the symbol of his death, for he confessed to me that, though he had heard of Brister's Spring, he had never seen it; and soiled cards, kings of diamonds spades and hearts, were scattered over the floor. One black chicken which the administrator could not catch, black as night and as silent, not even croaking, awaiting Reynard,[66] still went to roost in the next apartment. In the rear there was the dim outline of a garden, which had been planted but had never received its first hoeing, owing to those terrible shaking fits, though it was now harvest time. It was overrun with Roman wormwood and beggar-ticks,[67] which last stuck to my clothes for all fruit. The skin of a woodchuck was freshly stretched upon the back of the house, a trophy of his last Waterloo; but no warm cap or mittens would he want more.

Now only a dent in the earth marks the site of these dwellings,[68] with buried cellar stones, and strawberries, raspberries, thimble-berries, hazel-bushes, and sumachs growing in the sunny sward there; some pitch-pine or gnarled oak occupies what was the chimney nook, and a sweet-scented black-birch, perhaps, waves where the door-stone was. Sometimes the well dent is visible, where once a spring oozed; now dry and tearless grass; or it was covered deep, — not to be discovered till some late day, — with a flat stone under the sod, when the last of the race departed. What a sorrowful act must that be, — the covering up of wells! coincident with the opening of wells of tears. These cellar dents, like deserted fox burrows, old holes, are all that is left where once were the stir and bustle of human life, and "fate, free-will, foreknowledge absolute,"[69] in some form and dialect or other were by turns discussed. But all I can learn of their conclusions amounts to just this, that "Cato and Brister pulled wool;"[70] which is about as edifying as the history of more famous schools of philosophy.

Still grows the vivacious lilac a generation after the door and lintel and the sill are gone, unfolding its sweet-scented flowers each spring, to be plucked by the musing traveller; planted and tended once by children's hands, in front-yard plots,—now standing by wall-sides in retired pastures, and giving place to new-rising forests;—the last of that stirp,[71] sole survivor of that family. Little did the dusky children think that the puny slip with its two eyes only, which they stuck in the ground in the shadow of the house and daily watered, would root itself so, and outlive them and house itself in the rear that shaded it, and grown man's garden and orchard, and tell their story faintly to the lone wanderer a half century after they had grown up and died,—blossoming as fair, and smelling as sweet, as in that first spring. I mark its still tender, civil, cheerful, lilac colors.

But this small village, germ of something more, why did it fail while Concord keeps its ground? Were there no natural advantages,—no water privileges, forsooth? Ay, the deep Walden Pond and cool Brister's Spring,—privilege to drink long and healthy draughts at these, all unimproved by these men but to dilute their glass. They were universally a thirsty race. Might not the basket, stable-broom, mat-making, corn-parching, linen-spinning, and pottery business have thrived here, making the wilderness to blossom like the rose,[72] and a numerous posterity have inherited the land of their fathers? The sterile soil would at least have been proof against a low-land degen-

who had gone far astray from steady habits and the village, crossed my bean-field with empty jugs towards Quoil's. But what for? Did they sell rum there? I asked. "Respectable people they," "Know no harm of them," "Never heard that they drank too much," was the answer of all wayfarers. They went by sober, stealthy, silent, skulking (no harm to get elm bark Sundays); returned loquacious, sociable, having long intended to call on you. [J 1:414–16]

60 Belgian village, site of Napoléon's defeat by the British in 1815. After his defeat, Napoléon was exiled to the island of St. Helena in the South Atlantic.

61 One who digs or repairs ditches.

62 Coyle's obituary appeared in the *Concord Freeman* of 3 October 1845: "Mr. Hugh Coyle, a man of intemperate habits, residing in the vicinity of Walden pond, in this town, was found dead on the road near his house on Wednesday afternoon last. As he was seen on his way home a short time before he was found dead, with his features very much distorted and in a feeble state, he is supposed to have died in a fit of *delirium tremens*. He was an old campaigner and fought at the Battle of Waterloo."

63 A revision to this passage in Thoreau's journal indicates that it was the local Irishmen who called it an "unlucky castle" and avoided it.

64 Pun on the name Quoil (coil).

65 Allusion to Ecclesiastes 12:6–7: "Or ever the silver cord be loosed, or the golden bowl be broken, or the pitcher be broken at the fountain, or the wheel be broken at the cistern. Then shall the dust return to the earth as it was: and the spirit shall return unto God who gave it."

66 Traditional literary name for a fox, from the medieval French beast epic *Le Roman de Renart*.

67 Weed, the seeds of which, as a method of dissemination, catch on clothes or fur.

68 In a journal entry of 11 January 1857, Thoreau compared his explorations of cellar holes with Austen Henry Layard's (1817–1894) archaeological

digs in Mesopotamia: "These are our Ninevehs and Babylons. I approach such a cellar-hole as Layard the scene of his labors, and I do not fail to find there relics as interesting to me as his winged bulls" [J 9:214].

69 Quoted from Milton's *Paradise Lost* 2.557–61:

> Others apart sat on a hill retir'd,
> In thoughts more elevate, and reason'd high
> Of providence, foreknowledge, will, and fate,
> Fix'd fate, free-will, foreknowledge absolute;
> And found no end, in wand'ring mazes lost.

Thoreau wrote in a letter to Lidian Emerson (1802–1892) on 16 October 1843: "I suppose that the great questions of Fate, Freewill, Foreknowledge absolute, which used to be discussed in Concord are still unsettled" [C 143].

70 Pulled wool from the pelts of sheep, with a possible reference to the phrase "pull the wool over one's eyes" (deceive someone).

71 A line of descent from a common ancestor.

72 Allusion to Isaiah 35:1: "The wilderness and the solitary place shall be glad for them; and the desert shall rejoice, and blossom as the rose."

73 Thoreau read and had made several references to Layard's *Nineveh and Its Remains* (New York, 1849) and *Discoveries Among the Ruins of Nineveh and Babylon* (New York, 1853) in his journals, including June 1850 and December 1853 while he was writing *Walden*. It was in his journal of 9 December 1853 that he wrote in response to Layard: "Above all, deliver me from a city built on the site of a more ancient city, the materials of the one being the ruins of the other. There the dwellings of the living are in the cemeteries of the dead, and the soil is blanched and accursed" [J 6:15].

74 Although it is probably true that Thoreau had fewer visitors at Walden during the winter, George Hoar wrote that he "used to go down to see him in the winter days in my vacations in his hut near Walden. He was capital company."

75 Such an account is found in the *History of the Town of Sutton, Massachusetts, from 1704 to 1876*

eracy. Alas! how little does the memory of these human inhabitants enhance the beauty of the landscape! Again, perhaps, Nature will try, with me for a first settler, and my house raised last spring to be the oldest in the hamlet.

I am not aware that any man has ever built on the spot which I occupy. Deliver me from a city built on the site of a more ancient city,[73] whose materials are ruins, whose gardens cemeteries. The soil is blanched and accursed there, and before that becomes necessary the earth itself will be destroyed. With such reminiscences I re-peopled the woods and lulled myself asleep.

At this season I seldom had a visitor.[74] When the snow lay deepest no wanderer ventured near my house for a week or fortnight at a time, but there I lived as snug as a meadow mouse, or as cattle and poultry which are said to have survived for a long time buried in drifts, even without food; or like that early settler's family in the town of Sutton, in this State, whose cottage was completely covered by the great snow of 1717 when he was absent, and an Indian found it only by the hole which the chimney's breath made in the drift, and so relieved the family.[75] But no friendly Indian concerned himself about me; nor needed he, for the master of the house was at home. The Great Snow! How cheerful it is to hear of! When the farmers could not get to the woods and swamps with their teams, and were obliged to cut down the shade trees before their houses, and when the crust was harder cut off the trees in the swamps ten feet from the ground, as it appeared the next spring.

In the deepest snows, the path which I used from the highway to my house, about half a mile long, might have been represented by a meandering dotted line, with wide intervals between the dots. For a week of even weather I took exactly the same number of steps, and of the same length, coming and going, stepping deliberately and with

the precision of a pair of dividers[76] in my own deep tracks,
—to such routine the winter reduces us,—yet often they
were filled with heaven's own blue.[77] But no weather in-
terfered fatally with my walks, or rather my going abroad,
for I frequently tramped eight or ten miles through the
deepest snow to keep an appointment with a beech-tree,
or a yellow-birch, or an old acquaintance among the pines;
when the ice and snow causing their limbs to droop,
and so sharpening their tops, had changed the pines into
fir-trees; wading to the tops of the highest hills when
the snow was nearly two feet deep on a level, and shaking down another snow-storm on my head at every step;
or sometimes creeping and floundering thither on my
hands and knees, when the hunters had gone into winter quarters. One afternoon I amused myself by watching a barred owl (*Strix nebulosa*)[78] sitting on one of the
lower dead limbs of a white-pine, close to the trunk, in
broad daylight, I standing within a rod of him. He could
hear me when I moved and cronched[79] the snow with my
feet, but could not plainly see me. When I made most
noise he would stretch out his neck, and erect his neck
feathers, and open his eyes wide; but their lids soon fell
again, and he began to nod. I too felt a slumberous influence after watching him half an hour, as he sat thus
with his eyes half open, like a cat, winged brother of the
cat.[80] There was only a narrow slit left between their lids,
by which he preserved a peninsular relation to me; thus,
with half-shut eyes, looking out from the land of dreams,
and endeavoring to realize me, vague object or mote that
interrupted his visions. At length, on some louder noise
or my nearer approach, he would grow uneasy and slug-
gishly turn about on his perch, as if impatient at having
his dreams disturbed; and when he launched himself off
and flapped through the pines, spreading his wings to unexpected breadth, I could not hear the slightest sound
from them.[81] Thus, guided amid the pine boughs rather

(p. 18), of an Elisha Johnson who left his cabin to get supplies on the morning of the great snow: "He was seen on his way by a friendly Indian, who, when the storm had subsided, started on snow-shoes for the little settlement, and found the cabin of Mr. Johnson by the hole which the smoke from the fire-place had made through the snow. His family would doubtless have perished had it not been for the kind forethought of this friendly Indian. Mrs. Johnson said 'no human voice ever sounded half so sweet as did that.'"

76 Used for measuring distance on a map.
77 Ellery Channing noted in his copy of *Walden* that Thoreau "often made holes in the snow to see the blue—bluing he called it—in the air."
78 Now *Strix varia*.
79 Thoreau's variant spelling of craunch, mean-ing crunch.
80 Although Thoreau here made an associa-tion between the barred owl and the cat, it was the great horned owl (*Bubo virginianus*) which he called the cat owl.
81 Owl wings are virtually silent; fringes on the leading edge of the wings muffle the sound of their flapping.

82 Because the owl is nocturnal, its day begins at dusk.

83 Possible connection with the definition Thoreau wrote in a late December 1860 journal entry: "As in old times they who dwelt on the heath remote from towns were backward to adopt the doctrines which prevailed there, and were therefore called heathen in a bad sense, so we dwellers in the huckleberry pastures, which are our heath lands" [J 14:299]. This came from his reading in Richard Chenevix Trench's (1807–1866) *The Study of Words,* in which the term is traced back to the introduction of Christianity in Germany, where "the wild dwellers on the 'heaths' longest resisted the truth" of the Church.

84 Allusion to Matthew 5:39: "But I say unto you, That ye resist not evil: but whosoever shall smite thee on the right cheek, turn to him the other also."

85 Probably Alek Therien.

86 In his Bibliophile Edition, Sanborn identified the farmer as Edmund Hosmer. Phrenology, a popular pseudo-science in Thoreau's day, held that the degree of a person's mental development was supposedly revealed by the shape of the skull, which reflected the underlying parts of the brain. A long head was an indication of shrewdness and talent. Phrenology was popularized in America by George Combe's (1788–1858) *Constitution of Man* (1829), which Emerson called "the best Sermon I have read for some time." Emerson was later more circumspect in his praise: "The attempt was coarse and odious to scientific men, but had a certain truth in it; it felt connection where professors denied it, and was a leading to a truth which had not yet been announced."

87 Colloquial: cozy chat.

88 In "The American Scholar" Emerson made a distinction between "man on the farm" and the farmer: "The planter, who is Man sent out into the field to gather food, is seldom cheered by any idea of the true dignity of his ministry. He sees his bushel and his cart, and nothing beyond, and sinks into the farmer, instead of Man on the farm."

by a delicate sense of their neighborhood than by sight, feeling his twilight way as it were with his sensitive pinions, he found a new perch, where he might in peace await the dawning of his day.[82]

As I walked over the long causeway made for the railroad through the meadows, I encountered many a blustering and nipping wind, for nowhere has it freer play; and when the frost had smitten me on one cheek, heathen as I was,[83] I turned to it the other also.[84] Nor was it much better by the carriage road from Brister's Hill. For I came to town still, like a friendly Indian, when the contents of the broad open fields were all piled up between the walls of the Walden road, and half an hour sufficed to obliterate the tracks of the last traveller. And when I returned new drifts would have formed, through which I floundered, where the busy north-west wind had been depositing the powdery snow round a sharp angle in the road, and not a rabbit's track, nor even the fine print, the small type, of a deer mouse was to be seen. Yet I rarely failed to find, even in mid-winter, some warm and springy swamp where the grass and the skunk-cabbage still put forth with perennial verdure, and some hardier bird occasionally awaited the return of spring.

Sometimes, notwithstanding the snow, when I returned from my walk at evening I crossed the deep tracks of a woodchopper leading from my door, and found his pile of whittlings on the hearth, and my house filled with the odor of his pipe.[85] Or on a Sunday afternoon, if I chanced to be at home, I heard the cronching of the snow made by the step of a long-headed farmer,[86] who from far through the woods sought my house, to have a social "crack;"[87] one of the few of his vocation who are "men on their farms;"[88] who donned a frock instead of a professor's gown, and is as ready to extract the moral out of church or state as to haul a load of manure from his barnyard. We talked of rude and simple times, when men sat about large fires in cold bracing weather, with clear heads; and when other dessert failed, we tried our teeth on many a nut[89] which wise squirrels have long since abandoned, for those which have the thickest shells are commonly empty.

The one who came from farthest to my lodge, through deepest snows and most dismal tempests, was a poet.[90] A farmer, a hunter, a soldier, a reporter, even a philosopher, may be daunted; but nothing can deter a poet, for he is actuated by pure love. Who can predict his comings and goings? His business calls him out at all hours, even when doctors sleep. We made that small house ring with boisterous mirth and resound with the murmur of much sober talk, making amends then to Walden vale for the long silences. Broadway was still and deserted in comparison. At suitable intervals there were regular salutes of laughter, which might have been referred indifferently to the last uttered or the forth-coming jest. We made many a "bran new"[91] theory of life over a thin dish of gruel, which combined the advantages of conviviality with the clear-headedness which philosophy requires.

I should not forget that during my last winter at the pond there was another welcome visitor, who at one time came through the village, through snow and rain and darkness, till he saw my lamp through the trees, and shared with me some long winter evenings.[92] One of the last of the philosophers,—Connecticut gave him to the world,—he peddled first her wares,[93] afterwards, as he declares, his brains. These he peddles still, prompting God and disgracing man, bearing for fruit his brain only, like the nut its kernel. I think that he must be the man of the most faith of any alive. His words and attitude always suppose a better state of things than other men are acquainted with, and he will be the last man to be disappointed as the ages revolve. He has no venture in the present. But though comparatively disregarded now,

89 A conundrum, from the early 18th century, as in a hard, or tough, nut to crack.

90 Ellery Channing. Sanborn's Bibliophile Edition reported that Channing was "accustomed to walk in all weathers, he made nothing of the six-mile detour [from Punkatasset Hill, where he was then living] which brought him to the cabin in the Emerson pinewood."

91 More properly "brand new," although commonly spelled "bran new" in the 19th century, from the 16th-century usage meaning fresh or new from the fire.

92 Bronson Alcott, of whom Thoreau wrote in his journal on 8 May 1853:

> I have devoted most of my day to Mr. Alcott. He is broad and genial, but indefinite; some would say feeble; forever feeling about vainly in his speech and touching nothing. But this is a very negative account of him, for he thus suggests far more than the sharp and definite practical mind. The feelers of his thought diverge,—such is the breadth of their grasp,—not converge; and in his society almost alone I can express at my leisure, with more or less success, my vaguest but most cherished fancy or thought. There are never any obstacles in the way of our meeting. He has no creed. He is not pledged to any institution. The sanest man I ever knew; the fewest crotchets, after all, has he. [J 5:130]

93 Alcott, born in Wolcott, Connecticut, on 29 November 1799, was an unsuccessful Yankee peddler in the South in 1817–23.

94 Quoted from Thomas Storer's (1571–1604) "The Life and Death of Thomas Wolsey, Cardinal" (London, 1599); according to a note by Ellery Channing, Thoreau took the quote from Thomas Park's (1759–1834) *Heliconia: Comprising a Selection of English Poetry of the Elizabethan Age Written or Published Between 1575 and 1604* (London, 1815).

95 Nickname of Robert Paterson (1715–1801), who wandered through Scotland cleaning and repairing gravestones of the Covenanters. The antiquary in Sir Walter Scott's novel *Old Mortality* (1816) is based on Paterson.

96 Allusion to Genesis 1.26: "And God said, Let us make man in our own image, after our own likeness."

97 "Entertainment for man and beast" was a common sign hung at inns.

98 Eccentric, highly individual opinion or preference.

99 Latin: befitting a freeborn or noble, thus frank and honest.

100 The wood from first-growth white pine has a yellowish color. George B. Emerson (1797–1881) wrote in *A Report on the Trees and Shrubs Growing Naturally in the Forests of Massachusetts* (1846): "The white pines receive different names, according to their mode of growth and the appearance of the wood. When growing densely in deep and damp old forests, with only a few branches near the top, the slowly-grown wood is perfectly clear and soft, destitute of resin, and almost without sap-wood, and has a yellowish color, like the flesh of a pumpkin. It is then called pumpkin pine." In "The Ponds" Thoreau called it "yellow-pine."

101 Flocks, or locks, of wool, not flocks of sheep.

102 Much of this description came from Thoreau's journal reflections on Bronson Alcott after a day spent together on 9 May 1853.

103 In "Conclusion" Thoreau wrote: "If you have built castles in the air, your work need not be lost; that is where they should be. Now put the foundations under them."

104 Echo of the title *Arabian Nights' Entertainments*, a collection of Indian, Persian, and Arabic

when his day comes, laws unsuspected by most will take effect, and masters of families and rulers will come to him for advice. —

"How blind that cannot see serenity!"[94]

A true friend of man; almost the only friend of human progress. An Old Mortality,[95] say rather an Immortality, with unwearied patience and faith making plain the image engraven in men's bodies,[96] the God of whom they are but defaced and leaning monuments. With his hospitable intellect he embraces children, beggars, insane, and scholars, and entertains the thought of all, adding to it commonly some breadth and elegance. I think that he should keep a caravansary on the world's highway, where philosophers of all nations might put up, and on his sign should be printed, "Entertainment for man, but not for his beast."[97] Enter ye that have leisure and a quiet mind, who earnestly seek the right road." He is perhaps the sanest man and has the fewest crotchets[98] of any I chance to know; the same yesterday and to-morrow. Of yore we had sauntered and talked, and effectually put the world behind us; for he was pledged to no institution in it, freeborn, *ingenuus*.[99] Whichever way we turned, it seemed that the heavens and the earth had met together, since he enhanced the beauty of the landscape. A blue-robed man, whose fittest roof is the overarching sky which reflects his serenity. I do not see how he can ever die; Nature cannot spare him.

Having each some shingles of thought well dried, we sat and whittled them, trying our knives, and admiring the clear yellowish grain of the pumpkin pine.[100] We waded so gently and reverently, or we pulled together so smoothly, that the fishes of thought were not scared from the stream, nor feared any angler on the bank, but came and went grandly, like the clouds which float through the western sky, and the mother-o'-pearl flocks[101] which sometimes form and dissolve there.[102] There we worked, revising mythology, rounding a fable here and there, and building castles in the air for which earth offered no worthy foundation.[103] Great Looker! Great Expecter! to converse with whom was a New England Night's Entertainment.[104] Ah! such discourse we had, hermit and philosopher, and the old settler I have spoken of,[105] — we three, — it expanded and racked my little house; I should not dare to say how many pounds' weight there was above the atmospheric pressure on every circular inch; it opened its seams so that they had to be calked with much dulness thereafter to stop the consequent leak; — but I had enough of that kind of oakum[106] already picked.

There was one other[107] with whom I had "solid seasons,"[108] long to be remembered, at his house in the village, and who looked in upon me from time to time; but I had no more for society there.

There too, as every where, I sometimes expected the Visitor who never comes. The Vishnu Purana says, "The house-holder is to remain at eventide in his court-yard as long as it takes to milk a cow, or longer if he pleases, to await the arrival of a guest."[109] I often performed this duty of hospitality, waited long enough to milk a whole herd of cows, but did not see the man approaching from the town.[110]

tales, written in Arabic, and also known as *The Thousand and One Nights.*

105 In "Solitude" and "The Ponds."

106 Picking the hemp fiber, oakum, out of old rope, to use as caulking, was a dull and monotonous job often used to keep sailors busy. Thoreau's Harvard classmate Richard Henry Dana (1815–1882) explained in *Two Years Before the Mast* that sailors are kept "picking oakum—ad infinitum. This is the usual resource upon a rainy day, for then it will not do to work upon rigging; and when it is pouring down in floods, instead of letting the sailors stand about in sheltered places, and talk, and keep themselves comfortable, they are separated to different parts of the ship and kept at work picking oakum. I have seen oakum stuff placed about in different parts of the ship, so that the sailors might not be idle in the snatches between the frequent squalls upon crossing the equator."

107 Emerson.

108 Possible allusion to Emerson's letter of February 1843 to Thoreau in which he described the friendships he was developing in New York: "I see W. H. Channing and Mr. James at leisure & have had what the Quakers call 'a solid season' once or twice. With Tappan a very happy pair of hours & him I must see again."

109 Quoted from *The Vishnu Purána: A System of Hindu Mythology and Tradition,* translated from the original Sanscrit, and illustrated by notes derived chiefly from other Puránas, by H. H. Wilson (London, 1840), 305.

110 Allusion to the old English ballad "The Children in the Wood":

> These pretty babes, with hand in hand,
> Went wandering up and down,
> But never more could see the man
> Approaching from the town. [ll. 113–16]

Of animals that endure the winter, Thoreau wrote: "Insects, it is true, disappear for the most part, and those animals which depend upon them; but the nobler animals abide with man the severity of winter" [J 3:70].

1 Part of the Arctic Ocean, between Greenland and Canada.
2 Thoreau lectured at the Lincoln Lyceum on 19 January 1847 while living at Walden Pond, and twice more—on 6 March 1849 and 30 December 1851—while composing *Walden*. He is known to have delivered at least 75 lectures all told.
3 First of only two references (both in this chapter) to his house as a hut.
4 Tramped-down area, made by moose and deer in deep snow, where they can be comfortable and fed, as in "moose-yard" in the following sentence.

Winter Animals

When the ponds were firmly frozen, they afforded not only new and shorter routes to many points, but new views from their surfaces of the familiar landscape around them. When I crossed Flint's Pond, after it was covered with snow, though I had often paddled about and skated over it, it was so unexpectedly wide and so strange that I could think of nothing but Baffin's Bay.[1] The Lincoln hills rose up around me at the extremity of a snowy plain, in which I did not remember to have stood before; and the fishermen, at an indeterminable distance over the ice, moving slowly about with their wolfish dogs, passed for sealers or Esquimaux, or in misty weather loomed like fabulous creatures, and I did not know whether they were giants or pygmies. I took this course when I went to lecture in Lincoln in the evening,[2] travelling in no road and passing no house between my own hut[3] and the lecture room. In Goose Pond, which lay in my way, a colony of muskrats dwelt, and raised their cabins high above the ice, though none could be seen abroad when I crossed it. Walden, being like the rest usually bare of snow, or with only shallow and interrupted drifts on it, was my yard,[4] where I could walk freely when the snow was nearly two feet deep on a level elsewhere and the villagers were confined to their streets. There, far from the village street, and except at very long intervals, from the jingle of sleigh-bells, I slid and skated, as in a vast moose-yard well trodden, overhung by oak woods and solemn pines bent down with snow or bristling with icicles.

For sounds in winter nights, and often in winter days, I heard the forlorn but melodious note of a hooting owl indefinitely far; such a sound as the frozen earth would yield if struck with a suitable plectrum, the very *lingua vernacula*[5] of Walden Wood, and quite familiar to me at last, though I never saw the bird while it was making it. I seldom opened my door in a winter evening without hearing it; *Hoo hoo hoo, hoorer hoo,* sounded sonorously, and the first three syllables accented somewhat like *how der do;* or sometimes *hoo hoo* only. One night in the beginning of winter, before the pond froze over, about nine o'clock, I was startled by the loud honking of a goose, and, stepping to the door, heard the sound of their wings like a tempest in the woods as they flew low over my house. They passed over the pond toward Fair Haven, seemingly deterred from settling by my light, their commodore honking all the while with a regular beat. Suddenly an unmistakable cat-owl[6] from very near me, with the most harsh and tremendous voice I ever heard from any inhabitant of the woods, responded at regular intervals to the goose, as if determined to expose and disgrace this intruder from Hudson's Bay[7] by exhibiting a greater compass and volume of voice in a native, and *boo-hoo* him out of Concord horizon. What do you mean by alarming the citadel[8] at this time of night consecrated to me? Do you think I am ever caught napping at such an hour, and that I have not got lungs and a larynx as well as yourself? *Boo-hoo, boo-hoo, boo-hoo!* It was one of the most thrilling discords I ever heard. And yet, if you had a discriminating ear, there were in it the elements of a concord[9] such as these plains never saw nor heard.

I also heard the whooping of the ice[10] in the pond, my great bed-fellow in that part of Concord, as if it were

5 Latin: native language.

6 Great horned owl (*Bubo virginianus*), which Thoreau sometimes referred to as the cat owl.

7 Hudson Bay: inland sea in north-central Canada named for the explorer Henry Hudson (ca. 1565–1611), who discovered it in 1610.

8 Allusion to the sacred geese in Juno's temple that alarmed the citadel when the Gauls attacked Rome in 390 B.C.E. The story is told by several ancient Roman authors: Livy, Virgil, Lucretius, Ovid, and Martial.

9 Used as a common noun and as reference to the town of Concord.

10 Caused by expansion and contraction of the ice, described more fully in the "Spring" chapter.

restless in its bed and would fain turn over, were troubled with flatulency and bad dreams; or I was waked by the cracking of the ground by the frost, as if some one had driven a team against my door, and in the morning would find a crack in the earth a quarter of a mile long and a third of an inch wide.

Sometimes I heard the foxes as they ranged over the snow crust, in moonlight nights, in search of a partridge or other game, barking raggedly and demoniacally like forest dogs, as if laboring with some anxiety, or seeking expression, struggling for light and to be dogs outright and run freely in the streets; for if we take the ages into our account, may there not be a civilization going on among brutes as well as men? They seemed to me to be rudimental, burrowing men,[11] still standing on their defence, awaiting their transformation. Sometimes one came near to my window, attracted by my light, barked a vulpine curse at me, and then retreated.

Usually the red squirrel (*Sciurus Hudsonius*)[12] waked me in the dawn, coursing over the roof and up and down the sides of the house, as if sent out of the woods for this purpose. In the course of the winter I threw out half a bushel of ears of sweet-corn, which had not got ripe, on to the snow crust by my door, and was amused by watching the motions of the various animals which were baited by it. In the twilight and the night the rabbits came regularly and made a hearty meal. All day long the red squirrels came and went, and afforded me much entertainment by their manœuvres. One would approach at first warily through the shrub-oaks, running over the snow crust by fits and starts like a leaf blown by the wind, now a few paces this way, with wonderful speed and waste of energy, making inconceivable haste with his "trotters,"[13] as if it were for a wager, and now as many paces that way, but never getting on more than half a rod at a time; and then suddenly pausing with a ludicrous expression and a gra-

11 Thoreau made the same allusion in a December 1845 journal entry in which he described the fox as "but a faint man, before pigmies; an imperfect, burrowing man" [J 1:396].
12 Now *Tamiasciurus hudsonicus.*
13 Hind legs.

tuitous somerset, as if all the eyes in the universe were fixed on him,—for all the motions of a squirrel, even in the most solitary recesses of the forest, imply spectators as much as those of a dancing girl,—wasting more time in delay and circumspection than would have sufficed to walk the whole distance,—I never saw one walk,—and then suddenly, before you could say Jack Robinson,[14] he would be in the top of a young pitch-pine, winding up his clock[15] and chiding all imaginary spectators, soliloquizing and talking to all the universe at the same time,—for no reason that I could ever detect, or he himself was aware of, I suspect. At length he would reach the corn, and selecting a suitable ear, frisk about in the same uncertain trigonometrical way to the top-most stick of my wood-pile, before my window, where he looked me in the face, and there sit for hours, supplying himself with a new ear from time to time, nibbling at first voraciously and throwing the half-naked cobs about; till at length he grew more dainty still and played with his food, tasting only the inside of the kernel, and the ear, which was held balanced over the stick by one paw, slipped from his careless grasp and fell to the ground, when he would look over at it with a ludicrous expression of uncertainty, as if suspecting that it had life, with a mind not made up whether to get it again, or a new one, or be off; now thinking of corn, then listening to hear what was in the wind. So the little impudent fellow would waste many an ear in a forenoon; till at last, seizing some longer and plumper one, considerably bigger than himself, and skilfully balancing it, he would set out with it to the woods, like a tiger with a buffalo, by the same zig-zag course and frequent pauses, scratching along with it as if it were too heavy for him and falling all the while, making its fall a diagonal between a perpendicular and horizontal, being determined to put it through at any rate;—a singularly frivolous and whimsical fellow;—and so he would get off with it to where he

14 From a popular 18th-century song written by a London tobacconist named Hudson: "A warke it ys as easie to be done / As tys to saye *Jacke! robys on*." According to Francis Grose's *Dictionary of the Vulgar Tongue* (1811), however, Jack Robinson was a "very volatile gentleman of that appellation, who would call on his neighbours, and be gone before his name could be announced."

15 In *A Week on the Concord and Merrimack Rivers* Thoreau described the red squirrel's "peculiar alarum . . . like the winding up of some strong clock" [W 1:206].

16 Blue jay (*Cyanocitta cristata*).

17 "The scream of the jay is a true winter sound," Thoreau wrote on 2 February 1854 [J 6:91]. He made several references in his journals to the screams of the blue jay, but his most vitriolic came on 12 February 1854: "the unrelenting steel-cold scream of a jay, unmelted, that never flows into a song, a sort of wintry trumpet, screaming cold; hard, tense, frozen music, like the winter sky itself. . . . Like the creak of a cart-wheel. There is no cushion for sounds now. They tear our ears" [J 6:118].

18 Black-capped chickadee (*Parus atricapillus*), which, as indicated in the next sentence, belongs to the titmouse family.

19 In a post-Walden journal entry Thoreau described the sound as *"tche de de de"* [J 13:87].

20 In his journal of 10 March 1852 Thoreau referred to the "phœbe note of the chickadee" [J 3:345].

lived, perhaps carry it to the top of a pine tree forty or fifty rods distant, and I would afterwards find the cobs strewn about the woods in various directions.

At length the jays[16] arrive, whose discordant screams[17] were heard long before, as they were warily making their approach an eighth of a mile off, and in a stealthy and sneaking manner they flit from tree to tree, nearer and nearer, and pick up the kernels which the squirrels have dropped. Then, sitting on a pitch-pine bough, they attempt to swallow in their haste a kernel which is too big for their throats and chokes them; and after great labor they disgorge it, and spend an hour in the endeavor to crack it by repeated blows with their bills. They were manifestly thieves, and I had not much respect for them; but the squirrels, though at first shy, went to work as if they were taking what was their own.

Meanwhile also came the chicadees[18] in flocks, which, picking up the crumbs the squirrels had dropped, flew to the nearest twig, and, placing them under their claws, hammered away at them with their little bills, as if it were an insect in the bark, till they were sufficiently reduced for their slender throats. A little flock of these tit-mice came daily to pick a dinner out of my wood-pile, or the crumbs at my door, with faint flitting lisping notes, like the tinkling of icicles in the grass, or else with sprightly *day day day*,[19] or more rarely, in spring-like days, a wiry summery *phe-be*[20] from the wood-side. They were so familiar that at length one alighted on an armful of wood which I was carrying in, and pecked at the sticks without fear. I once had a sparrow alight upon my shoulder for a moment while I was hoeing in a village garden, and I felt that I was more distinguished by that circumstance than I should have been by any epaulet I could have worn. The squirrels also grew at last to be quite familiar, and occasionally stepped upon my shoe, when that was the nearest way.

When the ground was not yet quite covered, and again

near the end of winter, when the snow was melted on my south hill-side and about my wood-pile, the partridges came out of the woods morning and evening to feed there. Whichever side you walk in the woods the partridge bursts away on whirring wings, jarring the snow from the dry leaves and twigs on high, which comes sifting down in the sun-beams like golden dust; for this brave bird is not to be scared by winter. It is frequently covered up by drifts, and, it is said, "sometimes plunges from on wing into the soft snow, where it remains concealed for a day or two."[21] I used to start them in the open land also, where they had come out of the woods at sunset to "bud"[22] the wild apple-trees. They will come regularly every evening to particular trees, where the cunning sportsman lies in wait for them, and the distant orchards next the woods suffer thus not a little. I am glad that the partridge gets fed, at any rate. It is Nature's own bird which lives on buds and diet-drink.[23]

In dark winter mornings, or in short winter afternoons, I sometimes heard a pack of hounds threading all the woods with hounding cry and yelp, unable to resist the instinct of the chase, and the note of the hunting horn at intervals, proving that man was in the rear. The woods ring again, and yet no fox bursts forth on to the open level of the pond, nor following pack pursuing their Actæon.[24] And perhaps at evening I see the hunters returning with a single brush[25] trailing from their sleigh for a trophy, seeking their inn. They tell me that if the fox would remain in the bosom of the frozen earth he would be safe, or if he would run in a straight line away no fox-hound could overtake him; but, having left his pursuers far behind, he stops to rest and listen till they come up, and when he runs he circles round to his old haunts, where the hunters await him. Sometimes, however, he will run upon a wall many rods, and then leap off far to one side, and he appears to know that water will not retain his scent. A

21 In a journal entry from 1850 [PJ 3:54–55], Thoreau identified this quotation as coming from the works of John James Audubon, but it does not appear in Audubon's works. Audubon described the ruffed grouse, which is often called a partridge, as having this same characteristic: "When the ground is covered with snow sufficiently soft to allow this bird to conceal itself under it, it dives headlong into it with such force as to form a hole several yards in length, re-appears at that distance, and continues to elude the pursuit of the sportsman by flight."

22 Feed on the tree's buds. Jacob Post Giraud (1811–1870) wrote in *Birds of Long Island* (1844): "During winter, when the ground is covered with snow, it [the ruffed grouse] resorts to the orchards, and feeds on the buds of apple trees . . . 'budding,' as it is termed."

23 A decoction, often of guaiacum, sarsaparilla, or sassafras, taken either singly or in combination as normal drink throughout the day, usually for months, to change the habit of the body. Thoreau wrote in his journal: "Live in each season as it passes; breathe the air, drink the drink, taste the fruit, and resign yourself to the influences of each. Let these be your only diet drink and botanical medicines" [J 5:394].

24 In Greek mythology, a hunter who, having spied on the bathing Artemis, was changed into a stag and then hunted and eaten by his own hounds.

25 Fox tail.

26 Town east of Concord.

27 A fuller transcription of the conversation is given in Thoreau's journal:

> "Have you seen my hound, sir? I want to know!—what! a lawyer's office? law books?—if you've seen anything of a hound about here. Why, what do you do here?" "I live here. No, I have n't." "Have n't you heard one in the woods anywhere?" "Oh, yes, I heard one this evening." "What do you do here?" "But he was some way off." "Which side did he seem to be?" "Well, I should think he [was] the other side of the pond." "This is a large dog; makes a large track. He's been out hunting from Lexington for a week. How long have you lived here?" "Oh, about a year." "Somebody said there was a man up here had a camp in the woods somewhere, and he'd got him." "Well, I dont know of anybody. There's Britton's camp over on the other road. It may be there." "Is n't there anybody in these woods?" "Yes, they are chopping right up here behind me." "How far is it?" "Only a few steps. Hark a moment. There, do n't you hear the sound of their axes." [J 1:398–99]

28 Possibly George Minott, of whom Thoreau wrote in his journal of 8 July 1852: "M—— was telling me last night that he had thought of bathing when he had done his hoeing,—of taking some soap and going down to Walden and giving himself a good scrubbing,—but something had occurred to prevent it, and now he will go unwashed to the harvesting, aye, even till the next hoeing is over. . . . Men stay on shore, keep themselves dry, and drink rum. . . . One farmer, who came to bathe in Walden one Sunday while I lived there, told me it was the first bath he had had for fifteen years" [J 4:202].

29 An inspection of woods to estimate its potential lumber yield, but probably used here in its more general meaning of moving or traveling about, often with the purpose of discovery.

hunter told me that he once saw a fox pursued by hounds burst out on to Walden when the ice was covered with shallow puddles, run part way across, and then return to the same shore. Ere long the hounds arrived, but here they lost the scent. Sometimes a pack hunting by themselves would pass my door, and circle round my house, and yelp and hound without regarding me, as if afflicted by a species of madness, so that nothing could divert them from the pursuit. Thus they circle until they fall upon the recent trail of a fox, for a wise hound will forsake every thing else for this. One day a man came to my hut from Lexington[26] to inquire after his hound that made a large track, and had been hunting for a week by himself. But I fear that he was not the wiser for all I told him, for every time I attempted to answer his questions he interrupted me by asking, "What do you do here?"[27] He had lost a dog, but found a man.

One old hunter who has a dry tongue, who used to come to bathe in Walden once every year when the water was warmest,[28] and at such times looked in upon me, told me, that many years ago he took his gun one afternoon and went out for a cruise[29] in Walden Wood; and as he walked the Wayland road he heard the cry of hounds approaching, and ere long a fox leaped the wall into the road, and as quick as thought leaped the other wall out of the road, and his swift bullet had not touched him. Some way behind came an old hound and her three pups in full pursuit, hunting on their own account, and disappeared again in the woods. Late in the afternoon, as he was resting in the thick woods south of Walden, he heard the voice of the hounds far over toward Fair Haven still pursuing the fox; and on they came, their hounding cry which made all the woods ring sounding nearer and nearer, now from Well-Meadow,[30] now from the Baker Farm. For a long time he stood still and listened to their music, so sweet to a hunter's ear, when suddenly the fox

appeared, threading the solemn aisles with an easy coursing pace, whose sound was concealed by a sympathetic
rustle of the leaves, swift and still, keeping the ground,
leaving his pursuers far behind; and, leaping upon a rock
amid the woods, he sat erect and listening, with his back
to the hunter. For a moment compassion restrained the
latter's arm; but that was a short-lived mood, and as quick
as thought can follow thought his piece was levelled, and
whang!—the fox rolling over the rock lay dead on the
ground. The hunter still kept his place and listened to
the hounds. Still on they came, and now the near woods
resounded through all their aisles with their demoniac
cry. At length the old hound burst into view with muzzle
to the ground, and snapping the air as if possessed, and
ran directly to the rock; but spying the dead fox she
suddenly ceased her hounding, as if struck dumb with
amazement, and walked round and round him in silence;
and one by one her pups arrived, and, like their mother,
were sobered into silence by the mystery. Then the hunter
came forward and stood in their midst, and the mystery
was solved. They waited in silence while he skinned the
fox, then followed the brush a while, and at length turned
off into the woods again. That evening a Weston[31] Squire
came to the Concord hunter's cottage to inquire for his
hounds, and told how for a week they had been hunting
on their own account from Weston woods. The Concord
hunter told him what he knew and offered him the skin;
but the other declined it and departed. He did not find his
hounds that night, but the next day learned that they had
crossed the river and put up at a farm-house for the night,
whence, having been well fed, they took their departure
early in the morning.

The hunter who told me this could remember one Sam
Nutting, who used to hunt bears on Fair Haven Ledges,[32]
and exchange their skins for rum in Concord village; who
told him, even, that he had seen a moose there. Nut-

30 On the shore of Fair Haven Bay, approximately one mile south of Walden.

31 Village southeast of Concord, but with a possible pun on Squire Western from Henry Fielding's (1707–1754) novel *Tom Jones*.

32 On Fair Haven Hill, southwest of Walden. In his journal of 10 March 1853, Thoreau wrote: "Minott says that old Sam Nutting, the hunter,—Fox Nutting, Old Fox, he was called,—who died more than forty years ago (he lived in Jacob Baker's house, Lincoln; came from Weston) and was some seventy years old then, told him that he had killed not only bear about Fair Haven among the walnuts, but *moose!*" [J 5:16].

33 "Bug*ī*ne" in Thoreau's journal of 30 May 1851
[J 2:223].

34 Account book.

35 "I have an old account-book," Thoreau wrote
in his journal on 27 January 1854. "Its cover is
brown paper, on which, amid many marks and
scribblings, I find written:—

   'Mr. Ephraim Jones
   His Wast Book
   Anno Domini
   1742'

It extends from November 8th, 1742, to June 20th,
1743 (inclusive)" [J 6:77]. Ephraim Jones (1705–
1756) was a captain during the Battle of Concord,
town clerk in 1749–54, and a representative in the
General Court of the Massachusetts legislature for
the years 1745–50 and 1753. Thoreau's journal contains four separate entries recording details from
and comments on this and two other of Jones's
account books: 27 January, 31 January, 5 February,
and 5 February (P.M.) 1854.

36 These and the following figures represent
pounds, shillings, and pence.

37 Although Thoreau questioned this in his copy
of *Walden* after publication—"can it be calf?"—he
did not question it in his original journal passage:
"Hezekiah Stratton has credit in 1743, 'Feb. 7 by
$\frac{1}{2}$ a Catt skinn 0—1—4$\frac{1}{2}$,'—of course a wild-
cat" [J 6:95]. Wildcats, such as the bay lynx, had
been killed in eastern Massachusetts, and Thoreau wrote as much in his "Natural History of
Massachusetts": "It appears from the Report that
there are about forty quadrupeds belonging to the
State, and among these one is glad to hear of a
few bears, wolves, lynxes, and wildcats" [W 5:114].
In a letter of 13 October 1860 to the Boston Society
of Natural History, Thoreau wrote "that some of
the Lynxes killed in this vicinity of late years, and
called the Bay Lynx, were the Canada Lynx" [C 592].
A post-*Walden* journal entry confirms the presence
of wildcats in the area: "Spoke to Skinner about

ting had a famous fox-hound named Burgoyne,—he pronounced it Bugine,[33]—which my informant used to borrow. In the "Wast Book"[34] of an old trader of this town,
who was also a captain, town-clerk, and representative,[35] I
find the following entry. Jan. 18th, 1742–3, "John Melven
Cr. by 1 Grey Fox 0—2—3;"[36] they are not now found
here; and in his ledger, Feb. 7th, 1743, Hezekiah Stratton
has credit "by $\frac{1}{2}$ a Catt[37] skin 0—1—4$\frac{1}{2}$;" of course,
a wild-cat, for Stratton was a sergeant in the old French
war,[38] and would not have got credit for hunting less
noble game. Credit is given for deer skins also, and they
were daily sold. One man still preserves the horns of the
last deer that was killed in this vicinity,[39] and another has
told me the particulars of the hunt in which his uncle
was engaged. The hunters were formerly a numerous and
merry crew here. I remember well one gaunt Nimrod[40]
who would catch up a leaf by the road-side and play a
strain on it wilder and more melodious, if my memory
serves me, than any hunting horn.

At midnight, when there was a moon, I sometimes met
with hounds in my path prowling about the woods, which
would skulk out of my way, as if afraid, and stand silent
amid the bushes till I had passed.

Squirrels and wild mice disputed for my store of nuts.
There were scores of pitch-pines around my house, from
one to four inches in diameter, which had been gnawed
by mice the previous winter,—a Norwegian winter[41] for
them, for the snow lay long and deep, and they were
obliged to mix a large proportion of pine bark with their
other diet. These trees were alive and apparently flourishing at mid-summer, and many of them had grown a
foot, though completely girdled; but after another winter
such were without exception dead. It is remarkable that a
single mouse should thus be allowed a whole pine tree for
its dinner, gnawing round instead of up and down it; but

perhaps it is necessary in order to thin these trees, which are wont to grow up densely.

The hares (*Lepus Americanus*)[42] were very familiar. One had her form[43] under my house all winter, separated from me only by the flooring, and she startled me each morning by her hasty departure when I began to stir, — thump, thump, thump, striking her head against the floor timbers in her hurry. They used to come round my door at dusk to nibble the potato parings which I had thrown out, and were so nearly the color of the ground that they could hardly be distinguished when still. Sometimes in the twilight I alternately lost and recovered sight of one sitting motionless under my window. When I opened my door in the evening, off they would go with a squeak and a bounce. Near at hand they only excited my pity. One evening one sat by my door two paces from me, at first trembling with fear, yet unwilling to move; a poor wee thing, lean and bony, with ragged ears and sharp nose, scant tail and slender paws. It looked as if Nature no longer contained the breed of nobler bloods,[44] but stood on her last toes. Its large eyes appeared young and unhealthy, almost dropsical. I took a step, and lo, away it scud[45] with an elastic spring over the snow crust, straightening its body and its limbs into graceful length, and soon put the forest between me and itself, — the wild free venison, asserting its vigor and the dignity of Nature. Not without reason was its slenderness. Such then was its nature. (*Lepus, levipes,* light-foot, some think.)[46]

What is a country without rabbits and partridges? They are among the most simple and indigenous animal products; ancient and venerable families known to antiquity as to modern times; of the very hue and substance of Nature, nearest allied to leaves and to the ground, — and to one another; it is either winged or it is legged. It is hardly as if you had seen a wild creature when a rabbit

the wildcat he says he heard a month ago in Ebby Hubbard's woods. He was going down to Walden in the evening, to see if the geese had not settled in it (with a companion), when they heard this sound, which his companion at first thought was a coon, but S. said no, it was a wildcat. He says he has heard them often in the Adirondack region, where he has purchased furs" [J 10:212–13].

38 French and Indian War of 1754–63.

39 During Thoreau's day, deer had been hunted nearly to extinction in the vicinity of Concord.

40 Allusion to Genesis 10:9: "Nimrod the mighty hunter before the Lord."

41 Refers to the long, cold, snowy, and dark winters of Norway.

42 Snowshoe, or American, hare, but Ebenezer Emmons (1799–1863) in his *Report on the Quadrupeds of Massachusetts* (1840), which Thoreau ostensibly reviewed in "Natural History of Massachusetts," also equated the Latin name with the American rabbit. It is uncertain whether Thoreau made a distinction between the rabbit and the hare—he used the terms interchangeably in the next paragraph—and it is possible he may have been referring to the common gray rabbit (*Lepus floridanus transitionalis*).

43 Seat or bed of a hare or rabbit. In the original journal passage, the rabbit was male: "A whole rabbit-warren only separated from you by the flooring. To be saluted when you stir in the dawn by the hasty departure of Monsieur, —thump, thump, thump, striking his head against the floor-timbers" [J 1:425].

44 Allusion to Shakespeare's *Julius Caesar* 1.2.152: "Rome, thou hast lost the breed of noble bloods."

45 Moved swiftly, with haste.

46 Allusion to Varro's *Rerum Rusticarum* 3.12: "Lucius Aelius thought that the hare received its name *lepus* because of its swiftness, being *levipes,* nimble-foot."

47 Small fence of twigs used to divert a rabbit from its run into a snare.

48 A snare, or gin, set with horsehair used to catch birds and small animals.

or a partridge bursts away, only a natural one, as much to be expected as rustling leaves. The partridge and the rabbit are still sure to thrive, like true natives of the soil, whatever revolutions occur. If the forest is cut off, the sprouts and bushes which spring up afford them concealment, and they become more numerous than ever. That must be a poor country indeed that does not support a hare. Our woods teem with them both, and around every swamp may be seen the partridge or rabbit walk, beset with twiggy fences [47] and horse-hair snares,[48] which some cow-boy tends.

The Pond in Winter

1 Thoreau's translation from Langlois' French edition of the *Harivansa, ou Histoire de la Famille de Hari* 2:361.

After a still winter night I awoke with the impression that some question had been put to me, which I had been endeavoring in vain to answer in my sleep, as what—how—when—where? But there was dawning Nature, in whom all creatures live, looking in at my broad windows with serene and satisfied face, and no question on *her* lips. I awoke to an answered question, to Nature and daylight. The snow lying deep on the earth dotted with young pines, and the very slope of the hill on which my house is placed, seemed to say, Forward! Nature puts no question and answers none which we mortals ask. She has long ago taken her resolution. "O Prince, our eyes contemplate with admiration and transmit to the soul the wonderful and varied spectacle of this universe. The night veils without doubt a part of this glorious creation; but day comes to reveal to us this great work, which extends from earth even into the plains of the ether."[1]

Then to my morning work. First I take an axe and pail and go in search of water, if that be not a dream. After a cold and snowy night it needed a divining rod to find it. Every winter the liquid and trembling surface of the pond, which was so sensitive to every breath, and reflected every light and shadow, becomes solid to the depth of a foot or a foot and a half, so that it will support the heaviest teams, and perchance the snow covers it to

2 Heavy-set burrowing rodent belonging to the genus *Marmota*, but Thoreau was probably specifically referring to the *Marmota monax*, or woodchuck, also known as the groundhog.

3 Heavy cloth coat, often woolen, also called a dreadnought. In "A Winter Walk" Thoreau wrote: "Far over the ice, between the hemlock woods and snow-clad hills, stands the pickerel-fisher, his lines set in some retired cove, like a Finlander, with his arms thrust into the pouches of his dreadnaught" [W 5:180].

an equal depth, and it is not to be distinguished from any level field. Like the marmots[2] in the surrounding hills, it closes its eye-lids and becomes dormant for three months or more. Standing on the snow-covered plain, as if in a pasture amid the hills, I cut my way first through a foot of snow, and then a foot of ice, and open a window under my feet, where, kneeling to drink, I look down into the quiet parlor of the fishes, pervaded by a softened light as through a window of ground glass, with its bright sanded floor the same as in summer; there a perennial waveless serenity reigns as in the amber twilight sky, corresponding to the cool and even temperament of the inhabitants. Heaven is under our feet as well as over our heads.

Early in the morning, while all things are crisp with frost, men come with fishing reels and slender lunch, and let down their fine lines through the snowy field to take pickerel and perch; wild men, who instinctively follow other fashions and trust other authorities than their townsmen, and by their goings and comings stitch towns together in parts where else they would be ripped. They sit and eat their luncheon in stout fear-naughts[3] on the dry oak leaves on the shore, as wise in natural lore as the citizen is in artificial. They never consulted with books, and know and can tell much less than they have done. The things which they practise are said not yet to be known. Here is one fishing for pickerel with grown perch for bait. You look into his pail with wonder as into a summer pond, as if he kept summer locked up at home, or knew where she had retreated. How, pray, did he get these in mid-winter? O, he got worms out of rotten logs since the ground froze, and so he caught them. His life itself passes deeper in Nature than the studies of the naturalist penetrate; himself a subject for the naturalist. The latter raises the moss and bark gently with his knife in search of insects; the former lays open logs to their core with his axe, and moss and bark fly far and wide. He gets his living by barking trees.[4] Such a man has some right to fish, and I love to see Nature carried out in him. The perch swallows the grub-worm, the pickerel swallows the perch, and the fisherman swallows the pickerel; and so all the chinks in the scale of being[5] are filled.

When I strolled around the pond in misty weather I was sometimes amused by the primitive mode which some ruder fisherman had adopted. He would perhaps have placed alder branches over the narrow holes in the ice, which were four or five rods apart and an equal distance from the shore, and having fastened the end of the line to a stick to prevent its being pulled through, have passed the slack line over a twig of the alder, a foot or more above the ice, and tied a dry oak leaf to it, which, being pulled down, would show when he had a bite. These alders loomed through the mist at regular intervals as you walked half way round the pond.

Ah, the pickerel of Walden! when I see them lying on the ice, or in the well which the fisherman cuts in the ice, making a little hole to admit the water, I am always surprised by their rare beauty, as if they were fabulous fishes, they are so foreign to the streets, even to the woods, foreign as Arabia to our Concord life. They possess a quite dazzling and transcendent beauty which separates them by a wide interval from the cadaverous cod and haddock whose fame is trumpeted in our streets.[6] They are not green like the pines, nor gray like the stones, nor blue like the sky; but they have, to my eyes, if possible, yet rarer colors, like flowers and precious stones, as if they were the pearls, the animalized *nuclei*[7] or crystals of the Walden water. They, of course, are Walden[8] all over and all through; are themselves small Waldens in the animal kingdom, Waldenses.[9] It is surprising that they are caught here,—that in this deep and capacious spring, far beneath the rattling teams and chaises and tinkling sleighs that travel the Walden road, this great gold and emerald fish

4 Stripping or removing a ring of bark from a tree to kill it.

5 Also known as the great chain of being, the doctrine that all natural entities, animal, mineral, and vegetable, are linked in a continuous, unbroken sequence. This theological and social concept originated with Plato and represented a never-changing hierarchy joining the lowest natural form with all others, ultimately to God. The chain of being was the single most important unifying concept in biology through the early part of the 19th century.

6 Fish sellers in the nineteenth century blew "fish horns" as they peddled in the streets, as in Hawthorne's "The Village Uncle": "After innumerable voyages aboard men-of-war and merchantmen, fishing schooners and chebacco boats, the old salt had become master of a hand cart, which he daily trundled about the vicinity, and sometimes blew his fish horn through the streets of Salem."

7 Bodies about which matter is collected, the focal point.

8 Pun: being fish they have Walden water around and through them, but also they are "walled in" by the ice.

9 Sect of religious dissenters founded by the 12th century French merchant Peter Waldo (d. 1218). For rejecting the authority of the pope and various rites, they were excommunicated in 1184 and subjected to persecution, which continued through the 16th and 17th centuries and eventually reduced the Waldensian communities to remote niches in the Alps of Italy and France. Although partisans of the 16th-century Reformation recognized them as early defenders of a true and pure religion, repression and persecution did not abate. In the middle of the 17th century, the Duke of Savoy unleashed a campaign to suppress the communities living in the Piedmont region of his domains, about which John Milton wrote in his sonnet "On the Late Massacre at Piedmont." Thoreau was also punning on the Latin suffix *-ensis*, meaning an inhabitant of, thus, inhabitants of Walden.

swims. I never chanced to see its kind in any market; it would be the cynosure of all eyes there. Easily, with a few convulsive quirks, they give up their watery ghosts, like a mortal translated before his time to the thin air of heaven.

As I was desirous to recover the long lost bottom of Walden Pond, I surveyed it carefully, before the ice broke up, early in '46, with compass and chain and sounding line.[10] There have been many stories told about the bottom, or rather no bottom, of this pond, which certainly had no foundation[11] for themselves. It is remarkable how long men will believe in the bottomlessness of a pond without taking the trouble to sound it. I have visited two such Bottomless Ponds[12] in one walk in this neighborhood. Many have believed that Walden reached quite through to the other side of the globe. Some who have lain flat on the ice for a long time, looking down through the illusive medium, perchance with watery eyes into the bargain, and driven to hasty conclusions by the fear of catching cold in their breasts, have seen vast holes "into which a load of hay might be driven," if there were any body to drive it, the undoubted source of the Styx and entrance to the Infernal Regions from these parts. Others have gone down from the village with a "fifty-six"[13] and a wagon load of inch rope, but yet have failed to find any bottom; for while the "fifty-six" was resting by the way, they were paying out the rope in the vain attempt to fathom their truly immeasurable capacity for marvellousness. But I can assure my readers that Walden has a reasonably tight bottom at a not unreasonable, though at an unusual, depth. I fathomed it easily with a cod-line and a stone weighing about a pound and a half, and could tell accurately when the stone left the bottom, by having to pull so much harder before the water got underneath to help me. The greatest depth was exactly one hundred and two feet; to which may be added the five feet which

---

10 The line attached to a sounding lead or weight, used to determine the depth of a body of water by lowering the weight to the bottom and measuring the line.

11 Pun: foundation as the solid bottom of the pond as well as the fundamental explanations supporting a hypothesis.

12 In his journal of 15 September 1850, Thoreau noted one such visit: "Yesterday, September 14, walked to White Pond in Stow, on the Marlborough road, having passed one pond called sometimes Pratt's Pond, sometimes Bottomless Pond, in Sudbury. Saw afterward another pond beyond Willis's also called Bottomless Pond, in a thick swamp. To name two ponds bottomless when both have a bottom! Verily men choose darkness rather than light" [J 2:68].

13 A 56-pound iron weight, which was half a hundredweight (a hundredweight being 112 pounds in his day).

it has risen since, making one hundred and seven. This is a remarkable depth for so small an area; yet not an inch of it can be spared by the imagination. What if all ponds were shallow? Would it not react on the minds of men? I am thankful that this pond was made deep and pure for a symbol. While men believe in the infinite some ponds will be thought to be bottomless.

A factory owner,[14] hearing what depth I had found, thought that it could not be true, for, judging from his acquaintance with dams, sand would not lie at so steep an angle. But the deepest ponds are not so deep in proportion to their area as most suppose, and, if drained, would not leave very remarkable valleys. They are not like cups between the hills; for this one, which is so unusually deep for its area, appears in a vertical section through its centre not deeper than a shallow plate. Most ponds, emptied, would leave a meadow no more hollow than we frequently see. William Gilpin, who is so admirable in all that relates to landscapes, and usually so correct, standing at the head of Loch Fyne, in Scotland,[15] which he describes as "a bay of salt water, sixty or seventy fathoms deep, four miles in breadth," and about fifty miles long, surrounded by mountains, observes, "If we could have seen it immediately after the diluvian crash, or whatever convulsion of Nature occasioned it, before the waters gushed in, what a horrid chasm must it have appeared!

So high as heaved the tumid hills, so low
Down sunk a hollow bottom, broad, and deep,
Capacious bed of waters—."[16]

But if, using the shortest diameter of Loch Fyne, we apply these proportions to Walden, which, as we have seen, appears already in a vertical section only like a shallow plate, it will appear four times as shallow. So much for the *increased* horrors of the chasm of Loch Fyne when emptied.

14 Probably Calvin Carver Damon (1803–1854), who in 1835 bought a failing mill in West Concord that he turned into a very successful enterprise manufacturing flannel. In 1859 Damon's son Edward (1836–1901) commissioned Thoreau to survey "Damon's Mills."

15 Loch Fyne lies in the extreme southwest of the Scottish Highlands. It is the longest of all Scotland's sea lochs, running more than 40 miles from Kilbrannan Sound, opposite the Isle of Arran, to the foot of the big mountains of north Argyll.

16 Quoted from William Gilpin's *Observations on Several Parts of Great Britain* 2:4. Gilpin quoted from Milton's *Paradise Lost* 7.288–90.

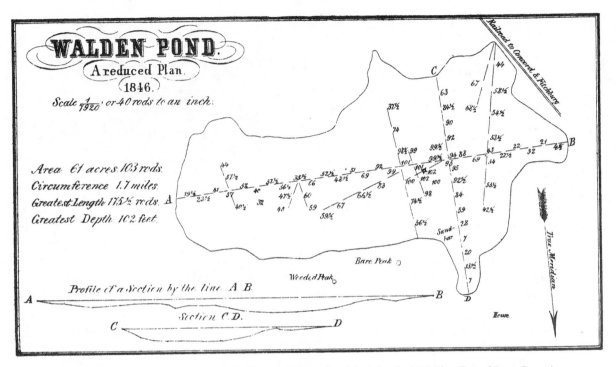

Thoreau's survey, *Walden Pond, A Reduced Plan, 1846* (lithograph; original plate by S. W. Chandler and Bros., Boston). Thoreau's survey was printed opposite page 307 in the first edition. His original 16-by-21-inch drawing, which was on a scale of 10 rods per inch, was reduced for publication to 40 rods per inch (the same scale it appears at here).

No doubt many a smiling valley with its stretching corn-fields occupies exactly such a "horrid chasm," from which the waters have receded, though it requires the insight and the far sight of the geologist to convince the unsuspecting inhabitants of this fact. Often an inquisitive eye may detect the shores of a primitive lake in the low horizon hills, and no subsequent elevation of the plain has been necessary to conceal their history. But it is easiest, as they who work on the highways know, to find the hollows by the puddles after a shower. The amount of it is, the imagination, give it the least license, dives deeper and soars higher than Nature goes. So, probably, the depth of the ocean will be found to be very inconsiderable compared with its breadth.[17]

As I sounded through the ice I could determine the shape of the bottom with greater accuracy than is possible in surveying harbors which do not freeze over, and I was surprised at its general regularity. In the deepest part there are several acres more level than almost any field which is exposed to the sun wind and plough. In one instance, on a line arbitrarily chosen, the depth did not vary more than one foot in thirty rods; and generally, near the middle, I could calculate the variation for each one hundred feet in any direction beforehand within three or four inches. Some are accustomed to speak of deep and dangerous holes even in quiet sandy ponds like this, but the effect of water under these circumstances is to level all inequalities. The regularity of the bottom and its conformity to the shores and the range of the neighboring hills were so perfect that a distant promontory betrayed itself in the soundings quite across the pond, and its direction could be determined by observing the opposite shore. Cape becomes bar, and plain shoal, and valley and gorge deep water and channel.

When I had mapped the pond by the scale of ten rods to an inch, and put down the soundings, more than a

17 The average depth of the Atlantic Ocean is 12,877 feet; the width of the Atlantic varies from 1,769 miles between Brazil and Liberia to about 3,000 miles between the United States and northern Africa.

18 The five coves of Walden were referred to by
Thoreau in his journals as: "My" cove [J 8:56],
adjacent to Wyman Meadow, mentioned by
Herbert Gleason (1855–1937) and now known
as Thoreau's Cove; Ice Fort, or Ice Heap, Cove
[J 9:190, 8:168], which Hawthorne described as
"the most beautiful cove of the whole lake" in his
notebooks; Long Cove [J 8:211]; Deep Cove [J 5:28,
9:190, 11:433], called South East Cove by Gleason;
and Little Cove [J 11:433].

hundred in all, I observed this remarkable coincidence. Having noticed that the number indicating the greatest depth was apparently in the centre of the map, I laid a rule on the map lengthwise, and then breadthwise, and found, to my surprise, that the line of greatest length intersected the line of greatest breadth *exactly* at the point of greatest depth, notwithstanding that the middle is so nearly level, the outline of the pond far from regular, and the extreme length and breadth were got by measuring into the coves; and I said to myself, Who knows but this hint would conduct to the deepest part of the ocean as well as of a pond or puddle? Is not this the rule also for the height of mountains, regarded as the opposite of valleys? We know that a hill is not highest at its narrowest part.

Of five coves,[18] three, or all which had been sounded, were observed to have a bar quite across their mouths and deeper water within, so that the bay tended to be an expansion of water within the land not only horizontally but vertically, and to form a basin or independent pond, the direction of the two capes showing the course of the bar. Every harbor on the sea-coast, also, has its bar at its entrance. In proportion as the mouth of the cove was wider compared with its length, the water over the bar was deeper compared with that in the basin. Given, then, the length and breadth of the cove, and the character of the surrounding shore, and you have almost elements enough to make out a formula for all cases.

In order to see how nearly I could guess, with this experience, at the deepest point in a pond, by observing the outlines of a surface and the character of its shores alone, I made a plan of White Pond, which contains about forty-one acres, and, like this, has no island in it, nor any visible inlet or outlet; and as the line of greatest breadth fell very near the line of least breadth, where two opposite capes approached each other and two opposite bays receded, I ventured to mark a point a short distance from the latter line, but still on the line of greatest length, as the deepest. The deepest part was found to be within one hundred feet of this, still farther in the direction to which I had inclined, and was only one foot deeper, namely, sixty feet. Of course, a stream running through, or an island in the pond, would make the problem much more complicated.

If we knew all the laws of Nature, we should need only one fact, or the description of one actual phenomenon, to infer all the particular results at that point. Now we know only a few laws, and our result is vitiated, not, of course, by any confusion or irregularity in Nature, but by our ignorance of essential elements in the calculation. Our notions of law and harmony are commonly confined to those instances which we detect; but the harmony which results from a far greater number of seemingly conflicting, but really concurring, laws, which we have not detected, is still more wonderful. The particular laws are as our points of view, as, to the traveller, a mountain outline varies with every step, and it has an infinite number of profiles, though absolutely but one form. Even when cleft or bored through it is not comprehended in its entireness.

What I have observed of the pond is no less true in ethics. It is the law of average. Such a rule of the two diameters not only guides us toward the sun in the system and the heart in man, but draw lines through the length and breadth of the aggregate of a man's particular daily behaviors and waves of life into his coves and inlets, and where they intersect will be the height or depth of his character. Perhaps we need only to know how his shores trend and his adjacent country or circumstances, to infer his depth and concealed bottom. If he is surrounded by mountainous circumstances, an Achillean shore,[19] whose peaks overshadow and are reflected in his bosom, they suggest a corresponding depth in him. But a low and smooth shore proves him shallow on that side. In our bodies, a bold projecting brow falls off to and indicates

19 The Greek hero Achilles was born in Thessaly, a mountainous region of northeastern Greece.

20 Another reference to phrenology, as in "Former Inhabitants" (note 86).

21 A narrow bend or baylike indentation. In his copy of *Walden,* Thoreau placed a question mark in the margin beside the lines "bights of the bays of poesy, or steer for the public ports of entry, and go into the dry docks of science, where," although it is unclear which word or words he was questioning.

22 Only known written use of this term. Leaching is the passing, or percolating, of a liquid through a solid. The term may come from the opening at the bottom of a "leach-tub," a vat used for leaching ash in the making of lye.

a corresponding depth of thought.[20] Also there is a bar across the entrance of our every cove, or particular inclination; each is our harbor for a season, in which we are detained and partially land-locked. These inclinations are not whimsical usually, but their form, size, and direction are determined by the promontories of the shore, the ancient axes of elevation. When this bar is gradually increased by storms, tides, or currents, or there is a subsidence of the waters, so that it reaches to the surface, that which was at first but an inclination in the shore in which a thought was harbored becomes an individual lake, cut off from the ocean, wherein the thought secures its own conditions, changes, perhaps, from salt to fresh, becomes a sweet sea, dead sea, or a marsh. At the advent of each individual into this life, may we not suppose that such a bar has risen to the surface somewhere? It is true, we are such poor navigators that our thoughts, for the most part, stand off and on upon a harborless coast, are conversant only with the bights[21] of the bays of poesy, or steer for the public ports of entry, and go into the dry docks of science, where they merely refit for this world, and no natural currents concur to individualize them.

As for the inlet or outlet of Walden, I have not discovered any but rain and snow and evaporation, though perhaps, with a thermometer and a line, such places may be found, for where the water flows into the pond it will probably be coldest in summer and warmest in winter. When the ice-men were at work here in '46–7, the cakes sent to the shore were one day rejected by those who were stacking them up there, not being thick enough to lie side by side with the rest; and the cutters thus discovered that the ice over a small space was two or three inches thinner than elsewhere, which made them think that there was an inlet there. They also showed me in another place what they thought was a "leach hole,"[22] through which the pond leaked out under a hill into a neighboring meadow, pushing me out on a cake of ice to see it. It was a small cavity under ten feet of water; but I think that I can warrant the pond not to need soldering till they find a worse leak than that. One has suggested, that if such a "leach hole" should be found, its connection with the meadow, if any existed, might be proved by conveying some colored powder or sawdust to the mouth of the hole, and then putting a strainer over the spring in the meadow, which would catch some of the particles carried through by the current.

While I was surveying, the ice, which was sixteen inches thick, undulated under a slight wind like water. It is well known that a level cannot be used on ice. At one rod from the shore its greatest fluctuation, when observed by means of a level on land directed toward a graduated staff on the ice, was three quarters of an inch, though the ice appeared firmly attached to the shore. It was probably greater in the middle. Who knows but if our instruments were delicate enough we might detect an undulation in the crust of the earth? When two legs of my level were on the shore and the third on the ice, and the sights were directed over the latter, a rise or fall of the ice of an almost infinitesimal amount made a difference of several feet on a tree across the pond. When I began to cut holes for sounding, there were three or four inches of water on the ice under a deep snow which had sunk it thus far; but the water began immediately to run into these holes, and continued to run for two days in deep streams, which wore away the ice on every side, and contributed essentially, if not mainly, to dry the surface of the pond; for, as the water ran in, it raised and floated the ice. This was somewhat like cutting a hole in the bottom of a ship to let the water out. When such holes freeze, and a rain succeeds, and finally a new freezing forms a fresh smooth ice over all, it is beautifully mottled internally by dark figures, shaped somewhat like a spider's web, what you may call

23 Allusion to Matthew 6:20: "But lay up for yourselves treasures in heaven."

24 With one sawyer standing in a pit below the log while another stands above, sometimes on a raised platform.

25 In Greek mythology, a race living beyond the north wind, but meaning also, as used here, frigid or extremely cold.

26 It is uncertain how this implement for planting seed would have been used in harvesting ice.

27 The agricultural journals *New England Farmer* (1822–71) and *Boston Cultivator* (1839–76).

28 Sown in the autumn for spring or summer harvest, but called winter rye because it survives through the winter.

29 Less than 1 percent of Iceland is cultivated and grain is difficult to grow there because of the climate, so it is clear that "grain recently introduced from Iceland" was not literal but a pun referring to the grain in the ice, as in the "Spring" chapter: "Ice has its grain as well as wood."

30 As Thoreau explained in "The Bean-Field": "I planted about two acres and a half of upland; and as it was only about fifteen years since the land was cleared, and I myself had got out two or three cords of stumps, I did not give it any manure."

31 Frederic Tudor (1783–1864), who became known as the "ice king." Although he spent the latter part of his life farming the family property in Lynn, Massachusetts, in 1805 he devised a method for sending 130 tons of ice to Martinique. Over the next fifteen years Tudor worked on perfecting the shipping of ice without loss, experimenting with insulating materials and building icehouses that decreased the loss from melting by more than 50 percent. His assistant Nathaniel Jarvis Wyeth (1802–1856) developed the horse-drawn ice plow to easily cut large quantities of ice. When Tudor and Wyeth had a falling out, a trade war began during which no source of ice was left untouched, including, for a very brief period, Walden Pond. In 1847 approximately 1,000 tons of ice were harvested from the pond daily.

ice rosettes, produced by the channels worn by the water flowing from all sides to a centre. Sometimes, also, when the ice was covered with shallow puddles, I saw a double shadow of myself, one standing on the head of the other, one on the ice, the other on the trees or hill-side.

While yet it is cold January, and snow and ice are thick and solid, the prudent landlord comes from the village to get ice to cool his summer drink; impressively, even pathetically wise, to foresee the heat and thirst of July now in January,—wearing a thick coat and mittens! when so many things are not provided for. It may be that he lays up no treasures in this world[23] which will cool his summer drink in the next. He cuts and saws the solid pond, unroofs the house of fishes, and carts off their very element and air, held fast by chains and stakes like corded wood, through the favoring winter air, to wintry cellars, to underlie the summer there. It looks like solidified azure, as, far off, it is drawn through the streets. These ice-cutters are a merry race, full of jest and sport, and when I went among them they were wont to invite me to saw pit-fashion[24] with them, I standing underneath.

In the winter of '46–7 there came a hundred men of Hyperborean[25] extraction swoop down on to our pond one morning, with many car-loads of ungainly-looking farming tools, sleds, ploughs, drill-barrows,[26] turf-knives, spades, saws, rakes, and each man was armed with a double-pointed pike-staff, such as is not described in the New-England Farmer or the Cultivator.[27] I did not know whether they had come to sow a crop of winter rye,[28] or some other kind of grain recently introduced from Iceland.[29] As I saw no manure, I judged that they meant to skim the land, as I had done, thinking the soil was deep and had lain fallow long enough.[30] They said that a gentleman farmer,[31] who was behind the scenes, wanted to double his money, which, as I understood, amounted to half a million already; but in order to cover each one of his dollars with another, he took off the only coat, ay, the skin itself, of Walden Pond in the midst of a hard winter. They went to work at once, ploughing, harrowing, rolling, furrowing, in admirable order, as if they were bent on making this a model farm; but when I was looking sharp to see what kind of seed they dropped into the furrow, a gang of fellows by my side suddenly began to hook up the virgin mould itself, with a peculiar jerk, clean down to the sand, or rather the water,—for it was a very springy soil,—indeed all the *terra firma* there was, and haul it away on sleds, and then I guessed that they must be cutting peat in a bog. So they came and went every day, with a peculiar shriek from the locomotive, from and to some point of the polar regions, as it seemed to me, like a flock of arctic snow-birds. But sometimes Squaw Walden had her revenge, and a hired man, walking behind his team, slipped through a crack in the ground down toward Tartarus,[32] and he who was so brave before suddenly became but the ninth part of a man, almost gave up his animal heat, and was glad to take refuge in my house, and acknowledged that there was some virtue in a stove; or sometimes the frozen soil took a piece of steel out of a ploughshare, or a plough got set in the furrow and had to be cut out.

To speak literally, a hundred Irishmen, with Yankee overseers, came from Cambridge[33] every day to get out the ice. They divided it into cakes by methods too well known to require description,[34] and these, being sledded to the shore, were rapidly hauled off on to an ice platform, and raised by grappling irons and block and tackle, worked by horses, on to a stack, as surely as so many barrels of flour, and there placed evenly side by side, and row upon row, as if they formed the solid base of an obelisk designed to pierce the clouds. They told me that in a good day they could get out a thousand tons, which was the

32 In Greek mythology, the lowest region of the underworld, as far below Hades as heaven is above the earth.

33 City on the Charles River, fifteen miles east of Concord.

34 Version 5 of *Walden* included a description, which Thoreau subsequently removed. Franklin Sanborn edited the passage for his Bibliophile Edition of *Walden* (2:207–8), as follows:

> When Walden was covered with snow, a dozen men were incessantly engaged in scraping it off, over an area of several acres, with various kinds of scrapers drawn by horses. Two men followed with a horse and a slight cutter,— one carefully leading the horse, while the other guided the cutter within a few inches of a rope drawn straight across the ice for ten or a dozen rods. Thus a groove was made on two sides of a parallelogram. Then, with various kinds of gauge-cutters,—that is, cutters connected by a frame with parallel marks or toothless plates, at a proper distance on one or both sides, running in the last-made groove,—the whole area was finally grooved in squares of twenty-two, on an average.
>
> I was told that the best ice-cutters or plows cost over a hundred dollars, and cut four inches at a bout, but it was hard work for a horse. And then men were employed with whip-saws cutting this area into long strips the width of a cake; half a dozen poling the strips along a narrow canal to the loading place, near which one stood with a spade-like chisel to cut off the "cake," which consisted of two squares, and therefore measured twenty-two by twenty-four inches. These cakes were to be finally divided by the shallow groove at the loading aboard ship, so that one man might handle them.
>
> At the end of the canal were a dozen or fifteen men, half on each side, incessantly hauling the cakes up a narrow iron framework or railway, sunk at one end on wood and resting

on a sled at the other, with pike-staffs which had a double point, one bent for hauling, the other straight for pushing. Each sled held fourteen or fifteen cakes which weighed about two tons and were drawn by one horse over the ice to the shore where they were rapidly hauled off on to an ice platform, and raised by grappling irons and block and tackle, worked by horses, on to a stack, as surely as so many barrels of flour, and there placed evenly side by side, and row upon row, as if they formed the solid base of an obelisk designed to pierce the clouds. There were sixty men employed at the stacks, about thirty above and thirty below,—about twenty in loading and sledding, and about twenty in scraping, grooving, sawing and poling.

35 Small depressions or ruts in a roadway, particularly in snow or ice covering a road.

36 The *Old Farmers Almanac,* in the 1850s, depicted winter on the January page as an old man. In "A Winter Walk" Thoreau wrote that "winter is represented in the almanac as an old man, facing the wind and sleet, and drawing his cloak about him" [W 5:182].

37 Pass the summer in a state of dormancy, as do certain snails and mollusks.

38 When the trade war between Tudor and Wyeth ended, the need for the Walden ice was eliminated.

39 The Goose Ponds, east of Walden.

yield of about one acre. Deep ruts and "cradle holes"[35] were worn in the ice, as on *terra firma,* by the passage of the sleds over the same track, and the horses invariably ate their oats out of cakes of ice hollowed out like buckets. They stacked up the cakes thus in the open air in a pile thirty-five feet high on one side and six or seven rods square, putting hay between the outside layers to exclude the air; for when the wind, though never so cold, finds a passage through, it will wear large cavities, leaving slight supports or studs only here and there, and finally topple it down. At first it looked like a vast blue fort or Valhalla; but when they began to tuck the coarse meadow hay into the crevices, and this became covered with rime and icicles, it looked like a venerable moss-grown and hoary ruin, built of azure-tinted marble, the abode of Winter, that old man we see in the almanac,[36]—his shanty, as if he had a design to estivate[37] with us. They calculated that not twenty-five per cent. of this would reach its destination, and that two or three per cent. would be wasted in the cars. However, a still greater part of this heap had a different destiny from what was intended; for, either because the ice was found not to keep so well as was expected, containing more air than usual, or for some other reason, it never got to market.[38] This heap, made in the winter of '46–7 and estimated to contain ten thousand tons, was finally covered with hay and boards; and though it was unroofed the following July, and a part of it carried off, the rest remaining exposed to the sun, it stood over that summer and the next winter, and was not quite melted till September 1848. Thus the pond recovered the greater part.

Like the water, the Walden ice, seen near at hand, has a green tint, but at a distance is beautifully blue, and you can easily tell it from the white ice of the river, or the merely greenish ice of some ponds,[39] a quarter of a mile off. Sometimes one of those great cakes slips from the ice-man's sled into the village street, and lies there for a week like a great emerald, an object of interest to all passers. I have noticed that a portion of Walden which in the state of water was green will often, when frozen, appear from the same point of view blue. So the hollows about this pond will, sometimes, in the winter, be filled with a greenish water somewhat like its own, but the next day will have frozen blue. Perhaps the blue color of water and ice is due to the light and air they contain, and the most transparent is the bluest. Ice is an interesting subject for contemplation. They told me that they had some in the ice-houses at Fresh Pond[40] five years old which was as good as ever. Why is it that a bucket of water soon becomes putrid, but frozen remains sweet forever?[41] It is commonly said that this is the difference between the affections and the intellect.[42]

Thus for sixteen days I saw from my window a hundred men at work like busy husbandmen, with teams and horses and apparently all the implements of farming, such a picture as we see on the first page of the almanac;[43] and as often as I looked out I was reminded of the fable of the lark and the reapers,[44] or the parable of the sower,[45] and the like; and now they are all gone, and in thirty days more, probably, I shall look from the same window on the pure sea-green Walden water there, reflecting the clouds and the trees, and sending up its evaporations in solitude, and no traces will appear that a man has ever stood there. Perhaps I shall hear a solitary loon laugh as he dives and plumes himself, or shall see a lonely fisher in his boat, like a floating leaf, beholding his form reflected in the waves, where lately a hundred men securely labored.

Thus it appears that the sweltering inhabitants of Charleston and New Orleans,[46] of Madras and Bombay and Calcutta,[47] drink at my well. In the morning I bathe my intellect in the stupendous and cosmogonal philosophy[48] of the Bhagvat-Geeta, since whose composition

40 In Cambridge, Massachusetts.

41 As the action of bacteria had not yet been discovered, Thoreau's question was real, not rhetorical.

42 Emerson explained in his essay "Intellect": "Intellect is void of affection, and sees an object as it stands in the light of science, cool and disengaged."

43 Probably the *Old Farmers Almanac*, which featured this type of illustration on its front cover.

44 Fable found in various forms. It appeared as "The Lark and Her Young Ones" in *The Fables of Æsop and Others* (Newcastle, 1818), and in La Fontaine as "The Lark and Her Young Ones with the Owner of the Field." Thoreau knew the fable as "The Lark and Her Family" in ballad form by Arthur Bour, or Bourcher, several verses of which he copied in his commonplace book as "The Lark and the Reapers."

45 Allusion to several parables in Matthew, such as:

> Hear then ye the parable of the sower. When any one heareth the word of the kingdom, and understandeth it not, then cometh the evil one, and catcheth away that which hath been sown in his heart. This is he which received seed by the way side. But he that received the seed into stony places, the same is he that heareth the word, and anon with joy receiveth it; Yet hath he not root in himself, but dureth for a while; for when tribulation or persecution ariseth because of the word, by and by he is offended. He also that received seed among the thorns is he that heareth the word; and the care of this world, and the deceitfulness of riches, choke the word, and he becometh unfruitful. But he that received seed into the good ground is he that heareth the word, and understandeth it; which also beareth fruit, and bringeth forth, some an hundredfold, some sixty, some thirty. [Matthew 13:18–23]

46 In South Carolina and Louisiana, respectively.

47 Three major cities in India, where ice from New England was shipped.

48 Thoreau used this same epithet in *A Week on the Concord and Merrimack Rivers* [W 1:149] to describe the Bhagavad Gita.

49 In the Hindu cycle of time, one year of the gods is equivalent to 360 human years.

50 Echoes in minor details the story of Rebecca and the servant of Abraham at the well in Genesis 24.

51 Three major Hindu deities.

52 Island that according to legend lay at the bottom of the Atlantic Ocean off the Straits of Gibraltar. Plato described it in the *Timaeus* and *Critias* as beautiful and prosperous, and said that it ruled part of Europe and Africa, but the Athenians defeated its kings when it attempted to conquer the rest, and the sea overwhelmed it.

53 In Greek mythology, paradisiacal islands of the blessed located in the far west.

54 Account of a voyage around an island or coast.

55 Follows the route of the Carthaginian explorer Hanno, who traveled to West Africa. Ternate and Tidore are two of the Spice Islands, paired in Milton's *Paradise Lost* 2.639–40: "Of Ternate and Tidor, whence merchants bring / Their spicy drugs."

56 Alexander the Great extended his empire into northwestern India, where he heard stories of the Ganges, an area he was unable to reach.

years of the gods⁴⁹ have elapsed, and in comparison with which our modern world and its literature seem puny and trivial; and I doubt if that philosophy is not to be referred to a previous state of existence, so remote is its sublimity from our conceptions. I lay down the book and go to my well for water,⁵⁰ and lo! there I meet the servant of the Bramin, priest of Brahma and Vishnu and Indra,⁵¹ who still sits in his temple on the Ganges reading the Vedas, or dwells at the root of a tree with his crust and water jug. I meet his servant come to draw water for his master, and our buckets as it were grate together in the same well. The pure Walden water is mingled with the sacred water of the Ganges. With favoring winds it is wafted past the site of the fabulous islands of Atlantis⁵² and the Hesperides,⁵³ makes the periplus⁵⁴ of Hanno, and, floating by Ternate and Tidore⁵⁵ and the mouth of the Persian Gulf, melts in the tropic gales of the Indian seas, and is landed in ports of which Alexander only heard the names.⁵⁶

Spring

The opening of large tracts by the ice-cutters commonly causes a pond to break up earlier; for the water, agitated by the wind, even in cold weather, wears away the surrounding ice. But such was not the effect on Walden that year, for she had soon got a thick new garment to take the place of the old. This pond never breaks up so soon as the others in this neighborhood, on account both of its greater depth and its having no stream passing through it to melt or wear away the ice.[1] I never knew it to open in the course of a winter, not excepting that of '52–3, which gave the ponds so severe a trial. It commonly opens about the first of April, a week or ten days later than Flint's Pond and Fair Haven, beginning to melt on the north side and in the shallower parts where it began to freeze. It indicates better than any water hereabouts the absolute progress of the season, being least affected by transient changes of temperature. A severe cold of a few days' duration in March may very much retard the opening of the former ponds, while the temperature of Walden increases almost uninterruptedly. A thermometer thrust into the middle of Walden on the 6th of March, 1847, stood at 32°, or freezing point; near the shore at 33°; in the middle of Flint's Pond, the same day, at 32½°; at a dozen rods from the shore, in shallow water, under ice a foot thick, at 36°. This difference of three and a half

Spring was an important symbol for Thoreau as well as a favorite season. He wrote on 22 March 1853:

> As soon as those spring mornings arrive in which the birds sing, I am sure to be an early riser. I am waked by my genius. I wake to inaudible melodies and am surprised to find myself expecting the dawn in so serene and joyful and expectant a mood. I have an appointment with spring. She comes to the window to wake me, and I go forth an hour or two earlier than usual. It is by especial favor that I am waked,—not rudely but gently, as infants should be waked. Though as yet the trill of the chip-bird is not heard,—added,—like the sparkling bead which bursts on bottled cider or ale. When we wake indeed, with a double awakening,—not only from our ordinary nocturnal slumbers, but from our diurnal,—we burst through the thallus of our ordinary life with a proper exciple, we awake with emphasis. [J 5:36]

1 The depth of Walden Pond at this time was 102 feet according to Thoreau's survey.

degrees between the temperature of the deep water and the shallow in the latter pond, and the fact that a great proportion of it is comparatively shallow, show why it should break up so much sooner than Walden. The ice in the shallowest part was at this time several inches thinner than in the middle. In mid-winter the middle had been the warmest and the ice thinnest there. So, also, every one who has waded about the shores of a pond in summer must have perceived how much warmer the water is close to the shore, where only three or four inches deep, than a little distance out, and on the surface where it is deep, than near the bottom. In spring the sun not only exerts an influence through the increased temperature of the air and earth, but its heat passes through ice a foot or more thick, and is reflected from the bottom in shallow water, and so also warms the water and melts the under side of the ice, at the same time that it is melting it more directly above, making it uneven, and causing the air bubbles which it contains to extend themselves upward and downward until it is completely honey-combed, and at last disappears suddenly in a single spring rain. Ice has its grain as well as wood, and when a cake begins to rot or "comb," that is, assume the appearance of honey-comb, whatever may be its position, the air cells are at right angles with what was the water surface. Where there is a rock or a log rising near to the surface the ice over it is much thinner, and is frequently quite dissolved by this reflected heat; and I have been told that in the experiment at Cambridge to freeze water in a shallow wooden pond, though the cold air circulated underneath, and so had access to both sides, the reflection of the sun from the bottom more than counterbalanced this advantage.[2] When a warm rain in the middle of the winter melts off the snow-ice from Walden, and leaves a hard dark or transparent ice on the middle, there will be a strip of rotten though thicker white ice, a rod

2 The *Concord Freeman* reported on 30 September 1842: "They are building a reservoir on a very large scale at Fresh Pond, for the purpose of *manufacturing ice,* the coming winter. It is intended to pump up the water into the basin and allow it to freeze, which it will more readily do, than in the pond, as the depth will be but little, and it can be but slightly disturbed. — *Charlestown Chronicle.*"

or more wide, about the shores, created by this reflected heat. Also, as I have said, the bubbles themselves within the ice operate as burning glasses to melt the ice beneath.

The phenomena of the year take place every day in a pond on a small scale. Every morning, generally speaking, the shallow water is being warmed more rapidly than the deep, though it may not be made so warm after all, and every evening it is being cooled more rapidly until the morning. The day is an epitome of the year.[3] The night is the winter, the morning and evening are the spring and fall, and the noon is the summer. The cracking and booming of the ice indicate a change of temperature. One pleasant morning after a cold night, February 24th, 1850,[4] having gone to Flint's Pond to spend the day, I noticed with surprise, that when I struck the ice with the head of my axe, it resounded like a gong for many rods around, or as if I had struck on a tight drum-head.[5] The pond began to boom about an hour after sunrise, when it felt the influence of the sun's rays slanted upon it from over the hills; it stretched itself and yawned like a waking man with a gradually increasing tumult, which was kept up three or four hours. It took a short siesta at noon, and boomed once more toward night, as the sun was withdrawing his influence. In the right stage of the weather a pond fires its evening gun with great regularity. But in the middle of the day, being full of cracks, and the air also being less elastic, it had completely lost its resonance, and probably fishes and muskrats could not then have been stunned by a blow on it.[6] The fishermen say that the "thundering of the pond" scares the fishes and prevents their biting. The pond does not thunder every evening, and I cannot tell surely when to expect its thundering; but though I may perceive no difference in the weather, it does. Who would have suspected so large and cold and thick-skinned a thing to be so sensitive? Yet it has its law to which it

3 As Thoreau wrote in his journal of 23 August 1853: "I am again struck by the perfect correspondence of a day—say an August day—and the year. I think that a perfect parallel may be drawn between the seasons of the day and of the year" [J 5:393].

4 No journal entry is extant to corroborate this date.

5 Another example of how intrigued Thoreau was by the music he found outdoors, which he mentioned in "The Bean-Field" (note 31); he called a vibrating telegraph wire the "telegraph harp" [W 3:11], and a friend called pebbles thrown on the frozen pond an "Ice-Harp" [J 1:14].

6 Striking the ice sharply would sometimes stun the fish and make them easier to catch.

7 Tiny sensitive protruding cells, as in any small nipplelike protuberance of the body or small fleshy projection on a plant.

8 Thoreau's journals are filled with entries marking the first signs of spring, as the following exemplify:

17 April 1852: The odor of spring, of life developing amid buds, of the earth's epithalamium. The first flowers are not the highest-scented,— as catkins,—as the first birds are not the finest singers,—as the blackbirds and song sparrows, etc. The beginnings of the year are humble. But though this fragrance is not rich, it contains and prophecies all others in it. [J 3:432]

3 March 1859: How imperceptibly the first springing takes place! In some still, muddy springs whose temperature is more equable than that of the brooks, while brooks and ditches are generally thickly frozen and concealed and the earth is covered with snow, and it is even cold, hard, and nipping winter weather, some fine grass which fills the water like a moss begins to lift its tiny spears or blades above the surface, which directly fall flat for half an inch or an inch along the surface, and on these (though many are frostbitten) you may measure the length to which the spring has advanced,—has *sprung*. Very few indeed, even of botanists, are aware of this growth. Some of it appears to go on even under ice and snow, or, in such a place as I have described, if it is also sheltered by alders, or the like, you may see (as March 2d) a little green crescent of caltha leaves, raised an inch or so above the water, with leaves but partially unrolled and looking as if it would withdraw beneath the surface again at night. This, I think, must be the most conspicuous and forward greenness of the spring. The small reddish radical leaves of the dock, too, are observed flat on the moist ground as soon as the

thunders obedience when it should as surely as the buds expand in the spring. The earth is all alive and covered with papillæ.[7] The largest pond is as sensitive to atmospheric changes as the globule of mercury in its tube.

One attraction in coming to the woods to live was that I should have leisure and opportunity to see the spring come in. The ice in the pond at length begins to be honeycombed, and I can set my heel in it as I walk. Fogs and rains and warmer suns are gradually melting the snow; the days have grown sensibly longer; and I see how I shall get through the winter without adding to my wood-pile, for large fires are no longer necessary. I am on the alert for the first signs of spring,[8] to hear the chance note of some arriving bird, or the striped squirrel's[9] chirp, for his stores must be now nearly exhausted, or see the woodchuck venture out of his winter quarters. On the 13th of March,[10] after I had heard the bluebird, song-sparrow, and red-wing,[11] the ice was still nearly a foot thick. As the weather grew warmer, it was not sensibly worn away by the water, nor broken up and floated off as in rivers, but, though it was completely melted for half a rod in width about the shore, the middle was merely honey-combed and saturated with water, so that you could put your foot through it when six inches thick; but by the next day evening, perhaps, after a warm rain followed by fog, it would have wholly disappeared, all gone off with the fog, spirited away. One year I went across the middle only five days before it disappeared entirely. In 1845 Walden was first completely open on the 1st of April; in '46, the 25th of March; in '47, the 8th of April; in '51, the 28th of March; in '52, the 18th of April; in '53, the 23d of March; in '54, about the 7th of April.[12]

Every incident connected with the breaking up of the rivers and ponds and the settling of the weather is particularly interesting to us who live in a climate of so great extremes. When the warmer days come, they who dwell near the river hear the ice crack at night with a startling whoop as loud as artillery, as if its icy fetters were rent from end to end, and within a few days see it rapidly going out. So the alligator comes out of the mud with quakings of the earth. One old man,[13] who has been a close observer of Nature, and seems as thoroughly wise in regard to all her operations as if she had been put upon the stocks[14] when he was a boy, and he had helped to lay her keel, — who has come to his growth, and can hardly acquire more of natural lore if he should live to the age of Methuselah,[15] — told me, and I was surprised to hear him express wonder at any of Nature's operations, for I thought that there were no secrets between them, that one spring day he took his gun and boat, and thought that he would have a little sport with the ducks. There was ice still on the meadows, but it was all gone out of the river, and he dropped down without obstruction from Sudbury,[16] where he lived, to Fair Haven Pond, which he found, un-expectedly, covered for the most part with a firm field of ice.[17] It was a warm day, and he was surprised to see so great a body of ice remaining. Not seeing any ducks, he hid his boat on the north or back side of an island in the pond, and then concealed himself in the bushes on the south side, to await them. The ice was melted for three or four rods from the shore, and there was a smooth and warm sheet of water, with a muddy bottom, such as the ducks love, within, and he thought it likely that some would be along pretty soon. After he had lain still there about an hour he heard a low and seemingly very distant sound, but singularly grand and impressive, unlike any thing he had ever heard, gradually swelling and increas-ing as if it would have a universal and memorable ending, a sullen rush and roar, which seemed to him all at once like the sound of a vast body of fowl coming in to settle there, and, seizing his gun, he started up in haste and ex-

snow has melted there, as if they had grown beneath it. [J 12:8]

9 Any of several small rodents with striped mark-ings on the back, but Thoreau used the name in its most common sense, to mean the Eastern chip-munk. He identified it more specifically in *A Week on the Concord and Merrimack Rivers*—"The chip-ping or striped squirrel, *Sciurus striatus* (*Tamias Lysteri*, Aud.)" [W 1:205]—and in "The Succes-sion of Forest Trees": "How commonly in the fall you see the cheek-pouches of the striped squir-rel distended by a quantity of nuts! This species gets its scientific name, *Tamias*, or the steward, from its habit of storing up nuts and other seeds" [W 5:198].

10 In 1846.

11 Red-winged blackbird (*Agelaius phoeniceus*).

12 These dates are further proof that *Walden* is not, nor should be taken as, a strict account of Thoreau's time at Walden Pond. According to his journal, Thoreau received proofs of *Walden* on 28 March 1854, so his including "the 7th of April" here shows that he was still revising and updating the text up until he returned the proofs to the publisher. There are no extant journal entries to in-dicate whether he recorded the opening of Walden in 1848–50.

13 Unidentified.

14 The frame or timbers on which a ship rests during construction.

15 According to Genesis 5:27: "All the days of Methuselah were nine hundred sixty and nine years and he died."

16 Town immediately southwest of Concord.

17 Technical term used to describe large sheets of ice in the Arctic regions.

18 This is related to humanity, through Thoreau's question later in this chapter: "What is man but a mass of thawing clay?" The image of a personal thawing is found in an early poem, "The Thaw": "Fain would I stretch me by the highway-side / To thaw and trickle with the melting snow" [W 5:409].

19 Botanical term: edges fringed or cut into deep, irregular lobes.

20 Botanical term: overlapping like the scales of a snake.

21 Simple plants with a body undifferentiated into stem, root, or leaf.

cited; but he found, to his surprise, that the whole body of the ice had started while he lay there, and drifted in to the shore, and the sound he had heard was made by its edge grating on the shore,—at first gently nibbled and crumbled off, but at length heaving up and scattering its wrecks along the island to a considerable height before it came to a stand still.

At length the sun's rays have attained the right angle, and warm winds blow up mist and rain and melt the snow banks, and the sun dispersing the mist smiles on a checkered landscape of russet and white smoking with incense, through which the traveller picks his way from islet to islet, cheered by the music of a thousand tinkling rills and rivulets whose veins are filled with the blood of winter which they are bearing off.

Few phenomena gave me more delight than to observe the forms which thawing sand and clay assume[18] in flowing down the sides of a deep cut on the railroad through which I passed on my way to the village, a phenomenon not very common on so large a scale, though the number of freshly exposed banks of the right material must have been greatly multiplied since railroads were invented. The material was sand of every degree of fineness and of various rich colors, commonly mixed with a little clay. When the frost comes out in the spring, and even in a thawing day in the winter, the sand begins to flow down the slopes like lava, sometimes bursting out through the snow and overflowing it where no sand was to be seen before. Innumerable little streams overlap and interlace one with another, exhibiting a sort of hybrid product, which obeys half way the law of currents, and half way that of vegetation. As it flows it takes the forms of sappy leaves or vines, making heaps of pulpy sprays a foot or more in depth, and resembling, as you look down on them, the laciniated[19] lobed and imbricated[20] thalluses[21] of some lichens; or you are reminded of coral, of leopards' paws or birds' feet, of brains or lungs or bowels, and excrements of all kinds. It is a truly *grotesque* vegetation, whose forms and color we see imitated in bronze, a sort of architectural foliage more ancient and typical than acanthus, chiccory, ivy, vine, or any vegetable leaves;[22] destined perhaps, under some circumstances, to become a puzzle to future geologists. The whole cut impressed me as if it were a cave with its stalactites laid open to the light. The various shades of the sand are singularly rich and agreeable, embracing the different iron colors, brown, gray, yellowish, and reddish. When the flowing mass reaches the drain at the foot of the bank it spreads out flatter into *strands,* the separate streams losing their semi-cylindrical form and gradually becoming more flat and broad, running together as they are more moist, till they form an almost flat *sand,* still variously and beautifully shaded, but in which you can trace the original forms of vegetation; till at length, in the water itself, they are converted into *banks,* like those formed off the mouths of rivers, and the forms of vegetation are lost in the ripple marks on the bottom.

The whole bank, which is from twenty to forty feet high, is sometimes overlaid with a mass of this kind of foliage, or sandy rupture, for a quarter of a mile on one or both sides, the produce of one spring day. What makes this sand foliage remarkable is its springing into existence thus suddenly. When I see on the one side the inert bank,—for the sun acts on one side first,—and on the other this luxuriant foliage, the creation of an hour, I am affected as if in a peculiar sense I stood in the laboratory[23] of the Artist who made the world and me,—had come to where he was still at work, sporting on this bank, and with excess of energy strewing his fresh designs about. I feel as if I were nearer to the vitals of the globe, for this sandy overflow is something such a foliaceous mass as the vitals of the animal body. You find thus in the very sands an anticipation of the vegetable leaf. No wonder

22 These are all leaves that have been used as architectural decorative motifs. The acanthus leaf was featured in classical architecture on, among others, the capital of Corinthian columns; the chicory leaf appeared in 15th-century Gothic ornamentation; the ivy leaf was used in Etruscan and Greco-Roman design; and the vine was popular in early Christian and Byzantine architecture. The United States Capitol building was decorated with corn and tobacco.

23 Appropriate terminology relating to Thoreau's description of life, in "Economy," as an experiment.

that the earth expresses itself outwardly in leaves, it so labors with the idea inwardly. The atoms have already learned this law, and are pregnant by it. The overhanging leaf sees here its prototype. *Internally,* whether in the globe or animal body, it is a moist thick *lobe,* a word especially applicable to the liver and lungs and the *leaves* of fat, (λείβω, *labor,*[24] lapsus, to flow or slip downward, a lapsing; λοβος, *globus,* lobe, globe; also lap, flap, and many other words,)[25] *externally* a dry thin *leaf,* even as the *f* and *v* are a pressed and dried *b.* The radicals of *lobe* are *lb,* the soft mass of the *b* (single lobed, or B, double lobed,) with the liquid *l* behind it pressing it forward. In globe, *glb,* the guttural *g* adds to the meaning the capacity of the throat. The feathers and wings of birds are still drier and thinner leaves. Thus, also, you pass from the lumpish grub in the earth to the airy and fluttering butterfly. The very globe continually transcends and translates itself, and becomes winged in its orbit. Even ice begins with delicate crystal leaves, as if it had flowed into moulds which the fronds of water plants have impressed on the watery mirror. The whole tree itself is but one leaf, and rivers are still vaster leaves whose pulp is intervening earth, and towns and cities are the ova of insects in their axils.

When the sun withdraws the sand ceases to flow, but in the morning the streams will start once more and branch and branch again into a myriad of others. You here see perchance how blood vessels are formed. If you look closely you observe that first there pushes forward from the thawing mass a stream of softened sand with a droplike point, like the ball of the finger, feeling its way slowly and blindly downward, until at last with more heat and moisture, as the sun gets higher, the most fluid portion, in its effort to obey the law to which the most inert also yields, separates from the latter and forms for itself a meandering channel or artery within that, in which is seen a little silvery stream glancing like lightning from one stage

---

24 The Latin verb *labor.*

25 Thoreau's etymologies owe much to Emerson's chapter "Language" in *Nature:* "1. Words are signs of natural facts. 2. Particular natural facts are symbols of particular spiritual facts. 3. Nature is the symbol of spirit."

of pulpy leaves or branches to another, and ever and anon swallowed up in the sand. It is wonderful how rapidly yet perfectly the sand organizes itself as it flows, using the best material its mass affords to form the sharp edges of its channel. Such are the sources of rivers. In the silicious matter which the water deposits is perhaps the bony system, and in the still finer soil and organic matter the fleshy fibre or cellular tissue. What is man but a mass of thawing clay?[26] The ball of the human finger is but a drop congealed. The fingers and toes flow to their extent from the thawing mass of the body. Who knows what the human body would expand and flow out to under a more genial heaven? Is not the hand a spreading *palm*[27] leaf with its lobes and veins? The ear may be regarded, fancifully, as a lichen, *umbilicaria*,[28] on the side of the head, with its lobe or drop. The lip (*labium* from *labor* (?)) laps or lapses from the sides of the cavernous mouth. The nose is a manifest congealed drop or stalactite. The chin is a still larger drop, the confluent dripping of the face. The cheeks are a slide from the brows into the valley of the face, opposed and diffused by the cheek bones. Each rounded lobe of the vegetable leaf, too, is a thick and now loitering drop, larger or smaller; the lobes are the fingers of the leaf; and as many lobes as it has, in so many directions it tends to flow, and more heat or other genial influences would have caused it to flow yet farther.

Thus it seemed that this one hill-side illustrated the principle of all the operations of Nature. The Maker of this earth but patented a leaf. What Champollion[29] will decipher this hieroglyphic for us, that we may turn over a new leaf at last?[30] This phenomenon is more exhilarating to me than the luxuriance and fertility of vineyards. True, it is somewhat excrementitious in its character, and there is no end to the heaps of liver lights[31] and bowels, as if the globe were turned wrong side outward; but this suggests at least that Nature has some bowels,[32] and there

26 Allusion to any of several biblical passages, such as "We are the clay" [Isaiah 64:8], and "Behold, I am according to thy wish in God's stead: I also am formed out of the clay" [Job 33:6].

27 The word "palm," in its meanings as both the flat of the hand and the tree, derives from the Latin word *palma*.

28 A genus of foliose umbilicate lichens (from the Latin word for navel, *umbilicus*).

29 Jean-François Champollion (1790–1832), French Egyptologist who deciphered the Rosetta stone, providing a key to Egyptian hieroglyphics.

30 This expression from the 16th century originally referred to the turning of a page, or leaf, in a book.

31 Lungs.

32 The bowels were considered the seat of compassion and sympathy, as in Colossians 3:12: "bowels of mercies, kindness, humbleness of mind, meekness, longsuffering."

33 Allusion to Mother Nature, not to the epithet Mother of Humanity used for Eve as the first woman, or later to Mary, the mother of Jesus, as the new Mother of Humanity.

34 At full power, from the currents of hot air used in blast furnaces.

35 Possible allusion to Jeremiah 18:6: "As the clay is in the potter's hand, so are ye in mine hand."

36 In Norse mythology, god of thunder. A New England pronunciation, making "Thor" and "thaw" sound almost alike, would have added to its value as a pun.

again is mother of humanity.[33] This is the frost coming out of the ground; this is Spring. It precedes the green and flowery spring, as mythology precedes regular poetry. I know of nothing more purgative of winter fumes and indigestions. It convinces me that Earth is still in her swaddling clothes, and stretches forth baby fingers on every side. Fresh curls spring from the baldest brow. There is nothing inorganic. These foliaceous heaps lie along the bank like the slag of a furnace, showing that Nature is "in full blast"[34] within. The earth is not a mere fragment of dead history, stratum upon stratum like the leaves of a book, to be studied by geologists and antiquaries chiefly, but living poetry like the leaves of a tree, which precede flowers and fruit,—not a fossil earth, but a living earth; compared with whose great central life all animal and vegetable life is merely parasitic. Its throes will heave our exuviæ from their graves. You may melt your metals and cast them into the most beautiful moulds you can; they will never excite me like the forms which this molten earth flows out into. And not only it, but the institutions upon it, are plastic like clay in the hands of the potter.[35]

Ere long, not only on these banks, but on every hill and plain and in every hollow, the frost comes out of the ground like a dormant quadruped from its burrow, and seeks the sea with music, or migrates to other climes in clouds. Thaw with his gentle persuasion is more powerful than Thor[36] with his hammer. The one melts, the other but breaks in pieces.

When the ground was partially bare of snow, and a few warm days had dried its surface somewhat, it was pleasant to compare the first tender signs of the infant year just peeping forth with the stately beauty of the withered vegetation which had withstood the winter,— life-everlasting, golden-rods, pinweeds, and graceful wild grasses, more obvious and interesting frequently than in summer even, as if their beauty was not ripe till then; even cotton-grass, cat-tails, mulleins, johnswort, hard-hack, meadow-sweet, and other strong stemmed plants, those unexhausted granaries which entertain the earliest birds, —decent weeds,[37] at least, which widowed Nature wears. I am particularly attracted by the arching and sheaf-like top of the wool-grass; it brings back the summer to our winter memories, and is among the forms which art loves to copy, and which, in the vegetable kingdom, have the same relation to types already in the mind of man that astronomy has. It is an antique style older than Greek or Egyptian. Many of the phenomena of Winter are suggestive of an inexpressible tenderness and fragile delicacy. We are accustomed to hear this king described as a rude and boisterous tyrant; but with the gentleness of a lover he adorns the tresses of Summer.

At the approach of spring the red squirrels got under my house, two at a time, directly under my feet as I sat reading or writing, and kept up the queerest chuckling and chirruping and vocal pirouetting and gurgling sounds that ever were heard; and when I stamped they only chirruped the louder, as if past all fear and respect in their mad pranks, defying humanity to stop them. No you don't—chickaree—chickaree.[38] They were wholly deaf to my arguments, or failed to perceive their force, and fell into a strain of invective that was irresistible.

The first sparrow of spring! The year beginning with younger hope than ever! The faint silvery warblings heard over the partially bare and moist fields from the blue-bird, the song-sparrow, and the red-wing, as if the last flakes of winter tinkled as they fell! What at such a time are histories, chronologies, traditions, and all written revelations? The brooks sing carols and glees to the spring. The marsh-hawk sailing low over the meadow is already seeking the first slimy life that awakes. The sinking sound of

37 Pun: any plant that crowds out cultivated plants, but also widow's mourning clothes.

38 Common 19th-century name for the red squirrel (*Tamiasciurus hudsonicus*) from the sound it makes. In *A Week on the Concord and Merrimack Rivers,* Thoreau described the chickaree's "warning of our approach by that peculiar alarum of his, like the winding up of some strong clock, in the top of a pine tree, and dodged behind its stem, or leaped from tree to tree with such caution and adroitness, as if much depended on the fidelity of his scout, running along the white pine boughs sometimes twenty rods by our side, with such speed, and by such unerring routes, as if it were some well-worn familiar path to him; and presently, when we have passed, he returns to his work of cutting off the pine cones, and letting them fall to the ground" [W 1:206].

39 Latin: "the grass which is called forth by the early rains is just growing" from Varro's *Rerum Rusticarum* 2.2.14.
40 Pun: crack the ice, i.e., start a conversation.
41 Echo of biblical resurrection, such as Luke 15:24 ("For this my son was dead, and is alive again"), and Revelation 2:8 ("And unto the angel of the church in Smyrna write; These things saith the first and the last, which was dead, and is alive").

melting snow is heard in all dells, and the ice dissolves apace in the ponds. The grass flames up on the hill-sides like a spring fire, — "et primitus oritur herba imbribus primoribus evocata,"[39] — as if the earth sent forth an inward heat to greet the returning sun; not yellow but green is the color of its flame; — the symbol of perpetual youth, the grass-blade, like a long green ribbon, streams from the sod into the summer, checked indeed by the frost, but anon pushing on again, lifting its spear of last year's hay with the fresh life below. It grows as steadily as the rill oozes out of the ground. It is almost identical with that, for in the growing days of June, when the rills are dry, the grass blades are their channels, and from year to year the herds drink at this perennial green stream, and the mower draws from it betimes their winter supply. So our human life but dies down to its root, and still puts forth its green blade to eternity.

Walden is melting apace. There is a canal two rods wide along the northerly and westerly sides, and wider still at the east end. A great field of ice has cracked off from the main body. I hear a song-sparrow singing from the bushes on the shore, — *olit, olit, olit, — chip, chip, chip, che char, — che wiss, wiss, wiss.* He too is helping to crack it.[40] How handsome the great sweeping curves in the edge of the ice, answering somewhat to those of the shore, but more regular! It is unusually hard, owing to the recent severe but transient cold, and all watered or waved like a palace floor. But the wind slides eastward over its opaque surface in vain, till it reaches the living surface beyond. It is glorious to behold this ribbon of water sparkling in the sun, the bare face of the pond full of glee and youth, as if it spoke the joy of the fishes within it, and of the sands on its shore, — a silvery sheen as from the scales of a *leuciscus,* as it were all one active fish. Such is the contrast between winter and spring. Walden was dead and is alive again.[41] But this spring it broke up more steadily, as I have said.

The change from storm and winter to serene and mild weather, from dark and sluggish hours to bright and elastic ones, is a memorable crisis which all things proclaim. It is seemingly instantaneous at last. Suddenly an influx of light filled my house, though the evening was at hand, and the clouds of winter still overhung it, and the eaves were dripping with sleety rain. I looked out the window, and lo! where yesterday was cold gray ice there lay the transparent pond already calm and full of hope as on a summer evening, reflecting a summer evening sky in its bosom, though none was visible overhead, as if it had intelligence with some remote horizon. I heard a robin in the distance, the first I had heard for many a thousand years, methought, whose note I shall not forget for many a thousand more, — the same sweet and powerful song as of yore. O the evening robin, at the end of a New England summer day! If I could ever find the twig he sits upon! I mean *he;* I mean *the twig.* This at least is not the *Turdus migratorius.*[42] The pitch-pines and shrub-oaks about my house, which had so long drooped, suddenly resumed their several characters, looked brighter, greener, and more erect and alive, as if effectually cleansed and restored by the rain. I knew that it would not rain any more. You may tell by looking at any twig of the forest, ay, at your very wood-pile, whether its winter is past or not. As it grew darker, I was startled by the *honking* of geese flying low over the woods, like weary travellers getting in late from southern lakes, and indulging at last in unrestrained complaint and mutual consolation. Standing at my door, I could hear the rush of their wings; when, driving toward my house, they suddenly spied my light, and with hushed clamor wheeled and settled in the pond. So I came in, and shut the door, and passed my first spring night in the woods.[43]

In the morning I watched the geese from the door through the mist, sailing in the middle of the pond, fifty

42 American migratory thrush, commonly called a robin.

43 Since Thoreau moved to Walden in July 1845, this would be the year 1846. The preceding passage is dated 26 March 1846 in his journal.

rods off, so large and tumultuous that Walden appeared like an artificial pond for their amusement. But when I stood on the shore they at once rose up with a great flapping of wings at the signal of their commander, and when they had got into rank circled about over my head, twenty-nine of them, and then steered straight to Canada, with a regular *honk* from the leader at intervals, trusting to break their fast in muddier pools. A "plump"[44] of ducks rose at the same time and took the route to the north in the wake of their noisier cousins.

For a week I heard the circling groping clangor of some solitary goose in the foggy mornings, seeking its companion, and still peopling the woods with the sound of a larger life than they could sustain. In April the pigeons were seen again flying express in small flocks, and in due time I heard the martins twittering over my clearing, though it had not seemed that the township contained so many that it could afford me any, and I fancied that they were peculiarly of the ancient race that dwelt in hollow trees ere white men came.[45] In almost all climes the tortoise and the frog are among the precursors and heralds of this season, and birds fly with song and glancing plumage, and plants spring and bloom, and winds blow, to correct this slight oscillation of the poles and preserve the equilibrium of Nature.

As every season seems best to us in its turn, so the coming in of spring is like the creation of Cosmos out of Chaos[46] and the realization of the Golden Age. —

> "Eurus ad Auroram, Nabathæaque regna recessit,
>   Persidaque, et radiis juga subdita matutinis."[47]

> "The East-Wind withdrew to Aurora and the Nabathæan kingdom,[48]

---

44 Small flock.

45 There are several antecedents for living in a hollow tree of which Thoreau may have been aware. The 7th-century saints Bavo of Ghent and Kevin of Glendalough, and the 13th-century St. Simon Stock, each lived for a while in a hollow tree. In medieval legend, Merlin was imprisoned in a hollow tree in the Forest of Broceliande. Pioneers would sometimes sleep in a hollow tree until a more permanent shelter could be built. Thoreau describes the lumbermen's shanties in "Chesuncook" as being but "a slight departure from a hollow tree" [W 3:139]. He also referred to the hollow-tree residence in "Brute Neighbors" and "Conclusion." In a journal entry of 15 May 1858, Thoreau wrote:

> Measured two apple trees by the road from the middle of Bedford and Fitch's mill. One, which divided at the ground, was thirteen and a half feet in circumference there, around the double trunk; but another, in a field on the opposite side of the road, was the most remarkable tree for size. This tree was exceedingly low for the size of its trunk, and the top rather small. At three feet from the ground it measured ten and a quarter feet in circumference, and immediately above this sent off a branch as big as a large apple tree. It was hollow, and on one side part of the trunk had fallen out. These trees mark the residence of an old settler evidently. [J 10:422]

46 In Greek mythology, the universe, Cosmos, was created out of an unformed original state, Chaos.

47 Quoted from Ovid's *Metamorphoses* 1.61–62.

48 Nabataean: area between Syria and Arabia, from the Euphrates to the Red Sea, independent from 312 B.C.E. to 105 C.E., when taken by the Romans.

And the Persian, and the ridges placed under the
    morning rays.[49]

          *   *   *   *

Man was born. Whether that Artificer of things,
The origin of a better world, made him from the
    divine seed;
Or the earth being recent and lately sundered
    from the high
Ether, retained some seeds of cognate heaven."[50]

A single gentle rain makes the grass many shades
greener. So our prospects brighten on the influx of better
thoughts. We should be blessed if we lived in the present[51]
always, and took advantage of every accident that be-
fell us, like the grass which confesses the influence of the
slightest dew that falls on it; and did not spend our time
in atoning for the neglect of past opportunities, which we
call doing our duty. We loiter in winter while it is already
spring. In a pleasant spring morning all men's sins are for-
given. Such a day is a truce to vice. While such a sun holds
out to burn, the vilest sinner may return.[52] Through our
own recovered innocence we discern the innocence of our
neighbors. You may have known your neighbor yesterday for a thief, a drunkard, or a sensualist, and merely
pitied or despised him, and despaired of the world; but
the sun shines bright and warm this first spring morning, re-creating the world, and you meet him at some
serene work, and see how his exhausted and debauched
veins expand with still joy and bless the new day, feel the
spring influence with the innocence of infancy, and all
his faults are forgotten. There is not only an atmosphere
of good will about him, but even a savor of holiness groping for expression, blindly and ineffectually perhaps, like a
new-born instinct, and for a short hour the south hill-side
echoes to no vulgar jest. You see some innocent fair shoots

49 Thoreau's translation of the preceding Latin
couplet.
50 Thoreau's translation of Ovid's *Metamorphoses* 1.78–81.
51 Thoreau wrote an early poem that began:

    I seek the present time,
    No other clime,
    Life in to-day, — [J 1:409]

52 Allusion to Isaac Watts (1674–1748), *Hymns
and Spiritual Songs* 1.88: "And while the lamp holds
out to burn / The vilest sinner may return."

53 Allusion to Matthew 25:21 and 25:23: "Enter thou into the joy of thy lord."
54 Thoreau's translation of Mencius, from Pauthier's French translation in *Confucius et Mencius.*

preparing to burst from his gnarled rind and try another year's life, tender and fresh as the youngest plant. Even he has entered into the joy of his Lord.[53] Why the jailer does not leave open his prison doors, — why the judge does not dismiss his case, — why the preacher does not dismiss his congregation! It is because they do not obey the hint which God gives them, nor accept the pardon which he freely offers to all.

"A return to goodness produced each day in the tranquil and beneficent breath of the morning, causes that in respect to the love of virtue and the hatred of vice, one approaches a little the primitive nature of man, as the sprouts of the forest which has been felled. In like manner the evil which one does in the interval of a day prevents the germs of virtues which began to spring up again from developing themselves and destroys them.

"After the germs of virtue have thus been prevented many times from developing themselves, then the beneficent breath of evening does not suffice to preserve them. As soon as the breath of evening does not suffice longer to preserve them, then the nature of man does not differ much from that of the brute. Men seeing the nature of this man like that of the brute, think that he has never possessed the innate faculty of reason. Are those the true and natural sentiments of man?"[54]

> "The Golden Age was first created, which
> without any avenger
> Spontaneously without law cherished fidelity and
> rectitude.
> Punishment and fear were not; nor were
> threatening words read
> On suspended brass; nor did the suppliant crowd
> fear
> The words of their judge; but were safe without
> an avenger.

Not yet the pine felled on its mountains had
    descended
To the liquid waves that it might see a foreign
    world,
And mortals knew no shores but their own.

        *   *   *   *

There was eternal spring, and placid zephyrs with
    warm
Blasts soothed the flowers born without seed." [55]

On the 29th of April,[56] as I was fishing from the bank of the river near the Nine-Acre-Corner bridge,[57] standing on the quaking grass and willow roots, where the muskrats lurk, I heard a singular rattling sound, somewhat like that of the sticks which boys play with their fingers,[58] when, looking up, I observed a very slight and graceful hawk,[59] like a night-hawk,[60] alternately soaring like a ripple and tumbling[61] a rod or two over and over, showing the underside of its wings, which gleamed like a satin ribbon in the sun, or like the pearly inside of a shell. This sight reminded me of falconry and what nobleness and poetry are associated with that sport. The Merlin[62] it seemed to me it might be called: but I care not for its name. It was the most ethereal flight I had ever witnessed. It did not simply flutter like a butterfly, nor soar like the larger hawks, but it sported with proud reliance in the fields of air; mounting again and again with its strange chuckle, it repeated its free and beautiful fall, turning over and over like a kite,[63] and then recovering from its lofty tumbling, as if it had never set its foot on *terra firma*. It appeared to have no companion in the universe, — sporting there alone, — and to need none but the morning and the ether with which it played. It was not lonely, but made all the earth lonely beneath it. Where was the parent which hatched it, its kindred, and its father in the heavens? The tenant of the air, it seemed related to

55 Thoreau's translation of Ovid's *Metamorphoses* 1.89–96, 107–8.
56 There is no extant journal entry to identify the year.
57 In the southwestern part of Concord.
58 Clappers or bones, sticks used as rhythmic instruments.
59 Male marsh hawk (*Circus cyaneus*).
60 *Chordeiles minor.*
61 Behavior exhibited during the mating season.
62 Pigeon hawk (*Falco columbarius*).
63 Any of various predatory birds of the hawk family Accipitridae, having a long, often forked tail and long pointed wings.

64 Copper-colored.

65 Allusion to 1 Corinthians 15:55: "O death, where is thy sting? O grave, where is thy victory?"

66 "How near to good is what is *wild!*" Thoreau wrote in "Walking." "Life consists with wildness. The most alive is the wildest. Not yet subdued to man, its presence refreshes him" [W 5:226].

67 American bittern (*Botaurus lentiginosus*), which Thoreau often called the "stake-diver" in his journals.

68 Thoreau identified the meadow-hen as the Virginia rail (*Rallus virginianus*) [J 5:259], now *Rallus limicola*.

69 Sound made by the snipe during its mating ritual as it circles and dives through the air. Of this booming Thoreau wrote in his journal of 9 April 1858:

> I hear the booming of the snipe this evening, and Sophia says she heard them on the 6th. The meadows having been bare so long, they may have begun yet earlier. Persons walking up or down our village street in still evenings at this season hear this singular *winnowing* sound in the sky over the meadows and know not what it is. This "booming" of the snipe is our regular village serenade. I heard it this evening for the first time, as I sat in the house, through the window. Yet common and annual and remarkable as it is, not one in a hundred of the villagers hears it, and hardly so many know what it is. [J 10:363]

70 Turkey vulture (*Cathartes aura*).

the earth but by an egg hatched some time in the crevice of a crag;—or was its native nest made in the angle of a cloud, woven of the rainbow's trimmings and the sunset sky, and lined with some soft midsummer haze caught up from earth? Its eyry now some cliffy cloud.

Beside this I got a rare mess of golden and silver and bright cupreous[64] fishes, which looked like a string of jewels. Ah! I have penetrated to those meadows on the morning of many a first spring day, jumping from hummock to hummock, from willow root to willow root, when the wild river valley and the woods were bathed in so pure and bright a light as would have waked the dead, if they had been slumbering in their graves, as some suppose. There needs no stronger proof of immortality. All things must live in such a light. O Death, where was thy sting? O Grave, where was thy victory, then?[65]

Our village life would stagnate if it were not for the unexplored forests and meadows which surround it. We need the tonic of wildness,[66]—to wade sometimes in marshes where the bittern[67] and the meadow-hen[68] lurk, and hear the booming of the snipe;[69] to smell the whispering sedge where only some wilder and more solitary fowl builds her nest, and the mink crawls with its belly close to the ground. At the same time that we are earnest to explore and learn all things, we require that all things be mysterious and unexplorable, that land and sea be infinitely wild, unsurveyed and unfathomed by us because unfathomable. We can never have enough of Nature. We must be refreshed by the sight of inexhaustible vigor, vast and Titanic features, the sea-coast with its wrecks, the wilderness with its living and its decaying trees, the thunder cloud, and the rain which lasts three weeks and produces freshets. We need to witness our own limits transgressed, and some life pasturing freely where we never wander. We are cheered when we observe the vulture[70] feeding on the carrion which disgusts and disheartens us and deriving health and strength from the repast.[71] There was a dead horse in the hollow by the path to my house, which compelled me sometimes to go out of my way, especially in the night when the air was heavy, but the assurance it gave me of the strong appetite and inviolable health of Nature was my compensation for this.[72] I love to see that Nature is so rife with life that myriads can be afforded to be sacrificed and suffered to prey on one another; that tender organizations can be so serenely squashed out of existence like pulp,—tadpoles which herons gobble up, and tortoises and toads run over in the road; and that sometimes it has rained flesh and blood![73] With the liability to accident, we must see how little account is to be made of it. The impression made on a wise man is that of universal innocence. Poison is not poisonous[74] after all, nor are any wounds fatal. Compassion is a very untenable ground. It must be expeditious. Its pleadings will not bear to be stereotyped.

Early in May, the oaks, hickories, maples, and other trees, just putting out amidst the pine woods around the pond, imparted a brightness like sunshine to the landscape, especially in cloudy days, as if the sun were breaking through mists and shining faintly on the hill-sides here and there. On the third or fourth of May I saw a loon in the pond, and during the first week of the month I heard the whippoorwill, the brown-thrasher, the veery, the wood-pewee, the chewink, and other birds. I had heard the wood-thrush[75] long before. The phœbe[76] had already come once more and looked in at my door and window, to see if my house was cavern-like enough for her, sustaining herself on humming wings with clinched talons, as if she held by the air, while she surveyed the premises. The sulphur-like pollen of the pitch-pine soon covered the pond and the stones and rotten wood along the shore, so that you could have collected a barrel-ful. This is the "sulphur showers" we hear of.[77] Even in Cali-

71 Thoreau was able to get beyond the fact of the carrion by placing it in a more universal context. As Emerson wrote in "The School," a lecture in his series *Human Life:* "The detached fact is ugly. Replace it in its series of cause and effect, and it is beautiful. Putrefaction is loathsome; but putrefaction seen as a step in the circle of nature, pleases. . . . The laws of disease are the laws of health masked."

72 In "Former Inhabitants" Thoreau briefly described "the marks of some homestead of the Stratton family," which he referred to in his journal of 11 January 1857 as "a mere dent in the earth there, to which, from time to time, dead horses or hogs were drawn from the village and cast in" [J 9:214].

73 Probable allusion to Pliny the Elder, who wrote in *Naturalis Historia* 2.57: "In the consulship of Manius Aciliius and Gaius Porcius it rained milk and blood, and . . . frequently on other occasions there it has rained flesh." Thoreau may also have been aware of local reports of showers of flesh and blood, such as one in a letter by W. Fitts on 8 September 1841 to the Boston *Daily Mail* regarding this phenomenon in Kensington, New Hampshire, or another in the *Concord Freeman* of 8 March 1844 reporting a similar incident in Jersey City, New Jersey.

74 Rhetorically similar to a passage in "Conclusion": "In proportion as he simplifies his life, the laws of the universe will appear less complex, and solitude will not be solitude, nor poverty poverty, nor weakness weakness."

75 Thoreau often used "wood-thrush" to include all thrushes, but here, given its appearance long before the beginning of May, he is referring to the hermit thrush (*Hylocichla guttata*).

76 Eastern North American bird that searches barns and sheds for a site for its nest.

77 Showers of yellow pollen, resembling sulfur in appearance, often carried a great distance by the wind from the pine forests.

78 Quoted from Calidas (sometimes Kalidasa, 5th-century Hindu poet and dramatist), *Sacontala, or The Fatal Ring,* translated by Sir William Jones in 1789, speech of Dushmanta, emperor of India, in act 7: "I see with equal amazement both the pious and their awful retreat.—It becomes, indeed, pure spirits to feed on balmy air in a forest blooming with trees of life; to bathe in rills dyed yellow with the golden dust of the lotos, and to fortify their virtues in the mysterious bath; to meditate in caves, the pebbles of which are unblemished gems; and to restrain their passions, even though nymphs of exquisite beauty frolick around them: in this grove alone is attained the summit of true piety, to which other hermits in vain aspire." Thoreau also quoted from *Sacontala* in *A Week on the Concord and Merrimack Rivers* [W 1:183].

79 It was hardly similar in that during Thoreau's second year he spent his famous night in jail, journeyed to Katahdin in Maine, built a summerhouse for Emerson with the help of Bronson Alcott, and lost his beans, tomatoes, squash, corn, and potatoes to a late frost on 12 June. As he has done elsewhere, Thoreau makes the sentence here stand as a reminder that he was condensing the two-year experience into one for literary purposes.

das' drama of Sacontala, we read of "rills dyed yellow with the golden dust of the lotus."[78] And so the seasons went rolling on into summer, as one rambles into higher and higher grass.

Thus was my first year's life in the woods completed; and the second year was similar to it.[79] I finally left Walden September 6th, 1847.

Conclusion

To the sick the doctors wisely recommend a change of air and scenery. Thank Heaven, here is not all the world. The buck-eye[1] does not grow in New England, and the mocking-bird[2] is rarely heard here. The wild-goose is more of a cosmopolite than we; he breaks his fast in Canada, takes a luncheon in the Ohio, and plumes himself for the night in a southern bayou. Even the bison, to some extent, keeps pace with the seasons, cropping the pastures of the Colorado only till a greener and sweeter grass awaits him by the Yellowstone. Yet we think that if rail-fences are pulled down, and stone-walls piled up on our farms,[3] bounds are henceforth set to our lives and our fates decided. If you are chosen town-clerk, forsooth, you cannot go to Tierra del Fuego this summer: but you may go to the land of infernal fire[4] nevertheless. The universe is wider than our views of it.

Yet we should oftener look over the tafferel[5] of our craft, like curious passengers, and not make the voyage like stupid sailors picking oakum. The other side of the globe is but the home of our correspondent. Our voyaging is only great-circle sailing,[6] and the doctors prescribe for diseases of the skin merely.[7] One hastens to Southern Africa to chase the giraffe; but surely that is not the game he would be after. How long, pray, would a man hunt giraffes if he could? Snipes and woodcocks[8] also may af-

1 Thoreau was most likely thinking specifically of the species of buckeye of the Midwest that gave Ohio its nickname of "the Buckeye State," although technically it refers to any of various deciduous trees or shrubs of the genus *Aesculus*, including the horse chestnut, which grew in Concord.

2 Thoreau's journal of 18 August 1854 recorded his only reference to the mockingbird, which was rare in his day, and this was only a possible sighting: "I think I saw a mockingbird on a black cherry near Pedrick's. Size of and like a catbird; bluish-black side-head, a white spot on closed wings, lighter breast and beneath; but he flew before I had fairly adjusted my glasses" [J 6:453].

3 Stone walls would form a more permanent barrier than a wood rail fence.

4 Hell.

5 Taffrail: the guardrail around the stern of a ship.

6 Navigation along the arc of any great circle, the shortest distance between two points, on the earth's surface, a great circle being formed on the surface of a sphere by a plane that passes through the center of the sphere. Thoreau is bemoaning the fact that for most people the shortest distance between two points is the best.

7 Not holistically or deeply, but on the surface only.

8 Two common game birds.

ford rare[9] sport; but I trust it would be nobler game to shoot one's self. — [10]

> "Direct your eye sight inward, and you'll find
> A thousand regions in your mind
> Yet undiscovered. Travel them, and be
> Expert in home-cosmography."[11]

What does Africa,—what does the West stand for?[12] Is not our own interior white on the chart? black though it may prove, like the coast, when discovered.[13] Is it the source of the Nile, or the Niger, or the Mississippi, or a North-West Passage[14] around this continent, that we would find? Are these the problems which most concern mankind? Is Franklin the only man who is lost, that his wife should be so earnest to find him?[15] Does Mr. Grinnell[16] know where he himself is? Be rather the Mungo Park,[17] the Lewis and Clarke[18] and Frobisher,[19] of your own streams and oceans; explore your own higher latitudes,—with shiploads of preserved meats to support you, if they be necessary; and pile the empty cans sky-high for a sign.[20] Were preserved meats invented to preserve meat merely?[21] Nay, be a Columbus[22] to whole new continents and worlds within you,[23] opening new channels, not of trade, but of thought. Every man is the lord of a realm beside which the earthly empire of the Czar is but a petty state,[24] a hummock left by the ice.[25] Yet some can be patriotic who have no *self*-respect, and sacrifice the greater to the less.[26] They love the soil which makes their graves, but have no sympathy with the spirit which may still animate their clay. Patriotism is a maggot in their heads. What was the meaning of that South-Sea Exploring Expedition,[27] with all its parade and expense, but an indirect recognition of the fact, that there are continents and seas in the moral world, to which every man is an isthmus or an inlet, yet unexplored by him, but that

---

9 In the sense of unusually excellent, or valuable to a degree seldom found, due not to scarcity but to the bird's natural camouflage.

10 Pun: commit suicide, but also with the meaning of to shoot (i.e., hunt) for one's true self.

11 Quoted from William Habbington's (1605–1664) "To My Honoured Friend *Sir* Ed. P. *Knight*." Thoreau modernized the spelling.

12 In "Walking" Thoreau explained what the West represented for him:

> We go eastward to realize history and study the works of art and literature, retracing the steps of the race; we go westward as into the future, with a spirit of enterprise and adventure. . . .
> The West of which I speak is but another name for the Wild; and what I have been preparing to say is, that in Wildness is the preservation of the World. [W 5:217–18, 224]

In "Life Without Principle," Thoreau made it clear that the West of which he spoke was not a geographical compass point: "Men rush to California and Australia as if the true gold were to be found in that direction; but that is to go to the very opposite extreme to where it lies. They go prospecting farther and farther away from the true lead, and are most unfortunate when they think themselves most successful. Is not our *native* soil auriferous?" [W 4:466].

13 Coastal charts in the 19th century, the primary function of which was to map the coast, often left the unexplored interior blank, or white. For Africa in particular, the coast was "black" not only in that it had been explored but also in relation to the skin color of the inhabitants.

14 Symbols of the quests for hidden sources. The Nile and the Niger are rivers in Africa; the Mississippi, in the United States. The Northwest Passage is an Arctic sea route between the Atlantic and Pacific oceans.

15 Sir John Franklin (1786–1847), an English explorer last seen in Baffin Bay, disappeared in 1847 in the Arctic attempting to find the Northwest Passage. His remains were discovered in 1859. In the late 1840s and early 1850s the *Boston Evening Transcript* contained several items describing the efforts of Lady Franklin to enlist ships to search for her husband. Sir John's fate and his wife's grief inspired several ballads, such as "Lady Franklin's Lament," of which there were many variations, and George Boker's (1823–1890) "A Ballad of Sir John Franklin" published in the May 1850 issue of *Sartain's Union Magazine.*

16 Henry Grinnell (1799–1874), New York merchant, who financed two searches for Franklin, in 1850 and 1853.

17 Scottish explorer (1771–1806) who traced the course of the Niger River and published *Travels in the Interior of Africa* in 1799. Park was drowned on his second expedition to the Niger (1805–6) in a conflict with natives at Boussa.

18 Meriwether Lewis (1774–1809) and William Clark, sometimes Clarke (1770–1838), explored the territory acquired in the Louisiana Purchase of 1803 and discovered a land route to the Pacific Ocean.

19 Martin Frobisher (1535–1594), English navigator and explorer who made three attempts to find the Northwest Passage.

20 Elisha Kent Kane (1822–1857) discovered Franklin's winter encampment and a pile of more than 600 empty cans that had held preserved meat. Kane had been lecturing about his discoveries since his return in 1851, accounts of which were widely published. Thoreau's first mention of the cans appeared in Version 6, written between the end of 1853 and the beginning of 1854. Although Kane's book was officially issued in March 1854 after a warehouse fire delayed publication, it could have been Thoreau's source as several copies of it had already been disseminated in 1853. The first published notice of the cans appeared in the *Illustrated London News* for 4 October 1851.

21 Pun: preserving meat for food, and preserving the life of the meat (i.e., the human body). Equating the human body with meat has many literary antecedents, as in John 6:55: "For my flesh is meat indeed" and *Romeo and Juliet:* "They have made worms' meat of me."

22 Christopher Columbus (1451–1506), Genoan explorer sailing under the Spanish flag who "discovered" the New World in 1492.

23 Possible echo of Byron's *Don Juan* 14:101:

> The new world would be nothing to the old,
> If some Columbus of the moral seas
> Would show mankind their souls' antipodes.

24 The Russian empire, ruled by the czar, was the largest body of land under one dominion.

25 A small hill or knoll moved by ice. Thoreau recorded several observations of this phenomenon in his journals. On 1 March 1855 he "saw some very large pieces of meadow lifted up and carried off at mouth of G. M. Barrett's Bay. One measured seventy-four by twenty-seven feet" [J 7:222–23].

26 Sacrifice the self (the greater) to politics (the lesser), or, as in the next line, sacrifice the spirit to the soil.

27 Expedition led by Lieutenant Charles Wilkes (1798–1877) of the U.S. Navy to explore the South Pacific and Antarctic Ocean in 1838–42, called variantly the South Sea Exploring Expedition, the Wilkes Expedition, and the United States Exploring Expedition. His five-volume *Narrative of the United States Exploring Expedition* appeared in 1844.

28 From the Roman poet Claudian's (ca. 370–ca. 404) *Carmina Minores* 20: "De Sene Veronensi." Thoreau wrote in his journal of 10 May 1841: "A good warning to the restless tourists of these days is contained in the last verses of Claudian's 'Old Man of Verona'" [J 1:259–60]. In "A Yankee in Canada" he was reminded "of those lines in Claudian's 'Old Man of Verona,' about getting out of the gate being the greater part of a journey" [W 5:26].

29 Thoreau substituted, in his translation, Australians for Iberians, making it more relevant to his readers as representative of a distant land.

30 Island off the coast of eastern Africa. Thoreau read about Zanzibar in Charles Pickering's (1805–1878) *The Races of Man* (London, 1851), which he was reading in August and September 1853, although this does not contain any reference to counting cats.

31 John Cleves Symmes (1779–1829), a retired army captain, tried from 1818 to his death in 1829 to raise money for an expedition to prove his theory that the earth was hollow. His pamphlet, "The Symmes Theory of Concentric Spheres, demonstrating that the earth is hollow, habitable, and widely open about the poles," published in 1818, stated: "To all the World I declare the earth is hollow and habitable within, containing a number of solid, concentric spheres, one within the other, and that it is open at the poles twelve or sixteen degrees. I pledge my life in support of this truth, and am ready to explore the hollow if the world will support and aid me in this undertaking." The *Boston Evening Transcript* of 14 October 1851 carried an account suggesting that the missing Sir John Franklin's ship may have been sucked into the opening Symmes proposed.

32 Both names refer to the north shore of the Gulf of Guinea in western Africa, famed as a source of gold and slaves from the 16th to the 18th centuries.

33 The direct way to India from America, chronologically in reverse through recorded history, from

it is easier to sail many thousand miles through cold and storm and cannibals, in a government ship, with five hundred men and boys to assist one, than it is to explore the private sea, the Atlantic and Pacific Ocean of one's being alone. —

> "Erret, et extremos alter scrutetur Iberos.
> Plus habet hic vitæ, plus habet ille viæ." [28]

Let them wander and scrutinize the outlandish Australians.[29]
I have more of God, they more of the road.

It is not worth the while to go round the world to count the cats in Zanzibar.[30] Yet do this even till you can do better, and you may perhaps find some "Symmes' Hole"[31] by which to get at the inside at last. England and France, Spain and Portugal, Gold Coast and Slave Coast,[32] all front on this private sea; but no bark from them has ventured out of sight of land, though it is without doubt the direct way to India.[33] If you would learn to speak all tongues and conform to the customs of all nations, if you would travel farther than all travellers, be naturalized in all climes, and cause the Sphinx to dash her head against a stone,[34] even obey the precept of the old philosopher, and Explore thyself.[35] Herein are demanded the eye and the nerve. Only the defeated and deserters go to the wars, cowards that run away and enlist.[36] Start now on that farthest western way,[37] which does not pause at the Mississippi or the Pacific, nor conduct toward a worn-out China or Japan,[38] but leads on direct a tangent to this sphere, summer and winter, day and night, sun down, moon down, and at last earth down too.

It is said that Mirabeau[39] took to highway robbery "to ascertain what degree of resolution was necessary in order to place one's self in formal opposition to the most sacred laws of society."[40] He declared that "a soldier who fights in the ranks does not require half so much courage as a foot-pad,"[41] — "that honor and religion have never stood[42] in the way of a well-considered and a firm resolve." This was manly, as the world goes; and yet it was idle, if not desperate. A saner man would have found himself often enough "in formal opposition" to what are deemed "the most sacred laws of society," through obedience to yet more sacred laws, and so have tested his resolution without going out of his way. It is not for a man to put himself in such an attitude to society, but to maintain himself in whatever attitude he find himself through obedience to the laws of his being, which will never be one of opposition to a just government, if he should chance to meet with such.[43]

I left the woods for as good a reason as I went there.[44] Perhaps it seemed to me that I had several more lives to live, and could not spare any more time for that one. It is remarkable how easily and insensibly we fall into a particular route, and make a beaten track for ourselves. I had not lived there a week before my feet wore a path from my door to the pond-side; and though it is five or six years since I trod it, it is still quite distinct. It is true, I fear that others may have fallen into it, and so helped to keep it open. The surface of the earth is soft and impressible by the feet of men; and so with the paths which the mind travels. How worn and dusty, then, must be the highways of the world, how deep the ruts of tradition and conformity! I did not wish to take a cabin passage,[45] but rather to go before the mast[46] and on the deck of the world, for there I could best see the moonlight amid the mountains.[47] I do not wish to go below now.[48]

I learned this, at least, by my experiment; that if one advances confidently in the direction of his dreams, and endeavors to live the life which he has imagined, he will

one of the most modern civilizations to one of the most ancient, would be through the civilizations of Europe and Africa. India also represented to Thoreau a place where much of the external was stripped away to get at the "inside at last." In "The Bean-Field" he associated India with contemplation.

34 In Greek mythology, a monster with the body and paws of a lion, the wings of an eagle, a serpent's tail, and the head and breasts of a woman. The Sphinx destroyed anyone who failed to guess her riddle. Oedipus finally solved the riddle, and the Sphinx killed herself by dashing her head against a rock. After explicating Emerson's poem, "The Sphinx," in his journal, Thoreau wrote: "When some Œdipus has solved one of her enigmas, she will go dash her head against a rock" [J 1:237].

35 Thoreau is probably referring to Socrates (469–399 B.C.E.) as the "old philosopher," one of many to whom this dictum, "Gnothi se auton" (Know thyself), has been attributed, although its origin is unknown. It is found chiseled over the portals of the ancient Greek temple of Apollo at Delphi. *Demosthenes* 3 in Plutarch's *Lives,* which Thoreau is known to have read, contains the line: "If the 'Know thyself' of the oracle were an easy thing for every man, it would not be held to be a divine injunction." Emerson, in "The American Scholar," wrote, "And, in fine, the ancient precept, 'Know thyself,' and the modern precept, 'Study nature,' become at last one maxim."

36 Cowards in that they are not brave enough to explore themselves. As Thoreau wrote earlier in this chapter, "Yet some can be patriotic who have no *self*-respect, and sacrifice the greater to the less."

37 Thoreau was writing *Walden* at the height of the migration to the American West.

38 Worn-out in that their cultures seemed ancient and static.

39 Honoré-Gabriel Victor Riqueti, Comte de Mirabeau (1749–1791), French revolutionary statesman.

Thoreau read about Mirabeau in an 1851 *Harper's New Monthly* article, "Mirabeau, An Anecdote of His Private Life," from which he copied several brief excerpts into his journal of 21 July 1851.

40 As described in "Mirabeau, An Anecdote of His Private Life," after being confronted by his brother-in-law about a robbery, Mirabeau claimed: "Do you imagine that it was for the sake of his money that I stopped this poor country squire? I wished to put him to the proof, and to put myself to the proof. I wished to ascertain what degree of resolution was necessary in order to place one's self in formal opposition to the most sacred laws of society: the trial was a dangerous one; but I have made it several times. I am satisfied with myself." The point of the exercise, Mirabeau explained in his defense, was to follow his reason even if it led to conflict with society or laws.

41 Robber on foot.

42 Slightly variant from the original: "about honor—about religion; but these have never stood."

43 On the possibility of a government acting justly, Thoreau wrote in "Civil Disobedience": "I please myself with imagining a State at last which can afford to be just to all men, and to treat the individual with respect as a neighbor; which even would not think it inconsistent with its own repose if a few were to live aloof from it, not meddling with it, nor embraced by it, who fulfilled all the duties of neighbors and fellow-men" [W 4:387].

44 Emerson was leaving for a lecture tour in Europe the first week in October, and his wife, Lidian, asked Thoreau to stay with the family while her husband was away. Emerson wrote to his brother William on 30 August 1847: "Lidian has invited Henry Thoreau to spend the winter here." A week later, on 6 September, Thoreau moved into the Emersons' household. On 22 January 1852, he wrote in his journal:

> But why I changed? why I left the woods? I do not think that I can tell. I have often wished myself back. I do not know any better how I

ever came to go there. Perhaps it is none of my business, even if it is yours. Perhaps I wanted a change. There was a little stagnation, it may be. About 2 o'clock in the afternoon the world's axle creaked as if it needed greasing, as if the oxen labored with the wain and could hardly get their load over the ridge of the day. Perhaps if I lived there much longer, I might live there forever. One would think twice before he accepted heaven on such terms. [J 3:214–15]

45 Although Thoreau rarely used the word "cabin" to describe his house, it is likely that he is punning on the term "cabin passage," referring to passage on a ship in a cabin as opposed to steerage or as a sailor, and his passage through life in his Walden cabin.

46 Common sailors slept before the mast, that is, between the mast and the bow.

47 Ellery Channing noted in his copy of *Walden* that this refers to an 1844 boat excursion he and Thoreau took together up the Hudson, where Thoreau spent the night in the bow of the boat under bright moonlight.

48 Below deck on a ship, to a cabin.

meet with a success unexpected in common hours. He will put some things behind, will pass an invisible boundary; new, universal, and more liberal laws will begin to establish themselves around and within him; or the old laws be expanded, and interpreted in his favor in a more liberal sense, and he will live with the license of a higher order of beings. In proportion as he simplifies his life, the laws of the universe will appear less complex, and solitude will not be solitude, nor poverty poverty, nor weakness weakness. If you have built castles in the air, your work need not be lost; that is where they should be. Now put the foundations under them.[49]

It is a ridiculous demand which England and America make, that you shall speak so that they can understand you. Neither men nor toad-stools grow so. As if that were important, and there were not enough to understand you without them. As if Nature could support but one order of understandings, could not sustain birds as well as quadrupeds, flying as well as creeping things, and *hush* and *who*,[50] which Bright can understand, were the best English. As if there were safety in stupidity alone. I fear chiefly lest my expression may not be *extra- vagant*[51] enough, may not wander far enough beyond the narrow limits of my daily experience, so as to be adequate to the truth of which I have been convinced. *Extra vagance!* it depends on how you are yarded.[52] The migrating buffalo, which seeks new pastures in another latitude, is not extravagant like the cow which kicks over the pail, leaps the cow-yard fence, and runs after her calf, in milking time. I desire to speak somewhere *without* bounds;[53] like a man in a waking moment, to men in their waking moments;[54] for I am convinced that I cannot exaggerate enough even to lay the foundation of a true expression.[55] Who that has heard a strain of music feared then lest he should speak extravagantly any more forever? In view of the future or possible, we should live quite laxly and undefined in front,

49 Similar to Thoreau and Alcott's "revising mythology, rounding a fable here and there, and building castles in the air for which earth offered no worthy foundation" in "Former Inhabitants."

50 Commands meaning "go" and "stop," respectively, for an ox.

51 Thoreau split the word to emphasize its Latin roots: *extra* (outside), and *vagari* (to wander). Possibly a reaction to William Ellery Channing's "Likeness to God" in which he wrote: "I exhort you to no extravagance."

52 Enclosed or limited, as in a yard.

53 Possible allusion to Thoreau's earlier statement in "Economy": "but I think that I speak within bounds."

54 Possible echo of Richard Baxter's (1615–1691) *Love Breathing Thanks and Praise:* "I preached as never sure to preach again, / And as a dying man to dying men."

55 Thoreau wrote in his journal of 7 September 1851 that life "is an experience of infinite beauty on which we unfailingly draw, which enables us to exaggerate ever truly" [J 2:469]. He wrote H. G. O. Blake, "I trust that you realize what an exaggerater I am,—that I lay myself out to exaggerate whenever I have an opportunity,—pile Pelion upon Ossa, to reach heaven so. Expect no trivial truth from me, unless I am on the witness-stand. I will come as near to lying as you can drive a coach-and-four" [C 304].

56 Used in both its simple meaning of rendered into another language and that of removed to a higher plane, as in Enoch's translation to Heaven in Hebrews 11:5. In a journal entry on 18 February 1852, Thoreau noted the difference between fact and poetry, finding it "difficult always to preserve the vague distinction which I had in my mind, for the most interesting and beautiful facts are so much more poetry and that is their success. They are *translated* from earth to heaven" [J 3:311].

57 An aromatic gum used as incense. In early Christian tradition, it was one of the three gifts of the Magi, or kings, to the baby Jesus, and thus a symbol of divinity.

58 Thoreau used the term here not as practical sense but in the meaning that came out of the Scottish common sense school of philosophy, in particular Thomas Reid's (1710–1796) *An Inquiry into the Human Mind, on the Principles of Common Sense*, which emphasized common sense as natural judgment from a set of innate principles of conception and belief implanted in the human mind by God. This is the antecedent of the concept of inspiration, of which Emerson wrote in "Self-Reliance": "the essence of genius, of virtue, and of life, which we call Spontaneity or Instinct. We denote this primary wisdom as Intuition. . . . In that deep force, the last fact behind which analysis cannot go, all things find their common origin."

"The wildest dreams of wild men, even," Thoreau wrote in "Walking," "are not the less true, though they may not recommend themselves to the sense which is most common among Englishmen and Americans to-day. It is not every truth that recommends itself to the common sense" [W 5:233]. More concretely, in "Ktaadn" from *The Maine Woods*, three words—solid, actual, common—share equal emphasis: "Talk of mysteries! Think of our life in nature,—daily to be shown matter, to come in contact with it,—rocks, trees, wind on our cheeks! the *solid* earth! the *actual* world! the *common sense!*" [W 3:79].

59 Peace-loving Indian mystic (1440–1518), who

our outlines dim and misty on that side; as our shadows reveal an insensible perspiration toward the sun. The volatile truth of our words should continually betray the inadequacy of the residual statement. Their truth is instantly *translated;*[56] its literal monument alone remains. The words which express our faith and piety are not definite; yet they are significant and fragrant like frankincense[57] to superior natures.

Why level downward to our dullest perception always, and praise that as common sense?[58] The commonest sense is the sense of men asleep, which they express by snoring. Sometimes we are inclined to class those who are once-and-a-half-witted with the half-witted, because we appreciate only a third part of their wit. Some would find fault with the morning-red, if they ever got up early enough. "They pretend," as I hear, "that the verses of Kabir[59] have four different senses; illusion, spirit, intellect, and the exoteric doctrine of the Vedas;"[60] but in this part of the world it is considered a ground for complaint if a man's writings admit of more than one interpretation. While England endeavors to cure the potato-rot,[61] will not any endeavor to cure the brain-rot, which prevails so much more widely and fatally?

I do not suppose that I have attained to obscurity, but I should be proud if no more fatal fault were found with my pages on this score than was found with the Walden ice. Southern customers objected to its blue color, which is the evidence of its purity, as if it were muddy, and preferred the Cambridge ice, which is white, but tastes of weeds.[62] The purity men love is like the mists which envelop the earth, and not like the azure ether beyond.

Some are dinning in our ears that we Americans, and moderns generally, are intellectual dwarfs compared with the ancients, or even the Elizabethan men. But what is that to the purpose? A living dog is better than a dead lion.[63] Shall a man go and hang himself because he belongs to the race of pygmies,[64] and not be the biggest pygmy that he can? Let every one mind his own business, and endeavor to be what he was made.

Why should we be in such desperate haste to succeed, and in such desperate enterprises? If a man does not keep pace with his companions, perhaps it is because he hears a different drummer. Let him step to the music which he hears, however measured or far away. It is not important that he should mature as soon as an apple-tree or an oak. Shall he turn his spring into summer? If the condition of things which we were made for is not yet, what were any reality which we can substitute? We will not be shipwrecked on a vain reality. Shall we with pains erect a heaven of blue glass over ourselves, though when it is done we shall be sure to gaze still at the true ethereal heaven far above, as if the former were not?

There was an artist in the city of Kouroo[65] who was disposed to strive after perfection. One day it came into his mind to make a staff. Having considered that in an imperfect work time is an ingredient, but into a perfect work time does not enter, he said to himself, It shall be perfect in all respects, though I should do nothing else in my life. He proceeded instantly to the forest for wood, being resolved that it should not be made of unsuitable material; and as he searched for and rejected stick after stick, his friends gradually deserted him, for they grew old in their works and died, but he grew not older by a moment. His singleness of purpose and resolution, and his elevated piety, endowed him, without his knowledge, with perennial youth. As he made no compromise with Time, Time kept out of his way, and only sighed at a distance because he could not overcome him. Before he had found a stock in all respects suitable the city of Kouroo was a hoary ruin, and he sat on one of its mounds to

tried to reconcile the religions of the Hindus and Muslims.

60 Thoreau's translation of Garcin de Tassy's *Histoire de la Littérature Hindoui et Hindoustani* 1:279.

61 The potato blight, which had affected the potato crop in England in 1845, devastated Ireland the following year.

62 After Frederic Tudor and Nathaniel Jarvis Wyeth, partners in the largest ice-harvesting operation in Massachusetts, had a disagreement in 1840, Wyeth continued to harvest "Cambridge ice" at Fresh Pond, to which he had secured rights, forcing Tudor to go elsewhere. With the railroad's expansion to Concord, Tudor began to harvest "Walden ice," which he could ship directly from Walden to Boston for exporting.

63 Allusion to Ecclesiastes 9:4: "For to him that is joined to all the living there is hope: for a living dog is better than a dead lion."

64 Possible allusion to the statement by the Orphic Poet in Emerson's *Nature:* "Man is the dwarf of himself."

65 An echo of Kuru (alternately Kooroo or Curu), the legendary hero of India, the contests of whose descendants form the subject of the *Mahabharata*. It is generally agreed that the following fable is by Thoreau.

66 An echo of the city name Kandahar, the capital of Afghanistan from 1748 to 1773.

67 Not a star but a period of time, in Hinduism and Buddhism, between the beginning and the end of the world, which is one day for Brahma, equivalent to 4.32 billion human years. Quoting Hugh Murray's (1779–1846) *Historical and Descriptive Account of British India*, Thoreau wrote in his journal in 1842: "4,320,000,000 years says Murray form 'the grand anomalistic period called a calpa, and fantastically assigned as a day of Brahma'" [PJ 1:413]. Thoreau mistakenly wrote the word "fantastically" for Murray's "fancifully."

68 Brahma slept at the end of the day. His nights were equal to his days: 4.32 billion human years. One day-and-night cycle would last for 8.64 billion years.

69 Thoreau expressed a similar idea in the beginning of "Life Without Principle": "I take it for granted, when I am invited to lecture anywhere, — for I have had a little experience in that business, — that there is a desire to hear what *I think* on some subject, though I may be the greatest fool in the country, — and not that I should say pleasant things merely, or such as the audience will assent to; and I resolve, accordingly, that I will give them a strong dose of myself" [W 4:455–56]. Emerson, in "Self-Reliance," explained the consequences of not expressing your own thoughts: "Else, to-morrow a stranger will say with masterly good sense precisely what we have thought and felt all the time, and we shall be forced to take with shame our own opinion from another."

70 Possible allusion to the proverb, traceable to at least the early 18th century, "The tailor that makes not a knot loses a stitch." The antecedents of Thoreau's Tom Hyde story have not been satisfactorily identified. In an October 1849 journal entry containing a variant of the story, Thoreau wrote:

> You Boston folks & Roxbury people
> Will want Tom Hyde to mend your kettle
> [PJ 3:37].

peel the stick. Before he had given it the proper shape the dynasty of the Candahars[66] was at an end, and with the point of the stick he wrote the name of the last of that race in the sand, and then resumed his work. By the time he had smoothed and polished the staff Kalpa[67] was no longer the pole-star; and ere he had put on the ferule and the head adorned with precious stones, Brahma had awoke and slumbered many times.[68] But why do I stay to mention these things? When the finishing stroke was put to his work, it suddenly expanded before the eyes of the astonished artist into the fairest of all the creations of Brahma. He had made a new system in making a staff, a world with full and fair proportions; in which, though the old cities and dynasties had passed away, fairer and more glorious ones had taken their places. And now he saw by the heap of shavings still fresh at his feet, that, for him and his work, the former lapse of time had been an illusion, and that no more time had elapsed than is required for a single scintillation from the brain of Brahma to fall on and inflame the tinder of a mortal brain. The material was pure, and his art was pure; how could the result be other than wonderful?

No face which we can give to a matter will stead us so well at last as the truth. This alone wears well. For the most part, we are not where we are, but in a false position. Through an infirmity of our natures, we suppose a case, and put ourselves into it, and hence are in two cases at the same time, and it is doubly difficult to get out. In sane moments we regard only the facts, the case that is. Say what you have to say, not what you ought.[69] Any truth is better than make-believe. Tom Hyde, the tinker, standing on the gallows, was asked if he had any thing to say. "Tell the tailors," said he, "to remember to make a knot in their thread before they take the first stitch."[70] His companion's prayer is forgotten.

However mean your life is, meet it and live it; do not

shun it and call it hard names. It is not so bad as you are. It looks poorest when you are richest. The fault-finder will find faults even in paradise. Love your life, poor as it is. You may perhaps have some pleasant, thrilling, glorious hours, even in a poor-house. The setting sun is reflected from the windows of the alms-house as brightly as from the rich man's abode; the snow melts before its door as early in the spring. I do not see but a quiet mind may live as contentedly there, and have as cheering thoughts, as in a palace. The town's poor seem to me often to live the most independent lives of any. May be they are simply great enough to receive without misgiving. Most think that they are above being supported by the town; but it oftener happens that they are not above supporting themselves by dishonest means, which should be more disreputable. Cultivate poverty like a garden herb, like sage. Do not trouble yourself much to get new things, whether clothes or friends. Turn the old; return to them. Things do not change; we change. Sell your clothes and keep your thoughts. God will see that you do not want society. If I were confined to a corner of a garret all my days, like a spider, the world would be just as large to me while I had my thoughts about me. The philosopher said: "From an army of three divisions one can take away its general, and put it in disorder; from the man the most abject and vulgar one cannot take away his thought."[71] Do not seek so anxiously to be developed, to subject yourself to many influences to be played on; it is all dissipation. Humility like darkness reveals the heavenly lights. The shadows of poverty and meanness gather around us, "and lo! creation widens to our view."[72] We are often reminded that if there were bestowed on us the wealth of Crœsus,[73] our aims must still be the same, and our means essentially the same. Moreover, if you are restricted in your range by poverty, if you cannot buy books and newspapers, for instance, you are but confined to the most significant and

71 Thoreau's translation of Confucius, *Analects* 9:25, from the French translation in Pauthier's *Confucius et Mencius* 149.

72 Misquotation of Joseph Blanco White's (1775–1841) sonnet "Night and Death" ("To Night"): "And lo! Creation widened in man's view." Both night and death, according to White, reveal knowledge of a wider universe.

73 King of Lydia (6th century B.C.E.) in western Asia Minor, considered the wealthiest of men.

74 Proverb dating back at least as early as the 15th century: "The nearer the bone, the sweeter the flesh." Also in "The Old Marlborough Road," where Thoreau wrote, addressing Elisha Dugan:

> O man of wild habits,
> Partridges and rabbits,
> Who has no cares
> Only to set snares,
> Who liv'st all alone,
> Close to the bone,
> And where life is sweetest
> Constantly eatest. [CP 17]

75 A type of bronze consisting of 60–85 percent copper alloyed with tin, used for its sonorous or musical quality.

76 Thoreau often complained about such noise. In "A Winter Walk" he "shut out the gadding town" [W 5:168], and in "Natural History of Massachusetts" he wrote of "this din of religion, literature, and philosophy, which is heard in pulpits, lyceums, and parlors" [W 5:106]. In his journal he wrote of his generation's "hip-hip-hurrah and mutual-admiration-society style" [J 2:170] and that "men are constantly dinging in my ears their fair theories and plausible solutions of the universe" [J 1:54]. In his poem "Cliffs," Thoreau wrote that "Tongues were provided / But to vex the ear with superficial thoughts" [CP 104].

77 Echo of Lucian (ca. 170) as quoted by Erasmus in his *Adagia* 1.7.11: "An ape is still an ape even thought he wears an insignia of gold."

78 Possibly Robert Augustus Toombs (1810–1885), a vehement defender of slavery who served as congressman from Georgia (1846–52) and U.S. senator (1853–61), attracting much public attention in the North.

79 Probably Daniel Webster, who is mentioned by name a few lines later.

80 An officer of the Mamelukes, a military caste in Egypt. In 1811, Mehemet Ali (Muhammad Ali Pasha), viceroy of Egypt, ordered the massacre of the Mamelukes, but a tradition exists that one

vital experiences; you are compelled to deal with the material which yields the most sugar and the most starch. It is life near the bone where it is sweetest.[74] You are defended from being a trifler. No man loses ever on a lower level by magnanimity on a higher. Superfluous wealth can buy superfluities only. Money is not required to buy one necessary of the soul.

I live in the angle of a leaden wall, into whose composition was poured a little alloy of bell metal.[75] Often, in the repose of my mid-day, there reaches my ears a confused *tintinnabulum* from without. It is the noise of my contemporaries.[76] My neighbors tell me of their adventures with famous gentlemen and ladies, what notabilities they met at the dinner-table; but I am no more interested in such things than in the contents of the Daily Times. The interest and the conversation are about costume and manners chiefly; but a goose is a goose still, dress it as you will.[77] They tell me of California and Texas, of England and the Indies, of the Hon. Mr. —— of Georgia[78] or of Massachusetts,[79] all transient and fleeting phenomena, till I am ready to leap from their court-yard like the Mameluke bey.[80] I delight to come to my bearings,—not walk in procession with pomp and parade, in a conspicuous place, but to walk even with the Builder of the universe,[81] if I may,—not to live in this restless, nervous, bustling, trivial Nineteenth Century, but stand or sit thoughtfully while it goes by. What are men celebrating? They are all on a committee of arrangements, and hourly expect a speech from somebody. God is only the president of the day,[82] and Webster is his orator. I love to weigh, to settle, to gravitate toward that which most strongly and rightfully attracts me;—not hang by the beam of the scale and try to weigh less,—not suppose a case, but take the case that is; to travel the only path I can, and that on which no power can resist me. It affords me no satisfaction to commence to spring an arch[83] before I have got a solid foundation. Let us not play at kittlybenders.[84] There is a solid bottom everywhere. We read that the traveller asked the boy if the swamp before him had a hard bottom. The boy replied that it had. But presently the traveller's horse sank in up to the girths, and he observed to the boy, "I thought you said that this bog had a hard bottom." "So it has," answered the latter, "but you have not got half way to it yet."[85] So it is with the bogs and quicksands of society; but he is an old boy that knows it. Only what is thought said or done at a certain rare coincidence is good. I would not be one of those who will foolishly drive a nail into mere lath and plastering; such a deed would keep me awake nights. Give me a hammer, and let me feel for the furring. Do not depend on the putty. Drive a nail home and clinch it so faithfully that you can wake up in the night and think of your work with satisfaction,—a work at which you would not be ashamed to invoke the Muse.[86] So will help you God,[87] and so only. Every nail driven should be as another rivet in the machine of the universe, you carrying on the work.

Rather than love, than money, than fame, give me truth. I sat at a table where were rich food and wine in abundance, and obsequious attendance, but sincerity and truth[88] were not; and I went away hungry from the inhospitable board.[89] The hospitality was as cold as the ices.[90] I thought that there was no need of ice to freeze them. They talked to me of the age of the wine and the fame of the vintage; but I thought of an older, a newer, and purer wine, of a more glorious vintage, which they had not got, and could not buy. The style, the house and grounds and "entertainment" pass for nothing with me. I called on the king, but he made me wait in his hall, and conducted like a man incapacitated for hospitality. There was a man in my neighborhood who lived in a hollow tree.[91] His manners were truly regal. I should have done better had I called on him.

man escaped by leaping, mounted on his horse, from a wall.

81 Epithet associated with God as the builder, or master builder, used particularly in Freemasonry, in the Sufi "Prayer for the Universel" ("O Thou, Who art the Maker, Molder, and Builder of the universe"), and in the Gnostic concept, developed from Plato's *Timaeus*, of the demiurge as the builder of the universe. Thoreau here describes himself as someone who can walk even with (equal to) God, which all people are capable of doing, as at the end of this paragraph: "you carrying on the work."

82 Master of ceremonies.

83 Architectural term for building an arch.

84 Thin or weak ice that bends when one goes across it, or the game in which children try to run or skate across thin ice without breaking it. The term has many variants, such as "kiddly-benders," "kettle-benders," and "tickly-benders." Thoreau used it in his journal of 4 February 1857: "Sometimes when, in conversation or a lecture, I have been grasping at, or even standing and reclining upon, the serene and everlasting truths that underlie and support our vacillating life, I have seen my auditors standing on their *terra firma*, the quaking earth, crowded together on their Lisbon Quay, and compassionately or timidly watching my motions as if they were the antics of a rope-dancer or mountebank pretending to walk on air; or here and there one creeping out upon an overhanging but cracking bough, unwilling to drop to the adamantine floor beneath, or perchance even venturing out a step or two, as if it were a dangerous kittly-bender, timorously sounding as he goes" [J 9:237–38].

85 Thoreau's source may have been the 22 November 1828 issue of the Concord *Yeoman's Gazette*, which contained the following:

A young fellow, riding down a steep hill, and doubting the foot of it was boggish, called out to a clown that was ditching, and asked if it was hard at the bottom?—"Aye," answered the countryman, "it is hard enough at the bottom I'll warrant you." But in a half dozen steps, the horse sunk up to the saddle skirts, which made the young gallant whip, spur, curse and sware. "Why thou lying rascal?" said he to the clown, "didst thou not tell me it was hard at the bottom?" "Aye," replied the other, "but you are not half way to the bottom yet."

86 In Greek mythology, one of the nine goddesses of the arts. Epic poems often opened with an invocation of the Muse.

87 The interrogatory part of an oath, the answer to which is "So help me God."

88 Allusion to 1 Corinthians 5:7–8: "For even Christ our passover is sacrificed for us: Therefore let us keep the feast, not with the old leaven, neither with the leaven of malice and wickedness; but with the unleavened bread of sincerity and truth."

89 Probably the Emerson household, at which he was a regular guest, and where he lived from April 1841 to May 1843, and again from September 1847 through July 1848. There are several references in Emerson's journal about drinking wine, such as: "Wine is properly drunk as a salutation; it is a liquid compliment." This passage was added in *Walden* Version 4 (ca. 1852), when Thoreau was feeling disillusioned with Emerson. On 31 January 1852 he wrote in his journal that Emerson "is too grand for me. He belongs to the nobility and wears their cloak and manners. . . . I should value E.'s praise more, which is always so discriminating, if there were not some alloy of patronage and hence of flattery about [it]" [J 3:256]. Emerson, in his 1853 journal, took the opposite course: "H.T. sturdily pushes his economy into houses & thinks it the false mark of the gentleman that he is to pay much for his food. He ought to pay little for his food."

90 Frozen confections of sweetened fruit juice or sweetened and flavored cream, milk, or custard.

91 Although Thoreau made a similar statement in his journal—"My neighbor inhabits a hollow sycamore, and I a beech tree" [J 1:133]—and also

How long shall we sit in our porticoes practising idle and musty virtues, which any work would make impertinent? As if one were to begin the day with long-suffering, and hire a man to hoe his potatoes; and in the afternoon go forth to practise Christian meekness and charity with goodness aforethought![92] Consider the China pride and stagnant self-complacency of mankind.[93] This generation reclines a little to congratulate itself on being the last of an illustrious line; and in Boston and London and Paris and Rome, thinking of its long descent, it speaks of its progress in art and science and literature with satisfaction. There are the Records of the Philosophical Societies,[94] and the public Eulogies of *Great Men!*[95] It is the good Adam contemplating his own virtue. "Yes, we have done great deeds, and sung divine songs, which shall never die"[96]—that is, as long as *we* can remember them. The learned societies and great men of Assyria,[97]—where are they?[98] What youthful philosophers and experimentalists we are! There is not one of my readers who has yet lived a whole human life. These may be but the spring months in the life of the race. If we have had the seven-years' itch,[99] we have not seen the seventeen-year locust[100] yet in Concord. We are acquainted with a mere pellicle[101] of the globe on which we live. Most have not delved six feet beneath the surface, nor leaped as many above it. We know not where we are.[102] Beside, we are sound asleep nearly half our time. Yet we esteem ourselves wise, and have an established order on the surface. Truly, we are deep thinkers, we are ambitious spirits! As I stand over the insect crawling amid the pine needles on the forest floor, and endeavoring to conceal itself from my sight, and ask myself why it will cherish those humble thoughts, and hide its head from me who might perhaps be its benefactor, and impart to its race some cheering information, I am reminded of the greater Benefactor and Intelligence that stands over me the human insect.

referred to the hollow tree as a residence in "Brute Neighbors" and "Spring," it is not known whether there was a local Concordian he had in mind. Emerson, in a December 1841 journal entry, likewise wrote, although in language that seems less literal: "Seemed to me that I had the keeping of a secret too great to be confided to one man[,] that a divine man dwelt near me in a hollow tree."

92 Reversal of the term "malice aforethought." In the Sermon on the Mount (Matthew 5:5), Jesus extolled meekness as a virtue: "Blessed are the meek; for they shall inherit the earth."

93 The Chinese empire was thought in Thoreau's day to be based on pride in its own perception of its self-sufficiency and its position as a great power.

94 The American Philosophical Society was founded in 1743, and its *Proceedings* were published quarterly since 1838, although Thoreau may have meant this in a general sense.

95 Possible reference to "Uses of Great Men," Emerson's introductory essay to *Representative Men*.

96 Unidentified allusion.

97 Ancient empire in western Asia.

98 Literal translation of the opening words of a type of medieval Latin poem beginning "Ubi sunt." The theme was taken up in several Old and Middle English works, such as *Beowulf* and "The Wanderer," and most prominently in the 14th-century lyric beginning, "Where beth they, beforen us weren."

99 Scabies, contagious and extremely itchy skin irritation caused by a mite.

100 Thoreau learned of this species of cicada in Staten Island in 1843. He wrote to his mother on 7 July 1843: "Pray have you the Seventeen year locust in Concord? The air here is filled with their din. They come out of the ground at first in an imperfect state, and crawling up the shrubs and plants, the perfect insect bursts out through the bark. They are doing great damage to the fruit and forest trees. . . . They bore every twig of last year's growth in order to deposit their eggs in it. In a few weeks the eggs will be hatched, and the worms fall to the ground and enter it—and in 1860 make their appearance again" [C 121–22]. The locust was known in other areas of Massachusetts, though not in Concord.

101 Skin.

102 Possible answer to Emerson's query opening "Experience": "Where do we find ourselves?"

103 Muskrat nests, or dens, are built with an upper chamber above water level and an entrance below. In extremely high water during spring freshets, muskrats, particularly the young, could drown inside their nest.

104 Thoreau would have known the story from Timothy Dwight's *Travels in New England and New York* (New Haven, 1821), and John Warner Barber's *Historical Collections,* where it began: "In 1806, a strong and beautiful *bug* eat out of a table made from an apple-tree, which grew on the farm of Maj. Gen. Putnam, in Brooklyn, Con[necticut]." It went on to relate essentially the same tale Thoreau tells here, giving specific years and dates provided by Putnam's son, the owner of the table.

105 Between the inner bark and the hard wood, the white and softer part of the wood of a living tree.

There is an incessant influx of novelty into the world, and yet we tolerate incredible dulness. I need only suggest what kind of sermons are still listened to in the most enlightened countries. There are such words as joy and sorrow, but they are only the burden of a psalm, sung with a nasal twang, while we believe in the ordinary and mean. We think that we can change our clothes only. It is said that the British Empire is very large and respectable, and that the United States are a first-rate power. We do not believe that a tide rises and falls behind every man which can float the British Empire like a chip, if he should ever harbor it in his mind. Who knows what sort of seventeen-year locust will next come out of the ground? The government of the world I live in was not framed, like that of Britain, in after-dinner conversations over the wine.

The life in us is like the water in the river. It may rise this year higher than man has ever known it, and flood the parched uplands; even this may be the eventful year, which will drown out all our muskrats.[103] It was not always dry land where we dwell. I see far inland the banks which the stream anciently washed, before science began to record its freshets. Every one has heard the story which has gone the rounds of New England, of a strong and beautiful bug which came out of the dry leaf of an old table of apple-tree wood, which had stood in a farmer's kitchen for sixty years, first in Connecticut, and afterward in Massachusetts,—from an egg deposited in the living tree many years earlier still, as appeared by counting the annual layers beyond it; which was heard gnawing out for several weeks, hatched perchance by the heat of an urn.[104] Who does not feel his faith in a resurrection and immortality strengthened by hearing of this? Who knows what beautiful and winged life, whose egg has been buried for ages under many concentric layers of woodenness in the dead dry life of society, deposited at first in the alburnum[105] of the green and living tree, which has been gradually converted into the semblance of its well-seasoned tomb,—heard perchance gnawing out now for years by the astonished family of man, as they sat round the festive board,—may unexpectedly come forth from amidst society's most trivial and handselled furniture, to enjoy its perfect summer life at last!

I do not say that John[106] or Jonathan will realize all this; but such is the character of that morrow which mere lapse of time can never make to dawn. The light which puts out our eyes is darkness to us.[107] Only that day dawns to which we are awake.[108] There is more day to dawn. The sun is but a morning star.[109]

THE END.

106 John Bull.

107 There are many antecedents to the concept of being blinded by the light, as in Luke 11:35: "Take heed therefore that the light which is in thee be not darkness."

108 One must be awake to the possibilities in order to perceive them. In "Autumnal Tints" Thoreau wrote: "We cannot see anything until we are possessed with the idea of it, take it into our heads,—and then we can hardly see anything else" [W 5:286]. And in his journal: "How much more game he will see who carries a gun, *i.e.* who goes to see it! Though you roam the woods all your days, you never will see by chance what he sees who goes on purpose to see it. One gets his living by shooting woodcocks; most never see one in their lives" [J 8:192]. A similar idea was expressed in John Donne's *Devotions upon Emergent Occasions* Devotion 17: "The bell doth toll for him that thinkes it doth."

109 There are several literary antecedents, any one of which may have helped Thoreau to realize the symbolic potential of the morning star. Emerson wrote in "Politics": "We think our civilization near its meridian, but we are yet only at the cockcrowing and the morning star." The final images of dawn, along with the opening motto on the title page about bragging like chanticleer, emphasize that *Walden* was written as a wake-up call to his neighbors.

Bibliography

For as murder will out so will a man's reading. — Thoreau in his journal, 9 November 1851

Æsthetic Papers. Edited by Elizabeth P. Peabody. Boston: The Editor; New York: G. P. Putnam, 1849.

Albee, John. *Remembrances of Emerson.* New York: Cooke, 1903.

Alcott, Amos Bronson. *The Journals of Bronson Alcott.* Selected and edited by Odell Shepard. Boston: Little, Brown, 1938.

———. *The Letters of A. Bronson Alcott.* Edited by Richard L. Herrnstadt. Ames: Iowa State University Press, 1969.

Ammer, Christine. *The American Heritage Dictionary of Idioms.* Boston: Houghton Mifflin, 1997.

Angelo, Ray. *Botanical Index to the Journal of Henry David Thoreau.* Salt Lake City: Peregrine Smith, 1984.

Audubon, John James. *The Birds of North America, From Drawings Made in the United States and Their Territories.* New York: J. J. Audubon; Philadelphia: J. B. Chevalier, 1840–44.

Barber, John Warner. *Connecticut Historical Collections, Containing a General Collection of Interesting Facts, Traditions, Biographical Sketches, Anecdotes, etc., Relating to the History and Antiquities of Every Town in Connecticut, with Geographical Descriptions.* New Haven: Durrie & Peck & J. W. Barber, [1838].

———. *Historical Collections, Being a General Collection of Interesting Facts, Traditions, Biographical Sketches, Anecdotes, &c., Relating to the History and Antiquities of Every Town in Massachusetts, with Geographical Descriptions.* Worcester: Dorr, Howland, 1841.

Bartram, William. *Travels Through North and South Carolina, Georgia, East and West Florida, The Cherokee Country, the Extensive Territories of the Muscogulges, or Creek Confederacy, and the Country of the Cherokees.* Philadelphia: Printed by James and Johnson, 1791.

Bickman, Martin. *Walden: Volatile Truths.* New York: Twayne, 1992.

Borst, Raymond. *Henry David Thoreau: A Descriptive Bibliography.* Pittsburgh: University of Pittsburgh Press, 1982.

———. *The Thoreau Log: A Documentary Life of Henry David Thoreau, 1817–1862.* New York: G. K. Hall, 1992.

Botkin, Benjamin Albert, ed. *A Treasury of American Folklore: Stories, Ballads, and Traditions of the People.* New York: Crown, 1944.

Brown, Mary Hosmer. *Memories of Concord.* Boston: Four Seas, 1926.

Buel, Jesse. *The Farmer's Companion; or, Essays on the Principles and Practice of American Husbandry.* Boston: Marsh, Capen, Lyon, and Webb, 1840.

Cameron, Kenneth Walter. *The Massachusetts Lyceum During the American Renaissance.* Hartford: Transcendental, 1969.

Canby, Henry Seidel. *Thoreau.* Boston: Houghton Mifflin, 1939.

Carew, Thomas. *The Poems of Thomas Carew with His Masque Coelum Britannicum.* Edited by Rhodes Dunlap. Oxford: Clarendon, 1957.

Carlyle, Thomas. *Critical and Miscellaneous Essays.* Boston: James Munroe, 1839.

———. *On Heroes, Hero-Worship, and the Heroic in History.* Notes and introduction by Michael K. Goldberg; text established by Michael K. Goldberg, Joel J. Brattin, and Mark Engel. Berkeley: University of California Press, 1993.

———. *Past and Present.* Boston: Little, Brown, 1843.

———. *Sartor Resartus: The Life and Opinions of Herr Teufelsdröckh in Three Books.* Introduction and notes by Rodger L. Tarr; text established by Mark Engel and Rodger L. Tarr. Berkeley: University of California Press, 2000.

Channing, William Ellery. *The Works of William E. Channing.* Boston: American Unitarian Association, 1901.

Channing, William Ellery II. *The Collected Poems of William Ellery Channing the Younger, 1817–1901.* Facsimile reproductions with an introduction by Walter Harding. Gainesville, Florida: Scholars' Facsimiles & Reprints, 1967.

———. *Thoreau, the Poet-Naturalist: With Memorial Verses.* New edition, enlarged and edited by F. B. Sanborn. Boston: C. E. Goodspeed, 1902.

Christie, John Aldrich. *Thoreau as World Traveler.* New York: Columbia University Press, 1965.

Christy, Arthur. *The Orient in American Transcendentalism: A Study of Emerson, Thoreau, and Alcott.* New York: Columbia University Press, 1932.

Clapper, Ronald E. *The Development of Walden: A Genetic Text.* Ph.D. diss., University of California, Los Angeles, 1967.

Collections of the Massachusetts Historical Society for the Year 1794. Boston: Massachusetts Historical Society, 1794; reprinted by Munroe and Francis, 1810.

Collier, J. Payne. *Old Ballads from Early Printed Copies of the Utmost Rarity.* London: Printed for The Percy Society by C. Richards, 1840.

Commager, Henry Steele. *Theodore Parker.* Boston: Little, Brown, 1936.

Concord, Massachusetts: Births, Marriages, and Deaths, 1635–1850. Concord: Printed by the Town, 1895.

The Concord Freeman: Thoreau Annex. Concord [Mass.]: Concord Freeman; Marlboro, Mass.: Pratt Brothers, 1880.

Conway, Moncure Daniel. *Autobiography: Memories and Experiences.* Boston: Houghton Mifflin, 1904.

Cook, Reginald. *The Concord Saunterer (Including a discussion of the nature mysticism of Thoreau, original letters by Thoreau, and a check list of Thoreau items in the Abernethy Library of Middlebury College compiled by Viola C. White).* Middlebury, Vt.: Middlebury College Press, 1940.

———. *Passage to Walden.* Boston: Houghton Mifflin, 1949.

Cooper, Susan Fenimore. *Rural Hours.* New York: George P. Putnam, 1850.

Critical Essays on Henry David Thoreau's Walden. Edited by Joel Myerson. Boston: G. K. Hall, 1988.

Cummings, Richard O. *The American Ice Harvests: A Historical Study in Technology, 1800–1918.* Berkeley: University of California Press, 1949.

Curtis, George William. *Early Letters of George Wm. Curtis to John S. Dwight: Brook Farm and Concord.* Edited by George Willis Cooke. New York: Harper and Brothers, 1898.

Darwin, Charles. *Journal of Researches into the Natural History and Geology of the Countries Visited During the Voyage of H.M.S. Beagle Round the World, Under the Command of Capt. Fitz Roy, R.N.* New York: Harper and Brothers, 1846.

The Dial: A Magazine for Literature, Philosophy and Religion. Boston: Weeks, Jordan, 1840–44; reprinted, New York: Russell and Russell, 1961.

Dykes, Oswald. *English Proverbs.* London: Printed by H. Meere, 1709.

Eidson, John Olin. *Charles Stearns Wheeler: Friend of Emerson.* Athens: University of Georgia Press, 1951.

Emerson, Edward. *The Centennial of the Social Circle in Concord: March 21, 1882.* Cambridge, Mass.: Printed at the Riverside Press, 1882.

———. Edward Emerson to Harry McGraw on 22 October 1920. The Raymond Adams Collection/Thoreau Society Collections at The Thoreau Institute at Walden Woods.

———. *Henry Thoreau as Remembered by a Young Friend.* Boston: Houghton Mifflin, 1917.

———. "Underground Railroad, Concord Station and Division." Typescript, 1915, The Raymond Adams Collection/Thoreau Society Collections at The Thoreau Institute at Walden Woods.

Emerson, George B. *A Report on the Trees and Shrubs Growing Naturally in the Forests of Massachusetts.* Boston: Dutton and Wentworth, 1846.

Emerson, Ralph Waldo. *The Collected Works of Ralph Waldo Emerson.* Cambridge: Harvard University Press, 1971–.

———. *The Complete Works of Ralph Waldo Emerson.* Centenary ed. Boston: Houghton Mifflin, 1903.

———. *The Correspondence of Emerson and Carlyle.* Edited by Joseph Slater. New York: Columbia University Press, 1964.

———. *Early Lectures of Ralph Waldo Emerson.* Edited by Stephen E. Whicher and Robert E. Spiller. Cambridge: Harvard University Press, 1959–72.

———. *The Journals and Miscellaneous Notebooks of Ralph Waldo Emerson.* Edited by William H. Gilman et al. Cambridge: Harvard University Press, 1960–82.

———. *The Letters of Ralph Waldo Emerson.* Edited by Ralph L. Rusk and Eleanor Tilton. New York: Columbia University Press, 1939–95.

———. *Nature; Addresses, and Lectures.* Boston: James Munroe, 1849.

Evelyn, John. *Sylva, or, A Discourse of Forest-Trees and the Propagation of Timber in His Majesties Dominions . . . Terra, a Philosophical Essay of Earth . . . Also, Kalendarium Hortense, or, The Gard'ners Almanac.* London: Printed for John Martyn, printer to the Royal Society, 1679.

———. *Terra: A Philosophical Discourse of Earth.* London, 1729.

Fénelon, François de Salignac de La Mothe. *The Lives and Most Remarkable Maxims of the Antient Philosophers.* London: Printed for B. Barker and R. Francklin, 1726.

Fink, Steven. *Prophet in the Market-Place.* Princeton: Princeton University Press, 1992.

Fleck, Richard. *Henry Thoreau and John Muir Among the Indians.* Hamden, Conn.: Archon, 1985.

Forbes, James D. *Travels Through the Alps of Savoy.* Edinburgh: A. and C. Black, 1843.

Fuller, Margaret. *Summer on the Lakes in 1843.* Introduction by Susan Belasco Smith. Urbana: University of Illinois Press, 1991.

Garcin de Tassy, Joseph Héliodore. *Histoire de la Littérature Hindoui.* Paris: Oriental Translation Committee of Great Britain and Ireland, 1839–47.

Gilpin, William. *Observations on Several Parts of Great Britain.* London, 1808.

———. *Remarks on Forest Scenery and Other Woodland Views, Relative Chiefly to Picturesque Beauty.* 1791.

———. *Three Essays: On Picturesque Beauty; On Picturesque Travel; and on Sketching Landscape.* 1792.

Giraud, Jacob Post. *The Birds of Long Island.* New York: Wiley and Putnam, 1844.

Goethe, Johann Wolfgang von. *Conversations with Goethe in the Last Years of His Life.* Translated from the German of Eckermann by S. M. Fuller. Boston: Hilliard, Gray, 1839.

Gookin, Daniel. *Historical Collections of the Indians in New England.* Boston: Massachusetts Historical Society, 1792.

Greeley, Horace. *Hints Toward Reforms.* New York: Harper and Brothers, 1850.

Greenough, Horatio. *Letters of Horatio Greenough, American Sculptor.* Edited by Nathalia Wright. Madison: University of Wisconsin Press, 1972.

Gross, Robert. *Books and Libraries in Thoreau's Concord: Two Essays.* Worcester: American Antiquarian Society, 1988.

———. "The Great Bean Field Hoax: Thoreau and Agricultural Reformers." *Virginia Quarterly Review,* Summer 1985.

Harding, Walter. *The Days of Henry Thoreau.* Enlarged and corrected ed. New York: Dover, 1982.

Harivansa, ou Histoire de la Famille de Hari, Ouvrage formant un appendice du Mahabharata, et traduit sur l'original Sanscrit. Translated by Simon Alexandre Langlois. Paris: Printed for the Oriental Translation Fund of Great Britain and Ireland, 1834–35.

Harlan, Richard. *Fauna Americana, Being a Description of the Mammiferous Animals Inhabiting North America.* Philadelphia: A. Finley, 1825.

Hawthorne, Nathaniel. *The American Notebooks.* Edited by Claude M. Simpson. Columbus: Ohio State University Press, 1972.

The Heetōpadēs of Veeshnoo-Sarmā, in a Series of Connected Fables, Interspersed with Moral, Prudential, and Political Maxims. Bath: R. Cruttwell, 1787.

Hemans, Felicia. *The Poetical Works of Mrs. Felicia Hemans.* Philadelphia: Grigg & Elliot, 1844.

Higginson, Samuel Storrow. "Henry D. Thoreau." *Harvard Magazine,* May 1862.

History of the Town of Sutton, Massachusetts, from 1704 to 1876. Worcester: Pub. for the Town by Sanford and Company, 1878.

Hoar, George F. *Autobiography of Seventy Years.* New York, 1903.

Hosmer, Horace. *Remembrances of Concord and the Thoreaus: Letters of Horace Hosmer to Dr. S. A. Jones.* Edited by George Hendrick. Urbana: University of Illinois Press, 1977.

Hosmer, Joseph. "Henry D. Thoreau." *Concord Freeman: Thoreau Annex.* 1880.

Howarth, William L. *The Book of Concord: Thoreau's Life as a Writer.* New York: Viking, 1982.

———. *The Literary Manuscripts of Henry David Thoreau.* Columbus: Ohio State University Press, 1974.

Hudspeth, Robert N. *Ellery Channing.* New York: Twayne, 1973.

Jarvis, Edward. *Traditions and Reminiscences of Concord, Massachusetts, 1779–1878.* Edited by Sarah Chapin; introduction by Robert A. Gross. Amherst: University of Massachusetts Press, 1993.

Johnson, Edward. *A History of New-England from the English Planting in the Yeere 1628 untill the Yeere 1652.* London: N. Brooke, 1654.

Johnson, Linck C. *Thoreau's Complex Weave: The Writing of A Week on the Concord and Merrimack Rivers, with the Text of the First Draft.* Charlottesville: Published for the Bibliographical Society of the University of Virginia, by the University Press of Virginia, 1986.

Jones, Samuel Arthur. *Thoreau: A Glimpse.* Concord: A. Lane, The Erudite Press, 1903.

Kane, Elisha Kent. *The United States Grinnell Expedition in Search of Sir John Franklin: A Personal Narrative.* New York: Harper and Brothers, 1854.

Kirby, William, and William Spence. *An Introduction to Entomology, or Elements of the Natural History of Insects.* Philadelphia: Lea and Blanchard, 1846.

Krutch, Joseph Wood. *Henry David Thoreau.* New York: W. Sloane, 1948.

La Fontaine, Jean de. *Fables of La Fontaine.* Translated from the French by Elizur Wright, Jr. Boston: Tappan and Dennet, 1842.

Laing, Samuel. *Journal of a Residence in Norway During the Years 1834, 1835, & 1836, Made with a View to Enquire into the Moral and Political Economy of that Country, and the Condition of its Inhabitants.* London: Printed for Longman, Orme, Brown, Green, and Longmans, 1837.

Lemprière, John. *Bibliotheca Classica, or, A Dictionary of all the Principal Names and Terms Relating to the Geography, Topography, History, Literature, and Mythology of Antiquity and of the Ancients: with a chronological table.* Revised and corrected, and divided, under separate head into three parts . . . by Lorenzo L. Da Ponte and John D. Ogilby. New York: W. E. Dean, 1837.

The Library of Entertaining Knowledge: The Hindoos. London: Charles Knight, 1834–35.

Liebig, Justus von. *Chemistry in Its Applications to Agriculture and Physiology.* 4th ed. London, 1849.

McGill, Frederick T., Jr. *Channing of Concord: A Life of William Ellery Channing II.* New Brunswick, N.J.: Rutgers University Press, 1967.

Meltzer, Milton, and Walter Harding. *A Thoreau Profile.* New York: Crowell, 1962.

Michaux, François André. *The North American Sylva, or, A Description of the Forest Trees of the United States, Canada, and Nova Scotia.* Paris: Printed by C. d'Hautel, 1818–19.

Miller, Perry, ed. *The Transcendentalists: An Anthology.* Cambridge: Harvard University Press, 1950.

Mott, Wes, ed. *Biographical Dictionary of Transcendentalism.* Westport, Conn.: Greenwood, 1996.

———. *Encyclopedia of Transcendentalism.* Westport, Conn.: Greenwood, 1996.

Myerson, Joel, ed. *Transcendentalism: A Reader.* New York: Oxford University Press, 2001.

O'Callaghan, Edmund Bailey. *The Documentary History of the State of New York.* Albany: Weed, Parsons, 1849–51.

Ogden, Marlene, and Clifton Keller. *Walden: A Concordance.* New York: Garland, 1985.

Ossian. *The Genuine Remains of Ossian.* Literally translated with a preliminary dissertation by Patrick MacGregor. London: Smith, Elder, 1841.

Paul, Sherman. *The Shores of America: Thoreau's Inward Exploration.* Urbana: University of Illinois Press, 1958.

Pauthier, Jean-Pierre-Guillaume. *Confucius et Mencius: Les Quatre Livres de Philosophie Moral et Politique de la Chine.* Paris: Bibliothèque-Charpentier, 1841.

Pellico, Silvio. *My Prisons: Memoirs of Silvio Pellico of Saluzzo.* Cambridge, Mass.: Printed by C. Folsom, 1836.

Percy, Thomas. *Reliques of Ancient English Poetry or A Collection of Old Ballads.* Philadelphia: James E. Moore, 1823.

Pfeiffer, Ida. *A Lady's Voyage Round the World: A Selected Translation from the German of Ida Pfeiffer by Mrs. Percy Sinnett.* New York: Harper and Brothers, 1852.

The Phenix: A Collection of Old and Rare Fragments. New York: W. Gowan, 1835.

Poirier, Richard. *A World Elsewhere: The Place of Style in American Literature.* New York: Oxford University Press, 1966.

Prescott, William Hickling. *History of the Conquest of Mexico.* New York: Harper and Brothers, 1854.

Raleigh, Walter, Sir. *The Works of Sir Walter Raleigh.* Oxford: The University Press, 1829.

Reports of the Selectmen and Other Officer of the Town of Concord. Concord: The Town, 1847–.

Richardson, Robert D., Jr. *Emerson: The Mind on Fire.* Berkeley: University of California Press, 1995.

———. *Henry Thoreau: A Life of the Mind.* Berkeley: University of California Press, 1986.

Ricketson, Anna, ed. *Daniel Ricketson and His Friends: Letters, Poems, Sketches, etc.* Edited by his daughter and son, Anna and Walton Ricketson. Boston: Houghton Mifflin, 1902.

Robbins, Roland Wells. *Discovery at Walden.* Stoneham, Mass.: G. R. Barnstead & Son, 1947.

Rohman, David Gordon. *An Annotated Edition of Henry David Thoreau's Walden.* Ph.D. diss., Syracuse University, 1960. Ann Arbor, Mich.: University Microfilms, 1978.

Rose, Mildred Alma. *A Borrowed Axe: A Study of Henry David Thoreau's Use of Literary Allusions and Quotations in Walden.* Master's thesis, University of Saskatchewan, 1969.

Roy, Rajah Rammohun. *Translation of Several Principal Books, Passages, and Texts of the Veds and of Some Controversial Works of Brahmunical Theology.* London, 1832.

Rusk, Ralph L. *The Life of Ralph Waldo Emerson.* New York: Charles Scribner's Sons, 1949.

Sadi. *The Gulistan, or Flower-garden, of Shaikh Sadī of Shiraz.* Translated into English by James Ross. London: J. M. Richardson, 1823.

Salt, Henry S. *Life of Henry David Thoreau.* Edited by George Hendrick, Willene Hendrick, and Fritz Oehlschlaeger. Urbana: University of Illinois Press, 1993.

Sanborn, Franklin Benjamin. *The Life of Henry David Thoreau: Including Many Essays Hitherto Unpublished, and Some Account of His Family and Friends.* Boston: Houghton Mifflin, 1917.

———. *The Personality of Thoreau.* Boston: C. E. Goodspeed, 1901.

———. *Recollections of Seventy Years.* Boston: Gorham, 1909.

———. "An Unpublished Concord Journal." *Century Magazine,* April 1922.

Sattelmeyer, Robert. *Thoreau's Reading: A Study in Intellectual History with Bibliographical Catalogue.* Princeton: Princeton University Press, 1988.

Sayre, Robert. *Thoreau and the American Indian.* Princeton: Princeton University Press, 1977.

Scudder, Townsend. *Concord: American Town.* Boston: Little, Brown, 1947.

Sears, Clara Endicott, compiler. *Bronson Alcott's Fruitlands.* Boston: Houghton Mifflin, 1915.

Seybold, Ethel Thoreau. *Thoreau: The Quest and the Classics.* New Haven: Yale University Press, 1951.

Shakespeare, William. *The Norton Shakespeare Based Upon the Oxford Edition.* Stephen Greenblatt, gen. ed. New York: W. W. Norton, 1997.

Shanley, J. Lyndon. *The Making of Walden, with the Text of the First Version.* Chicago: University of Chicago Press, 1957.

Shattuck, Lemuel. *A History of the Town of Concord, Middlesex County, Massachusetts: From its earliest settlement to 1832; and of the adjoining towns, Bedford, Acton, Lincoln, and Carlisle; containing various notices of county and state history not before published.* Boston: Goodspeed's Book Shop, [1973].

Smith, John. *Travels and Works of Captain John Smith, President of Virginia and Admiral of New England, 1580–1631.* Edited by Edward Arber; a new edition, with a bibliographical and critical introduction, by A. G. Bradley. Edinburgh: John Grant, 1910.

Stowell, Robert F. *A Thoreau Gazetteer.* Edited by William L. Howarth. Princeton: Princeton University Press, 1970.

Studies in the American Renaissance. Edited by Joel Myerson. Charlottesville: University Press of Virginia, 1977–96.

Swift, Lindsay. *Brook Farm.* New York: Macmillan, 1908.

Terry, Charles E., and Mildred Pellens. *The Opium Problem.* New York: Committee on Drug Addictions, Bureau of Social Hygiene, 1928.

Thoreau, Henry D. *The Annotated Walden: Walden, or, Life in the Woods.* Edited, with an introduction, notes, and bibliography by Philip Van Doren Stern. New York: Clarkson N. Potter, 1970.

———. *Collected Poems of Henry Thoreau.* Enlarged ed. Edited by Carl Bode. Baltimore: Johns Hopkins University Press, 1965.

———. *The Correspondence of Henry David Thoreau.* Edited by Walter Harding and Carl Bode. New York: New York University Press, 1958.

———. *Early Essays and Miscellanies.* Edited by Joseph J. Moldenhauer and Edwin Moser, with Alexander Kern. Princeton: Princeton University Press, 1975.

———. *Huckleberries.* Edited, with an introduction, by Leo Stoller. Iowa City: Windhover Press of the University of Iowa, 1970.

———. *Journal.* Edited by John C. Broderick et al. Princeton: Princeton University Press, 1981–.

———. *The Journal of Henry Thoreau.* Edited by Bradford Torrey and Francis H. Allen. Boston: Houghton Mifflin, 1906.

———. *Thoreau on Birds.* Compiled and with commentary by Helen Cruickshank; foreword by Roger Tory Peterson. New York: McGraw-Hill, 1964.

———. *Thoreau's Fact Book in the Harry Elkins Widener Collection.* Hartford: Transcendental, 1966.

———. *Thoreau's Literary Notebook in the Library of Congress.* Edited by K. W. Cameron. Hartford: Transcendental, 1964.

———. *The Variorum Walden.* Annotated and with an introduction by Walter Harding. New York: Twayne, 1962.

———. *Walden.* Edited by J. Lyndon Shanley. Princeton: Princeton University Press, 1971.

———. *Walden.* With an introduction, notes, and bibliography by Ramesh K. Srivastava. Delhi: Oxford University Press, 1983.

———. *Walden: An Annotated Edition.* Foreword and notes by Walter Harding. Boston: Houghton Mifflin, 1995.

———. *Walden, or Life in the Woods.* Boston: Ticknor and Fields, 1854.

———. *Walden, or, Life in the Woods.* Edited by Franklin Sanborn. Boston: Bibliophile Society, 1909.

———. *Walden, or Life in the Woods.* Edited with introduction and notes by Byron Rees. New York: Macmillan, 1910.

———. *Walden, or Life in the Woods.* With an introduction and notes by Francis H. Allen. London: George G. Harrap, [1910].

———. *Walden, or Life in the Woods.* Illustrated with 142 photographs, an introduction, and interpretive comments by Edward Way Teale. New York: Dodd, Mead, 1946.

———. *Walden; and, Resistance to Civil Government: Authoritative Texts, Thoreau's Journal, Reviews, and Essays in Criticism.* Edited by William Rossi. New York: W. W. Norton, 1992.

———. *The Writings of Henry D. Thoreau.* Walden edition. Boston: Houghton Mifflin, 1906.

Thoreau Society Bulletin. Geneseo, N.Y.: Thoreau Society, 1941–.

Treasury of New England Folklore: Stories, Ballads, and Traditions of the Yankee People. Edited by B. A. Botkin. New York: Crown, 1947.

Trench, Richard Chenevix. *The Study of Words.* New York: Redfield, 1852.

Van Doren, Mark. *Henry David Thoreau: A Study.* Boston: Houghton Mifflin, 1916.

Walker, Eugene Hoffman. "Walden's Way Revealed." In *Man & Nature,* 11–20. Lincoln: Massachusetts Audubon Society, 1971.

Walker, John. *A Critical Pronouncing Dictionary, and Expositor of the English Language.* Boston: Lincoln and Edmands, 1829.

West, Michael. *Transcendental Wordplay: America's Romantic Punsters and the Search for the Language of Nature.* Athens: Ohio University Press, 2000.

Wheeler, Ruth. *Concord: Climate of Freedom.* Concord: Concord Antiquarian Society, 1967.

White, John H. *The American Railroad Passenger Car.* Baltimore: Johns Hopkins University Press, 1978.

Wildman, Thomas. *A Treatise on the Management of Bees.* London: T. Cadell, 1768.

Wilkin, Charles, translator. *Mahābhārata: Bhagvat-gēētā, or Dialogues of Kreeshna and Arjoon.* London, 1785.

Wilkinson, John Gardner. *Manners and Customs of the Ancient Egyptians, Including Their Private Life, Government, Laws, Arts, Manufactures, Religion, and Early History.* London: J. Murray, 1837.

Willis, Frederick L. H. *Alcott Memoirs.* Posthumously compiled from papers, journals, and memoranda of the late Dr. Frederick L. H. Willis by E. W. L. & H. B. Boston: R. G. Badger, 1915.

Wordsworth, William. *The Complete Poetical Works of William Wordsworth Together with a Description of the Lakes in the North of England.* Edited by Henry Reed. Boston: James Munroe, 1837.

The Works of the English Poets, from Chaucer to Cowper. Edited by Alexander Chalmers. London: J. Johnson, 1810.

Notes on the Text

Choice of Copy Text

The text for this edition of *Walden* has been newly established based on the following principles. The basic copy text is the first edition of *Walden* as published on 9 August 1854 in Boston by the firm of Ticknor and Fields. As the book never reached a second edition in Thoreau's lifetime, this is the only edition published with authority. The 1854 text as printed has been emended where any of the following circumstances apply:

- Where Thoreau made corrections in the page proofs of *Walden,* now in the Henry E. Huntington Library, San Marino, California (referred to as Huntington below). His corrections to the proofs were not always followed, however, and in certain cases, where this was apparently to conform to the practice of the publisher, and where it does not affect or alter the intention of the author, the text as printed in the first edition has been retained.
- Where Thoreau made corrections in his copy of the first edition, now in the Abernethy Library, Middlebury College, Middlebury, Vermont (referred to as Abernethy below).
- Where obvious errors have occurred in the printed text but were not corrected by the author: Flints' for Flint's, for example.
- Where inconsistencies in spelling or word division exist.

In certain cases, reference has been made to manuscript drafts of *Walden* in the Henry E. Huntington Library, San Marino, California. These drafts have been referenced as Versions 1–7, following J. Lyndon Shanley in *The Making of Walden with the Text of the*

First Version (Chicago: University of Chicago Press, 1957). Their dates of composition, as established by Shanley, are:

Version 1	1847
Version 2	1849
Version 3	1849
Version 4	1852
Version 5	late 1852–53
Version 6	1853–54
Version 7	1854

Textual Notes and Emendations

The following have been regularized throughout the text:

- corn-field(s) for cornfield(s) in "Economy" (2 occurrences); "The Pond in Winter" (1 occurrence)
- hill-side(s) for hillside(s) in "Economy" (2 occurrences); "Spring" (2 occurrences)
- woodchopper(s) for wood-chopper(s) in "Visitors" (1 occurrence); "House-Warming" (3 occurrences)
- Fair Haven for Fair-Haven in "The Village" (1 occurrence); "The Ponds" (3 occurrences); "Baker Farm" (1 occurrence); "Spring" (2 occurrences)
- Flint's for Flints' in "The Ponds" (7 occurrences); "Baker Farm" (1 occurrence); "House-Warming" (1 occurrence); "Winter Animals" (1 occurrence)

The following are specific emendations that have been made, or explanations of spellings that have been retained. The numbers at left refer to page number followed by line number in this edition.

iii:1 Title: *Walden,* corrected from *Walden; or, Life in the Woods* in the first edition, following Thoreau's intention as outlined in a letter to Ticknor and Fields (4 March 1862): "leave out from the title the words 'Or Life in the Woods'" [C 639].

ECONOMY

2:23 *Bramins:* Thoreau's spelling is less common but acceptable, and is retained here. It is found in Webster's 1828 *American Dictionary of the English Language,* and was used sometimes by Emerson in his journals, his essay "The Poet," and *English Traits.*

3:3 *Iolas:* More commonly Iolaus, however, this is the spelling found in Lemprière's *Bibliotheca Classica,* Thoreau's primary classical dictionary, and is retained here.

17:5 *well nigh:* hyphen deleted from *well-nigh* for consistency with usage elsewhere in "Economy" and "House-Warming."

20:13 *port:* corrected from *post* (to follow Versions 1 and 2). Although Thoreau did not correct the word "post" in Huntington, it was apparently a misreading by the typesetter, as the word was clearly "port" in Versions 1 and 2—later versions of this passage are not extant.

24:26 *is said to have been:* corrected

from *was* to follow Abernethy (further explanation appears in "Economy" at note 141).

32:30 *shoe-strings:* corrected from *shoe-strings* to be consistent with usage later in this chapter.

32:32 *springe:* It is possible that the word "springe" was an error not caught by Thoreau in Huntington and that the proper word should be "spring," as Thoreau had in the early draft versions of *Walden,* meaning that the trap is lightly set so that the slightest touch will trip it.

37:20 *fail? or of the three:* corrected from *fail, or the three* to follow Huntington.

42:16 *coffee-mill:* not hyphenated in first edition but hyphenated here for consistency, following usage later in this paragraph and in Version 3.

46:26 *carpenter:* comma following carpenter removed, to follow Version 6, as being grammatically unnecessary.

50:7 *Rodgers':* corrected from *Rogers'* to follow the correct spelling of the corporate name.

52:27 *manure:* corrected from *manure whatever* to follow Huntington.

WHERE I LIVED, AND
WHAT I LIVED FOR

79:14 *place:* although "place" is capitalized in Version 6 and in "A Poet Buy's a Farm" [*Sartain's Union*

Magazine 11 (1852): 127], the lowercase form is retained here in accordance with Thoreau's usage in Huntington, as well as in a pre-*Walden* journal passage [PJ 4:358]. It is also consistent with his similar usage, "Hollowell farm," on the next page.

79:35   *My right:* indentation of the second line of the poem corrected from no indentation in the first edition, to follow Huntington as well as the indentation in standard editions of Cowper's poems.

81:29   *Day:* capitalization corrected from *day* to follow Huntington.

90:7   *Irish-man:* although Thoreau failed to change "Irishman" to "Irish-man" in Huntington, in accordance with his hyphenation in Version 1 and to emphasize, as the context would indicate, the word "man," the hyphenated form is used here.

93:22   *Kieou-pe-yu:* corrected from *Kieou-he-yu* to follow the correct form from Thoreau's source.

93:28   *accomplish it:* corrected from *come to the end of them* to follow Abernethy.

95:13   *which:* corrected from *that* to follow Huntington.

READING

102:22   *"Little Reading":* quotation marks added to be consistent with use later in this chapter.

SOUNDS

110:29   *pitch-pines:* hyphen added to be consistent with Thoreau's spelling elsewhere in *Walden*.

110:34   *Cerasus:* capitalized as indicated in Huntington and to be consistent with the form of plant names in *Walden*.

111:4   *Rhus:* capitalized as indicated in Huntington and to be consistent with the form of plant names in *Walden*.

113:21   *to men:* added to follow Huntington where it had not been marked for deletion by Thoreau.

114:2   *plough, plough:* comma added as indicated in Huntington although Thoreau's spelling—plow, plow—has been disregarded here to be consistent with "plough" elsewhere in *Walden*.

114:35   *were:* corrected from *are* to follow Abernethy.

115:1   *rang:* corrected from *rings* to follow Abernethy.

118:23   *bell-wether:* corrected from the mistaken *bell-weather* used in the first edition.

121:7   *wood-side,:* punctuation changed from *wood-side;* to follow Huntington.

121:31   *gl:* non-italicized form *gl* but corrected here to be consistent with similar text in "Spring": "The radicals of *lobe* are *lb*, the soft mass of the *b* (single lobed, or B, double lobed,) with the liquid *l* behind it pressing it forward. In globe, *glb,* the guttural *g* adds to the meaning the capacity of the throat."

122:11 *double:* corrected from *single* to follow Abernethy. The single spruce does not grow in Concord.

124:27 *gate,:* comma added to follow Huntington and to be consistent with punctuation in this sequence.

SOLITUDE

129:20 *issue;:* corrected from *issue,* to follow Huntington.

131:28 *remunerate:* comma after remunerate, as in first edition, removed to follow Abernethy.

132:6 *tolerable,:* comma added to follow Huntington.

132:8 *fire-side:* hyphen added for consistency with usage in "House-Warming" and "Former Inhabitants; and Winter Visitors."

133:5 *northstar:* corrected from *north star* to follow Huntington and consistent with its use in the "Visitors" chapter.

VISITORS

147:25 *occasionally:* corrected from *occca-sionally.*

THE BEAN-FIELD

151:36 *shrub-oak copse:* corrected from *shrub oak copse* in first edition for consistency.

152:26 *begun:* corrected from *began* to follow Version I as being grammatically correct.

153:4 *Colman:* Thoreau's misspelling of the name as *Coleman* has been corrected (also at 157:22).

158:3 *":* ditto marks inserted to follow Huntington; comma after *small* removed to be consistent with other lists.

159:6 *orchards?:* punctuation corrected from *orchards,* to follow Huntington.

THE VILLAGE

165:1–2 *invariably,:* punctuation added to follow Abernethy.

THE PONDS

173:11 *neighborhood:* corrected from *neihhorhood.*

176:12 *pitch-pines:* not hyphenated in first edition but hyphenated here for consistency.

178:18 *(Pomotis obesus,):* inserted to follow Huntington; comma added to be consistent with (*Leuciscus pulchellus,*).

179:15–16 *kingfishers dart away from its coves,:* inserted to follow Huntington; punctuation added to set off phrase.

181:6 *skater insects:* Thoreau lightly wrote *(Hydrometer)* under *skater insects* in Abernethy. As his intention is unclear, that reading has not been adopted here.

187:26   *State Street:* corrected from *State-street* for consistency with the form used in "The Village."

BAKER FARM

194:10   *black-spruce trees:* corrected from *white-spruce trees* to follow Abernethy.

195:8   *Celtis:* corrected from *celtis* to follow Huntington.

200:23   *farmers':* punctuation restored; the apostrophe, present in Huntington, was left off in the first edition.

HIGHER LAWS

207:5   . . . : third ellipsis dot added to follow standard punctuation.

207:29   *carnivorous:* corrected from *carniverous* in the first edition, which is neither a correct nor a variant spelling.

213:12   *recreate:* Thoreau corrected the end-of-line hyphenation from "rec-reate" to "re-create" in Abernethy. Following this correction some editions have retained the hyphenated form, but none of the draft versions of *Walden* indicates that Thoreau intended to use a hyphenated form in the text. It is clear from the change that Thoreau was using this word to mean create anew rather than revive or refresh.

BRUTE NEIGHBORS

214:25   *sweet-briars:* corrected from *sweet-briers* to follow Huntington.

216:26   *wild native kind:* in Abernethy Thoreau added *(Mus leucopus)* but as this was apparently in error it has not been incorporated here (further explanation in "Brute Neighbors," note 16).

216:31   *crumbs:* corrected from *crums* to follow Thoreau's spelling in the extant draft versions of *Walden* for this chapter and "Winter Animals."

219:5   *nearer,:* comma inserted to follow Huntington.

219:7   *attention:* comma removed to follow Huntington.

HOUSE-WARMING

228:22   *red squirrels:* hyphen deleted from *red-squirrels* to be consistent with the form found elsewhere in *Walden.*

231:33–34   *masonry.:* punctuation restored. The period, present in Huntington, was left off in the first edition.

234:17   *fireplace:* hyphenated in first edition, but unhyphenated here (also at 244:16) for consistency with the form used elsewhere in this chapter and in "Economy."

239:36–240:1   *driftwood:* hyphen deleted to be consistent with the form found elsewhere in *Walden.*

245:14   *Mrs. Hooper:* unattributed, Thoreau added the poet's name in Abernethy.

FORMER INHABITANTS; AND
WINTER VISITORS

247:6–7   *Stratton:* corrected from *Stratten* to follow Thoreau's correction of the second instance of this name in Abernethy (also at 248:18–19).

255:19   *them:* comma removed to follow Huntington.

258:19   *deer:* corrected from *meadow* to follow Abernethy.

WINTER ANIMALS

264:36–265:1   *gratuitous:* corrected from *gratui tous* to follow Huntington; the hyphen was left off at the end of the line in the first edition.

265:13   *frisk:* corrected from *brisk* to follow Huntington and also as it appeared in Versions 1 and 6.

266:18, 23   *crumbs:* corrected from *crums* to follow Thoreau's spelling in the extant draft versions of *Walden* for this chapter and "Brute Neighbors."

270:7   *ledger:* corrected from *leger.* Although Thoreau left this uncorrected in Huntington, and there are rare instances of the form "leger" as in Emerson's "The American Scholar" and Webster's 1828 *Dictionary of the English Language,* usage here follows Thoreau's in Version 7 and his correction in Abernethy.

THE POND IN WINTER

279:7   *has:* corrected, for grammatical accuracy, from *have.* The original journal passage of 1 September 1852 [J 4:339] and Version 4 had "was necessary," but "was" was inadvertently corrected to "have been" in Version 6 and carried through to publication.

285:11   *was,:* corrected from *was, —* to follow Huntington.

287:36   *Bhagvat-Geeta:* not hyphenated in first edition, but hyphenated here to be consistent with form used in "Economy."

SPRING

297:16   *(labium from labor (?)):* dashes setting off the entire phrase changed to parentheses to follow Huntington.

299:17   *red squirrels:* hyphen deleted from *red-squirrels* to be consistent with the form found elsewhere in *Walden.*

301:9   *on:* corrected from *in* to follow Huntington.

302:30   *Nabathæaque:* corrected from *Nabathacaque* in first edition, to follow Huntington and original Latin form.

CONCLUSION

310:4   *sight:* corrected from *right,* which may have been a printer's misreading. Thoreau often underscored

intentional changes for emphasis,
which was not done here, and the
line is quoted correctly in Versions
6 and 7 of *Walden,* as well as in
his commonplace book.

319:2   *fault-finder:* extra space deleted
following the hyphen.

321:14   *furring:* corrected from *furrowing.*
Thoreau mistakenly used the word
"furrowing" for "furring": thin
strips of wood nailed to the studs
to even a surface prior to plastering or to which laths are nailed.
In *Walden* Version 4, "furrowing" was followed by the canceled
word "stud." Edward Emerson
silently corrected the word to furring when quoting this passage in
*Henry Thoreau as Remembered by a
Young Friend.*

322:33   *might perhaps:* Punctuation corrected from *might, perhaps,* to
follow Huntington.

End-of-Line Hyphenation

The two lists below record end-of-line hyphenations.
The first list shows the form adopted in this edition for
compound words that were hyphenated at the end of
a line in the first edition. Judging by the predominant
usage in Thoreau texts published in his lifetime, he
most likely intended these compounds to be printed
as shown on this list.

2:25	downward
5:17	cannot
6:23	overseer
6:26	highway
13:13	night-clothes

16:22–23	turtle-dove
17:13	manna-wise
20:33	dress-maker
21:20	scarecrow
23:20–21	empty-handed
26:20	skin-deep
26:28	Therefore
28:27	railroad
28:36	whenever
33:33	almshouse
35:2	woodchuck
35:11	glow-shoes
35:22	housewife
37:15	twenty-five
39:6	shellfish
39:10	to-day
42:1	Door-sill
42:19	to-night
42:31–32	cart-loads
45:21	mother-o'-pearl
48:8–9	shortcomings
51:22	railroad
57:16	woodchuck
57:22	woodchucks
60:1	bread-making
60:22	housewives
64:9	to-day
75:20	mankind
82:34	wood-thrush
84:21	overcast
86:1	forever
89:12	quicksands
90:7	Irish-man
90:24	to-morrow
93:13	newspapers
93:34–35	draggle-tail
95:5–6	outskirts
95:34	downward
102:11	tip-toe

103:3–4	weathercocks		178:34	blood-red
103:10	Tittle-Tol-Tan		179:18	white-pine
105:2	low-lived		180:4	overlap
109:23	to-morrow		181:21	hill-top
110:12	three-legged		184:3	skylight
110:32	golden-rod		187:26	State Street
110:33	ground-nut		187:29–30	outlet
113:11	cloud-compeller		191:17	pitch-pine
114:4	drill-barrow		192:15	waterlogged
118:9	township		194:10	toad-stools
118:17	cow-yards		194:12	butterflies
120:18–19	whippoorwills		194:23	black-birch
121:7	wood-side		196:28–29	pickerel-weed
121:12	night-walked		197:10	sibyl-like
122:22–23	wine-bibbers		199:6	a-huckleberrying
123:1	*tr-r-r-oonk*		202:8	half-starved
123:13–14	cock crowing		204:35	phil-*anthropic*
123:24	drumsticks		212:19	overcome
124:26, 27	front-yard		214:18	woodpecker
125:7	bullfrogs		215:29	Methinks
129:24	townsmen		221:20	first-mentioned
130:6	workman		221:31	saddle-bow
130:31	driftwood		223:31	flying-squirrel
134:19	noon-day		224:6	spy-glasses
140:1–2	white-oak		231:26	pitch-pine
140:24	bean-field		232:14, 16	fireplace
140:36	woodchucks		233:29	keeping-room
142:23	demigods		239:11	pond-hole
143:28	home-made		240:7	piecemeal
151:25	shrub-oaks		242:13	sap-wood
155:31	woodchuck		242:21–22	wood-chopper's
155:35	elm-tree		243:11	housekeeper
163:20	fire-engine		247:21	golden-rod
164:33	cart-path		248:20	pitch-pines
166:5	headlands		254:20	beggar-ticks
166:22	senate-house		255:10–11	sweet-scented
171:28	railroad		255:31	linen-spinning
175:26	overflow		257:7	yellow-birch
178:14–15	fisherman		257:10	fir-trees

260:21	yesterday		122:22–23	wine-bibbers
261:21	court-yard		122:36–123:1	*tr-r-r-oonk*
263:31	*boo-hoo!*		123:13–14	cock-crowing
264:30	shrub-oaks		129:17–18	school-house
291:24	withdrawing		134:5–6	great-grandmother
291:30	fishermen		140:1–2	white-oak
294:22	railroads		140:25–26	a-going
299:2	johnswort		143:17–18	close-fitting
303:28	re-creating		146:18–19	weak-headed
307:33	sulphur-like		152:29–30	hard-featured
309:4	wild-goose		152:36–153:1	Fellow-travellers
316:13	half-witted		176:30–31	pow-wow
322:3	long-suffering		181:14–15	thistle-down

The following list shows words hyphenated at the end of a line in this edition that should be considered intentionally hyphenated compounds. All other words that are hyphenated at the end of a line in this edition but do not appear on this list should be considered as a single word.

3:19–20	seventy-five		181:28–29	water-bug
7:1–2	Self-emancipation		182:17–18	mid-afternoon
9:21–22	vegetable-made		188:10–11	ninety-seven
16:22–23	turtle-dove		191:7–8	dog-day
23:20–21	empty-handed		191:12–13	sand-paper
32:12–13	ninety-seven		196:28–29	pickerel-weed
42:31–32	cart-loads		197:10–11	cone-headed
60:27–28	bottle-full		197:34–35	broad-faced
64:2–3	compact-looking		200:6–7	bog-holes
80:22–23	house-dog		205:10–11	wood-chopping
90:27–28	bell-rope		208:15–16	sweet-scented
93:34–35	draggle-tail		208:30–31	opium-eater's
103:22–23	rye-and-Indian		220:15–16	hill-side
104:25–26	class-books		221:12–13	three-penny
105:8–9	tit-men		221:18–19	window-sill
107:7–8	"Olive-Branches"		223:14–15	farm-houses
110:31–32	life-everlasting		223:16–17	a-hunting
			230:28–29	corn-field
			234:36–235:1	trap-door
			236:2–3	hasty-puddings
			237:35–36	forty-eight
			241:8–9	gun-stocks
			242:9–10	hill-side
			248:2–3	apple-trees
			254:19–20	over-run

255:10–11	sweet-scented		292:7–8	honey-combed
255:31–32	stable-broom		296:29–30	drop-like
258:35–36	barn-yard		310:21–22	sky-high
262:25–263:1	sleigh-bells		312:29–30	worn-out
263:30–31	*boo-hoo*		316:12–13	once-and-a-half-witted
279:1–2	corn-fields		322:21–22	seven-years'
280:31–32	forty-nine		324:12–13	seventeen-year

Index

a b abs (school ABCs), 102
Abelard, Peter, 106
account books, old, 11–12, 270
accounting, 102
Achilles and Patroclus, 220
across-lot routes, 17–18
Actaeon, 267
action: and contemplation, 109; must
    follow thought, 14
Acton (Mass.), 119
actual vs. ideal: in Thoreau's life, xviii–xx;
    in Transcendentalism, 16
Adam, 10, 95, 322; "Adam's grandmother,"
    201; and Eve, 27, 174
Addison, Joseph, 7
Adelaide, Princess, 51
Admetus, 67–68
Aeneas Silvius (Pius II), 222
aes alienum (debt), 6
Aeschylus, 98, 101
African Americans and Africans, 147,
    247–50. *See also* anti-slavery; slaves and
    slavery; Underground Railroad
Agassiz, Louis, 177, 216
Albee, John, 200
Alcott, (Amos) Bronson, 24, 56, 69, 70, 81,
    308; and Fruitlands, 54; lends axe, 39;
    lends books, 81, 97; refuses tax, 166; "re-
    vising mythology" with Thoreau, 315; at
    Thoreau's house-raising, 43; Thoreau's
    praise of, 259–61; vegetable theory of, 15;
    "welcome visitor" at Walden house, 259
alertness, 7, 102, 108, 292
Alexander the Great, 288; and *Iliad*, 100–
    101
Algonquins, 204
alms-house, 145, 319

Alms House Farm (Concord), 247
America, United States of, 197–98, 324; In-
    dependence Day, 43, 81, 83; intellectual
    capacity, 316–17; Irish coming to, 197;
    "the only true," 198; Revolution, 84. *See
    also* democracy; society
American Philosophical Society, 323
American Whig Review, 209
amusements and entertainment, 109, 203,
    251, 260, 321; despair beneath, 7
analogy, 13; actual world as "language
    without metaphor," 108, 297; basis of
    Thoreau's art, xxiii; circle as straight
    line, 309; exploration as introspection,
    310–12; measuring ethics (character),
    281–82; Pond mirrors nature, 182; sand
    foliage as archetypal, 294–97
ancient authors and authorities: Aeschylus,
    98, 101; Aesop, 46, 63; Apollodorus, 3;
    Aratus, 231; Aristotle, 12, 13; Bias, 23–24;
    Cato the Elder, 61, 81–82, 233–34, 241;
    Cato the Younger, 247; Cicero, 12, 37;
    Claudian, 312; Diodorus Siculus, 3, 59;
    Diogenes, 12; Euripides, 121; Gnostics,
    321; Hanno, 20, 288; Heraclitus, 100;
    Hesiod, 174, 249; Hipparchus, 70; Hip-
    pocrates, 9–10; Homer, 8, 101; Livy, 263;
    Lucian, 320; Lucretius, 263; Martial,
    263; Ovid, 4, 71, 263, 302–3; Plato, 101,
    104–5, 275, 288, 321; Pliny the Elder, 231,
    307; Plutarch, 12, 100, 220, 313; Scipio
    Africanus, 249; Simonides, 3; Socrates,
    313; Solon, 9; Stoics, 100; Tibullus, 167;
    Varro, 271, 300; Virgil, 101, 114, 231, 263;
    Vitruvius, 56; Xenophanes, 100
animals: as food, objections to, 206–10;
    health and vigor of, 210; heat of, 12–

bonfire, 65

books, 97–107, 110, 113, 319; "treasured wealth of the world," 100. *See also* reading; writers and writing

Bose, name for dog, 214, 222

Boston (Mass.), 111, 168, 228, 322; "I was brought from," 151; "skip the gossip of," 107

Boston Cultivator, 81, 284

Boston Evening Transcript, 112, 311

botanists and botany, 25, 75, 194–95, 292

Bottomless Ponds (Sudbury), 276

bounds, 55; speaking within, 29; speaking without, 315. *See also* extravagance

Brahma and Brahminism, 2, 94, 288, 317–18

bread, 58, 214; baking at Walden, 44, 59; grain vs. chestnut and ground-nut, 230; unleavened, 60

Breed, John, 248, 249–50; death of, 250; son of, 252–53

bricks, 247, 252; second-hand used in Walden house, 231–33

Bright, name for ox, 129, 315

Brighton (Mass.), cattle market, 129

Brister, Scipio, 249. *See also* Freeman, Brister

Brister's Hill (Walden Woods), 218, 247, 258

Brister's Spring, 178, 254

British Empire, 324

"broad margin to my life," 108

Broadway (N.Y.), 259

Brook Farm, xvii, 49

Brown, Deacon Reuben, effects auctioned, 65

Browne, Sir Thomas, 7, 103

Brownson, Orestes A., 67

Bryant, William Cullen, 46

Buel, Jesse, 114

Buena Vista (Mexico), Battle of, 115

"bug, a strong and beautiful," story of, 324

Bunker Hill, Battle of, 221

Bunyan, John, 6

burning glass (magnifier), 238

Burns, Robert, 46

business: as self-enslavement, 67–68; Thoreau's idea of, 19–20, 67; Thoreau's private, 19; Walden a good place for, 20. *See also* commerce; trade

busk (purifying new-year celebration), 65

Buttrick, Maj. John, 221

Byrd, William, 114

Caatskill (Catskill) Mountains (N.Y.), 83

Cabot, James Elliot (naturalist), 216

Calidas (Kalidasa), 308

Calpa (Kalpa), a day of Brahma, 318

Cambridge (Mass.), 285, 287; ice made at, 287, 316–17

Cambridge College. *See* Harvard College

Cambridge ice, vs. Walden ice, 316–17. *See also* ice; ice trade

Canada, 104; Thoreau visits, 18, 25

Carew, Thomas, verse by, 76–77

Cargill, Hugh, and Stratton Farm, 247

Carlyle, Thomas, xvi, xxii, 21, 23, 44, 134, 213

carpentry, 44, 46, 56–57

Cassiopeia's Chair, 85

castles in the air, 261, 315

Cato, M. Porcius (the Elder), 61; *De Agri Cultura,* 61, 81–82, 233–34, 241

cats, 42; wild, 223; winged, 223

Cattle Show, Middlesex (Concord), 32

caves, 27, 91

Cawtantowwit (Wampanoag crow deity), 230–31

Celestial Empire (China), 36. *See also* China and Chinese empire

cellars and cellar-holes: dents still mark sites of, 254–55; of former inhabitants, 247–48; of Walden house, 43, 234, 243

Cellini, Benvenuto, 195–97

Flying Childers (racehorse), 51

food, 11, 12, 52–53, 56–58. *See also* cooking at Walden; diet

Forbes, James D., 171

"Forefathers' Song," 61, 89

former inhabitants of Woods, 246–56; "this small village, germ of something more," 255. *See also* Breed, John; Brister, Scipio; Freeman, Brister; Ingraham, Cato; LeGrosse, Francis; Nutting; Quoil, Hugh; Stratton family and farm; White, Zilpha; Wyman, John

foundations, 37, 45, 49, 315, 321

Fourier, Charles, 68

Fourth of July (Independence Day), 43, 81, 83

fox, 29, 63, 114, 254–55, 264, 267, 270

France, revolutions in (1840s), 93

frankincense, 316

Franklin, Benjamin, 70

Franklin, Sir John, 310–12

freedom, 85, 90, 200, 202. *See also* individual and individualism

Freeman, Brister, 247–49; confused with Scipio Brister, 249; Fenda his wife, 248; "pulled wool," 255

Freeman, Concord (journal), 25, 39, 91, 255, 290, 307

Fresh Pond ice-houses (Cambridge), 287, 290, 316–17

"fried rat with a good relish, eat a," 208

friends and friendship, xviii, 258–61; Alcott, 259–61; Channing, 259; Emerson, 261; G. Hoar, 256; Hosmer, 258–59

Frobisher, Martin, 310–11

frogs: herald of spring, 302; as topers, 122–23

Frost, John N., assimilated into John Field character by Thoreau, 197–98

Fruitlands (Harvard, Mass.), xvii, 49; and Alcott, 54

fruits, 59, 66, 74, 75, 78, 194, 207, 209; "noble," 59; in wholesome diet, 207; "wild forbidden," 194. *See also names of particular fruits*

Fry, Elizabeth, 73

fuel: food as, 12; a necessary of life, 12, 62, 256; Thoreau's at Walden, 52–53, 239–40, 241–42

Fugitive Slave Bill, 202, 222–23

Fuller: Ellen, 80; Margaret, 2, 17, 168

furniture, 62–65, 89, 112; commonly a burden, 63; Thoreau's minimal, 62–64, 110

Ganges River (India), 288

"Gazette, the," 17

gazettes (Native American records), 27

geese, migrating, 301–2, 309; "intruder from Hudson's Bay," 263

Geneva (N.Y.) *Gazette,* 225

genius (individual sense or guiding spirit), 54, 55, 70, 87, 101, 109, 200, 208–9, 211; defined, 87; "Genius" (essay by Emerson), 87; as "irresistible voice," 10; "I would not stand between any man and his," 87; "Oration on Genius" (S. Reed), 87

Georgia, 320

German Confederacy, 89

Gilpin, William, 46, 79, 240, 277

giraffe hunting in Africa, 309

Giraud, Jacob Post, 267

girdling, 270

glacier, 177

Gleason, Herbert W., xxi, 280

God, ideas of, 88, 95, 211, 295, 320–22. *See also* divinity; religion

Goethe, Johann Wolfgang von, 2, 168

Gold Coast (Africa), 312

Golden Age, 174, 234, 302

Golden Rule, 71–72

good and goodness, 71–76, 159–60, 304;

Hoar: Edward S., 19, 91; Elizabeth, 18, 110; George F., 253, 256; John, 249; Squire Samuel, 18

Holbrook, Josiah, 105

holiness and the sacred, 211, 240, 303. *See also* divinity; nature

Hollowell place, 78–80; picturesque beauty of farm at, 80

hollow trees, dwellers in, 302, 321, 322–23

Homer, 219; *Iliad*, 44, 55, 87, 98, 100–101, 220

Hooper, Ellen Sturgis, 244–45

horizon, 84–85, 112, 201

horses, 51, 54–55; dead horse reassures Thoreau, 307; lost bay, 16; used in ice-cutting at Walden, 284–86

Hosmer family, 58; Abigail and Jane, 18; Abner, 221; Alfred, 146; Andrew, John, and Edmund, Jr., 43; Edmund, Sr., 43, 53, 251, 258; Horace, 24, 135; Joseph, 217; Mary H. Brown, 135

hospitality, 18, 135–49, 235, 260, 261, 321; "hospitalality," 146

Hotel des Invalides (old soldiers' home), 222

Hottentots, 88

hounds, 202, 267–70; lost (parable by Thoreau), 16; lost, other stories of, 268–69

houses, 34–39; beauty in, 45–46; expense of, 29–32, 33–35, 37, 39, 47–48; modern, 33; as oppressive, 28; as "porch at the entrance of a burrow," 43; as "seat," 78; Thoreaus' Texas house, 40; Thoreau's vision of a, 235; tool box as a, 28. *See also* Walden house

Howard, John, 71, 73

Hubbard's Bridge, 78

Huber, Pierre, 219, 222

huckleberries, 67, 166, 168; hills stripped by commerce, 112

Humane Society, 203

humanity (humane feelings), 203–4

humility, 319

hummock left by ice, 310–11

Hunt, Leigh, 222

hunters and hunting, 63, 114, 210, 219, 267, 293–94; bear, moose, 269–70; duck, 293; familiarizes boys with nature, 202–3; fox killed, 269; giraffe (Africa), 309; "the hunter stage of development," 205; Indian "best men," 204; loon, 224–25; "Mill-dam sportsmen," 224; as murder, 204–5

"hurry and waste of life," 89–91; and railroad, 51–52, 114–15

Hyde, Tom, 318

I (first person): Thoreau and, 2, 48; Transcendentalists on, 2. *See also* self

Icarian Sea, 190

ice (cover on ponds), 262, 273–74; cracking and whooping of, 238, 263–64, 291–94; cutting of, for ice trade, 72, 282, 284–86; formation of, 236–38, 239; grain and structure of, 290–91; ice fishing, 274–75; melting and thawing of, 40, 289–94, 300–301; Thoreau examines, 237–38. *See also* ice trade

ice trade, 89–90, 284–87, 316–17

ideal ("real") realm: vs. actual, xviii–xx; reality of, for Thoreau, 16; in Transcendentalism, 16

Iliad (Homer), 55, 87, 100–101; frame for ant-war description, 220; Thoreau's copies of, 44, 98

illiteracy, 104, 105

Illustrated London News, 311

imagination, xxiii, 79–80, 85, 206–7, 233, 277, 294–97; "dives deeper and soars higher than nature goes," 279; vs. fancy, in Coleridge and Ruskin, 8

immortality, 306

India, 52, 58, 74, 288; direct way to, 312;

language, 103–4, 235, 315–16; ancient, study of, 98–99; "dead to degenerate times," 98; "*lingua vernacula* of Walden Woods," 263; of literature, 99; our mother and father tongues, 99; of reality, 108

Laplanders, 26–27

lark and the reapers, fable of the, 287

"Laws of Menu, The" (Thoreau), 212

Layard, Austen Henry, 255–56

leaf, as prototypical form in nature, 295–97

lecturing and oratory, deprecated by Thoreau, 100

legends. *See* fables and fabulists; myths

LeGrosse, Francis, 253

Lemprière, John, 3, 33, 219

lethargy, a Thoreau "family complaint," 250–51

Lewis and Clarke (Meriwether Lewis and William Clark), 310–11

Lexington (Mass.), 106, 197, 268

liberality, follows from wisdom, 105

library, 97; Concord's, 97, 102, 106; Emerson's personal, 97; Harvard College, 97; Vatican, 101

Liebig, Justus von, 12

life, 94; basically means keeping warm, 13; "broad margin to my," 108; changes in, our denial of, 11; earth's "great central," 298; essential laws, 11; as experiment, xxii, 9, 15, 201, 295, 313; "front only the essential facts of," 88; fundamental facts of, xviii, 49, 88; marrow of, 88; meanness of, 88, 210, 213, 318; morality of, 210; nature rife with, 307; necessaries of, 9, 11–15; "our life in nature," 316; poverty and simplicity in, 14; in primitive ages, 36; simple and innocent as Nature, 86; successful, 18; "take life bravely," 199; varies with individuals, 10; whole ground of, 9. *See also* living

light, 195; halo of, 195–96; pure and bright,

"proof of immortality," 306; "puts out our eyes," 325. *See also* sun and sunlight

"Light-winged smoke, Icarian bird" (verse by Thoreau), 242–43

lilac, overgrows house ruins, 255

lime and limestone, 236

Lincoln (Mass.), 119, 197, 223, 228, 246, 249, 269; hills of, in winter, 262; Lyceum, Thoreau lectures at, 262, 308; Precinct Burial Ground, 219

Little Reading, Much Instruction from, 102, 104

livelihood, 56–68, 197–201; man's complicated solution to problem of, 32; Thoreau earns his, while at Walden, 57, 66

living: deliberation in, 8, 95; nation "lives too fast," 89; our anxiety in, 11; "we should live quite laxly . . . ," 315

Loch Fyne (Scotland), 277

locust, seventeen-year, 322–23

London (England), 322

Longfellow, Henry Wadsworth, 114

loon, 179; hunted for sport, 224–25; Thoreau chases a, 224–26; wild laughter of, 224, 226

Lord Warden (forest protection authority), 240

Loudon, John Claudius, 46–47

Louisiana, 227

love, poet actuated by pure, 259

Lovelace, Richard, 29

Lowell Institute (Boston), 50

luxury and convenience, 36

lyceum: Boston, 50; Concord, xxiii, 1, 105–6; first in U.S., 105; Lincoln, 262, 308

Lynn (Mass.), 284

lynx, 270–71

machines and machinery, 32, 89, 102, 114, 285–86

MacPherson, James, 46
Madison, James, 54
Maine, 29, 50, 116, 308
Mameluke bey, 320
Mammoth Cave (Ky.), 92
Man, Isle of, 235
"Man of the Age, come to be called working-man," xxii
Mann, Horace, 106
mapping: of ponds, 279–80; of Walden Pond, 151, 278
marrow: eaten raw, 88; of life, 88
Marryat, Capt. Frederick, 247
Marshman, Joshua, 11
marten, 223
Martineau, Harriet, 50
Marvell, Andrew, 188
Mason, James M., and Fugitive Slave Bill, 223
masonry. *See* bricks
Massachusetts, 320, 324
Mather, Cotton, 70, 116
maturation, human: comes in its own time, 317; compared with autumn, 228
Maya, unveiling of, in Hindu scripture, 97
meat-eating. *See* animals
meditation, 214. *See also* contemplation
"melancholy accident," end result of progress, 51–52
melons, 81
Melven, John, 270
Melville, Herman: *Moby-Dick,* 93; *Typee,* 26
Melvin, George (Concord trapper), 63
Memnon, singing statue of, 87–88
Mencius (Meng-tze, Confucian philosopher), 210–11, 304
"Men say they know many things" (verse by Thoreau), 41
Menu (Manu), legendary Hindu lawgiver, 212–13
Mesmer, Friedrich Anton, 75
Mesopotamia, 232, 256

messenger sent to Khoung-tseu (Confucian parable), 93–94
Mexicans and Mexican-American War, 60, 66, 115
Michael Angelo (Michelangelo), 172
Michaux, François André, 241
Middle Ages, 103
Middlesex Cattle Show (Concord), 32
Middlesex Mutual Fire Insurance Co., 250–51
migration, 301–2, 309
Mill Brook (Concord), 251
Mill-dam (Concord), 94
Milton, John, 73; "Lycidas," 168; "On the Late Massacre at Piedmont," 275; *Paradise Lost,* 7, 70, 255–56, 277
mink, 111, 306
Minott: George, 14, 24, 32, 251, 268; Mary (seamstress), 23–24; Thomas, 178
Mirabeau, Comte de, 312–14
miracles, 11
Mîr Camar Uddîn Mast (Qamar-uddin Minnat, poet), 97
Mississippi frontier, 92
Mississippi River, 310, 312
Moby-Dick (Melville), 93
molasses, 61, 234; in slave-trade triangle, 250
moles, in Thoreau's cellar, 243
"monarch of all I *survey,*" 79
Montaigne, Michel de, 12, 23
monuments, 55; vanity of hammered stone, 55–56
moods, poet's, xviii
moon and moonlight, 88, 196, 270, 313
Moore, Thomas, 16, 114, 182, 231
More, Sir Thomas, 106
morning (dawn), 7, 16, 82, 84, 86, 101, 108, 273, 296, 316, 325; "brings back the heroic ages," 86; cars (railroad train), 113; courage, 115; hours (reading), 98; "an infinite expectation of the dawn," 88;

morning (dawn) (continued)
spring, 289, 306; star, 114, 325; vigor, 95;
wind, 82; work, 16, 273

Morse, Samuel F. B., 50

mortgages and rent, 31–32, 78

Morton, Thomas, 62

mosquito: heralds vigor and fertility, 86;
Homeric celebration of, 87

moulting season, our, like fowls', 22

mouse: killed pines, 270; Thoreau observes, 216–17; Thoreau sends specimen
to Agassiz, 216; wild or white-bellied
(deer mouse), 243, 258

"mummy wheat," 24–25

music, 82, 94, 95, 107, 153, 210, 213, 298,
315, 317; Aeolian music, 127; "carols and
glees to the spring," 299; "let him step
to the music which he hears," 317

"Musketaquid" (Thoreau's boat), 83

muskrats (musquash), 208, 262, 305;
"drown out all our," 234; heroic virtue
of, 63

mussels, 179, 236

Myrmidons, 219

myths, 83, 261, 298, 302; in *Walden,* xx,
xxiii, 113. *See also* classical myths and
legends; fables and fabulists; parables

nakedness, 20, 27; Thoreau and, 22

Napoléon I, emperor of France, 56, 115

narcolepsy (sleeping disorder). *See* lethargy

natural philosophy (natural science), 107

nature, xviii, 99; becoming part of, 202–3;
equilibrium of, in spring, 302; laws of,
281; "living poetry" of, 298; "mother of
humanity," 298; operations of, 293, 297;
study of, 107

navigation, 50, 68, 89, 199, 282

Nebuchadnezzar, 232

necessaries of life, 11–15, 62; food, 11–12;
necessaries of the soul, 320; "next to

necessary" tools, books, etc., 13; shelter,
clothing, fuel, 12

Neva marshes (Russia), 20

Newell, John C., 249

New England, 22, 38, 94; can hire wise
teachers, 107; climate of extremes,
292–93; rum in, 268, 269

New England Farmer (journal), 284

"New England Nights' Entertainment, A,"
261

New Forest (England), 240

New Hollander (native Australian), 12

New Jersey, 51; shipwrecks, 19; showers of
flesh and blood reported in, 307

news and newspapers, 41, 91, 103, 105, 319–
20; *Concord Freeman,* 25, 39, 91, 255,
290, 307; as gossip, 91–92, 107

Niger River (Africa), 310–11

night (darkness), 70, 87, 91, 319

Nile River (Egypt), 310

Nilometer, 96

Nine-Acre-Corner Bridge (Concord), 305

nineteenth century, 106, 320

"noise of my contemporaries, the," 320

Norris, Rev. Thomas F., 107

North American Review, 13

northstar (fugitives' guide), 147

Northwest Passage, 310

Northwest Territory, 235

novels, popular, satirized by Thoreau,
102–3

Nutting: Sam, 269; Stephen, 253

oakum, 261

O'Callaghan, Edmund Bailey: *Documentary History of New York,* 38, 230

odors. *See* scents and odors

Olaus Magnus, 222

old, the, useless advice to the young, 9–10

Old Farmers Almanac, 286–87

Old Marlboro Road (Concord), 246

plants (continued)
blueberry, 110, 168, 176; blue flag (iris),
192; caltha (marsh marigold), 292;
cattail, 299; cotton-grass, 299; dock,
292; dogwood (poison sumach), 194;
goldenrod, 110, 247, 298; ground-nut,
110; hard-hack, 299; hazel-bush, 254;
huckleberries, 67; johnswort, 110, 215,
299; life-everlasting, 110, 298; lilac,
255; meadowsweet, 299; mullein, 299;
pickerel-weed, 196; pinweed, 298;
purslane, 59; raspberry, 254; Roman
wormwood, 254; shrub-oak, 110, 264,
301; skunk-cabbage, 258; strawberry, 110,
254; sumach, 214, 247, 254; swamp-pink
(azalea), 194; sweetbriar, 214; sweet flag,
192; thimble-berry, 254; toadstools and
fungi, 194; usnea lichen, 194; waxwork
(climbing bittersweet), 194; white lily
(water lily), 192; wild-holly (mountain
holly), 194. *See also* grasses; trees
Plato, 101, 104–5, 275, 288, 321
Pleasant Meadow (Baker Farm), 196
plowing: earth, 52–53; snow, 115
Plutarch, 12, 100, 186, 220, 313
poets and poetry, 94, 203, 209
polestar, sailor's and fugitive's true guide,
68
Polk, James K., 222
poorhouse and the poor, 33–34, 145–46,
319. *See also* poverty
Pope, Alexander, translation of *Iliad,* 98
post office, 91–92
potatoes, 230, 234, 243, 244, 250–51, 322;
potato-rot, 316
potter, 253
poverty, 5, 76–77, 197–201, 319; "the
degraded poor," 34; essential to philosophers, 14; material and spiritual, of some
readers, 5. *See also* poorhouse and the
poor

prairies, 85, 203
preachers and preaching, 93–94, 147;
Edward Thompson Taylor, 93
Prescott, William Hickling, 66
present moment, 97, 108, 303; "God himself culminates in the," 95; "gospel
according to this moment," 82; as line
between past and future, 16
"Pretensions of Poverty, The" (Carew),
76–77
progress, 322
publishers: as arbiters of literary choice,
107; "the modern cheap and fertile
press," 98; of *A Week on the Concord and
Merrimack Rivers,* 19, 67
Punkatasset Hill (Concord), 214
Puri (native Brazilians), expressions of
time, 109
purity, 211–12, 316; in parable of Kouroo,
318; "the purity men love," 316; of
Walden water and ice, 316, 318
Putnam, Gen. Israel, 324
Pyramids, 55

Quakers, 261
Quarles, Francis (verse by), 159
Quoil (Coyle), Hugh, 1, 253–55; death and
ruined house of, 254–55

rabbits, 207, 264, 271
raccoon, 218
railroads, 32, 51, 52, 89, 111–12, 228; call
of the freight train, 112; causeway, 112,
195, 196; connection with ice trade, 317;
Fitchburg Railroad, 41, 51, 112; "it rides
upon us," 90; "last improvement of
civilization," bordered by shanties, 34;
as modern myth, 113; and punctuality,
114–15; *Railroad Journal,* 95; thawing of
sand in railroad cut, 294–97; Western
Railroad (Mass.), 91

rainbow, 195, 199, 208, 306

rain and rainstorms, 17, 84, 196, 290, 303, 306; "inspector of rainstorms," 17; rain of flesh and blood, 307

Raleigh, Sir Walter, 5

Rans des Vaches, 153

reading, xx, 97–107; a noble exercise, 99, 102; reading "language without metaphor," 108; we should read the best, 102. *See also* classics of literature

reality: "Be it life or death, we crave only reality," 96; "a hard bottom and rocks in place," 96; vs. illusion, 94–96; intuiting or knowing, 108, 297; real vs. actual, xviii–xx, 16; "Realometer," 96; vehicle of the "sublime and noble," 95

reason vs. understanding, 11; Emerson and Ripley on, 11–12

rebirth, renewal, and resurrection, 300, 303–4, 306–7, 324; in parable of Kouroo, 318; recovered innocence, 303; victory over death, 306; "Walden was dead and is alive again," 300–301

recreation and relaxation, 108

Redding, George W., Co. (Boston newsdealer and publisher), 107, 162

reform and reformers: reform of oneself, xvii, 87; temperance reformers, 250; Thoreau's objections to, 73–76

Reid, Thomas, 316

religion, 101, 209, 288. *See also* Asian belief systems; Bible; Christianity, traditional; divinity; God, ideas of; scriptures; spirit and spirituality

Reynard the Fox (medieval tale), 82

Reynolds, Sir Joshua, 46

Ricardo, David, 50

rice, 58, 234

rich, the, 319; "accidental possession of wealth," 22; "the degraded," 34; "A man is rich in proportion to the number of things which he can afford to let alone," 79; as self-enslaved, 16

Ricketson, Daniel, 25

Ripley, George, 11, 49, 153

roads and paths (Walden Woods), 256–57; in winter, 246

Robbins, Roland W., 53

Robin Goodfellow, 70

Robinhood, 241

Robinson Crusoe (Defoe), 16

Rodgers penknife, handmade knife preferable to, 50

Rome and Romans, 3–4, 322; "a new Rome in the West," 4

rooster, crowing of, 81, 82–83, 123–24

root meanings of words, important to Thoreau, 29, 36–37, 296

Rosetta stone, 297

rum, New England, 268, 269; "demon rum," a robber and murderer, 248; in slave-trade triangle, 250

Rumford fireplace, 30

Rusk, Ralph Leslie, 43

Ruskin, John, on fancy vs. imagination, 8

Russell, Chambers, 251

rye, 103, 111, 234, 284

sabbath, 72; as seventh, not first, day of week, 93; Thoreau proposes six per week, 66

Sacontala, or The Fatal Ring (Calidas), 308

Sadi (Saadi, poet), 75–76

Sahara desert, 71

St. Angelo, castle of (Rome), 195–96

St. Helena, Napoléon exiled to, 253

St. Petersburg (Russia), 20

Saint Vitus' dance, 90

Salem (Mass.), 20

salt, 59, 62

Salt, Henry S. (biographer), 39

Sanborn, Franklin B.: Bibliophile Edition of *Walden,* 63, 114, 209, 210, 285; describes E. Hosmer, Sr., 53; on former inhabitants of Woods, 246–47, 249; on Thoreau, 24; Thoreau's description of ice-cutting restored by, 285–86

sand: thawing in railroad cut, 294–97; used in mortar and plaster, 232, 236–67

Sankhya Karika of Iswara Krishna, 94

Sartain's Union Magazine, 79, 111, 311

satyrs and fauns, 211

sauntering, 108, 260

Say, Jean-Baptiste, 50

scale of being (great chain of being), 275

scarecrow, 21, 22

scents and odors, 208, 254–55, 316

school-keeping, Thoreau's career in, 66–67

science, 204, 258; corroborates human experience, 203. *See also* astronomers and astronomy; botanists and botany; natural philosophy; nature; navigation; philosophical instruments

Scientific American, 51, 95

scimitar, 96

Scotland and Scots, xvi, 260, 277; common sense school of philosophy, 316

Scott, Sir Walter, 260

Scribner, Ira (miller in Catskills), 83

scriptures, 72, 103–4; "the architects of our bibles," 46. *See also* Asian belief systems; Bible; Christianity, traditional; divinity; God, ideas of; religion

seasons, 78; autumn, 228–38; Indian summer, 238; spring (1845), 39–43, 52–53; spring (1846), 289–308; summer, 43, 81–88, 308; winter, 239–88

seeds, 81, 103, 114, 287, 299; of a better life, 205; divine, 303

seeing, 85, 94, 102, 325; discipline of, 108

Seeley, nail-thief, 42; represents "spectatordom," 43

seer (visionary), 64, 108

self, xvii; "a dose of myself," 318; exploration of one's, 310, 312; idea of, in Transcendentalism, 2; as opposed to society, 312–14; our confinement within the, 10. *See also* individual and individualism

Selkirk, Alexander, 79

serenity, 260, 274, 301

"settler, the old," 133, 177, 261

seventeen-year locust (cicada), 323–24

seven-years' itch, 323

"several more lives to live," 313

Seward, William H., on higher law, 202

shadows, 195–96, 201, 233, 319; double shadow, 284

Shakespeare, William, 73, 101; *Hamlet,* 6, 8, 23, 149; *Julius Caesar,* 65, 271; *King Lear,* 217; *A Midsummer Night's Dream,* 70, 103; *Richard III,* 40

shanties, xvi, 1, 41–42, 47; "human beings living in sties," 34

Shattuck, Lemuel, 179

shelter, a necessary of life, 26–30. *See also* houses

shepherds, 86; the Good, 205; "Shepherd's Love for Philiday," 86. *See also* herds and herdsmen

Sheridan, Richard Brinsley, 71

shiners, 178–79, 199

shingles: shingle-tree, 195; of thought, 260; of Walden house, 46

shipwrecks: on Jersey shore, 19; metaphorical in life, 19–20, 24, 89, 306, 317

shirt, "our true bark," 23

shoe-strings, 32

silk, 112

simplicity and simplifying, 88–89

skating and sledding, 240, 262–63

slaves and slavery, 5, 7–8, 147, 198, 247–50, 312, 320; metaphorical in society, 6; slave-breeding, 34, 72; slave-trade triangle, 250